FACILITIES MANAGER'S DESK REFERENCE

Jane M. Wiggins

WILEY-BLACKWELL

A John Wiley & Sons, Ltd., Publication

This edition first published 2010

© 2010 by Jane M. Wiggins

Blackwell Publishing was acquired by John Wiley & Sons in February 2007. Blackwell's publishing
programme has been merged with Wiley's global Scientific, Technical, and Medical business to form
Wiley-Blackwell.

Registered office
John Wiley & Sons Ltd, The Atrium, Southern Gate, Chichester, West Sussex, PO19 8SQ, United Kingdom

Editorial offices
9600 Garsington Road, Oxford, OX4 2DQ, United Kingdom
2121 State Avenue, Ames, Iowa 50014-8300, USA

For details of our global editorial offices, for customer services and for information about how to
apply for permission to reuse the copyright material in this book please see our website at www.wiley.
com/wiley-blackwell.

Library of Congress Cataloging-in-Publication Data

Wiggins, Jane M.
  Facilities manager's desk reference / Jane M. Wiggins.
    p. cm.
  Includes index.
  ISBN 978-1-4051-8661-2 (pbk.: alk. paper)   1. Facility management—Handbooks, manuals, etc.   I. Title.
  TS155.W536 2010
  658.2—dc21

                                                                              2009046207

A catalogue record for this book is available from the British Library.

Set in Minion 10/12 pt by MPS Limited, A Macmillan Company.

Printed and bound in Malaysia by Vivar Printing Sdn Bhd

3   2012

Contents

List of Abbreviations

AC	air conditioning
AC/DC	alternating current/direct current
ACM	asbestos-containing material
ACoP	Approved Code of Practice
ACPO	Association of Chief Police Officers
ACPOS	Association of Chief Police Officers Scotland
ACT	advanced corporation tax
ADSL	asymmetric digital subscriber line
AFM	Association of Facilities Managers
AGA	Authorised Guarantee Agreement
AHU	air handling unit
AIB	asbestos insulating board
AMR	automatic meter reader
ASCII	American Standard Code for Information Interchange
AVAB	Automatic Vending Association of Britain
BACS	British Association for Chemical Specialities
BALI	British Association of Landscape Industries
BCM	business continuity management
BCP	business continuity planning/plan
BE	built environment
BICS	British Institute of Cleaning Science
BIFM	British Institute of Facilities Management
BMI	building maintenance information
BMS	building management system
BOO	build, own, operate
BOT	build, operate, transfer
BPA	British Parking Association
BRE	Building Research Establishment
BREEAM	Building Research Establishment Environmental Assessment Method
BRERR	Business Enterprise and Regulatory Reform
BS	British Standard
BSIA	British Security Industry Association Ltd
BSRIA	Building Services Research and Information Association
CAD	computer-aided drafting/design
CAFM	computer-aided facilities management
CAR	Control of Asbestos Regulations
CAWR	Control of Asbestos at Work Regulations 2006

CBA	cost benefit analysis
CCIA	Computer Communications Industry Association
CCITT	Comité Consultatif Internationale de Télégraphique et Téléphonique
CCTV	closed circuit television
CD	compact disc
CDG – CPL	Carriage of Dangerous Goods – Classification Packaging and Labelling Regulations
CDM	Construction Design and Management Regulations
CEA	cost effectiveness analysis
CFM	Centre for Facilities Management
CHAS	Contractors Health and Safety Assessment Scheme
CHIP	Chemicals (Hazard Information and Packaging or Supply) Regulations
CHP	combined heat and power
CIAT	Chartered Institute of Architectural Technologists
CIBSE	Chartered Institution of Building Services Engineering
CIOB	Chartered Institute of Building
CIPS	Chartered Institute of Purchasing and Supply Management
CIS	Construction Industry Scheme
CMMS	computer-based maintenance management system
COSHH	control of substances hazardous to health
CPA	critical path analysis
cps	characters per second
CPU	central processing unit
CRC	Carbon Reduction Commitment
CRM	customer relationship management
CSR	corporate social responsibility
CV	constant volume
DBFO	design, build, finance, operate
DCF	discounted cash flow
DCLG	Department of Communities and Local Government
DCMF	design, construct, manage, finance
DDA	Disability Discrimination Act
DEC	Display Energy Certificate
DECT	Digital Enhanced Cordless Telecommunications
DHWS	Domestic Hot Water System
DNO	distribution network operator
DoE	Department of Environment in Northern Ireland
DPC	damp proof course
DSL	digital subscriber line
EA	Environment Agency
ECA	enhanced capital allowance
EDMS	electronic document management system
EFQM	European Foundation of Quality Management
EHO	Environmental Health Officer

EIA	Electronic Industries Association
EIA/TIA	Electronic Industry Association/Telecommunications Industry Association
EMI	electromagnetic interference
EPBD	Building Energy Performance Directive
EPC	Energy Performance Certificate
ERP	enterprise resource planning
EU	European Union
FAQs	frequently asked questions
FCSI	Food Service Consultants Society International
FF&E	fittings and equipment
FM	Facilities Management *or* Facilities Manager
FMA	Facilities Management Association
FMI	Facility Management Institute
FTSE	Financial Times Stock Exchange
GCW	General Contract Works
GDO	General Development Order
GEA	gross external area
GIA	gross internal area
GNP	gross national product
GPRS	general packet radio service
GPS	global positioning system
GSM	global system for mobile communication
HACCP	hazard analysis critical control points
HCIMA	Hotel and Catering International Management Association
HIV	human immunodeficiency virus
HMIP	Her Majesty's Inspectorate of Pollution
HMRC	Her Majesty's Revenue & Customs
HQ	head quarters
HR	Human Resources
HSE	Health and Safety Executive
HVAC	heating, ventilation, air conditioning systems
IAM	Institute of Administrative Management
IBM	International Business Machines
ICA	Institute of Chartered Accountants
ICE	Institute of Civil Engineers
IDC	IBM data connector
IEE	Institute of Electrical Engineers, *now part of the IET*
IEEE	Institute of Electrical and Electronics Engineers
IET	Institute of Engineering & Technology
IFM	Institute of Facilities Management
IFMA	International Facility Management Association
IFRS	International Financial Reporting Standards
IiP	investors in people
IOSH	Institute of Occupational Safety and Health
IP	internet protocol

IPC	integrated pollution control
IPPC	Integrated Pollution Prevention Control
IPSA	International Professional Security Association
IPSOTEK	Intelligent Pedestrian Observation Technologies
IRR	internal rate of return
ISA	Individual Savings Account
ISDN	integrated services digital network
ISO/IEC	International Organisation for Standardisation/International/ Electrotechnical Commission
ISP	internet service provider
IStructE	Institute of Structural Engineers
IT	information technology
ITU-T	International Telecommunications Union
JCT	Joint Contract Tribunal
KPI	key performance indicator
LA	local authority
LAN	local area network
LCC	life-cycle costing
LCD	liquid crystal display
LCR	least cost routing
LEED	Leadership in Energy and Environmental Design
LEO	low earth orbit
LNG	liquefied natural gas
LOLER	Lift Operations and Lifting Equipment Regulations
LPA	local planning authority
LPG	liquefied petroleum gas
M&E	mechanical and electrical
MDHS	method for determining hazardous substances
MEL	maximum exposure limits
MERS	most economical route selection
MFD	multi-function device
MICC	mineral insulated copper cable
MIS	management information system
MMS	multimedia services
MS	Microsoft
NACOSS	National Approval Council for Security Systems
NEBOSH	National Examination Board in Occupational Safety and Health
NEC	New Engineering Contract
NFMA	National Facility Management Association
NHBC	National House-Building Council
NHSS	National Highways Sector Scheme
NIA	net internal area
NPV	net present value
NRA	National Rivers Authority
NSI	National Security Inspectorate
NUA	net usable area

NVQ	National Vocational Qualification
O&M	Operating & Maintenance
ODP	Ozone Depletion Potential
OES	occupational exposure limits
OGC	Office of Government Commerce
OHP	overhead projector
OJEU	Official Journal of the European Union
PACE	Property Advisers to the Civil Estate
PAN	personal area network
PAT	portable appliance testing
PBX	private branch exchange
PC	principal contractor *or* personal computer
PDA	personal digital assistant
PDCA	plan, do, check, action
PEEP	personal emergency evacuation plan
PERT	program evaluation and review technique
PFI	Private Finance Initiative
PIA	Post Implementation Analysis
PIN	prior information notice *or* personal identification number
PIP	Pricing in Proportion
PIR	passive infra red
PLC	public limited company
PPP	public-private partnerships
PM	project manager
PMSPA	Park Mark Safer Parking Award
POE	Post Occupation Evaluation
PPE	personal protective equipment
PQQ	pre-qualification questionnaire
PRINCE	projects in controlled environments
PSTN	public switched telephone network
PUWER	Provisions for Use of Work Equipment Regulations 1999
PV	photovoltaic
PVC	polyvinyl chloride
PZB	Parasuraman, Zeithaml and Berry
QM	quality management
QMS	quality management system
RAM	random-access memory
RCDs	residual current devices
REIT	Real Estate Investment Trust
REP	Real Estate Partnership
RF	radio frequency
RFI	requests for information
RFID	radio frequency identification
RH	relative humidity
RIBA	Royal Institute of British Architects
RICS	Royal Institution of Chartered Surveyors

RIDDOR	Reporting of Injuries, Diseases and Dangerous Occurrences Regulations 1995
RIFD	radio frequency identification
ROCE	return on capital employed
ROI	return on investment
ROLO	Registration of Land based Operatives
ROM	read-only memory
RRO	Regulatory Reform Order
SCS	structured connectivity solutions
SENDA	Special Educational Needs and Disabilities Act
SEPA	Scottish Environment Protection Agency
SEPA	Scottish Environment Protection Agency
SERVQUAL	service quality
SIA	Security Industry Authority
SIC	Standard Industrial Classification
SIM	subscriber identity module
SLA	service level agreement
SMEs	small- and medium-sized enterprises
SMS	short messaging service
SOR	statement of requirements
SPC	statistical process control
SPS	Safer Parking Scheme
SPV	special purpose vehicle
STP	shielded twisted pair
STS	customer (student/patient/resident) telephony service
SWOT	strengths, weaknesses, opportunities and threats
TAC	trunk access class
TDS	total dissolvable solid
TFM	Total Facilities Management
TIA	Telecommunications Industry Association
TOR	terms of reference
TPO	tree preservation order
TPS/FPS	telephone/fax preference service
TQM	total quality management
TSB	Technical Systems Bulletin
TUPE	Transfer of Undertakings (Protection of Employment) Regulations
UBR	uniform business rate
UDP	unitary development plan
UPS	uninterruptible power supply
UPVC	unplasticised polyvinyl chloride
UTP	unshielded twisted pair
VAT	value added tax
VAV	variable air volume
VDT	visual display terminal (computer screen)
VE	value engineering
VIP	very important person

VoIP	Voice over Internet Protocol
VPN	virtual private network
WAN	wide area network
WAP	wireless application protocol
WC	water closet
WEEE	Waste Electrical and Electronic Equipment Directive *or*
	Waste Electrical and Electronic Equipment Regulations
WiFi	wireless fidelity
WLAN	wireless local area network
WMS	Water Management Society
WPA	WiFi protected access
WRAs	waste regulation authorities
WSL	water supply licensing

Introduction

Facilities management (FM) covers a wide range of disciplines – often referred to as the jack of all trades or the Cinderella function in an organisation. Many employees will turn to the Facilities Manager (FM) to sort out their workplace problems so that a competent FM must be able to turn their hand to practically anything. With constant changes to legislation, advances in the use of technology in the workplace, organisations are striving to maintain their competitive advantage. FMs are frequently expected to ensure compliance, provide opportunities for the organisation to adopt new ways of working and other creative ways to reduce operational occupancy cost yet maintain the working environment standards.

Facilities Manager's Desk Reference will provide a useful reference as a source of information to help in the daily activities of FM, specifically helping any person who is responsible for the management of premises and provision of business support services. Many doing this role may not consider themselves 'facilities managers', and may work under titles such as office manager, practice manager, warehouse manager, leisure centre manager, etc. It will be useful for people working at all levels of FM, but especially those starting their careers in FM, such as the team leader of a group of operatives. Supervisors, FM co-ordinators and assistant FMs will also find this resource helpful as they gain more experience across the wide roles of FM.

Students will also find the desktop companion text useful for their studies, helping with key aspects of various topics in the syllabus of many FM courses, or FM modules in property management and business management courses.

1 History of Facilities Management

1.1 Origins of facilities management

The origins of facilities management (FM) can be traced to an era of scientific management and the subsequent explosion in office administration in the early 1900s. The main catalyst in the 1960s towards FM was the introduction of computers in the workplace. The energy crisis in the 1970s brought home the importance of cost-in-use and the need to better manage costs associated with premises that support the organisation's business. As the pace of change has speeded up and as new technologies have been adopted, FM has developed and expanded in the more recent decades.

1.2 A Brief history of FM

FM owes its origin to the growth of office administration – bringing together large groups of people into buildings. The introduction of computers into the workplace was a major catalyst for change in the workplace.

1960s era

The 1960s could claim to be the first period in the history of FM. This was when the term 'Facilities Management' was first coined by Ross Perot of EDS in the USA. At that time, it was associated with the trends affecting the management of IT systems and networks. However, quite soon, the scope of FM had expanded to include system/modular furniture and office design.

1970s era

The energy crisis of the 1970s forced organisations to analyse critically their true cost base. Also during the 1970s, office furniture manufacturers, such as Herman Miller and Steelcase, were developing ever more sophisticated furniture systems. The problem was that the new office furniture was ahead of office design. It was certainly ahead of the thinking of the average office manager, who was typically responsible for procuring new 'desks and chairs', rather the 'systems furniture'.

Herman Miller, realising that the market was being supply led, concluded that it needed to interact with knowledgeable clients – clients who understood the importance of space planning and value of space, and who could consequently understand the relevance of the permutations which could be contrived from the new furniture systems.

1

Herman Miller brought together a group of would-be knowledgeable property users and various property advisers in 1979. It was only at this point that the importance of FM in the process of strategic organisational planning was recognised, and discussed openly at senior management level. Very quickly this group established itself as the Facility Management Institute (FMI) and it is the FMI that is generally credited with the coining of the term 'Facilities Management'. One member, Dave Armstrong, a leading proponent of the FMI, is recognised by many as the unofficial 'father' of FM.

The FMI was founded in Ann Arbor, Michigan, in 1979 as an offshoot of parent company Herman Miller Inc. The aim was to establish and advance FM as a new management science and professional activity. FMI laid the groundwork for organisational recognition of the importance of facilities in corporate strategic planning (although there was much emphasis on utilisation of space).

1980s era

A year later, in 1980, the National Facility Management Association (NFMA) came into existence, born of the need to create independence from a furniture/space planning commercial parent in order to allow FM's full potential to develop. NFMA very quickly evolved into the IFMA. The year 1980 is therefore a key date in the development of FM generally.

This era is a period of great change, with more organisations outsourcing to specialist providers. Many new laws were introduced in the UK, affecting employees, working practices and contracts. Large scale infrastructure projects linked with the operational services in 'Private Finance Initiative' schemes raised the awareness of FM across a wider population of users and customers.

2000s era

In this era, the FM profession has raised its profile in many organisations. Issues such as business continuity, security threats, risk management, corporate social responsibility and financial instability have put increasing pressure on FMs to deliver efficiencies in the workplace. Pan European and Global FM contracts have become a reality, supported with an increasing use of technologies in all facets of FM.

1.3 Growth of the FM profession

International Facility Management Association (IFMA)

The IFMA is based in the USA, and also operates internationally via chapters or groups in overseas countries. There are approximately 19,500 members in 60 countries worldwide in 2009. It is estimated that in excess of 60,000 people use the job description of Facilities Manager (FM) in the USA. They have their own education programme, awarding the designation CFM and FMP to their members who have been tested in their knowledge of FM.

FM in the UK

In the UK, FM developed ahead of the rest of Europe. Major strides in FM development were made in the UK particularly in the early 1990s. Until 1993 there were two organisations competing for members and status in the FM market, resulting in many people waiting until they merged before they joined.

❏   The Association of Facilities Managers (AFM).
❏   The Institute of Facilities Management (IFM).

Association of Facilities Managers (AFM)

The AFM was registered in 1985 and launched in 1986 by a small group of 10 FMs as the first such body in the UK, formed to support the professional practising FM.

Institute of Facilities Management (IFM)

The IFM was launched in June 1990. It grew out of the Facilities Management Group and Office Design Group (of the Institute of Administrative Management, IAM). The ODG had been active within the IAM for 25 years. This institute also owned and ran the Office of the Year Awards, the precursor to today's British Institute of Facilities Management (BIFM) Awards for Excellence. The IFM developed qualification examinations with the IAM's support.

British Institute of Facilities Management (BIFM)

The merger of these two organisations was formalised on 1 September 1993, and in January 1994, this merged organisation was named the British Institute of Facilities Management (BIFM). By 2002, membership had grown to around 7300. In 2009, there are some 12,500 members and it is often quoted as the fastest growing membership association. There are four categories of member – associate, member, certified and fellow. The new certified category, agreed in June 2009, replaces the former Qualification status, and recognises the achievements of members who have successfully demonstrated their professional competence in FM.

Facilities Management Association (FMA)

The Facilities Management Association (FMA) is the UK's leading representative trade body for employers engaged in delivering non-core services in the FM sector.

The FMA represents employers of those engaged in the provision of services for companies' non-core business and activities. The need to establish the association arose as a result of peer pressure and popular demand. As the professional disciplines of the individuals are represented by institutions to cherish and voice their needs, so there is an association to represent the employers.

Against this background, many employers in FM have requested that their interests are represented by an association, and that is precisely what the FMA aims to do. One common aspiration unites the FMA membership, and that is 'service provision and fair reward'. One noteworthy contribution by the FMA is the Young Managers Forum, nurturing new and young FMs to develop their career.

Action FM

Action FM is a collaboration of the leading FM organisations in the UK, who have come together to promote FM with a single, unified voice. Their primary objective is to raise the profile of FM to the widest audience possible, targeting UK companies, government and influencers by communicating to the business media, as well as the trade and national media, as appropriate. They aim to ensure that FM is understood as a vital business process that can provide strategic advantage and at the same time encourage the sector to be seen as a career of choice.

EuroFM

EuroFM is a network of more than 75 organisations, all focused on FM. They are based in more than 15 European countries and represent professional (national) associations, education and research institutes and corporate organisations.

The open network of professionals, academics and researchers generates a rich mix of activity, initiated by three network groups: the Practice Network Group, the Education Network Group and the Research Network Group. These network groups form the core of EuroFM. The EuroFM members are involved in an open exchange of information and experience through meetings, seminars and workshops, through collaboration in research projects, sometimes funded by EC and through the development of joint educational programmes. Proceedings of these activities are disseminated through the network via the EuroFM website, an annual conference and through newsletters, research papers and publications.

Global FM

Global FM is a worldwide federation of member-centred organisations committed to providing leadership in the FM profession. Global FM is a formal alliance of FM-related associations, an international association of associations. The founding members are the BIFM, the Facility Management Association of Australia and the IFMA. Global FM builds on the work done through the BIFM International Memorandum of Understanding to promote collaboration between the three bodies in the interests of their members and to extend such benefits to the wider FM community around the world.

As a single, united entity promoting FM, Global FM is a conduit for furthering the knowledge and understanding of FM, sharing of best practices and resulting in added value to the individual members of each member organisation.

The vision of Global FM is 'to be the worldwide community of organisations that provides leadership in facilities management'.

Asset Skills

This is one of many Sector Skills Agencies appointed by the UK government. Asset Skills represent the housing, cleaning, property and FM sectors. The aim is to improve productivity, efficiency and effectiveness. Their key purpose is to work with employers to ensure their staff and potential staff have the skills they need to do their work well. There are three core activities – qualifications, employer engagement and labour market information. Asset Skills have developed the new national occupational standards for FM.

1.4 Defining FM

It has been difficult to establish a standard definition due to lack of commonality between organisations teaching FM, practising FM and representing FM. Currently there are as many definitions as there are different types of organisation in the industry. This emphasises the very dynamic nature of FM and its rapid development as a profession. It really depends on where you come from and your viewpoint as to which one you find the most acceptable and suitable in your organisation.

Many definitions are very general, whilst others are very specific. This restricts their use and gives rise to a limited view of the FM industry and profession. The most widely accepted definitions of FM are as follows.

International Facility Management Association (IFMA)

'The practice of co-ordinating people and the work of an organisation into the physical workplace.'

'An integrated management process that considers people, process and place in an organisational context.'

Association of Facilities Managers (AFM)

'... the management of premises and buildings together with the facilities, services and people contained therein; this has implications in respect of initial design, maintenance, the day-to-day administration and control of manpower, energy and related resources' (1986).

Strathclyde Centre for Facilities Management (CFM)

'Facilities Management is a process by which an organisation delivers and sustains agreed support levels within a quality environment to provide full values in use to meet strategic objectives.'

Chartered Institute of Building (CIOB)

This institute avoids the issue of providing a definition with the following statement in their Technical Information Service paper:

'To be more specific is not easy. It is a sign of prevailing uncertainty that confer-ence speakers and other authorities usually feel it necessary to offer guidance of one sort or another. In consequence, definitions [FM] and lists of responsibilities and activities abound.'

Royal Institution of Chartered Surveyors (RICS)

'Facilities Management (FM) involves the total management of all services that support the core business of an organisation. It deals with those areas that the managers of the organisation consider to support their fundamental activities. FM focuses on the interaction between the core business, the support functions, and the facilities throughout all sections of industry, commerce, and services.'

British Institute of Facilities Management (BIFM)

The former definition used by the Institute, which represents the FM profession in the UK, is:

'Facilities Management is the integration of multi-disciplinary activities within the built environment and the management of their impact upon people and the workplace.'

Box 1.1   Extract from the BIFM website

BIFM has formally adopted the definition of FM provided by CEN, the European Committee for Standardisation, and ratified by BSI British Standards:

'Facilities management is the integration of processes within an organisation to maintain and develop the agreed services which support and improve the effectiveness of its primary activities.'

FM encompasses multi-disciplinary activities within the built environment and the management of their impact upon people and the workplace. Effective FM, combining resources and activities, is vital to the success of any organisation. At a corporate level, it contributes to the delivery of strategic and operational objectives. On a day-to day level, effective FM provides a safe and efficient working environment, which is essential to the performance of any business – whatever its size and scope.

Within this fast growing professional discipline, FMs have extensive responsibilities for providing, maintaining and developing myriad services. These range from property strategy, space management and communications infrastructure to building maintenance, administration and contract management.

This definition has been replaced and enhanced by the adoption of the new European definition.

The BIFM have provided supplementary explanations to help members and others understand the new European definition of FM. Critically, there is mention of a safe and efficient working environment, and also some examples of likely services provided to support a business (see Box 1.1).

Broad definition

FM is about taking control, adding value, supporting the business, ensuring that the space and working environment enhance not impede the productivity of the core activity and the staff. Each of the many definitions of FM can be applied in an organisation. Indeed an organisation may wish to develop its own definition to ensure that it fully scopes the mission and vision of FM.

Professional management

FM is the professional management of the built environment. FM is the champion of the occupant or end-user who requires the services and facilities to get their work done. FM is also about getting the maximum efficiency and effectiveness of the space, or working environment, that an organisation owns or leases.

A supporting role

Every organisation relies on a mix of functions and services to provide the support essential to its core business operations. Ensuring that this support is available in the right form, at the right quality and for the right cost is the task of FM. A proactive approach is required ensuring that the most appropriate support is provided. FM is the process by which an organisation delivers and sustains agreed levels of support services in a quality environment at appropriate cost to meet the business need.

Control of non-core activities

FM is about taking control, freeing organisations to do what they do best while the FMs take care of the rest. Defining the core and non-core activities in some organisations can be difficult. In many cases the productivity of staff and the satisfaction of customers will depend on critical FM services – such as reception or catering.

A business enabler

FM is a business enabler, and it bridges the gap between the physical environment of the workplace and the occupants. FMs work with suppliers, customers, neighbours, contractors and community members to ensure that the workplace is safe, secure and fit for its purpose.

1.5 Development of FM

Essentially there are four types of organisation offering FM services and these groups are based on the original business of the organisation.

(i) Construction.
(ii) Property development.
(iii) Technical.
(iv) Service providers.

Market size

The FM market ranges from £4.5 to £187 billion (depending on what is measured by whom).

The FM market is a large and increasingly important industry, and in recent times the advent of Private Finance Initiatives (PFI) and Real Estate Partnership schemes have helped to highlight the importance of managing operating and maintenance costs. The problem with identifying the size of the market is determining which services and functions to include in any assessment, and indeed in identifying the FM function within different organisations. According to research by Barbour Index plc in 2000, fewer than four in 10 managers fulfilling FM responsibilities actually held the FM job title, with more than 40 different titles having been recorded. More recent studies by Asset Skills reveals some 2000 job titles held by employees carrying out FM roles.

The Centre for Facilities Management (CFM) at Strathclyde estimated the value of commercial and industrial FM services at £130 billion in 1998. Bernard Williams estimated that the value of facilities services in the European Union Member States is €1000 billion. The most recent survey in 2009 by MBD gives a UK FM market value of £116.8 billion. The problem is what is included in 'facilities services' when trying to estimate the market size.

Measurement of FM market

In the future, understanding and measurement of the FM market should be made easier in Europe with the advent of a new code for classification of business. The new FM code, 81.10, was introduced in January 2008 across Europe (see Box 1.2).

Box 1.2   81.10 Combined facilities support activities

> This class includes the provision of a combination of support services within a client's facilities. These services include general interior cleaning, maintenance, trash disposal, guard and security, mail routing, reception, laundry and related services to support operations within facilities. These support activities are performed by operating staff who are not involved with or responsible for the core business or activities of the client.

Market growth

While the various functions of FM have always existed within an organisation, prior to the 1980s they were not commonly brought together under one manager, but rather managed separately. There are a number of factors contributing to the growth of FM, including:

❑ Global competition forcing companies to re-trench to core business areas and seek cost-driven competitiveness.
❑ High cost of space and premises focuses attention on the cost of occupying, servicing and maintaining space. Premises' costs are second only to the payroll on many balance sheets.
❑ Employees' rising expectations of work and their local working environments.
❑ Cost of mistakes – health, safety and environment in particular.
❑ Information technology (IT) and the growth of technologies used in the operation of buildings. Technologies are changing the way we work and how we can control working environments.
❑ Public sector policy – the competitive tendering, best value, Private Finance Initiatives and European procurement regulations.
❑ The investment focus of the property market, with little concern for the needs of tenant occupants.

1.6 European standard

A new European standard has been established, EN 15221.1. This new standard defines FM as:

> 'the integration of processes within an organisation to maintain and develop the agreed services which support and improve the effectiveness of its primary activities'.

2 Key Drivers of FM

2.1 The business organisation

An organisation relies on its primary processes in order to achieve its strategic objectives. Changing market forces and developments coming from legislation, technology, mergers, etc. influence these processes constantly. These changes must be managed and structured at strategic, tactical and operational levels throughout the organisation in order to remain viable and compliant.

The support processes, which can be a part of the organisation or be delivered by external service providers, have a direct impact on the efficiency and effectiveness of the primary activities. The distinction between the primary activities and support services is decided by each organisation individually; this distinction has to be continuously updated. Some organisations in the UK refer to the support services as non-core and the primary activities as core. What is considered core in one organisation may be considered non-core in another.

2.2 Demand and supply

FM aims at balancing the demand for supporting services with supply of an optimised mix between needs/service levels and capabilities/constraints/costs. This is illustrated in Table 2.1. To maximise performance and value, it is crucial to align demand and supply based on the economic, organisational and strategic objectives. Figure 2.1 shows the demand supply model of FM, which is described below.

Table 2.1 Demand and supply of FM services

Demand	The internal need of the primary activities for facility services (space and infrastructure and/or to people and organisation)
	Driven by the primary activities of organisation
	Responsibility of the client (at a corporate level) to clearly define the FM strategy and requirements
	Generated from client, customer, consumer, end-user
	Specified and defined in a service level agreement (SLA) that can change over time
Supply	Providing a broad scope of services as defined in the FM specification and agreement
	Managed and delivered by internal and/or external service providers
	Performance measured via key performance indicators (KPIs)

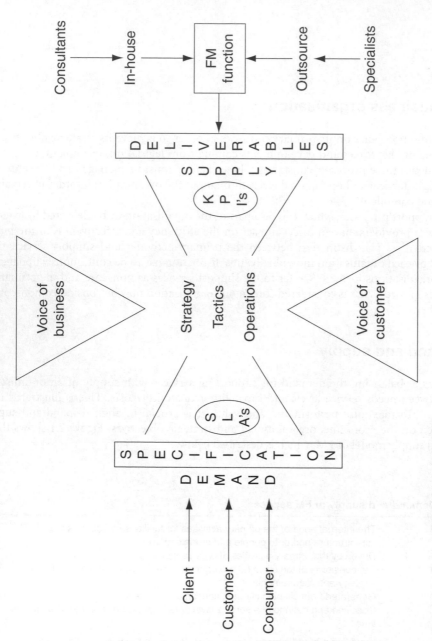

Figure 2.1   Demand supply model of FM

The organisation can be viewed as being made up of client (corporate level), customer (business unit level) and end-users. It's the task of the client to specify their needs and to procure the required FM services. The business units or departments will request the delivery of these services within the conditions of an FM agreement. Finally, end-users or consumers then receive these support services. These various levels of interaction from clients, consumers, and customers in the demand side of FM create many challenges in expectation management and communication. To succeed and deliver required results, the FM should be working in harmony and in close synchronisation with the mission and vision of the organisation and its objectives. The FM must work hard at relationship management with the demand side of the business to be effective.

2.3 Roles of FM

The role of FM can be considered at the three levels of the organisation as shown in Table 2.2.

Table 2.2   FM functions in an organisation

1	Strategic level	Defining the overall FM strategy Policy making, setting guidelines for space, assets, processes and services Active input and response at corporate level Initiating risk analysis and providing the direction to adapt changes in the organisation Initiating and monitoring KPIs Managing the impact of facilities on the primary activities, external environment and community Maintaining relations with authorities, landlords and tenants, strategic partners, associations, etc.
2	Tactical level	Implementing and monitoring guidelines to follow strategies Developing budget plans Translating business objectives to operational level Defining and interpreting KPIs (performance, quality, risk and value) Monitoring compliance to laws and regulations Managing projects, processes and agreements Managing the FM team Optimising the use of resources Interpreting, adapting and reporting changes Communicating with internal or external service providers on a tactical level
3	Operational level	Delivering services Monitoring and checking the service delivery processes Monitoring the service providers Receiving requests for service, e.g. via help desk or service centre Collecting data for performance evaluations, feedback and demands from end-users Reporting to tactical level Communicating with internal or external service providers on an operational level

Effective and efficient provision of FM in an organisation will therefore:

❑   Enable integration of the different services processes across the organisation.
❑   Provide the link between the strategic, tactical and operational levels of activity within the organisation.
❑   Ensure consistent communication (bottom up and top down) in the organisation.
❑   Develop a partnership relationship between clients/end-users and suppliers/service providers.

2.4 Drivers of FM

The development of FM has been driven by many internal and external factors. These are summarised in Table 2.3.

2.5 Champion of end-user

The role of FM as the champion of the user or occupier of buildings can be traced back to a time when traditionally the landlord and/or the landlord's agent was focused on rent recovery rather than tenant satisfaction. Property is viewed as a product or investment by a landlord – who and how it is used does not really concern the landlord too much. Agents were appointed for rent reviews, service charge administration and resolution of disputes between the landlord and tenant. The conflict of interest

Table 2.3   Factors driving development of FM

Global change	Reduction in trade barriers Resultant government policy Compulsory competitive testing Market testing
Global competition	Customer-focused Quality/cost/change-orientated
Impact of IT	Connectivity of systems Reporting of information
PFIs and other service-based property market products	New procurement methods Service availability
Cost implications of physical resources	The search for a competitive edge
More sophisticated user and stakeholder expectations	Workplace quality Accountability Quality control Raised standards
Growing recognition and acceptance of environmental issues	Legislation Regulation Corporate risk Sustainable development Corporate responsibility

meant that the agents could only really act for the landlord, and not the tenant. The role of a customer-focused FM was created to champion the needs of the occupiers. Professional FMs can offer the kind of impartiality and confidentiality required of the tenants and occupiers. This has lead to more important strategic planning roles within client/customer organisations and ultimately to a more structured and better-informed occupier-led property market.

2.6 Flexibility in office space

The economy requires corporate business plans to change direction quickly, if they are to survive in a highly competitive market. The fixed and highly specialised corporate head-quarters building is often a constraint on a business. Buildings and their layout have traditionally been an obstacle in the need to change the working environment, but with new types of buildings, the space can be more flexible and adaptive to an organisation's current and future needs. Shorter leases and more flexible open plan offices suit the majority of modern businesses. The corporate campus with multiple interconnected buildings may become the location of choice for many corporations. Each building can operate independently if required. These building clusters can readily respond to shrinking business plans by allowing the subleasing of a floor, or an entire building. Conversely, demands for more space can be met by adding buildings or more intensive occupation.

2.7 A recruitment differentiator

Salary is not the only way to attract and retain new employees. The image that the organisation conveys through its working environment is an essential feature in how companies attract and retain staff. The physical environment is one of the first points of contact with prospective employees and customers. It is often the first opportunity for a company to make an impression on their customers, either good or bad.

2.8 Scope of services

Organisations will find that the range of supporting services in the workplace will become increasingly important as staff compare employment and career prospects of one organisation against another. Competition for skilled employees will force companies to provide an ever-greater array of amenities and services. HR and FM professionals will need to work more closely together.

The restaurants, canteens and vending spaces offer the socialisation spaces in corporate buildings – encouraging individuals to meet casually, access the intranet or Internet, exchange ideas, be creative and be productive. The trends on the high street have come into the corporate environment. A full range of support and employee services may continue to be developed to meet the demands and expectations of occupants. These could include child-care centres, fitness centres, retail outlets, car maintenance and valeting, order and delivery points for Internet shopping at the workplace, etc. FMs with health and safety remits could also find themselves dealing with audits of the home workplace.

2.9 Impact of work space on productivity

Workplace quality has become increasingly important to employers: a well-designed and strategically considered office creates a happier, more productive and empowered workforce. An efficient, pleasant, dynamic workplace improves performance and productivity; it fosters happier staff and, ultimately, better business.

As more people are working at home, at client sites or in transit, they will require a new range of support services. These staff will expect to use a range of FM services accessible from various locations and settings. The FM needs to respond to these demands in cost effective ways.

Buildings influence the culture of organisations. The quickest way to change people's behaviour is to change the space they're in. Organisations frequently modify and change the workspaces in order to change the behaviour and culture of their employees.

Companies articulate and express corporate values and goals in their property, real estate and FM decisions. Companies in many sectors use their work environments as a source of competitive advantage. The workplace is changing, and companies are responding to these changes and the role of 'place' in competitive business strategy.

2.10 The virtual office

Working virtually – from anywhere connected via the Internet or email systems – will not completely eliminate the need for corporate office space. Working on the move is increasing. For the actual FM and their teams, they have to be present to manage the actual building and the services, but in time, even these roles may be more flexible as technology develops further. Some would argue that office buildings will continue to be required because complex knowledge relies on face-to-face communication, and innovation occurs through spontaneous interaction between people. But as technology improves, this preference for face-to-face interaction and a place for work may change. Pressures to reduce the carbon footprint of an organisation will also favour greater use of alternative working spaces and modes.

2.11 Technology systems integration

Different information and technology systems can be brought together by the integration of building systems with general management IT systems.

Voice, data and electrical distribution systems, together with lighting and temperature controls are becoming more integrated. Ideally, users need greater individual control of their working environment, via their own computers, mobile phones or personal digital assistants (PDAs). This demand, however, conflicts with the need to set one standard for everyone, with better efficiency of building plant and services. Security monitoring can now be introduced across a global organisation via fibre optics, digital cameras and using the Internet. This approach can be applied to one-off buildings as well as whole communities. Cities can be reconfigured with wireless fidelity (WiFi) to create new types of connected living and working spaces.

2.12 Building designs

Buildings of tomorrow will need to be smarter to ensure that the traditional downtime associated with the process of reconfiguring office space is minimised. Building mechanical and electrical services will be linked via Internet and intelligent controls to allow the services to be easily configured and reconfigured.

The operation and maintenance of modern complex buildings requires information about many areas and on several levels. Information comes from many diverse building systems such as fire alarms, access control systems, closed circuit television (CCTV) and security systems, all from different manufacturers and communicating in different languages, as well as from the general management information residing in various IT systems. The integration and merging of the technologies and protocols will support the step change required to raise both the profile and the performance of FM and their teams.

The advances of energy efficiency and renewable energy technologies have also made an impact in building design, construction and operations. Greater pressures from environmentalists to address sustainability issues, together with increasing legislation to increase the standards of building environmental performance, will also impact on the development of FM.

2.13 Financial performance

Building design, technology, telecommunications and space utilisation offer the means to gain a competitive advantage. Organisations need to think differently about workplaces and look at how their physical space positively impacts the corporate financial performance.

(i) It is evident that the workplace environment can affect employee behaviour.
(ii) Reductions in facilities and property costs have a direct impact on overheads and the bottom line.
(iii) Corporate performance measures will include aspects of building performance, in particular sustainability, energy and community performance.

2.14 Ownership of the property

The move away from ownership of corporate real estate to leasing or buy-back deals will continue. Companies are under pressure to release and re-use the capital tied up in real estate, putting this money to better use often through investment in their core business.

Private PFI deals and sale/leaseback of corporate office space will continue to be an attractive option for many organisations. Owner-occupiers of buildings are generally less effective in space utilisation (and associated FM costs) than those who lease their property. The effect of rent and service charges in the balance sheet brings more sharply into focus the relationship between space and its impact on both productivity and overhead costs. The issues of legacy leases on empty premises will require organisations to ensure that the estate is well managed as a strategic asset. Changes in taxation and rates will also require closer co-operation between the financial and property teams in organisations.

2.15 Value added

The value chain, as originated by Michael Porter, in his seminal text in 1985, *Competitive Strategy*, gives rise to the concept of value added. In the value chain, the supporting services of HR, FM, IT and Finance are challenged to ascertain if they add or detract from the value of the primary or core processes of the business. It is imperative therefore that FM continually tests the value contribution of its services to the organisation it serves. One challenge is to continually add value to the business processes by proactively initiating change programmes that impact on the margins or profit. FM performance measures need to be directly related to organisational deliverables such as customer retention, service delivery and level of production or market share. Intermediate performance measures such as productivity, adaptability, speed of response and performance resilience will still be recognised but ultimately it is the bottom line impact of the FM services that will judge whether FM is delivering added value to the business.

2.16 FM's contribution

During more recent times, informed senior management now recognise the contributions that efficiently and effectively run buildings make to a healthy and sustainable business. At last the people who have been managing buildings – with or without the title of FM – are being recognised, and more importantly appreciated. The FM must therefore argue that he can contribute to corporate success at a strategic level. The FM must deploy his managerial skills to step back from day-to-day tasks and find time to look longer term, into the future, to ensure that the buildings he manages today are the buildings that will suit the organisation tomorrow.

FMs will need to demonstrate the buildings and the FM services are contributing to business objectives on three levels:

(i) efficiency;
(ii) effectiveness;
(iii) economy.

Efficiency of service is increasingly seen as an absolute necessity and given in terms of performance. It is something that is expected as the norm by all service providers, whether internal or outsourced. FMs must become professionally recognised experts in operational management of buildings and services. It will become a given requirement that all FMs understand both the hard and soft aspects of FM.

2.17 Performance measurement

In both outsourced FM contracts and PFI/PPP relationships, there is an ongoing need to be able to measure performance against the contract SLAs. Payments to the service provider depend on performance levels. Performance in many of these areas needs to be monitored by an integrated performance measurement system using real time data. Data can be from individual sub-systems such as access control, CCTV, building management system

(BMS) and fire alarms, as well as from general management IT systems such as enterprise resource planning (ERP), MIS packages or individual accounting or human resources systems. Developing technologies such as radio frequency (RF) tagging allow many new areas of performance to be measured objectively in real time and have the data made available to other systems.

The potential benefits of real time data are reduced administration costs and manual input, reduced frequency of disputes on data availability or interpretation and reduction in failures to meet service levels. With truly integrated performance measurement systems, the various parties involved in service provision will be able to develop a more effective management of the contract; continuous improvement and better partnerships.

2.18 Benchmarking

As FMs raise their value and contribution in organisations, they will need to use building performance information as a powerful resource. As with all data care needs to be exercised in data interpretation. The key categories of information for comparison are:

- ❑ **Property costs** – Rent, rates and service charges are usually one of the highest costs.
- ❑ **Maintenance costs** – This is a major area of building expenditure that should be proactively managed. A Planned Preventative Maintenance (PPM) programme ensures balance is achieved between cost and building performance.
- ❑ **Cleaning** – This can be a high cost in many buildings, especially if the design is such that the decorative finishes and internal surfaces require a lot of attention. For example, glass atria, vast common areas and wooden floors require specialist equipment and trained staff.
- ❑ **Utilities** – An energy audit and active energy management policies should ensure that costs are as efficient as building operation will allow.

2.19 Future trends

Predictions for the future of FM include:

- ❑ More global outsourcing of business support services to countries such as India and other developing countries.
- ❑ Less property and real estate needed for a shrinking workforce.
- ❑ Facilities with more enticing amenities to attract the best class of employees and get the best out of them.
- ❑ More integrated workspaces to foster creativity and innovation.
- ❑ Infrastructure to support 'working on the move' as businesses have to react more quickly to market changes and customer demands.
- ❑ Multiple work locations for employees to increase flexibility of the workforce.
- ❑ Closer integration with other business support services such as HR and IT.
- ❑ Larger integrated FM contracts as more organisations are operating across international boundaries.
- ❑ Longer contracts, with reward linked to performance.

The external influences bringing about these future developments are:

- ❏ Labour skills and availability of suitable entrants to FM, including competition from other professions.
- ❏ Changing demographics with ageing western populations, and migrations across borders.
- ❏ Corporate cultures and governance influencing the structure of business.
- ❏ Political impact of business across national boundaries – the future composition of the European Union (EU).
- ❏ Global competition, including the rise of China, India, Russia and Brazil as major players in the industrialised economy.
- ❏ Maturity of PFI/PPP market.
- ❏ Converging technologies (video, voice, data, satellite, IP, radio).
- ❏ Legislation to protect the environment and the people in it.
- ❏ Global terrorism and fundamentalism.
- ❏ Maturing FM industry and increasing competition to win business.
- ❏ Global financial situation – cost of money, availability of credit and worldwide debt.
- ❏ World power – shift of power from older western economies to new emerging economies.
- ❏ Climate change – impact of weather, natural disasters, food production, use of natural resources.

3 Key Activities in FM

3.1 Introduction

FMs are responsible for many diverse functions and activities. FM entails the development, co-ordination and management of all the non-core, support services of an organisation, together with the buildings, including their systems, plant, IT equipment, fittings and furniture, in such a way as to positively assist an organisation in achieving its strategic objectives.

3.2 Facilitation of services and information

Often the senior management of the organisation does not understand the full scope and range of these responsibilities. FMs need to see that their role is not just the provider of services, but also as a strategic planner and provider of information to facilitate the efficient utilisation of resources and the running of an organisation. Although frequently labelled as non-core, FM in reality is a core service to the business, featuring in most organisations' business continuity plan. The development of the services to support an organisation may involve setting up contracts, identifying roles, potential improvements and the delivery of services, as well as managing change, key relationships and possible closure of services. These are shown in Figure 3.1.

3.3 Management functions

FM is a management function concerning three interrelated elements of business:

❑ Premises.
❑ Support services.
❑ Information technology.

For each of these three categories there are two aspects:

❑ Management – strategy or 'the thinkers'.
❑ Operation – implementation or 'the doers'.

FM covers an extremely wide range of activities that are dependent on the type of business, the sector and the organisation's structure.

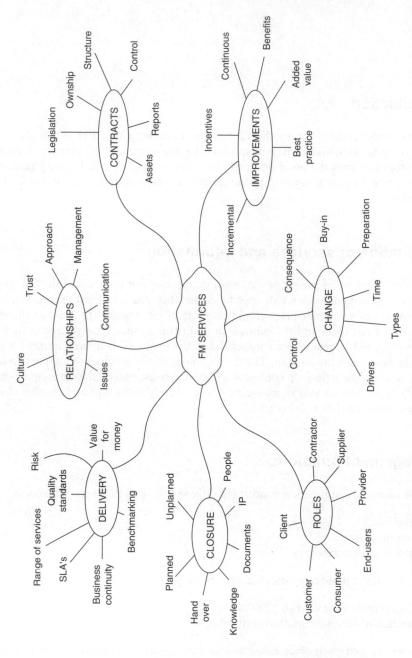

Figure 3.1   Factors involved in the provision of FM services

3.4 Premises and building management

Often referred to as Hard FM, this involves the mechanical, electrical and fabric element of buildings. It may also include the IT and other technologies used in the whole organisation or at the very least, the technologies used in the FM department. The range of services covers:

- ❑ mechanical systems and services;
- ❑ electrical systems and services;
- ❑ HVAC (heating, ventilation, air conditioning);
- ❑ public health services;
- ❑ control systems;
- ❑ utility services;
- ❑ property management;
- ❑ fabric maintenance;
- ❑ external areas, grounds and landscaping.

Generally, hard FM services may include:

- ❑ HVAC;
- ❑ lifts (passengers, goods);
- ❑ escalators;
- ❑ lighting and emergency lighting;
- ❑ plumbing/sanitary services;
- ❑ kitchen extraction systems;
- ❑ security systems – CCTV;
- ❑ acoustics;
- ❑ television/radio/satellite services;
- ❑ data (coaxial, fibre optics);
- ❑ fire protection;
- ❑ BMS;
- ❑ IT structured cabling;
- ❑ public address systems;
- ❑ power supplies (electricity, gas, oil, wind, solar, solid fuel, CHP);
- ❑ small power distribution system;
- ❑ standby supplies (generator/UPS);
- ❑ waste compactors;
- ❑ conveyors and mechanical handling systems;
- ❑ gases (laboratory, medical, tools).

Electrical systems:

- ❑ mains distribution system;
- ❑ power supply services;
- ❑ lighting systems;
- ❑ emergency and critical systems;
- ❑ heating/cooking;
- ❑ IT networks/server rooms;
- ❑ standby systems and supplies.

Mechanical systems:

❑ hot water systems/boilers;
❑ cold water services;
❑ drainage;
❑ HVAC;
❑ natural ventilation;
❑ mechanical ventilation;
❑ comfort cooling;
❑ air conditioning.

Public health services:

❑ plumbing;
❑ drainage;
❑ sanitation;
❑ water supplies.

Control systems:

❑ comfort control;
❑ alarm/fire monitoring;
❑ security – access/egress;
❑ lone working controls;
❑ maintenance systems;
❑ energy monitoring;
❑ energy management.

Utilities:

❑ electricity;
❑ solar, wind, ground, coal-fired, nuclear, hydro, combined heat and power (CHP) systems;
❑ oil;
❑ gas;
❑ water;
❑ air;
❑ waste/sewerage.

3.5 Business support services

FMs will provide and manage a full range of support services, which are usually referred to as the Soft FM activities. The range may include:

❑ Meeting and room bookings.
❑ Exhibition space and conference facilities.
❑ Video conferencing.

❑ Audio visual equipment services.
❑ Mail, post and courier services.
❑ General office equipment, such as printers, shredders and copiers.
❑ Computing equipment and data services.
❑ Reprographics and printing services.
❑ Stationery and consumables purchasing.
❑ Newspapers and publications services.
❑ Wireless, fixed and mobile telephony and broadband services.
❑ Central switchboard services.
❑ Pagers and short-wave radios, including licenses.
❑ Information centres, common area noticeboards.
❑ Signage and legal notices.
❑ Helpdesk services.
❑ First-aid services.
❑ Occupational health services.
❑ Building services.
❑ Fabric maintenance services.
❑ Cleaning and housekeeping services.
❑ Vending of personal hygiene consumables.
❑ Catering and vending services.
❑ Security and business continuity services.
❑ Car parking, car valet and car servicing schemes.
❑ Green travel plan services, e.g. shuttle buses, bicycle share schemes and car sharing services.
❑ Company vehicles and car fleet management.
❑ Hair and beauty services.
❑ Sports, fitness and leisure facilities.
❑ Merchandising, retail and Internet shopping services.
❑ Personal purchases (energy, stationery, cars).
❑ Business travel services.
❑ Residential accommodation services.
❑ Landscaping and grounds maintenance.
❑ Internal planting.
❑ Floral arrangements including florists for staff purchases.
❑ Office furniture and equipment.
❑ Secretarial services.
❑ Library services.

3.6 Range of FM activities and services

As an alternative, the services provided and managed by the FM can also be clustered into three main groups as listed in Table 3.1:

  (i) support;
 (ii) information;
(iii) premises.

Table 3.1   Potential FM services

Support services	
Mail services	Refuse disposal
Vehicle fleet	Reprographics
Catering	Security
Reception	Stationery
Housekeeping	Travel
Office administration	Vending
Furniture	Document management
Information services	
Data network	Wiring installation
Systems integration	Planning and design studies
Voice and data network	Software development
Network management	
Premises services	
Property asset management	Lease management
Site selection	Relocation
Acquisitions and disposals	Structure and fabric maintenance
Energy management	Infrastructure
Security infrastructure	M&E services maintenance
Space management	Capital works
Project management	Property development

4 Delivering FM – FM Strategy

4.1 Introduction

In the determination of how to deliver the FM services in an organisation, an understanding of general business strategy and management concepts is useful. The starting point for establishing an FM strategy is to understand the organisation's business plan, its defined strategy and high-level goals. This is shown in Figure 4.1.

No function or department in an organisation works in isolation – in real terms, they all exist to fulfil the organisation's overall mission and goals and should work together to deliver the strategic direction set by senior management level. The strategic apex in Figure 4.2 shows the relationship of the FM strategy between the end-users and the organisation.

4.2 Business strategy

A defined strategy is necessary for every organisation that wishes to achieve its goals, or for successfully completing a specific project. The strategy defines the long-term lines of action that an organisation will take to achieve its goals. It is based on two elements:

 (i) **Vision** – The desired future of the organisation, taking into account the needs of both staff and users.
(ii) **Mission** – Justifies the existence of the organisation in the eyes of its users. The mission explains the scope and goals of the institution's services to its users.

4.3 Identifying the needs

When developing a strategic plan, an FM must first identify the needs and the demand levels for services, and then determine how to meet them:

❑ Define the vision and the mission of the organisation according to stakeholders, both internal and external.
❑ Identify and analyse the Strengths and Weaknesses of the organisation as well as the external Opportunities and Threats. This can be done by using the force field technique or the SWOT analysis.
❑ A strategic plan must be designed that systematises the various steps to achieve the mission and reach the vision, taking into account the forces that promote and impede reaching the goal. Brainstorming will help generate four or five lines of action. These strategies should be fine-tuned by analysing their technical, economic and political viability.

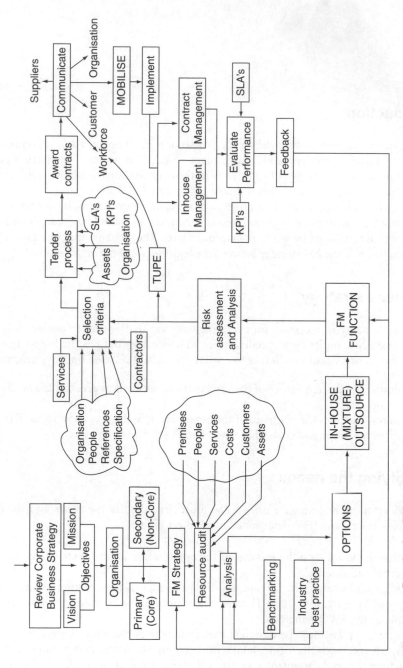

Figure 4.1 Developing FM strategies

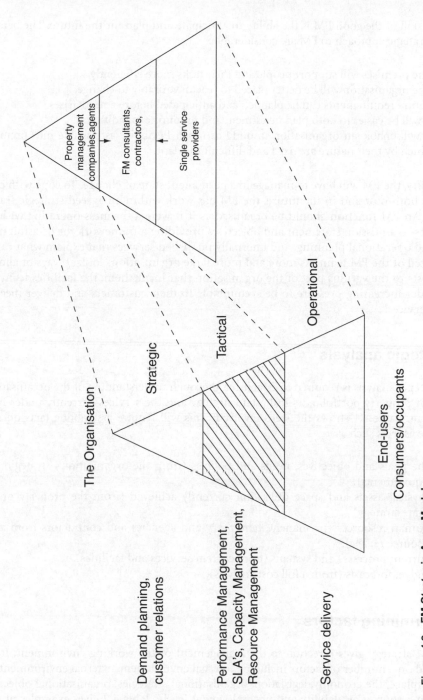

Figure 4.2   FM Strategic Apex Model

4.4 Benefits of a strategic approach

A key skill of the good FM is the ability to anticipate and plan for the future. The benefits of a strategic approach to FM are considerable:

❑ The premises will support people and their tasks more efficiently.
❑ The organisation will be better placed to react favourably to change.
❑ Future requirements can be planned and anticipated before a need arises.
❑ It will be easier to both plan investment and monitor expenditure.
❑ It will enable an organisation to build as much flexibility as possible into premises, which by their nature are fixed and difficult to adapt.

In reality, the FM will have to manage in a permanent state of change. To cope with challenges both now and in the future, the FM has work within an agreed strategic framework. An FM function should be organised as if it were a business operating within a business – a mission statement and objectives providing a framework for decision making and operational planning, and internally published services that explain what can be expected of the FM team. As more and more large organisations look at ways of allocating costs to the various part of the organisation that incur them, the facilities team will be under increasing pressure to be accountable to their customers and deliver measurable services.

4.5 Strategic analysis

A strategic analysis is required to establish a thorough understanding of the organisation's current property portfolio, its real estate strategy and the services currently under management. Table 4.1 shows the steps involved. This will require assembling facts on such diverse aspects such as:

❑ The goals and objectives, needs and policies (from the organisation's strategic plan requirements).
❑ Physical assets and space utilisation currently achieved (from the property or real estate strategy).
❑ Human resources (permanent, temporary and agencies and contractors from a full resource review).
❑ Current processes and systems (from current services and facilities).
❑ Budget forecasts (from a full cost analysis).

4.6 Determining factors

An FM strategy gives direction to the management of the working environment. It will depend on a number of factors including internal environment, external environment, the marketplace, the economy, legislation, organisational strategies, organisational objectives, human resources availability and unemployment levels. Table 4.2 gives examples of such factors or conditions.

Table 4.1   Steps in a strategic analysis

1	Idea generation	Brainstorming, PEST, SWOT, 'what if' scenarios
2	Portfolio audit	Spaces analysis Estates register Maintenance plans Maintenance audit Risk audit
3	Services review/audit	Current SLAs/performance analysis Benchmarking Customer satisfaction levels
4	Resource audit	People training/skills audit Existing internal service provision audit Business process mapping or analysis Zero-based analysis
5	Market audit	External service providers intelligence review Suppliers' competences Suppliers' management analysis, e.g. IiP, ISO 9000, ISO 14000 Availability of premises Market trends
6	Organisational fit	Current management functions and expertise Stakeholders' determination and requirements
7	Regulatory and statutory compliance	Accidents statistics and environmental violations analysis Claims history

Table 4.2   Conditions affecting an FM strategy

Internal conditions	External conditions
The buildings themselves – types and uses	Economic environment
Condition and location of the buildings and estate	Interest rates – the cost of money
Client services requirements	Unemployment rates – affecting availability of labour
Political conditions (the status of FM in the hierarchy of an organisation)	Political environment – taxes, legislation
Client relationships	Tariffs and trade conditions
Culture of an organisation	Political stability
Finances – amount of money available	Market conditions
Attitude of an organisation to improve or maintain a good standard of working environment	Needs, desires and aspirations of customers
Value added tax (VAT) status	Compulsory competitive market testing and procurement rules in public sector

FM strategy is influenced by:

- External and internal conditions.
- Success of current strategy.
- Direction of core business.
- Development of property and premises policy.

4.7 Premises policy

The starting point for the FM strategy is the premises policy. This in turn will be aligned with the corporate business plan. It should be a written document that articulates all the factors relating to the buildings the company occupy and own. It should also be forward-looking and identify future requirements, particularly in relationship to people, location and information technology. The policy may include standards of accommodation, charging methods, references to other company policies and targets for improvements.

A premises policy document should be approved and supported by the senior management. It will be a document unique to each organisation.

The premises policy should establish the current situation, with future projections for 5 and 10 years. Table 4.3 lists some of the considerations involved in the determination of a premises policy.

Table 4.3 Premises policy contents

1	Location preferences	Property or land choices Accessible to appropriate skilled employees and customers/clients.	City centre, business park, rural, transport links
2	Property	Financing implications of any acquisition/ disposal, whether property is leased or owned, valuation of property, impact on profit/loss and balance sheet.	Types of premises, uses, sizes, features, legal obligations and constraints
3	Space	Workplace space standards to ensure that space use can be maximised, that employees are provided with appropriate workspace and that expansion or contraction can be managed.	Space standards, allocation policy, furniture system, range of space uses, costs of space
4	Quality	Agreed quality standards to ensure that the premises and general business and support services meet the appropriate quality levels, that planned maintenance will be of required quality.	BS or ISO standards, quality management standards, benchmarks and best practice models
5	Image	Premises will reflect a corporate identity. Outward tangible appearances communicate much about a company and its culture.	Reputation, risk profile
6	Information technology	IT can enhance or hinder effective performance of an organisation. IT is playing an important role in FM: to provide management information, to monitor building efficiency and to increase facilities efficiency.	System integration, protection, security, confidentiality, resilience

4.8 Facilities audit

The next stage in creating an FM strategy is an audit of the current situation. The audit will examine information about the organisation:

❑ **Policy requirements** in terms of standards, guidelines, working procedures perform-ance standards, quality standards, health and safety, manning levels, financial and other approvals.
❑ **Processes and procedures** will enable a full understanding of how these business areas work today including budgets, procurement, purchasing approvals and payments.
❑ **Service delivery audits** of the existing property portfolio and service deliveries will tease out relationships with customers.

4.9 Audit process

The audit is a two-stage process to fully understand the organisation and its current facili-ties operation. Understanding the cost of facilities is the fundamental requirement of an audit. The audit will seek to find out the following:

❑ Exactly what facilities exist?
❑ What facilities services are offered?
❑ The effectiveness and efficiency of the management systems employed by the FM team.
❑ The current mode of service delivery.

4.10 Awareness

It is common for the senior management team of an organisation not to know how much space it occupies. In some cases, it is even a question of not knowing how many buildings are occupied. Examples to illustrate this are:

❑ Organisations approaching agents to acquire property they do not need.
❑ Subsidiary firms or business divisions looking for new space on the open market while similar space is vacated to another part of the company.
❑ Tenders for services quoting buildings no longer occupied, or missing out buildings that are now used.

4.11 Space audit

The space audit – part of a full facilities audit – is often required to determine the true use and ownership of space. Very often, spare space only becomes identifiable when an 'internal charge' for occupied space is levied. When space is 'free', occupiers (e.g. indi-vidual departments) are often spread out, build empires and defend their boundaries. When a charge per square metre is imposed, the 'shrink' in the space required can be dramatic.

The FM needs to prepare an outline plan of how the audit will be carried out. This is because it is very time consuming, and may involve others (internal and external). The plan needs to show:

❑ Likely extent of investigation.
❑ Probable resources required.

4.12 Audit stage 1 – fact finding

1	Establish the extent (the boundaries/the parameters)	Number and size of buildings Use of buildings (and subcategories of use) The facilities support services provided The role of facilities in providing IT/IS to the organisation Does a facilities policy exist?
2	Collect the organisation's existing cost data	
3	Reallocate this cost data under meaningful facilities cost centres	These cost centres must relate directly to services for comparison purposes. This could be the client's departments or cost codes
4	Analyse each cost per unit	Could be per unit of floor area or per capita or other appropriate parameter
5	Check actual performance against the SLAs	
6	Review the results of any user satisfaction surveys	Check validity of questions
7	Identify if the costs are above or below average	External benchmark costs or comparison across the estate may be needed
8	Check if performance matches the specification	Could be higher or lower than specified
9	Check that specifications (service levels) are appropriate for obtaining the desired performance level	Could be higher or lower than needed
10	Identify the cost centres or services which warrant more detailed examination	

4.13 Audit stage 2 – further investigation

Having carried out the first stage of data gathering and initial analysis, the FM should be able to identify the areas of concern which need further investigation and analysis. It is likely that the next stage includes:

❑ A detailed space planning audit.
❑ A detailed energy audit.
❑ Other experts and specialists, such as surveyors for a full condition survey of the estate.

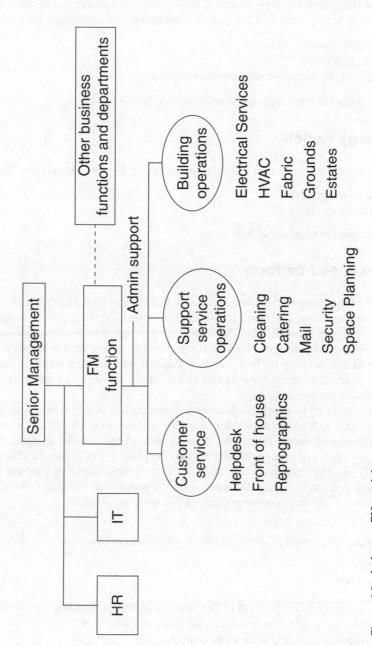

Senior Management

HR

IT

Other business functions and departments

FM function

Admin support

Customer service

Helpdesk
Front of house
Reprographics

Support service operations

Cleaning
Catering
Mail
Security
Space Planning

Building operations

Electrical Services
HVAC
Fabric
Grounds
Estates

Figure 4.3   In-house FM model

4.14 Audit benefits

The results of the audit have to be looked at holistically – not just cost, but also efficiency and effectiveness. Savings may well come from identifying, and acting upon, e.g.:

❑   Poorly written specifications.
❑   Inappropriately drafted SLAs.
❑   Inefficient management systems as well as cost issues.

The audit gives the FM a baseline upon which to base future FM strategies.

4.15 FM strategy models

There are a two principle ways that an organisation can arrange its FM services. These are:

(i)   Inhouse or self-perform
(ii) Outsource to specialist

These are described in more detail below.

4.16 In-house or self-perform

The structure of the in-house team will depend on the services that are offered, the number of sites and their locations. The team may need to be structured to match the organisation, with a representative to liaise with key departmental representatives on all aspects of FM.

Alternatively, the team may be structured functionally, giving each member a specialist area, such as 'soft' services or 'hard' services. Each of these in turn will have functional areas such as cleaning, security, projects and so on. Figure 4.3 shows a typical structure of an in-house FM department.

This option can often be overlooked, as the focus of both general managers and current FM practitioners is to look externally for solutions and services. The in-house option of directly employed staff across the whole service provision needs to be compared against the costs of any other FM strategy model. In some organisations, it may be more appropriate to keep the FM team in-house due to security, commercial or pastoral reasons. Another aspect to consider is the VAT status of an organisation. If exempt, then the VAT charged on services will increase the real cost of FM quite significantly.

Advantages
Total control over the work and close alignment with the core business.

Disadvantages
The in-house team:

❑   Requires a remuneration package in line with the core staff package.
❑   Requires management effort to be diverted from core activities.
❑   Can be inflexible, slow and difficult to change.
❑   Can be costly to keep staff trained and competent to carry out specialist roles.

Implication
Cost and manpower savings are unlikely to be achievable.

4.17 Single or packaged services

This is a term used to describe the separate contracts for each service line, i.e. one contractor for catering, another separate contractor for cleaning and so on.

Advantages
The advantage of this type of FM strategy is the closeness to the experts of the particular service, the direct control of the relationship and the reduced risks if there is a need to change a particular service. The phasing of contracts can be easier. The cancellation of individual contracts is easier. This strategy is particularly beneficial when commissioning a new building, when there is a need to get all the services operating efficiently and effectively. There are many contractors and suppliers to choose from.

Disadvantages
Disadvantages arise due to the lack of staff development in small contracts, and the potential loss of good staff to other sites run by the contractor. This option requires more in-house management and support to monitor, manage and administer the range of single contracts. There is limited scope for economies of scale.

Implication
Opportunity for manpower and cost reductions likely from the temptation to merge contracts together. Often a short term strategy.

4.18 'Bundled' services

Bundled services are where contracts are grouped together. A bundle is where one contractor will be supplying cleaning, catering and security as one contract, for example. Another is grouping the M&E and building fabric and grounds maintenance together. Services can be bundled into either a Hard FM cluster or a Soft FM cluster depending on what services are required, and what is suitable for the organisation.

Advantages
The advantage of bundling comes from the economies of scale, the reduced administration of contracts and invoices, reduction in time to manage the many services and a more consistent approach to a range of services from one contractor. Staff may be able to move with the bundle of contracts which can be good for career development for the individual.

Disadvantages
A disadvantage arises if one service line is weak or needs changing, which may create difficulties in other services that are working effectively.

Implication
A bundled approach can be seen as a mid-term solution to gain economies of scale and uniformity of services. It may lead to the next stage of one all-encompassing FM contract.

4.19 Total facilities management

Total facilities management (TFM) is used to describe the total outsourcing of all facilities services to one provider. The client has just one relationship with this provider, typically an account manager or director, and will receive one invoice to cover all services. There are relatively few organisations that can provide or self-deliver all FM services. Many FM contractors will actually need to have subcontractors in place to provide the full range of services.

Advantages
The contract is more easily managed by the organisation. In theory, there should be economies of scale which should lead to cost savings. It is up to the supplier to ensure roles and jobs are always staffed. There will be fewer bills to process and less HR issues to resolve. The client gains access to higher levels of expertise from the TFM contractor, who is expected to innovative and be creative in raising FM service standards as well as cost reductions. The outsourced staff get better access to training and development via their employer, with increased career opportunities.

Disadvantages
There is only one contract and the customer is totally reliant on one supplier. It might be difficult to change if delivery of part of the contract is unsatisfactory, particularly if all services are contracted to be delivered for the same period from the same date. The client can lose control of FM and lose valuable knowledge about their estate, the FM services and their employees requirements. There is a limited choice of organisations that are capable of TFM.

Implication
In-house FM staff cease to manage the people doing the job and are not responsible for the way the job is done. They manage the performance contract and the service delivery.

4.20 Managing agent

A managing agent solution for FM services is potentially the most expensive option. It is typically provided by the property management and FM management companies, who have management skills, as opposed to the operational service providers. In this model, the managing agent does not self-perform any services – they simply provide the monitoring and management services, acting as a go-between link between client and the contractor. The organisation is buying in others to oversee the services delivered by others, and this is where the extra cost lies. The fee paid to the managing agent can be linked to the monitoring performance and relationship management of the service providers. It can be used in start-ups of new buildings, or when the organisation has no internal FM expert or intelligent client function, or when relationships need a neutral broker.

Advantages
Professional management of services.

Disadvantages
Relationship is managed via a third-party, extra layer of management and costs, possible time delays and misinterpretation of requirements and issues.

Implication
This is a short-term strategy that is very useful when establishing FM for the first time, and it tends not to be a long-term solution or strategy due to its high cost.

4.21 Private Finance Initiative (PFI)

This model of FM developed in the 1990s in the UK as a result of the Government agenda to find new sources of finance and expertise in managing its estate. There are more details on this type of contract in Chapter 14.

Advantages
One point of contact for the organisation for the full service operation, including the construction phase. Payments are linked to availability of the services.

Disadvantages
Very long term contracts, which may cost more than other modes of FM in the long term. Few organisations operate in this market, so restricted choice for the client organisation.

Implications
The organisation needs to be clear in the early stages of its requirements and a rigorous change process, and many other processes, must be clearly agreed at the start of the contract.

4.22 Corporate PFI

This model of FM is based on the public sector PFI concept. Where extensive property portfolios are involved, finance directors and chief executives may choose to raise large sums for core business investment through what are effectively sale and leaseback or 'Property Outsourcing Schemes', while simultaneously reducing exposure to the risks of ownership of property. Abbey Bank (now part of Santander), Norwich Union (now trading as Aviva) and British Telecom are examples of large organisations that have adopted this strategy.

Such schemes have become known as corporate PFIs or real estate partnerships (REPs).

4.23 Special purpose vehicles (SPVs)

The large number of public and private sector PFI schemes have also created new types of TFM contractor and consortia working partnerships. The latter are often established in response to PFI customer requirements and specifications needed for large Build and Operate projects to draw on different strengths from the various parties. These consortia are generally referred to as SPVs. Some of these contractors and SPVs offer a wide and comprehensive range of sophisticated services from FM consultancy through to more traditional 'hands-on' service delivery, as well as providing construction and project management capabilities.

5 Outsourcing

5.1 Introduction

Historically, the desire to reduce operating costs has been the primary reason for outsourcing. Cost efficiencies have been the driving force behind FM outsourcing. By outsourcing, companies can take non-core activities off the balance sheet and concentrate on their core business. Companies recognise that outsourcing offers powerful forces for change through the innovations that outside specialists can bring. The typical FM services that have been outsourced to specialist contractors are catering, cleaning and security.

Companies can pick and choose from a sophisticated marketplace of suppliers for a diverse range of services from property management, space management and communications infrastructure to building maintenance, administration and contract management. Cost efficiencies are still critical in outsourcing the services to others; however, there is an increasing need for the outsourced contractor to innovate and add value to their service delivery.

FM services are not the only areas of outsourcing by an organisation. Other functions could be customer call centres, car fleet management, information management, human resource (personnel) management, financial management, training, payroll administration.

Where it suits a company to outsource, FM services can be arranged in any number of permutations. Some companies will manage as many as 50 or 60 outsourced service lines; others will bundle a group of services into a single contract. By consolidating a number of contracts, an organisation can expect real cost benefits, a more streamlined administration and a greater degree of flexibility. Integrated FM – where a provider takes on the entire outsourcing operation – takes this consolidation one stage further.

5.2 Multi-service contracts

Multi-service contracts dominate the FM market over single service contracts for several reasons. Significant cost savings can be made through the improved economies of scale, and a single point of contact gives a higher degree of accountability for the delivery of services. Reducing the number of suppliers reduces the administrative burden of procurement and contract administration for the organisation.

5.3 Best value

The UK public sector is made more attractive to FM companies by the government's desire to access private sector efficiency, competition and innovation. The concept of 'best value', for example, puts as much emphasis on quality as price. (Best Value in the public sector embraces the concepts of economy, efficiency and effectiveness.)

5.4 Longer contracts

The UK FM contracts are estimated to have an average duration of 4 years, with the research body Mintel estimating that around 50% of contracts are signed for over 4 years. The move for longer contracts is driven by the development of the PFI market, where the levels of commitment and capital are greater. Longer contracts allow more time for innovation to show benefits and reap the rewards and returns on the larger investments by the contractor(s).

5.5 Integrated FM solutions

The UK market has seen more 'single solution' FM companies targeting the strategic FM functions, such as property strategy, in their bid to win more contracts. The relationships between parties have become risk/reward sharing rather than traditional fee-based contracts. Advances in information technology allow payments to be tuned more finely to performance measurements. In addition, performance-based contracts are becoming more common. These contracts are where there is no service fee but performance is guaranteed and the savings are shared between operator and client.

5.6 Benefit analysis

There are advantages and disadvantages in contracting, outsourcing or using directly employed labour to deliver a maintenance service. The choice will depend on the location, the types of buildings, type and volume of work and the current workforce. Appropriate arrangements for emergency and out-of-hours call-outs need to be put in place. SLAs, KPIs and other methods of performance management may be introduced to effectively deliver the required level of service by the staff and contractors. Figure 5.1 shows that

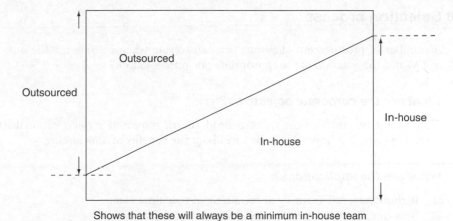

Shows that these will always be a minimum in-house team
retained for control and direction of outsourced organisation

Figure 5.1   Relationship between in-house and outsourced operations

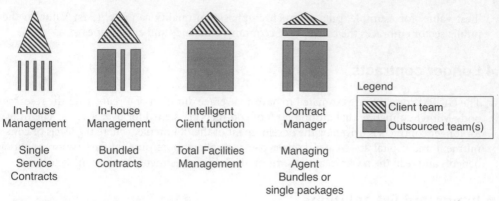

Figure 5.2   Outsourcing FM models

there will always be a minimum in-house team retained for control and direction of outsourced organisation.

5.7 FM outsourcing models

There are several stages or models that can be developed, as described in Chapter 4. Figure 5.2 shows the stages from the in-house management of single service contracts, through to the use of a management agent. The figure shows the relative size of the in-house FM function change in shape and size according to the model and the shift of management towards the outsourced provider. Some organisations may move progressvely through the various models, others will go directly from in-house to the PFI or the Total FM model.

5.8 Selection process

A number of procurement questions need answering when considering the outsourcing of FM and the selection of the appropriate outsourcing model.

What are the corporate objectives?

They might be cost cutting, reduced head count, improved service, rationalisation or something else. It is important to be sure about the benefits of outsourcing.

What are the implications?

❑   Redundancy, restructuring or retraining of redeployed staff.
❑   New or different monitoring and control systems.
❑   There is a need to be clear about the level of service required. An outsourced service might be quite different from that presently provided.

❏   An assessment of whether the costs incurred in tendering would be better spent on achieving improvements in a different way using the existing in-house team.
❏   Treatment of VAT.

What are the risks?

❏   Security.
❏   Loss of direct control of labour.
❏   Implications if a contractor fails to deliver.

The service specification

Getting the specification right is critical. The specification should emphasise the results required, not the methods the contractor should use to achieve them. The specification should incorporate a management structure and chain of command with the client organisation. **Appropriate** quality and **appropriate** performance measurement and review procedures should be included. Where possible, payment should be linked to performance improvement over time.

The theme of partnership should be developed with a view to a long term, mutually beneficial relationship.

What are the contractual issues?

The ability to terminate for non-performance must be built into an outsourcing contract. The advantages and disadvantages of long-term contracts should be borne in mind. Longer-term contracts should generate a better relationship but might lead to complacency, unless quality and performance are strictly monitored. Flexibility is important – not just in terms of break clauses – but in terms of delivery location and numbers served.

What are the considerations concerning potential suppliers?

As a part of the pre-tender process, a 'long' list of suppliers should be assessed as to their suitability for inclusion on a 'short' list to be invited to tender. The track record of any potential supplier should be examined. References should be taken both from customers and suppliers. These should give a lead as to the business ethics of contractors being considered as well as to their performance.

Quality assurance

BS 5750 registration provides evidence that the contractor's quality management system has been assessed as being effective and that there is evidence of a responsible attitude to quality prior to registration. It does not, however, provide evidence of a permanent quality culture. For larger organisations, a supplier with a geographical spread relative to their own spread may have economic and serviceability attractions.

Are there any particular tendering considerations?

❏   A simple system should be developed for objectively scoring tender submissions.
❏   Contract costs elements should be easily identifiable.

6 Financial Management

6.1 Introduction

FMs are usually responsible for budgets representing a significant percentage of an organisation's total expenditure. Financial information and performance is required by FMs in order to:

❑ Trend and benchmark information.
❑ Inform decisions.
❑ Prepare future budgets and requests for investment via business cases.
❑ Allocate funding to give appropriate services.
❑ Make allowances for the depreciation of assets.
❑ Repair or renew decision points.

The typical financial challenges faced by FMs include:

❑ Reducing overhead costs.
❑ Improving services, with same or less funds.
❑ Negotiating discounts from suppliers.
❑ Negotiating contracts for services with contractors and consultants.
❑ Value for money analysis.
❑ Business case preparation.
❑ Project budget management.
❑ Ensuring accurate charges for services on account (such as utilities, service fees, rates).

6.2 Financial systems and process

All managers should have a thorough understanding of financial systems and processes used in their organisation. Table 6.1 shows a glossary of financial terms frequently used. An organisation's finance department will be dealing with the forecasting and managing of cash flow, keeping track of income and expenditure, organising longer-term funding for new assets, recording financial information and providing monthly and annual financial statements. The main financial statements in business are the profit and loss account, the balance sheet and the cash flow statement. Managers should be aware of how the funds for their business are obtained, and how these are then used in that business.

The first aim of any business is to make a profit and increase the wealth of its owners, the shareholders. To do this, its income must be enough to cover all its daily costs and tax bills. In addition, it should have surplus income to spend on investment projects in future years. These could be the purchase of new equipment, new campaigns, or the modifications to the premises to ensure productive and safe working environments are provided. The generation of surplus income will enable the business to grow and improve its market position or provide more services to the community in the case of the public sector or a charity organisation. All organisations should also want to please their customers and reward their employees to ensure the loyalty of both.

6.3 The finance department

The organisational structure of the finance department and their interface with support and operational business departments will affect how the relationship is managed and nurtured. In some FM departments, there is sufficient volume of business to justify a dedicated member of staff dealing with financial matters. In either case, it is important there is an understanding of the FM issues by the finance staff, and equally an appreciation of financial matters by the FM.

The job of the finance department is to manage the organisation's money, and to ensure good governance and accountability of the financial transactions. Their principal activities are:

- ❏ Forecasting how profits or surplus are going to be made.
- ❏ Credit control and debt collection to keeping track of the income to ensure profits are made, or reserves are created in a not-for-profit organisation.
- ❏ Cash flow management to make sure that the organisation has sufficient cash to pay its bills (salaries, utilities, contract fees, supplier invoices, tax demands, expenses, rent and rates).
- ❏ Organising longer-term funding for new assets.
- ❏ Financial control by recording financial information (payments made, requests for payment).
- ❏ Producing monthly and annual financial statements.
- ❏ Production of management accounts.
- ❏ Monitoring variance against budget predictions.
- ❏ Assistance with preparation of business cases.
- ❏ Review of business cases.
- ❏ Investigation into suppliers' financial stability.
- ❏ Tax records and returns.
- ❏ Maintenance of asset inventory.

6.4 Financial controls

Control systems will increase the probability of an organisation achieving its objectives and encountering no unpleasant surprises. Without financial management controls, organisations may experience the impairment of assets, deficient revenues, excessive costs, inaccurate records and reports, legal sanctions and business interruption.

Controls can affect the inputs and outputs of business operations as well as the behaviour of employees. Managers as an intrinsic part of an organisation are both part of the problem and also the solution of management control. There are many alternatives for achieving good financial management control in organisations. Their selection is based on feasibility, degree of control needed, costs and management style. For controls to work, staff need to know what the desired actions or results are expected of them, and they need to be able to influence the outcome. Good control is said to exist when failure is possible, but detected in a timely and unbiased way to ensure corrective action can be taken. Controls should therefore be future orientated and objective driven. Clearly, it is therefore important for the competent FM to develop a good working relationship with the finance department, to understand the control measures in place to ensure that the right infrastructure services are delivered at the right time, place and price.

6.5 Financial statements

These are produced by organisations to show shareholders, owners and investors the financial status of the business. Not-for-profit organisations also use these standard methods to record their financial status:

❑ The profit and loss account.
❑ The balance sheet.
❑ The cash flow statement.

6.6 Finance and the FM

The FM needs to understand these company financial documents because:

❑ The costs of facilities may affect the profitability of the business. Facilities costs in many organisations represent the second largest cost after the payroll for staff. Much of the facilities costs are considered an overhead, which reduces the margins and scope for profit from the activities of the organisation.
❑ The discretionary nature of some facilities services results in frequent requests for reductions in services to generate savings on the budget expenditure.

This means FMs have to develop good working relationship with colleagues in their finance departments. Collaboration will be more productive if managers understand what finance does, why certain information is needed and what it is used for. Table 6.2 shows the users and purposes of financial information.

6.7 Sources of funding

An organisation needs funds, known as capital, to start a business. This is because the business will need to spend money at the outset in order to generate income. Typical start-up costs are the rent of premises, advertising, raw materials and wages.

If the person starting the business has enough money, they will probably use some of it. If they don't have enough, they will probably approach:

❑ Other people who may be invited to become shareholders. They put in capital and receive shares in return. This funding is known as share capital.

Table 6.2   Users of financial information

User	Purpose
The shareholders (owners) of the business	To find out if the business is doing well, and whether the directors are doing a good job running it.
Banks and lenders	To find out whether the business can manage its finances and is profitable. This would be important if the business was asking for a loan.
Creditors (trade suppliers)	To find out if the firm pays its bills on time and has good cash flow. This will help them decide whether or not to give credit.
Company management	To control and manage the business.
Analysts and advisors	To assess the business in order to advise potential new shareholders and lenders whether to invest money in the company.
Employees and their representatives	To assess the firm's potential for continuous and profitable employment.
The government, and their representative agencies	Financial statements are a legal obligation, and are also the starting point for tax calculations
Customers and other business contacts	To find out how well the firm is performing when trying to decide whether to do business with the organisation.

❑ Banks or other lenders of funds.
❑ Suppliers who can offer credit as a source of funding.
❑ Venture capital providers.
❑ Government agencies for grants.

Once the business is making profits, it can use these profits to reinvest in the business. This source of funding is known as retained profits.

6.8 Use of funding

Once the business has got funding, it will use it:

❑ To purchase fixed assets – these are the large items such as equipment and machinery.
❑ To stay afloat until customers start paying – this 'float' money is known as working capital and will be spent on paying wages, buying stocks, paying for advertising, rent and all the day-to-day costs of running a business.

In the longer term, funding may also be used for investment in other profitable activities.

6.9 Fixed assets

Fixed assets are purchased and owned by the business to generate profits. They are not likely to be sold in the normal course of business, hence the name 'fixed'. The fixed assets can be either 'tangible' or 'intangible'.

Tangible assets are ones that can be seen and touched such as land and buildings. Intangible assets cannot be seen or touched. The most common intangible fixed asset is goodwill. This is often bought when purchasing another business, as part of getting the trade and custom that the owner has built up, and a monetary value is often agreed for that goodwill. Patents, trademarks and brand names are other examples of intangible assets.

6.10 Working capital

Working capital is the 'float' funding which is used to keep a business going until they generate cash. A certain amount of the organisation's money will always be tied up in its 'float'. At any point in time these funds are likely to be invested in:

❑   Stocks or inventories of products (manufacturing companies).
❑   Customers who owe money, known as trade debtors.
❑   Cash deposits in the bank account.

However, organisations also get short-term credit to help the cash flow and management of the working capital. Sources of this credit are:

❑   The bank (an approved overdraft or loan).
❑   Creditors – those to whom money is owed.
❑   Suppliers – when payment terms are longer than the sales of the goods to customers.
❑   Inland revenue – payment of taxes in arrears.
❑   Shareholders who are owed dividends.

These creditors reduce the need for working capital. The precise definition of working capital used by accountants is therefore:

Current Assets less Current Liabilities = Net Current Assets (net working capital).

6.11 Investments

These are assets which don't relate to the business's normal activities but still generate income such as:

❑   Shares in other companies.
❑   Other companies that have been purchased outright.
❑   Loans to others which generate interest charges as an income.

6.12 The balance sheet

Funding and assets are put together to make up the balance sheet. The balance sheet shows both where the funds have come from and how they have been used. Funding should equal assets otherwise the balance sheet does not 'balance'.

Investors and lenders use the balance sheet to see how much debt and cash the company has, and to find out whether it is managing money efficiently.

6.13 The profit and loss account

This shows all the income and expenditure for a given period. It will show whether the company has made a profit or loss.

Start-up organisations often make a loss in the first few years until they become established, but in the long term, a business must make a surplus or profits. Lenders and investors may not be prepared to continue investing in the organisation without getting a dividend or return on their investment.

The profit and loss account shows income and expenditure but does **not** indicate if that income has been received or those expenses paid. Thus it does not give an entire picture of a company's financial health. A company could have a huge overdraft and be unable to pay its employees, due to not having received payment from customers, yet it could still show a profit in theory but not in reality.

6.14 Cash flow statement

This shows how much cash the business has generated in the year and what it has been spent on. The business will generate cash from:

- ❑ Trading (after paying all trading expenses).
- ❑ Selling fixed assets.
- ❑ New borrowings or taking credit from suppliers.
- ❑ New money invested by shareholders.
- ❑ Receiving interest.
- ❑ Selling part of the business.

Cash is spent on:

- ❑ Fixed assets.
- ❑ Repaying debt and giving loans to customers.
- ❑ Paying dividends.
- ❑ Paying interest.
- ❑ Investments.

The difference between these two is the net increase or decrease in cash for the year.

Investors and lenders are very interested to see where their money has gone and the cash flow statement has become very strict in its format to give a complete picture.

6.15 Performance measurement

FMs may need to look at a set of accounts for new suppliers or new contractors to make decisions on current and future relationships with these organisations. It is important to determine how well the business has performed in the past to inform decisions about risks in relationships with suppliers that support the FM function. Two key aspects to look for in any performance analysis or financial comparison are:

- ❑ profitability;
- ❑ liquidity (how well they are managing cash).

6.16 Profitability

Profits in general should be increasing year on year. However, just looking at the profit figures doesn't indicate how much money has been invested to generate those profits. There are number of key profitability ratios used to determine the profitability of an organisation:

❑ Return on capital employed (ROCE).
❑ Gross profit margin.
❑ Net profit margin.

Return on capital employed
'Return' is the net profit (before interest and tax). Capital employed is the total long-term investment in the company.

$$\text{ROCE} = \frac{\text{Net profit (before interest and tax)}}{\text{Long-term debt} + \text{shareholders funds (includes reserves)}} \times 100$$

Gross profit margin
This can be calculated from the profit and loss account.

$$\text{Gross profit margin} = \frac{\text{Gross profit}}{\text{Sales}} \times 100$$

Net profit margin
This can also be calculated from the profit and loss account as follows:

$$\text{Net profit margin} = \frac{\text{Net profit}}{\text{Turnover (sales)}} \times 100$$

6.17 Liquidity

Liquidity ratios are used to indicate how well an organisation is managing their day-to-day cash. A business must have enough money to pay its debts. A common cause of business failure is simply running out of cash and being unable therefore to pay the bills. There are several ratios that indicate the ability of organisations to meet their debts:

❑ Current ratio.
❑ Quick ratio.
❑ Interest cover.

Current ratio
This looks at the assets which an organisation could quickly turn into cash, and compares it with the short-term debts to see if there is enough cash to meet the debts. This can be calculated from the balance sheet as follows:

$$\text{Current ratio} = \frac{\text{Current assets}}{\text{Current liabilities}}$$

Quick ratio

This is similar to the current ratio, but ignores stock as it is argued that this cannot always be turned into cash quickly.

$$\text{Quick ratio} = \frac{\text{Current assets} - \text{Stock}}{\text{Current liabilities}}$$

A ratio of less than 1 is often seen as being too low, because not enough cash could be raised quickly to pay current liabilities. Despite this, it is not uncommon in certain industries.

The main cause of liquidity problems is the inability to manage debtors. By allowing customers too long to pay for the services or goods supplied, the organisation can run out of cash. When investigating the cause of cash flow problems, the accountants can review how long customers are taking to pay, and compare this to previous years or to competitors figures. A credit control management system is required to follow up late payments and ensure payments are collected on time. A typical measure is the number of debtor days.

$$\text{Debtor days} = \frac{\text{Debtors}}{\text{Turnover (if all sales are on credit)}} \times 365$$

6.18 Liquidity issues

Another cause of liquidity problems is when an organisation pays their creditors too quickly, before the due date of payment.

Consider this scenario:

An FM does a large one-off deal with a stationery supplier, agreeing to receive a 1% discount if payment is made within 7 days. The offer seems too good to refuse and the FM agrees over the phone.

This could cause serious cash flow problems if the business normally pays its suppliers on 30-day terms, since the cash may not be available until then. If the large payment has to be brought forward then other more important payments, such as wages, may have to be put back, causing widespread concern amongst employees.

A business will keep track of how long it is taking to pay creditors using creditor days.

$$\text{Creditor days} = \frac{\text{Creditors}}{\text{Cost of sales}} \times 365$$

6.19 Annual reports of accounts

It is a legal obligation to keep records on the financial transactions of an organisation. These are known as the accounts. All limited companies must keep accounts and send them to the Registrar at Companies House, each year. For most companies, these accounts will include:

❑ A balance sheet.
❑ A profit and loss account.

and in addition:

❑   An auditors' report.
❑   A directors' report.
❑   Notes to the accounts.

The auditors' report

Most companies have to have their accounts audited by a chartered or certified accountant. The auditors' report is crucial. If the auditors are satisfied that the accounts give a 'true and fair' view of the company's affairs, then the report will be 'unqualified'.

If they are not satisfied, they may 'qualify' the report and state what issues they are concerned about. If the auditors are concerned then this will clearly cause concern amongst shareholders and lenders.

The directors' report

This gives summary information about the company relating to the accounting period. This could include issues such as corporate responsibility, environmental performance, market changes, remuneration of directors, bonus and share save schemes, acquisitions and disposals.

Notes to the accounts

The notes give more detailed analysis of some figures in the profit and loss account and balance sheet. The notes must also include a description of accounting policies and indicate the general accounting methods and assumptions used in preparing the accounts.

Third parties use the notes to see:

❑   How much was paid to directors?
❑   Any future commitments that have been made by the company that will not show up in the accounts.
❑   Any legal action that is ongoing and may result in financial penalties.
❑   Other 'contingent liabilities', i.e. sums of money that will be incurred if certain events happen.

6.20 Recent developments in financial accounting

It is now a legal obligation for companies listed on a European Stock Exchange to prepare their financial statements in line with the new International Financial Reporting Standards (IFRS).

IFRS and FM

For FMs, the most significant issue is the treatment of leases in the accounts. The international standard (IAS 17) excludes leases for investment property but covers all other leases.

FMs may come across building leases, equipment leases (such as photocopiers) and even vehicle leases, and the rules are relevant for all of these.

Under the IFRS rules, different treatment is required for 'finance leases' which are used to ultimately purchase an asset, and 'operating leases' where the asset is returned to the leasing company after a certain period of time. Auditors will thus pay particular attention to these leases and how they have been dealt with in the accounts. These rules may be subject to change in the future, so FMs need to keep up to date through regular dialogue with colleagues in the finance department.

6.21 Budgets

Management cannot control the future progress of a business without a plan of action and the constant efforts to find out whether the plan is being achieved. A budget is a financial plan. Budgetary control is concerned with the fixing of the plan and the use of controlling efforts to achieve it with constant comparisons of actual performance to the budget. For budgetary control to be successful, the organisation needs good communications, appropriate decision making at the right levels and acceptance by the managers concerned for the responsibility of the results.

An organisation will have a master budget, summarising the overall financial plan. This will be made up of departmental operational (or revenue) budgets and capital budgets. Revenue (operational) expenditure deals with the short-term purchase of goods and services required to keep the business going, and occurs within one financial year. Capital expenditure is associated with fixed assets, which tend to have a value over several years. Both types of costs will be managed on a monthly basis to monitor the impact on the organisation's cash flow, and the funding to service these costs in the form of borrowing or loans. After all the costs have been determined by the organisation, cost apportionment or absorption costing is then applied. Departments will then be allocated their operational monthly budget.

Facilities-related budgets often represent a significant proportion of an organisation's total expenditure, on average 10–15% of the turnover. In some sectors, such as student accommodation, catering operations and conference management in the university sector, the FM budget also represents a significant income to the organisation too.

6.22 Roles of budgets

Budgets may have a number of different roles within an organisation. If a budget takes on more than one role in an organisation, then this may lead to conflict.

Table 6.3 shows the range of roles. This is particularly relevant if the same budget is used for both performance evaluation and for planning. Budgets set for performance will be set at an achievable target, whereas budgets set for motivation will be set at a difficult target. Using such budgets for planning and forecasting will be of little use due to the variances.

Table 6.3   Roles of budgets

1	A system of authorisation
2	A means of forecasting and planning
3	A channel of communication and co-ordination
4	A motivational device
5	A means of performance evaluation and control
6	A basis for decision making

Budget preparation tends to follow the structure of an organisation, although the amount of consultation and ownership by managers varies both within organisations and from one company to another. Typically, departments or functions within an organisation will be set up as responsibility centres, and these may be cost, profit or investment centres. If set up correctly, then the efficiency and effectiveness of such centres can be measured via the accounting data.

Budget setting

Research has found that managers tend to set easier rather than more difficult budgets as they see this as in their own interest to incorporate a bit of slack into the budget estimates. It has also been found that some managers may agree budgets that are impossible to achieve just to gain senior management approval. Bias in the budget setting process may be caused by the type of reward system, past history of budget achievement and the insecurity of managers.

Budgetary control

Budgetary control determines the financial plan and then monitors it with constant comparisons of actual performance to the expected budget. Budgetary control requires the full range of general management skills, including:

❑ Planning.
❑ Preparation, administration and co-ordination.
❑ Communication.
❑ Reporting.
❑ Reconciliation and analysis.
❑ Change management.
❑ Evaluation and review.

Planning is about forecasting, gathering information on the services required and their likely costs. Budgeting is an annual process, often starting 6 months prior to the new financial year. In some organisations, budgets are prepared on a rolling basis and so the budgetary planning is a recurring activity at predetermined intervals in the business calendar.

6.23 Budget design

The process of budget design will depend on the certainty of objectives in an organisation and the ability to identify results. Costs are required as part of the budget design process and the preparation of the budgets. Budgets can be prepared in two ways. The first way requires a previous budget, and involves looking at the previous and current year and then using an agreed index to increase (or decrease) each budget line. An alternative method, referred to as a zero-based budgeting, is when a budget is built up from nothing or a zero basis. Using the previous year's budget, and an inflationary percentage, is not good practice as it can lead to inaccurate forecasts and budgets. The advantage of the zero-based budgetary approach is that it focuses attention on actual need and appropriate costs. It encourages an examination of the reasons why services are provided, and the true costs of all services. A zero based budget is required if starting up a new building or new service.

Table 6.4   Examples of FM costs

Capital costs	Revenue or operational costs
Plant	Service contract
Equipment	Employees and employment costs
Construction projects	Consumable
Vehicles	Rent, rates, service charges
IT equipment	Travel
	Depreciation
	Energy
	Insurance

6.24 Capital or revenue

Preparation of budgets involves the use of the appropriate cost centres for recording the financial information. There are two main types of expenditure, capital and revenue. Table 6.4 shows the range of costs. Revenue expenditure typically deals with the purchase of goods and services and tends to be in the short term, and with the purchase or expense made within a single financial year. Capital expenditure is associated with fixed assets which tend to have a value over several years, and the spend profile tends to occur over more than one financial year.

6.25 Property costs

There are two major elements to property costs – the costs of occupation and the cost of the property itself. Occupation costs will be the primary concern to FMs, and may include rents, rates, leases, service charges, service contracts or maintenance costs. In most cases, the amount of space determines the occupancy costs, so it is important to appreciate the link between space management, the estate role and financial control.

Normally the FM budget will have several functional groupings such as property and premises costs, business support costs and staff support costs. These could be further sub-divided as shown in Table 6.5.

6.26 Budget variances

Managers use budgets to ensure that their costs do not exceed their income or revenue. The difference between target and actual is called a 'variance'. If the variance is less than has been budgeted – it is a 'favourable' variance. If it is over the budget, it is an 'adverse' variance. Adverse variances need drastic action and may be investigated by the finance department. Variation reports are outputs of budgetary control, informing managers of financial performance. Budget variances may be caused by:

❑   Inefficiency of operation.
❑   The plan being incorrect originally.
❑   Poor communication of the budgetary goals.

Table 6.5   FM cost categories

Main category	Service or activity	Average (%)
Property and premises	Rent, rates, insurance	33
	Building services	7
	Fabric maintenance	1
	Grounds	0.5
	Minor works	5
	Cleaning	8
	Security	5
	Utilities	10
Business support	Archiving	0.5
	Reprographics	5
	Stationery	2
	Voice services	1
	Data services	1
	Post and mailroom	1
	Transport and fleet	0.5
	Porterage	0.5
	Business travel	0.5
	Furniture	0.5
	Office equipment	0.5
Staff support	Catering	16
	Fitness	0.5
	Well-being services	0.5
	Help desk	0.5

❑ Actions of other departments and external forces.
❑ Random fluctuations in prices from suppliers
❑ Clerical or typographical errors.

6.27 Cost data

Obtaining good quality data and inputs into the budgetary planning process is critical. Sources of data to help the FM include prices and schedules in contracts, pricing books, staff costs from payroll and contractor budgets. Costs are required in business to make a decision and to provide a means of control. Costs can be described in two ways:

❑ Fixed and variable costs.
❑ Direct and indirect costs.

Table 6.6 shows examples of fixed and variable costs.

Fixed costs
Every organisation, and indeed every department, has 'fixed costs', which are incurred whether or not the services are used. A good example is the cost of the property that an organisation is renting and paying rates for. The lease is a fixed cost, regardless of whether the premises are actually used or not. These costs are called 'fixed', because they do not change with the amount of use.

Table 6.6   Examples of fixed and variable costs in the FM budget

Fixed costs	Variable costs
Rent	Consumables
Rate	Maintenance
Service charges	Repairs
Leases	Energy
Contracts	Reprographics
Tax	Travel and transport
Insurance	Post/couriers
Employment costs of staff	IT – telephone fax mobiles

Here are some other examples of 'fixed costs'.

❑   Mortgage.
❑   Maintenance service contracts.
❑   Employment or salary costs.
❑   Hire purchase costs on equipment.

Variable or marginal costs
'Variable or marginal costs' are those that increase with usage. In the production department of an organisation, direct costs are the basic wages and variable costs are the overtime and bonuses that may be needed to meet particular manufacturing or operation schedules.

Ordering materials is another example. Usually the more materials that are purchased in bulk, the better the discount from the supplier. Materials or consumables are therefore considered variable as they can be increased or decreased depending on the requirement and usage.

6.28 Cost accounting

Cost accounting is required in an organisation to set prices of services and products and to measure efficiency. Costs are determined by identifying what resources are used to provide the product or service. Costs are said to be variable or fixed. The variable costs change with volume, whereas the fixed costs tend to vary with time. Total costs are the sum of both fixed and variable costs. Costs are also classified as direct and indirect. Cost allocation will attribute the direct costs of a function to that function, e.g. salaries of staff solely employed in that function. Cost apportionment is required to charge the indirect costs to a function; these are typically overheads. There are two main costing methods – marginal and absorption.

(1) Absorption costing
The absorption rate that best measures the consumption of overhead resources by the product or service should be chosen. Usually time is used to measure the use of overheads – such as labour hours or machine hours. It is important to use the appropriate constraint that limits the production capacity – i.e. labour or equipment. Absorption costing implies that fixed costs behave in a similar way to variable costs.

(2) Marginal costing
It is argued by some that because fixed overhead costs are time based and variable costs are volume based they should be treated differently. In the marginal costing method, overheads

are ignored as the cost of one more unit is its marginal cost. Marginal costs are perhaps of more use to management decision making. However, absorption costing is still much used in business as the preferred method because in the long term, all costs are variable.

Overhead costs

If a department or function of an organisation were to be independent then overheads such as the building, equipment and administration would be required. Apportionment of the overhead is an attempt to approximate these costs across the organisation. The charge to occupiers for space utilisation which includes rent, rates, utilities and service costs is a typical application of apportionment costing in the FM context. Apportioning costs can be a substitute for market forces. If an external supplier provides services, then the manager is aware of costs and could change supplier if dissatisfied. When these services are provided in-house, they will be cheaper, but there is a reduced freedom of choice. By apportioning costs of these services, managers are made aware of the costs, and they can put pressure on the service provider if quality or price deteriorates. This in turn instils a discipline into the service providers that may be less likely if costs are not apportioned in the organisation.

Impact of costing methods selected

The apportionment of costs is said to simplify complex accounting issues, motivate decision makers and co-ordinate decisions in a decentralised organisation. Such costs serve as a constraint on a manager's consumption of prerequisites and an approximation of the 'difficult to observe' costs. Apportionment costs can be considered as a lump sum tax to reduce the profitability or increase the costs of a unit. They act as a restraint on discretionary expenditure.

There are, however, negative aspects of absorption and apportionment costing methods. Managers are judged on costs that they have little or no control over. Managers may waste time and effort trying to control the uncontrollable. Some managers may ignore all costs on the basis that they have no control over them. In some cases, it can lead to increased production and higher volumes irrespective of the consequences of other departments. It is important to maintain sight of the cause–effect relationship of overheads to a product or service.

6.29 Cost centres

A service department is a department that makes no profit, but provides a service to the whole organisation. Examples include payroll, personnel, facilities, IT and finance departments. They are a cost that the company incurs in order to provide a service that is both internal and external to the organisation. Departments that are directly involved in the primary activities of an organisation are known as profit centres. Examples include manufacturing, production departments, sales and marketing departments. However, these departments need the service departments in order to operate.

Indirect costs/overheads

As every department uses service departments, most organisations charge the running costs of service departments to profitable departments or profit centres. This is an 'indirect cost' that profitable departments incur, sometimes referred to as the overhead. This is called 'cost apportionment'.

The cost apportionment can be based on a number of factors:

❏ Usage of service, based on preceding year.
❏ Number of employees.
❏ Floor space occupied.

Using floor space factor, indirect costs for cleaning would be based on the square footage. Where an organisation only charges those departments that are responsible for the overheads or indirect costs, the method is termed 'absorption costing'.

Example – effluent waste treatment is an overhead created by the manufacturing and production departments. Absorption costing will share out the cost between these departments evenly, depending on the amount of use by each.

Direct costs

These are the costs directly attributable to that department's operation and would typically include:

❏ Wages for labour.
❏ Overtime/bonuses.
❏ Machine breakdown maintenance.
❏ Equipment.
❏ Purchases.

In general, every department has direct costs and some also have indirect costs. Most direct and indirect costs are also occasionally 'variable' costs. An example of this is overtime/bonuses in a production department. It is a direct cost as it is directly attributable to production, but it is also a variable cost as it will change with use.

The FM department indirectly does not make money as a cost centre. Therefore it is an indirect cost to all departments and will be recovered by cost apportionment or absorption costing. However, some FM departments may run as a profit centre and will charge out their services with an extra margin to cover all incidentals. When user departments are charged for the use of FM services, the occupant users take a keener interest in the costs of the services and their impact. When company wide budget cuts occur, there is a need to renegotiate provision of services and service levels so that each department can meet their new budget constraints.

6.30 Cash flow

Cash flow is concerned with the cash generated and spent in any given period. The flow of cash may be monitored daily or less frequently depending on the size and type of organisation. Key principles involved are knowing whether costs are fixed or variable; being aware of the timing of payments (such as utility, rates and rent bills), ensuring there is enough cash to meet commitments (such as the payroll and suppliers) and knowing what is owed to creditors and owing from debtors.

Cash flow forecasting

This requires the following:

- ☐ Monitoring the outgoing expenditure.
- ☐ Knowing fixed and variable costs.
- ☐ Being aware of the timing of payments.
- ☐ Matching incoming payments against outgoing expenditure.
- ☐ Ensuring enough funds to meet commitments.
- ☐ Knowing what is owed to creditors, and owing from debtors.

The cash budget is a vital forecasting tool. When a cash shortage in the coming months is foreseen, an organisation may be able to do something about it. Many businesses fail because they either don't foresee cash flow problems or see them too late. They may be making a profit but the money is not being received quickly enough to balance the payments. Unless they can manage the cash flow, they will run out of cash and be forced into liquidation.

Elements of the cash budget

- ☐ Receipts – including sales and other cash receipts such as rent from a tenant, sales of fixed assets, shareholder cash input.
- ☐ Expenses – including trade purchases and other payments such as tax and dividends, purchases of fixed assets and loan repayments.
- ☐ The opening bank balance shows what is expected in the current account at the start of the month.
- ☐ The net cash flow is totalled receipts less totalled payments.
- ☐ The closing balance is the sum expected in the current account at the end of the month.
- ☐ Each month's closing balance is next month's opening balance.
- ☐ Brackets indicate an overdraft or negative balance.

Corrective action

As long as a company is profitable, most cash flow problems can be dealt with given sufficient notice. Possible corrective action that could be taken may include:

- ☐ Negotiate a higher overdraft limit.
- ☐ Reduce credit terms to customers to 30 days or less.
- ☐ Ensure purchase payments are paid at due date and not before.
- ☐ Sell an asset that is no longer needed.
- ☐ Negotiate credit terms to extend payments.
- ☐ Defer purchase of equipment (capital expenditure).
- ☐ Renegotiate interest on loans.
- ☐ Delay salary and expenses payments to staff.

Using cash forecasts

It is important to understand that the cash flow forecast is only a forecast, and that even if the cash manager has taken every step to ensure that the business has enough cash, there can still be cash shortages. The basic causes are:

❑ Sales income does not arrive on time.
❑ Sales revenue falls suddenly.
❑ The business has to make unexpected cash payments.

Cash management options

It is not usually possible to extend the overdraft at short notice, although banks will sometimes agree to a temporary extension. This option cannot therefore be relied on. If sales income does not arrive on time, and the overdraft is already at its limit, accountants can:

❑ Decide on what is essential to be paid.
❑ Delay or cut non-essential payments.
❑ Delay essential payments, such as salaries and taxes.

If sales revenue falls suddenly the business should:

❑ Reduce purchases in line with sales.
❑ Reduce expenses and overtime.

6.31 Tax

The UK Government's annual budget and its attendant Finance Act incrementally change the tax rules each year. FMs do not need to be tax experts but they do need at least a basic understanding of the tax system. This is essential if tax efficient facilities budgets are to be prepared and managed. Activities such as food sales in catering and vending services, provision of uniform and company cars to employees and funding of capital and disability projects have taxation implications.

There are several taxes that could impact on FM:

❑ Income Tax and Corporation Tax.
❑ Capital Gains Tax.
❑ Value Added Tax.
❑ Stamp Duty.
❑ Inheritance Tax.

6.32 Value Added Tax (VAT)

VAT is a purchase and sales tax charged by the government on the supply of goods, services and imports or acquisitions into the UK. It was introduced in 1973 when the UK joined the European Community. It is a self-assessed tax and stringent rules for registration based on taxable supplies exceeding, or being expected to exceed, a prescribed annual limit. The seller collects the tax on behalf of the government and sends quarterly VAT returns to the Customs and Excise computer centre. HM Customs and Excise (HMCE) through local Valuation Offices administer VAT. There are heavy penalties for persistent late submissions of returns. VAT has applied to construction and property matters since 1988. Unless the goods or services supplied to their customers are zero-rated, or their turnover is very small (the threshold changes each year in the annual budget round in the Finance Act), most organisations are required to register for VAT and charge their customers VAT. The tax on a taxable supply is known as **output tax**. The tax paid on supplies received is **input** tax.

VAT liability is categorised as follows:

Taxable

VAT is normally liable at the standard rate of 17.5%. The taxpayer (defined by HMCE as 'The Trader') must add 17.5% to the disposal price or other income. However, the trader can offset the VAT paid on business expenditure against the tax due to HMCE. Examples of taxable supplies are construction services and goods, the services provided by a professional team (architect, etc.) and specialists such as M&E consultants and so on. There are complex rules relating to the sale of interests in buildings and land, and the grant of leases. Note that under certain circumstances, these may be exempt from tax. A reduced rate of 5.0% is charged on the installation of certain energy-saving materials to the supply of domestic fuel and power used in the home and by charities. Reduced rates are also applicable to car child seats and smoking cessation products. VAT tax rates must be subject to change in future years.

Zero-rated supplies

These supplies are taxed at zero, 0%. This category enables a trader to recover from HMCE the VAT that he suffers on expenditure, even though he does not have to charge his customer VAT. Zero-rated supplies are taxable supplies, even though no tax is payable by the customer. Some examples of zero-rated supplies are:

❑ Food and drink (but not confectionery, meals in restaurants and hot food take-aways).
❑ Young childrens' clothing and footwear.
❑ Books, newspapers and journals.
❑ Stamps.
❑ Drugs and medicines on prescription.
❑ Equipment for the disabled.
❑ Passenger travel and transport (but not taxis or hire-cars).
❑ Exports and services to overseas traders.
❑ New domestic buildings, mobile homes and houseboats.

Note that for the purpose of VAT, residential buildings include a 'home' or other institution, accommodation for school pupils and students, monasteries or nunneries.

Exempt supplies

These are supplies not within the VAT system. An exempt trader does not have to charge VAT to his customers but pays VAT on expenditure. Examples of exempt supplies are those made by banks, charities and educational bodies, and include:

❑ Most sales, leases and lettings of land and buildings.
❑ Financial services.
❑ Insurance.
❑ Certain educational services and training.
❑ Most health care.
❑ Postal services.

❑   Most betting, gaming and lotteries.
❑   Certain supplies by undertakers.
❑   Membership of professional bodies and trade unions.

The makers of exempt supplies cannot recover input tax, that is to say, any VAT they have paid to their suppliers. Under certain circumstances, there may be eligibility to exercise an option to tax otherwise exempt supplies, depending on the type of disposal or category of use. Examples are qualifying buildings, the freehold sale of undeveloped land or land with mature development. The effect of exercising the option is that taxable inputs relating to that particular supply may be recovered from the date the option was exercised. Where rent is a consideration for exempt supply, then service charges are also a consideration for exempt supply. Where rent is a consideration as a standard rated supply under the 'option to tax', then service charges are a further consideration for standard rated supply. Landlords are advised to warn tenants well in advance if they intend to exercise an 'option to supply' because the VAT arising from the exercise of the option will be a new charge to tenants, who may not be able to claim it as input tax. It may also have an adverse affect on cash flow.

This means that the organisations that supply exempt supplies do not have to charge VAT on these goods and services. However, these organisations cannot claim back VAT on expenses either.

NB: There have been recent appeals by leading organisations to the HMCE to change the way VAT is charged on business catering and hospitality. FMs are advised to check the situation regarding issue of free food or accommodation to particular groups of staff as this may be considered as a taxable benefit in kind that has to be declared.

It is important to appreciate the difference between zero rating and VAT exemption. Zero rating carries a theoretical rate of VAT, which just happens to be 0%. Exemption means that no VAT applies at all.

On the face of it there appears to be no difference between the two, but there is a significant one. If the goods sold are zero-rated, the seller can still claim VAT on their purchases. However, if a seller's organisation is exempt, they cannot reclaim the VAT on their inputs (purchases) because they cannot register for VAT.

VAT on rent, leases and service charges

Many FMs may be surprised to see lettings listed as an exempt supply, knowing that they are charged VAT on rent.

Since 1989 landlords have had the option to charge VAT on rent and leases relating to land and buildings. Once having opted to tax, every subsequent sale must be taxed and the option is irrevocable.

Some landlords choose this option because it means they can claim back VAT on supplies. This is often VAT which they would be charged anyway but cannot reclaim as long as their rental income is exempt.

If a tenant is charged VAT on the rent, then the tenant will also be charged VAT on their service charges due to the landlord.

6.33 Landfill Tax

Landfill Tax applies to waste disposed of at landfill sites in the UK licensed under environmental law. Liability rests with the landfill site operators who in turn pass on the costs to their customers by way of commercial disposal rates.

6.34 Climate Change Levy

This tax was first introduced in 2001, and has thresholds reset each year. It was established in response to the Kyoto Agreement, to reduce impacts on climate change. To reduce carbon emissions, businesses are taxed depending on how much fossil fuel they use. The levy is charged on taxable supplies of a taxable commodity. Taxable commodities are as follows:

❑   Electricity.
❑   Natural gas as supplied by a gas utility.
❑   Petroleum and hydrocarbon gas in a liquid state.
❑   Coal and lignite.
❑   Coke and semi-coke of coal or lignite.
❑   Petroleum coke.

The levy is charged at a specific rate per unit of energy. There is a separate rate for each category of taxable commodity. The rates are based on the energy content of each commodity and are expressed in kilowatt-hours (kWh) for gas and electricity, and in kilograms for liquid petroleum gas and other taxable commodities.
    Rates in 2009 (and likely to be continued in 2010/11) are:

❑   Gas 0.16 p/kWh.
❑   Coal 1.17 p/kg (equivalent to gas levy).
❑   Liquefied petroleum gas (LPG) 1.05 p/kg (equivalent to 0.07/kWh).
❑   Electricity 0.47 p/kWh.

The levy does not apply to fuels used by the domestic or transport sector, or fuels used for the production of other forms of energy or for non-energy purposes. The levy does not apply to energy used by registered charities for non-business uses and energy used by very small firms.
    The levy does not apply to oils, which are already subject to excise duty. Certain renewable energy forms are exempt from the levy.

6.35 Business rates

Within the UK, a uniform business rate (UBR) is tax charged to every business organisation based upon the value of the property that they occupy. All commercial properties are assessed at the prevailing market rent levels by the Inland Revenue Valuation Office, and a rateable value calculated and fixed for a certain period of time. For occupied property, the UBR is added to this value to calculate the total sum payable for rates. In recent years, the UK government has changed the rules on UBR for empty and unoccupied premises.
    The FM should be aware of these rules, together with the following opportunities for effective financial management:

❑   Unoccupied offices and retail property are no longer entitled to a 50% reduction in rates – the full sum is required.

❑ Unoccupied industrial properties and warehouses have 6 months exemption from the rates and thereafter, they pay the full rateable sum.
❑ Unoccupied listed buildings still qualify for exemption status, and pay no rates when empty.
❑ Appeals may be made against rating assessments, for which an expert surveyor's services should be sought.
❑ Where the property assets have changed materially – through part demolition, for example – then rate liability may be reduced.
❑ External factors such as neighbouring road works or building works can reduce the rateable value.

6.36 Stamp duty

Stamp duty has been in existence since the 17th century. It is payable on legal documents associated with property transactions or company share dealings. However, it also applies to the surrender of a lease where no document exists. Examples of documents in property transactions are a conveyance or transfer on sale and leases. Rates of stamp duty vary upwards from 1%. FMs should be aware that it applies not only to the purchase of property but also to new leases. The rates of this duty are subject to change in the annual Government budget announcements.

6.37 Income Taxes

Personal Income Tax is charged on the annual income of individuals. The UK enjoys the dubious honour of being the first country to introduce income tax. It was in 1799 that a tax at the rate of 2 shillings in the pound (10%) on all incomes in excess of £200, with lower rates applying to incomes between £60 and £200 was introduced. The tax was introduced to finance the Napoleonic Wars. The tax was allowed to lapse for a while after the end of the wars but became a permanent feature of the UK tax system as far back as 1880.

Corporation Tax is charged on the profits of companies and unincorporated bodies such as members clubs. 'Profits' include all sorts of income surplus (other than dividends) and also capital gains. Corporation Tax is charged on the world profits of resident companies. Non-UK companies with subsidiaries in the UK are charged on the profits arising in the UK. Double taxation relief is available where profits are taxed twice (i.e. in both the UK and the home nation).

Examples of UK Income Tax on which liabilities arise as a result of income are:

❑ Rents from leases. Premiums may also be liable for Capital Gains Tax.
❑ Dealing in property, which is assessed on the basis of annual profit.
❑ Dividends received from shares in property companies. The basic rate of income tax is deducted at source and then allowed as Advanced Corporation Tax (ACT) against any liability a company has for Corporation Tax.

Capital Gains Tax

The tax was effective from 6 April 1965. Although mainly a personal tax, the rules broadly apply to companies but the gains are charged to corporation tax. The Taxation of Chargeable Gain Act of 1992 consolidated the law on the matter but the Finance Act of 1998 caused some significant changes to be effective.

The liability arises if any capital gain accrues as a result of a disposal relating to a period of ownership since 1982. Exceptions include when the gain accrues to property developers who 'deal' in property.

Inheritance Tax

The tax object is the bequest made to a person or organisation. The system includes provision to circumvent the avoidance of Inheritance Tax by the making of gifts (such as land and buildings) between living persons. It used to be called Capital Transfer Tax and was introduced in 1975 to replace Estate Duty. The relevant law is the Inheritance Tax Act of 1984.

6.38 Corporation Tax

Corporation Tax is only payable by limited companies. The owners of sole trader businesses and partnerships are taxed on their profits through the personal taxation system.

The provisions for Corporation Tax are somewhat complicated, but the essential elements are as follows. The full rate (currently 30%) is charged to companies whose annual profits exceed £1,500,000. A small company's rate (currently 19%) is charged to businesses whose profits fall between £50,000 and £300,000. Marginal relief is given on taxable profits falling between these bands. There are plans to change both the rates and the thresholds and these changes will be phased.

Taxable profits

The taxable profits of the company are calculated by adding:

❑   Trading income.
❑   Capital gains (called chargeable gains).
❑   Rents and interest on other investments.

Trading income is calculated by taking profit derived from the accounts and then adjusting it, adding back certain costs which are not allowable and adding other costs which are. There are two types of FM expenditure that can be taken into account for tax purposes.

Revenue expenditure
Revenue expenditure embraces routine premises costs such as rent, rates, cleaning, energy, routine maintenance, repairs and service charges. As a general rule, all the premises costs incurred in the normal running of the business can be offset against income before calculating taxable profit.

Capital expenditure
Expenditure on capital items cannot be deducted from profits all at once, but will be spread over a number of years.

Capital allowances

Capital allowances are amounts that can be deducted from profits in respect of capital expenditure.

To calculate taxable profits, depreciation is added back to trading profit and capital allowances are deducted – in this way the cost of the capital expenditure is not deducted twice. This is an area of frequent lack of understanding resulting in many organisations not claiming for the allowances or under claiming. There are various allowances for plant and machinery (such as IT, heating and ventilation, and specialist mechanical and electrical installations), energy saving and environmentally friendly plant and machinery, hotels, industrial and agricultural buildings and research and development innovation facilities. Specialist advice on these complex allowances should be sought.

6.39 Tax status of construction workers

The objective of the Construction Industry Scheme (CIS) tax scheme is to stop casual and part-time construction workers abusing the benefits system. Previously, construction industry workers could register for a tax exemption certificate that allowed them to draw gross pay. Non-production of a certificate meant that the employer deducted the basic rate of income tax from the employees' wages. Problems included high earners being able to pay only the basic rate of tax and some casual workers drawing benefits as well as their pay.

The rules require all construction industry workers to have a Tax Registration Card. Without one, they cannot be paid. Under the scheme, organisations may be deemed to be 'contractors' and outside bodies hired to carry out construction services deemed to be 'sub-contractors'. Under the scheme, payment may not be made to any 'sub-contractor' unless they are registered with the scheme and hold a valid registration card (CIS4) or a valid gross payment certificate (CIS5 or CIS6).

It is the responsibility of the 'contractor' to check the validity of registration cards and certificates and to have procedures in place for the management of the system. The procedures must cover dealing with invoices and the submission of payment vouchers to the Inland Revenue and subcontractors at the end of each tax period.

The CIS sets out the rules for how payments to subcontractors for construction work must be handled by contractors in the construction industry and certain other businesses.

Under the Scheme, all payments made from contractors to subcontractors must take account of the subcontractor's tax status as determined by HMRC. This may require the contractor to make a deduction, which they then pay, from that part of the payment that does not represent the cost of materials incurred by the subcontractor.

In 2007 a new CIS was launched, with specific aims:

❑ To reduce the regulatory burden of the Scheme on construction businesses.
❑ To improve the level of compliance by construction businesses with their tax obligations.
❑ To help construction businesses to get the employment status of their workers right.

The deduction rates for this scheme are 20% for subcontractors registered with HMRC for payment under deduction and 30% for those not registered.

All contractors will have to:

❑ Be able to *demonstrate* that the employment status of each subcontractor has been reviewed each month.

❏   Provide to HMRC (within 14 days of the end of each month) a return detailing every
    payment made to every subcontractor.
❏   Provide (again within 14 days) a monthly declaration confirming every subcontractor
    has been verified.

If an organisation cannot prove that they have both verified each subcontractor and
considered his/her employment status monthly. The organisation may be liable to
penalties of:

❏   Up to a £3000 for every month.
❏   100% of any tax underpaid.
❏   Loss of their own gross payment status.

6.40 Depreciation

Fixed assets are normally discounted in the accounts in order to show the true (reducing)
value of the capital investment over a period of years. There are two common methods for
calculating depreciation.

❏   *The straight-line method*: This divides the capital sum (less final salvage value) by
    the useful economic life of the asset.
❏   *The reducing instalment method*: This is when a fixed percentage is applied to the
    reducing balance year on year.

6.41 Financial business cases

FMs will often have to prepare accurate and resilient financial cases to secure access to
funds for projects and new initiatives. Organisations will have a finite amount of funding. All applications for capital funding will therefore need to be appraised to decide
which projects to support and which to reject. Appraisal techniques include payback
period, discounted cash flow (DCF), return on capital employed (ROCE), internal rate of
return (IRR).

   Each organisation will have a process for submitting business case applications, usually determined by the value of the project. Some organisations have investment boards
or capital investment committees that meet at predetermined times. It is important for
the FM to find out when these are, the date for submission of papers and who sits on the
committee. In some case, influencing and lobbying is required to gain support for a particular project so that the appropriate approval is achieved.

   A business case will need to state:

❏   The purpose of the project/investment.
❏   The need.
❏   The benefit.
❏   The financial impact.
❏   The options available – including the 'do nothing' option.
❏   A recommendation for the preferred option.

Examples

Typical FM capital projects include the following examples:

❑ Purchase of a new fleet of cars or vehicles.
❑ Extension of existing building.
❑ Refurbishment of existing building.
❑ Relocation.
❑ Implementation of a new computer system.
❑ Replacement of building equipment such as boilers, chillers, lifts.
❑ Replacement of building infrastructure services such as power supplies, network cabling, lighting distribution system, fire alarm systems.

6.42 Investment appraisal methods

There are a number of methods of investment appraisal used to establish where the estimates of benefits from an investment compensate for the initial outlay. The main methods used are:

❑ Payback period.
❑ Return on capital employed.
❑ DCF and net present value (NPV).
❑ Internal rate of return.
❑ Cost/benefit analysis.

Each method has its advantages and disadvantages as shown in Table 6.7. It is important that the FM establishes which type is used in their organisation, and what evaluation criteria are used – such as the cost of money to that organisation, the period for payback and so on.

Table 6.7   Project financial appraisals

Type of appraisal method	Advantage	Disadvantage
Payback period	Quick, easy to understand, data often readily available. Focus on cash flows. Suitable for simple projects.	Not suitable for complex projects. No account of the value of money over time.
ROCE	Simple, quick to calculate. Results shown in % format.	Value is relative not absolute. Does not take into account the cash flow or liquidity. Needs a clear and exact definition of profit and capital employed across all projects compared.
DCF	Allows comparison of projects over a time period which accounts for time value of cash flows.	Need to use present value tables to convert cash flows. More complicated than other methods. Consultation with the finance department is essential to ascertain the appropriate discounted rate is used in the calculation.

Some organisations will require all three types of appraisal to be applied to the project business case so that all aspects of the project's costs are considered.

6.43 Cost benefit analysis

This technique is often used in case studies. Table 6.8 gives examples of the costs and the benefits in an analysis.

Costs

All the known and likely costs must be listed, e.g.:

❑   Cost of the replacement equipment.
❑   Cost of installation.
❑   Cost of training staff to use it.

Benefits

All the known and anticipated benefits need to be listed and, where possible, stated in monetary terms, e.g.:

❑   Continued production versus average lost time this year = £x value.
❑   Improvements to service.
❑   Faster turnaround or improved completion or production rates.
❑   Opportunity costs.
❑   Improved productivity.
❑   Increased sales.

Table 6.8   Cost Benefit Analysis

Costs	Benefits
Contract negotiation and set up (opportunity costs of x amount of manager's time = £a)	Reduction in managerial time of y hours per month = £b
Less direct control over the work done on a daily basis	Bulk purchasing ability for cleaning fluids so £c saving made per month

If the overall costs or investment are paid back by the benefits over a short period of time, the budget holder will see that it makes good sense to invest.

6.44 Payback period

This is a very simple method. It measures the number of years that it is expected to take to recover the cost of the original investment. It is good indicator of risk but best used with other methods. There are numerous disadvantages of this method:

❑   Cash received after pay back is completed is completely ignored.
❑   It does not relate the total cash earned on the investment to the amount invested.
❑   It does not measure the total profitability over the whole life of the investment.

6.45 Discounted cash flow

All items of income and expenditure resulting from the investment are clearly and separately identified. The different rates of interest can be used to discount different items of income or expenditure back to their present values. Items of income and expenditure can be allocated to the precise dates when they will occur (rather than assuming it is at the end of the year). Comparisons can be readily made between alternative investments.

6.46 Net present value

This investment appraisal technique takes into account the value of money over time. The underlying principle of the technique is that an amount of money earned in a year's time will be worth less than the same sum earned now. It is related to the DCF method of expressing future cash inflows in present values. The NPV technique assumes a minimum desired rate of return that is used as the discount factor. All inflows and outflows are totalled, outflows are deducted from inflows and the chosen discount rate applied in order to arrive at the present value of the cash flow. When making comparisons, the project with the largest positive total NPV is the most desirable. Present value tables are available and are generally used to identify a range of discount rates across a number of years. NPV is used to compare different investments to determine which one will, for any given interest rate, produce the greatest NPV.

NPV can also be used directly as a method of valuation omitting purchase price and purchase costs from the calculations. The total excess of the discounted net inflows over the discounted net outflows will then represent the price (excluding the costs of acquisition) that could be paid for the item assuming a particular interest rate.

6.47 Internal rate of return

Every organisation will have an internal interest rate to compare investments against. This is the percentage earned on the amount of capital invested each year of the life of the project after allowing for the repayment of the sum originally invested. This method finds the rate of interest that equalises the discounted net inflows and outflows (that will give an NPV of zero). The IRR indicates the exact rate at which an investment will earn money.

6.48 Preparing a financial proposal

Any financial proposal, if it is to succeed, will need to set out the business case for the proposed course of action. Whether presented verbally or in writing (and often proposals involving significant sums will demand both), the presentation will need to convey clearly what is suggested and the benefits to the business. Table 6.9 shows the contents with likely headings and areas to be covered.

Given that the proposal is likely to involve capital investment, the commitment of additional resources and perhaps incurring increased costs in advance of future savings, the case will need to be convincing and well argued.

Table 6.9   Contents of a business case

1	Introduction	Scope and background Contents
2	Clarify need	Briefly describe the present situation Highlight the problems that currently exist Explain why the status quo is unsatisfactory
3	Match need	Outline the proposal or ideas Mention alternatives that have been considered and discarded Explain in detail what is required and why
4	State benefits	Explain the benefits that will flow from the proposal Say what the benefits will mean for the organisation, employees and customers Quantify the positive impact on the business
5	Summarise	The current situation The solution and its key features The business benefits that will result

6.49 Submission

FMs will need to know the action, processes, procedures, protocols and key dates required to obtain the necessary approvals and signatures for the business case.

6.50 Building life cycle costs

Between first occupancy and demolition a building will undergo many changes. The interior fabric and fittings in a building can be expected to undergo significant change every 5–7 years in the life of the building. The mechanical and electrical services can expect to survive from 10 to 20 years. Any estimates such as these are, of course, generalisations, as many buildings do not survive even to maturity, never mind old age, whilst others seem to have eternal life.

Building life cycle costs, sometimes called 'whole life costs' are:

❑ Pre-occupancy costs
   o   As well as the costs associated with the acts of construction, fitting out and commissioning of the building, these costs will include fees and finance charges incurred in the feasibility and pre-production stages of building life. Land is not usually included, as it is not considered to be a wasting asset.
❑ Occupancy costs
   o   These include the majority of FM costs – such as reactive and proactive maintenance, as well as rents, rates, service charges, utilities, FM services costs, insurance costs, and all day to day costs of occupation of a building. Management costs and the likely impact of inflation can also be included here.
❑ Costs associated with adaptation, extension, refurbishment or subdivision
   o   Most life cycle cost forecasts will ignore these unless they are part of a phased programme.
❑ Demolition costs.

6.51 Life cycle costing methodology

Conventional life cycle cost analysis is concerned with tangible costs, such as the income and expenditure arising as a result of the physical performance of buildings. Cost benefit analysis (CBA) can be used for the purpose of appraising options. The effect of using CBA would be to bring together the physical and all the functional aspects of building performance.

There are six stages in a life cycle CBA.

(i) Definition of the project and its overall objectives (the benefits).
(ii) Preparation of a list of the likely costs and benefits. Social and other intangible benefits and costs are included in a CBA. For example, in the public sector the CBA for a road bypass might include benefits such as noise reduction, local environmental considerations, accessibility and travel time, while the costs might include a wider environmental impact or the effects on other populated areas on the route.
(iii) The list of costs and benefits, either direct or indirect are given a monetary value. While the social/intangible costs must depend on judgement to a degree, providing there is consistency in their assessment they do provide a basis for comparing the total costs and benefits of alternative projects – which is the purpose of a CBA.
(iv) The net benefit for each year of the analysis is predicted. These are the value of the benefits less the costs and will be expressed as positive or negative cash flow, depending on whether benefits exceed costs or vice versa.
(v) The stream of annual net benefits is compared with the capital cost. Various mathematical methods are used but not all are satisfactory insofar as property investments are concerned.
(vi) The final appraisal is made. Fairly obviously, if costs exceed benefits, the option should be rejected.

Cost effectiveness analysis (CEA) is an alternative method for life cycle costing. CEA compares alternative courses of action in terms of their costs and their effectiveness in achieving specific objectives.

6.52 Evaluating life cycle costs

In evaluating the life cycle costs of a building, the calculations can be to the power of any number up to the anticipated life of the building, e.g. n^{50} where n is the number of years being used in the calculation.

Three principal methods are used for evaluating the life cycle costs of buildings. Provided a consistent approach is used, the calculations can either ignore or take account of inflation and tax. The methods are:

(i) **Simple aggregation** – A useful rule of thumb sometimes used by the design team in the very early stages of evaluation. The forecast total capital costs and total revenue costs (operating costs, expenditure on repairs, maintenance and renewals) are added together. It is important that the forecasts should detail the basis for calculating component life cycles and operating costs.

The method can make the point that life cycle costs are greater than the initial costs and the method can also be used to demonstrate that greater expenditure on capital items will reduce revenue expenditure. However, it is as well to be aware that a building which is of a better quality and thus requires less annual revenue expenditure will eventually require greater capital expenditure on replacements/renewals, albeit later than would be the case of a lower quality building. Simple aggregation ignores the significant effect of discounting future cash flows.

(ii) **Annual equivalent (AE) and sinking funds** – This is the annual rate of interest per £1 added to a sinking fund to be set aside to provide each £1 of capital by the end of the period. A sinking fund used for the calculation of depreciation is also calculated using the formula.

(iii) **Net Present Value (NPV)** – See section 6.46.

6.53 Sinking funds

The above example is the investor or developer's choice for evaluating whole life costs. Occupiers should note that landlords may choose to set up a sinking fund for major expenditure – lift replacement for example – and this will be included in service charges. Sinking funds are not popular. Key considerations are:

❑ The sinking fund charge should be separately itemised.
❑ The operation of the sinking fund must be monitored.
❑ Legal advice should be sought to ensure that the fund does not belong to the landlord.
❑ If taking an assignment of a lease, the new tenant must ensure that the previous tenant has made the correct sinking fund contributions, otherwise the new tenant might be liable for them.
❑ If disposing of a lease by assigning it, the outgoing tenant must ensure that proper recognition is given to the sinking fund contributions already made and if appropriate, a refund is paid by the incoming tenant.

6.54 The impact of inflation

Inflation is often left out of most financial equations because it is not easily predicted. However, there are arguments for and against, largely based on whether or not the inflated sums to be paid will be in a similar relationship to the finances of an organisation as a whole.

The UK government and the Bank of England use interest rates as a way of curbing inflation. This policy is effective because as rates rise companies and individuals see the cost of their borrowings increase. This can affect not only the costs of servicing mortgage finance but also bank overdrafts. However, high interest rates make borrowing expensive and may reduce investment. Economic activity falls and as a consequence companies shed employees and workspace. At the same time banks may reduce their exposure to commercial property, particularly when the reduction in activity causes business failure and loan default.

When inflation is under control and interest rates become stable or reduce, economic activity should increase. Any increase will be evident from a growth in employment, and general confidence. As the economy picks up bank lending increases to fund an improved level of investment in the economy. Eventually, this will result in an increased demand for commercial premises for occupation.

Building cost data

Successful life cycle costing in FM depends on the quality of the data generally available for:

- ❑ Overall building life.
- ❑ The life of systems within buildings.
- ❑ Component and element life.
- ❑ Maintenance and repair costs.
- ❑ Replacement costs.

Computerised management systems now generate much information on the physical, financial and functional performance of buildings. The objective of the new computer-based maintenance management system (CMMS) tools is to improve life cycle prediction and to better inform both FMs and designers of the consequences of selecting particular materials and systems in buildings. This in turn will help to produce better financial management reports and better informed decisions.

Table 6.1   Glossary of financial terms

Accruals	Estimates made of costs incurred but not yet invoiced. They are charged to the profit and loss account and also appear as liabilities in the balance sheet.
Allocated Cost	Indirect cost which is shared out over products or departments using some basis of allocation (e.g. hours worked, headcount, square footage).
Assets	The value of items owned by the business which are shown on the balance sheet.
Auditors	There are External and Internal Auditors. External Auditors are External Accountants who report on the 'truth and fairness of the published financial statements. Internal Auditors co-operate with the External Auditors but also review operational aspects of the business.
Balance Sheet	A financial statement which records assets, liabilities and shareholders' investment in the business at a point in time, normally the end of an accounting period.
Book Value	The value at which assets are stated in the balance sheet, i.e. cost less any depreciation (also called net book value).
Borrowings	Total amounts owing to those who have lent money to the company. This is often split in the balance sheet into short term, i.e. due within 1 year and long term, i.e. due in more than 1 year.
Break-Even Point	Level of sales or volume where sales and the sum of variable and fixed costs are exactly even, i.e. profit is zero.
Budget	General term for a short-term (normally 1 year) financial plan.
Capital Employed	The amount of finance (share capital or loan capital) put into a company and on which the management must make a return.
Capital Expenditure	Amounts spent on items of a long-term nature, i.e. which will be used in the business for more than 1 year which are classed as fixed assets in the balance sheet. Also called Capital Investment.
Cash Flow	The change in the cash position of a business during an accounting period or as a result of a particular event.

(Continued)

Table 6.1   (Continued)

Costs	Charges incurred, whether spent or accrued for, by a company which are charged to the profit and loss account because they refer to the current year's operations.
Creditors	Amounts owing to suppliers for bills unpaid at a point in time, e.g. at the end of a financial period. (Also see payables.)
Current Assets	Those assets which are constantly moving around in the business and are therefore relatively easy to turn into cash or realise, i.e. stocks, debtors and cash.
Current Liabilities	Amounts owing at the period end which will or could be required to be paid within 12 months.
Debtors	An asset in the balance sheet which represents amounts owing by customers. (Also see receivables.)
Depreciation	A book entry spreading capital expenditure over the estimated life of an asset by means of a charge which reduces profits in the profit and loss account and the value of assets in the balance sheet.
Direct Costs	Those costs which can be directly identified with a brand, business unit, department or other part of the business.
Discounted Cash	A method of evaluating projects by flow (DCF) discounting their projected future cash flows to their present values.
Dividend	Amounts of cash paid or payable to shareholders as a distribution of profits.
Equity	The investment in the business by shareholders.
Expenses	Another term for costs, more usually applied to those below the gross profit level.
Financial Accounts	The accounts prepared for inclusion in the Annual Report to Shareholders.
Fixed Assets	Those assets which are retained for long-term use in the business.
Fixed Costs	Costs where the total amount spent does not vary directly with volume in the short term.
Historical Cost	The original cost of an asset.
Incremental Cost	Another term for Marginal Cost.
Indirect Costs	Costs which cannot be classified as directly attributable to a product, process or department.
Interest Payable	Interest paid on borrowings.
Interest Receivable	Interest received from investment of surplus funds.
Internal Rate of Return	The IRR, expressed as a percentage, is the (IRR) discount rate (see DCF) which would cause a project to have a zero net present value (NPV). A project with an IRR lower than the cost of capital should not be accepted on financial grounds. Often used as an alternative to the NPV.
Inventories	The US American term for stock.
Liabilities	Amounts owed by the business.
Loan Capital	Long-term capital put into the business by lenders rather than shareholders.
Management Financial information	Information produced for the Accounting purpose of management decision making and control, rather than for reporting to shareholders.
Margin of Safety	The amount by which sales can fall before profit equals zero, i.e. at the Break-Even Point.
Marginal Cost	The increase in total cost as a result of a particular event or decision.

Net Assets	Total assets in the balance sheet less liabilities. Sometimes applied to total assets less current liabilities; also applied to total assets less current and long-term liabilities, in which case it can be described as Net Worth.
Net Current Assets	Current assets less current liabilities. (See Working Capital.)
Net Present Value (NPV)	The net amount of a project cash flow, after discounting at the appropriate cost of capital, i.e. after allowing for the time value of money.
Opportunity Cost	The amount foregone by utilising a resource, i.e. its cost plus any profit it might otherwise have generated.
Overdraft	Facility for short-term borrowing available from bankers.
Payables	The US American term for Creditors.
Payback	The number of years it takes to recover an initial amount invested.
Profit and Loss Account	A financial statement which records the sales, the costs and therefore the profit for a stated accounting period.
Profit Margin	Profit as a percentage of sales.
Provision	Estimate of expenditure which is not yet fully ascertainable, but which is charged as a cost in the profit and loss account, such as a provision for Bad Debts.
Receivables	The US term for debtors.
Reserves	Another phrase for retained profits; also used to describe retained profits plus capital reserves.
Retained Profits	All profits made since the company was formed which have not yet been distributed as dividends.
Revenue Expenditure	Another term for Expenses.
Sensitivity Analysis	The calculation of the impact on profit of changing assumptions.
Share Capital	Money put into the business by shareholders by means of direct investment.
Shareholders' Capital	Another term for Shareholders' Equity Employed.
Shareholders' Equity	Share Capital plus retained profits and other reserves.
Shareholders' Funds	Another term for Shareholders' Equity.
Short-Term Borrowing	Borrowing which will or could need to be repaid within 12 months.
Stock	The amount of money tied up in Raw Materials, Work in Progress and Finished Goods.
Sunk Cost	A cost which has already been paid and which therefore should be ignored when considering future actions.
Trade Creditors	Amounts owing to suppliers in the normal course of trading.
Trade Debtors	Amounts owing by customers in the normal course of trading.
Trading Profit	Sales less all normal costs of running the business.
Variable Costs	Costs where the total amount spent varies directly with volume in the short term.
Working Capital	Stocks plus Debtors less Creditors. It does not include cash. (Operating definition.)
Working Capital	Current Assets less Current Liabilities, i.e. another term for Net Current Assets (Bankers definition).
Written Down Value	The book value of fixed assets at historical cost less depreciation.

7 Property and Estates Management

7.1 Introduction

The property portfolio or estate is a major element of cost for all organisations. It is often quoted as the second largest cost to an organisation, with the staff payroll as the largest expense in most organisations. Estate management may be the responsibility of a separate department in an organisation, or outsourced to a specialist. Either way, it is an area in which FMs need to gain an overall understanding, as the nature of the property portfolio will have an impact on the facilities operation. At a basic level, the FM needs to know whether the buildings are leased or owned, the restrictions or rules of their occupation and the sizes of the buildings.

If an FM is to effectively manage the property portfolio on behalf of their organisations, they need to understand the organisational objectives so that the portfolio meets the infrastructure needs of the business. This requires understanding how the properties are used, the nature of leases and covenants that may restrict use and the future needs of the organisation in terms of space and location.

7.2 Property industry

The UK property industry is closely linked with the FM industry; however, it has its own drivers and characteristics. There are many specialists and professionals (such as agents, solicitors and surveyors) in this sector and it is useful to know what they do and how they affect the work of FMs. Financial institutions, pensions fund managers, the church, the government and the crown as well as private and public companies use property as an investment tool. In recent years, the awareness of property as an investment tool has grown because of various reasons. These include the increased uptake of the buy-to-let residential market, the launch of Real Estate Investment Trusts in the UK and the more recent global recession caused by dubious financial transactions in the property mortgage market.

The UK, in common with other market economies, has a sophisticated commercial property market. The market exists because companies and individuals require property for occupation or for business purposes. Investors purchase property in order to benefit from rental income obtained from tenants. Firms of estate agents and surveyors operate in this market and act as brokers for sales and letting of commercial property. They also carry out professional duties such as formal valuation of property or dealing with disputes or complex negotiations.

7.3 Market influences

The property market is driven by economic factors; values fall and rise dependent upon a range of issues – such as general market confidence, the costs and availability of finance, the level of inflation and the strength of sterling or local currency as well as the balance of a supply and demand market. International factors of a strategic or financial nature are also important considerations, as recently demonstrated with the global credit crisis.

The market is not uniform in its performance across the UK as a whole. Different types of property may show growth in value and others a fall. Economic factors vary from region to region. Demand for certain types of premises may reduce because of changes in employment or changes in the type of work and use of premises. Technological change may render some properties obsolescent. New transport infrastructure may improve access to an area and generate demand for space, with an upward impact on values. Regeneration by government agencies can also be beneficial, providing grants for new buildings, assisting with decontamination of land and offering incentives to organisations relocating or establishing in particular areas.

7.4 The cyclical nature of the market

Property prices rise and fall in reaction to changes in the overall economic market but lag to some extent due to the relatively long timescales involved in buying and selling property. The simple pressures of supply and demand are important considerations in understanding the property market.

An economic slowdown results in larger volumes of floor space coming onto the market. Values fall and incentives may be offered to tenants to induce them to take space. The property market will follow the general economic cycle as a whole. In a buoyant economy, property prices rise both in the commercial and residential market and then fall as activity decreases.

7.5 A property portfolio

A portfolio is a list of investments held by an individual or organisation. An investment is an outflow of funds needed to acquire an asset. A property portfolio is the investment made in land and buildings. Investors invest to make money. Investors put their money into property for a number of reasons. Either they want the property for their own operational use, as is the case with some commercial and industrial organisations, or they expect to make money as a result of the property being rented to users, or from selling it on. Property investors put their money into property because they predict that it will provide a better return than it would elsewhere.

7.6 The investment market

Property as an investment medium is just one of several choices open to the investor. Other investment methods include shares, gilts (government stock), unit trusts, commodities, currency, bonds, ISAs, insurance policies and works of art. Property is an investment that is illiquid, in that buying and selling it takes time and its cash value cannot be quickly converted to cash.

It is expensive to trade in property. It is now possible to buy shares in a property, in the same way that shares in a PLC company can be bought. These investment vehicles are known as Real Estate Investment Trusts (REITs) – allowing organisations and individuals to trade in shares in property companies. Market knowledge remains in the hands of a few expert valuers and it is not readily available. There is no FTSE 100 for property. However, the number of countries that now have REIT funds is growing. Property offers an attractive prospect to investors due to rental growth because of the regular rent reviews and security of income particularly at the prime end of the market. Investment property is also tangible and provides the benefit of visible status and prestige.

Property is management intensive and requires input from the owner or his representatives to collect rent, ensure that the lease is complied with and that the building remains in good repair. Property is an investment that is illiquid, in that buying and selling it takes time and its value cannot be quickly converted into cash.

The 'prime' investment market

The UK has a highly developed investment market; this market deals in the sale and purchase of properties that are let to tenants that are income producing in the same way that shares produce annual dividends. Prices for investment properties are dependent upon the security of the income stream from rents, the length of the lease and the frequency of rent reviews. Thus the ideal property investment will be one where a quality building is let to a large and secure company for a long lease with regular rent reviews. Such investments are called 'prime'. A typical investment lease will be for 20 or 25 years, with regular rent reviews every 5 years.

The major pension funds and property investment companies dominate this market. Major landmark buildings in London and other city centres such as Canary Wharf Tower or Centre Point are examples of prime office investment property. The market will also include prime shopping centre property, such as Bluewater and well-located retail and distribution warehouses. Prices paid can run in some circumstances to many millions of pounds.

The secondary investment market

The secondary investment market would include property of lower capital values and whilst still of interest to some larger investors, may have a wider audience for private investors and family trusts. Unit sizes vary but they are normally from £250,000 to £5,000,000. The market is often conducted by auction.

Speculative/tertiary investments

Increasingly, many individual investors have seen both commercial and residential property as part of a wider investment portfolio. The residential property 'buy to let' market has increased in size significantly in the last few years. Again auctions are an important part of the market. Lot sizes are normally from £10,000 to £250,000. Many small investors now see property investment as an alternative to other forms of personal investment such as the more traditional pension fund.

7.7 Property investors

Setting aside the development of property for owner occupation, owning property to let to tenants is a well-established alternative to investing in stocks and shares. Examples of major UK property investors are described in the following sections.

Private sector

These are individuals or private organisations. For example:

❑ Grosvenor Estate – Held by the Duke of Westminster's family for over 500 years. Extensive holdings of prestigious assets in London and also in Chester.
❑ Insurance companies and pension funds who invest to achieve capital growth in the long term. The property investment may only be in the region of 5–15% of the organisation's total investments but can still be measured in many millions of pounds overall. Scottish Widows, Liverpool Victoria Friendly Society, and the Prudential are examples of these types of private investor.

Public sector and quasi public bodies

❑ Central government: Traditionally owns much of its older operational stock but has moved away from ownership since the extensive development of the PFI procurement strategy for building and managing public buildings.
❑ Church Commissioners.
❑ Crown Estate.
❑ Local Authorities.
❑ Universities.

Before a property crash that took place in 1990, holdings of English and Welsh local authorities were estimated to have a capital value of some £100 billion. This did not include housing and about a quarter of this sum was estimated to be investment stock. More recently there has been a significant move away from ownership. Health authorities particularly have moved away from public funded development. The first PFI development, a 400-bed hospital, was reported by the National Audit Office as making savings of some £5 million. While savings were not as great as expected (£17 million), the development has been held by the health authority and the NHS executive as being good value for money and offering significant health benefits. As well as the construction, the contract included maintenance and the provision of non-clinical support services.

Investors in property are as much at risk as any other investor. Some banks, major office space users and leading retailers still own their own premises. However, there has been a trend by some organisations to sell their properties and then lease them back, thus freeing up capital for other purposes. One such example is British Telecom, whose property is now owned by a consortium, Telereal. The deal, negotiated in 2001, raised £2.4 billion for BT, involved the transfer of 6,700 properties covering some 5.5 million square feet. BT now pay a rental charge for the use of the properties.

7.8 Property management

There are four approaches to the management of property portfolios:

(i) Management by an in-house team
Property companies and larger organisations usually apply this approach. However, such an approach ensures a high degree of confidentiality and needs an in-house team to respond

quickly to provide an effective and efficient response to investment decisions. Even so, it would be unusual for any organisation to have the complete range of expertise required for property investment transactions in-house and will require the services of external agents for specialist services.

(ii) The use of a property agent
Agents are widely used. They offer extensive expertise and experience of the property market, especially in local markets. Agents will compete for appointments, which can be made for from 3 to 5 years.

(iii) A combination of in-house team and appointed agent
The success of these arrangements relies on the ability, expertise and commitment of both parties and good team dynamics.

(iv) A hierarchy of management
In this arrangement, the in-house team maintains overall responsibility for the management of the portfolio and uses an appointed agent for the more mundane property management tasks. (This is a variation on the theme of outsourcing.) Over time such arrangements have the potential to develop into the previously mentioned combination arrangement.

7.9 Property professionals and specialists

There are many specialists and professionals who operate in the property industry. They are often appointed and remunerated on the basis of fees calculated as a percentage of all or part of the project cost. Disciplines most likely to be used are as follows.

Architects

Architects will be members of the Royal Institute of British Architects (RIBA). Responsibilities can include:

❑ Design of the appearance and construction of new buildings and building refurbishment.
❑ Administration of a building contract on behalf of a developer or other type of client.
❑ Certification of the completion of the work.
❑ Obtaining any necessary planning permission when a planning consultant is not employed.
❑ Project management.
❑ Interior design.

Some key considerations in selection of an architect include:

❑ Early selection of the architect is important.
❑ References from clients of previous commissions.
❑ Site visits.
❑ Good communication between client and the architect is essential.

- ❏ The objective is good architecture that provides a cost-effective design attractive to the occupier. Care must be taken to ensure chosen architects have a satisfactory track record, the experience, and resources that are appropriate for the work to be undertaken.
- ❏ Some larger organisations have their own in-house architects and designers.

Building surveyors

Qualified building surveyors will belong to the Royal Institute of Chartered Surveyors (RICS). Typical responsibilities can include:

- ❏ Survey of existing buildings and advising on alterations.
- ❏ Advising on defects, repair, service charge issues and dilapidation schedules.
- ❏ Reviewing technical documentation, e.g. schedules of conditions and building specifications.
- ❏ Working closely with the agent or other property adviser to ensure appropriate terms in building transactions.
- ❏ Undertaking a project management role in some cases that can include managing the tender process.

Some key considerations in the selection and appointment of a surveyor include:

- ❏ Early selection of the building surveyor is important for refurbishment projects.
- ❏ Good communication between client and the surveyor is essential.
- ❏ Some larger organisations have their own in-house building surveyors, as well as architects and designers.

Engineers

There are many different disciplines within engineering. Civil engineers or highway engineers will be responsible for major infrastructure work (roads and ground works). Mechanical and electrical engineers will be responsible for the design of all the building's mechanical and electrical services. Structural engineers will work with the architect and quantity surveyor advising on the design of the structural elements of a building. They will also have some supervisory responsibility for structural elements of the construction.

Financial advisers

These are likely to be internal staff in an organisation. Specialist financial responsibilities can include:

- ❏ Advising on the complex tax and VAT regulations that impact on property development, property leases and service charges and the financial standards that must be observed.
- ❏ Analysis of the market prior to consideration of funding proposals.

They may also advise on the structuring of partnership, consortium and other financial arrangements, such as PFI or PPP schemes.

Quantity Surveyors

Quantity surveyors will also be members of the RICS; however, their role is quite different to the building surveyor. They are the accountants or cost managers for the project or property development. They will typically report directly to the client and their responsibilities may include:

- ❑ Advising on the most appropriate form of building contract.
- ❑ Advising on the cost of the building contract and associated works.
- ❑ Costing the designs presented by the architect.
- ❑ Administering the contract tender process.
- ❑ Monitoring the financial aspects of the construction work and approving stage payments.
- ❑ Suggesting cost-effective alternatives to those proposed by the architect.
- ❑ Preparation of financial reports to the client.

Lawyers and solicitors

These could be appointed by the client for various legal transactions in property management.

Some organisations may have an internal legal team, whilst others may appoint a legal practice to advise on all property law matters. Responsibilities can include preparation of legal documentation in connection with:

- ❑ Acquisition and development of a site.
- ❑ Completion of leases and contracts for sale.
- ❑ Funding or other financial arrangements for the project.

Building contractors

Building contractors are employed by the client to carry out the construction work.

Some property development companies have their own contracting division. There are numerous types of contract used to engage a building contractor in the property industry. It is important to ensure the capacity and capability of the contractor to carry out the work. This can mean striking a balance between the lowest tender and quality of performance.

The planning authority

With certain exceptions, planning permission will be required if any works come within the definition of 'development' given in the Town and Country Planning Act 1990. Development is 'the carrying out of building operations, engineering operations, mining operations or other operations in, on, over or under any land or, the making of any material change in use of a building'. The definition therefore covers a wide range of building activities from the erection of a new building to the demolition of buildings and any other significant building works in between. Independent consultants in planning matters can be used to assist in the complex process of obtaining the relevant permissions from the Local Authorities and agents such as English Heritage.

The client (or FM)

The client or their representative will need to be able to demonstrate the following skills and attributes when assembling a team of property specialists:

- ❑ Financial management and access to funds.
- ❑ Leadership and team building skills.
- ❑ Appointment and development of a professional advisory team.
- ❑ Efficient and effective communication of client strategy and objectives.

❑   Clear instructions about the expectations of the team and consultants.
❑   Ability to involve the professional team in the client decision-making process.

Others

There are other specialists involved in property management and property transactions. These include archaeologists if the site has any historical significance, land surveyors and landscape architects if there are extensive grounds to be designed and planted. Marketing consultants may be required if a sale is involved. Public relations consultants would be used particularly if a development proposal is controversial. Environmental specialists would be used to deal with any ground or water contamination and to prepare or comment on an Environmental Impact Analysis.

7.10 Developing a property strategy

Property represents the largest asset of an organisation. Property and occupancy costs come second only to the organisation's staff costs. In all sectors, public and private, savings in the costs of owning and occupying property can generate funds that can be used elsewhere in the business. A robust strategic property management can have a significant impact on profitability and share value.

FMs must strike a fine balance between observing any financial constraints and satisfying real (and to some extent, perceived) operational needs of staff and external stakeholders. At a strategic level, the need is for a coordinated property strategy that enables overall business needs to be met effectively.

There are several objectives for all occupiers and owners of property:

❑   Providing only the space essential for the conduct of the core business and any essential support space in terms of its size, type, condition and specification at an appropriate location and on satisfactory financial terms by way of leasing or purchase.
❑   Disposal of surplus space by way of sale or subletting.
❑   Setting and meeting realistic occupancy cost objectives.
❑   Enhancing asset value of the property, by re-development (if appropriate).
❑   Releasing asset value of property by sale and leaseback transactions.
❑   Maximize commercial income from surplus property.
❑   Ensure compliance to relevant property, planning and safety legislation.

The property strategy is driven by organisational strategic objectives. These have to be translated into property objectives. This is illustrated in Table 7.1.

Table 7.1   Comparison of objectives

Corporate objectives	Property objectives	Property strategy
Profit up by x%	Property costs down by x%	Relocate head office
Turnover up by x%	Expand property portfolio by x square metres	Initiate benchmarking of occupancy costs
Costs down by x%	Rationalise portfolio and dispose of surplus space	Introduce flexible working arrangements
Share price up by x%	Maximise capital value of portfolio	Review portfolio for value enhancement potential

7.11 Property and asset register

It is a requirement of the Companies Act that a property and asset register is kept for audit purposes. This responsibility may fall to the FM, who needs to understand the benefits and costs of creating the register, how technology can assist with the task and how the information from the register can be used for management purposes and to maintain asset value. The purpose of an asset register is to:

❑ Record details of physical assets.
❑ Provide a basis for maintenance plans and activities.
❑ Inform replacement decisions.
❑ Communicate tasks.
❑ Provide information for management to use as a basis for action.

Typically, the register will include details of the asset description, location, ownership, initial cost, warrantee details, rent reviews, service charges, condition of asset, compliance and statutory regulations pertaining to that item, safety precautions and so on. Typical sources of information for asset registers are:

❑ Operating and maintenance (O&M) manuals.
❑ Construction Design and Management Regulations (CDM) files.
❑ Building logbook.
❑ Drawings and schematic plans.
❑ Site and condition surveys.
❑ Delivery notes and invoices for goods received.
❑ Catalogues, particularly for furniture and consumables.
❑ Licensing details in the case of motor vehicles.
❑ Leases on property and equipment
❑ Service contracts

Assets may include:

❑ Buildings.
❑ Furniture and fittings.
❑ Office equipment.
❑ Building plant and machinery.
❑ Vehicles.
❑ Operational plant, equipment and machinery.

Many organisations use a computerised maintenance management system (CMMS) to manage the asset register, recording faults and maintenance work against each asset. Key considerations are:

❑ A proper evaluation of the requirement.
❑ Appropriate hardware and software.
❑ Adequate training for users.
❑ Data must be accurate, timely and relevant.

Larger organisations may have separate registers – one for the property and another for the inventory of plant and equipment within each property. This is especially important in a mixed portfolio of owned and leased premises where some assets are part of the landlord's demise.

A property database would be expected to include information that is relevant and to provide output that is capable of being summarised into meaningful management reports. Examples of input requirements are:

- ❑ Site details and address.
- ❑ Name.
- ❑ Reference number.
- ❑ Location.
- ❑ Type (e.g. office, school, hospital and so on).
- ❑ Constraints (e.g. it is a listed building).
- ❑ Size (e.g. GEA, GIA, NUA, NIA in either square feet or metres).
- ❑ Number of floors and floor areas.
- ❑ Space usage.
- ❑ Age.
- ❑ Replacement value.
- ❑ Occupation costs.
- ❑ Service details.
- ❑ Dates of purchase or sale.
- ❑ Build completion date.
- ❑ Date of occupation.
- ❑ Lease start, break and end.
- ❑ Rent review dates.
- ❑ Insurance renewal dates.
- ❑ License renewals.
- ❑ Overall building value or costs.
- ❑ Cleaning, catering and security costs.
- ❑ Communications costs (e.g. landline and mobile phones).
- ❑ Energy costs.
- ❑ Fabric maintenance costs.
- ❑ Furniture and office equipment maintenance costs.
- ❑ M&E maintenance costs.
- ❑ Personnel details and costs.
- ❑ Printing and reprographic costs.
- ❑ Professional fees.
- ❑ Rates.
- ❑ Rent.
- ❑ Service charges.
- ❑ Changes.
- ❑ Insurance costs and licence fees.

The output of a facilities asset management database will:

- ❑ Assist with benchmarking (e.g. rent, rates, service charges and other costs).
- ❑ Enable financial modelling and 'what if' scenarios.
- ❑ Enable the production of forward maintenance plans.
- ❑ Make life cost and element replacement projections.

❑   Prompt the payment of fees and invoices such as rent, rates, goods and services.
❑   Provide budgeting and accounting information.
❑   Provide historical financial information.
❑   Signal maintenance requirements and produce job sheets.
❑   Signal upcoming rent reviews, lease breaks or lease ends.

7.12 Dilapidations

Dilapidations are items of disrepair, which arise through breach of contract in a lease. The breach of contract, in such instances, normally relates to a failure on the part of the tenant or the landlord to repair the property in accordance with the terms of the lease.

A schedule of dilapidations is a list of all elements of a property that require repair or in some cases maintenance at the end of a lease. It may also be served during the lease term, when it is called an interim schedule.

The extent of repairing liability will depend upon the wording of the lease, and tenants should be wary of phrases such as 'to put and keep in repair' in a lease which imply a significant liability on the tenant.

Out of repair

For property to be 'out of repair', it must be damaged or have deteriorated to a state below that which occurred at the beginning of the lease. There can be prolonged dispute over the condition of the property at the beginning of the lease and this is perhaps quite understandable. The lease may have begun many years ago, and if the standard of repair at that time was not recorded in either photographs or in a schedule of condition, either party may be at a disadvantage.

Procedure

A schedule of dilapidations is drawn up by a surveyor before the end of the lease to establish through inspection if there has been a diminution (reduction) in value in the freehold interest as a result of the tenant's failure to repair and maintain the property. The standard of repair required should be reasonable. The premises must be fit for occupation by the type of tenant who would occupy such a property. Although either party in a lease can draw up the schedule, it is most commonly done by the landlord's surveyor. There are three schedules that could be produced and issued with a claim letter. These are:

❑   Interim – produced any time during the lease.
❑   Terminal – produced towards the end of the lease (likely to be the more significant breaches of the lease).
❑   Final – produced after the end of the lease term.

The reduction in value will be defined as the costs incurred in carrying out any works and any subsequent loss in rent. A technical argument between the tenant and the landlord may arise. Other specialists may be required including mechanical or electrical engineers. Many of the debates over dilapidations will centre on the merits of replacement or repair or of the quality of materials to be used and so on. Normally, an agreement can be negotiated but if not the matter may go to court.

The Property Law Association's protocol should be used to resolve a claim for dilapidations. RICS also issue a Guidance Note to help ensure that matters are dealt with correctly.

Quantifying the claim

Section 18 (S18) of the Landlord and Tenant Act 1927 sets a ceiling on the amount of damages that may be recovered. The damages or claim cannot exceed the amount by which the landlord's 'reversion' (property) is diminished by the breach.

No damages can be claimed if the landlord intends to demolish or substantially alter the premises, and so render the repairs valueless. This is an important factor because where a landlord terminates a lease for development purposes under the Landlord and Tenant Acts no claim for dilapidations can be made.

In addition, the Leasehold Property (Repairs) Act 1938 gives the tenant protection against a landlord who is intent on pursuing a dilapidations claims for an improper motive.

Like many aspects of property management, dilapidations claims are settled by negotiation. The landlord's surveyor will inspect the property and draw up a schedule showing all the elements of the property which are 'out of repair' and the costs of restoring the property to an appropriate condition. The tenant is given an opportunity to comment on the schedule and the costs.

Negotiations will not only concern what repairs are to be undertaken, but also relate to the costs involved. There may be discussions concerning the best or most economic way of undertaking repairs. A tenant will be expected to respond to a dilapidations claim within 56 days. It is expected that the surveyors representing both parties will meet on site to discuss the issues. If the matter cannot be agreed then the dispute may be referred to court or to an arbitrator.

At this stage, the landlord's surveyor will submit a fully detailed and costed claim to which the tenants' surveyor will add his own costings and comments. This is known as a 'Scott Schedule' after a case concerning Mr Scott. The judge or arbitrator will then decide on the actual claim. In many cases by the time the dispute reaches the court, some items will have been agreed.

The diminution in value

The actual claim is often reduced by S18 as stated above. A summary of a typical claim is shown in Table 7.2 and Table 7.3. This shows the impact of the diminuition in value of the claim when the value of the property is taken into account.

It is important to understand that the cost of the works do not necessarily equate to value, and by undertaking works up to a certain sum it does not follow that the value of the property will be increased by that sum.

An extreme example of S18 in action is where a property with a low value, say, in a declining seaside town may only be worth £50,000 in its current condition and £60,000 when repairs have been finished. However, the cost of repairs is £30,000. The landlord could not claim £30,000, only the diminution in value of £10,000.

Dilapidations and good estate management practice

At the beginning of the lease both parties should agree the condition of the property to be let, unless the tenant is taking responsibility for putting the property into good repair. This is undertaken by agreeing and attaching a schedule of condition to the lease. Such a schedule is set out in plain English stating what defects exist at the beginning of the lease.

Table 7.2   Dilapidations section 18 claim

Claim on cost basis	£
Cost of works of repair	18,000
Supervision, say 12%	2,160
VAT at 17.5%	3,528
Loss of rent during repair	£3,000
Total claim	**26,688**

Table 7.3   Dilapidation claim devalued by diminuition in value

Valuation of property in good repair	110,000
Valuation in current condition	100,000
Diminution in value	10,000
Therefore claim limited to	**10,000**

This may be backed up by dated photographic records of the building, which can be used in the future when a dispute may arise.

It is usual for certain major items of repair to be removed from a tenant's repairing liability where they are of significant cost to the tenant and are already in poor repair. This could relate to walls that have been subject to settlement over a protracted period and where the disrepair clearly occurred well before the commencement of the lease.

This course of action should have the effect of preventing the level of repairs at the end of the lease being such that the building is given back to the landlord in better condition than at the commencement of the lease.

8 Property Legislation and Leases

Property law in the UK is one of the most complex and difficult fields of law, and a high volume of litigation in this area is constantly underway, leading to new precedents and rulings on a frequent basis. Managers need a broad understanding of property law, contract law, planning legislation, leases and licences, and landlord and tenant issues. The main legislation is the Landlord and Tenant Act, The Town and Country Planning Act, The Building Act with associated Building Regulation, Defective Premises Act and the Occupiers Liability Act.

8.1 Ownership and tenure

Freehold

The most common forms of property tenure in the UK are freehold and leasehold. There is a separate legal system in Scotland. Freehold is the most secure form of ownership in that it is in perpetuity and there are relatively few limits to the rights of a freeholder to deal with his property. A freeholder will hold Title Deeds to prove ownership and by undertaking enquiries about the property before purchase will be aware of any rights held by third parties over the land. Examples of third-party rights could include a public footpath across land or a restriction placed on the use of property by a former owner known as a Restrictive Covenant and which is legally enforceable in most cases.

Leasehold

Standard commercial leases
Leasehold interests are created out of freehold interests. Leaseholders can also create leasehold interests by subletting or assigning their interests. In the commercial property market, occupational leases are normally granted for any period from 1 to 25 years. The length of the lease depends upon the respective requirements of the owner and the potential tenant.

There is often a conflict in the requirements of a lease between the landlord and the tenant. Landlords seek security and growth in income, which can be achieved by letting to an established tenant for a lease of reasonable length. Tenants may see things rather differently. In selecting premises for occupation they may be concerned with issues of flexibility in their leasing arrangements, and may be looking for clauses in the lease which allow it to be ended at short notice before the contractual term expires.

Long leasehold interests
Longer leasehold interests are common in the residential market and leases of 99–125 years are often found, particularly for flats or maisonettes.

Leases of similar length are found in commercial property. Long leases are granted on land and property because the lease covenants allow the freeholder to exercise more control over the use of the property than if it were freehold. This is because the lease will comprise a series of agreements known as covenants, which are enforceable between the parties. The freeholder will in such cases draft the lease to control the use of the land, the size of buildings and even the quality of tenants. Lease covenants can also be used to control the maintenance of service roadways.

Long leases are acceptable to some developers because the period of 99 or 125 years is long enough to use the lease as a security for loan finance – these types of leases are known as ground or building leases.

For example, many industrial estates are developed on land whereby the freehold is owned by a person or firm who then grants a long building lease for a nominal rent. Buildings are constructed and then let on standard 25-year commercial leases to tenants. Once completed and let, the investment can then be sold on the investment market. Thus it can be seen that out of the freehold, several legal interests can be created.

For example:

❑ Owner A is a local authority. They own a piece of land on the outskirts of a town that is ripe for development. They do not wish to develop it themselves, but will sell a long lease-hold interest in the land to a developer, owner B. B will normally pay a sum of money for the long lease and also a nominal annual rental often known as a peppercorn rent.
❑ B then develops industrial units in accordance with the terms of the ground lease.
❑ B lets the buildings on 25-year leases to business occupier C and receives an annual rental.
❑ B will then sell the completed and let development to D, an investor, for a capital sum.
❑ It should be borne in mind that other arrangements could take place in future. Occupier C may sublet or assign his interest to another.

Licences

It is important to distinguish between a lease and a licence because a lease can often give rights of security of tenure and prevent the landlord from gaining occupation except on certain limited grounds.

An agreement has to be carefully drawn to constitute a licence, and many licences will in fact be leases.

A lease is a proprietary right, whereas a licence is a mere personal arrangement. The nature of the agreement together with the intentions of the parties, rather than any name attaching to the agreement is crucial. The interpretation of commercial occupation as a lease or licence is often unclear. Professional legal advice should be sought.

Examples of typical licence agreements

These can be personal or inter-family arrangements. They may be temporary, e.g. to permit access to land to do certain tasks for a certain time in a day.

In business they may allow various occupiers into the premises for a limited and restricted purpose. For example, in shopping centres to sell from market stalls, or to occupy serviced offices where facilities in terms of clerical or reception are shared, but where the arrangement is clearly transitory. Serviced offices are increasingly important in the UK and provide affordable and flexible accommodation, particularly for start-up businesses.

8.2 The Estate Agents Act 1979

This legislation was effected to protect the public from malpractice by estate agents. There is in any event a duty for the agent to act in the best interests of the client in terms of achieving the best price, and in providing appropriate advice. There is no specific duty to act, but if he does so it must be in the client's best interest. The above Act sets out the specific duties that relate to estate agency as opposed to any other agent–client relationship.

The principal requirements of the Act relate to the following:

(i) The agent must disclose any personal interest to his client irrespective of whether he is acting on a disposal or acquiring a property.

This means that if he is acting for a vendor (seller) he must confirm in writing if he or any of his family or business associates are interested in the property.

If the agent is selling a property on his own behalf he must disclose in writing, usually on the sales particulars that he or associates or family members have an interest in the property.

(ii) The agent must give full details to his client in writing of the basis of the appointment in terms of fees, advertising costs and the nature of the appointment whether it is one of the following:

– *sole selling agency*

Where a client appoints one agent to act on his behalf to the exclusion of all others. The type of agreement normally encountered in this context is very restrictive and would mean that even if the client sold the property to a relative he would be responsible for agent's fees.

– *sole agency*

As above but less restrictive, the agreement would normally not extend to payment of fees for a sale by the vendor to family members or persons introduced to the client before the agreement commenced.

– *joint sole agency*

As above but where two or more firms are instructed to market a property on a cooperative basis, and where a joint and equal commission is payable upon completion.

– *multiple agency*

Where several non-cooperating firms are independently instructed to act on the sale. Only the firm that introduces the buyer is paid commission.

(iii) The agent should confirm details of the timescale of the appointment and the procedure for termination of the appointment by either party, or if the seller wishes to vary the basis of the appointment.

Contract letters

The letter must define the agency appointment and explain when commission becomes payable. Particular care should be taken with sole selling and sole agency appointments. This is because it is the agent's duty to clarify with the client in what circumstances commission is payable.

Normally commission is payable out of completion monies and is invoiced upon exchange of contracts. Some firms add the clause to the effect that 'commission is payable upon the introduction of a ready, willing and able purchaser'. This means that the vendor becomes liable to pay commission when a deposit and a signed contract is deposited with the sellers solicitor. There has been case law surrounding this wording, which confirms that if the vendor withdraws from the transaction before exchange but after the buyer has lodged his deposit and signed the contract then he is liable to the agent, even if that particular transaction becomes abortive. Therefore, at this stage, the agent has carried out his duty in accordance with the contract, between himself and the seller.

The Act also deals with the holding of deposits and the passing on of interest to the client.

8.3 The Property Misdescriptions Act 1991

The Act covers statements and written information about property that are inaccurate and/or misleading. Statements made by sellers themselves are not covered by the Act but may fall under legislation covering misrepresentation generally. Such statements are known as specified matters and are set out in the specified orders of the Property Misdescriptions (specified matters) Order 1992. Specified matters include information such as details on location, services, accommodation, room sizes, state of repair, tenure, council tax, planning permission and price.

Statements like 'wonderful view', when the property backs onto an industrial or manufacturing establishment should be avoided. Such statements are likely to attract complaints and result in possible referrals to the local Trading Standards Department, the body with responsibility for administering the law. Penalties for a misdescription are unlimited and quite trivial errors have been met with heavy fines. The firm and/or individual will receive a criminal record. In extreme cases, the person or firm may be banned from practising as estate agents.

There is a limited defence if the agent can prove all due diligence. The agent must be able to show:

 (i) That all staff are aware of the implications of the Act.
 (ii) That adequate staff training procedures are in place with appropriate induction for new staff.
(iii) That all complaints received and mistakes made are picked up on internal audit and are recorded, investigated and rectified as soon as possible.
(iv) That written guidance material covering procedures is provided to all staff. Staff must by implication check all statements and information received about a property prior to disseminating information to the public.

Estate agents have reacted to this legislation by largely reducing the amount of information made available to the public in particulars. This has led to some adverse effects such as interested parties not receiving sufficient guidance on the property's pre-inspection, for example, when agents protect themselves from potentially serious legal proceedings.

8.4 Defective Premises Act

The Defective Premises Act imposes duties on those who undertake works in connection with the provision of most types of building, including houses and commercial premises. This would include architects, builders and designers.

Section 1 of the Act states that work should be done in a workmanlike manner with appropriate materials. The work should result in the building being fit for habitation when completed. Examples of unfitness for habitation are obviously quite wide but could include poor ventilation specifications that result in excess condensation and damp.

The Act is limited to defects, which render the building unfit for habitation. Defects that do not render the building unfit for habitation do not give rise for a claim under the Act. In recent times, potential litigation over defective premises in terms of residential property has been covered by claims under National House-Building Council (NHBC) certificates, which guarantee standards of construction to purchasers.

8.5 Occupiers Liability Act

This Act applies to owners who have liability to those who come onto their land with express or implied permission. It imposes a duty on the owner or occupier to take care to ensure that the visitor will be safe in using the premises for the purposes for which they were invited or permitted. The term 'premises' includes all buildings and land whether in use or not.

Section 2 of the Act reverses the Unfair Contracts Term Act 1977. This enables those who permit access to land for recreational or educational uses to seek to exclude liability for any injuries caused as a result of gaining access to premises.

For example, visitor safety can be maintained by ensuring adequate signage is available indicating wet or slippery surfaces when cleaning operations are in progress. In buildings where potentially hazardous processes are being undertaken, protective equipment should be provided, or safety helmets worn by all visitors on building sites.

Occupiers and trespassers

The situation regarding trespassers is also of relevance.

Owners or occupiers may be liable to the trespassers, who gain access to premises and injure themselves as a result. This is of particular relevance with disused properties where juveniles or vandals are concerned. Properties that are particularly prone to trespassers are derelict, abandoned premises and building sites. The building owner or FM must ensure that fences and gates are secure, that notices are displayed on dangerous properties and that reasonable steps have been taken to prevent entry.

8.6 Landlord and tenant legislation

Landlord and tenant legislation has evolved to regularise the relationship between landlords and tenants in commercial leases, most of which are subject to this legislation.

8.7 The contents and terms of a commercial lease

Modern commercial leases tend to follow a broadly similar format. The lease is issued in duplicate. The landlord's copy is known as the counterpart. The tenant's copy is normally known as the lease. Leases are divided into several sections. Each section will comprise certain clauses and each section will be numbered as will each clause within it. These sections and all the various clauses vary from lease to lease.

Introductory

This section will set out the names of the landlord (lessor) and tenant (lessee) otherwise known as the 'parties' to the lease; the premises or land to which the lease refers, the contractual term, the rent commencement date, the initial rent, rent review intervals, permitted user and any other items such as details on parties' liability to repair.

Landlord
The landlord is the owner of the land or buildings to which the lease applies. He receives a rent or other payment and in return for this payment, grants the right to exclusive possession of the land or buildings to the tenant for a specific period of time.

Tenant
The tenant is the person or firm who, by agreement with the landlord, is granted exclusive possession of land or buildings for a period of years in return for payment of rent.

Ground lease
A long lease granted at a ground rent, this disregards the value of any buildings on the site, but may reflect any right to develop land. Developers may lease a site on a ground lease for 99 or 125 years. A developer constructs a building and then grants a standard 25-year commercial lease to an occupier. Thus the developer is in effect a landlord to his new tenant, and the original landlord who granted the long lease is the landlord to the developer. It can be seen that various interests in land can be arranged, with a head landlord, a ground landlord and a tenant.

Headlease
In the above scenario where a developer took a long leasehold interest, held directly from the freeholder, he becomes what is known as a headlessee. The lease could be subject to one or more underlease(s) or sublease(s). In the above example, the occupier of the property built by the developer is the underlessee.

Sublease
Tenants can sublet property, if the lease allows it. Subleases are for a period of time less than the remainder of the lease. The sublessee will pay rent to the tenant, who will continue to keep up his payments to the landlord. The sublessee normally has no direct contract with the landlord. There are normally special clauses in a lease, which will set out conditions for subletting. The tenant is not usually allowed to sublet without the landlord's consent.

The premises
Usually at the beginning of the document the address of the subject premises is stated. However, further information will be given later in the document including a plan, which is normally a marked up extract from an ordnance survey map.

(Contractual) Term
The lease is agreed as a contract between the parties. The 'term' is the number of years for which the lease will run. Most commercial leases have terms from 3 to 25 years, depending upon what is agreed between the parties.

Rent commencement date

In some leases rent will not be paid immediately from the commencement of the term. This may be because there is an agreement to fit out the premises by the tenant and in return the landlord will grant a 'holiday' on rent, normally called a rent-free period.

Initial rent

The amount of rent to be paid during each year up until the rent review date.

The permitted use

Most leases will specify what use(s) the tenant may put the premises to. Normally there will be a separate clause under tenants covenants setting this out in more detail.

Repair

All leases state which of the parties should undertake repairs of the building. Normally the tenant will be responsible for both internal and external repairs if he occupies the whole of a building. This is then known as a full repairing lease. If the tenant is also responsible for insuring the building then it will be known as a full repairing and insuring lease. Where the tenant is one of several in a multi-occupied building, then the landlord may be responsible for the repair of the exterior. This is known as an internal repairing lease. The landlord may then levy a service charge to cover a percentage of their costs for the common parts and external areas. When this occurs, the charge is divided up between the various tenants. Landlords and tenants may agree to an internal repairing lease even if the tenant occupies the whole. Much depends upon the negotiating position of the parties.

Definitions

In order to avoid repetition, it is usual for the definitions of various phrases and words used in the lease to be set out close to the beginning of the document.

Interpretation

(i) In the duration of a lease, the landlord may change, and it is important to set out expressions relating to the current landlord and tenant that will apply to their successors.
(ii) The lease may also refer to gender, or singular or plural. For the avoidance of doubt the lease would normally state that words importing one gender include all genders and words importing the singular include the plural.
(iii) In addition, where the term development is used it must be given the correct interpretation; normally this would mean development under the Town and Country Planning Acts

Demise

The phrase 'The landlord demises to the tenant the premises together with any rights specified...........' in plain English means that the landlord grants the exclusive right of occupation of the property to the tenant, or more properly, the granting of a right to exclusive possession of a property for a term of less than that held by the landlord. Demise is commonly used by FMs to mean the area covered by the lease.

Yielding and paying

This term relates to the payment of rent and such sums of insurance that may be required as well as the intervals at which they are paid (normally quarterly in advance).

8.8 Tenant's covenants

A covenant is a written obligation made between the landlord and tenant by a party and effected by the signed lease. The lease covenants will set out what obligations are to be met by both the landlord and tenant. In most leases there will be many more covenants for the tenant when compared with the number for the landlord.

Covenants can be:

❑ Absolute, i.e. a complete undertaking not to do something.
❑ Qualified, i.e. not to do something without the landlord's consent.
❑ Fully qualified covenants, i.e. not to do something without the landlord's consent. Such consent not to be unreasonably withheld.

Examples of covenants include:

(i) A covenant to pay rent, rates taxes and other outgoings. This phrase would cover rent, insurance costs, business rates and other charges levied on the business.
(ii) To repair. The extent to which the tenant will be liable for repair is set out in the lease. The wording can be very important. Contrast the impact on expenditure by a tenant between the following: the following wording is commonly found in lease documents.

   – 'To put and keep and well and substantially repair and keep the premises in a good and tenant like condition throughout the term.'

   or

   – 'To keep all parts of the interior including plate glass windows in repair.'

   It is clear that the first example (i) is the more onerous repairing obligation. The repairing obligations agreed will have cost implications for both the landlord and the tenant.
(iii) To clean the premises. A relatively minor covenant.
(iv) To redecorate internally and externally. The tenant will be obliged to redecorate at set intervals throughout the lease. These are normally every 3–5 years, but depend upon the type of premises. The quality of the building and its finishes will have a cost implication for the tenant.
(v) Not to make alterations without landlord's consent. Alterations are normally physical changes to a building or structure, which may or may not involve improvements. Landlords normally consent to alterations or improvements which add to the value of their property. The question of whether these affect rent is considered below.
(vi) To comply with statutory obligations, i.e. to undertake works to ensure that the premises comply with statutory requirements. This could include Town Planning, Building Regulations, Disability Discrimination, for example. Government legislation controls all business uses to a greater or lesser degree. Some uses such as restaurants or hotels have wider concerns over food safety legislation. The tenant agrees to ensure the building is compliant with this legislation if it is appropriate to the property he occupies.
(vii) Access by landlord. Landlords or their agents will have the right with reasonable notice to enter the premises to view the state of repair and to ensure that covenants have been complied with.
(viii) Alienation/Assignment. Alienation is the legal name for the transfer of an interest in property to another. The assignment (transfer) of the leasehold interest to another is a complex aspect of the lease. Legal advice should be sought. Further information can be found later in this chapter on page 102.

Most leases do not permit assignment of part of the premises. Assignment of the whole is usually granted with the landlord's consent. Consent is required in order that the landlord can control the quality of the tenants. The landlord can refuse to grant a licence to assign but there must be reasonable grounds for so doing. For example – a poor business reference from a prospective assignee.

The legal position at assignment has been changed for leases that have commenced since 1996, as a result of the Landlord and Tenant (Covenants) Act 1995. This new law was introduced as a response to growing concerns over the number of former tenants that were being pursued by landlords for breaches of contract by their successors. They were able to take action against former tenants under the principle of Privity of Contract, which makes the first tenants responsible for the actions of his successors. Therefore if a company assigns its lease to another company and the assignee fails to pay rent or goes bankrupt, then the landlord, if unsuccessful in suing the assignee, can look to the original assignor for damages. This is seen as being unfair and as a result of the above Act, a tenant's liability now ceases on assignment. In return landlords can now be more robust in dealing with applications for assignment and have wider grounds for refusal.

The Act does provide for tenants to provide guarantees known as Authorised Guarantee Agreements (AGAs) which effectively ensure that the outgoing assignor retains liability for the duration of the first assignment. The imposition of an AGA is quite common in leases and is effectively a compromise between the complete cessation of liability and the position prior to the new law.

(ix) To pay landlords costs in relation to an application for a licence or consent in respect of the lease or in the preparation of any notice or proceedings against the tenant. This is largely self-explanatory; however, proceedings are often brought against tenants. The circumstances in which these could be brought are as follows:
   – Serving a notice in respect of the commencement of forfeiture proceedings.
   – A licence to assign or vary a clause in the lease.

(x) Forfeiture. If a tenant breaches covenants in the lease and fails to remedy the breach then the landlord may apply to the court to forfeit the lease. This action ends the lease, although case law surrounding forfeiture is complicated and there are various other issues to consider. The landlord, if successful in these proceedings, can re-enter the property and can claim damages for any breach. Damages are particularly relevant if the tenant has failed to carry out repairs and the property has deteriorated. But the landlord must have a covenant in the lease allowing re-entry into the property in such circumstances. In most instances, the tenant can remedy any breach, by paying rent arrears or by repairing the building. The law tends to give the tenant the opportunity to remedy his breach.

Where a landlord brings a claim for breach of covenant to repair, the Leasehold Property Repairs Act 1938 provides relief against enforcement of the covenant to repair in most leases where there is more than 3 years unexpired.

The courts will only permit enforcement if the landlord can prove one of the following:

❑   Immediate remedy is necessary to prevent substantial diminution of the reversion; this means that if the landlord does not obtain possession, the value of the buildings will reduce.

❑   Immediate remedy is necessary because the tenant has ignored statutory legislation, such as food safety or lift safety, for example.
❑   Where the lessee does not occupy the whole property, immediate remedy is required in the interests of another occupier, who may be suffering as a result of this tenant's breach of the repair covenant.
❑   The breach is capable of remedy at small cost now, but if deferred, the costs could increase, an argument used if the building was deteriorating due to the tenant's neglect.
❑   Not to commit waste. 'Waste' is a legal term for an unlawful act in relation to the property; usually involving deterioration, but it can be an unlawful improvement known as ameliorating waste. The term voluntary waste implies a deliberate act of a tenant in damaging the property.

8.9 Landlord's covenants

(i) Quiet enjoyment. This means that the tenant will be given possession of the premises and an entitlement to receive damages if there is substantial interference by acts of the lessor or persons claiming by the lessor.
(ii) Other landlord's covenants may include such items as: to insure the premises, to maintain estate roads or to repair the whole or part of the premises.

8.10 Schedules

A schedule is a list or plan of intended events in the lease. It will include such things as future rent reviews or any rights that the landlord may wish to reserve in terms of re-entry in the case of an emergency.

Landlords rights reserved
This gives the landlord the right to enter the premises in case of emergency to undertake works of repair, or to inspect, or to take schedules of fixtures and fittings to be yielded up at the end of the lease. This could be where sudden or unforeseen damage to the property has occurred.

The rent review clause
The commercial purpose of the rent review clause is to keep the rent in line with property values. They are perhaps the most difficult part of landlord and tenant relations. Rent reviews on modern leases are normally at 3, 5 or 7 yearly intervals. Rent review clauses contain assumptions, which can be different from the actual circumstances of the lease. This can be confusing initially, but are commonly followed in modern leases and allow for consistency in approach to lease drafting.
    Examples of such clauses can include:
    'That the property is:

 (i) let in the open market and assumed to be vacant;
 (ii) on a particular date;
(iii) on a lease of a certain duration, and this may be actually longer than the number of years left on the lease;
(iv) ignoring any increase in rent by virtue of that particular tenants occupation;
 (v) and that the building is in good repair'.

Thus a rent review clause can assume:

❑   That at rent review a property is vacant (which it is not).
❑   That it has been repaired to a certain standard which it may or may not have been.
❑   That the lease may have 5 years remaining but the rent review assumes that it is for the same term as at the beginning of the lease.

Disregarded matters at rent review

The Landlord and Tenant Act 1954 sets out statutory disregards for ascertaining the rent at lease renewal. These are set out in Section 34 of the above Act. These are now incorporated into modern rent review clauses. These disregards include:

❑   Tenant's goodwill.
❑   Tenant's occupancy.
❑   Tenant's improvements carried out with landlord's consents.

The disregards tend to favour the tenant to some extent by protecting his investment in the property if he has improved it. Similarly, if the tenant is successful, he is not penalised at rent review, if he has a successful business. This latter situation is covered by the disregard of the value of tenant's goodwill and also his occupation.

Repairs and improvements

It is important that the difference between repairs and improvements is understood. Repairs are undertaken to maintain the condition of the building as a covenant in the lease. Improvements will add to the building in terms of extra floor space or additional amenities and may add to the rental value of the premises.

Improvements carried out by the tenant as a condition of the lease are normally subject to rent, but discounts on initial rent at the commencement of the lease may be given. Thus the landlord is granting a concession to the tenant for improving the property. The landlord will benefit from an increase in value of his property as a result of these improvements and a subsidised rent for a period of time will be some form of compensation to the tenant for his expenditure.

If a tenant improves the property without landlord's consent, then he must expect these works to be taken into consideration at rent review. If the tenant improves the property with the landlord's consent then these improvements are excluded at review. Thus sometimes a valuer is calculating the rent of a building but excluding part, if it is an authorised tenant's improvement. This is not a straightforward task!

The proper procedure is for the tenant to obtain the landlord's written consent to undertake works to improve the holding, prior to commencing the works. Plans and costs may be submitted to support the request and work should only be commenced by the tenant when formal written consent is obtained. The consent may be in the form of a Licence to Alter.

Remember, if a tenant improves the property without obtaining consent then the improvement will be included at rent review. Major extensions or the installation of costly plant or fixtures may add value to the building, and contribute significantly to the rental value.

8.11 Trigger notices

Starting rent review negotiations

There is a different procedure for rent review clauses than for lease renewals.

Rent reviews may incorporate a trigger notice under an express covenant. A trigger notice initiates the start of rent review negotiations. It is often in the form of a letter stating the details of the property and the amount of rent claimed. There has been considerable litigation over rent review trigger notices. In order to avoid uncertainty and costly litigation, notices should be in writing and sent by recorded delivery.

The term 'without prejudice' is used in correspondence when negotiations have commenced to protect the position of the negotiating parties who do not wish their correspondence used in court. If this term is used on a rent review notice, it may be misconstrued as a negotiating position and not a notice. This is important; a demand for a revised rent should be in open correspondence and entirely unambiguous.

8.12 Time limits

In commercial leases, certain events that are to occur are dictated by strict timescales. Failure to comply with these timescales can result in one of the following:

❑ Landlords could lose the opportunity to review the rent, if they fail to serve a notice on time.
❑ Tenants could be obliged to accept an excessive rent increase if they fail to respond to a notice within a proscribed timescale.

Thus, where strict adherence timescales are found in a lease, time is of the essence. Some leases will establish clear timescales for the serving of notices for revised rents and for the serving of a tenant's counter notice.

It is good practice always to check, record and diarise the dates of reviews and dates for serving counter notices. A missed notice can be potentially expensive.

Clauses regarding the timing of notices, particularly in old leases, may not be immediately obvious. It is good estate management practice to record all terms of the lease in a précis form in a card index system or by utilising database software.

Time of the essence can interact with other aspects of the lease and the rent review. There may be deadlines set for the appointment of an arbitrator, which if missed may prejudice the right to make an application to The Royal Institution of Chartered Surveyors to appoint an arbitrator to resolve a dispute.

The type of phrase to look for is, for example:

'either party may make reference to a third party (arbitrator or independent expert) within 3 months, but not otherwise.'

Such a wording makes time of the essence and a late notice would be out of time. In many instances, particularly with modern leases, the rent review clause will provide for the rent to be settled at any time, but not normally 6 months before the review date. This is clearly not a problem if a date is missed and in a poor letting market rents are simply not reviewed and the date of review will pass without action. Modern drafting has therefore led to less litigation. However, there are many old leases still in operation with arcane and sometimes bizarre wording which can catch out the unwary FM or estate manager.

8.13 User

A user clause that restricts the use of the premises can affect rental value. In some leases, the landlords have chosen to restrict the permitted use of a property. As an example, a user clause that restricts the use of a property to 'an architect's office only' can arguably be seen to have a downward impact on rental value. Only a limited number of architect tenants would be interested in renting the property. Contrast this with a user clause that permits the use of the property for offices in general. The latter is likely to have a far wider appeal to a greater range of office occupiers in general and as a consequence of this would have a higher rental value.

Normally a clause will not seek to restrict the use of a property too significantly because the tenant can justifiably argue that the range of prospective occupiers will be limited and this will impact on rental growth.

Good drafting of user clauses is good estate management practice. The estate manager should keep the user clause separate from the rent review clause. The rent review should concentrate on the open market rent and the wording should disregard the user clause. This is particularly appropriate in modern shopping centres where the tenant mix is crucial to the overall performance of the centre, but rent review uplift on individual units would otherwise be poor if lease rents were restricted to specific trades only.

8.14 Alienation or assignment

Alienation as far as commercial leases are concerned is the term used to cover the right of the tenant to assign (transfer) his interest to another company or individual. Most commercial leases place a complete bar on the assignment of part of the premises but not the whole of the premises. Consent can be withheld but not unreasonably. A complete bar on alienation will have a downward impact on rent at rent review. Most firms would not even consider taking a lease, which bars assignment, because they could not transfer their lease. They would have to wait for their lease to end before their liability ceased. Such an arrangement is too inflexible and not commercially viable. Banks will be reluctant to use the lease as security against a loan if alienation is restricted.

8.15 Arbitration

In many instances, if the landlord and tenant cannot settle a rent review by negotiation then the lease will provide for the appointment of an arbitrator or an independent expert to settle the matter. Arbitration is a legal process under the Arbitration Act. The Arbitrator will reach a decision based on evidence presented to him by both the parties to the dispute. He is normally only allowed to consider evidence placed before him. This is important because he cannot use his own knowledge of the type of property in making his decision. The award will normally be called a reasoned award and will state why he has come to his conclusions.

The Arbitrator's decision is final as if it were a decision by a Court. There are limited grounds for setting aside an Arbitrator's award, and normally only on grounds of misconduct.

As an alternative, the lease may provide for the appointment of an Independent Expert to settle the review. The Expert generally has to use his own expertise and knowledge in arriving at his decision. He can be sued for negligence and misconduct by either of the parties. This dispute procedure is generally quicker and cheaper than arbitration.

Arbitrators or Experts are either appointed by agreement between the parties or in the absence of agreement by the Royal Institution of Chartered Surveyors.

8.16 Additional covenants

Certain additional tenant's covenants may be placed in a schedule. Examples could be:

❑ To use the premises for the permitted user only.
❑ Not to bring objects or plant and machinery into the buildings that may place strain on the floors.

If the tenant is to undertake works at the commencement of the lease, these should be set out in a schedule. This schedule will be specific to those works being undertaken and set out the obligations of the respective parties in undertaking these works and also the nature and extent of them. Any rent 'holiday' over and above an initial rent-free period will normally be set out in the schedule that relates to rent review and payment of rent.

8.17 Lease renewals

The Landlord and Tenant Act 1954 (part II) and subsequent amendments gives security of tenure to tenants and controls the procedure of lease renewal and termination for commercial property.
There are exceptions:

❑ Serviced offices which offer an all inclusive package of rent, rates and some services are almost always outside the 1954 Act. These arrangements tend to be licences – see earlier.
❑ Some leases are contracted-out of the 1954 Act. Both the landlord and the tenant have agreed to exclude the renewal and compensation provisions of the 1954 Act. This is normally the case where short-term leases are agreed and where renewal rights are not appropriate or where development will take place in the near future and compensation to the tenant is to be avoided. Contracting out can only take place with the agreement of the Court.

The 1954 Act and subsequent amendments are important pieces of legislation and establish a statutory framework for ending and renewing leases. There are many sections to this Act and each deals with a certain part of the process of lease renewal.

8.18 Security of tenure

The Landlord and Tenant Act applies to business premises that are widely defined. It includes commercial enterprises and also voluntary societies, clubs, doctors' surgeries and institutions. The Act excludes tenancies of agricultural holdings, mining leases, service tenancies and tenancies on a fixed term of 6 months or less, in most instances. The initiation of the process for renewing or ending a lease is governed by certain sections of the Act, which are described below.
Where this machinery is not implemented, that is no action is taken by either party, then a lease will continue until the process of termination/renewal is implemented.

The way an organisation reacts to the process will depend upon the circumstances – are you a landlord or are you a tenant? For example, if the property let is required for development the landlord will wish to commence the termination procedure as soon as possible.

In a rising market and where a new lease is acceptable, the landlord will also seek to obtain the notice served to commence discussions for a new lease, in order to benefit from the higher rent. Conversely, if the market is falling then there is less incentive for the landlord to start negotiations as this may result in a lower rent than under the old lease.

The tenant who wants a new lease, especially when the market rents are less, can start the process by serving a notice on the landlord requesting a new lease, or may serve a notice stating that he does not want a new lease.

8.19 The machinery for termination – Sections 24–28

Sections 24–28 of the Landlord and Tenant Act 1954 set out the way in which leases are terminated by either party. The notices are legal documents, and therefore legal advice should be sought when serving or receiving one of these notices. These sections are listed below:

❑ Section 24 provides that no tenancy of more than 6 months to which the Act applies can be terminated unless in accordance with the Act.
❑ Section 25 Landlords notice to terminate.
❑ Section 26 Tenants request for a new tenancy.
❑ Section 27 Tenants notice to terminate.
❑ Section 28 Renewal of tenancies by agreement.

8.20 Landlord's grounds for opposing a new tenancy – Section 30

The 1954 Act provides limited grounds that the landlord can use in order to prevent the tenant from obtaining a new tenancy. The grounds under Section 30 are stated as follows:

(a) Breach of repairing obligations. Landlord must be able to show that this breach is of a serious nature. The Courts may accept an undertaking by the tenant to remedy the breach.
(b) Persistent delay in paying rent.
(c) Other serious breach of covenant. Discretion given to courts to interpret what constitutes a serious breach.
(d) The landlord is willing and able to provide a suitable alternative accommodation on reasonable terms including protection of goodwill.
(e) Possession is required of a subtenancy in order to let the premises as a whole. This ground is only relevant when the interest of the tenant's immediate landlord is shortly to end.
(f) The landlord intends to demolish, reconstruct or carry out substantial works of construction and these could not be undertaken without gaining possession.
(g) The landlord intends to occupy the premises either for business or residential purposes but the landlord must have held the superior interest for at least 5 years. There must be proof of the requirement to occupy the premises, e.g. evidence of financial planning, acquisition of specialist trading expertise, the raising of finance.

If the landlord is successful in refusing a new lease on the grounds (d) to (g), then compensation to the tenant will be expected from the landlord. If the landlord is successful in opposing a new tenancy, Section 31 provides that the court will not grant a new tenancy.

8.21 The new tenancy

Where the parties to the new lease cannot agree to the terms, the courts can make an order for a new tenancy in the absence of agreement. The terms of the new lease are normally similar to those in the old and the Section 34 disregards apply to the setting of the rent.

There must be good grounds for varying the terms of a new lease. These terms are usually controlled by Sections 32–35 of the 1954 Act.

The new lease will normally be:

❑ The same property.
❑ A lease of similar length.
❑ At the open market rent excluding:
  o Any effect on rent of the tenant's occupation.
  o Any goodwill attaching to the property.
  o The effect on rent of tenant's improvements provided that these were carried out with the permission of the landlord and within the last 21 years or during the current tenancy regardless of its duration.
  o Any other terms that may be agreed between the parties or determined by the courts.

8.22 Section 32 Rule

There are limits to the ability of either the landlord or tenant to achieve a variation in the terms of a new lease without agreement between the parties. This sets out four tests in Section 32:

  (i) There must be valid reasons for the change on estate management grounds.
 (ii) The change must be compensatable by a change in rents.
(iii) The tenant's security of tenure must not be adversely affected.
(iv) The change must be fair and reasonable in the view of the court.

Exceptions to the Section 32 Rule

If the tenant occupies only part of the original demise, the landlord could force the tenant to take a lease on the whole property or demise or permit him to renew in relation to that part of the property which he occupying only.

In most instances, the courts will try to establish a reasonable position between the parties and look closely at the tenant's intention to his business as well as the length of time he was previously in occupation.

Following an award for a new tenancy, the tenant may decide not to take on the lease by repudiating the proposed lease within 14 days. This would occur typically where the tenant cannot afford the new rent. The lease will then terminate at the next quarter day.

8.23 Market forces and lease renewal

In poor rental markets, tenants have challenged the upward-only rent review terms of older leases and there have been cases where at renewal both upward and downward provisions in rent reviews have been established by the courts.

Compensation for termination of the lease

This is available to the tenant only under grounds –(e), (f), (g) (see above). The amount of compensation for termination is based on a multiplier of rateable value and depends upon the date of termination in relation to the current rating system at the time.

Compensation on quitting

The basis for compensation for quitting, where improvements have been undertaken, is set out under Section 1 and Section 2 of the Landlord and Tenant Act 1927.

If the landlord is successful in obtaining possession on one of the above grounds as set out above under Section 30 of the 1954 Act then the Court will not grant a new lease under Section 31.

The compensation for quitting a lease is payable only under grounds (v), (vi) and (vii). The amount of compensation is dependent upon the time the tenant has been in occupation and is based on a multiplier of rateable value. Currently, if the tenant has been in occupation for more than up to 7 years then it is calculated on $1 \times$ the rateable value. If occupation has been for more than 7 years then it is based on $2 \times$ the rateable value. Where the tenant has been in occupation for less than 5 years, compensation can be excluded under Section 37 of the Act. It should be noted that the amount of compensation can be changed by legislation, normally concurrent with any rating revaluation.

Improvements qualify for compensation if they were undertaken with the landlord's consent and if the improvement undertaken by the tenant has added value to the property. However, the effect of improvements depends upon the landlord's intentions following occupation at the end of the lease. If these include demolition, refurbishment or structural alterations or change of use, or where the improvements do not add value, then these changes will be reflected to the detriment of the tenant.

8.24 Repairs

Section 4 of the Landlord and Tenant Act states that landlords who are responsible for repairs to premises are liable for personal injury or damage to property due to a defect in repair. This liability could extend to passers by as well as occupants and visitors. Examples of defects that could cause accidents to passers by would be falling masonry or roof tiling occasioned by poor workmanship. Occupants could be put at risk by poorly installed gas boilers, or by defective electrical wiring, as well as a host of general structural problems.

The landlord is liable if he knows or ought to have known of the defect. The Act goes further in imputing knowledge to the landlord where he is given an express or implied right to enter premises and carry out repairs.

The landlord will not be liable in respect of any defect in the state of the premises arising because the tenant had failed to carry out a repairing obligation imposed on him. This latter point could become quite contentious. Consider a situation whereby the tenant has an obligation to repair the interior of the property and the landlord the exterior. A defect arising out of the tenants liability if left unremedied could result in a spread of damage that could then cause damage to the external fabric, and become partly the landlord's liability, if a claim arose.

9 Developing New Buildings

9.1 The development process

Property development is a high-risk, complex activity that is directly influenced by global, national and local economics. It involves changing or intensifying the use of land. It also involves tying up large sums of money in a lengthy production process.

The development process can be considered in three main stages and a number of sub-stages.

Stage 1 – Feasibility

A site is considered appropriate for development or re-development, or a suitable site is sought. Reasons may be: demand for the development or in anticipation of enhanced value of the site due to changing economic, social, technical or other circumstances. Market research will take place at this stage and the potential for obtaining any necessary planning consent will be investigated.

Evaluation

The results of the feasibility study will guide development decision making throughout the process. The evaluation includes the financial appraisal of the development proposal, which must establish the value of the site and ensure that development costs are reasonable. In the private sector, it indicates the anticipated level of profit. In the public sector and non-profit organisations, it sets out to ascertain whether costs can be recovered. The developers' professional team should be involved at this stage.

Acquisition

Given a decision to proceed, two key activities will be:

Legal investigation
If the developer does not already own the site, it will be essential for the investigation to establish existing planning permissions and other consents (e.g. concerning the alteration or demolition of a listed building), light, ownership and any rights-of-way across the site. Government departments may become involved if, for example, compulsory purchase has to be a feature of the project. Failure to conduct a meticulous and detailed legal investigation can endanger the viability of the proposed development.

Ground investigation
This will include investigations into:

❏ Access.
❏ Assessing the load-bearing capacity of the land or existing building(s).
❏ Drainage.

❏ Establishing the ability of existing services (electricity, gas, water, sewage and telephones) to meet the requirements of the completed development. In the event of non-availability of essential services, assessing the cost of their provision.
❏ Site survey to establish the actual site measurements.
❏ Archaeological artefacts (e.g. Roman remains), or geological faults, site contamination, underground services or storage tanks.
❏ Environmental and ecology issues.

Stage 2 – Pre-production

Design and costing
Design and costing is a continuous process that extends from the initiation stage and continues during construction. In some circumstances the team involved will produce the design likely to be required because they are working with the eventual occupier. A building pre-let to an industrial or commercial concern, a private finance initiative project to construct a hospital or military installation are examples. The key to success is the design brief document because it gives the architect the various parameters within which to work.

Initial cost estimate
In the early stages of the development process, before the developer is committed, design work will only be sufficient to enable a quantity surveyor to produce an initial cost estimate. It is this cost estimate that is used in the preparation of an initial financial evaluation.

Initial design phase
The early design will include:

❏ Scaled drawings showing the position of the building on the site, the site plan.
❏ Drawings of the main elevations.
❏ Floor plans showing only the internal arrangement of the building(s).
❏ An outline specification of the building materials and finishes.

Detailed design information
Later in the process, more detailed plans and specifications will progressively be required. These will enable:

❏ The creation of a detailed estimate of building costs by the quantity surveyor.
❏ The submission of requests for planning permission.
❏ Improvement in the quality of the financial appraisal.
❏ Preparation of specifications and plans, which will be required in the construction tendering process and for the building contract.

Once committed, the developer must ensure that significant and potentially costly changes to the design are avoided. Incremental design activities do, inevitably, take place during the production phase.

Permissions
Planning consent will be required for anything but minor schemes and it is prudent, even for a small refurbishment scheme that entails alterations, to establish whether it is necessary. Professional advice is essential for obtaining planning consent. Obtaining permissions can be a complex, lengthy and expensive process for which adequate provision must be made in the financial evaluation.

Outline planning consent
To obtain outline planning consent, the developer submits only sufficient information about the purpose to which the site will be put and the proposed density of the scheme. Outline planning consent cannot be obtained for a change of use, e.g. from an office block to housing or from a house to an office. Outline planning consent is only valid for a fixed period of time, usually 5 years. If the development has not occurred in this time, then it may be renewed after submission of the appropriate application. Outline planning consent does not give the developer the authority to proceed, only an agreement 'in principle' of the proposed scheme. Detailed planning consent is required to actually proceed with the development.

Detailed planning consent
Obtaining detailed planning consent entails the submission to the planning authority of detailed drawings and information about:

❑   Siting.
❑   Access.
❑   Design.
❑   External appearance.
❑   Landscaping.
❑   Environmental impact.
❑   Biodiversity.

If the development proposal changes after detailed planning consent is given, it will be necessary to obtain further consent. If the local planning authority (LPA) refuses planning consent, the developer has the right to appeal.

Legal consents
These include a requirement for:

❑   Listed building consent (permission to alter or demolish a listed building).
❑   Permission to divert or close a right of way.
❑   Agreements to secure the provision of the necessary infrastructure and services.
❑   Building Regulations approval.

Planning agreements
Also known as planning 'gains', these are contracts negotiated as part of a planning approval and deal with matters that are not part of the planning consent (e.g. the provision and maintenance of public facilities). These agreements must be signed before planning consent is given. Inevitably they will involve additional cost, which must be included in the financial evaluation. Section 106 Agreements are common in many development projects. They may be funds to support the local community (education, transport, etc.) or funding of improvements or changes in roadways, infrastructure, or environmental projects – the key is that the gain is linked to a benefit to the local community.

Commitment
To minimise cost and risk, it is essential that before a developer becomes liable for any outlay of money on anything other than preliminary work, the developer must be certain that all preliminary work has been satisfactorily completed. Completing the preliminary work can itself be a lengthy process and while it has been going on, things might have

changed, particularly if the economy is in a volatile state. At worst the scheme may no longer be viable. It is therefore critical that before committing to a scheme, the evaluation is up to date and soundly based.

Up to the time before commitment, the most likely costs are professional fees, general expenses, investigation costs and staff-related costs. In certain circumstances, professional teams may work during the preliminary stages of the scheme on a speculative basis or for a reduced fee. This is on the basis that they will be appointed for the development once the developer commits to it. In the case of major PFI projects, consortia bidding for the work can expend six and seven figure sums each in order to become the preferred bidder and only one out of perhaps three or four will get to that stage. Conditional contracts are sometimes a feature of a development project. As an example, the developer may be in possession of land for which planning consent has not been given. Contracts may then be made subject to the developer obtaining planning approval.

Stage 3 – Production

Construction, commissioning and fitting out take place during this phase, the objective of which must be completion on time and within budget, without detriment to quality. This phase will take upwards of 2 years and in that time things will change. The project must be promoted and where appropriate, marketed. Change must be minimised but at the same time the finished construction must be fit for purpose, which may involve changes to the specification along the way. Major development projects may of course take longer than the average 2 years.

Occupation considerations

The developer may have had the ultimate occupation of the building in mind from the start either as a pre-let or pre-sold arrangement or for the owner occupier. The other possibilities are letting or disposal. In these situations, the developer will need to:

❑ Secure a willing occupier at an acceptable rent or price within the period forecast in the evaluation. In the case of some developments there may be many occupiers (e.g. a retail shopping mall) or in some office developments, there may only be one.
❑ Appoint an agent or staff member responsible for letting or disposal in the development process from the start.
❑ Decide whether to try to let or dispose of the building before or after completion. The financiers of the development can greatly influence this decision.

9.2 Planning legislation

The system of planning and development control emerged from the rebuilding programmes following the Second World War, public concern over ribbon development in rural areas and urban slum clearance. The current system dates from laws made in the period 1944–1947.

The Town and Country Planning Act came into force on 1 July 1948. The Law was consolidated by the Town and Country Planning Act 1990, although some of the pre-1990 legislation is still operative. The procedure for obtaining planning permission and the rights of appeal against a refusal is set out together with the role of the Secretary of State. Most forms of development require planning permission. Important buildings and sensitive areas are protected. There are constraints on development of listed buildings and in conservation areas.

The planning legislation in the UK is a complex system of statutes, statutory instruments, and circulars, administered by Local Authorities (LAs), although in some urban areas the functions of the LA have been transferred to other institutions, such as Urban Development Corporations. Homes and Communities Agency is the new government agency to ensure sustainable development via regeneration projects. The Department for Communities and Local Government has responsibility for planning, building and environmental issues in the UK.

Planning legislation is made by central government and implemented at local level, with ministerial supervision. The High Court can intervene in certain circumstances. LAs are obliged to draw up development plans. They show how and where development in the future will occur. They will also indicate areas allocated for certain forms of development and others for conservation.

Guidance on standards for parking, the density of development and landscaping are examples of issues that are set out in the unitary development plan (UDP).

Administering the system

The abolition of the Greater London Council and the Metropolitan District Councils in 1985 led to the creation of a single tier planning system in most parts of the country, operated by London Boroughs or Metropolitan Councils and the recently formed Unitary Authorities.

Outside these areas in the rural 'Shire Counties' a two tier system of planning remains in force with both District Councils and County Councils having planning functions. County Councils have a limited planning role where matters of strategic importance are to be considered, which would include mineral-related developments, e.g. mining or the use of land for waste infill. District Councils fulfil the majority of planning functions.

Local government is controlled by a series of statutory directions, obligations procedures and consultations. The Secretary of State exercises ministerial control and the ways in which he may influence planning matters are considered later. In certain instances the courts will intervene.

9.3 The Town and Country Planning Act

The Town and Country Planning Act 1990 confers powers on County, District, Metropolitan, Borough and London Borough Councils. This Act is divided into many different sections. There are over 100 sections and some examples of these are shown below.

❑   Section 12 requires the preparation of a UDP by each metropolitan district and each London Borough Council.
❑   Section 36 requires preparation of district wide local plans by non-metropolitan district councils.
❑   Section 57 specifies that planning permission is required for the carrying out of any development on land.
❑   Section 77 specifies powers of the Secretary of State to 'call in' a planning application for a decision by him.
❑   Section 97 specifies powers to revoke or modify the grant of planning permission.
❑   Section 106 permits LAs to enter into obligations with applicants for planning permission.

9.4 Planning permission

Planning permission is required for the carrying out of any development on land.

The term development covers the carrying out of operations, such as an extension to a building and also the making of a material change of use.

Other examples of development include the construction of a car park or the erection of an advertising hoarding. Such activities normally require planning permission. Another example is the change of use from a small boarding house to a private dwelling.

Not all operations require planning permission. This is discussed further below in the section delegated legislation.

Making a planning application

Planning applications for change of use are submitted to the LA.

The application must be made in the correct manner. It may be made by the owner of land, i.e. the subject of the application. The application can be made by his agent or by a firm or an individual who is looking to obtain consent.

The planning application form must include the address of the site, an ordnance survey map to scale showing boundaries and in most cases scale floor plans of the development and details of access to the site. Applicants are also asked to state the present and previous uses of the site. There may be a presumption in the UDP or in a General Development Order (GDO) against turning certain uses into another. Additional information on such matters as tree felling, refuse collection provisions, drainage, vehicular access, access statements, environmental impact statements and parking may be requested depending upon the type of scheme applied for. The LPA must have regard to the impact of the scheme on services infrastructure, the amenity of the area and public safety.

Processing a planning application

Following the results of any informal discussions between the applicant and the planning officer, the application will be submitted with the appropriate fee, plans and any supporting information. It is then acknowledged by the LPA.

The accuracy of the form is then checked together with the practicality of the proposal. The proposal is then checked against the local plan and policy guidance. A site visit is made by the planning officer and copies of the application will be sent to highways authorities, utility providers, parish councillors if a rural proposal and, if it is an area of conservation importance, to civic societies or environmental organisations. A report sheet is completed following assembly of all the information including the results of consultations. The application forms and plans are now posted on the Planning Portal, for everyone to view.

Determination of the application

In the case of non-contentious applications, the planning committee have powers to delegate the decision-making process to a planning officer. An example of this would be a change of use from an office to a private dwelling, where the officer's report indicates no adverse impact on the locality in terms of employment loss, visual amenity or traffic congestion. Similarly, where the building is currently in a non-conforming use, such as a motor car spray shop in a residential area, a more environmentally acceptable use has been proposed.

In other instances, many applications are approved on the recommendation of the planning officer.

Where the application is contentious, the planning committee will discuss representations by pressure groups or neighbours. The committee may overturn the recommendation of the planning officer, grant permissions with conditions attached or refuse it. A formal decision notice is then sent to the applicant.

Outline planning permission

An application for outline planning permission is normally made to confirm the acceptability of a large-scale proposal, and to spare initial expense on detailed plans and investigations that may prove to be abortive. Matters left for future agreement such as the density of the built development, or landscaping or parking are known as reserved matters.

Planning appeals

An applicant may appeal to the Secretary of State if dissatisfied with a refusal or the imposition of an onerous condition. Information on how to appeal is set out in the decision notice. The appeal is sent directly to the Secretary of State with reasons. The appeal is dealt with by a planning inspector and normally by written representations. Significant weight is attached to Planning Policy Guidance Notes in arguing a case and by the inspector in arriving at a decision. In certain cases, a public enquiry or a hearing will be required. Either party may request to be heard, but this is a very expensive procedure and normally reserved for major schemes. The inspector can grant planning permission and can attach conditions. There is a further recourse to the courts if a point of law is at issue.

Delegated legislation

Delegated legislation in the form of statutory instruments is important in planning legislation. These are regulations issued by the Minister under the powers of an Act and come into force by being 'laid on the table' in the House of Commons.

The General Development Order (GDO) 1988 enables the LPA to grant planning permission for most forms of small-scale development. This would include painting a house, small-scale extensions to factories or replacing window frames.

The withdrawal of permitted development rights occurs in environmentally sensitive areas in both urban and rural settings. An example of this would be the use of similar materials in the replacement of a roof to those on existing surrounding buildings in order to preserve the character of the area.

The Secretary of State can withdraw permitted development rights for a particular area. For example, withdrawal could be in connection with a permitted house extension size in an urban conservation area.

9.5 The Town and Country Planning Use Classes Order 2005

The 2005 Use Classes Order controls the activities that take place in or on land as shown in Table 9.1. As an example, shops can also be suitable as restaurants or cafes. However, the characteristics of use in each case will be different, in terms of hours of opening and issues such as refuse collection and noise.

Table 9.1   List of classes of use permitted

A	Retailing
A1	Shops, e.g. clothes, grocer and so on
A2	Financial services, e.g. bank, estate agents
A3	Restaurants and cafes
A4	Drinking establishments
A5	Hot food takeaways
B	**Business**
B1	Business use offices and light industry
B2	General industrial
B3 to B7	Special industrial, e.g. oil refining
B4	Warehouses
C	**Residential**
C1	Hotels and institutions
C2	Residential institutions e.g. nursing homes, care homes, hospitals, boarding schools
C3	Private dwelling
D	**Other uses**
D1	Non-residential institutions
D2	Places of assembly and leisure, e.g. a bingo hall
Sui generis	Particular uses, such as petrol filling station, amusement arcade, etc.

The Use Classes Order places shops in Class A1. Premises used for food or drinking have their own categories. Planning permission is needed to change a shop into a restaurant and such applications are frequently refused. By contrast planning permission is not needed to change a restaurant back into a shop. Nor is it needed to change from one type of shop use to another.

The Use Classes Order adds a degree of flexibility to certain business uses by allowing movement between certain classes without planning permission. Permitted changes do not apply where the change would involve intensification of use on land or buildings or where the change would involve dangerous or hazardous processes.

The permitted changes are:

A5 to A1, A2, A3
A4 to A3, A2, A1
A3 to A1 or A2
A2 to A1
B2 or B8 to B1 Where the floor space does not exceed 235 m^2
B1 to B8

9.6 Planning policy guidance notes

Such documents explain the powers and duties of LPAs and the impact of new legislation and policy guidance on planning matters. LPAs must have regard to these when determining planning permissions and in many circumstances they will have a bearing on the success and failure of an appeal. Planning policy guidance notes of major importance are:

❑   PPG1 general policies and principles.
❑   PPG2 green belts.

❑ PPG4 industrial development in small firms.
❑ PPG13 out-of-town shopping.

9.7 Development plans

The 1990 Town and Country Planning Act (Section 12) obliges LAs to draw up plans in order that they may see how their areas are developing in future.

Structure plans are drawn up by shire councils and are broad brush statements concentrating mainly on major settlements and roads.

Local plans are drawn up at district level. They normally relate to a part of a town or an area of countryside.

Unitary Development Plans are prepared by LAs and replace structure and local plans in metropolitan areas.

Policies covered by plans would include:

❑ Settlement patterns and areas for growth or specific control.
❑ Areas earmarked for industrial or commercial development.
❑ Guidance on the future need for housing, favoured locations for such development and advice on unit size and supporting facilities.
❑ Areas for both rural and urban conservation.
❑ Social infrastructure.

9.8 Planning agreements

Planning agreements are often a solution where otherwise the LPA would be unable to grant a permission under Sections 106, 106A and 106B of the 1991 Planning and Compensation Act as amended from the 1990 Town and Country Planning Act.

A typical scenario would be where planning permission to develop a dwelling in the grounds of a hotel would limit the use of that dwelling to an employee of the hotel. It follows that if it were occupied privately a breach of the Planning Agreement would have occurred.

Such agreements are executed as deeds which:

❑ State that the obligation is a planning obligation.
❑ Identify the land and the person entering into the obligation.
❑ Identify the authority by whom the obligation is enforceable.

9.9 Breach of planning control

If development occurs without planning permission or in breach of a condition or limitation attached to a planning permission then a breach of Section 171A of the 1990 act occurs. The LA may then take enforcement action by issue of an enforcement notice or breach of condition notice.

Enforcement notice

This notice will require the breach to be remedied by issue of a notice, which will state the nature of the breach and the steps necessary to remedy it. An appeal to the Secretary of State can be made.

Breach of condition notice

This is served where there has been non-compliance with a condition attached to a planning permission. There is no right of appeal to the Secretary of State.

Planning contravention notice

Such a notice is issued where the LA wish to obtain information on the nature of operations being undertaken. Failure to comply is an offence.

Certificate of lawfulness

Unauthorised uses can become lawful when no enforcement action is taken once a limitation period has expired. In order to have a use certified as lawful through passage of time, the 1991 Planning and Compensation Act provides for a 10-year limitation rule after which enforcement action is banned.

A certificate of lawfulness is applied for to confirm that:

❑ An existing use is lawful.
❑ Operations undertaken are lawful.
❑ Whether any other matter constituting a failure to comply with a condition or limitation on a planning permission is lawful.

They are often applied for where a property has been in a certain use for many years but with no record of grant of planning permission.

9.10 Users pre-1964

Development control came into existence in 1948. Pre-1948 uses are normally granted an exemption from the need for planning permission. Uses between 1948 and 1964 without planning permission were unlawful prior to the 1991 Planning and Compensation Act, but at that time not necessarily subject to enforcement action.

9.11 Listed buildings

A building of special architectural interest will be protected from demolition or unauthorised extensions, additions and in certain cases internal alterations. Special features that could be listed include:

❑ External features such as a decorative façade, windows and doors.
❑ The spaces and internal layout – the plan of a building is one of its most important characteristics. Interior plans should be respected and left unaltered as far as possible.
❑ Internal features of interest such as decorated plaster surfaces, panelling, floors, window shutters, doors and doorcases.
❑ Details such as mouldings, stucco-work, wall and ceiling decorations can be just as valuable in simple vernacular and functional buildings as in grander architecture, and can be a building's most important features.

Listed buildings are not necessarily old. Certain factories and buildings from the 1930s as well as some even more contemporary have been listed. Buildings are graded to show their relative architectural or historic interest:

❑   Grade I buildings are of exceptional interest.
❑   Grade II* are particularly important buildings of more than special interest.
❑   Grade II are of special interest, warranting every effort to preserve them.

The Planning (Listed Buildings) Act 1990 places the Secretary of State under a duty to compile and maintain a list of such buildings in order to protect them. Owners of listed buildings have obligations to repair and maintain their buildings to certain standards. This will normally have significant cost implications. If the building is allowed to fall into dis-repair, then the LA will issue a Repairs Notice to the owner. It is a criminal offence to demolish or to carry out any works which would affect the character of a listed building. Fines of up to £20,000 or a prison sentence not exceeding 2 years were introduced under the 1991 Planning and Compensation Act.

9.12 Conservation areas

Local planning authorities are under a duty to determine which parts of their area are 'of special architectural or historic interest'. A conservation area could comprise a whole town or village, or just a street or square. It does not follow that all the buildings in a conservation area will be of historic or architectural interest, but as a group they will be worthy of atten-tion. There are 9,300 areas designated as conservation areas in the UK. English Heritage, Local Authorities and the Secretary of State share the responsibility for the compliance to the act. Typically the Act controls demolition of buildings, preservation of trees, and the nature of building works. The LPAs have a duty to preserve the character of conservation areas. Restrictive development control known as conservation area consent will apply and will be needed for demolition and most building operations. Regulations regarding the display of shop signs and advertising hoardings will be more stringent in the interests of amenity.

9.13 Building design

Whilst FMs rarely get the chance to be fully involved in a new building design, many wish they could. Many day-to-day management issues of buildings stem from the design stage, and there is an increased pressure for the future needs of maintenance and occupiers to be more closely considered by the design team. The increased use of PFI and PPP contract methods in large-scale infrastructure projects, such as the new Building Schools for The Future, is helping to raise the profile of FM in design matters.

   Case studies exist that show how ill-conceived building designs demonstrate a lack of forethought about post-occupancy maintenance. The studies indicate that these designs have significant implications for post-occupancy operating costs and safety. It is common knowledge that the ratio of design, construction and occupation costs is 1:5:200. The pre-occupancy or design phase is an appropriate time to:

❑   Ensure that early and adequate consideration is given to the influence of proposed design features on post-occupancy maintenance.

❑   Integrate key maintenance staff in the commissioning process.
❑   Develop the maintenance systems, procedures and measures to be adopted.
❑   Develop a training programme to ensure the smooth operation of the systems and procedures from handover stage.
❑   Set in place specialist service contracts.
❑   Establish how IT can help to manage maintenance and decide what IT systems can best meet the requirements.

9.14 Types and uses

There is a wide range of building types, from temporary to permanent, from small to large. Different uses can be made of the many different types, with some being naturally more suitable than others for specific functions. Buildings can be categorised as simple naturally ventilated, open plan naturally ventilated, standard air conditioned or prestige air conditioned. In addition they are hybrids of the aforementioned, as well as special purpose buildings such as hospitals, hotels, retail and warehousing.

Buildings provide space for user activities. They provide shelter and protection for their contents, e.g. goods, animals or people. Heating, ventilation and cooling helps to mitigate the effect of the external and internal environment.

Most buildings are permanent structures, although it is possible to find buildings that are temporary, erected for some specific purpose and able to be moved at a future date. Examples of these would include Porta Cabins which are often used as building site offices or prefabricated school classrooms.

9.15 Drivers of building design

The factors that must be considered in a building design project include:

❑   The treatment of time. In the short term, the building must contribute to meeting the current organisational objectives and requirements of the current working practices of the occupier. Longer-term considerations would include flexibility and adapt-ability, which can make a building more manageable over time. For example, to what extent will the building lend itself to refurbishment, or a different internal layout? Furthermore, will the building be capable of different uses in the future?
❑   The physical, functional and financial performance of the building based on the occupier's perception of need in terms of time, cost and quality. These considerations include:
    o   The suitability of the site, its shape, size and orientation, together with the likely impact of climate and any hazards either natural or man made. Site contamination by chemicals or substances from past uses could be an issue in this respect. The site must be suitable in terms of access and have ample parking and loading facilities.
    o   Locational factors are also important. Is the site in the right place in terms of the prestige and status of the occupiers business? Is the location too down or up market? Does the site benefit from good road and rail communications?

o The functions of the building and the tasks it carries out are major concerns. The needs of a high-tech software house are of course different from those of a manufacturer. Both will have different requirements in terms of the size and layout of the space they occupy. Occupiers increasingly realise that the nature of their business might change over time, due perhaps to technological innovation, changing staff needs or new legislation.

o Functional obsolescence can be a problem. Buildings can become outmoded or unsuitable for a use. They may become uneconomic to run or the location in which the building is situated may change in character due perhaps to local adverse economic circumstances.

o The expected contribution to the company's organisational performance and profitability can be supported by an evaluation of the life cycle costings and operating costs, as well as capital value increases or decreases.

9.16 Sustainable construction

Buildings and structures change the appearance of cities, towns and countryside. Construction and maintenance of buildings use resources and generate waste on a scale far greater than most other industrial sectors. For example, the construction industry is quoted as consuming 6 tonnes of resources and generating half a tonne of waste per citizen. It is also said that in the UK half of all CO_2 emissions arise from building energy consumption. It is therefore not surprising that over the last few years, sustainability has become an important construction issue. The concept covers development, resource use and sustainable material sources. Pressure on the industry to get leaner, to minimise waste, eliminate non-value adding activities and minimise resource use comes from central and local government, customers and building users.

New buildings can be designed to achieve the BREEAM standard. The Building Research Establishment (BRE) are responsible for the Building Research Establishment Environmental Assessment Method (BREEAM) – this is a framework to get better environmental friendly buildings. The standard was launched in 1990, and relaunched in 2008 to reflect changing views of the impact of a building on the environment. The areas of assessment include the overall management of the building, energy use, health and well being of occupants, pollution, transport, land use, ecology, materials and water use. Credits are awarded according to the performance of the building against specific criteria. The credits added together and the overall rating is based on a weighting system. Ratings range from Outstanding, Excellent, Very Good, Good or Pass. The Interim Certificate is awarded for Building Design and Construction – i.e. the intention of the building; whereas the Final Certificate is awarded for the Building Operation, reflecting how well the FM can actually manage the building. The new scheme is aligned with other standards such as the Energy Performance Certificates (EPCs) and Carbon Trust standard.

Leadership in Energy and Environmental Design (LEED) is the American standard in building design, launched in 1998. It assesses the design in six areas (sustainable sites; water efficiency; energy and atmosphere; materials and resources; indoor environmental quality; innovation and design process). There are four grades awarded as follows:

(i) Certified 40 – 49 points.
(ii) Silver 50 – 59.
(iii) Gold 60 – 79 points.
(iv) Platinum – 80 points and above.

Table 9.2   Building technologies

Building management	Space management	Business management
Climate control (HVAC systems)	CAD capabilities	Voice systems
Energy management	Building information	Data and image transfer
Fire safety	Cost monitoring systems	Cabling for LANs, WANs
Lighting	Cable management	Mobile communications
Maintenance management	Equipment databases	Video conferencing
Security, including access control		Meeting room management

9.17 Intelligent buildings

A definition of an intelligent building is:

'One which maximises the efficiency of the occupants while enabling the effective management of resources with minimum lifetime costs.'

A definition of building intelligence is that it:

'Enables the efficient use of buildings, space and business systems to support staff in the effective operating of the business.'

Both definitions imply a building that is both responsive to the needs of its users and inherently responsive to change and has a building shell that enables the incorporation of the technology to make it responsive.

The key to the ultimate intelligent building is one that has technology that integrates systems as listed in Table 9.2.

9.18 Structure and its effect on building use

The structure of buildings is a major determinant in the possible internal usage and layout. The envelope of the building is used to classify types of buildings – steel framed, concrete framed, preformed, space framed or timber framed. The types of materials used to construct a building will be determined by the intended use of the building, availability and cost of materials, location of building, local ground and weather conditions, size of building (height, width and span), internal layout requirements, the construction timescale and local planning restrictions. The internal structure features such as window mullions, span, floor depth, slab to slab dimensions, distances to the core and floor height will impact on the future use of the space.

9.19 Planning grids and the use of space

The planning grid is the term given to the way a commercial building is divided into squares or rectangles because of the way in which it is constructed. The pattern of the grid depends upon the following:

❑ The size and depth of the building.
❑ The distance between window mullions will dictate the size of each enclosed module of space, i.e. the location of partitions for individual offices will be dictated by the location of windows frames and supports, known as mullions.

❑   The structural columns supporting the building.
❑   The ceiling height of each floor in an office building will dictate the potential for installation of a raised floor or for a suspended acoustic tiled ceiling and can therefore have a bearing on how and where services are located.
❑   The eaves' height in a warehouse will dictate the height of the racking and also the vehicles that can be accommodated for loading and unloading.
❑   The length and width of the building. The need for circulation space and fire safety requirements will determine how the space is divided up.
❑   The ceiling and lighting grid should be co-ordinated with the window mullions to enable partitioning. The same would apply to cable systems for computer and other data services.
❑   The installation of computer suites into buildings may require air conditioning systems to be installed. The grid should allow for adaptation of the workspace to accommodate any such changes.

9.20 Developers' fit-out

The needs of occupiers vary significantly depending upon many factors and because of this, many buildings are constructed only to a 'shell finish', enabling the occupier to fit it out to their precise requirements. The occupier will then install their own partitions, service areas, such as kitchens, toilets and heating systems, in the case of an office building, or furnishings, racking and shelving and a shop front in the case of a retailer.

However, the main problem with such fittings is that they may not always suit the individual tenant. Costly alterations could result at some future date when the functional shortcomings of the speculative fit-out become apparent.

It is more prudent for an occupier to work with a developer in establishing the most suitable layout during the final construction phase, and before entering into a lease commitment.

Sometimes developers will undertake a large amount of the fitting out before the property is occupied. This could be a result of a tenant's requirement being incorporated into the building. If a building is constructed speculatively, the fit-out scheme is solely a marketing device to attract buyers or tenants. Some developers will attach great importance on good presentation of the buildings they are attempting to let. This may help where a tenant has to be enticed to sign up to a lease by a quality fit-out, including suspended ceilings, lighting and carpets. Terms used by developers are shell and core, category A and category B fit-outs. These are explained below.

Shell and core

Shell-and-core developments include fully finished landlord areas comprising main entrance and reception, lift and stair cores, lobbies and toilets. These areas are not part of the space rented to the tenant. The office floor areas are left as a shell, ready for category A fit-out by the tenant.

Category A fit-out

There is no standard definition for category A fit-out – it can vary between the different developers. Typically, category A is what the developer provides as part of the rentable office space and usually comprises the following:

- ❏ Raised floors.
- ❏ Suspended ceilings.
- ❏ Extension of the mechanical and electrical services above the ceiling from the riser across the lettable space.
- ❏ Finishes to the internal face of the external and core walls.
- ❏ Blinds.

It is also common for the developer to make a contribution to the tenant for the carpets, floor boxes and grommets, which are then installed as part of the tenant's category B fit-out, rather than installing them during the category A works, as they are subject to damage and may not complement the tenant's colour scheme. Typical levels of contribution that tenants can expect are:

- ❏ Carpet tiles £25/m².
- ❏ Floor boxes (1 per 20 m²) £75/unit.
- ❏ Grommets (1 per 20 m²) £10/unit.
- ❏ Category A fit-out £344–£377/m².

It should be noted that, typically, the landlord does not physically make the contribution until the tenant has installed the item.

Shell-and-core completion

This can occur when a large tenant moves into a new building and installs a complex kitchen, for example, which would need a very specialist category A fit-out. Often, a tenant will take a financial contribution for the landlord's entire category A fit-out on the affected floors to offset against their own fit-out costs.

Category B fit-out

Category B completes the fit-out to the occupier's specific requirements. It can typically comprise the following:

- ❏ Installation of cellular offices.
- ❏ Enhanced finishes.
- ❏ Conference/meeting room facilities.
- ❏ Reception area.
- ❏ Enhanced services/specialist lighting.
- ❏ IT and AV installations.
- ❏ Tea point/kitchen fit-out.
- ❏ Furniture.

9.21 Measuring building efficiency

Measuring terminology

Four terms are in general use. These are abbreviated as the GEA, GIA, NIA and NUA (gross external area, gross internal area, net internal area and net usable area) and described at the end of this section.

Technical drawings and plans

Technical drawings and plans are scaled representations of the designer's intentions, or a scaled historical record of changes. They may be larger or smaller than that which they represent.

Architectural drawings

Architectural drawings can be broadly classified as follows:

  (i) **Preliminary drawings** – These are often little more than sketches to help clarify the client's intentions and to point the way to possible design solutions.
 (ii) **Design drawings** – These may be development drawings requiring the collaboration of consultants and specialists (e.g. M&E and communications) aimed at getting the designers thoughts onto paper. They may also be a graphic representation of the finished product, showing a three-dimensional or perspective view.
(iii) **Production drawings** – These are sometimes called working drawings. They are used with other documents to provide precise information about the building and its services to the professional team (e.g. the quantity surveyor), contractors (which would include builders, M&E and specialists) and LAs. They can be used for tender purposes, as a part of contract documents. Working drawings will have a title block that will include the scale, production and revision details. They will normally be produced on cartridge paper and come in standard sizes from A0 downwards through A1 to A4. They can also come produced on tracing paper, cloth and film.

Drawings can be 'plan' (a horizontal view) or 'elevation' (a vertical view). Either can be 'cut' into 'sections' to show a horizontal or vertical sectional view. Drawings of buildings will usually have more than one plan view (e.g. one for each floor, the roof and foundations) or elevation (i.e. the external walls on each side of the building) and a number of sectional views created for important points requiring detailed emphasis.

As well as their importance during pre-occupancy, technical drawings and plans are essential tools for the efficient operation and maintenance of buildings. They are a vital element of building records and it is essential that they are kept up to date. The role and importance of building records will become apparent when maintenance is discussed. Many buildings will now have these drawings digitised in AUTOCAD, or similar software. However, it is important to have actual plans too.

9.22 Building efficiency

There are two views of building efficiency. One is that of the landlord, the other is that of the occupier. The landlord seeks to maximise the letting potential. From the landlord's point of view, the efficiency of the building is measured by the percentage of NIA to GIA. For example:

❑ 84–87% is considered to be excellent.
❑ 80–83% is considered to be good.
❑ Below 80% is considered to be poor.

Clearly, therefore, a tightly planned building core will be more efficient.

Table 9.3   Features of building structures and layouts

The shape, size and depth of the building	Glass to core depth 9–12 m. Glass to glass depth 13.5–18 m.
The window mullions	The distance between the vertical divisions of the windows, centre to centre will govern the degree of flexibility available.
The structural columns supporting floors above	The size, layout and number of columns within the space will govern the degree of flexibility available.
Floor loading	There is a tendency to over specify requirements. 4 kN/m is usually sufficient but there may be special requirements to support heavy furniture or equipment.
The distance from the floor to the underside of the floor above (slab to slab)	This will dictate the potential for the installation of a raised floor or false ceiling and thus influence how the services will be distributed. It should be considered in conjunction with the floor depth. Four to five metres provides maximum flexibility in larger buildings. Smaller, narrower buildings may not require such a generous height. With current technology, the need for false ceilings and raised floors should be carefully considered in the design. This will determine the overall height of the building and the consequent cost.
The size, shape and location of the building core	Smaller floors are inefficient in terms of the ratio of gross to net usable floor area. Landlord and tenant building efficiencies are a factor to be borne in mind.
The length and width of the building	The need for primary circulation space and other fire safety requirements will dictate how the space can be divided up.
The building skin	This should be considered as part of the servicing strategy, not just as a barrier to the weather. Building management systems should include solar control and openable windows. Should be linked to the building management system (BMS) to enable reconfiguration of the HVAC system.

The occupier seeks to get the highest possible percentage of NUA to the NIA. For example:

❑   85% or more is considered to be excellent.
❑   80–84% is considered to be good.
❑   75–79% is considered to be fair.
❑   Anything less than 75% is poor.

9.23 Layout impact

Significant factors that will affect both the size and arrangement of enclosed spaces and internal partitioning layouts are given in the guidelines shown in Table 9.3.

9.24 Building performance

The design and performance considerations of a building can be related to the diverse range of functions that it is intended for. This diversity is represented in commerce, education, health care, defence, nuclear power generation, travel and many others. There are three main considerations – physical, functional and financial.

Physical performance

Factors include accessibility, the building services, capacity of the building, its durability, energy efficiency, internal and external environmental considerations, maintainability, manageability over time and its structural integrity.

Assemblies, components, materials
All buildings can be specified in terms of the characteristics required for their elements of construction. The properties or criteria of construction components relevant to required performance standards are defined in the following Table 9.4, and explained in detail in the following sections.

Use and performance
A performance specification defines the expected performance of a building. Details of performance in use cover, among other things:

❑ Space requirements.
❑ Temperature and humidity control.
❑ Acoustic response.
❑ Access.
❑ Storage.
❑ Servicing.

This information can be used throughout a building's life:

❑ To develop a design brief.
❑ To advertise a building and, later, to form the basis of a lease.
❑ To assess a building's performance accurately towards the end of a lease or at review.
❑ To indicate the end of a building's life.

Security
Security includes physical and psychological protection of property and people. As buildings are bound to deteriorate, protection is designed for a specified period of time.

Strength
Depending on the application of the element, compressive, tension, shear, bending and torsional stress must be considered. Point loading will affect certain structures in a different way to uniform loading, e.g. a piece of furniture on legs will require different loading conditions from a wardrobe on a framed base.

Some materials, particularly mastics and flexible plastics, have low elastic stress. For stiffer materials, plasticity and ductility need to be considered as well as permanent deformation (known as 'creep').

Movement
Thermal and moisture movement may significantly affect the overall performance of a material.

Thermal properties
All construction systems allow the transmission of heat. This is measured in W/m^2K. The transmission calculated by taking the reciprocal of the total resistance of all elements

Table 9.4   Properties of elements of construction

Element	Performance criteria	Unit of measurement
Strength	– Uniform loads or point loads	N or kN
	– Compression	N or kN
	– Tension	N or kN
	– Bending	Nm or kNm
	– Shear	Nmm^2 or kN/mm^2
	– Bond	N/mm^2
Deformation by	– Deflection	mm
	– Buckling	mm^4
	– Thermal movement	$mm \times 10^{-4}/°C$
	– Moisture movement	$mm \times 10^{-3}/_5$ mc
Weathering by	– Moisture	g/m^2
	– Wind	N/mm^2 or kN/m^2
	– Frost	mm/°C
	– Abrasion	$mm \times 10^{-6}/m/year$
	– Thermal change	$mm \times 10^{-3}/°C$
Deterioration	– Corrosion	g or mm/year
through	– Chemical attack	g or mm/year
	– Moisture	N/mm^2
	– Abrasion	mm/year
	– Fire	Hour
	– Biological decay	N
Thermal response	– Heat loss	W/m^2K
	– Air temperature	°C
	– Mean radiant temperature	°C
	– Humidity	%mc
	– Reflectivity	%
	– Absorption	W/m^2K
Electrical	– Resistance	ohm
	– Power requirement	Watt
Acoustic	– Sound insulation	dB/freg
	– Reverberation	sec/freg
Optical	– Intensity	Lux
	– Glare	Unit
	– Colour balance	Lux/col
	– Shading	Lux/lux
Aesthetic	– Colour	CIE or Munsell code
	– Texture	Compare
	– Shape	Proportion
	– Security	Level

in the system is measured as U-value. This includes allowance for the surface conduction of reflective finishes and any reduced skin effect due to wind.

Although moisture content may affect conductivity by as much as 20%, this factor is not normally considered.

Optical properties

Translucency and transparency should be considered as well as the quantity of light transmitted at each frequency.

Acoustic properties

(i) If the noise level is above 70 dB, speakers will need to be as close as 150 mm to each other in order to speak normally and be understood.

(ii) If people are exposed to high noise levels for a long time they can suffer illness and hearing problems. The Health and Safety at Work Act 1974 and the Control of Noise at Work Regulations 2005 recognise this in laying down maximum levels of noise and exposure time in certain working situations.

(iii) If a telephone is used, the environment sound level must be below 75 dB. Even at 60 dB it can be difficult to be understood on the telephone.

(iv) Mass and density are important in preventing the passage of sound. Impact or structure-borne sound and airborne sound each needs to be considered in building construction and each needs a different treatment.

Fire

Fire requires fuel, oxygen and an initial source of heat.

(i) In a building, fuel is present in the materials which form the structure and the contents.

(ii) The ordinary materials used for the structure and finishings do not combine directly with oxygen when they burn. They give off flammable vapours when heated above a certain temperature, and it is these vapours which burn in the form of flames.

(iii) The initial source of heat is usually quite small, e.g. a lighted cigarette end. This small source of heat may, however, ignite some readily combustible material, such as waste paper, which is capable of generating sufficient heat to ignite adjacent, less combustible materials.

The intensity of fire depends on the nature of the materials and the supply of oxygen. Materials which have a high calorific value and those which have an open fibrous nature burn most fiercely. If all the combustible materials within a room are heated above their ignition temperature at the same time, the ensuing simultaneous ignition of the evolved vapours is termed a 'flash-over'.

Fire may spread to other parts of a building by one of the following processes:

(i) **Conduction** – Heat is conducted rapidly along steel members and may ignite combustible materials in other rooms. Other non-combustible materials may become so hot that heat is conducted through them. Although a reinforced concrete floor is fire-resisting, it may nevertheless conduct sufficient heat to ignite combustible materials on the side furthest from the fire.

(ii) **Convection** – The hot products of combustion rise and heat everything in their path. A burning waste paper basket at floor level may set fire to a combustible ceiling lining. Openings in floors permit fire to spread rapidly from floor to floor throughout the building.

(iii) **Radiation** – Fire radiates heat in all directions, the intensity varying according to the square of the distance from the source. Heat radiated through window openings may be sufficient to set fire to adjacent buildings.

Staircases and lift shafts leading to open windows act as flues, discharging hot gases and smoke and at the same time drawing more oxygen over the fire and thereby increasing its intensity.

The fire performance standards for buildings are usually measured in:

- ❑ Fire resistance.
- ❑ Resistance to passage of smoke.
- ❑ Combustibility/fire spread.

Functional performance

This is the performance of the building in terms of the quantity and quality of space, the building shape, orientation and layout. It includes the image the building reflects, and other locational considerations such as the availability of appropriate infrastructure and utilities, the amenities it offers and its inherent health, safety and security attributes. An important consideration is the avoidance of unnecessary, or inappropriate, functional performance. Other important functional considerations are the building's adaptability and flexibility. These two terms are sometimes used interchangeably. They should not be, for they are not synonymous as far as buildings are concerned. The definitions below are worth noting.

Adaptability
The extent to which the inherent versatility of a building makes it suitable for adaption to different forms of building use. (Examples are the adaption of a house to turn it into an office, an office block that is adapted to become housing or a disused power station adapted to become an art gallery or leisure centre.)

Flexibility
The extent to which a building will accommodate different internal layouts, e.g. different sizes of offices, reusable partitioning system and so on.

Financial performance

In the case of a building that is owned by the organisation, financial considerations are the preservation and enhancement of the building and the value by which it is expected to appreciate over time. Other considerations are capital and revenue expenditure, depreciation and the contribution it makes to profitability. In the event that the financial performance of a new building is not a consideration because the occupier is a tenant, then rent and service charges are some of the factors determining financial performance of a leased building.

9.25 Commercial building materials

The types of construction materials used in a building depend upon its proposed use. However, other factors may play an important role. For example, ground conditions, the availability and cost of materials and any requirements that may be placed on the designer in terms of planning and building regulations. Climate is also an issue, although in the UK the problems associated with climate can hardly be described as extreme. Building materials have different thermal insulation capacities; some conduct heat more than others. For example, buildings with a large amount of glazing can generate high temperatures in the warmer months and cause rapid heat loss in the winter.

Other important factors in terms of construction material selection relate to the size and use of the building. For example, with pressures on land availability and price in major city centres it is often necessary to build offices of 10 or more storeys. The growing requirement for open plan office floors will also influence the selection of building materials. Brick and masonry construction is not considered suitable for high-rise buildings due to its cost, weight and problems associated with movement. A steel frame is usually a more economic solution for a high-rise building with a series of external and internal columns supporting the structure.

As stated earlier, cost is also a factor. Some materials are more expensive than others and money can be saved by careful choice of materials. Designers and occupiers will carefully consider the 'trade-off' between cheap, lightweight construction and greater thermal variation, with the higher cost of a heavyweight brick and concrete structures. The latter are less prone to uncomfortable temperature spread, and may be more resilient. Increasingly, a number of building contractors offer prefabricated components that can reduce the construction period and in some cases actual building contract costs.

Prefabricated components can be quite large and include entire room suites that can be 'dropped' into a framed structure. External wall panels can be transported to a site and erected very quickly. The use of prefabricated components limits the amount of work that has to be undertaken on site. There is also a further advantage in this respect. Employment costs on site are reduced where prefabricated components are used. This is because fewer skilled trades are needed for assembly. The skilled work has taken place in the factory.

9.26 Building Regulations

The first Building Regulations came into force as a Statutory Instrument in 1966.
Areas covered at that time included:

❏   Structural fire precautions.
❏   Requirements for division or compartment walls.
❏   Sound insulation.
❏   A list of exempted buildings.

The Building Regulations are constantly being reviewed. The regulations are a Statutory Instrument stemming from the Building Act 1984.

The purpose of the Regulations was to establish standards in the construction and alteration of buildings to ensure health and safety of persons using them, energy efficiency and use by disabled persons. Thus, the Regulations by clear implication promote high standards of construction.

Enforcement

Building Control Inspectors employed by the LA undertake enforcement of the Regulations. The Regulations establish the standards required for the carrying out of building works. Failure to comply is an offence. The Regulations are supported by a series of Approved Documents. These provide guidance for the minimum expected standard, but are not mandatory.

Obtaining approval

Approval of works by building control officers can be through either a full plan application or a building notice. A full plan application seeks approval in advance of any works and gives greater certainty.

A building notice has to be served to the LA 48 hours in advance of works being undertaken.

The Regulations are divided into five parts including three schedules. These schedules are:

❑ A summary of the technical requirements set out in the Regulations.
❑ A list of exempt buildings such as nuclear installations, archaeological monuments, greenhouses and temporary or other non-habitable buildings.
❑ A list of revoked Regulations including past Building Regulations.

9.27 Approved Documents

Approved Documents provide guidance for most conventional building procedures. There are 13 Approved Documents – A to N, that cover such aspects of building as structure, fire safety, toxic substances and drainage and waste disposal. Approved Document B deals with the safety of buildings in respect of fire safety.

There is no obligation to adopt any particular solution contained in an Approved Document. However, where a contravention of the Regulations occurs and the document has not been followed, the onus is on the contractor to show that he has complied in other ways to the Regulations. Thus, it is recommended that Approved Documents are followed to reduce the potential for disagreement later.

Approved Documents refer to named standards for materials and components. The contractor should ensure that the correct components and materials are used to the stated standards. These standards include EU marks, British Standards, technical approvals such as Agreement Certificates and Building Regulations.

Part A   Structural stability
Part B   Fire safety
Part C   Site preparation and resistance to contamination and moisture
Part D   Toxic substances
Part E   Resistance to the passage of sound
Part F   Means of ventilation
Part G   Hygiene
Part H   Drainage and waste disposal
Part J   Combustion appliances and fuel storage systems
Part K   Protection from falling, collision and impact
Part L   Conservation of fuel and power
Part M   Access to and use of buildings
Part N   Glazing: safety in relation to impact, opening and cleaning
Part P   Electrical safety

10 Project Management

10.1 Introduction

FMs may need to act as project managers for a range of projects from small internal moves to major building works.

A project can be defined as a significant, non-routine change, with defined objectives, a clear start/end, which requires an investment decision. It needs to be planned, monitored and controlled. Typical facilities projects are minor refurbishment and repairs in buildings, relocation, major capital works or construction, design and build.

Projects need to be planned, monitored and controlled. They are about a need, a change programme and a plan of action. Projects need sponsors, owners, partners and of course a manager!

10.2 Project management process

   (i) Agree precise specification for the project.
  (ii) Plan the project – time, team, activities, resources, financials.
 (iii) Communicate the project plan to your project team.
 (iv) Agree and delegate project actions.
  (v) Manage, motivate, inform, encourage, enable the project team.
 (vi) Check, measure, review project progress; adjust project plans and inform the project team and others.
(vii) Complete project, review and report on project performance, give praise and thanks to the project team.

10.3 Fundamentals of project management

The fundamentals of a project are initiation, planning and control. Projects are controlled in three main areas – time, cost and quality. A system or method to monitor these aspects of a project needs implementing at the earliest possible stage.

Time is typically monitored via a programme plan, such as a Gantt chart.

Cost is typically monitored by a cost consultant or quantity surveyor and may include a detailed value for money or value engineering exercise. The project budget will be monitored by a programme plan, with regular prediction of final costs. All extras need to be priced and approved.

Quality can be monitored via use of approved standards such as the ISO 9000 series. Specifications need to be clear, consultants and contractors must be carefully selected, and the project output must be regularly checked and tested.

All aspects of control require regular feedback that is accurate and relevant at all stages of the project. The control mechanisms allow comparison between the actual and the proposed or planned. This allows adjustments so that the project keeps on track.

10.4 Project manager (PM) role

FMs are often expected to take on a project management role that has unique objectives and responsibilities. The role will include target setting, risk analysis, planning, controlling, monitoring and management. There is an expectation of technical competence that could include product or services knowledge, an ability to understand the overall process, how to avoid and mitigate problems, how to effectively overcome and rectify errors, when to seek expert advice and an awareness of new technology and methods in project management.

When initiating a project, it is a good practice to develop a document called the terms of reference (TOR) and establish a Steering Committee. Members of this group may include the sponsor, the client and the main supplier or provider. The project manager will need to identify, seek and manage the project finances and master budget. They will have to develop and manage project change control procedures, set up a master project file, define appropriate quality standards and monitoring procedures. The project manager must also undertake a project risk management study to ensure contingencies are mitigated in the overall project strategy.

10.5 Responsibilities

The project manager has a number of responsibilities including:

- ❏ Managing the project team.
- ❏ Selecting the project team members.
- ❏ Defining the project objectives and goals.
- ❏ Managing risk.
- ❏ Managing change.
- ❏ Negotiating with the client and the host organisation.
- ❏ Problem resolution.
- ❏ Financial management and reporting.
- ❏ Measuring progress.
- ❏ Completion and handover

There are four areas to consider:

(i) The customer who will receive or use the project's end result.
(ii) The project team.
(iii) The host sponsor or client organisation.
(iv) The project itself.

The project manager has a balancing act to perform – the end-user and the host organisation interests and needs versus the project team and the project itself. To be effective, the project manager must be able to communicate, delegate, lead and negotiate.

The FM project manager must therefore consider the issues of:

- End-user involvement.
- Security and privacy aspects of key information.
- Determine methodology to be used.
- Selection of appropriate planning and IT tools to use.
- Criteria for team selection.
- If and what the external resource requirements may be.
- How and when to brief the team.
- Team cohesion and team dynamics.
- Project performance.

10.6 Project briefs

The project brief is equivalent to a project specification. Problems could arise if there is no project brief. It is important to appreciate the role and benefit of a brief, the content and who is responsible for developing one. A project brief or specification should be an accurate description of what the project aims to achieve, and the criteria and flexibilities involved, its parameters, scope, range, outputs, sources, participants, budgets and timescales.

Usually, the project manager must consult with others and then agree the project specification with superiors or with relevant authorities. The specification may involve several drafts before it is agreed. A project specification is essential in that it creates a measurable accountability for anyone wishing at any time to assess how the project is going, or its success on completion. Project TOR also provide an essential discipline and framework to keep the project on track, and are concerned with the original agreed aims and parameters. A properly formulated and agreed project specification also protects the project manager from being held to account for issues that are outside the original scope of the project or beyond the project manager's control.

This is the stage to agree special conditions or exceptions with those in authority. Once the PM has published the TOR, a very firm set of expectations is created by which he will be judged. So if the PM has any concerns, or wants to renegotiate, now's the time to do it.

The largest projects can require several weeks to produce and agree project TOR. Most normal business projects, however, require a few days thinking and consulting to produce a suitable project specification. Establishing and agreeing a project specification is an important process even if the task is a simple one.

A template for a project specification:

- Describe purpose, aims and deliverables.
- State parameters (timescales, budgets, range, scope, territory, authority).
- State people involved and the way the team will work (frequency of meetings, decision-making process).
- Establish 'break-points' at which to review and check progress, and how progress and results will be measured.

For every project, a brief needs to be prepared which identifies and addresses the objectives, outcomes and critical success factors such as targets, risks, timing, customer requirements and dependencies. A brief will typically contain a TOR. The minimum TOR can be created using the mnemonic **BOSCAM**.

Background
Objectives
Scope
Constraints
Assumptions
Management

10.7 TOR

This document must use appropriate language for the reader, avoiding jargon and clearly written. It will include:

❑ Background of the project – This will put the project into context. For example 'Why do it and why now?' The background may include the business benefits from the project.
❑ Objectives of the project – These can be both business and project objectives. They should be SMART (Specific, Measurable, Achievable, Realistic and Timely).
❑ Scope of the project – This may include the business areas, business processes, geographical locations, interfaces, inclusions and exclusions.
❑ Constraints which may impact on the success of the project, such as limitations on time and cash flow, external agency approvals, legislation, technology, location, equipment, environment, landlord/tenant issues and experience of the project team.
❑ Assumptions surrounding the project such as funding, approvals, risk profile, co-operation and so on. It is important to check the assumptions with sponsor, end-user, client, stakeholders and partners.
❑ Reporting structure and the communication plan – This will detail how project progress is reported, in what format, to whom and how often. An escalation process should be documented in the event of problems that may arise.
❑ Deliverables or milestones in the life of the project – These are the 'physical outcomes of a piece of work'. Deliverables are the elements that can be checked to confirm that the work is done and if to the appropriate quality of work. The TOR must identify the major deliverables with when and who, state the quality required and confirm who accepts or approves the completion of that element.

10.8 Project programmes

Project programmes are the output of detailed planning of the various stages and activities of the project. A useful tip is to work backwards from the end aim, identifying all the things that need to be put in place and done, in reverse order. First, brainstorming (simply noting ideas and points at random) will help to gather most of the points and issues. For complex projects, or when the PM lacks experience of the issues, it may require the involvement of others in the brainstorming process. Thereafter it is a question of putting the issues in the right order, and establishing relationships and links between each issue. Complex projects will have a number of activities running in parallel. Some parts of the project will need other parts of the project to be completed before they can begin or progress. Some projects will require a feasibility stage before the completion of a detailed plan.

10.9 Project timescales

Most projects come in late – that's just the way it is – so don't plan a timescale that is over-ambitious. Ideally plan for some slippage. If the PM has been given a fixed deadline, they will usually plan to meet it earlier and work back from that earlier date. It is best practice to build some slippage or leeway into each phase of the project. It is better to err on the side of caution wherever possible, otherwise the PM could be setting themselves up to fail.

An FM acting as a project manager will organise a project programme to meet the requirements of the brief. Progress against the programme has to be monitored to ensure that deadlines are met and problems are addressed as they arise. Changes to the programme have to be agreed according to a predetermined process. Project sponsors and other interested parties also have to be kept informed. Change control mechanisms are intended to enable change, not to prevent or limit change, but not all changes are necessary or valid. The project manager must keep a change request register for future audit of acceptances, costs and rejections.

10.10 Quality plan

This is typically used in large projects or projects over 6 months duration. A quality plan is defined as a 'document created and maintained by the PM which describes the project and measures to be taken to ensure the project delivers a quality project'. It will include the TOR, risk summary, organisation, structure, quality standards, project programme and review dates, change control mechanisms, training and communications plan.

10.11 FADE project methodology

FADE is an example of one approach to project management as illustrated in Table 10.1. It is a problem-solving system in which each phase has an output. It can be applied to all problems or projects both small and large. There are three basic steps per phase which work for most projects/problems. Different tools can be used in each step/phase. These are:

❑ Brainstorming.
❑ Multi-voting selection grid.
❑ Impact analysis.
❑ Problem statement.
❑ Checklist.
❑ Data-gathering plan.
❑ Sampling.
❑ Survey.

❏ Pareto analysis.
❏ Fishbone diagram.
❏ Flowchart.
❏ Innovation transfer.
❏ Cost benefit analysis.
❏ Force-field analysis.
❏ Process description.
❏ Specifications.
❏ Action plan.

Table 10.1   The FADE project approach

Focus stage	Analysis stage	Develop stage	Execute stage
• Identify the project	• In-depth examination of 'as is'	• Confirm requirements	• Prepare site
• Clarify background	• Detailed requirements of 'to be'	• Negotiation	• Install equipment
• Investigate customer objectives	• Detailed cost benefit analysis	• Design solution	• Training
• Initial risk analysis	• Confirm project approach	• Build	• Implement product of the project
• Agree roles and responsibilities	• Plan next stage and update outline	• Internal test	• Gain acceptance/sign-off
• Create and agree quality plan	• Obtain approval to proceed	• Plan next stage	
• Plan next stage in detail, rest in outline		• Obtain approval to continue	• Review project

The FADE methodology could be applied to each stage or across the whole project. It is important to beware of expectations and staff awareness of the project and be capable of using these tools. One approach does not suit all projects and so the project manager may have to consider other methodologies or tune the method to suit the circumstances. For some large projects, it is possible to use more than one method.

Estimating techniques are common, and may involve guessing or personal experience (but this must be recent and relevant).

10.12 PRINCE

Projects In Controlled Environments (PRINCE) is a project management method and is based on the formal life cycle of a project. Its origin can be traced to computer systems projects and has since been applied to a wide range of projects in Government and commercial organisations. Project managers can attend courses and gain a qualification in the PRINCE project methodology. The fundamental concepts of PRINCE are: the separation of management and technical tasks; clear definition of the project team structure; integration of quality management; control mechanisms to keep the project on track and clear identification of activities needed to deliver the project.

PRINCE2 is a structured approach to project management and it is the second method established by the Office of Government Commerce (OGC). It provides a method for managing projects within a clearly defined framework. PRINCE2 describes procedures to coordinate people and activities in a project, how to design and supervise the project, and what to do if the project has to be adjusted if it doesn't develop as planned. In the method, each process is specified with its key inputs and outputs and with specific goals and activities to be carried out, which gives an automatic control of any deviations from the plan. Divided into manageable stages, the method enables an efficient control of resources. On the basis of close monitoring the project can be carried out in a controlled and organised way. Being a structured method that is widely recognised and understood, PRINCE2 provides a common language for all participants in the project. The various management roles and responsibilities involved in a project are fully described and are adaptable to suit the complexity of the project and skills of the organisation.

10.13 Project planning

The planning stage of a project is the most important aspect of all the managerial tasks that a project manager must do. A project manager is expected to:

❑   Forecast.
❑   Set objectives.
❑   Decide ways of achieving the targets.

To ensure the success of subsequent activities, the plan itself must be:

❑   Realistic and capable of achievement.
❑   Flexible and allow some contingency.
❑   Based on best available information.
❑   Able to identify critical events and set clear targets.

Planning a project involves identifying the steps and their sequence in a project and the use of appropriate scheduling techniques. There are now many software programmes to assist in this task. Project planning can be defined as 'the action taken now to arrange future events to bring about a desired conclusion'. It is about organising what is to be done, by whom and when to achieve success. It can be viewed as a positive step to control future events. The benefits of good planning are many and include:

❑   The consideration of alternative approaches and potential pitfalls.
❑   Seeing at the outset if the project has a chance of succeeding.
❑   Organisation in advance of resources required later.
❑   Communication with others about what is about to take place, and what is their part/role.
❑   Obtaining an agreement now on the subsequent involvement of others.
❑   Establishing a basis against which to plot progress.

So why does planning not always happen? Those opposed to planning may say that it:

❑   Takes time away from doing the project itself.
❑   Involves sticking neck out against the odds.
❑   It is difficult to produce plans to accurately predict the future.

But remember time spent planning is saved in future actions. A plan is a basis for future action which can be modified if necessary. Plans are destined to be modified!

The steps involved in creating a project plan or programme include:

❑ Agree TOR (quality plan).
❑ Identify work and effort required.
❑ Identify dependencies in the work and tasks.
❑ Schedule the work to clarify the appropriate sequence of tasks.
❑ Identify control measures and critical points in the programme.

The criteria of a good project plan include:

❑ All activities are included and considered.
❑ Resources required are shown.
❑ Dependencies of tasks and activities are clearly identified.
❑ Review dates are shown.
❑ The format is easy to communicate with all team members.
❑ Contingencies are considered and visible.
❑ It is easy to read, use and update.

10.14 Planning techniques

There are a number of techniques to help plan the project tasks. These include:

❑ Network analysis involving job sequence, scheduling and time analysis.
❑ Gantt (bar chart) programmes.
❑ PERT – an example is the US Navy Special Projects – saved 2 years on Polaris project.
❑ Critical path analysis (CPA) – Dupont used CPA and saved $1 million in first year of using this technique.
❑ PRINCE2 – this is a structured process, developed by UK Government for larger projects.
❑ Precedence diagrams.
❑ Linear programming.
❑ Computer modelling.

The software now available to help manage projects may include:

❑ Modelling the relationship between the task, time, cost and resource.
❑ Tracking progress.
❑ Task scheduling.
❑ Resource allocation.
❑ Project evaluation diagrams.
❑ Generating reports and project plans.
❑ General management documents.

10.15 Gantt charts

Gantt charts are extremely useful project management tools. A Gantt chart can be created using MS Excel or a similar spreadsheet. Every activity has a separate line. The first step is to create a timeline for the duration of the project (normally weeks, or for very big long-term projects, months). The next stage is to colour code the time blocks to denote type of activity (e.g. intense, watching brief, directly managed, delegated and left to run, and so on). All the project review and break points need to be added to the schedule. At the end of each line, cost columns for the activities can be added as needed. A Gantt chart can be used to keep track of progress for each activity and how the costs are running. The time blocks can be moved around to report on actuals versus planned, and to re-schedule, and to create new plan updates. Costs columns can show plan and actuals and variances, and calculate whatever totals, averages, ratios, etc. are needed. Gantt charts are the most flexible and useful of all project management tools. However, they do not show the importance and interdependence of related parallel activities, and they won't show the necessity to complete one task before another can begin.

10.16 CPA

This tool allows the PM to identify the critical path for getting a project done. It will identify those activities in the project that are dependent on others and those on the critical path will require careful management and scrutiny. CPA establishes which activities have to be completed first before the next activity at any stage in the project.

Each activity is assigned a time or duration, with earliest start date and earliest finish date. Once all the activities are mapped in order, then the latest finish date of each activity can be determined, and then new earliest start dates. If activities have no difference in the start/finish times, they will be on the critical path – there is no slippage or slack. The activities that have different times have a float or spare time so that there is time to delay the start without it impacting on other activities. In many projects, simultaneous activities will take place, and this tool allows the PM to focus on the activities that could jeopardise the overall project.

10.17 Project control

The key ingredients for a successful project include:

❑   Recognition of the key elements that will indicate success.
❑   Agreement on the criteria for success.
❑   A clear and well understood TOR.
❑   Effective planning and control procedures.
❑   Adequate resources.
❑   Continuous customer or end-user involvement.
❑   Roles and responsibilities of the project team members that are clearly understood.
❑   The adoption of a partnership concept.

10.18 Risk management

Projects are potentially risky activities. All projects should have a risk assessment carried out. The first stage is a risk analysis – this looks at the probability and the impact of business risks, and what mitigating factors or containment measures are in place. In analysing business risk, the project manager needs to ascertain what the risks of failure are likely to be, and to consider the impact of project failures or delays on:

❑   Organisation.
❑   People.
❑   Image.
❑   Performance/profit.
❑   Other projects.

This could be done in a forum, brainstorming the options and actions. The typical symptoms or outcomes of risky projects are:

❑   Late delivery.
❑   Over budget.
❑   Contain errors or omissions.
❑   Not working or functioning as expected.
❑   Difficult to operate or use.
❑   Costly to support, maintain or enhance.
❑   May never be implemented.

These outcomes can be prevented by managing the risks. The project manager can:

❑   Quantify the costs of failure.
❑   Quantify the cost of mitigation.
❑   Quantify the cost of management.

This information can provide information to undertake a cost/benefit analysis to find out if the project is worth doing and the steps to ensure its success are also worth doing.

Risk monitoring is an ongoing feature of project management. It should be built into every programme as it is essential to manage the project show-stoppers. Risk management reporting needs to be an agenda item for every project review meeting. This requires that the responsibility and accountability of monitoring tasks in the project is clearly identified to the:

❑   Project sponsor.
❑   Project owner.
❑   Project manager.

10.19 Project budget

Project budgets will reflect the project brief and programme. The budget must be managed using project control techniques, ensuring that cash flow is in line with the financial approvals. Financial reports on the project's status must be regularly issued to the project sponsor and other stakeholders. Project budget control is about knowing the current spend profile, the committed spend profile, the forecast outturn and variations up or down of actual expenditure against the budget estimates. The focus of effort should be on monitoring cash flows in and out and having the expertise to bring the budget back on track should the monitoring reveal deviations from the budget allocation.

10.20 Project teams

Another important part of the planning stage is selecting the right team. The PM must take great care, especially if the project has team members imposed by the project brief. Selecting and gaining commitment from the best team members – whether directly employed, freelance, contractors, suppliers, consultants or other partners – is crucial to the quality of the project, and the ease with which the PM is able to manage it. Generally it is recommended to try to establish the team as soon as possible. Identifying or appointing one or two people even during the TOR stage is possible sometimes. Appointing the team early maximises their ownership and buy-in to the project, and maximises what they can contribute. But be very wary of appointing people before you are sure how good they are, and not until they have committed themselves to the project upon terms that are clearly understood and acceptable. Don't imagine that teams need to be full of paid and official project team members. Some of the most valuable team members are informal advisors, mentors and helpers, who want nothing other than to be involved and a few words of thanks. Project management on a tight budget can be a lonely business – get some help from good people who can be trusted, whatever the budget.

The FM project team will be made up of several disciplines or specialists, often from different departments or organisations. The membership will reflect the nature and scope of the project. The team must be led and managed to ensure the desired outcome is achieved.

10.21 Project support

A project team will require support in both technology and administration. Software examples include MS Project and Project Commander. The general administrative support includes project documents, minutes of meetings, progress reports, programme charts, contacts, agendas and so on. Having good systems in place will give assurance to sponsors and clients that the project is in safe hands. It will ensure that a project history is maintained, that reporting is consistent and that review dates are kept to.

Ideally a spirit of partnership in a project needs to be nurtured to ensure that the team have common goals, total commitment, shared risk, responsibility and accountability. It is assumed that everyone in the team wants success!

The performance of the team will depend on effective team building, communications, well-managed meetings, shared information. Up-to-date contact details are essential.

Ways to create a good team may include team away days, a social event or celebration, co-location of the members into a project office and a project newsletter. A good team needs a supportive framework, prompt rectification of issues or show-stoppers. Their individual and collective contribution must be valued, recognised and rewarded. Members deserve to be treated with respect and will require regular contact with the project manager. Some projects or project teams are given specific names or brands making them more clearly identifiable to others. In some cases, the name may hide the real project purpose but nevertheless gives a sense of identity to those in the team and others externally.

10.22 Project handover

At the close of a project, all aspects must be properly completed including the customer sign-off. The pre-handover stage is critical to ensure that training, testing, witnessing and commissioning is carried out. Certification of compliance, the pre-paration of the O&M procedures, As-built drawings, the Health procedures and Safety File, and the Building Logbook are examples of documents that need to be ready for the formal practical completion stage. Project managers will also need to create the snagging list. The defects period, details of warranties or guarantees and the post-project defect or fault reporting procedure also need to be confirmed. At practical completion, there are several implications for FMs, including: insurance of site, building and equipment; responsibility for maintenance; site security; and transfer of responsibility for health and safety compliance.

It is important to evaluate and learn from completed projects, identifying successes and development needs which will improve performance next time. There are several evaluation methods:

❑   Post Implementation Analysis (PIA).
❑   Post Occupation Evaluation (POE).

A POE will assess the performance of a building. It will find out if occupiers are satisfied, gather any evidence of sick building syndrome, determine the effects of the building on staff productivity, check if the building supports occupants' functional performance, identify if the project purpose has been achieved and identify any management or personnel problems. POEs can be carried out via standard questionnaires, interviews, observations, physical monitoring, focus groups, analysis of energy consumption data and benchmarking with other organisations.

There are many benefits of POEs to client, designer and the FM. For example, project sponsors are assured that investment has been well spent, that the project aims have been met and that the views of end-users are valued and considered to improve future projects. It is useful to be aware of the typical reasons why projects fail to deliver the expectations of the sponsor or client. Reasons may include: project objectives not clearly specified; an inexperienced project manager; too few in the project team; lack of experienced team members; technology was new; inaccurate or restricted information; poor performance of suppliers; inadequate communications; and lack of control of decisions and changes.

11 Space Management

11.1 Introduction

Space management is a very practical skill. The need to be fully conversant with the space in the organisation's property portfolio is a fundamental aspect of FM. It brings the FM into contact with every person and every aspect of the organisation and the premises.

FMs are usually responsible for the use and management of space within their buildings. Space management covers many aspects such as the formulation of a space strategy or policy, consideration of the impact of structure and services on space use, preparing briefs for office layouts, managing changes in accommodation, keeping abreast of legislation, and new developments in the way space can be used to support an organisation and their employees.

As in all good management practices, a regular review is required to check that the working environment is providing the medium for the organisation to achieve its operational objectives. Policies and standards may have to be reviewed, moves and relocations managed and new ways of working introduced. The landscape of the working environment needs a good manager to keep it productive, creative and compliant.

11.2 Data and information gathering

A competent FM will need to know:

- The amount of space they manage, and the proportion of occupied and empty space – this could be in either square metres or square feet.
- The details and type of ownership (landlord, lease, license, etc.).
- The type or kind of space (industrial, office, residential, retail, leisure, etc.).
- Details of the occupiers and people who use it (department and/or functions).
- Details of the activities that take place in which areas (quiet work, meetings, creative, desk sharing, socialising, collaboration, team working).
- The utilisation of the space over time.
- The churn rate (how often do people move and how often is it reconfigured).
- The costs of occupying the space (often expressed as £ per square metre or foot).
- The costs of servicing the space (such as cleaning, security, energy, fit-out and maintenance).
- The impact of the space on the overall purpose of the business and its contribution to the organisations objectives.

11.3 Importance of space

Space is an expensive resource and has to be used effectively and efficiently. Space is expensive to buy, costly to maintain, slow to dispose of and can easily become ineffectively utilised. In today's competitive world, people work in a variety of ways and locations. FMs have to balance the needs of the user with the amount of space available. They have to maximise the user's opportunity to work effectively, whilst enabling the space to be used as efficiently as possible. With the increasing use of home working, desk sharing and remote working in client sites, the gathering of information about the true use of space is a challenge.

Space can also be: a valuable source of income (such as conference and accommodation lettings); it is a key resource for the organisation; it can provide a creative stimulus to the occupants and it will provide a tangible identity for the organisation.

Traditionally, the amount and quality of space allocated to a person at work was a function of a person's status and/or their job title. In traditional hierarchical organisations, the best space was given to the most important employees or the owners of the business. With the impact of new types of work and new organisational structures, the allocation of space is more likely to be based on type of work and the needs of the occupants.

FMs need to have space guidelines, which specify the organisation's space and furniture standards, to manage the allocation of space. These guidelines will reflect the culture and image of the organisation.

11.4 Space management policy

Key to successful space management is the organisational policy for space. The policy should include:

❏ A strategy for space which reflects the organisational culture and which will help to support the achievement of organisational objectives.
❏ Guidelines for the optimum use of buildings and the space in them, based on current knowledge and best practice.
❏ Proper provision for space costs in the organisational business plan.
❏ Proper provision for an efficient and effective space management component, such as AUTOCAD, in the computer-aided facilities management system (CAFM).

To be able to manage space effectively, it is necessary to understand the nature of organisations. The term 'organisational culture' is often described as:

'The way we do things around here' or 'It's what makes the organisation tick.'

The extent to which the organisation's culture will permit space to be properly managed will depend on:

❏ The degree to which the organisational strategy for space reflects the core assumptions and beliefs inherent in the organisation.
❏ The organisational attitude to space guidelines and standards.

❑   A willingness to make proper provision for space costs at both departmental and organisational levels.
❑   The ability of the facilities team to operate successfully within the organisational culture.

11.5 Space guidelines

Guidelines are defined as codes of practice to help decision making. Organisational space management policy requires a space strategy that reflects the organisational culture and defines the role of space in the achievement of corporate objectives. The policy should include guidelines for the optimum use of buildings and the space in them. Key features of best practice space guidelines are:

❑   The promotion of flexibility and an understanding of the constraints and opportunities afforded by the available space.
❑   A definition of the role of space in the achievement of organisational objectives, which as well as financial performance, includes consideration of social and environmental factors such as energy use and recycling.
❑   An appropriate corporate standard for space, equipment and furniture based on functionality in preference to standards based on status.
❑   Guidelines for the provision of ancillary space and common support space.
❑   A system for monitoring user attitudes to the space that feeds back to the space planning process.
❑   Measures that monitor space use, service provision and service delivery.
❑   Effective control mechanisms for space management and accountability. An example would be a well-managed system for the charging back of space and services to the users or occupiers.
❑   The use of technology as a space planning tool (AUTOCAD) within an integrated CAFM system.

Space standards

Space standards are measures applied to the provision of space, equipment, furniture and services. Key points are:

❑   They should be derived from organisational guidelines, which form part of the organisational strategy for space.
❑   There should be a minimum number of standards.
❑   The standards should be based on functionality, rather than status.
❑   The standards must comply with legislation – the Workplace (Health, Safety and Welfare) Regulations 1992 – each person requires $11\,m^3$. This is equivalent to $4.4\,m^2$ if the ceiling height is 2.5 m.

They should cover ancillary and common support space as well as workspaces.

11.6 Effective use of space

Matching supply and demand requires the FM to have an in-depth knowledge about the space, the organisation and its people. The first step in managing space is to understand how the business uses it, and what it requires to support its business objectives and needs.

Is the organisation:

❑ Expanding?
❑ Contracting?
❑ Merging?
❑ De-merging?

Does the organisation need:

❑ Innovative or creative space?
❑ Private space?
❑ Open planned, shared space?
❑ Public access or community space?
❑ Secure space?

FMs need to understand the building stock in their portfolio, and how this matches the requirements. Understanding the user's needs, what are the triggers for change, and the likely future demands are essential in developing a space brief, and informing longer-term plans. A rigorous and well-documented space policy with clear guidelines will enable the FM to manage the space. This will also enable measures of space utilisation and performance to be monitored.

Functionality and diversity

People, organisations and buildings are diverse as is the space used by people and organisations within buildings. In space management, the concept of diversity acknowledges that people are individuals and this could give rise to an alternative space management policy. Given that people work differently and that they have different personal and working environment-related needs in order to be effective and efficient, the space management policy needs to offer flexibility and choice. The concept allows individuals or groups to exercise choice within a decision framework. It is a sort of a 'free range' idea for using space, furniture and equipment. The framework is defined by the cultural attitude to status and functionality and one or more of the following:

❑ **Cost** – A limit will be placed on the amount of money that can be spent. Expenditure may be limited to making selections from a predetermined range of work surfaces, storage and equipment but may be extended to include carpets, curtains and finishes.
❑ **Quality** – Selection will be limited to a range of options and may be strongly influenced by status issues.
❑ **Footprint** – Groups or individuals may be able to exercise their cost/quality freedom of choice to organise their work areas on a functional basis, within a predetermined footprint or allocation of an area.

A key consideration is that, except for the most senior employees, choice is likely to be restricted to ranges of furniture, equipment or finishes adopted on an organisational basis. The reasons for this are:

❑ **Inventory control** – Overall control of the furniture and equipment inventory will need to be maintained. Items can be interchanged between individuals and work groups. The problems associated with the replacement or purchase of additional 'specials' will be reduced and possibly avoided.

❑ **Cost control** – Limiting choice to centrally selected and procured ranges will increase the opportunities for economically advantageous procurement decisions. In addition to economies of scale in procurement, closer and longer term relationships with suppliers will be possible. In some cases, the suppliers will be able to manage many of the aspects of space management for their client – such as layout plans, furniture moves and reconfigurations.

❑ **Image** – Although what might be termed 'free range' arrangements of space may reflect varying degrees of individuality, an appearance of chaos can be avoided by the uniform design, size and colour of the centrally procured ranges. In some organisations, the space needs to compliment the overall business brand and other design attributes.

The objective of diversity as a space management concept is to achieve the best possible use of people's talents and the available space, equipment and furniture. It encourages individuality, 'ownership', group and individual effectiveness and efficiency. However, the potential for chaos of excessive diversity is a danger not to be underestimated. Clear guidelines are required and it is important to ensure that the 'free range' space conforms to the minimum legislative and regulatory requirements.

11.7 The FM cost driver

There is a direct relationship in the amount of space and occupancy costs. All FM services, utilities and premises costs relate to the amount of space being managed. Space can be considered as the FM cost driver for both the premises (rent, rates and utilities) and the services (cleaning, maintenance). The cost of space can have a major impact on FM and the organisation. Typically, organisations will benchmark their costs per square foot, so accurate space occupancy data is essential. A recent RICS report suggests that owner occupied space is less effectively and efficiently used than leasehold space where the cost hits the organisation's balance sheet directly. The way space is used will also impact on other aspects of how space is managed.

❑ The housekeeping policy – clear desk policy.
❑ Document filing and archiving.
❑ Furniture procurement.
❑ Churn and office relocation management.
❑ Internal space charging policy.
❑ Treatment of surplus empty space.

11.8 Business performance

Space will also impact on business performance. Space affects staff morale, productivity and creativity. It is also known to impact on recruitment and retention of staff, and presents a powerful image to customers and suppliers. Most importantly, the way space is used and managed will determine whether the organisation complies with legislation governing the working environment.

Space is an expensive organisational resource. It must be flexible, encourage productivity by being aesthetically pleasing, be comfortable and conducive to individual and group interaction. Driven by status, headcount largely determined space requirements in the past. However, social, environmental and technological changes have combined with a lengthy worldwide recession to compel the rejection of the hierarchical legacy of traditional organisations in favour of the needs of a knowledge-based society. This means functionality and need are the way forward, not status, when it comes to space management. The principles of space allocation have to underpin the process of reconciling demand and supply. On the one hand, social, environmental and technological changes have increased the demand for more and better space. On the other hand, pressure to conserve resources and reduce costs requires more efficient and effective management of the available physical, environmental and financial resources in order to meet these increased expectations.

11.9 Space planning

Space planning is essentially the task of fitting an organisational structure into a building structure. To achieve this, the FM needs to determine how much space do a certain number of people need and how many people can the space hold. Space planning involves reconciliation of these opposite approaches to inform the detailed study of how the space can be effectively used. The space brief is a statement of intent developed during the design process, and forms the basis for initial space planning. Planning tools are typically schedules of accommodation, adjacency matrices, proportional bubble diagrams and flow diagrams.

Space estimates

At the feasibility stage, a rough estimate of the amount of space required by the organisation is needed. A simple method is to divide the net internal area (NIA) by an average gross area per person (say 15–20 m^2). This provides an indication of the number of people that a particular building or space can accommodate.

Another approach (the additive approach) is adding space needs together.

$$12–14 \text{ m}^2/\text{person} \times \text{working population} = \text{net usable area}$$

Add   20–30% primary circulation
             10% partition allowance
             10% building inefficiency factor

                                            = Total net internal area

Yet another approach is the subtractive method. This takes the gross internal area (GIA), and then deducts core area, and primary circulation to derive an NUA which can be used to determine the population that could be accommodated.

Gross internal area	100%
Less core area	(20)
Net internal area	80%
Less primary circulation	(15)
Net usable area	65%

Adjacency matrix

The next stage is to identify the needs of individuals, groups or teams of people. The needs of particular activities such as ancillary and support services (e.g. filing, processing, meeting, refreshments).

The relationships and linkages between and within departments and functions are essential components of space planning. Questions that need to be asked at this stage are:

❏   Does the relationship involve the physical movement of people or objects?
❏   How important is the relationship?
❏   How frequent is the linkage enacted?
❏   How many linkages make up the relationship?

With the increasing use of IT systems in many organisations, the physical linkage between and within organisational structures has meant there is less demand on physical adjacencies. The information gathered in an analysis of relationships can be used to create an adjacency or interaction matrix. The matrix will show the relationships between pairs of functions, showing which have important relationships, which functions could be further apart and the frequency of contact.

Proportional bubble diagram

The next stage is to create a bubble diagram which graphically shows how the various functions of an organisation are linked. When combined with an initial space analysis, the relative sizes of the functions can be shown to produce the outline space plan.

Zone and stacking plans

The next stage is to use broad brush tools that fit the functions into the available space. Zoning is the term used for planning in the horizontal plane whereas stacking relates to the vertical floor by floor plan. Together they produce block plans to show where functions can be best located in a building.

Circulation

Circulation forms the arteries of a building. Routes need to be wide enough for people and equipment, such as wheelchairs and trolleys. The primary circulation route will link the fire escapes and the core areas. It needs to be as wide as the fire doors, typically 1.2 m. Allowances of 1.5–2.0 m are used in planning. Depending on the depth of the space and shape of the space, secondary circulation routes may also be required. These will be a minimum of 0.9 m wide, and provide clear access to the primary circulation routes. Allowances of 0.9–1.5 m may be used in planning.

Distances to fire escapes will determine space layouts. The maximum distance to a single escape is 18 m, with the travel distance to an alternative escape of 45 m.

Planning grids

The planning grid governs how flexible the building is in relation to the organisation's needs for enclosed spaces and open areas. The grid is the division of the floor into a series of squares or rectangles. There are many grids that can be used in space planning. The most common are:

❑ Structure – the beams and columns.
❑ Shell – window mullions and spacings.
❑ Services – power services, heating, ventilation and air conditioning (HVAC) and lighting fittings.
❑ Settings – raised floor, partitioning and ceiling systems.
❑ Furniture – workstation components and layouts.

Significant factors that will affect both the size and arrangement of enclosed spaces and internal partitioning layouts are:

❑ The shape, size and depth of the building.
❑ The spacing between the window mullions. The distance between the vertical division of the windows, centre to centre, will govern the size of enclosed modules. For example, a 1.5 m × 1.2 m grid will mean that two window modules are at least 3 m wide. The larger (or smaller) the grid, the wider (or narrower) an enclosed two window module will be.
❑ The size, layout and number of structural columns and load-bearing walls supporting floors above.
❑ The distance from the floor to the underside of the floor above. This will dictate the potential for the installation of a raised floor or false ceiling and thus influence how the services will be distributed.
❑ The size, shape and location of the building core. Building core includes plant rooms, ducts and risers, toilets, lifts, staircases, lobbies – these are all fixed in the building design.
❑ The length and width of the building. The need for primary and secondary circulation space and other fire safety requirements will dictate how the space can be divided up.
❑ The size of the ceiling and lighting grid. The ability to partition the space will be inhibited if it is not co-ordinated with the window mullions.
❑ The availability of small power, voice and data services. Cable management systems are complex and they are expensive to install. Ideally, these services need to be easily relocatable to keep down the overall cost of moving or rearranging workstations. Options are delivery of services via surface trunking around the perimeter, from the ceiling or from under the floor. As wireless technology reduces in unit costs, there are more options to consider. Built-in services (for power and communications) may not offer as high a degree of flexibility as flood-wired or wireless options.
❑ The type and flexibility of the heating, ventilation and air conditioning systems (HVAC) – its ability to cope with the workspaces being rearranged and any variations in heat load arising from the proliferation of IT.

11.10 Impact of building structures on space use

The structural form of a building will impact on the way in which the space inside can be configured and used. The shell of the building has a number of criteria that directly affect space planning as shown in Table 11.1.

Table 11.1   Impact of building structures on space use

Shape	Buildings may be L-shaped, square, rectangular, H-shaped, curved, pointed, low storey, high storey, terraced. Many iconic buildings are remembered because of their external shape. Examples include the Ark in Hammersmith, the Dome in Greenwich, the Gherkin in the City.
Floor depth	The depth of the space will determine the planning grids and the potential layouts of offices, workstations, meeting and support spaces. Typically, the glass to core depth will range from 9 to 12 m and the glass to glass depth will range from 13.5 to 18 m.
Storey height (floor to underside of floor above)	This feature should be considered in conjunction with floor depth. A height of 4–5 m provides maximum flexibility in larger buildings. Smaller, narrower buildings may not require such a generous height.
Floor size and configuration	Small floors are inefficient in terms of a ratio of core to usable floor area. Landlord and tenants will be looking at the highest building efficiencies when buying or leasing space. Between 500 and 2500 m^2 will provide the most usable space. The positioning of core services (such as lifts, risers, toilets, stairwells) and the size of window mullions will also determine the way the space can be used.
Floor loadings	There is a tendency to over specify requirements. A loading factor of 4 kN/m is usually sufficient for most business functions. If floors are required to support heavy furniture or equipment, then strengthened floors will be required.

11.11 Impact of building services on space use

A wide range of building mechanical and electrical services may be required in a business or a building and both of these impact on the way space can be used in premises. Services that affect space include:

❑ Power distribution system – via perimeter, floor grommets, ceiling poles, integrated into systems furniture or partitioning systems.
❑ Lighting – numbers and sizes of lights and their fittings, relationships to ceiling grid, lux levels required.
❑ HVAC – location of ducts, vents, grilles, radiators, sensors, temperature, humidity and air changes required.
❑ Lifts/escalators – impact on vertical circulation and department adjacencies. Location of stairs and fire staircases.
❑ Voice and data services – location of cable runs, wireless transmitters, servers mainframe, UPS.

IT and the workplace

The impact of technological change on the office has been dramatic. Cheaper computing power and easier-to-use applications software have revolutionised office work. The digital revolution has included advances in the fields of voice, data and image transfer, information management, handling and storage of documents with advances in reprographics technology.

These changes have contributed to the premature obsolescence of some buildings and has significantly affected workplace ergonomics. Whilst technology has been changing

Table 11.2   Noise control principles

Separation	Planning and managing space so that the noise source is separated from the employees to whom it poses a nuisance or threat. The background sound level should be of a similar frequency to the offending source.
Enclosure of the noise source	An example would be to have a separate room for printers and/or photocopiers. Where complete enclosure is impractical, separation or partial enclosure using acoustic screens would be a helpful alternative.
Apply control at source	There are two options. One is to select quiet equipment, the other is to modify the equipment. A simple modification would be to put a sound absorbing pad under a noisy desktop printer and/or provide an acoustic cover for the equipment.
Local sound absorption	This can be achieved by the use of acoustic screens, either for separation, complete enclosure or partial enclosure of noisy areas.
Sound absorption at room boundaries	The use of sound absorbing materials to cover floors, walls, internal partitions and ceilings.

rapidly, the design of buildings is changing more slowly. This results in many buildings that cannot be adjusted to provide a suitable aural, visual and comfortable work environment.

Physical comfort

The desirable work environment is one where comfort is derived from there being an acceptable level of noise, adequate lighting, effective and suitable draught-free ventilation and conditions that are neither too hot nor too cold. There are two issues that concern space management. Firstly, the association between IT, noise, light, heat and how these affect the working space or environment. Secondly, the legislation and control principles which can be adopted to limit the negative impact on the space used by people.

Acoustics

Noise in the office is generally regarded as being unwanted sound that serves to distract, disturb or annoy. Noise can spoil concentration, be stressful and in extreme cases cause physical damage. It can also cause dissatisfaction with both the workplace and the job for an individual. Noise control principles are summarised in Table 11.2.

Research into office noise has found the most disturbing sources of noise to be telephones ringing, co-worker's conversations and visitors or passers-by. Another source of disturbing noise is office equipment. Computer printers and photocopying machines are prime examples. Other sources include the background noise from building services and externally generated noise (e.g. traffic noise or the noise created as a result of construction or other work).

Compliance

The Noise at Work Regulations set out to reduce damage to hearing arising from loud noise in the workplace. The Health and Safety (Display Screen Equipment) Regulations 1992 require that 'Noise emitted by equipment belonging to any workstation shall be taken

Table 11.3   Factors affecting light and its effectiveness in the workplace

The individual	Personal judgement as to what is suitable, sufficient, adequate or appropriate lighting will be different. Individual visual ability will change with age.
The task	The precise performance of particular tasks will not be the same for each individual. The degree of visual difficulty of the task will be a factor.
Daylight	The quality and quantity of daylight will depend on the orientation of the building, its depth and its fenestration, the weather, the season, the time of day (or night) when the task is being performed, the distance the individual is from the daylight source, the space layout, individual workstation design and the degree to which the daylight is, or can be internally or externally attenuated.
Glare	The reflectance properties and glare producing potential of the vertical, horizontal or other reference planes of the work surfaces and surrounding areas. Use of colour and texture. Wall finishes, equipment, work surfaces and lighting colour will be factors.
Direction	Shape of objects and shadows will be affected by the direction of light. Diffusers are typically used to give an even diffused light.
Appearance	Light can be of contrasting colours and rendition. Ideally, colours in a space need to appear as they would in natural daylight.

into account when a workstation is being equipped, with a view in particular to ensuring that attention is not distracted and speech not disturbed'.

Light

Light influences perception, mood and behaviour. It is an aspect of the design of space as shown in Table 11.3. There are two aspects of light to be considered – the ambient light that provides general lighting in a space, and the additional light that may be needed at the point of work to do it properly and safely. Light is therefore required to:

❑   Illuminate the task.
❑   Provide a desired ambience.
❑   Contribute to safety and security.

The principles that control lighting are summarised in Table 11.4.

Compliance

Many organisations install Category 2 lighting in spaces where there are computer screens or other display screen equipment in use. However, there is no legal requirement to do so. The Workplace (Health, Safety and Welfare) Regulations 1992 require that every workplace shall have suitable and sufficient lighting and that it shall, as far as is reasonably practicable, be by natural light. The Health and Safety (Display Screen Equipment) Regulations state that any room lighting or task lighting provided shall ensure satisfactory light conditions and an appropriate contrast between the screen and background, taking into account the type of work and the vision requirements of the user. There are other requirements for lighting such as the requirement for emergency lighting.

Table 11.4   Lighting control principles

Daylight is the preferred option	There must be a system for attenuating daylight. Horizontal or vertical blinds are one solution.
Local control	This is highly desirable in the interests of user satisfaction.
Illuminance levels (lux)	These should be checked by a competent person to see whether they conform to recommended design values for particular areas and any deviations corrected.
Glare	Distracting or disturbing reflections can come from room surfaces, work surfaces or lighting. Glossy work surfaces are to be avoided. Matt surfaces of light or neutral tone are required. N.B. Dark work surfaces are not a good option. They contrast sharply with white paper. Distracting or disturbing room surface reflectance may need to be overcome by decoration or screens.
Task lighting	Having task lighting, either table-mounted, free standing or screen-mounted, gives the worker performing the task a greater degree of local light control. It is important that it gives the best illumination for the task.
Source of lighting	The advantages and disadvantages of downlighting and uplighting or a combination of both should be assessed by a competent person. Downlighting should ideally enable flexibility in the deployment of workstations. One option would be the use of directional spot lights capable of being rotated through 360° to serve different layouts, while avoiding glare at the work surface. Uplighting, either free standing or wall-mounted, is an important alternative, or supplement, to overhead lighting. It can sometimes enable a degree of local control not available in large down-lit areas.

Table 11.5   Guidance on lux levels

Studios and drawing offices	Up to 750 lux
General office space	400–500 lux
Reception, kitchenettes, ancillary areas	300 lux
Corridors, toilets, changing rooms	100–200 lux
Store rooms	100–150 lux

There are several guidance notes available:

❑ LG3 The Visual Environment for Display Screen Use published by the Chartered Institution of Building Services Engineering (CIBSE).
❑ HS(G) 38 Lighting at Work published by the HSE.

Lighting levels for typical spaces is shown in Table 11.5. The Health and Safety (Display Screen Equipment) Regulations 1992 require that:

❑ Any room lighting or task lighting shall ensure satisfactory lighting conditions and an appropriate contrast between the screen and the background environment, taking into account the type of work and the vision requirement of the operator or user.

❑ Possible disturbing glare and reflections on the screen or other equipment shall be prevented by co-ordinating workplace and workstation layout with the positioning and technical characteristics of the artificial light source.
❑ Workstations shall be so designed that sources of light, such as windows and other openings, transparent or translucent walls and brightly coloured fixtures or walls, cause no direct glare and no distracting reflections on the screen.
❑ Windows shall be fitted with a suitable system of adjustable covering to attenuate the daylight that falls on the workstation.

Detailed guidance to lighting is given by the CIBSE. The CIBSE code for interior lighting provides general guidance.

Lighting guide LG3 gives guidance on areas for visual display terminals, including checking and solving existing problems. It provides a benchmark against which to judge existing lighting schemes.

LG7, Lighting for Offices, provides detailed guidance on office lighting design criteria, lighting systems, equipment and recommendations for specific office-based applications.

BS 7179: Part 6: 1990 (Code of Practice for the Design of VDT Work Environments) provides guidance based on ergonomic principles, for preferred levels of light, noise and heat in offices used for visual display terminal or computer screen (VDT) work.

Heat and workplace comfort

The principles that control thermal comfort in the workplace are shown in Table 11.6. Heat in any given workplace can be supplied by:

❑ The installed heating system.
❑ Heat given off by people.
❑ Heat produced by the local equipment.
❑ Heat given off by the artificial lighting.
❑ Heat from solar gain from the effect of the sun's rays on the fabric of the building and the glazing.

Compliance

The Workplace (Health, Safety and Welfare) Regulations 1992 require that temperatures in all workplaces inside buildings shall be reasonable. In static working areas of offices, a

Table 11.6   Thermal control principles

Appropriate settings for temperature and humidity should be maintained. Check that thermostats and thermometers are accurate and that they are located in the most appropriate position.
Control solar gain.
Energy efficient methods of lighting, heating and ventilation should be used. Same principle applies to air conditioned premises.
Use of high energy efficiency office equipment and equipment that automatically goes into standby mode when not in use.
Investigate causes of complaint about discomfort. If appropriate, arrange for a competent person to survey the thermal environment.

minimum of 16°C is required within 1 hour of operation. CIBSE recommends a reasonable temperature to be 19–21°C during winter and 20–22°C in summer for office workers. Although there is no maximum temperature stated in legislation, the employer has the standard duty of care to provide a safe and healthy place of work. Excessive thermal conditions of over 30–35°C may require action to reduce the impact on staff, processes and equipment.

The Health and Safety (Display Screen Equipment) Regulations 1992 require that 'Equipment belonging to any workstation shall not produce excess heat which could cause discomfort to operators or users'. These regulations also require that there be an adequate level of humidity. The recommended levels are 40–60% relative humidity (RH).

BS 7179: Part 6: 1990 (Code of practice for the Design of VDT Work Environments) provides guidance and recommendations concerning temperatures, heat build up around equipment and humidity.

11.12 Space allocation

FMs are often responsible for the development of a space allocation strategy. They will be expected to analyse the needs and priorities of the business and prepare a clear and concise strategy for space allocation, including space guidelines where appropriate. The impact of change within the space and premises has to be carefully managed to minimise its implications for the occupants and other customers.

Matching supply and demand requires the FM to have an in-depth knowledge about the space and organisation and its people. Space allocation policy will provide a framework for space planning. The policy should determine the standards in space, furniture, style and layout options. A housekeeping policy will determine how the space is used and a policy on furniture procurement will deter rogue purchases and one-off items appearing in the workspace.

Questions to consider are:

❏   Is the business expanding, contracting, merging or acquiring?
❏   Is space allocated on status, function or need of the user?
❏   Does the organisation, department or occupant need space that is innovative, creative, private, secret or at client sites?
❏   What are the space standards for particular uses and functions?
❏   How many types of space does the business need?
❏   Do job functions and type of work determine how the space is allocated?
❏   Is there a clear desk policy?
❏   What is the archiving and filing policy; how much personal filing is permitted; are there central files; is there an efficient off-site archiving service?
❏   How many furniture and equipment suppliers are used; how are new orders managed; does everyone have the same product; what are the options for ergonomic and special needs?

Traditionally, space allocation has been based on adjacencies so that communication and close working of departments is achieved. However, with the need to increase creativity and overall communication within an organisation, it may well be better to create disadjacencies so that more effort is made to communicate with sections and functions of the business. With increasing concerns about obesity and well-being of staff, space management can also be a tool to increase movement and circulation within the premises.

Space layout briefs

FMs need to be able to capture information about the space and operating requirements of customers and prepare clear briefs for layouts. Understanding the users' needs, what are the triggers for change and the likely future demands are essential in developing a space brief, and informing long-term plans. A rigorous and well-documented space policy with clear guidelines will enable the space to be managed and monitored over time.

11.13 Space utilisation

Organisations can use snapshots of the workplace to establish how the space is used. This could involve people walking around the building perhaps once an hour observing the use of each workstation, meeting rooms, classrooms, etc. An audit will determine what space the organisation has now, how it is used, by whom and why. Ideally, the audit will take place every year at the same time. An ideal time is in either November or February when fewer people are off sick or taking holidays. To gather sufficient data, the survey needs to last for 3 weeks and it will record who is doing what and where. One methodology uses the categories of hot, warm and cold to denote use of the space. Hot = someone sitting there, i.e. occupied; warm = evidence of occupation of space, e.g. jacket on chair, paper on desk and cold = unoccupied, e.g. the desk is completely free of all personal effects and is available for use.

This methodology has several drawbacks. Observations on how the space is used are for just a few seconds, and only over a fixed time period. So there is a limit to the accuracy of information and whether the data collected is truly representative of the behaviour and use of the space. The observation of whether someone is at a desk may not be indicative of their real activity or productivity. Someone sitting at the desk may in fact not be working at all. Employment of observers over a given period of time can be very expensive.

Space utilisation data typically shows that workspaces are frequently underused. Taking holidays, sickness, training, meetings and other absences into account, spaces may be unoccupied for a significant part of the working day. No organisation will ever get 100% but the aim may be to achieve 85% (this is the gap taken up by holiday, sickness or absence on business).

Space utilisation data can raise more key questions, for instance:

❑   How well are the workstations, meeting rooms and social spaces being used?
❑   When people are not at their desks, where are they?
❑   Who really needs to be closely located with whom?

Radio frequency identification (RIFD) tracking technology can be used to help measure space utilisation. The use of a credit card sized badge attached to an item or a person enables sensors in defined locations to track the exact location of the individual or item in real time. This technology gives a constant stream of information about the patterns of space use, and it is potentially cheaper than employment of observers and consultants conducting a space study.

11.14 Space audits

When setting up a space audit, it is important to establish its intention and purpose. Typically, a space audit will state the reasons for conducting the audit and it will provide a focus for the audit team.

Consider the following examples of space audit criteria:

❑ To propose actions to reduce costs by changing the amount, location and use of space.
❑ To review the impact of changing space requirements on the organisational premises policy and recommend appropriate changes.
❑ To establish the potential for the present building stock to meet strategic requirements for space over the next 5 years and propose how any deficiencies or oversupply will be dealt with.
❑ To propose action that would be necessary to respond to space requirements in the event of the sudden, unforeseen, loss of a building or part of a building.

Benefits of a space audit

Space audits present the FM team with a number of opportunities for reassessment. These are presented later using the mnemonic RESCUE, which in some cases might perhaps be an appropriate title for the auditing operation.

❑ Review the way work is organised, the patterns of work and the space used to perform the various work activities.
❑ Examine the suitability of existing building stock for the business operations.
❑ See whether space costs and use match best practice benchmarks.
❑ Critically review the organisation's space strategy.
❑ Use the audit to assess the real and perceived performance of the FM function with regard to space.
❑ Examine the demand for space arising from the impact of technological change, staff expectations and legislative/regulatory requirements.

The desirable outcome of the audit is that the audit team provides management with the feedback it requires for decision making. The space audit will provide up to date information on the available space, the way in which it is being used and what it costs. This is hard evidence, which can be used by the FM team to support judgement, and avoid controversy with regards to the use of space. Space-related databases and CAFM systems can be updated and the evidence can also help to bring about essential changes to the way space is managed, improve performance and reduce costs.

The space audit process

The audit should be arranged and conducted in such a way as to avoid generating mistrust or work group rivalries. The purpose of the audit and its ground rules need to be communicated to those on the receiving end to ensure no misunderstandings. The results of the audit should be communicated objectively and unambiguously so as to avoid the possibility of them being misinterpreted.

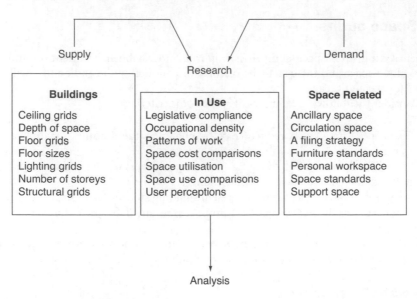

Figure 11.1   The space audit framework

The audit framework

The framework for the audit is the research and analysis of the space supply, demand and use characteristics in quantitative and qualitative terms. The audit research is conducted by means of investigative surveys (Figure 11.1). The aim of the audit is to establish a range of information as shown in Table 11.7.

The output of the research is analysed and related to the intention of the audit. It is unlikely that any one particular survey methodology will provide sufficient information. It is also unlikely that the audit process of research and analysis will be completed in one hit.

Methodology

There are five options for conducting the survey. It is unlikely than one option alone will satisfy the research requirement. The options are shown in Table 11.8.

11.15 Building efficiency

As explained in the earlier chapter, efficiency of a building is viewed quite differently from the landlord's or the tenant's perspective. In addition to the ratios or percentage of NUA to NIA, the following are also likely to be occupier concerns:

❑   The potential of the building for adaption for change of use.
❑   The potential for expansion or contraction offered by the building. What is the potential of the site and/or building to accommodate growth, or the ability to subdivide the building in order to let surplus space?
❑   The implications for space planning of the shape, size and depth of the building; the size and location of the building core; the planning grid; the columns supporting

Table 11.7   Critical examination of the organisation and use of space

What type of space there is	Simple, naturally ventilated Open plan, naturally ventilated Standard air conditioned Prestige air conditioned
Where the space is	The ad hoc acquisition of additional space to cope with unforeseen growth leading to disjointed core operations. Road, rail or air communication difficulties, or even the lack of public transport facilities or parking space. The deterioration of a location to the extent that it adversely affects organisational image, or affects recruitment and retention of staff. Environmental considerations – the control of pollution which might include the need, or otherwise, for air conditioning or problems associated with the disposal of hazardous waste.
When the space is used	If space is permanently allocated to staff who only use it for, say, 25% of their contracted time, might non-territorial use of space merit consideration? If a staff restaurant is under utilised because local facilities are perceived to offer greater choice or flexibility, might a financial incentive such as a lunch allowance, free up space for more productive use?
Who uses the space	There might be circumstances when it would be more effective if departmental or work group ownership of some ancillary areas such as meeting rooms and training space was terminated and the space became common support space, bookable centrally and available to everyone. Are there drawings that show occupational details?
How the space is used	The extent to which scientific or technological change has made the space inappropriate. Whether, or to what extent, organisational guidelines for the use of space have become eroded as incremental changes have taken place? The identification of discrepancies in the provision and use of space by departments and work groups. How often or for how long particular areas or workspaces are used. This might entail monitoring usage over more than one time frame – hourly, daily, weekly, seasonally. Numbers of individuals accommodated. The number of times individuals move over a given period of time.
How much it costs	Comparison of space costs against internal and external benchmarks. The cost of space per m^2, per workstation, per employee or per unit of organisational output.
Why it is used the way that it is	The extent to which the organisation's culture is inhibiting space utilisation. Factors would include outdated or unnecessary hierarchical conventions, historical considerations and resistance to change. The identification of wasteful workflow and/or duplication of effort. User perceptions of their workplace. However, the perception is not always the reality. Inefficient space, well managed by a responsive FM team, may not be perceived to be bad space by the users. On the other hand, a good building badly managed may not be perceived to be so by the user.

Table 11.8   Methods of data collection

Interviews	These can be structured or informal with the objective of obtaining hard and soft data from all categories of space users. The accuracy of existing drawings and the space database can be verified.
Observation	Informal observations about the way space is being used or arranged can provide the trigger for the formal recording of the level of space use and its operational relevance. The use of existing drawings to make an initial assessment the way space is used for core and support functions; the amount of space given over to circulation or the amount of space in non-productive use.
Recording	Can be used to provide hard evidence to confirm (or debunk) casual observations, or perceptions, about the what, where, when, who, how and why of space use. An accurate but time-consuming process.
Sampling	Thirty random samples in any given circumstance will give a good impression of what the situation is for the organisation as a whole.
User and in-use surveys	Well-designed questionnaires to get feedback about the degree of user satisfaction with the work environment or the service from the FM team. Relationship surveys to establish the broad requirements for space as a basis for the development of detailed recommendations. 'Walkabouts ' to identify areas of non-compliance with legislative or regulatory requirements, overcrowding, deviation from space guidelines/standards or departure from organisational space management policy.

the floors; the floor to ceiling height; the distribution of HVAC; small power, voice and data services and the ability of the building services to meet known requirements and their potential for expansion.

Building selection

Selection of a building is not as simple as choosing the one with the highest ratio of NUA to NIA. The potential occupier's selection is made against the background of the organisational policy for space, technological requirements, time, cost and quality imperatives and design considerations. In addition, the physical, functional and financial performance attributes of the building might outweigh the cost benefit of a higher ratio of NUA to NIA.

The cost of building inefficiency

Rent and the freehold value of the building are based on the NIA, not the NUA. In other words, a building advertised as being one of 10,000 m^2 NUA will actually be 10,000 m^2 NIA. On the basis that all other variables are taken into account and the choice is reduced to two apparently similar buildings offered at 10,000 m^2 NIA, the importance of the higher ratio of NIA to NUA is demonstrated in Figure 11.2 and the calculations below.

❑ Building 'A' yielding 7500 m^2 NUA. Using the rent, rates and operating costs from Figure 11.2, the NUA will cost £406.10/m^2. (The total costs divided by the yield.) The occupier's building efficiency is 75%.
❑ Building 'B' yielding 8500 m^2 NUA. Again, using the rent, rates and operating costs from Figure 11.2, the NUA will cost £358.33/m^2. The building efficiency is 85% and the NUA costs £47.77/m^2 per annum, less than the NUA in Building 'A'.

```
                    SPACE COST ILLUSTRATION

NIA                              10,000 square metres
(107,642.6 square feet)
Workspaces to be deployed     606

Rent @ £150.70 per square metre (psm)          £1,507,000
(£14 per square foot [psf])
Uniform Business Rate (UBR) @ £96.88 psm       £  968,800
(£9 psf)
Building Operating Costs @ £57 psm             £  570,000
Total rent, rates and building operating costs £3,045,800
Cost per workstation per annum  -  £5,026
Cost psm per annum              -  £ 304.58 (Approx. £28.30 psf)
```

Figure 11.2   Space cost illustration

Table 11.9   Operational costs

Cleaning and housekeeping	Internal and external general cleaning, internal window cleaning, external cladding and window cleaning, cleaning equipment and materials, toilet supplies, laundry. Pest control not included in grounds maintenance.
Energy	Electricity, gas, oil or other fuel.
Grounds	Internal and external landscaping, car parks, pest control.
Maintenance	Building fabric, internal and external decoration, fixtures and fittings, mechanical and electrical services, including plumbing, fire and safety equipment.
Management	Operating cost element of the cost of the staff compensation package.
Public health	Sewage and waste disposal, environmental testing.
Security	Staff costs, equipment, systems and systems maintenance costs.
Service charges	Where the cost, or part of the cost, of the above is included in the landlord's service charges and a management charge is levied.
Change	Elements of the above directly attributable to churn, minor modifications or improvement.

All other things being equal, Building 'B' would be the appropriate choice. Of course, all other things are not equal. There is 1000 m^2 difference in the NUA measurements between buildings A and B. It is therefore possible to either increase the building population or sublet the surplus space. Increasing the population would have an impact on the building operating costs.

11.16 Building operating costs

Operating costs can be categorised – the headings may vary from organisation to organisation. Examples are shown in Table 11.9.

Table 11.10   Examples of potential space and operating costs

Building size: 10,000 m² NIA					
Space per capita	Workspaces deployed	Operating cost per capita	Total operating costs	Assessed cost per square metre	Total cost per square metre
20 m²	500	£1300	£650,000	£50	£500,000
15 m²	666.66	£1050	£700,000	£60	£600,000

Strategies to reduce space costs

In addition to having buildings with the most efficient ratio of NUA to NIA, two other options will help to mitigate the high cost of space. Both are concerned with density:

(i) Devise and implement a strategy for non-territorial working. The strategy should take advantage of the opportunities available as a result of technological advances, particularly in the field of wireless and mobile communications.

(ii) Where non-territorial working is not an option, plan the available space on the basis of functionality and in consultation with the workforce. The objective must be the highest possible level of productive occupational density, commensurate with effective and efficient working conditions.

Increased density will result in increased wear and tear and higher energy consumption. There will be an increase in some cleaning and housekeeping costs. Some maintenance costs will increase and there will be increased security requirements. It is likely that the management and service charge cost elements will be higher. Churn costs are also likely to increase. Therefore, both the total operating costs and the cost per square metre NIA will increase. However, the operating cost per capita will come down and there will be a significant increase in productivity.

In Table 11.10, a reduction of 5 m² in NIA per person permits a 33% increase in the number of workspaces deployed for an increase in total operating costs of only 7.69%. While costs per square metre rise by 20%, the cost per capita reduces by 19.23%. These figures illustrate that density and thus productivity can be significantly increased for a proportionately smaller increase in total operating costs and cost per unit of space.

11.17 Measuring terminology

Gross external area*

Area of the building measured externally at each floor level.

Includes perimeter wall thickness and external projections, areas occupied by internal walls and partitions, columns, piers, chimney breasts, stairwells, lift wells, etc., atria measured at base level only, internal balconies, covered lift rooms, plant, etc., rooms, some outbuildings, loading bays, areas with less than 1.5 m headroom and pavement vaults.

Excludes open balconies, open fire escapes, open-sided covered ways and canopies, open car park areas.

Gross internal area*

Area of the building measured to the internal face of the perimeter walls at each floor level.

Includes areas occupied by internal walls and partitions, columns, piers, chimney breasts, stairwells, lifts, other internal projections, vertical ducts, etc., atria measured at base level only, internal open-sided balconies, fire corridors, smoke lobbies, lift rooms, plant rooms, etc., toilets, toilet lobbies, bathrooms, showers, changing rooms, cleaner's cupboards, voids over stairwells, lift shafts on upper floors, loading bays, areas with a headroom of less than 1.5 m and pavement vaults.

Excludes perimeter wall thickness, external projections, external open balconies, fire escapes and canopies.

Net internal area*

The usable area measured to the internal face of the perimeter walls at each floor level.

Includes atria measured at base level only, entrance halls, notional lift lobbies, kitchens, cleaner's cupboards accessed from usable areas, built-in units and cupboards, etc. which occupy usable area, ramps of lightweight construction to false floors, floor areas which contain ventilation, heating grilles, areas occupied by skirting and perimeter trunking, areas severed by non-structural walls, demountable partitions where the purpose is partition of use not support and providing the area beyond is not used in common, pavement vaults.

Excludes toilets, toilet lobbies, bathrooms, etc., lift, plant and tank rooms, fuel stores, stairwells, lift wells, permanent lift lobbies, those parts of entrance halls, atria, landings and balconies used in common for essential access, corridors and other circulation areas including fire corridors, smoke lobbies, etc., meter cupboards, etc., internal structural walls, walls enclosing excluded areas, columns, piers, chimney breasts, etc., space occupied by permanent air conditioning, heating or cooling apparatus and ducting, areas with headroom less than 1.5 m, parking areas.

Net usable area*

Includes gross workspace (which includes secondary circulation), ancillary space, common support space and any fit factor.

Excludes core areas, primary circulation space and any other non-usable areas included in the GIA or NIA.

11.18 New developments in space use

Space is usually one of the principal elements of cost to an organisation. More efficient ways of using space are constantly under review, and FMs need to keep up with innovations in use of space.

> 'Space is seen as a way of creating an environment that attracts the best people, keeps the best people and gets the best out of people, and markets the company as a good employer who values people' (Anon).

Source: RICS Code of Measuring Practice.

The introduction of new ways of working and new space standards are used by many organisations as a catalyst for large-scale transformation change and innovation. Examples include BA Waterside near Heathrow, GSK House in Brentford, Vodafone House in Newbury and Pfizer HQ at Walton Oaks. These new headquarter premises use space in many different ways to integrate the people with place and process.

There is a direct relationship between the amount of space and occupancy costs. All FM services, utilities and premises costs relate to the amount of space being managed. Space can be considered as the FM cost driver for both the premises (rent, rates and utilities) and the services (cleaning, maintenance).

Space will also impact on business performance. Space affects staff morale, productivity and creativity. It may impact on recruitment and retention of staff, and presents a powerful image to customers and suppliers. Most importantly, the way space is used and managed will determine whether the organisation complies with legislation governing the working environment.

The impact of change

Social, technological and economic changes have led to important changes in the ways organisations use space.

Firstly, there has been a move away from the functional hierarchies in organisational structures to networking matrix organisations. Secondly, a continuing trend towards non-territorial working in recent years has led towards flexible, shared and multi-use spaces. Some of the benefits and disadvantages of these dynamic changes are:

❑   Manpower and space savings, sometimes resulting in job losses and either surplus or redundant space in some sectors. The space requirements of non-territorial working and the use of interactive audio visual and broadband is resulting in demands for less, new and different space.
❑   An improved working environment, sometimes resulting from better overall space utilisation. At the same time, technological advances in communication and document management have led to the premature obsolescence of some space which cannot be easily adapted to new needs.
❑   Protective legislation aimed at improving employee health, safety, security and well-being increases the complexity of the space management task.

People like to work in a visually attractive space that is both comfortable and offers them some personal control over their environment. As well as responding to the pressure of legislation, employers appreciate that a good working environment helps to attract, retain and motivate staff. The provision of a staff restaurant, vending machines, crèches for working parents and social areas in workplaces are important facilities.

A deteriorating or unsatisfactory working environment may be a potent indicator for the need to conduct a space audit. Symptoms of space management problems include:

❑   An inability to maintain an appropriate aural, visual or comfortable environment.
❑   Inability to apply agreed space standards.
❑   Space guidelines are ignored.
❑   Overcrowding.
❑   Absenteeism and productivity issues.
❑   Long-term booking of meeting rooms and support space for departmental or individual use.

Status, power and space

Space can symbolise status and power. Traditionally, in a hierarchical organisation, the higher a person climbs up the organisational tree, the larger their office is likely to be, the more lavishly it will be furnished, and the more privacy will be enjoyed, relative to the individuals lower down the tree. Some organisations have an 'executive suite' which is virtually a no go area for those other than the board, their staff and VIP visitors (and of course, the facilities staff who maintain it).

Status can also be aligned with the actual building in which a person works – whether it is the corporate HQ or a less prestigious building. Even the floor on which a person works in any building can be a status marker. In an open-plan environment, status can be symbolised by the size of the workspace footprint, the amount and size of the furniture and location in the open-plan area. A workspace with an outside aspect is seen as more desirable than one with no view. As the trend towards flatter organisations continues as levels of management are reduced, space can no longer be used or viewed as a status symbol. However, space is still one of the things that visibly signifies individual rank and power, both within the organisation and to strangers who visit it. For many people, these symbols are important and in some cases will have been hard earned. It is not surprising therefore that there will be resistance to their surrender, even in the face of indisputable evidence that they are counterproductive or expensive. The removal of space-related status symbols is a challenge that has to be approached with great sensitivity and must have absolute and unequivocal top down support. Furthermore, it needs to be supported by a cost benefit analysis. As well as making a monetary assessment of the total costs and financial benefits of the proposed course of action, the analysis needs to pay particular attention to the social and psychological costs and benefits, which do not normally feature in costing exercises. Table 11.11 shows some of the resistance and concerns expressed by employers and employees.

Non-territorial working

Non-territorial working can be defined as 'where the responsibilities of the job can be fulfilled without a requirement for an individually dedicated space at an organisational base location'.

Various labels have been put on non-territorial working. These include out-working, teleworking, space sharing, hotelling, hot desking and home working. Each is covered by the above definition.

Table 11.11   Resistance to changes in space use

Employer concerns	An inability to release capital tied up in space and current IT-based systems. Existing employment practices will be difficult to change and may inhibit the process. Loss of control of staff and work.
Employee fears	That remote working will inhibit their employment and/or promotion prospects and training opportunities. Lack of social contact and the spontaneous interaction between colleagues. A feeling of isolation from the organisation and customers. Home may not be a suitable work environment. Lack of privacy may be a problem. There may not be space for any furniture or equipment appropriate for the job.

Not all jobs in an organisation will be suitable for non-territorial working. The ones that are likely to be suitable will include:

❑ Those dependent on the availability of information, not a full time physical presence at the point where the information is held. In such cases, the work would travel to and from the worker via a telephone line and the internet (usually broadband). Examples of tasks that can be carried out in this way are word processing, desk top publishing, computer software development, insurance claims processing, help desk or enquiry type operations, retail catalogue order taking, space planning.
❑ Those dependent on information but where a 'hands on' service is provided at a location remote from the employer's base. Examples would be financial auditors, some consultants, visiting salesmen and maintenance engineers.

Expected space-related benefits

Examples of space-related savings are reductions in work stations or work areas (savings of over 40% have been quoted), reduced numbers of car parking spaces, reduced cleaning, energy, maintenance and security requirements and costs, as well as a reduction in accommodation changes and associated churn costs.

Other benefits include recruitment/retention advantages, reduced sick leave absenteeism, reduced carbon footprint, improved work/life balance for employees, and flexible employment contracts.

Constraints and disadvantages

In some organisations the concept of space sharing to achieve non-territorial working is both costly and slow to introduce. It is likely to represent a significant cultural change and will be seen as a threat to the status of some supervisory and manager grades.

General enabling requirements

A detailed analysis of space use and work activities is necessary. A space audit framework could either provide essential information, or be adapted to do so. Key considerations and questions would be:

❑ How the available space is used, when it is used and by whom.
❑ What work is being performed and what is necessary to support it in terms of space and services.
❑ Why the space is used in the way that it is. Is its use geared to meeting client requirements and the formal or informal needs for interaction within the organisation.
❑ The development of organisational and individual remote working management techniques, including appropriate risk assessments. Both employer and employee concerns have to be satisfied.
❑ The provision of a workspace at home or at a base at a remote location such as a 'tele cottage' or serviced office, appropriately furnished and equipped would suit those peripatetic employees who are working on a variety of client sites (such as auditors, consultants and maintenance engineers).
❑ The provision of a suitably equipped drop-in or touch down working space in the organisation's premises to allow remote workers to occasionally come in to work.

In most cases these areas and services will be bookable in advance. There may also be a requirement for meeting spaces, a need for privacy, secretarial support or the need for presentation aids as opposed to the use of a desk space and communications links.

❑ For those working remotely, appropriate electronic voice, data and image interface technology must be provided – telephone, fax, email, video conferencing, voice messaging, access to intranet and electronic databases. A PC or laptop, mobile phone, fax, telephone, and answer machine are the likely minimum. Incidental to the IT requirement is the need for appropriate furniture and equipment.

❑ When the remote workers are working at the employer's base, then appropriate furniture and equipment needs providing. This will include individual mobile storage to enable the use of available space and a storage area to accommodate it when the 'owner' is away from the base.

❑ A significant investment in computer and communications convergence technology will be necessary. Employees must be able to perform equally well, whether operating remotely or back at base. It will be necessary to achieve a seamless transition of the employee operating requirements from the remote location to the base and back again.

11.19 Legislation and compliance

FMs must understand and comply with the legislation that impacts on space use. There is wide range of legal requirements to consider including building regulations, environmental legislation, fire safety legislation, health and safety legislation and disabled access legislation.

The particular Acts that affect space management are:

❑ The Building Act, Building Regulations and Approved Documents.
❑ The Health and Safety at Work Act with numerous Regulations such as Workplace (Health, Safety and Welfare) Regulations, Display Screen Regulations and various Approved Codes of Practice.
❑ Town and Country Planning Act, Listed Buildings Regulations and Classes Use Regulations.
❑ Disability Discrimination Act.
❑ Regulatory Reform (Fire Safety) Order.

12 Accommodation Management

12.1 Accommodation changes

FMs must ensure that changes in accommodation proceed smoothly, cost effectively and with minimal interruption to business. This requires careful planning and co-ordination of all the elements of the move and keeping the customers informed at all stages of the process. Accommodation moves need to be effective and efficient.

The average costs of accommodation moves in an office vary from £250 to £3500 per person or workstation. This cost variation is due to the nature of the move. The lower cost reflects moving just the person, their day to day files and personal effects, whereas the higher costs relate to a total workstation (furniture and equipment) relocation and the associated disruption.

As in all good management practices, a regular review is required to check that the space is providing the appropriate resource for the organisation to achieve its operational objectives. Policies and standards may have to be reviewed, moves and relocations managed and new ways of working introduced.

12.2 Planning a move

In addition to cost, aspects of accommodation moves to consider when planning changes are:

❑ Obtaining local authority building control and landlord planning permission (this will depend on the nature of business, scale of changes, and type of occupancy of the premises).
❑ Updating the lease documents, if appropriate.
❑ Updating the fire plans and risk assessments.
❑ Minimising the impact of the move on the business – i.e. reduce the downtime due to packing /unpacking. Agreeing the acceptable disruption in the business and the most appropriate time of week and time of day for a move.
❑ Ensuring customer or end-user satisfaction at all stages of the move – applying good communication skills, being approachable, and carrying out before and after customer care visits.
❑ Using reliable relocation specialists who have the correct equipment and trained labour.
❑ Ensuring project plans are drawn up to keep all those involved in the move appraised of the project.

12.3 Churn

Churn is a term used to describe the amount of moves in a building. Bernard Williams defines churn as:

'The facilities manager's jargon for the movement of personnel, groups and departments as a direct result of changed operational departments.'

Churn rate is the volume of office moves taking place in an organisation. It is the ratio between the number of workstation moves made in a year to the number of personnel working in the premises. Some organisations may have very high churn rates – up to 500%. The churn rate is indicative of the fluidity of an organisation. High churn rates will be costly to an organisation.

FMs can improve churn rates by persuading organisations to adopt more flexible space and accommodation offerings, so that the moves are only needed when a person is changing jobs, rather than the whole-scale upheaval of a department due to organisational structural changes. Some other ways to reduce the cost of churn include:

❏   Use of standard furniture throughout the organisation.
❏   Use of standard technology throughout the organisation.
❏   Full connectivity to voice and data services throughout the premises.
❏   Cross-charging the costs of moves to the department or function.
❏   Use of thresholds for internal moves for the local FM team to manage – say five people.
❏   Allocation of project status for accommodation moves of large groups – say more than five people – to a designated project team.
❏   Use of an agreed template for every move.
❏   Use of CAD for keeping accurate records of before and after the move.
❏   Planning moves in standard work rate time, rather than the more expensive prime time at the weekend or evenings.

12.4 Swing space

Swing space is the spare space in a building that can be used to facilitate accommodation changes. Some organisations keep a small percentage of their total space always empty. This helps to quickly facilitate a relocation or restacking of the building.

If there is sufficient capacity in the premises, then a permanent project office could be set up with say 10 workstations. This would allow capacity for moves, ad hoc projects and provide the swing space for enabling relocations. Such a facility is an expensive overhead, but can give the much-needed ability to respond quickly to accommodation changes.

13 Procurement

13.1 Introduction

FMs often manage the most dynamic purchasing budget in an organisation. Cost savings are required in procurement activities to ensure that value for money is achieved. FMs have traditionally been able to offer significant savings in corporate spend with the use of a range of procurement strategies. FMs need to develop a purchasing strategy for various goods and services, create appropriate specifications, appreciate the impact of contract terms and conditions, evaluate supplier proposals using suitable cost models and ensure compliance to relevant contract and procurement legislation.

The term 'procure' is defined as 'obtained by care or effort, to acquire or to bring about' whereas the term 'purchase' describes the transaction of buying and the items bought. Purchasing is therefore just one aspect of procurement. Many purchasing departments have changed their name to procurement to reflect the wider remit of their roles. The list of potential goods or services that are required in FM is endless. Table 13.1 shows a list of the range of goods and services that an FM may have to procure.

13.2 Purchase criteria

The key criteria to consider in procurement and purchasing include:

- ❏ The right product (or service).
- ❏ At the right place.
- ❏ In the correct quantity.
- ❏ At the right quality.
- ❏ Delivered when you need it.
- ❏ From a reliable source.
- ❏ At the right price.

13.3 Procurement policy

FMs have to consider whether they are buying a service or a product and are these one-off purchases or part of a continual supply. Procurement policy for a broad range of goods and services will be developed and implemented. Often this will involve liaison with colleagues in other parts of the organisation to ensure that there is a central database of information about suppliers and their performance, working together to leverage better terms from the supply chain.

Table 13.1   Examples of goods or services purchased by an FM

Stationery supplies	Printed materials
Vehicles/fuel	Signage
Uniforms	PPE and safety equipment
Furniture	Consumables like tissue, soap, sanitary products, light bulbs, bin liners, visitor pass systems
Catering items, vending supplies and equipment, cash tills	Specialist equipment – security, CCTV, audio visual
Computer supplies	Energy and utilities
Consultancy	Publications
Training courses	Travel and hotel accommodation
Car hire	Couriers
Mail services/post	Specialist service contracts, e.g. lift maintenance, fire alarm maintenance

Effective procurement requires:

❑ Detailed specifications of the products or services required.
❑ An investigation of the market and the potential suppliers.
❑ A process of selection and appointment.
❑ A performance monitoring scheme to evaluate the supplier and their goods or services.

In some cases, an FM may be procuring goods or services on behalf of the end-user. This could include stationery, travel, vehicles, accommodation, catering and hospitality. The procurement of all goods, services and items should be based on detailed specifications to ensure value for money and accountability.

13.4 Service contracts

FMs will be particularly concerned with contracts for services and maintenance. Critical assets supplied and supported by contracts should be identified, e.g. maintenance contracts on plant, equipment and IT systems. Issues to be identified include: manufacturers' warranties and guarantees; operational requirements; length of contract; location of supplier; call-out, attendance or travel fees; unique parts or software required; software licences; performance incentives and penalties and availability of other suppliers. Another aspect of such contracts is whether they are fully comprehensive including all labour, parts, consumables, and travel costs; or whether there are exclusions in the contract. Contracts can be set up for labour only, or labour and parts, to suit the particular situation.

13.5 Procurement strategy

An organisation's procurement strategy will be unique, reflecting the culture of that organisation. For example, in the public sector where accountability for the public purse is a key concern, the strategy is formal and highly procedural. By contrast, a small entrepreneurial business might treat each purchase individually and the only overarching strategy might be that goods purchased must be fit for the need.

As organisations get larger and more complex, FMs may have to contend with the issues of centralised versus decentralised purchasing. This is particularly important in a multi-site operation. Better deals from suppliers may be available via the economies of scale in national purchasing contracts of common products and services. In some sectors, the use of purchasing consortium can leverage even better deals with suppliers for the members of that consortium.

It is essential to determine the most appropriate policies, procedures and processes for acquiring the various categories of supplies on a day-to-day basis – which may involve call-off contracts, E-procurement, purchasing cards, or framework contracts as appropriate to the category of services or goods being procured. Plans also need to be developed for managing key suppliers; this might include partnering, joint ventures or strategic alliances. It is also the responsibility of the FM to ensure that benefits that are expected are monitored, measured and acted upon.

The supply matrix as illustrated in Figure 13.1 is a useful tool to determine the effort that must be afforded to the procurement for any particular item or service required by the business. Those items in the top right box will require most effort and resources.

It is important to analyse the current purchasing position – this may involve identifying the changing patterns of buying behaviour, marketplace trends (such as mergers reducing the number of suppliers) and the sources and types of funding (e.g. PFI). The options for the supply requirements with recommendations can then be generated.

13.6 Procurement stages

The typical stages of procurement are:

❑ Specification of requirements.
❑ Procurement strategy.
❑ Contract versus in-house option.
❑ Type of contract.
❑ Assessment of risks.
❑ Tender process.
❑ Contract duration and award.

13.7 Strategic sourcing

Strategic sourcing is a core activity in purchasing and supply management. The Chartered Institute of Purchasing and Supply Management (CIPS) define this activity as 'satisfying an organisation's needs from markets via the proactive and planned analysis of supply markets and the selection of suppliers with the objective of delivering solutions to meet predetermined and agreed organisational needs'.

It is important to identify the current purchasing position, which can be used as a starting point, or base line, for developing the strategic sourcing activity. Changing patterns of buying behaviour are examined to identify any trends in the marketplace (such as a reduction in the number of suppliers) and identify the sources and types of funding (e.g. PFI).

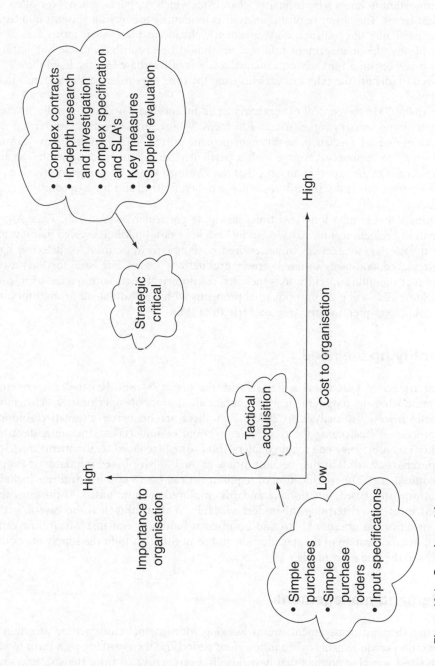

Figure 13.1   Supply matrix

13.8 Spend analysis

It is important to know who is buying what, from which suppliers, when, how often and on what terms. The objective of this analysis is to identify the buying patterns and trends and in particular the contracts and agreements already in place, their terms and expiry dates. Ideally, this management information should be instantly available but unfortunately many organisations rely on a manual analysis of purchase ledgers. In addition, FMs will need to identify the extent of variation and the time to reorder particular items in the workplace.

For many FMs, the control of maverick spend by end-users on various office artefacts, equipment and services is the first area to focus. Whilst some organisations have put an end to the one-off specials in senior management offices, many FMs still have to manage the urgent requests to engage with a particular consultant or contractor. The time taken to manage the variety is an issue that the FM must use as a leverage to insist on preferred supplier lists and standards for office supplies, fixtures and fittings, consultants and contractors.

Products that require long lead times also pose particular problems for FMs. A post-occupation evaluation study carried out in 1995 for a new building revealed that if it took more than 3 days for services to be restored, such as taps to be fixed, or defective lights to be replaced, end-users suffered serious productivity losses. The issue for FMs was to ensure that the future specifications included continuity of parts within a reasonable lead time. Some FMs will pre-empt potential problems with a call-off stock or inventory held on the suppliers' premises, for an agreed length of time.

13.9 Identifying the need

The first stage of purchasing is liaison with the person(s) who has the requirement to determine what the requirement is and obtain an appropriate specification. This should normally involve an analysis to ensure that there are no better alternative solutions. The process of challenging the requirement should be undertaken, including discussing whether it can be deferred (acquired later), diminished (reduced requirement) or deleted (the purchase avoided). It may be appropriate to use industry-based standards or simplify the requirements. The specification of requirement can take a number of forms including output/outcome based, functional, standards employed or input based. At the same time, the FM must also determine the budget available. Without this, it is too easy to get the ideal specification priced, only to find insufficient funds are available. Much time can be wasted in modification of the specification and re-negotiation to fit the supply of goods or services to the budget available.

13.10 Demand management

Proactive demand management means working with internal customers to ascertain the organisation's requirements over a future given period and then working with them to identify the best sourcing options that have, ideally, been generated from the strategic sourcing analysis as described earlier. Most organisations have broadly two types of requirement; direct and indirect.

Direct

Direct means those requirements for the core of the business; for example, in a car manufacturing plant it would be all the items, such as sub-assemblies, that are required for the production of the cars.

Indirect

Indirect generally refers to the rest of the organisation's requirements and includes many of the FM functions (such as cleaning, security, energy), insurance and IT. This indirect spend can be as high or even higher than direct spend in some organisations. Indirect spend is common across all organisations but in some cases it is the greater proportion of expenditure. It includes all the supplies necessary to run an organisation such as electricity, computers, furniture, capital expenditure works and is therefore a significant part of an organisation's turnover. Internal services like catering, FM, legal services and IT may be outsourced (increasing the indirect spend of many organisations even more). Many organisations will have hundreds if not thousands of suppliers, with possible duplications. The cost of managing so many supplier relationships with high transaction costs has led many organisations to review their supplier base and reduce the number of suppliers permitted.

13.11 Supplier selection

A supplier appraisal is necessary to evaluate and check suppliers' credentials. Supplier appraisal involves assessing the company profile, e.g. through their annual report and accounts, checking their financial standing, determining their capacity, assessing their quality procedures, taking up performance references, evaluating their policies, track record and attitude. This is where the analysis of the supply base is useful. A supplier appraisal is sometimes undertaken via a pre-qualification system, or when new suppliers respond to adverts or submit responses to requests for information (RFI), or even at the time their tenders are evaluated. It is usually more efficient to appraise a supplier's suitability prior to inviting them to tender. Pre-qualification questionnaires (PQQ) or RFI are tools used by FMs to do this. Suppliers and their own supply chains should be audited as part of this evaluation in respect of their ethical business practices.

13.12 Specifications

A critical aspect of procurement is the brief or the specification for the goods and services. Specifications define what is to be purchased, and what the items or services will be used for. The various types of specifications are shown in Table 13.2. Some specifications may be a hybrid, with elements of more than one type.

Standard specifications ensure that suppliers can be evaluated on a like-for-like basis, and avoid confusion over the assumed requirements. The ideal specification criteria are clear, concise, comprehensive and consistent.

FMs will use a variety of methods to investigate the market, such as word of mouth recommendations, exhibitions and networking events. It is important to find out who is the best or most suitable supplier to suit the specification.

Table 13.2   Comparison of specificiations

Type	Focus	Example	Issues
Input	Tools, skills, equipment, hours, and activities required	Cleaning, catering, security service contracts	Prescriptive and detailed. Relies on huge input from client to detail the how, why, when, who, how much and so on . . . . Contract performance based on ability to do exactly as prescribed. Costly and difficult to change, less flexible.
		Projects such as building refurbishment	
Output	The end product	A lunchtime food service	Output orientated – little detail on the how or who does the work or delivers the service. Agreement on standards (SLAs) is required for measurement.
Outcome	Results	Target % levels of satisfaction, 100% compliance	Focused on end-users expectations of products or service. Both qualitative and quantitative measures needed.
Function	Purpose	Computer system, machinery or equipment to do or make something	Useful for new design or service, when scope includes conceptual information and ideas. Fitness for purpose is the critical test.

Table 13.3   Stages in procurement

1	Specification of services
2	Prepare tender document
3	Pre-qualification process
4	Visits by contractors
5	Visits by client to contract/supply premises or sites
6	Evaluation of written documents
7	Presentations
8	Negotiation
9	Award
10	Mobilisation

13.13 Tendering process

There are several stages in the overall tender process when procuring most goods and services as shown in Table 13.3. Each stage is important in order to gather information and to test which contractor or supplier offers the best service or product to meet the specification.

Allocation of sufficient time for the tender process is critical if the process is to be well executed. An example of the schedule is shown in Table 13.4.

As with all projects, time can be reallocated from one area to another. However, it is important not to underestimate the time it takes to get replies to queries or to convene meetings with the stakeholders to discuss the options. At least 3 months is required; however, ideally 6 months is more realistic due to the time needed for exchange of information between parties involved in the process.

Table 13.4   Tender schedule

	Activity	Time required
1	Gather information and compile tender document	Weeks 1 and 2
2	Send tender document to contractors	Week 3
3	Contractors survey site	Week 4
4	Site visits	Weeks 5 and 6
5	Tender documents returned	Week 8
6	Presentations	Week 9
7	Tender evaluation	Weeks 10 and 11
8	Meetings to discuss evaluation	Week 12
9	Appoint successful contractor	Week 13
10	New contract commences	Week 17

Additionally, it is recommended that more than one person is involved in the exercise. Ideally, a small number of representatives with different skills or from different departments such as FM, finance, or client, can provide a broader input and feedback for the tender process.

13.14 The tender document

Once the specification is completed and agreed it can be inserted into a tender document. A basic structure of a tender and some of the headings is shown in Table 13.5.

13.15 Invitation to tender process

The short list

Some organisations have detailed knowledge concerning the contractors they wish to invite to tender. If this is not the case, an alternative is to hold a pre-qualification exercise to help identify those who have the necessary resources and attributes to supply the service satisfactorily.

Pre-qualification process and selection criteria

This is a matter of preference and perhaps deference to specific purchasing regulations within the organisation. The recommended minimum number of contractors to invite to tender is generally four. This is to optimise the choice of provider against the time taken to manage the tendering process and evaluate all the information collected.

The selection criteria used to identify appropriate contractors will be driven by the needs of the organisation.

Once preferred contractors have been selected and have confirmed they are interested in proceeding, the tender document can be dispatched.

Site survey

It is recommended that the shortlist of contractors is invited on site to view the current facilities and services. The positive side to inviting all parties together is that it saves time

Table 13.5   Tender document structure example

Introduction	• General background to the company
	• Overview of the services
	• The reason for tendering the service
General information given	• Timetable
	• Response format
	• Contract type
	• Costs to be included and not included
	• How Transfer of Undertakings (Protection of Employment) Regulations (TUPE) will be handled
Detailed specification	As identified in the earlier section
Information requested	• Descriptions of each service
	• Description of support resources
	• Job matrices, specifications, descriptions
	• Company policies
	• Service innovation and alternative options
Financial proformas	• Cost analyses relevant to the services specified
	• Labour schedule and costs
	• Equipment schedule and costs
	• Miscellaneous costs
	• Management fee
	• A total cost summary of the individual analyses

by not having to duplicate the process four times over and it also ensures that all contractors receive identical information.

The reason for them to view the site is fourfold, namely:

❑   To view the facilities, equipment, services and standards required.
❑   To test their understanding of the tender document and to clarify any points raised.
❑   To give the contractors an opportunity to ask questions about the organisation and its objectives.
❑   To establish a relationship and a knowledge of the contractor's management style.

The more the contractors have an understanding of the facilities and the culture of the company the more accurate and tailored their responses should be.

Site visits

It is strongly recommended that visits are arranged to view operations currently run by each contractor. Although this may appear as a heavy investment of time in the process, it will afford much greater understanding of the written tender responses and illustrate what is being described during the presentations.

These can take place while the contractors are completing the written response. This not only foreshortens the timetable but it also enables the contractors to tailor their responses to specific issues raised during the visits.

The visits should be *relevant* to the services specified within the tender document and bear a relation to how each particular contractor proposes developing the services at the site. There is a great temptation for contractors to escort potential clients to their biggest and best flagship operation. However, if the services bear no relation to the tender specification then the visit is wasted.

13.16 Cost models

FMs need to understand all the elements that make up the cost of contracts or goods. These may include labour, materials, design, management overhead, preliminaries, mobilisation, expenses, contingencies, VAT and other taxes. The implications of warranties, guarantees and exclusions, as well as issues such as whole life costing, value engineering (VE) and the price–quality relationship must also be understood.

13.17 Whole life costing

Life-cycle costing (LCC), also called whole life costing, is a technique to establish the total cost of ownership. It is a structured approach that addresses all the elements of this cost and can be used to produce a spend profile of the product or service over its anticipated lifespan. The results of an LCC analysis can be used to assist management in the decision-making process where there is a choice of options. The accuracy of LCC analysis diminishes as it projects further into the future, so it is most valuable as a comparative tool when long-term assumptions apply to all the options and consequently have the same impact.

The visible costs of any purchase represent only a small proportion of the total cost of ownership. In many organisations, different departments of an organisation hold the responsibility for acquisition cost and subsequent support funding and, consequently, there is little or no incentive to apply the principles of LCC to purchasing policy. Therefore, the application of LCC does have a management implication because purchasing departments are unlikely to apply the rigours of LCC analysis unless they see the benefit resulting from their efforts.

There are four major benefits of LCC analysis:

❑ Evaluation of competing options in purchasing.
❑ Improved awareness of total costs.
❑ More accurate forecasting of cost profiles.
❑ Performance trade-off against cost.

The types of costs incurred will vary according to the goods or services being acquired, some examples are given in Table 13.6.

13.18 Value engineering (VE)

Value engineering can be defined as the organised effort directed at analysing the functions of systems, equipment, facilities, services and supplies for the purpose of achieving the

Table 13.6   Cost examples

One-off costs	Recurring costs
Procurement	Retraining
Implementation and acceptance	Operating costs
Initial training	Service charges
Documentation	Contract and supplier management costs
Facilities	Changing volumes
Transition from incumbent supplier(s)	Cost of changes
Changes to business processes	Downtime/non-availability
Withdrawal from service and disposal	Maintenance and repair
	Transport and handling

Table 13.7   The value engineering approach to cost management

1	Life-cycle cost	The total cost of a system, building or other product computed over its useful life. It includes all relevant costs involved in acquiring, owning, operating, maintaining and disposing of the system or product over a specified period of time, including environmental and energy costs.
2	Cost savings	A reduction in actual expenditures below the projected level of costs to achieve a specific objective.
3	Cost avoidance	An action taken in the immediate time frame that will decrease costs in the future. For example, an engineering improvement that increases the mean time between failures and thereby decreases operation and maintenance costs is a cost avoidance action.

essential functions at the lowest LCC consistent with required performance, reliability, quality and safety.

In the construction industry, VE, value analysis and value management describes a structured process of examination of the function of a building to ensure that it is delivered in the most cost-effective way. Table 13.7 shows the benefits of this approach.

Value engineering is a systematic and function-based approach to improving the value of products, projects or processes. VE involves a team of people following a structured process. The process helps team members communicate across boundaries, understand different perspectives, innovate and analyse.

Good value is achieved when the required performance can be accurately defined and delivered at the lowest LCC.

Value engineering improves value by using a combination of creative and analytical techniques to identify alternative ways to achieve objectives. The use of function analysis differentiates VE from other problem-solving approaches. VE focuses on delivering the product or service at the best price by incorporating those value characteristics deemed most important by the customer. VE follows a structured thought process to evaluate options. Every VE session goes through a number of steps:

❑   Gather information.
❑   What is being done now?
❑   Measure performance.

❏ How will the alternatives be measured?
❏ Analyse functions.
❏ What must be done?
❏ What does it cost?
❏ Generate ideas (brainstorming).
❏ What else will do the job?
❏ Evaluate and rank ideas.
❏ Which ideas are the best?
❏ Develop and expand ideas.
❏ What are the impacts?
❏ What is the cost?
❏ What is the performance?
❏ Present ideas.
❏ Sell alternatives.

The benefits of VE

❏ Clarification of the brief separating needs from wants.
❏ Improved performance through efficiency savings.
❏ Identification of alternative designs, solutions or locations.
❏ Identification of alternative construction methods.
❏ Empowered staff through multidisciplinary teamwork.
❏ Enhanced service/product quality.
❏ Identification of risk.
❏ Identification of additional functions that improve the outcomes of the project.
❏ Improved staff morale, commitment and relationships.
❏ Rationalisation of the project programme.

Risks of VE

There are potential risks that must be guarded against. They can be managed effectively if recognised, identified and dealt with. These risks might include:

❏ The exercise undertaken too late for changes to be effective.
❏ Inadequate information causing incorrect assumptions.
❏ Insufficient participation by stakeholders.
❏ Insufficient time allocated for the process.
❏ Inadequate support by senior management.
❏ Unskilled facilitator using improper application of the methodology.

13.19 E-purchasing

The use of the Internet in purchasing activities has greatly impacted on FM. The use of E-procurement, e.g. desktop online ordering of stationery is now commonplace in many organisations. In addition, the increasing use of E-bidding to renew contracts of commodity supplies (e.g. energy and stationery) is threatening the more traditional forms of procurement.

13.20 Legislation

Supply of Goods and Services Act 1982

This Act requires that any person providing a service in the course of a business should provide that service with reasonable care and skill (Section 13).

Sale of Goods Act 1979

It is implied into the contract that the goods:

❑ Effectively belong to the seller and no third party has rights over them (Section 12).
❑ Will be as described by the seller (Section 13).
❑ Will be of satisfactory quality (Section 14[2]).
❑ Will be reasonably fit for any purpose made known to the seller (Section 14[3]).
❑ Will be delivered to the seller's place of business, if no place for delivery of the goods has been agreed (Section 29).

Unfair Contract Terms Act 1977

This Act states that any term which attempts to exclude or limit the following liability will be ineffective:

❑ Liability for death or personal injury caused by negligence (Section 2[1]).
❑ Liability for other negligence (unless the term satisfies the reasonableness test set out in the Act (Section 2[2]).

Housing Grants, Construction and Regeneration Act 1996

Part 2 of this Act was introduced to address two main issues within the construction industry – payment abuse and disputes. From 1998, all 'construction contracts' entered into have to be Act compliant. Many FM contracts are classified as construction contracts – these can include, but may not be limited to:

❑ New builds, extensions.
❑ Repair, maintenance and internal refurbishment.
❑ Cleaning of buildings.
❑ Alterations and renovations.
❑ Painting and decoration.

13.21 European procurement legislation

In January 2004, the European Union Parliament approved a new Consolidated Procurement Directive covering the purchase of Supplies, Services and Works by the public sector. The purpose of the EU procurement rules and legislation is to open up the public procurement market and to ensure the free movement of supplies, services and works within the EU. The EU rules reflect and reinforce the value for money (VFM) focus of the Government's procurement policy. VFM is defined as 'the optimum combination of whole-life cost and quality to meet the user's requirements'. Thresholds of supplies, services and works dictate if the procurement will have to comply with the formal EU procedures of advertising in the Official Journal of the European Union (OJEU). Thresholds are updated annually as shown in Table 13.8.

Under the EU regulations, there are three types of tender procedure available to buyers as shown in Table 13.9.

Table 13.8   EU public sector OJEU thresholds

2009 Thresholds	Supplies	Services	Works
Government bodies listed in Public Contracts Regulations 2006 (and their successors) 'Schedule 1'	£90,319 (€133,000)	£90,319 (€133,000)	£3,497,313 (€5,150,000)
Other public sector contracting authorities	£139,893 (€206,000)	£139,893 (€206,000)	£3,497,313 (€5,150,000)
Indicative notices	£509,317 (€750,000)	£509,317 (€750,000)	£3,497,313 (€5,150,000)
Small lots	£54,327 (€80,000)	£54,327 (€80,000)	£679,090 (€1,000,000)

Table 13.9   EU tender procedure types

1	The open procedure	This is available in all circumstances and involves a single-stage approach where all candidates may respond to the OJEU advertisement and all offers received must be considered.	Costly, lengthy process. Negotiations limited.
2	The restricted procedure	This is available in all circumstances and involves a two-stage approach where candidates who respond to the OJEU advertisement will be considered to have expressed an interest and, from these, the buyer will then shortlist a number of candidates to submit offers.	Preferred method. Only 37 days for receipt of expressions of interest, then 40 days must be allowed for offers to be returned from those shortlisted (could be 26 days if a prior information notice [PIN] is used).
3	The negotiated procedure	This is only available in a very limited number of circumstances and is subject to strict conditions.	

14 Contracts and Contract Management

14.1 Introduction

A contract may be defined as an agreement enforceable by the law, between two or more persons, to do or abstain from doing, some act or acts. Their intention must be to create legal relations and not merely to exchange mutual promises. Both parties must have given something or have promised to give something of value as consideration for any benefit derived from the agreement.

The essential elements of the formation of a valid and enforceable contract can be summarised under the following headings:

❑ There must be an offer and acceptance.
❑ There must be an intention to create legal relations.
❑ There must be an agreement about the same thing.
❑ The parties must have the capacity to contract.
❑ There must be possibility of performance.
❑ There must be certainty of terms.
❑ There must be legality of objects.
❑ In the case of simple contracts, there must be a consideration that has a value (i.e. the consideration is the exchange between two parties in a simple contract; there must be a loss to one party and a benefit to the other).

Most of the contracts entered into by FMs are 'simple contracts'.

Simple or 'parol' contracts are 'informal' contracts and may be made:

❑ Orally.
❑ By implication from conduct.
❑ In writing.

Most maintenance and service contracts are in writing.

Formal agreements, for example for the supply of electricity, are contracts 'under hand'.

14.2 Consideration

Consideration need not be adequate but must have some value, however slight. There would be no question of a contract being void because the payment agreed upon for the work or service to be provided was a very small sum.

❑ Consideration must also be sufficient. This situation arises, where the consideration offered by the provisor is an act which he/she is already bound to carry out.
❑ Consideration must be legal.

❏ Consideration must move from the promisee, i.e. the person to whom the promise is made, who must give some consideration for it to the promiser.

14.3 Communication of offer and acceptance

A contract is brought into existence upon communication of the acceptance. The posting of a letter of acceptance, where the post is the normal means of communication, brings a contract into existence even though it does not reach the other interested party/parties. Once accepted a contract cannot be retracted.

14.4 Acceptance to be identical with offer

It is important to be satisfied that the offer has been expressed with precision, and that the unqualified acceptance is in accordance with the requirements. Acceptance must be identical to the offer.

14.5 Withdrawal and revocation of offer

An offer can be revoked at any time before acceptance. To be effective, however, withdrawal and revocation must be brought to the knowledge of the other party before acceptance takes place.

14.6 Contracts by deed

Contracts of this class are made by employing a formal agreement, as opposed to a simple contract which is effected by the exchange of documents. Speciality contracts or contracts by deed are used in the following circumstances:

❏ Land.
❏ Leave of property.
❏ Articles of partnership.

A deed becomes operative when it is signed and dated. The signing in the case of an individual must be witnessed. Because of the form in which they are expressed, contracts by deed are legally enforceable even though they are made without valuable consideration, and the right of action arising out of such contracts is not barred for 12 years. Although deeds may be used if desired for any other contracts, however unimportant, in practice they tend to be confined to cases required by law.

14.7 Contracts which are not binding

Mistake

There are two legal categories of mistake.

(i) Where both parties make the same common mistake.
(ii) Where parties have different intentions.

Misrepresentation

The rights and remedies that flow from misrepresentation depend upon whether it was fraudulent or innocent.

Illegal contracts

Contracts that contravene the law are, in general, void and no action may be brought upon them. The illegality may involve doing an act prohibited by statute such as building contrary to the building regulations, or it may exist in a project which is prohibited, e.g. an agreement to commit a crime or a tort.

Incapacity of the parties

Certain parties are restricted in their contractual capacity and liability, e.g.:

❏ Crown or government departments.
❏ Minors (those under the age of 16).
❏ Infants.
❏ People who are diagnosed or certified as insane.

Privity

The common law rule of privity is that a contract cannot be enforced by or against a person not party to that contract.

14.8 Contract types

Trading contracts are called many different things, including: supply agreements, service agreements, services agreements, management contracts, service contracts, trading agreements, supply contracts, details of supply, details of services, schedule of services, services schedules and just about any other permutation of these words that you care to construct.

What matters is not what the contract is called – it is what the contract contains, and how the contents are worded, that count most. This is why for large important contracts, which carry significant legal responsibilities and potential liabilities, it is sensible to involve a solicitor or lawyer in producing the contractual documents.

Service contracts and supply agreements are used for all manner of trading and commercial arrangements and relationships, e.g:

❏ Provision of services from one organisation to another.
❏ Provision of services from an organisation to a private consumer.
❏ Management of services by an organisation or provider on behalf of a client organisation.
❏ Direct contracting of services.
❏ Sub-contracting of services.
❏ Licensing arrangements between two organisations or bodies.
❏ Franchising arrangements between a franchisor and franchisee or franchisees.

❏ Rental supply of products and/or service by a services provider to clients, either corporations or private individuals.
❏ Provision of equipment in conjunction with leasing or other financing arrangements.
❏ Many other types of supply agreements and commercial trading arrangements.

Trading and supply arrangements of these sort apply in all industry sectors, and can involve any type of service or product supply.

FMs will be particularly concerned with contracts for services and maintenance. Critical assets supported by contracts should be identified, e.g. maintenance contracts on plant, equipment and IT systems. As the scope of services delivered by the FM is so varied in nature, it is often difficult to find a form of contract that best fits the entire range of services provided.

14.9 Contract methods

There are a variety of ways to purchase involving formal contracts: call-off orders, preferred suppliers, term agreements and framework agreements. FMs will need to be familiar with the method most appropriate for the particular purchase, and if the organisation has any particular purchasing rules and regulations. For example, those working in the UK public sector will need to be aware of the EU public procurement rules on tenders for supplying services and goods.

Issues to be identified in service and maintenance contracts include: manufacturers' warranties and guarantees; operational requirements; length of contract; location of supplier; call-out, attendance or travel fees; unique parts or software required; performance incentives and penalties and availability of other suppliers.

There are many types of contracts that can be used in the purchase of FM services and products:

❏ Fixed price.
❏ Reimbursable.
❏ Schedule of rates.
❏ Reimbursable and fixed fee.
❏ Partnership.
❏ Lump sum.
❏ Measured time contract.
❏ Standard contract proforma.

Selection criteria

With so many different contract types available, FMs need to understand the advantages and disadvantages of contract agreements available so as to make a decision as to the most appropriate contract to use for a particular situation. Some points to consider when choosing a contract are:

❏ Flexibility – how rigid is the specification and how rigid are the service delivery timescales?
❏ Price – is a guaranteed or fixed price needed?

❑   Change – how likely is the organisation going to add to or reduce the scope of services in the future?
❑   Terms and conditions – the extent that a standard contract meets the needs of the parties in the contract – do any of the terms and conditions need rewriting?

Contract document checklist

The nature of the goods and/or services being supplied will dictate the content of the contract but the following key questions will always apply:

❑   Are the parties to the contract clearly named and identified?
❑   Does the contract set out (in sufficient detail) the goods or services to be supplied? Technical details may be incorporated into a schedule.
❑   Are there clear start and end dates? If there is no fixed end date, can the customer terminate the contract by giving reasonable notice (and without suffering unreasonable consequences)?
❑   Are all prices/fees clearly set out (and what rights does the customer have to withhold payment)?
❑   What provision does the contract make with regards to quality of the goods and/or services to be supplied?
❑   Are clauses excluding or limiting liability of the supplier reasonable (in the light of the potential damage which might be suffered by the customer if there is a serious breach of contract)?
❑   In what circumstances can the parties cancel or terminate the contract?
❑   If the customer cancels the contract/terminates early, what are the consequences (and are they reasonable)?

14.10 Contents of a contract

Trading and supply contracts come in all sorts of shapes and sizes, but essentially they contain the same fundamental elements, which are summarised in the listing below:

❑   Heading/title.
❑   Description/purpose/the service (basically the product/service description).
❑   Parties (supplier and client – including addresses).
❑   Date.
❑   Territory/geographical coverage.
❑   Definitions – essential glossary 'root' of frequently occurring items in the document.
❑   Term – period of agreement.
❑   Pricing (refer if appropriate to attached schedule).
❑   Pricing adjustment (e.g. annual increases linked to suitable index).
❑   Responsibilities of provider – include or append details of services and SLAs.
❑   Responsibilities of client.
❑   Payment terms.
❑   Confidentiality.
❑   Dispute and arbitration process.
❑   Termination and force majeure.

- ❑ Renegotiation/renewal.
- ❑ Prevailing laws.
- ❑ Signatures and witnesses.

14.11 Lump sum contract

A lump sum contract is essentially where the whole of the requirement to be supplied can be specifically defined, where a firm (not necessarily a fixed) price can be agreed in advance, and on what basis the contract will be awarded and paid can be agreed. The distinction of a fixed price is that the cost is not subject to increases due to fluctuations in the cost of materials and/or labour. It is therefore possible to have a fluctuation-based lump sum contract or a fixed price lump sum contract.

In summary, a lump sum contract has these features:

- ❑ Length of contract is relevant to the time required to complete the work. Original tender/contract price may change if variations apply.
- ❑ Suitable for one-off items of work.
- ❑ Pre-tender process allows control of quality.
- ❑ Quality may deteriorate as profit margin erodes.

14.12 Measured term contract

A measured term contract on the other hand is the 'best estimate' of the quantity of work that is likely to be done during a defined period of time, e.g. over the next 2 years. A schedule of items that is expected to be carried out are priced, along with some indication of the total amount of work that is likely to be undertaken over the period of time of the contract.

However, there is no guarantee to the contractor that all of the items will in fact be required or carried out. As such there is an element of risk in pricing the schedule for the contractor, where quantity discounts can skew a particular price significantly. Payment for work is made against actual work undertaken, i.e. the work is measured after it is done.

In summary, a measured term contract has the following features:

- ❑ Must have agreed schedule of rates.
- ❑ Work is measured and priced on completion.
- ❑ Each item of work ordered individually (specified).
- ❑ General specification (quality and so on) is already established.
- ❑ Set-up for specific period of time, i.e. the term of the contract.

14.13 Term contract

This type of contract is appropriate for a planned programme of work or call-off items. It is set up for a specific period of time (term), and is inflexible as the term is fixed. Known quality, timescales and price are a feature and so it is critical to have a clear understanding of requirements needed prior to negotiation of the contract.

14.14 Fixed price contract

In this type of contract, the customer describes what they want, gets quotes from the marketplace and chooses the best one. The work is done for the tendered price. This type of contract is typically used for simple purchases or requirements which are easy to describe and are not likely to alter.

14.15 Reimbursable contract

In this type of contract, the customer hires in resources from a supplier and gives instructions on what to do. The supplier is not pressured into finishing early at the expense of quality. The customer reimburses all the costs of labour and materials.

14.16 Schedule of rates

A schedule of rates is when a contractor or supplier gives the customer a menu of prices for all the standard tasks. There are standard schedules of prices published by industry, such as the BMI book. These prices are averages, and so may be greater or lower than a fixed price. Schedules of rates can be useful when work needs to proceed quickly with minimal time for estimates and pricing work before the job starts. Time is needed at the end of the project or activity, however, to agree the completed work. The contractors can gain greater profits from this method of contract if they can work more efficiently than the schedule agreed.

14.17 Reimbursable and fixed fee contract

In this contract, the customer pays the supplier's costs and a fixed fee for their profit. It can be used in circumstances where a reimbursable contract could be used but provides more support from the supplier. The supplier is not pressured into finishing early at the expense of quality.

14.18 Contract relationships

A well-designed service contract provides a really useful platform and constant reference point for good positive mutually beneficial trading relations, so it is worth thinking about it and getting it right at the outset. It is often said that contracts and agreements are usually shut away in a drawer and never looked at again after they are signed, and in many cases this is true. The supplier's and client's freedom to get on with the business is largely enabled because they have properly considered each other's position, and agreed the basis of supply in the form of a proper contract. They have no need to look at the agreement contract as the trading relationship has been properly established by the process of drawing up and agreeing a sound and suitable contract.

The process of agreeing a contract is, therefore, aside from anything else, an excellent way to flush out and make transparent all aspects of the supply or service arrangement, much of which is otherwise commonly 'taken for granted', usually including many wrong or mismatched assumptions on both sides. A good trading contract enables such risks to be averted.

14.19 Partnership

There are various types of partnership contract, where things are set up such that the supplier can only make money by achieving what the customer wants. The advantage for both parties is that no time or effort is wasted tendering for individual smaller jobs. These types of contracts also allows the supplier to get closer to the customer. Partnerships are not for the faint-hearted or for those afraid of innovation.

14.20 Contract extensions

Contracts can be extended for a limited period, for example a few months to bring the end time in line with other contracts or financial operating periods. Contracts could also be extended by longer periods if there is a good relationship between the parties – typically one or two years.

The benefits of contract extensions are:

❑ Extending the existing contract under the same terms and conditions.
❑ Could be used to employ the same contractor on a similar job.
❑ Alleviates the tender process, but removes competition.
❑ Allows continued use of a known contractor.

14.21 Service level agreement (SLA)

SLAs are basically detailed standards of performance for individual service aspects, e.g. response times, reporting and monitoring, liaison with other suppliers, and specific detailed deliverables. Large complex agreements might have many pages of complicated SLAs appended, which would be referenced in the service description section and responsibilities of the provider. These more complex agreements would also need to state the terms governing the alteration of SLAs – otherwise high legal costs will be incurred.

SLAs may or may not form part of the contract. SLAs tend to be used when the details in the contract need clarification. The SLA can be used to verify standards and performance measurement of key activities or services. If excluded from the main contract, then annual review and revisions can be applied with limited extra legal cost. In summary, a SLA can:

❑ Provide an agreed quality and performance standard.
❑ Include penalties for non-compliance.
❑ Be internal or external to the organisation.
❑ Form part of a contractual arrangement.
❑ Be used in benchmarking activities.

14.22 Standard contract forms

There are many standard contract documents written by various professional organisations and experts within the industry that can be purchased. It is important to choose the most appropriate standard contract to avoid too many costly amendments. Examples include:

- ❑ GC/Works/10 Facilities Management Contract (2000).
- ❑ BSRIA 'Soft landings'.
- ❑ CIOB Facilities Management Contract.
- ❑ BE Collaborative Contract.
- ❑ ICE (Institute of Civil Engineers).
- ❑ JCT (Joint Contract Tribunal) suite of contracts.
- ❑ NEC framework of contracts.

14.23 Chartered Institute of Building Facilities Management Contract

This contract was developed jointly between the CIOB and Cameron McKenna in 1999 and revised in 2004. It provides a simple-to-understand set of terms and conditions, to which a choice of specifications and pricing options can be easily appended. Pricing can be fixed fee, cost plus or index-linked. The contract includes Guidance notes, Facilities Management Contract Guidance which covers team working, plant maintenance and business transfers. The contract has three appendices as shown in Table 14.1. Caution is required in terms of the new CDM Regulations and TUPE which both impact on these large-scale project contracts.

14.24 Joint Contracts Tribunal (JCT) Forms of Contract

The JCT was established in 1931 and has for many years produced standard forms of contracts, guidance notes and other standard documentation for use in the construction industry. The JCT is an independent organisation representing all parts of the construction industry and is the leading provider of standard forms of building contract. A new suite of contracts – Revision 2 – are now available via various agents and bookshops. These include contracts for Construction Management, Design and Build, Framework Agreement, Measured Term, and Minor Works Building Contract, Standard Building Contract, Major Project Construction Contract, Repair and Maintenance Contract and many others.

Table 14.1   CIOB FM Contract appendices

Appendix 1	Identification of premises.
Appendix 2	A list of services – such as 'arrange, administer and manage all contracts and subcontracts for the provision of the Services at the Premises', and 'undertake the operational tasks and attendance requirements set out in the Specification'.
Appendix 3	Specification – a list of 32 FM services including building maintenance, energy management, landscaping, project management of refurbishment and space management.

14.25 General Contract Works (GCW) 10 Facilities Management (2000)

This contract owes its origination to PACE, the UK Property Advisers to the Civil Estate. It is a fixed-sum, fixed-term contract and includes for either: (a) unless expressly removed, the supplier to assume all costs, expenses and risk or; (b) where rates can be adjusted annually in line with agreed cost or price indices. This was first published in 2000 and it is retailed by HM Stationery Office. It is presented in two volumes. There is also very helpful guidance provided in a commentary and 11 model forms, including:

❑ Abstract of Particulars.
❑ Invitation to Tender.
❑ Tender and Tender Price Form.
❑ Adjudicator's Appointment.
❑ Subcontractor's Collateral Warranty.
❑ Contract Agreement.
❑ Employer's Representative Instruction.
❑ Payment Notice.
❑ Notice of Intention to Withhold Payment.

The contract is capable of wide application for FM services. It can be used for the appointment of an FM as a professional consultant, or where the client wishes to appoint an FM contractor, and it can be used for services at one or more sites. The contract comprises the following documents:

❑ Contract Agreement.
❑ General Conditions of Contract (and any supplementary and annexed conditions).
❑ Abstract of Particulars.
❑ Specification (either 'input' or 'output' type, or a hybrid).
❑ Schedule of Prices and Rates.

14.26 NEC Contract

The NEC Contract is a legal framework of project management procedures designed to handle all aspects of the management of construction projects. Its benefits include stimulus to good management, flexibility and simplicity and can be applied to any construction project, large or small. It comprises of a suite of contract documents and guidance books. The NEC family of contracts are an alternative set of standard contract documents to the JCT forms of contract used in the UK construction sector. The flexibility and simple language of the contract documents are some of the reasons for its use on a wide variety of projects nationally and internationally.

14.27 BSRIA Soft Landings

The 'soft landings' concept was first proposed several years ago by Mark Wey, and more recently BSRIA have developed the soft landings contract into a framework that can be used in new construction, refurbishment and alteration projects. There are five key stages

Table 14.2   Stages in the Soft Landings Contract

Inception and briefing	Clarification of duties of design, client and construction teams, manages expectations on future performance
Design development and review	Specification and construction, reviewing the likely performance against the original expectations
Pre-handover	Involvement of all parties (design, operators, builders, commissioning specialists) to ensure operational readiness of building
Initial aftercare	Resident representative on site to respond to queries, react to problems, ensure transfer of knowledge during first year of occupation – the settling-in period
Years 1–3 aftercare	Periodic monitoring and review of building performance

in the framework as shown in Table 14.2. The term 'soft landings' comes from the analogy of an aircraft landing with no bumps – the idea is that a successful project will be easily used by the customer at handover due to the terms of the contract.

14.28 BE Collaborative Contract

This type of contract is based on a collaborative approach. The contract consists of a purchase order and compatible set of terms and conditions that can be used in the appointment of professionals, contractors and subcontractors. The contract framework is shown in Table 14.3. This form of contract was developed to enable a less confrontational relationship between the parties in a construction contract.

14.29 Private Finance Initiatives (PFI)

The concept of PFIs was conceived during the early 1990s. It provides a mechanism for industry to partner government in long-term, high-cost projects and to share the potential benefits – as well as risks – of such 'partnering' opportunities. The idea is to use private sector finance and expertise to achieve better value for money; in this way, the UK government has become a purchaser of services rather than a commissioner of major capital projects.

There are a number of different partnering arrangements, depending on the nature of the project and the objectives of particular initiatives. The main categories are:

❑   Build, Operate, Transfer (BOT).
❑   Build, Own, Operate (BOO).
❑   Design, Build, Finance, Operate (DBFO).
❑   Design, Construct, Manage, Finance (DCMF).

For example, in a BOT project, the Government grants a private sector organisation the concession to build a facility, operate it during the concession period and then transfer it back at the end of the period. However, for a BOO project, the industrial partner finances,

Table 14.3   BE Contract features and framework

A purchase order	This sets out the key elements of the contract – the names of the parties, description of work/services, start date, completion date, insurance and security requirements
Contract terms	Written in plain English and aimed at supporting the underlying processes necessary for successful projects (primarily team working and proactive risk management)
A risk allocation schedule	Allows the flexible allocation of responsibility for the consequences of risks between the parties
Payment	Provisions based on a target cost arrangement (with provision for pain and gain share and subject to a guaranteed maximum sum with an alternative lump sum arrangement where appropriate)
Specification	Details of the works and/or services to be provided
Warranty	This identifies the third party/end-users who may have rights against designers and contractors if latent defects appear
Partnering charter	A project protocol written in the party's own words, of their personal aspirations for a particular project or longer-term partnership

designs, constructs and operates the facility over a given period but the facility does not revert back to the principal, the Government.

The principles of the PFI forms of contract are:

❑ The new building owner has a real incentive to design and construct a good-quality building in order that maintenance costs are kept to a minimum.
❑ The contractors take responsibility for revenue and replacement costs as well as their capital costs. Over the contract term, FM costs will accumulate to become an enormous sum, funded by future revenue, and therefore need to be predicted accurately during initial contractual negotiations.
❑ Comprehensive SLAs can help to ensure good maintenance of the facility and penalty clauses may provide further incentives for the private sector organisation to perform well.
❑ Construction or refurbishment costs, together with all FM costs, may be progressively recovered through staged payments during the period of concession.
❑ Risk is transferred to the private sector. Staff and equipment may be transferred from old to new property. Any risks associated with project slippage may be placed with the private sector. Some risks may be better managed and handled by the public sector, so it is not necessary to equate a PFI with transfer of all risks.

14.30 Terms and conditions

Purchase orders will state the buyer's conditions, and often the supplier will dispute these, requiring their conditions of sale to prevail. FMs will often be presented with the supplier's 'standard terms and conditions' in contract documents. FMs need to minimise risk by ensuring that suppliers work to the client organisation's terms wherever possible. Purchaser and supplier should agree upon reasonable terms and conditions.

The typical terms found in the small print on the reverse of purchase orders and included in the general terms of other types of contracts include:

- ❑ Payment terms.
- ❑ Responsibilities of both parties.
- ❑ Liabilities.
- ❑ Insurance.
- ❑ Penalties.
- ❑ Title of goods.
- ❑ Time periods.
- ❑ Force majeure.
- ❑ Termination/cancellation terms.
- ❑ Jurisdiction/legislation.
- ❑ Warranties/guarantees.
- ❑ Delivery terms.
- ❑ Intellectual property/copyright.

FMs should look out for the following words in supplier's terms and conditions:

- ❑ Any wording which turns on 'the sole opinion of the Supplier'.
- ❑ Any indemnities flowing from the customer to the supplier.
- ❑ Any reference to goods or services provided 'at the customer's additional expense' (particularly if unquantified).
- ❑ Any right of the supplier to vary the contract without the customer's consent.
- ❑ Any term which should apply to both parties but has been drafted so that it favours only one party.
- ❑ Any options which are exercisable by the supplier on a unilateral basis.

15 Legislation

FMs have many regulations and legislation to know and understand if they are to be competent in the discharge of their duties.

FMs need to look after the well-being of the employees working in the buildings and facilities, provide a safe place of work with safe equipment, as well as mitigate the risks of loss of productivity, prosecution, litigation and claims. It has been suggested that FMs need to be aware of up to 400 legal rules that are to be found in various Acts of Parliament, Regulations, Approved Codes of Practice and Guidance Notes.

The UK legal system has a long history, and although not based on a written constitution, it is based on the separate powers of:

❑ The legislature or rules made by Parliament.
❑ The executive agencies, departments and public bodies acting on behalf of the Government.
❑ The judiciary system, which comprises a range of courts and tribunals that checks everyone acts within the law laid down by legislature.

In the UK, there are three types of law as shown in the Table 15.1.

The legal justice system is based on a hierarchy of courts depicted in Figure 15.1. With more settlements made 'out of court', most cases are dealt with within the Magistrates' Courts.

The law is constantly changing to respond to different needs and circumstances. There is a time lag from the drafting of a new Bill to becoming a Statute or Act of Parliament and the legislation coming into force. There are about 60–70 new Bills each year. Courts interpret the law, and as new legislation is enacted, there may be changing emphasis in the interpretation. It is therefore very important to:

❑ Interpret the legislation by reading the Act or legal rule very carefully.
❑ Ensure that the legal source is completely up to date, ensuring that the particular legislation has not been amended, revised or repealed.

Table 15.1 Types of law

Type	Examples
1 Civil	Contract law, employment law, tort (civil wrongs)
2 Criminal	Breaches of regulations, enforcement of notices, punishment for acts (such as assault, burglary, murder), breaches of duty of care (such as waste management, water pollution, health and safety)
3 Public	Planning regulations, building regulations

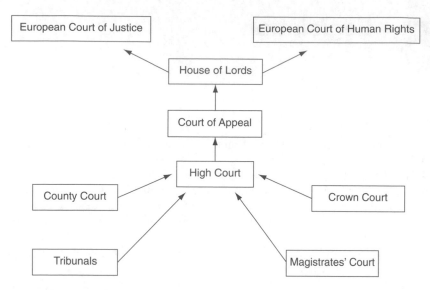

Figure 15.1   The UK justice system

❑   Determine where and when the breach of rights or legislation has occurred.
❑   Establish the causal links in the chain of events in the act or omission which has led to a failure to comply with legislation.
❑   Seek expert help early.

Civil law principles are based on a justice system designed to resolve disputes between two or more parties. It provides redress for damages suffered. The main remedy is compensation or injunctions to either prevent someone from doing something or to force an action to be carried out. In general, the claimant has to initiate proceedings, and to prove on a balance of probabilities (more than 50%) that they have a case.

Criminal law principles are based on the need to punish the wrongdoers, and impose sanctions on those who are in breach of regulations. Fines and imprisonment are typical sanctions imposed. The State will initiate proceedings via a number of public bodies – a few are listed in Table 15.2. The officers acting for the prosecuting authorities have more powers than the average police constable, and must comply with the PACE code of conduct.

Offences under criminal law are known as strict liability, which means that even though there was no intention to cause harm, the defendant will be guilty. In these cases, the State must prove beyond reasonable doubt (more than 95%) that the criminal act occurred. The defendant may be able to provide evidence in a number of ways, such as:

❑   That reasonable precautions were taken – this is sometimes referred to as 'due diligence'.
❑   That a reasonable excuse is afforded.
❑   That actions or activities were undertaken in an emergency to avoid harm to the public.
❑   That the best practical means were used to prevent or counteract the effects of the actions or activity.

Table 15.2   Government agents and areas of responsibility in law

Health and Safety Executive	Health and safety related offences
Environment Agency	Water related, more serious waste and integrated pollution control (IPC) matters
Local Authorities	Less serious waste offences, air pollution, planning control, food and hygiene, noise and general environmental health offences
Crown Prosecution Service	Offences against the state
Director of Public Prosecutions	Serious offences
TV Licensing Authority	License for television
Customs and Excise	Revenue fraud, tax evasion
Security Industry Association (SIA)	Security offences relating to Private Security Industry Act

Table 15.3   List of concerns listed in ranked order of importance

1	Contractors	6	Accident/incident investigation
2	Risk assessment	7	Lone working
3	DDA 1995	8	Workplace inspections
4	Asbestos	9	Enforcement
5	Fire	10	Competence

Criminal proceedings may result in sanctions imposed on the organisation, and if the offence was committed with the consent (knowledge and awareness of the risks), connivance (knowing but doing nothing about it) or neglect (unreasonable breach of duty of care) on an individual such as a director, manager or other officer.

Public law principles are based on judicial review and control. This is a way of ensuring everyone follows the law. This is particularly important for FMs with property management responsibilities because the main area of public law is the control of land use.

In most health, safety and environmental legislation, offences attract vicarious liability. This is when the liability falls on one person as a result of the actions of another. Typically, this is the liability of the employer for the acts and omissions of his employees.

Some of the main issues regarding legal compliance for FMs are shown in Table 15.3.

FMs cover such a broad range of responsibilities and so not surprisingly the knowledge areas of legislation are also very broad, and often extend beyond the normal health, safety and environment remit. Table 15.4 shows the range of legislation against the typical areas of responsibility.

In health and safety legislation, FMs have obligations as an employee. As with other employees, they cannot interfere or misuse safety equipment, they must observe instructions and cooperate with procedures and take reasonable care for themselves and others by their acts and omissions.

In addition, FMs have responsibilities as a duty holder for many of the regulations in health, safety and environmental legislation. This does depend on the exact nature of their role, and what other roles are held by other employees in the organisation. For example, does the organisation employ a Fire Officer, a Health and Safety Officer or a CDM Co-ordinator? FMs working in smaller organisations may find themselves with greater responsibilities than those in larger organisations. FMs will often find that they are respresenting or acting on behalf of the employer duties, e.g. the responsibility for the contractors, third parties and the public often comes under the FM function, the management of a safe place of work is ultimately the FM role, the issuing of personal protective equipment and so on.

There are three types of duties in health and safety legislation, these are:

(i) Absolute – this is something that must be done.
(ii) So far as is practicable – this is something that must be done if physically possible disregarding the costs involved.
(iii) So far as is reasonably practicable – this is something that can be done after a cost benefit analysis has been carried out.

15.1 Operational compliance

As custodian of the common spaces in most workplaces, FMs and their appointed contractors will be the duty holder in regulation 4 of the Workplace Regulations 1992. '... every employer or person who has to any extent control of the premises shall ensure that every workplace, modification, extension or conversion under their control and where any of their employees work complies with these regulations'. Many of the other specific regulations of the Workplace Regulations will feature in the daily work of a FM, and it is therefore essential to have a good level of understanding of this particular regulation and its many sections.

Dealing with non-employees and visitors is also a role that often falls to the FM team to manage. This will therefore include the giving of suitable information regarding health and safety arrangements to visitors, the assessment of risks and the issuing of permits to work.

As UK society becomes more litigious, with increasing expectations and demands, due diligence must be applied to all activities. Records of all incidents and near-misses must be kept. Records of investigations into breaches of company or statutory rules and regulations must be kept for a number of years. Employees and others may claim up to 6 years after an incident, so it is important to keep the evidence to assist or defend potential claims. There is also a direct impact on the organisations' insurance costs and their liabilities.

15.2 Strategic impact

There are some longer-term impacts of compliance affecting whole business activities, such as employment contracts, property acquisition and development, service contracts and continuity of business activities. Some organisations will be more risk averse than others, and have a different attitude to the management of uncertainties in their organisation. There needs to be an understanding of the impact of FM activities upon the business, and how these may support or jeopardise the business activities. Policies and procedures supporting the business goals of an organisation must take into account the relevant legislative duties and responsibilities.

In addition, the long-term implication of inappropriate operational activities that may lead to prosecution, fines, business closure and litigation must be considered. The reputation of the organisation to employees, suppliers and the general public needs to be considered. The time taken to defend cases as well as the cost of experts, potential hospital charges and compensation claims are other aspects to consider.

FMs and others with specific duties for providing a safe working environment will be under increasing pressure to keep their senior management as well as themselves out of jail.

Table 15.4   List of various FM activities and the relevant laws

Employment	Equal opportunities, discrimination, recruitment, pay, TUPE, part-time and fixed-term employees, termination of service, paternity and maternity rights, flexible working, disciplinary and grievance procedures	Disability Discrimination Act 2004; Employment Rights Act 1996; Public Interest Disclosure Act 1998; Employment Act 2002; Working Time Regulations 1998 (amended in 2002); Transfer of Undertakings (Protection of Employment) Regulations 1981; Acquired Rights Directive 2001 (2001/23/EC); Race Relations Act 1976; Employment Equality (Religion or Belief) Regulations 2003; Employment Equality (Sexual Orientation) Regulations 2003; National Minimum Wage Act 1998; Sex Discrimination Act 1975 (amended in 2003)
Health and Safety	Providing safe place, safe people, safe process and equipment	Health and Safety at Work Act 1974; Control of Asbestos Regulations 1987; Noise at Work Regulations 1989; The Six Pack Regulations 1992; Health and Safety (Safety Signs and Signals) Regulations 1996; Electricity at Work Regulations 1989; Lifting Operations and Lifting Equipment Regulations 1998 (LOLER); Gas Safety (Installation and Use) Regulations 1998; Provisions for Use of Work Equipment Regulations 1999 (PUWER); Health and Safety (Miscellaneous Amendments) Regulations 2002; Control of Substances Hazardous to Health Regulations 2002; Chemicals (Hazard Information and Packaging for Supply) (Amendment Regulations 2002; Confined Spaces Regulations 1997; Working at Height Regulations 2005
Environment	Waste management, environment protection, use of resources	Environment Protection Act 1990; Environmental Protection (Duty of Care) Regulations 1991; Waste Management Regulations 1996; Control of Pollution (Amendments) Act 1989; Controlled Waste Regulations 1992 (amended 1993); Special Waste Regulations 1996; Landfill (England and Wales) Regulations 2002; Waste Electrical and Electronic Equipment Directive (WEEE)
Human Rights	Privacy, information on people, monitoring employees	Human Rights Act 1998; Regulatory Investigative Powers Act 2000; Data Protection Act 1998; Freedom of Information Act 2000; Copyright, Design and Patents Act 1988

(Continued)

Table 15.4   (Continued)

Construction	New buildings, maintenance and refurbishment activities	Construction, Design and Management Regulations 2007; Construction (Head Protection) Regulations 1989
Property	Planning permission, ownership of property	Town and Country Planning Act 1990; Building Act 1984; Building Regulations 2002; Landlords and Tenants Act 1954, 1985, 1988; Occupiers Liability Acts 1957, 1984; Defective Premises Act 1972
Fire Safety	Fire risk assessment, equipment provision, training and maintenance	Regulatory Reform (Fire Safety) Order 2004
Welfare	First aid, accident reporting	Health and Safety (First Aid) Regulations 1981; Reporting of Injuries, Diseases and Dangerous Occurrences Regulations 1995 (RIDDOR); Control of Major Accidents Hazards Regulations 1999
Food	Catering, vending and hospitality services	Food Safety Act 1990; Food Safety (General Food Hygiene) Regulations 1995; Food Safety (Temperature Control) Regulations 1995; Food Premises (Registration) Regulations 1991; Food Labelling Regulations 1996 (amended in 1999 and 2003)
Security	Door supervision, wheel clamping, guards, key holding, consultants and investigators	Private Security Industry Act 2001
Purchasing	Buying of goods, contracts with suppliers, sale of goods and services	Arbitration Act 1996; Housing Grants, Construction and Regeneration Act 1996; Sale of Goods Act 1979; Supply of Goods and Services Act 1982; Unfair Contract Terms Act 1977; European Procurement Directive
Directors and Senior Management	Accountability and financial management	Companies Act 1985, 1989; Insolvency Act; Value Added Tax Act 1994; Corporate Manslaughter Act
Hand-held radio devices	Radio licensing	The Radio Equipment and Telecommunications Terminal Equipment Regulations 2000; Communications Act; Communications Act 2003

16 Legislation Affecting FM Activities

16.1 Introduction

FMs must be familiar with the legislation that affects FM services and activities. With much legislation impacting on the work of the FM, a qualification in Health and Safety is becoming more important to demonstrate competence. Qualifications that are often stated as requirements in job advertisements include the NEBOSH General Certificate or the IOSH Managing Safely qualifications.

FMs should be aware of the legislation, regulations and approved codes of practice that relate the buildings, the services and the employment of people providing those services. All managers must be aware of the basic principles of the Health and Safety at Work Act, as shown in Table 16.1.

16.2 Safety policy

A written safety policy is required by the Health and Safety at Work Act (section 2[3]) for organisations of five or more employees. Advice on drafting or checking a policy can be found in HSC6 and HSG65. There should be three parts:

(i) Intentions – Objectives of the policy.
(ii) Organisation – Responsibilities of who does what in the organisation.
(iii) Arrangements – How is safety actually managed, in terms of procedures, training, information and supervision?

The FM needs to know where they fit into the organisation's structure in terms of the safety policy. The organisation may be large enough to warrant a separate function, otherwise the facilities or personnel function may have the responsibility for safety. Either way,

Table 16.1   The Health and Safety at Work Act 1974

Employers responsibilities	Employees responsibilities
Safe place, safe people, safe process	No interference or misuse of safety equipment
Non-employees/third parties	Observe instructions and co-operate with procedures
Consultation, safety committees, safety policy	Take reasonable care for self and others by acts and omissions
Free personal protective equipment (PPE)	

the FM is frequently involved in many safety aspects of the organisation. They may be required to: set up, chair or attend safety committee meetings; draft, amend and publish the organisation's safety policy; determine appropriate procedures and systems of work. As the manager of the workplace, with particular responsibility for third parties such as visitors and non-employees, it is important that the FM understands the wide range of legislation that affects the workplace.

16.3 Enforcing authorities

Enforcing officers representing the local authority, the Health and Safety Executive (HSE) or other government agencies have many powers. It is important the FM team recognises this power, and that the front of house team alert the FM when they arrive on the premises. The powers of an enforcement officer include:

- ❑   Right of entry.
- ❑   To bring a policeman or other expert.
- ❑   Bring equipment, materials and use them.
- ❑   Examine, inspect, investigate, dismantle.
- ❑   Direct that things or places are left undisturbed.
- ❑   Require anyone to give facilities and/or assistance and to provide advice.
- ❑   Take measurements, photographs, recordings.
- ❑   Take samples from premises or atmosphere.
- ❑   Interview people and obtain signed statements of truth.
- ❑   Inspect and take copies of documents, entries in books and other paper or digital records.
- ❑   Issue enforcement notices.
- ❑   Initiate prosecution.
- ❑   Any other power to do their job.

The client or FM has limited rights when the enforcing officer enters the premises. They can check the identity/warranty of the Environmental Health Officer (EHO) or enforcement officer. They can query their powers by asking for a list of their powers and they can ask for a signed statement of the infringement.

16.4 Management of Health and Safety Regulations

The Health and Safety at Work Act requires employers to maintain a healthy and safe system of work, which, under the Management of Health and Safety at Work Regulations, should be achieved through risk assessment.

These Regulations are particularly important due to the section relating to risk assessment. They were amended in 1994 to include expectant/nursing mothers, young persons and fire; and again in 1999 to include the need for competent persons and arrangements for contacting emergency services.

Employers are required to carry out suitable and sufficient assessments of all the risks to employees and others affected by their work activities. This requires an ability to know what is wrong now or in the future and what could be done about it. The aim is to be proactive and deal with the hazards before they cause an accident. A competent person should have knowledge of the workplace and experience of the work being carried out – this gives them the ability and confidence to carry out risk assessments.

16.5 The HSE five-step approach

The HSE recommend a competent person uses the five-step approach when conducting a risk assessment.

❑ Identify the hazards.
❑ Identify those who may be harmed.
❑ Implement control measures.
❑ Record your findings.
❑ Review and revise.

A competent person is someone with sufficient training, experience and knowledge to properly assist the employer to undertake measures to comply with health and safety legislation.

16.6 Risk assessment standards

In order to be suitable and sufficient and to comply with other legal requirements, a risk assessment must:

❑ Identify all the hazards associated with the operation, and evaluate the risks arising from those hazards (taking account of relevant Acts and Regulations).
❑ Record the significant findings if more than five persons are employed (even if they are spread across two or more locations).
❑ Identify any group of employees (or single employees as the case may be) who are especially at risk.
❑ Identify others who may be especially at risk, e.g. visitors, contractors, members of the public.
❑ Evaluate existing controls, stating whether or not they are satisfactory, and if not what action needs to be taken. This should include training and information provision.
❑ Judge and record the probability or likelihood of an accident occurring as a result of uncontrolled risk. Also record the 'worst case' likely outcome.
❑ Record any circumstances arising from the assessment where serious and imminent danger could arise.
❑ Identify what information is needed for employees on the risks to their health and safety identified by the assessment, the precautions to be taken and any emergency arrangements.
❑ Provide an action plan giving information on implementation of additional controls, in order of priority, and with a realistic timescale.

16.7 Hazards

FMs need to be able to identify the hazards that have a potential to cause harm. These hazards may be people, things or places. As part of the identification process, a number of questions such as 'who, what, how, where' can be asked. The likelihood and the severity of the hazard(s) being realised will need quantifying. All risk assessments must be recorded and reviewed on a regular basis, but especially after an incident, change of personnel or equipment or change of process. Control measures to mitigate and reduce the risks need expert management, and in many cases, this falls to the FM and their specialist team.

16.8 Risk control

The risk control measures that can be applied to manage risks are known as the hierarchy of control measures. It is important to apply these in order as listed in Table 16.2, with the use of personal protective equipment (PPE) being only used as the last resort. It is more cost effective, and safer too, to undertake the control measures in this order to reduce the numbers of staff that have to be issued, trained and monitored in the use of PPE.

Health and safety management tasks that may be part of the operational role of FMs may include:

❑   Physical workplace inspections.
❑   Hazard spotting.
❑   Safety audits.
❑   Discussions with staff and contractors.
❑   Job safety analysis and/or task analysis.
❑   Study of past accidents, incidents and near-misses.
❑   Benchmarking.

16.9 Risk register

A risk assessment register must be maintained and updated. This means that any significant change to a process or activity, and any new process, activity or operation should be subject to new risk assessment, and that if new hazards or accidents or near misses come to light then these should also be subject to risk assessment.

In addition, the risk assessment should be periodically reviewed and updated. The frequency of review depends on the level of risk in the operation, and should normally not exceed 10 years. It may be found useful to carry out review of risk assessment as part of the safety policy annual review as the two activities are closely linked.

16.10 Definitions of hazard and risk

The terms 'hazard' and 'risk' are frequently used in the Regulations, Approved Code of Practice and Guidance. It is important to appreciate what these terms mean.

Hazard is the potential for harm. **Risk** is a function of the probability (or likelihood) of that harm actually occurring and the severity of its consequences.

Table 16.2   Hierarchy of control measures

1   Elimination
2   Substitution
3   Avoidance
4   Isolation
5   Segregation
6   Engineering controls
7   Procedures and safe systems of work
8   PPE

The extent of the risk should also take into account the number of people exposed to the harm. It should be carefully noted that this assessment does not need quantified probability except for higher risk activities where the outcome could be multiple fatalities.

16.11 Hazard identification

There are a number of simple ways in which hazards can be identified. In order to achieve a suitable and sufficient risk assessment, it is essential to identify all the hazards associated with the activity. Therefore all the methods of identifying hazards will need to be assessed and the most suitable mix used.

Before going to the next stage, a check needs to be made that all the hazards have been identified. In all cases, team consultation is a powerful aid. This can involve an appropriate selection from line management and safety representatives. Some people use a floor to ceiling approach to ensure all hazards in a given space are identified. Another approach is using the categories of biological, chemical, ergonomic, psychological and physical for identifying hazards.

For complex activities, it can be useful to break down the activity into its component parts, perhaps using job analysis or job descriptions. For example, the operation and use of a large machine could comprise:

❑ Normal operating.
❑ Breakdown.
❑ Cleaning/spillage.
❑ Lubricating.
❑ Setting/adjustment.
❑ Overhaul.
❑ Installation.
❑ Dismantling.

Potential hazards from an activity might include:

❑ Fall of a person from height.
❑ Fall of an object/material from height.
❑ Fall of a person on the same level.
❑ Manual handling.
❑ Use of machines.
❑ Operation of vehicles.
❑ Fire including static electricity.
❑ Electricity.
❑ Drowning.

16.12 Work activities

Examples of work activities that require risk assessment include:

❑ Excavation work.
❑ Handling stored energy.

❏   Work that may result in explosions (chemical dust).
❏   Contact with cold/hot surfaces.
❏   Using compressed air.
❏   Mechanical lifting operations.
❏   Activities that generate noise or occur in noisy environments.
❏   Work involving biological agents.
❏   Work using ionising radiation.
❏   Vibration from hand- and power-operated tools.
❏   Working in adverse weather.
❏   Working with chemicals and substances.
❏   Stacking and movement of materials.
❏   Housekeeping activities, such as bed changing, curtain hanging.
❏   Working in a confined space.
❏   Cleaning.
❏   Working on display screen equipment.

16.13 Risk assessment

For each activity, a risk assessment needs to be made. There are many techniques of risk assessment ranging from complex techniques such as fault-free analysis and reliability studies to simple subjective judgement.

In simple terms, if there is a risk of a single event or fault killing many people, then a complex assessment method is justified. On the other hand, if the worst case is a serious injury or a single fatality, then a simpler method is justified.

A judgement must be made as to whether or not a risk is acceptable. For each hazard identified for each activity/situation, the question 'what if?' must be asked to test the likely outcome of that risk being realised.

The FM must consider and investigate realistically what is the worst likely outcome? Is it:

❏   A fatality?
❏   Major injury/permanent disability including permanent ill health?
❏   A minor injury?
❏   Environmental/plant damage?

Two important laws of human nature should always be taken into account. First, never rely solely on common sense as it is much less common than is generally assumed. Second, always rely on Murphy's law—'if someone can do it, sooner or later someone will'.

Likelihood

A judgement of the probability or likelihood of harm occurring is needed, often using simple descriptions as shown in Table 16.3.

Best practice

A further crucial aspect is to bear in mind what is the best practice for controlling the hazard which is under consideration. This means that one needs to be aware of

Table 16.3 Probability outcomes

Probability/likelihood	Description
Likely/frequent	Occurs repeatedly/event only to be expected
Probable	Not surprised
	Will occur several times
Possible	Could occur sometime
Remote	Unlikely, though conceivable
Improbable	So unlikely that probability is close to zero

relevant practice in other employment sectors. This can best be done by reference to HSE Guidance Notes, the publications of Industry Advisory Committees, trade press, suppliers' manuals, etc.

16.14 Risk assessment records

In order to produce a suitable and sufficient assessment, the following points must be recorded in a retrievable format:

- ❑ The activity/situation.
- ❑ Number of persons at risk.
- ❑ Any group of persons especially at risk (e.g. specially vulnerable employees such as disabled or lone workers, young persons, visitors, members of the public, contractors).
- ❑ Any serious and imminent risk (in which case, written procedures are required and one or more competent persons appointed to carry out the procedure).
- ❑ Probability of harm occurring and the realistic worst-case outcome (e.g. fatality, major injury, minor injury, no injury, environmental/plant damage).
- ❑ Relevant health and safety information needed by employees/others (as a minimum, this would mean reviewing the provision of safety signs and audible/visual warnings).
- ❑ Any additional training needs.
- ❑ Reference to existing controls and whether or not these are satisfactory. (Existing controls need not be reproduced in full where they are documented elsewhere. Referring to these other documents as appropriate is sufficient.)
- ❑ Action required in order of priority with proposed timescale and who is responsible for action.

16.15 The Workplace (Health, Safety and Welfare) Regulations 1992 amended 2002

These Regulations are fundamental to the FM. As the name implies, these Regulations concern the workplace, and any person who has any control of the premises is the duty holder and must ensure compliance to the Regulations. Table 16.4 gives an outline summary of the main areas.

Table 16.4   Scope of the Workplace Regulations

Topic	Reg No.	Scope of requirement
Work space	10	Sufficient floor area and height, 11 m^3.
Workstations/seating	11	Suitable for any likely work or person.
Drinking water	22	Adequate supply of wholesome drinking water at readily accessible places, conspicuously marked. Sufficient number of drinking vessels, unless jet stream device.
Sanitary conveniences	20	Readily accessible, adequately ventilated and lit, separate for men and women unless in separate room, secured from inside, approximately 1/25 persons.
Workplace and equipment	5	Kept clean and maintained, efficient working order, good repair, suitable system of maintenance.
Lighting	8	Suitable and sufficient, if possible by natural light, emergency lighting if risk to safety when artificial light fails.
Windows, skylights, ventilators	15 and 16	Designed and constructed for safe cleaning. If openable, then safe for person opening, closing or adjusting.
Ventilation	6	Suitable and effective by fresh or purified air. Indication of failure.
Floors/traffic routes	12 and 17	Suitable for purpose, free from obstructions and anything that could cause a slip, trip or fall. Effective drainage. Assess and protect holes, slopes and slippery surfaces. Provide guard rails and handrails. Sufficient number, size and quantity of traffic routes, segregation from pedestrians.
Temperature	7	Reasonable temperature. Sufficient thermometers to be provided.
Washing facilities	21	Suitable and sufficient, accessible places, sufficiently ventilated and lit, clean, orderly and well maintained. Near toilets and changing rooms. Clean supply of hot and cold running water, soap and towels. Separate for men and women, unless designed for one person at a time and secured from inside.
Meals and restrooms	25	Suitable and sufficient restrooms, facilities with adequate tables and chairs with backs, suitable for disabled, pregnant women, nursing mothers, protection from tobacco smoke. Suitable and sufficient to eat meals.
Clothing	23 and 24	Suitable and sufficient location for clothing stored whilst at work. Secure and separate to avoid risks of contamination. Facilities for drying wet clothes. Suitable and sufficient facility, accessible, sufficient capacity, with seating, separate for men and women, to change into work clothing.

Table 16.4   (*Continued*)

Topic	Reg No.	Scope of requirement
Disabled persons	25A	Facilities to be organised to take account of disabled persons – access, workstations, washing facilities and sanitary conveniences.
Cleanliness and waste	9	Fixtures, fittings, walls, ceilings, floors and furniture kept sufficiently clean. Waste not allowed to accumulate except in suitable receptacles.
Falls/falling objects	13	Suitable and effective measures to prevent anyone being injured through falling or being stuck. Tanks, pits, structures to be securely covered or fenced.
Doors/gates	18	Safety catches and devices, clear view either side.
Transparent/translucent windows, doors, gates, walls	14	Safety material, protected against breakage. Appropriately marked or incorporate features which make it apparent.
Escalators	19	Function safely, safety devices, accessible safety stops.

The implications of the Workplace Regulations are diverse, affecting nearly every aspect of the FM function. Reference to the Regulations can help defend cleaning and maintenance budgets, help with space planning conflicts and ensure that suitable FM contractor accommodation and changing areas are provided.

16.16 Control of Substances Hazardous to Health

The Control of Substances Hazardous to Health (COSHH) Regulations cover practically all substances, including bacteria and organic matter, capable of causing harm to human health. There are eight principles to observe:

  (i) Processes and activities must be designed to minimise emission, release or spread of hazardous substances.
 (ii) All routes of exposure must be taken into account (inhalation, skin absorption, ingestion).
(iii) Exposure to be controlled by measures proportionate to the health risk.
 (iv) Most effective and reliable control options to be used to minimise and control spread.
  (v) Use suitable PPE.
 (vi) Check and review all control measures.
(vii) Inform and train all employees.
(viii) Ensure control measures do not increase overall risks to health and safety.

Substances can be chemicals, cleaning materials, metals, pesticides, biological agents or organisms. These can be in various forms such as solids, liquids, vapours, gases, dust, fibres, fumes, mist and smoke. Data sheets of products purchased and used are required as part of the risk assessment. The Regulations require the employer to set procedures to cover:

❑   Assessments.
❑   Prevention or control of exposure.
❑   Use, maintenance, examination and test of control measures.
❑   Monitoring.
❑   Health surveillance.
❑   Information, instruction and training.
❑   Exposure limits.
      o   MEL (maximum exposure limits)
      o   OES (occupational exposure limits)

16.17 Working at Height Regulations 2005

These Regulations require that all work at height is properly planned and organised, that the work is carried out safely, and that employees are trained and competent in their work. These regulations also cover falling objects, fragile roofs and equipment. The FM has a duty to do all that is reasonably practical to prevent someone from falling. The application of risk control and a hierarchy of measures is required. The first consideration is whether the work at height can be avoided altogether. If not, the FM must consider the most appropriate equipment and means of access for that activity. The FM should also consider when planning any work at height, the impact of adverse weather conditions, what to do in an emergency, and the steps needed to prevent objects falling. The use of scaffolding, access platforms, ladders and fall-arrest equipment requires specific competence, training, instruction and supervision. These Regulations also cover the maintenance of fragile roofs and other fragile surfaces.

The use of ladders is an area of particular concern. The HSE issues guidance notes – INDG402 and INDG405 – on the safe use of ladders and stepladders. The type of ladder recommended is EN131 or Class 1 Industrial.

16.18 Provision and Use of Workplace Equipment Regulations 1998 (PUWER)

First introduced in 1992 alongside five other significant Regulations that impact on the FM these Regulations cover all types of equipment used for work, such as hand tools, ladders, power tools, lifting equipment, machinery, computers, vehicles and so on. Some equipment may also be covered by LOLER too. Work equipment is defined as any machinery, appliance, apparatus, tool or installation for use at work (whether exclusively or not). Such a wide definition therefore extends to desks, chairs, pens, trolleys and employee's own equipment that they use to do their job.

The Regulations require the employer to ensure that the equipment is suitable for the task, that it is maintained and that it is inspected, with suitable records kept. Users must be given instruction, information and training on its use, especially the correct use of safety features/controls.

16.19 Manual Handling Regulations 1992

These Regulations were introduced to reduce the risk of injuries to the upper body through lifting, lowering, pushing, pulling, reaching, twisting, turning, holding and carrying activities. Repetitive strain injuries and other disorders could result if people continue to do their work in a way that puts strain on their arms and back. In FM operations, there are many activities requiring manual handling – cleaning, document distribution, deliveries, maintenance and porterage. In many cases, the nature of the activity can be changed by use of equipment and technology to reduce the load and method of handling. It is important to have a good regime of health surveillance, training and awareness for all the team in best practice manual handling operations. If possible, the best approach is to eliminate or avoid the need for manual handling, or to use alternative methods. If equipment is provided, then it will be covered by the PUWER legislation. When assessing the risks of manual handling, the FM must consider the tasks, the loads, the working environment and the individual (age, gender, prior injuries).

16.20 Personal Protective Equipment at Work Regulations 1992 (PPE)

These Regulations concern the provision and use of protection work equipment that may be provided by the employer and used by people to protect their health and safety at work. Amendments to the Regulations in 2002 concern the manufacturers and providers of equipment – such as the need for a CE quality safety mark on all new PPE. Protective clothing can include aprons, gloves, safety footwear, safety helmets, high-visibility jackets and waistcoats. Protective equipment can include eye protectors (glasses, goggles, masks), life jackets, respirators, underwater breathing apparatus, safety harness, fall arrest equipment, etc. There is also specific protective equipment required in other legislation, and so the PPE Regulations are therefore not applicable in these cases. Other legislation includes the Noise at Work Regulations, Control of Asbestos Regulations, Control of Lead at Work, Ionising Radiations Regulations, Construction (Head Protection) Regulations, COSHH. In cases where a worker's activities also requires PPE, then the equipment must be compatible.

Employers must decide if PPE is necessary, and if so, must select suitable PPE, issue it free of charge, and then maintain it and replace as necessary. Employers must also provide suitable space or lockers to keep the PPE safe, and also information, instruction and training on its safe use. A system for reporting PPE defects and losses must also be established. The issue of PPE is the last resort in the hierarchy of risk control measures. Employees must take reasonable care of the PPE that they are issued with, and they have a duty to use it too.

16.21 Lifting Operations and Lifting Equipment Regulations 1998 (LOLER)

The LOLER Regulations cover a wide range of equipment used in buildings. For example passenger and goods lifts, cranes, hoists, scissor lifts, cherry pickers, cradles and so on. Equipment and accessories attached to lifting machinery, for anchoring, fixing or supporting (such as shackles, clamps, swivels, slings, and eyebolts), are also included in the Regulations. Lifting is defined as an operation that lifts or lowers a load.

Equipment must be marked clearly with a safe working load (SWL). It must be inspected when first put into service, and then regularly checked. Passenger lifts need to be examined every 6 months, as do lifting equipment accessories. Other types of lifts can be examined every 12 months. These examinations must be carried out by a competent person, who will report the defects identified to the owner of the equipment. Copies of these reports must also be sent to the relevant enforcing authority with in a month. This equipment may be used in many FM activities such as cleaning, general access, maintenance, deliveries and inspection. There is a statutory requirement for insurance inspections and checks. Accidents in passenger lifts are reportable under RIDDOR (see Chapter 20).

16.22 Control of Noise at Work Regulations 2005

Originally introduced in 1999, these Regulations were updated in 2005, with new threshold levels, as shown in Table 16.5. Employers have a legal duty to safeguard their employees' hearing. They must assess the risks of hearing loss and implement risk control measures. The action level at which employers must make hearing protection available is 80 dB(A). There are two further action levels, over an 8-hour day, of 85 dB and 87 dB.

Steps to reduce noise exposure may include personal ear protection, soundproofing structures and enclosures, buying quieter equipment or changing processes to make them quieter. A regime of regular surveillance of those likely to be exposed to noise is required.

Zones where ear protection is required must be clearly demarcated and signed. An ACoP is provided by the HSE – reference L108.

16.23 Confined Spaces Regulations 1997

Many FM controlled spaces in buildings can be defined as confined. Typically, these may be the lift shafts, lift motor rooms, plant rooms, tunnels, access chambers, risers and other chambers. In some premises, there may also be operational business process equipment that is defined as confined. The characteristics of a confined space are that

Table 16.5 Noise levels requiring action to safeguard hearing

80 dB(A) daily personal limit	Peak value of 112 pascals	Suitable and sufficient ear protection, but individual may choose not to use it
85 dB(A) daily personal limit	Peak value of 140 pascals	Noise must be reduced, ear defenders and ear protection compulsory
Limit of 87 dB(A)	Peak value of 200 pascals	

there is only one way in or out, and the activities in the space may result in a change in the composition of the air (depleting oxygen). These Regulations require a risk assessment before work in a confined space is permitted. A critical aspect is planning communications throughout the duration of the work between those operating in the confined space and those external to the area, such as a foreman or banksman. Plans for dealing with an emergency rescue must also be considered prior to the work commencing. Work in confined spaces must be controlled by a permit to work system.

16.24 Part L Building Regulations 2006

FMs responsible for buildings over $1000\,m^2$ which are being improved, refurbished and updated need to comply with the amended 2006 Regulations. Examples of actions required include:

❑ Ensure boilers are assessed by a competent person and obtain a certificate of compliance.
❑ Ensure that the air conditioning system is checked by a competent person and obtain a certificate.
❑ Ensure that a building air lightness test is carried out and a certificate is obtained.
❑ Update the building logbook.
❑ Implement an energy policy and plan to ensure energy costs are reduced.
❑ Achieve 10% of energy supplies via renewable sources.
❑ Work with supply chain and partners to develop carbon reduction in all activities and projects.
❑ Enhance the air supply rate from 8 litres/second per person to 10 litres/second per person.

16.25 Data Protection Act 1998

This gives protection to individuals and requires organisations to protect information they have on individuals. It requires users of personal information and their employer to:

❑ Obtain and process information fairly and lawfully.
❑ Limit disclosure to the right people.
❑ Ensure information is relevant, adequate but not excessive in relation to purpose in holding information.
❑ Ensure its accuracy and where necessary keep up to date.
❑ Keep data secure.
❑ Give individuals the right to know/have access/correct or erase data held on them.
❑ Obtain consent of the individual if processing certain sensitive data (e.g. ethnic origin, political affiliation, criminal convictions, health, religion and sexuality).
❑ Not transfer the data to countries outside the EU without adequate protection.

16.26 Regulation of Investigatory Powers Act 2000 (RIPA)

This gives a legal basis for monitoring employees telecommunications and emails. The recording and monitoring of telephone calls can only be carried out:

❑ If it can be useful in establishing facts relevant to the business.
❑ To monitor standards and compliance to standards or procedures.
❑ To test security or operation.
❑ To investigate and/or detect unauthorised use of the telecommunications system.
❑ To prevent and/or detect crime.

16.27 Human Rights Act 1998

Under Article 8, everyone has the right to respect for his/her private and family life, his/her home and correspondence.

16.28 Transfer of Undertakings (Protection of Employment) Regulations

This legislation applies in many situations in FM where the in-house team is being transferred to a contractor or when outsourced staff are transferred to a new contractor after a retendering of those services. The legislation is based on the EC Acquired Rights Directive 2001. It concerns the rights of staff to the same terms and conditions of employment if they are still performing the same job. There are a number of issues to address in the application of these regulations.

❑ The type of undertaking being transferred.
❑ Whether tangible assets are transferred.
❑ Whether intangible assets are transferred.
❑ Whether the majority of employees are taken on by the new employer.
❑ Whether the customers are transferred.
❑ The degree of similarity in the activities carried on before and after the transfer.

The provision of information and consultation with employees is required. Sufficient time must be allowed for this process. During this period, there will be issues of loyalty and performance that may impact on the services to occupants in the premises.

16.29 Working Time Regulations 1998

These Regulations affect the workers in many FM services. They have been updated in 2001, 2003 and 2007 to reflect new sectors affected. They implement the European Working Time Directive, that regulates hours worked, rest breaks and holidays. It states that a person should not be required to work more than 48 hours per week – this includes all employment for all employers. This can be averaged over a 17-week rolling reference period. The Regulations also state that a 20-minute break every 6 hours is provided to staff, that they have an 11-hour rest between work periods, that they have 5.6 weeks paid holiday and that there must be a 24-hour uninterrupted rest period every 7 days. Records need to be kept to show compliance. There are special cases in which a worker can continue to work without breaks and also for the reference period to be extended to 26 weeks. Staff may choose to opt out of these regulations as either an individual or as a member of a collective group. There is some concern that UK employees work the longest hours per week in Europe. Changes to the EU Directive concerning the opt out procedures have been suggested which would bring the UK into line with the other European States. The issues for FM include:

❑ The arrangements for payment of out of hours attendance and call out arrangements.
❑ The treatment of on call/duty cover in the hours of working.
❑ Workers who may have several jobs with other organisations that all count towards the total working time.
❑ Giving more breaks when the work is monotonous, such as security surveillance.

17 Fire Safety and Legislation

17.1 Introduction

Fire safety and legislation is an area in which the FM needs a good working knowledge. Firstly, the FM needs to be aware of the safety aspects in terms of design and space planning, and secondly, the FM is often the duty holder for general fire safety of occupied space. Fire needs three things present – fuel, ignition source and oxygen – as illustrated in Table 17.1. Fire prevention depends on avoiding these three elements coming together. The absence of one of these elements can prevent a fire starting.

The main consequences of fire are:

- Death.
- Personal injury.
- Building damage.
- Flora and fauna damage.
- Loss of business and jobs.
- Disruption to transport.
- Environmental contamination.

Fires can be extinguished by four main methods:

- Cooling.
- Smothering.
- Starving.
- Chemical reaction.

Table 17.1   The components of a fire

Sources of ignition	Naked flames External sparks Internal sparks Hot surfaces Static electricity
Sources of fuel	Solids (paper, wood, plastics) Liquids (paint, varnish, adhesives, petrol, paraffin, acetone) Gases (LPG, acetylene, hydrogen)
Oxygen	Air Chemicals (nitrates, oxides, chlorates)

Table 17.2   Classes of fire

Class	Nature of fire	Extinguishing method
Class A	Solid materials	Water
Class B	Liquids	
	B1 soluble liquids	Carbon dioxide, dry powder, water spray, foam
	B2 non-soluble liquids	Carbon dioxide, dry powder, foam
Class C	Gases	Foam, dry powder
Class D	Metals	Special dry powder
Class F	Cooking fats or oils	Wet chemical
Electrical	Electrical	Carbon dioxide, dry powder

Heat is transmitted in fires by several means – convection, conduction, radiation or direct burn-ing. These principles govern how buildings are designed to prevent and control fires. Fires are classified according to the fuel source and the means of extinguishing them – see Table 17.2.

17.2 Legislation and standards

The main standards in building design to observe are:

BS 5839: Fire Detection and Alarm Systems.
BS 7273: Part 1:2000 Code of practice for the Operation of Fire Protection Measures.
BS EN 54 Fire Detection and Fire Alarm Systems.

17.3 Building design

When designing a new space for an organisation, or refurbishing an existing space, the FM and design team must observe the legislation governing how the space can be safely used to meet various standards and Approved Documents. Three objectives to be achieved in effective building design are:

 (i) It must be possible for everyone to leave the building quickly and safely.
 (ii) The building must remain standing as long as possible.
(iii) The spread of fire and smoke must be reduced.

Fire safety engineering has emerged as a building discipline in response to the need to provide fire safe solutions for larger and more complex buildings.

17.4 Building Regulations

The Building Act requires buildings to comply with various standards, which are published in the Approved Documents, to ensure health and safety compliance, energy conservation and the welfare and convenience of disabled people. Whilst there is no obligation to adopt

Table 17.3   Building Regulation Part B

B1	Means of warning and escape	Ensures satisfactory provision of means of giving an alarm of fire. Ensures a satisfactory standard of means of escape for persons in the event of a fire in a building.
B2	Internal fire spread (linings)	Ensures that fire spread over internal linings of buildings is inhibited.
B3	Internal fire spread (structure)	Ensures the stability of buildings in the event of fire; ensure that there is a sufficient degree of fire separation within buildings and between adjoining buildings. Inhibits the unseen spread of fire and smoke in concealed spaces in buildings.
B4	External fire spread	Ensures that the external walls and roofs have adequate resistance to the spread of fire over the external envelope. Ensures that the spread of fire from one building to another is restricted.
B5	Access and facilities for the fire service	Ensures satisfactory access for fire appliances to buildings and the provision of facilities in buildings to assist firefighters in the saving of people's lives in and around buildings.

any particular solution contained in the Approved Document, as there may be other ways of achieving compliance, it is a minimum standard. The Building Regulations Approved Document B requires that the building is designed and constructed so that there are means of escape in case of fire from the building to a place of safety. It comprises five main sections as shown in Table 17.3.

In most buildings, the place of safety would be a secure area outside the building. The Approved Document acknowledges that in certain circumstances a place of safety may be reached within some buildings, if suitable planning and protective measures are in place.

Other issues taken into account by this Approved Document include:

❑   Measures required to prevent the spread of fire within the building. This requires the use of linings that will resist the spread of flames, but if ignited must have a reasonable rate of heat release.
❑   Design in buildings must allow for the stability of the structure to be maintained for a reasonable period and also to retard as far as possible the spread of flames from building to building.
❑   The design should allow the satisfactory access to the building by fire appliances.
❑   The escape routes should be free from all obstacles that might impinge movement, e.g. ironmongery, steps or raised thresholds.

17.5 Designing space

In general terms, good building design will reduce the spread of fire from one area of a building to another. Logically, it would seem that large open spaces within buildings are more hazardous because there is a large area to burn and draughts through open areas may fan flames. Buildings with a large number of compartments are less vulnerable to fire spread than open plan offices or factories. However, heavily compartmented buildings may have problems with clear means of escape.

Certain materials used within buildings are more combustible than others. Buildings with a large amount of timber within their construction are more likely to combust than those made of concrete. Steps can of course be taken to reduce the risks, for example: the isolation of a fire within a timber framed building could be achieved by ensuring that the floors are constructed with a high degree of flame-resistant panels, thus isolating a fire onto the floor where the fire originated.

17.6 Standards

Guidance on fire safety engineering for buildings is given in British Standard BS 7974 Part 1 – Application of Fire Safety Engineering Principles to the Design of Buildings, BSI 2001 – which is supported by seven guidance documents on various aspects of fire safety engineering. For large, complex and innovative buildings, fire engineering can be used to develop a fire strategy that considers the building holistically, including how its occupants are likely to respond in a fire, to develop the fire strategy and determine appropriate fire safety measures. However, a fire engineer's involvement in a project will more typically involve looking at an aspect of a building that cannot easily comply with one aspect of building regulations, such as extended travel distances. The fire safety engineering solution, therefore, requires sufficient compensatory features to justify the extended travel distances, but the rest of the building can be designed and constructed in accordance with the requirements of Approved Document B – Fire Safety 2000, DETR.

17.7 Balanced solution

A fire safety solution will look at providing a combination of active, passive and design features that achieve the required balance between the needs of the building design and those of safety. The features that need to be considered include.

❑ Means of escape.
❑ Fire alarm and automatic fire detection.
❑ Behavioural response of the occupants.
❑ Measures taken to prevent fire.
❑ Spread of smoke and fumes and if necessary measures to control it.
❑ Fire development and its containment.
❑ Structural response to fire.

17.8 Fire separation

Facilities for the fire services and the standard of fire safety management are both aspects of achieving fire separation. Fire engineering can also be useful in determining the fire safety requirement for existing buildings. In general, any new build element should achieve the current standard of safety, but the rest of the building does not have to comply as long as the alterations have not made the existing standard worse. The exception to this is if a serious fire safety issue is identified in the refurbishment project, and that if it can be rectified as part of the building work, then it must be done.

17.9 Classification of materials, buildings and fixtures

The principal document concerned with the fire rating of materials is BS 476 Parts 6 and 7 (Fire Test on Building Material and Structures; Method of Test for Fire Propagation for Products, 1989; Method of Test to Determine the Classification of Surface Spread of Flame, 1997). It details how the tests are undertaken and the method of classifying products by the results achieved. The following notes outline some of the terminology used in fire tests.

Fire ratings

Approved Document B limits the flammability of ceiling linings and walls to prevent rapid fire spread affecting escape in the early stages. However, the flammability of floor linings is not controlled by Building Regulations. The flammability of linings is established by subjecting samples to a surface spread of flame test, as defined in BS 476 Part 7. Depending on the extent of fire spread across the sample, the lining is classified as follows:

❑ Class 1 (best performance and required by Approved Document B for linings of rooms).
❑ Class 2.
❑ Class 3.
❑ Class 4 (unclassified).

In addition to their surface spread of flame characteristic, materials can be subjected to testing under BS 476 Part 6, which measures their likely contribution to the intensity of fire. Samples that exhibit low fire propagation indices along with a Class 1 surface class of flame characteristic are classified as Class 0.

Class 0 is the highest material classification and is required by Approved Document B for the linings on all escape routes. Certain products such as plasterboard are accepted as achieving the Class 0 classification because of their proven performance in fire.

Roof ratings

Under BS 476 Part 3, two letters are quoted:

(i) First letter – time to penetrate.
(ii) Second letter – measure of spread of flame.

The scale is from A to D (A being the best performance). Table A5 in Section B of the Building Regulations gives design ratings for common types of roof construction. For example:

Natural slate on a timber-constructed roof with an underfelt – designation = AA.

Fire resistance

Building structures and components within it must have fire resistance to ensure that their premature failure in fire does not endanger the building's occupants or the attending fire brigade. The element of fire resistance of a material or component is established by subjecting it to a furnace test.

The three criteria used to assess the fire resistance of a material are:

(i)   Ability to support its load, by retaining its strength in fire.
(ii) Resistance to fire penetration (integrity).
(iii) Insulation.

Some elements have to exhibit all of the above characteristics, while others only have to achieve one, e.g. fire doors only have to exhibit fire resistance in terms of maintaining integrity. Guidance on the periods of fire resistance required for building structures and components are given in Appendix A of Approved Document B.

Fire doors

Fire doors are self-closing doors, with high fire resistance properties. They are installed in areas to provide fire compartments, and to protect the means of escape. Doors can give either 1 or 2 hours of structural integrity, and are classified accordingly. Manufactured fire doors are tested to conform to BS 476-3:2004 for the whole door (the frame, door, glazing and door ironmongery). Fire doors are fitted with intumescent edge strips around the door or the doorframe lining. The strip expands in heat or flame, and fills in the gaps around the doors to create a barrier.

Electromagnetic door releases can be used to control frequently used fire doors. These will be linked to the automatic fire detection system, and on activation will close shut. This helps to minimise the problems that may arise when fire doors are propped open for ease of circulation around busy areas of a building.

Glazing

If fire-resistant glass is required in windows, doors or partitions, there are several types available:

❏   Georgian wired glass.
❏   Copper light glazing.
❏   Borosilicate glass.
❏   Laminated float glass.

17.10 Building classifications

Approved Document B divides buildings into different purpose groups, for example residential, institutional, office, industrial and so on, dependent on the nature of the occupants and what a building is being used for. The purpose group then determines the construction requirements for the building, such as maximum fire compartment size.

The required period of fire resistance for a building is partially governed by its purpose group, but is also dependent on its height. Buildings with occupied storeys higher than

18 m require a longer period of fire resistance as they will take longer to evacuate and the fire brigade may face increased difficulties.

17.11 Furnishings

The furnishings of a room are likely to make the greatest contribution to fire growth and fumes in a fire. The ease of ignition and rate of burning of flames are controlled by the Fire Safety Regulations 1988 and 1989.

The Building Regulations do not attempt to control the furnishings within buildings, because it is recognised that this cannot realistically be achieved or enforced. However, in premises subjected to a greater central control, for example hospitals and certain government buildings, they do impose internal standards on the ignitability and flammability of the furnishings.

17.12 Means of escape

The fundamental objective of fire precaution and safety is to ensure that there are adequate provisions and time to ensure safe evacuation of the premises. This requires a means of giving a warning of fire, adequate signage, illumination of escape routes and, most importantly, the means of escape are suitably protected from the effects of fire. There is also a requirement that there are routes of sufficient number and capacity which are suitably located to enable persons to escape to a place of safety in the event of a fire.

Guidance on achieving adequate means of escape relative to a building's occupancy and size is given in Approved Document B. Guidance is also provided in the BS 5588 code of practice, which can be used instead of the Approved Document. BS 5588 sometimes has to be used to determine the means of escape requirements for more specific building types, such as those given in Part 10 for enclosed shopping centres. The common terms used in the design and specification of means of escape are shown in Table 17.4.

Factors influencing the design of a means of escape

There are many factors that will determine the requirements for an adequate means of escape, as shown in Table 17.5.

Design features of a means of escape

The objective is to ensure that a building's occupants have a sufficient number of escape routes within reasonable travel distances. For a simple building, with escape routes in two directions, the maximum recommended travel distance is generally in the order of 45 m. When escape is in only one direction, that is the occupants are not able to turn their backs on fire, the recommended maximum is shorter, typically only 18 m.

Typical features of a means of escape strategy or design include:

❑   All escape routes should be provided with adequate fire signage indicating final exits and directional signs leading to them. In addition, fire action notices giving instructions on what actions to take in a fire should be displayed throughout the building.
❑   All escape routes should be adequately illuminated and for many buildings it is necessary to ensure that this is backed up with emergency lighting, which comes on if the mains power fails.

Table 17.4   Common Means of Escape Terminology

Access room	A room that forms the only escape route from an inner room.
Accommodation stairway	An open staircase used for general circulation that cannot be counted as part of the means of escape, except in conditions of limited, non-public occupancy and short travel distances.
Circulation space	A space (including a protected stairway) mainly used as a means of access between a room and an exit from a building or compartment.
Escape lighting	Part of the emergency lighting provided to ensure that the escape route is illuminated at all material times.
Escape route	Route forming part of the means of escape from any point in a building to a final exit.
Evacuation lift	A lift that may be used for the evacuation of disabled people in the event of a fire.
Final exit	The termination of an escape route from a building giving direct access to a street, passageway, walkway or open space, and sited to ensure the rapid dispersal of persons from the vicinity of a building so that they are no longer in danger from fire and/or smoke.
Firefighting shaft	A protected enclosure containing a firefighting stair, firefighting lobbies and, if provided, a firefighting lift, together with its machine room.
Firefighting stair	A protected stair communicating with the accommodation area only through a firefighting lobby.
Means of escape	Provision, such as emergency exits and protected stairs, which ensures that in the event of fire the occupants can leave the building in a reasonable time.
Pressurisation	A method of protecting escape routes against the ingress of smoke by maintaining an air pressure difference between the protected area and the adjoining accommodation.
Protected corridor/lobby	A corridor or lobby which is adequately protected from fire in adjoining accommodation by fire-resisting construction.
Protected entrance hall/landing	A circulation area in a dwelling consisting of space enclosed with fire-resisting construction (other than any part which is an external wall of a building).
Protected shaft	A shaft which enables persons, air or objects to pass from one compartment to another, enclosed with fire-resisting construction.
Protected stairway	A stair discharging through a final exit to a place of safety (including any exit passageway between the foot of the stairs and the final exit) that is adequately enclosed with fire-resisting construction.
Single direction of travel	Part of a room or building from which escape is possible in one direction only.

Table 17.5   Means of escape

Nature of occupancy	The type of occupancy is a major factor in deciding appropriate measures for escape. Buildings containing sleeping risks demand a high standard of compartmentation, and buildings serving the public require a large capacity of escape routes because they can often be crowded. In comparison, the means of escape requirements for offices are relatively simple.
Type of building	Its construction, degree of openness, fabric fire rating and ability of fire to spread throughout the premises.
Degree of risk	Are flammable materials stored in the building? What types of manufacturing processes are undertaken? If there was a fire, what would be the likely consequences?

❑ Lifts and escalators are not normally considered as part of the means of escape, unless the former are provided with the additional measures recommended in BS 5588 Part 8, to enable them to continued to be used in a fire by disabled people.

❑ Exits must be sized to ensure that occupants can leave the building. This typically involves allowing 5 mm of exit width per occupant. A typical 750 mm door allows 40 people to exit per minute.

❑ Exits should be reached within a reasonable travel distance of 45 m when there are two directions of escape; 45 m is measured as the actual distance an occupant will have to travel to reach the exit allowing for the internal layout. When a building is being designed and the internal room layout is not known, the codes recommend that exits are set out so that occupants can reach them within two-thirds of the actual distance, i.e. 30 m.

❑ If only one escape route is provided, then the maximum travel distance in one direction to the one escape route is 18 m. In assembly areas, or areas with rows of seating, this distance reduces to 15 m and also reduces further to 9 m in plant rooms.

❑ In premises with no more than 60 people, it may be sufficient to provide one escape route. A minimum of two routes is required for premises with a capacity of up to 600 people. At least three escape routes must be provided for buildings with over 600 occupants.

❑ Escape from upper stories should be via a protected stair that leads directly to outside; and double door protection should be provided in some instances to protected staircase shafts (via a protected lobby).

❑ Tall and large buildings can follow phased evacuation, where the fire floor and the one above are evacuated first, followed progressively by the rest of the building as required. For phased evacuation to be permissible, the building must be constructed with compartment floors and have an automatic fire detection system, a method of internal communication between floors and a central control point/room.

❑ Services such as gas pipes should not pass through protected stairs, unless they are fire clad.

❑ Protected routes should be kept free from all obstructions at all times and all doors should be readily openable without having to manipulate one simple device, such as 'panic bolts'. For some escape routes, typically in residential buildings, it is necessary to provide smoke clearance, including smoke ventilators at the top of stairs.

17.13 Fire signage

Exit signs on doors or indicating exit routes should be provided where they help people to find a safe escape route. Signs on the exit routes should consist of directional arrows, using the conventional white or green colour scheme, to comply with the Health and Safety (Safety Signs and Signals) Regulations 1996. Emergency exit signs must include a running man symbol. In assembly rooms, theatres and lecture rooms, signs are illuminated. In high risk areas, such as plant rooms in basement or roof areas, signs could be luminescent making them easier to see in lower light levels.

17.14 Fire detection and fire alarms

Fire detection and alarm systems are complex and often interact with other building service systems, such as air conditioning, ventilation systems and lifts. There may be conditions imposed by the organisation's insurer and the local fire authority that determine the nature of the detection and alarm system.

17.15 Fire detection system categories

The British Standard BS 5839 gives details of the requirements. The specific capabilities of a system will depend on many factors including building size, budget, type of occupants, complexity of the premises and essential safety requirements. There are five broad categories of system as shown in Table 17.6.

More complex and more capable systems will be addressable – this allows each detector or call point to send a signal to the control panel to allow each to be individually identified. Addressable systems can be analogue or non-analogue. The analogue system will mean that the output signal from each device will vary in proportion to the amount of smoke, heat or flame, giving an early indication of fire. These systems allow detection of defects with particular detectors, and can help to reduce the number of false alarms.

17.16 Control panels

A control panel is the heart of all fire alarm systems. Their function is to provide the means of control of the system, and provide a user interface to display the status of the system, and to allow regular tests to be carried out. It is best practice for the control panel to be installed near the entrance to the building, allowing easy access by the fire emergency services. A control panel needs to:

❑   Provide information on the status of the detection line that connects the detectors and manual call points.
❑   Activate the sounders if an alarm condition occurs.
❑   Indicate which zone is the source of the alarm signal.
❑   Indicate if a fault occurs with the sounder or detection line.
❑   Indicate the condition of the system's backup power supply.
❑   Provide a means of activating and silencing the sounders.

Table 17.6   Fire detection systems

L	Automatic fire detection systems to protect life		
	L1	Installed throughout the building	Residential care home, hotel, buildings with specific access or structural risks
	L2	Only installed in defined parts of a building	Large complex office, older buildings with many corridors and small rooms
	L3	Give early warning	Medium-sized office, retail or factory, large numbers of people, with relative easy escape
	L4	Installed in circulation spaces in escape routes, such as corridors and stairways	
	L5	Specific fire risks	
M	Manual systems, no automatic fire detectors	Small office buildings with clear escape routes and occupants who know the building	
P	Automatic fire detection systems to protect property		
	P1	Installed throughout the building	Complex office building, high risk profile, small fire could be easily spread
	P2	Installed only in defined parts of a building	Listed building, older style of premises, fire damage would be expensive to rectify

In more complex and large fire alarm systems, there will be repeater panels. These could be installed in the lobbies of each floor, in a central control room or other strategic locations. In some instances, an alarm system may be installed with radio links for communication between the various system components. This eliminates the need for hard-wired circuits, and reduces installation time and costs. Such systems could be useful when connecting separate buildings on a campus.

17.17 Zoning

An important aspect of building design and fire safety is the ability to locate the fire and smoke as quickly as possible. A building can be divided into zones to make this identification easier and quicker. Guidance on zoning can be found in the BS 5839. There are some general principles to consider when zoning a fire alarm system:

❑   The floor area of a zone should not exceed 2000 m^2.
❑   A zone must not cover more than one floor (unless the whole building is less than 300 m^2).
❑   A zone cannot be divided between different tenants in multiple-occupancy buildings.

Table 17.7   Fire detector types

Fixed-temperature heat detectors	Alarm triggered when fixed temperature is exceeded. Useful in areas when temperatures fluctuate significantly, such as kitchens, plant areas, boiler rooms.
Rate of rise heat detectors	These react to the rate of temperature increase. Suitable in spaces which could be dusty or contain high airborne pollution.
Flame detectors	These sense the flicker of the non-visible light produced by flames. Used in dusty or smoky environments. Could be sensitive to either infrared or ultraviolet light.
Ionisation smoke detectors	An alarm is triggered when the current between two electrodes in the detector chamber is disturbed. These are very sensitive detectors.
Optical smoke detectors	These rely on the change of light reflection onto a device that is monitoring beams of infrared light transmitted across an area. Suitable in areas with fabrics, furnishings and foams.
Optical beam smoke detectors	These detect smoke across the length of a beam of infrared light.

17.18 Fire, smoke and heat detectors

There are two basic types of heat and smoke detector used in fire alarm systems. Table 17.7 gives a summary of the range of systems in use.

(i) Linear heat detection – these respond to changes in the temperature along the whole length of the installed cable.
(ii) Point detection – these respond to smoke, flame or changes in temperature in the vicinity of the detector.

Point detectors may use a variety of techniques to detect the presence of smoke, heat or flame and this gives rise to a variety of detectors that can be installed. The environment being protected and the type of combustible materials contained in that area will determine the choice of detector.

17.19 Sounders

These can be bells, sirens and klaxons. The requirements are detailed in the BS 5839 standard. They are installed for both property protection and life protection. The number of sounds in a life protection system should be sufficient to produce a minimum sound level in accessible parts of the building of 65 dBA or 5 dBA greater than any background noise which may last more than 30 seconds.

In areas where people sleep, the sounder should produce at least 75 dBA at the bedhead. Normally, two sounders are installed even if one sounder would be sufficient to produce the required level of sound. At least one sounder must be installed per compartment.

Voice evacuation systems can be installed as a means of alerting people. Various systems of pre-recorded messages can be selected.

Fire alarm warnings for people with impaired sight or hearing may be required. These can be fixed, movable or portable tactile alarm systems and they need to be interfaced with the fire detection and alarm control equipment.

17.20 Call points

Manual call points will be the primary means of triggering an alarm condition in a manual fire alarm system. They can also be included into automatic systems. Basic guidance on call points includes:

- All call points must operate in the same way.
- Only 3 seconds delay is permitted between operation of the call point and the alarm sounding.
- Call points must be located in staircases, landings, exit routes and exits from buildings.
- Travel distance to a call point must be 30 m or less.
- A call point must be mounted at 1.4 m above the floor.
- Call points must be well-lit, easily accessible and free from obstructions.

Depending on the location and environment, call points can be weatherproof or specially designed to cope with flammable or explosive environments. They can be fitted with a striker to assist in the breaking of the glass and a light diode to indicate their activation.

17.21 Cabling

The connection of the various components of a fire alarm system must be made via fire-resistant cables. The types of cabling are shown in Table 17.8.

17.22 Suppression systems

Depending on the equipment and environment for fire protection, a fire suppressant system may be used to protect delicate or irreplaceable data and equipment or for certain hazardous processes. Table 17.9 gives a list of those used.

Gas-based suppression systems work on the basis of flooding the space or equipment with an inert gas extinguishing medium. Since the ban of halon, other gas systems have had to be developed and used. If people work in the same space, then a warning system is required for evacuation of occupants before the suppression system operates.

17.23 Fire extinguishers

The most common type is the water extinguisher or hose reel. Generally, one water extinguisher covers 200 m² of floor space, with a minimum of one per floor. Portable

Table 17.8   Fire cabling types

Type	Features	Description
Mineral insulated copper cable (MICC)	Very robust, has a long service life, does not burn or emit smoke or gases	Copper sheath on outside
	Care in termination to prevent ingress of moisture	Inner insulation of magnesium oxide
		Copper conductors
Soft skinned cable	Can be rigid or flexible	Thermoplastic sheath on outside
	Quick and easy to install	Aluminium screen in rigid format
		Heat-resistant insulation around conductors

Table 17.9   Fire suppression systems

FM–200	Liquid, used in low concentrations, takes up little storage space, zero ODP	
Argonite	A blend of nitrogen and argon, zero ODP	
Inergen	High pressure agent, stored in banks of cylinders. Natural substance, zero ODP	Used in computer and data-processing equipment
Carbon dioxide	Control systems needed	Used in electrical switchgear, generator or transformer rooms

Table 17.10   Fire extinguishers

Water	Red	Class A
Foam	Red with 5% cream	Class A, Class B
Powder	Red with 5% blue	Class B, Class C, Class D
Carbon dioxide	Red with 5% black	Electrical
Vaporising liquid	Red with 5% green	Class B

fire extinguishers operate by releasing the medium under pressure. Some extinguishers contain a gas cartridge, which is activated to expel the contents. Fire extinguishers can be identified by their colour, in accordance with BS 7863: 1996 as shown in Table 17.10.

All extinguishers should be affixed to walls, so that the carrying handle is approximately 1 m from the floor. They should be in conspicuous positions such as escape routes, near exits or in the line of an exit. In larger premises, it is good practice to group the firefighting equipment into fire points. Such a point should be clearly visible, conspicuously signed and be in similar positions on each floor.

17.24 Hose reels

Large premises may be equipped with hose reels. They may be used in addition or instead of portable water extinguishers. Table 17.11 shows their benefits and disadvantages. They will be operated by a valve and will be various lengths and diameters depending on the floor areas. They are usually installed in corridors or on escape routes, in recessed areas. They need regular maintenance, and must conform to BS EN 671-1:2001.

Table 17.11   Use of hose reels

Advantages	Disadvantages
Cost-effective maintenance	Hard to use due to pressure
Easy to use	Trip hazards
Unlimited supply of water	Need water pressure in mains supply
Reach fires at some distance	Hose may deteriorate over time
Usable by fire service	

17.25 Fire blankets

These are normally located in areas where smothering is required as a extinguishing method. This could be in kitchens or laundries where cooking oils, pan fires or clothing is ignited. Heavy-duty blankets are used in manufacturing operations.

17.26 Sprinklers

These could be in buildings of a certain size or a requirement of the insurer, and will conform to BS 5306. Typical criteria for sprinklers include:

❑   Buildings over 30 m high.
❑   Unpartitioned areas of more than 2000 m^2 in shops, commercial and industrial premises.

There are several types of sprinkler systems as shown in Table 17.12.

17.27 Fire hydrants

Fire hydrants are standard fittings provided in buildings to allow the emergency fire services to attach their equipment to the public water supply. A private hydrant system may be installed in a large business campus or complex site. Hydrants need to comply with BS 5306, and will need to be tested annually. Foam inlets may also be installed to allow the fire services to apply firefighting foam to burning flammable liquid fire.

17.28 Dry and wet risers

The dry or wet risers are essentially pipes that run vertically through the core of the building. These risers are found in high-rise buildings to provide fire services easier means to tackle fires on upper floors. The essential difference is whether the riser is primed with water or kept dry. Both types require regular maintenance, and in the case of wet risers, checks on water pressure and leaks are essential.

Table 17.12   Fire sprinkler systems

Wet pipe	Most commonly used, fast to operate as water always present in pipework above heads. Only feasible where no chance of freezing is likely.
Alternate systems	Have water only in summer season. System drained and filled with air in winter. Used in unheated buildings.
Dry pipe	Pipes are filled with air under pressure, control value holds back the water until sprinkler head opens.
Pre-action	Similar to above, but sprinkler head relies on activation by detectors. Useful when it is not possible to have water-filled pipes.
Deluge	These are firefighting systems in industrial areas, such as manufacturing and workshop areas.

17.29 Regulatory Reform (Fire Safety) Order 2005

The Regulatory Reform Order (RRO) governs the fire protection and means of escape in all buildings in England and Wales. It requires a continuous compliance and is therefore of significant importance to maintenance regimes. The main effect of the new legislation is the greater emphasis on prevention and life safety, putting greater responsibility on building owners and users. Fire certificates are now abolished, having no legal status. Changes to the fire legislation in Scotland and Northern Ireland have also occurred, with their own local legislation. FMs working in other regions and countries will obviously need to check their local legislation.

Responsible person

The RRO requires the appointment of a responsible person for each premises. This person must carry out a fire risk assessment and take reasonable steps to reduce or remove that risk. Article 3 of the RRO defines the responsible person as someone who has control of the workplace in connection with the job or role. This could be the owner or employer if there are no premises or FMs. A competent person may have to be appointed to assist the responsible person in carrying out their duties.

Emergency plan

A written emergency plan is created to provide information to others on the arrangements for fire safety. The plan is normally kept on the premises, and can be inspected by fire authority personnel. In premises that are shared with other users, the plan may be created in consultation with neighbours. The plan will contain clear information on the following:

❑ The method of communication to warn the occupants if there is a fire.
❑ Details on how the evacuation should be carried out.
❑ Details and locations of the assembly points.
❑ Details of how the workplace is checked for complete evacuation.
❑ Identification of key fire escape routes – often best shown in a drawing.

❑   Details on how occupants gain access to the escape routes.
❑   Duties of competent persons.
❑   Identification of competent persons.
❑   Arrangements for high risk occupants such as visitors, contractors, disabled, members of the public.

Fire precautions

These are defined in the RRO as measures to:

❑   Reduce risk of fire.
❑   Reduce risk of spread of fire.
❑   Provide a means of escape.
❑   Ensure that the means of escape can be used safely and effectively at all times.
❑   Detect fire.
❑   Give a warning in the case of fire.
❑   Fighting fire on the premises.
❑   Instruction and training of employees in the action to be taken in the event of fire.
❑   Action to be taken in the event of fire to mitigate the effects of fire.

Types of buildings and activities

The Regulations affect various types of buildings which FMs could be responsible and these include:

❑   Sleeping accommodation.
❑   Organisations that provide care or treatment.
❑   Places of entertainment, instruction, recreation.
❑   Teaching, training or research.
❑   Any place where people work.
❑   Premises which permit the public access.

Maintenance activities

Fire risk assessment and codes of practice may specify the requirements to comply with the Regulations, and the maintenance activities may include:

❑   Maintenance of means of escape.
❑   Maintenance of fire protection systems, e.g. sprinklers and alarms.
❑   Maintenance of firefighting equipment, e.g. fire extinguishers, blankets and hoses.
❑   Record keeping of the above activities.

17.30 Risk assessment

A fire risk assessment needs to specifically address the following issues:

❑   Risks arising from young people.
❑   Risks arising from dangerous substances.

❑ Evaluation of disabled people.
❑ Firefighting equipment.
❑ Fire detection equipment.

There are five main hazards produced by fire to consider when conducting the risk assessment:

(i) Oxygen depletion.
(ii) Flames and heat.
(iii) Smoke.
(iv) Gaseous combustion products.
(v) Structural failure of buildings.

Evaluation of existing fire precautions needs to be undertaken in order to address the extent of available measures to offset identified risks.

There are 11 guidance documents produced by the UK government to help with specific types of premises, such as schools and hospitals.

Assessment of precautions can be undertaken using any of the three assessment methods outlined below.

17.31 Assessment methods

There are essentially three means of evaluating risks: probabilistic, quantified or equivalency assessment. These methods vary in complexity and in the expertise necessary to utilise them properly, yet the objective is always identification of what is likely to happen and what the consequences of an incident will be. The choice of assessment method will depend on the nature of the case to be analysed and in some circumstances a combination of one or more methods may be appropriate. It is considered that for ease and practicability, most premises will benefit by application of equivalency assessment with either probabilistic or quantified methods being used when equivalency is impossible or inappropriate. The methods are outlined below.

Equivalency assessment

Equivalency assessment, or comparative analysis, is a method of evaluation based on comparing one element (of the building, e.g. wall, window, floor, fabric and so on) or set of elements with another providing the same function. Thus, in fire safety and risk assessment terms, one or more precautions or risk reduction measures which are lacking may be compensated for by providing one or more substitutes which will perform the same or equivalent task. In other words, can the bits that make up the built environment be substituted with something that is less hazardous when ignited but will give the same functional performance, e.g. vinyl versus carpet, paint versus wallpaper?

Probabilistic assessment

Probabilistic risk assessment is a methodology which is used to identify that the likelihood of a certain event occurring is sufficiently small to be acceptable. It can be complex in that it involves a number of other individual methodologies within which specific probabilities are considered. Furthermore, it normally requires, as a basis for probabilities to be determined, sufficient statistical or anecdotal information from which to evaluate similar occurrences in similar situations. This is using complex statistical methods to calculate the probabilities of hazards being realised. Probability is a measure of uncertainty – measuring the chance or likelihood that a particular event will occur—usually on a scale of 0–1, with 0 being no chance, 0.5 being likely to happen or not happen and 1 as will happen. Fire engineers will have a wealth of data to use to do accurate calculations based on all the fires that have occurred so that they can see the likelihood of particular elements in buildings becoming a fire risk.

Quantified risk assessment

Quantified risk assessments are based on physical relationships derived from scientific theories and empirical results, and are intended to show that a given set of conditions will always produce the same outcome (simply $2 + 2 - 1 = 3$). This may be commonly regarded as the quantification of risk by examination of each element in detail for each set of circumstances. In some situations, this method can predict the worst-case scenario by calculating the outcome and effect on persons, premises and business. This is the Monte Carlo simulation when all the data is entered into the computer and an answer is produced. This is complex and expensive to undertake, and is only carried out on very big projects, where there are very many variables to consider.

The Monte Carlo simulation is a technique which randomly generates values for uncertain variables over and over to simulate a model. The name Monte Carlo derives from the games of chance for which the principality is famous, such as roulette and baccarat.

On first hearing the notion of a simulation based on chance, you may think of never winning at roulette. However, the technique should be viewed from the point of the casino. They also have no idea which number the ball is going to land on next. Even the next 100 rolls will be difficult to predict.

What the casino does know though is that if the wheel is spun 30 million times, there will be one million each of 1, 2, 3, etc. As each spin is an independent act of chance, it is impossible to predict in which order the numbers will come. This predictability allows us to generate transactions that mirror the real world. The randomness displayed on the roulette table can be displayed in many situations including stock prices, weather and behaviour of hazards in the workplace that may create a fire risk.

17.32 Training records

A record of all fire safety training given to staff needs to be kept to demonstrate compliance with the Management of Health and Safety at Work Regulations. The details should include:

❑ Dates of the instruction or exercise.
❑ Duration of training.
❑ Names of attendees.
❑ Details of trainer or instructor.
❑ Details of the instruction, exercise or drill.

17.33 Fire-trained staff

The responsible person can appoint others to help in the implementation of fire safety measures. These could include a designated fire safety manager, fire marshals or fire wardens. Each will need to be appropriately trained to ensure competence. Security personnel who are often required to patrol buildings and premises will also need a higher level of training in fire safety.

Training in fire safety should include:

❑ Action to take on discovering a fire.
❑ Instructions on how to raise an alarm.
❑ Action to take on hearing an alarm.
❑ Arrangements for calling the fire brigade.
❑ Procedures for alerting visitors or members of the public.
❑ Evacuation procedures.
❑ Location of fire assembly point.
❑ Location and use of firefighting equipment.
❑ Location of escape routes.
❑ How to open exit doors and the use of emergency fastenings.
❑ The importance of fire doors and why they must be completely shut and kept closed.
❑ Details on how to switch off equipment and processes.
❑ Information on how to isolate power supplies.
❑ Reasons for not using lifts.
❑ Good housekeeping and being vigilant.
❑ Specific measures relating to specific hazards at the workplace.

Training is usually best given at the new employee or staff induction. Written instructions may need to be adapted for people whose first language is not English, and for those with hearing or sight impairments and learning difficulties. Fire safety briefings are also required for contractors and third parties on the premises, such as visitors. Fire safety training will need to be repeated as refresher training on an annual basis or more frequently if the risk assessment identifies specific issues – such as changes to the procedures, staff turnover, changes to the building that affect the evacuation process or level of risk in the workplace. Practical training should be conducted twice a year.

17.34 The fire drill

It is important to plan ahead so that the annual or 6-monthly evacuation drill is conducted in a professional manner to reduce the inconvenience and interruption to business. Ideally, the date is set about 3 months ahead. Only a few people need to be involved in the planning, such as fire wardens. The drill is similar to an audit and helps to identify improvements. The drill is an opportunity to evaluate the effectiveness of the responsible person and the appointed fire wardens.

The existing procedures must be checked for their relevance and if they are up to date. Aspects to consider include evacuation routes, risk assessment findings, number of

Table 17.13 Fire evacuation strategies

1	Single stage	This is a total evacuation
2	Horizontal	This is when evacuation is from fire affected areas only in the initial stages
3	Staff alarm	This is when there is a controlled evacuation by staff (such as shops, theatres, cinemas)
4	Two stage	This is when there is a warning or alert signal which is then followed, if necessary, by an evacuation signal
5	Phased	This is when the evacuation is controlled in phased sequence

employees and new personal emergency evacuation plans (PEEPs). Changes identified will require an update on the procedures and communication with all those affected.

Evacuation methods may be via several methods, depending on the type and use of the premises concerned as illustrated in Table 17.13.

The outcome of the risk assessment and advice from local fire authority officers will determine the most suitable method. Ideally, everyone in the building should be able to get to the nearest place of safety in 2 to 3 minutes. If premises have only one escape route, or there is a higher risk of fire, this evacuation time is reduced to 1 minute. Some areas will require more time to prepare for evacuation, such as visitor areas or workshops where machinery has to be switched off.

The responsible person has a duty to make adequate provision for the safe evacuation of all personnel, not the emergency fire and rescue services. This includes the safe evacuation of people who need extra help. Fire wardens may need additional training and support to assist those people who require assistance. A PEEP will be required for each individual who needs special assistance.

During the evacuation drill itself, it is important to have sufficient support and observers to check for backlogs and the overuse or under use of escape routes. Information about the drill needs to be recorded, such as:

- The timings of 'all clear' reports to the chief warden at the assembly point.
- Areas not checked.
- Areas not accessible.
- Visitors.
- Contractors.
- Supervision at the assembly point.
- Overall time for complete evacuation.
- Successful grounding of lifts.
- Successful switching off – air conditioning, gas supplies.

After the drill, a debrief meeting should be held with the fire wardens and others involved in the drill, such as security personnel, other tenants, adjacent neighbours or maintenance staff. This is an opportunity to review the positive aspects and identify areas for improvement. A summary report may be necessary, with changes to the procedure for the next drill.

17.35 Refuges

A refuge is a place of safety in which a disabled person can wait for assistance in the event of an evacuation of a building. The assistance could be the use of an evacuation chair, lift or a buddy to help them up or down the stairs. The location of a refuge will depend on the fire safety design of the building. A refuge could be in a lobby, corridor, stairway or open space and will depend on the fire compartmentalisation and protection system in place. Refuges need a method of communication, such as telephone, radio or mobile phone, so that the person waiting there can be informed of the situation.

Evacuation chairs or lifts need to be regularly tested and checked for safe use.

18 Electrical Supplies and Electrical Safety

18.1 Introduction

There are many different ways to make electricity. Each method involves the use of a turbine to spin and convert kinetic energy into electricity. A turbine is a type of engine that can extract energy from a fluid, such as water, steam, air or combustion gases. Electricity is made when a turbine moves a large magnet around a very large wire. Three coils are set around the magnets. This movement serves to electrify the wire. This generates three-phase supplies – referred to as red, blue and yellow. Each phase is 230 V supply. Electricity is then pushed away from this generator through special transformers. Steam, combustion gases and water are commonly used to turn industrial turbines for the creation of electricity.

Electricity behaves like water – it flows. It therefore follows the path of least resistance. If resistance is encountered, then the energy is discharged. The further the electricity has to travel from where it is made to where it is used, the more resistance and loss of energy occurs. It is more efficient to create electricity nearer to the point of use. Combined heat and power (CHP) plant, solar panels and photovoltaics are examples of locally produced electricity.

Electricity is provided to buildings as either low voltage supplies or high voltage supplies. Low voltage is a term to describe the 400 V three-phase and 230 V single-phase supplies. These low voltage supplies are normally direct from the electricity supplier via an underground cable. There will be a fused unit to protect the consumer's installation. Supplies will be metered for billing purposes, and the meter normally belongs to the supplier of electricity. The meter will measure the kilowatt-hours (kWh) consumed. Electricity is typically supplied on maximum demand basis, so that if an organisation goes over the agreed load, then penalties are charged. The mains switch will be connected via the meter to the supplier's 'cut-out'. The mains switch is capable of handling the full load of the electrical installation.

The Electricity at Work Regulations 1989 states the duties and responsibilities of the duty holder who must ensure that all electrical installations and equipment is selected, installed and maintained in a safe condition to prevent danger. Only competent persons with technical and appropriate practical knowledge of electrical equipment can work on electrical equipment and installations.

18.2 Single-phase supply

Most domestic and small commercial buildings will be supplied with single-phase 230 V, and this will be suitable for all the electrical equipment in the building. Other properties in the locality are likely to be supplied by single-phase supplies but perhaps another phase to ensure that the three phases are evenly distributed to balance the overall load.

18.3 Three-phase low voltage supply

Larger buildings will often receive their electrical power supplies in three-phase 400 V, as there is too much demand or load for a single phase. Typically, a building will be divided up into three zones which have approximately the same load. Each zone can then be provided with one phase (red, yellow or blue) of 230 V. Heavy-duty equipment (e.g. compactor, air handling unit [AHU], some catering equipment, air conditioning plant and lift motors) will require a direct three-phase 400 V supply and these will be connected to the incoming mains distribution board.

Safety issues and problems will arise if there are two phases on one floor, and equipment is plugged into both phases at the same time, which could then allow a 400 V to pass through a person/equipment. Sockets of different phases on the same floor must be marked to warn potential users of the danger of connecting their electrical equipment to such sockets. There may also be problems of over- or underloading of the electrical supplies on any particular floor if the building is not evenly occupied or used. One phase may get overloaded, become hot, possibly resulting in arching of electricity across the phases.

18.4 High voltage three-phase supply

Industrial sites and buildings with loads greater than 1000 kVA will usually require a high voltage three-phase supply. The supply is typically 11 kV. Such supplies require specialist management and therefore incur higher capital and operating costs than a low voltage supply. There are several reasons for this:

❑ The consumer has to purchase and maintain the high voltage equipment.
❑ Space in the building must be dedicated to the high voltage equipment, known as the substation.
❑ Transformers which step the supplies down to usable low voltage loads will not be 100% efficient and these losses are borne by the consumer.
❑ Trained competent electricians (an authorising person and an authorised engineer) qualified in high voltage switching are required to operate the high voltage equipment.
❑ Access to the substation must be managed via a permit to work system.

18.5 Wiring

In the UK, different coloured wiring insulation is used to differentiate the phases of the three-phase supply. Old wiring was coloured red, yellow and blue to indicate the three phases, with black for neutral. In April 2004, there were changes in the identification of power cables to conform to European standards and this is now a safety issue for FMs and others responsible for premises. Harmonisation of colour codes of three-phase cabling has resulted in the following changes to the wiring colours:

red to brown; yellow to black; blue to grey; and neutral black to blue

As neutral is a different colour (from black to blue) there is a potential danger. Some deaths have occurred as a result of the changes. It is permitted to use different colour schemes in the same building, but not in the same installation. Great care in refurbishment and labelling of electrical supplies is required. It is essential that suitable warning and safety notices are fixed in distribution boards.

18.6 Inspection and testing

Every electrical installation must be inspected and tested to ensure safety, preventing injury and fire. Inspection and testing of the fixed wiring must occur regularly, typically every 5 years, or more frequently if high risk activities and operations take place (e.g. hospitals, factories, swimming pools). An inspection of joints, conductors, cables, cords, switchgear, labelling, protective devices and measures, enclosures, sockets, etc. is required. Qualified electrical engineers will conduct tests on continuity, resistance, polarity, impedance and earthing. A schedule of remedial work will be created indicating the priorities for work to bring the power installation up to standard. The reliability and safety of electrical installations can be improved by more frequent inspections, using techniques such as thermal imaging.

18.7 Standards – 17th Edition

BS 7671: 2008 Requirements for Electrical Installations (17th Edition) was issued in 2008. All domestic and industrial electrical installations and wiring must conform to these standards. Compliance to these standards demonstrates conformity to the Electricity at Work Regulations. There are several significant changes to the earlier 16th Edition standards. Residual current devices (RCDs) must now be installed on socket outlets and tested annually. Emergency escape and warning systems must be considered in electrical installations. Services to life-support systems must include back-up power. Equipment must not emit dangerous levels of magnetic fields. Documents must be kept up to date. Disconnection times have been reduced to reduce the exposure to electric shock and fire risk. A socket outlet can now be installed in bathrooms subject to being 3 m from the edge of a shower or bath and it must be protected by an RCD. 'Special Locations' such as photo-voltaic power supplies, fairgrounds and amusement parks, marinas, exhibitions and floor and heating systems are now covered in the 17th Edition.

18.8 Portable electrical equipment

Portable equipment is defined by the HSE as 'equipment that is not part of a fixed installation but may be connected to a fixed installation by means of a flexible cable and either a socket and plug or a spur box or similar means'. This means that extension leads are included. The Electricity at Work Regulations 1989 requires that portable electrical equipment is tested at appropriate regular intervals. The intervals are not prescribed, but should be based on a risk assessment by competent persons. The frequency of portable appliance testing (PAT) should reflect the usage of the equipment, the nature of the task and the environmental conditions. The users of the portable devices could carry out simple visual checks.

18.9 Safety

All electrical installations deteriorate over time. The factors affecting the rate of deterioration include: the environment (dust, moisture, vibration and temperature); loading; utilisation of plant; mechanical damage; general wear and tear and the level of maintenance. The harm from faulty electrical installations and equipment can vary – a personal injury or damage to property. The typical causes of electrical faults are:

- ❑ Damaged or weak insulation.
- ❑ Inadequate or inappropriate systems and standards of work.
- ❑ Overrated protection (fuses, circuit breakers).
- ❑ Poor earthing of appliances.
- ❑ Complacency of user.
- ❑ Overheating of apparatus.
- ❑ Earth leakage.
- ❑ Loose contacts and connectors.
- ❑ Inadequate ratings of circuit components.
- ❑ Unprotected connectors.
- ❑ Inadequate maintenance and testing.

18.10 Electric shock

The danger of electricity is the potential electric shock from faulty installations, connections or misuse of equipment. It is important to protect people from shock. Shock can arise from either:

- ❑ Direct contact with live components or;
- ❑ Indirect contact if an object is live.

The body is a conduit or conductor of electricity either allowing electricity to flow to earth or to another object. Depending on which part of the body comes into contact with the current and the overall health of the person, some people will survive an electric shock and others will be severely injured or die.

The levels of danger from electricity depend on magnitude of current and the path through the body as shown in Table 18.1. If electricity passes via vital organs, it is more dangerous. The impact to the human body also depends on the duration of contact, the frequency of voltage (50–60 Hz is very dangerous), the resistance of body mass and the percentage of water/moisture in the body.

18.11 Earthing

Electricity will naturally follow a path to earth. To protect against the risk of indirect contact, all exposed conductive parts of an electrical installation must be earthed. This will include the metal casings, trunking and conduit. Earthing will ensure that if a fault occurs, and

Table 18.1   Dangers of electricity to people

Current level	Human impact
1–5 mA	Discernible, but no danger
5–15 mA	Pain, muscular contraction, repulsion from equipment
15–20 mA	Person unlikely to release from power source
20–50 mA	Extreme pain, loss of consciousness, unable to release grip
50–75 mA	Paralysis, no pulse or respiration
Over 100 mA	Ventricular fibrillation, instant death

Table 18.2   Electrical faults

Overcurrent	Current in circuit exceeds maximum safety level	Overheating of equipment, installation damage
Short-circuit	A phase conductor connects to another phase or neutral	Overheating of cables, potential fire
Earth fault	Live conductor contacts metalwork	Electric shock

an item of equipment becomes live, the current flows directly to earth rather than via the person touching it. Earthing is intended to limit the duration of touch voltages.

A protective earth conductor is an integral part of the electrical distribution system in all buildings. The conductor can be attached to various sources of earth – e.g. the metal sheath of the supply cable, an earth electrode inserted into the ground or connections to incoming gas and water pipes that are in the ground.

18.12 Bonding

Bonding is intended to limit the magnitude of touch voltages. In theory, all metal service pipes, such as gas or water, that enter a building should have the same earth potential. To ensure that there is no differential between them, all these pipes are bonded via connections to the mains earthing terminal. This is known as mains bonding. Metal frameworks and metal building structures may also have to be bonded. Extra or supplementary bonding in wet areas such as kitchens or bathrooms is required.

18.13 Circuit protection

Circuit protection devices and systems are an essential part of the electrical installation in all buildings. They detect and isolate faults as soon as they occur. This reduces the risk of damage and electric shock to occupants.

There are three basic types of electric fault as shown in Table 18.2.

Circuit protection devices are used to detect and isolate these faults. There are several types – fuses, circuit breakers, RCDs.

18.14 Cable management

The management of power cables in buildings is critical. Busbars are often used for power distribution – these give flexibility in the configuration. Power can be supplied into the perimeter trunking; under raised floors to floor boxes or via a skirting trunking system. Cable trays, baskets, ladders, conduits or cable trenches, trunking and modular wiring are features of a power distribution system.

18.15 Power quality

The quality of power supplies and energy consumption may be affected by a number of factors. These include the generation of power itself, the demand from equipment, and the weather. A review of power usage in a building may identify problems with the equipment, the installation and the tariffs of supply.

The efficiency of an electrical system is measured using a power-factor rating – a number between 0 and 1 representing the ratio of the real power flowing to the load compared with the apparent power. If the rating is lower than 1, then the building is losing power to absorption by cables and switchgear and more energy is required to transfer the same amount of useful power. The supplying authorities will charge for the extra energy, and will also levy a premium on that extra energy. Power-factor correction equipment can overcome this problem, reducing energy demand and lowering the electricity bill.

Another problem that may result in higher energy consumption is due to harmonic distortion of the electricity supplies. Filters can be used to balance the loads and identify if equipment needs replacing.

18.16 Power failures

Power interruptions can vary from a brief 'flicker' to more than 24 hours' duration. The impact of such interruptions needs to be considered. For example, an operating theatre in a hospital cannot afford to have lights and power to critical equipment fail. Such life-critical systems would need to be supported by an uninterruptible power supply (UPS) and a standby generator. A business which relies on computers cannot suffer a prolonged power failure without a serious impact on the business, so consideration needs to be given to the impact of power interruptions to IT systems. Duration of support is ultimately decided by battery size or fuel shortage capacity. Businesses may require standby power for 10 minutes or 25 hours and longer.

(i) A **UPS** consists mainly of a set of batteries and will give a constant ('no-break') supply until the batteries run down. The support from a UPS depends on the number of batteries installed and this determines how many 'hours' are provided. A UPS provides an additional, continuous function of protecting the electrical supply from external disturbances such as harmonic distortion and transient voltages. UPS systems can, however, be very expensive, heavy and space consuming. Batteries need to be replaced roughly every 3–5 years, which is also expensive.

(ii) **Standby generators** are comparatively cheaper, with fuel being replaced as it is used. The big drawback is that there is a break of up to 40 seconds between the mains supply failing and the generator coming online.

(iii) **Combination approach** – It is usual to take a layered approach and support only critical equipment on a UPS (e.g. main computers and operating theatre equipment). Less important equipment can be supported by a generator, and some electrical loads ignored completely. This is generally referred to as 'load shedding'.

18.17 Assessing the need

The first stage is to list all the electrical loads in the building(s), which could include ventilation plant, lifts, lighting, general office power and special IT loads. The next step is to decide which loads cannot be interrupted, e.g. special IT loads such as servers. The loads that an organisation considers cannot be interrupted are the loads that should be supported by a UPS. Any of the remaining loads that can be interrupted briefly, but still need to run, will be generator loads, e.g. life safety systems such as fire alarms. The remaining loads can be load shed. Once priorities have been decided, a specialist should be consulted to manage the underlying levels of detail.

All standby systems will require space. It may be possible to purchase systems in containers, which can be accommodated in car parks. Structural loads for systems within buildings should be considered and expert advice should be sought on system sizes and structural capacities. In addition to the UPS or generator, the additional costs of switchgear, fuel storage, running costs (such as fuel and competent personnel to operate the equipment) and maintenance need to be considered. Fuel systems have to be agreed with the local planning authority at design stage. Requirements will vary depending on the amount of fuel stored. Generally, it is unusual to have bulk fuel storage above basement level, because of the risk of leaks. There may also be requirements for bonding, leak detection and spill back lines.

18.18 Uninterruptible power supplies (UPS)

These generally consist of banks of batteries supplied by an inverter/rectifier unit. The batteries store energy and allow an uninterrupted supply to be given to the load if the mains fail. The length of time the batteries can maintain a load is called the 'autonomy'. This will vary with the load. As the load increases, autonomy falls. The relationship is non-linear. Careful management of loads connected to a USP is necessary to ensure that it will perform its desired function. Various types are shown in Table 18.3.

18.19 Generators

Generators are generally equipped with diesel engines. The concept of adapting the standard road transport container system for use in housing noisy equipment such as diesel generator sets is quite common. This product can be applied to a variety of requirements where robustness, ease of transport as a one-piece system, good weather protection and a neat external appearance are required. Usually they are equipped with a daily service tank (typically with 8 hours' capacity), simple controls and mounted in an acoustic container. One issue with generators is the noise level. A limit of 45 dBA at the boundary of the property for daytime – or 35 dBA for night-time operation can be used as a guide, where business or residential neighbours are likely to be affected.

Table 18.3   UPS examples

(i)	Static UPS	This is the most widely used type of UPS. It uses solid-state electronics to convert mains power to DC for battery charging and then convert and condition DC back to AC for use by the load. It can impose harmonic distortion (power quality problems) on the supply network.
(ii)	Rotary UPS	A rotary UPS consists of rectification equipment, which converts the normal AC mains to DC. This is then used to drive a motor mounted on a common shaft with a generator (AC generator). Mostly supplanted by static systems, the rotary UPS still has some uses where isolation of the load from the supply network for electrical reasons is a consideration.
(iii)	Online/offline	Online systems operate constantly 'in line' between the supply and load, conditioning the voltage to the load. Offline systems 'switch in' to supply a load when the supply fails. They do this very quickly so the effect appears to be uninterrupted. There may be a brief 'flicker' which IT loads in particular can be sensitive to.
(iv)	Gas turbines	Normally used to support very large loads. Where such installations exist, it is assumed specialist staff will be available.
(v)	CHP	Some CHP systems may serve a dual function as a source of standby supply.
(vi)	Fuel cells	This is an embryonic technology, which may become more prominent in the future.
(vii)	IPS interface	UPS can usually be regarded as an 'in line device such that if the input supply fails, the integral battery will maintain the output for a finite period known as autonomy'. Depending on their size and sophistication, UPS can provide a number of information outputs, including 'mains-healthy'/'mains-fail', self-diagnostic reports, associated cooling equipment failure and so on. Where necessary these can be used to start generators if these are available. An adequate number of emergency stop buttons will be required in a standby generator house or UPS room, which when operated stop the machine(s). Releasing the buttons must not allow the machine to restart; there must be a separate reset facility elsewhere. Provision of emergency stops should be decided by experts.

The main characteristics of generating sets are described below:

(i) Generating sets – The most common type of standby power supply is the diesel engine standby generator. The diesel engine drives an alternator, which generates the power. They are simple reliable devices, which with proper maintenance and regular testing should last for very many years.

(ii) High or low voltage generators – Standby generators most commonly operate at low voltage (230/400 V). For very large buildings and loads, it is often considered more advantageous to use high voltage (3.3–11 kV) machines. These have the benefit of saving space, but need to have a load supplied from the high voltage side of the main transfers. The decision as to which is most appropriate is normally taken at design stage. It should be remembered that specially qualified (and thus more expensive) staff are required to maintain high voltage machines.

(iii) Diesel no-break set – The main supply drives a motor mounted on a common shaft with a generator, flywheel and diesel engine (via a clutch). When the mains fails, the fly wheel keeps the shaft and alternator rotating, the clutch is engaged and the flywheel starts the diesel. The diesel then maintains the rotation of the generator.

(iv) Diverse power supplies – Larger and more complex buildings and sites may enjoy electrically separate electrical supplies, each capable of supplying the total load. This type of supply would need to be negotiated with the local supplier and a significant premium paid for it. FMs would need to check regularly with their supplier to confirm the arrangement is still valid.

(v) Generator interface – All standby generator systems will require interfacing with the normal mains supply. This will enable failure of the normal supply to cause the generator to automatically start, changeover switchgear to operate and the generators to be connected to the building load. In addition, the generator will need to provide an electrical supply to battery charges and any fuel transfer pumps. Possible air supply and exhaust fans may also require a supply. Alarms can include oil pressure, coolant temperature, voltage, frequency, 'mains-healthy'/'mains-fail', starter battery condition, fuel level, etc. Generators can be 'held off' by operation of emergency power off push-buttons or fire alarms if required.

19 Accessibility

19.1 Introduction

The provision of inclusive services and buildings will help the FM and their employing organisation meet legal and moral duties in terms of accessibility and anti-discrimination. There is a broad range of legislation that needs to be consulted including:

- ❑ Employment law.
- ❑ Disability Discrimination Act (DDA).
- ❑ Health and safety regulations.
- ❑ Planning and highways legislation.
- ❑ Listed buildings consent.
- ❑ Building Regulations.
- ❑ Fire safety regulations.
- ❑ Licensing laws.
- ❑ The Occupier's Liability Act.

19.2 Inclusive FM

This is an approach that is more far reaching than simply compliance to legislation. Given the need to meet the needs of a wide range of customers, most organisations would ideally like to recruit employees from a similar wide range of people. Given that there are over 11 million disabled people in the UK, this is a large pool of both customers and employees. One issue that has restricted the mindset of some is the use of the wheelchair symbol for disabled. In fact only 5% of disabled people use wheelchairs to assist with their mobility impairments. For FMs and others tasked with roles in the built environment, it is easy to become too concerned with the physicality of access and forget other issues such as the management processes. Many disabilities arise due to age, injury, disease or accident – over 70% of disabled people have acquired their disability during their working life. As many as 50% of disabled people do not consider themselves disabled, perhaps because their disability is not apparent or they wish not to declare it to others.

The adoption of a universal inclusive approach to both premises and workplace design and to services provision ensures that everyone benefits from great accessibility as shown in Table 19.1.

19.3 The Disability Discrimination Act (DDA) (1995)

This Act was introduced to give improved access for the disabled to employment, services, goods and facilities. It became law on 2 December 1996 and applies to employees, applicants,

Table 19.1   Principles of accessibility

Inclusive principle	Areas of concern and attention
Flexibility in use Minimum physical effort Sufficient space for approach and use	Physical environment – room sizes, space allocation, furniture, decoration, finishes, lighting, acoustics, surfaces, handrails, ramps, steps, doorways, door furniture, car parking, catering services, vending machines, lifts, reception, wash and shower facilities, security access, etc.
Perceptible information	Information – format, tactile, notices, signage
Intuitive use	Communication modes – written, telephone, face-to-face, electronic, assistive technology
Simplicity of use	
Use by all	Management practices – policy, rules, regulations, forms, processes
Tolerance for error	Attitudes – prejudice, stereotypes, assumptions

job apprentices and people who contract personally to provide services. The DDA 1995 was extended by the Special Educational Needs and Disabilities Act SENDA 2001 and the DDA 2005. To be protected by this legislation, a disabled person must satisfy the following criteria:

❑   There must be a physical or mental impairment.
❑   The impairment must adversely affect ability to carry out normal day-to-day activities.
❑   The adverse effect must be substantial (not minor or trivial and effects can be cumulative).
❑   The adverse effect must be long term (likely to last at least 12 months, or recurring qualifying impairments).

Discrimination occurs when a disabled person is treated less favourably for a reason that relates to their disability and the treatment cannot be justified on objective grounds. Normal day-to-day activities include: mobility, manual dexterity and physical co-ordination; continence; ability to lift, carry or move everyday objects; speech, hearing or eyesight; memory or ability to concentrate, learn or understand, and perception of risk or physical danger.

FMs' responsibilities fall into two distinct areas:

(i) Employment.
(ii) Service provision.

Duties of employers (Part II)

Employers are required to make reasonable adjustments to their premises, including appropriate management arrangements. This duty is often triggered when a disabled person applies for a job or is employed, or becomes disabled whilst employed.

Disabled employees must be afforded equal opportunities to other staff in the working environment including training, safety and benefits. Some examples of adjustments that may be considered reasonable are shown:

❑ Allowing flexibility in working style or hours.
❑ Making physical adjustments to the building.
❑ Assigning the person to a different workplace.
❑ Allow absence for assessment, treatment or rehabilitation.
❑ Tailoring testing or assessment procedures.
❑ Acquiring or modifying equipment.
❑ Providing auxiliary aids and services (e.g. text phones, induction loops, accessible formats).
❑ Transferring the disabled person to fill an existing vacancy.
❑ Adjusting in-house health and safety policies and procedures.
❑ Providing a reader or interpreter.
❑ Training of managers, co-workers and disabled workers.
❑ Modification of working manuals or instructions.
❑ Providing additional support or supervision.

Employers may be held responsible for acts of discrimination by their employees, unless it can be demonstrated that the employer has taken reasonable steps to prevent this taking place. Evidence of the reasonable steps is required, such as an access assessment.

Duties of service providers (Part III)

The prime duty for service providers is to offer an environment that allows independent access and use by disabled people. Most facilities and organisations are 'service providers', as defined in the Act. They have two principal duties:

(i) Anticipatory duty – a proactive approach to making changes.
(ii) Continuing duty – once adjustments have been made, they must be reviewed often and further enhanced, if appropriate.

Discrimination can arise if:

❑ A disabled person is treated less favourably, is provided with a lower standard of service or is refused service.
❑ Reasonable adjustments to the delivery of a service have not been made in order to allow disabled people to use them.

Consideration should also be given to the time and effort a disabled person would need to spend in order to access a service, compared with a non-disabled user. These duties apply even where the service is provided without payment.

The Act overrides lease covenants not to make alterations so that landlords cannot stop tenants making changes to a property to help them comply with the Act. In multi-occupancy buildings, the landlord may be responsible for making alterations, so FMs will need to check the lease to establish whether the landlord or the tenant is liable.

19.4 Special Educational Needs and Disabilities Act 2001

Special Educational Needs and Disabilities Act (SENDA) provisions affect all education and training provision, including admissions to courses and the provision of other 'student services' such as residential accommodation, leisure facilities, catering, library facilities and welfare services. SENDA places various duties on colleges and post-16 education establishments that are quite similar to those placed on service providers and employers:

❑   Not to treat disabled students less favourably, without justification, for a reason which relates to their disability.
❑   To make reasonable adjustments to ensure that disabled people are not at a substantial disadvantage in accessing education.

The duty is anticipatory and evolving – responsible bodies need to anticipate the kind of adjustments that disabled students might need and not simply wait for disabled students to apply for a place. They need continually to review arrangements and have a rolling improvement plan. Some adjustments will be very specific to individuals. However, there are many adjustments that can be pre-empted as they apply to everyone, such as:

❑   Ensuring all buildings are generally accessible to people with mobility problems.
❑   Ensuring all handouts are accessible electronically in different formats (font size, coloured backgrounds).
❑   Having additional support services in place.
❑   Having pre-vetted interpreters, sign language translators, and other specialists available.

19.5 Planning and Compulsory Purchase Act 2004

Access and Design statements are now required in the standard planning application process for new buildings or major refurbishment works. Property developers now need to include accessibility and inclusive design from the concept stage of their project.

19.6 Disability Discrimination Act 2005

The DDA 2005 introduced a duty on all public bodies to consider disability equality at the beginning of all activities and processes, rather than making adjustments at the end. It changes the emphasis from individuals having to make a complaint regarding accessibility, to a public sector becoming a proactive agent of change. Public sector bodies, such as local authorities, universities, hospitals and regulatory bodies, need to apply the principles of equality of opportunity to meet their general duty under the Act:

❑   Promote equality of opportunity between disabled people and other people.
❑   Eliminate discrimination that is unlawful under the Act.
❑   Eliminate harassment of disabled people that is related to their disabilities.
❑   Promote positive attitudes towards disabled people.
❑   Encourage participation by disabled people in public life.
❑   Take steps to take account of disabled people's disabilities, even where that involves treating disabled people more favourably than other people.

In addition, they must produce a disability equality scheme which must:

❑ Involve disabled people in producing the scheme and developing the action plan.
❑ Identify how they gather and analyse evidence to inform their actions and track progress.
❑ Set out how they assess the impact of their existing and proposed activities on disabled people.
❑ Produce an action plan for the next 3 years.
❑ Report on their progress every year and review and make appropriate revisions to this scheme at least every 3 years.

19.7 Disability awareness

Disability awareness training is essential in dealing with visitors with disabilities or special needs. Reception staff will benefit from disability awareness training, and learning some of the main signing phrases in an established sign language to communicate with deaf or hearing impaired visitors and staff. Sign language is a visual means of communicating using gestures, facial expression and body language. The most useful languages include finger spelling or the British Sign Language. The Employer's Forum on Disability is a useful source of advice and booklets for greeting disabled visitors. In particular the booklet 'Welcoming disabled customers' provides excellent guidance on best practice. For large organisations, the booklet can be personalised for the organisation (www.employers-forum.co.uk).

19.8 Front of house services

Providers of goods, services and facilities are required to take reasonable steps to remove, alter or provide reasonable means of avoiding physical features that make it impossible, or unreasonably difficult, for disabled people to access or use a service. Physical features include steps, stairways, kerbs, exterior services and paving, parking areas, building entrances and exits, toilets, public facilities (including telephones, counters, reception desks) and so on.

Access to reception and waiting areas will be of paramount importance to disabled people. The ease of approaching the reception desk, and the type of welcome received, will have a major impact on a disabled person's initial perception of an organisation, as well as being a statutory requirement.

A management system to check correct use of designated car parking spaces and the pre-booking of visitors, capturing special needs will ensure a professional welcome to all disabled and able-bodied visitors. It is good practice to have a regular check of external areas and routes to ensure debris, overhanging foliage, damaged pavements and other obstacles and hazards are promptly dealt with. Internal corridors must also be checked for obstacles, trip and slip hazards. Much of this is just good practice operational FM. Regular checks in the accessible WC or shower facilities are needed, especially if infrequently used, to include the alarms or call points and supplies of soap and tissue products.

19.9 Personal Emergency Evacuation Plans (PEEP)

There is a duty of care on employers to have an emergency evacuation plan in place for each disabled person which takes account of their individual needs and circumstances.

A PEEP will help the disabled person, their colleagues and the FM to know the needs of disabled people in the event of an evacuation. It is best to prepare a PEEP in a face-to-face meeting to encourage full involvement of disabled people in the planning of their evacuation strategy. A PEEP is similar to a risk assessment and should contain this information:

- ❏ Details of disabled person (name, job title, location, department, contact details, manager details).
- ❏ The procedures to follow:
  - o The alarm system – how to raise an alarm?
  - o Activation of alarm – how the disabled person is alerted?
  - o Egress procedure
- ❏ The assistance to provide:
  - o Buddy
  - o Equipment
  - o Methods of assistance
- ❏ Safe routes
- ❏ The level of staff training is required to provide appropriate assistance:
  - o Frequency
  - o Testing and drills
  - o Refresher
- ❏ Signature (disabled person, buddy or carer, manager, safety adviser, FM, etc.)
- ❏ Review date (at least annual, or after event).

A suitable alerting system needs to be provided to visually or hearing impaired people. These could be vibrating pagers, or pagers with flashing lights. Some people may have guide dogs that are trained to respond to the building alarm. A recording of the various alarms and sounds will be required for training the guide dogs.

19.10 Communication

Here are a few simple tips for effective communication:

- ❏ Smile, relax and ask how you can help.
- ❏ Be patient and give extra help and time if needed.
- ❏ If you do not understand a request or information given, then ask the visitor to repeat.
- ❏ Do not interrupt if the person has a stammer or is slow with speech.
- ❏ Continue to use everyday phrases such as 'see you later'.
- ❏ Avoid using words such as 'invalid' or 'victim of' or 'suffering from'.
- ❏ Speak clearly, facing the light and keep hands away from the mouth so that lip readers can understand.
- ❏ Do not shout when someone has not heard.
- ❏ Offer pen and paper if communication is becoming difficult.
- ❏ Speak directly to someone in a wheelchair at their level.
- ❏ Move around the desk to a lower level or in front of the desk to assist them.

19.11 Physical adjustments

FMs will need to consult the Approved Document Part M of the Building Regulations, and the British Standard (BS 8300) for design of buildings. These provide standards that will help to meet the requirements of disabled users of buildings. There are no buildings that can be totally 'DDA compliant' nor are there any products or adjustments that make a building DDA compliant. This is because it is virtually impossible to demonstrate due to the individual adjustment needs of an individual disabled person. Adjustments that could be made in a building or a work space to allow better access and usability include:

❑   Widening of doorways and corridors.
❑   Provision or modification of lifts with audio guidance.
❑   Installation of ramps.
❑   Adaptable WC, shower and changing facilities.
❑   Induction loops (either permanent installation or portable devices).
❑   Improved design of signs and directional signs.
❑   Designated car spaces of the correct size.
❑   Non-slip surfaces in wider use.
❑   Handrails in rooms and corridors.
❑   Tactile surfaces when height changes.
❑   Retention of heavy fire doors via magnetic devices until fire activation.
❑   Proximity of security access readers.

19.12 Claims

Any disabled person may take civil action against an employer (usually in an employment tribunal) or service provider (in a County Court), if they feel they have been discriminated against. Aside from the financial implications of any compensation awarded (the level of which is unlimited), the following potential hidden costs may be awarded in the compensation, which should also be borne in mind:

❑   Effect upon staff morale, and increased stress levels.
❑   Damage to reputation and corporate image within the local community.
❑   Public relations and time lost to staff involved.
❑   Legal costs.

Employee claims

If an employee who is disabled complains that an employer has breached a duty in the Act, then a claim can be brought to an Employment Tribunal.

Claims could arise from the failure to make changes in work practices to support a disabled person, in respect of the provision of wheelchair access to the building, or from a deaf person not being provided with appropriate telephone hand sets. There is a broad test of reasonableness within the Act, but the Tribunal will decide if an employer's failure to Act is unreasonable. The Tribunal can either uphold or reject a complaint. It may recommend that an employer carry out works to a building to accommodate the needs of the disabled person. It cannot order that work, but if it is not carried out the level of compensation payable may increase. In addition, compensation may be payable to the person bringing the complaint. It may also order a dismissed person to be reinstated.

Landlords can also be brought to account in claims. For example, if a landlord refuses consent for alterations on premises required under the Act, then the Tribunal can make an order authorising the occupier to make the alterations and in some cases obtain an order for the landlord to pay compensation.

Time limits are in force, and complaints should be instigated within 3 months of the actual cause of the complaint.

Service claims

Where a service provider has breached the Act, a claim can be made in the County Court. An example of this could be when a disabled person visits a restaurant and is not given the same courtesy as an able-bodied person. The same could apply if a person could not enter a building due to a failure by the owner to provide disabled access.

20 First Aid at Work

People at work can suffer injury or sudden illness at any time, and this may be in the workplace. It is important that employers have made arrangements to ensure their employees receive immediate attention if they are injured or taken ill at work.

People with first-aid training may have a positive influence on health and safety in the workplace. First-aiders may be in an advantageous position to help spread positive, basic health and safety messages throughout their organisation. The UK Health and Safety Executive (HSE) has provisionally estimated that at least 1.4 million workers have an up to date certificate in first aid at work or have recently completed first-aid training for appointed persons.

20.1 Definition of first aid

When employees become ill or suffer injuries at work, it is important that immediate first-aid attention is obtainable and, if necessary, an ambulance called. First aid given promptly and effectively can save lives; often it can assist in the prevention of minor injuries deteriorating into serious injuries. In many incidents/accidents, it is the only treatment necessary.

It is recommended that organisations develop a first-aid policy that covers the arrangements required to ensure that appropriate first-aid provision be situated in all places of work throughout the organisation. Depending on the size and structure of the organisation, this policy may be managed by the occupational health, human resources or health and safety functions, or it may be one of the many aspects of the FM function.

20.2 Health and Safety (First-Aid) Regulations 1981

The Health and Safety (First-Aid) Regulations 1981 require employers to provide adequate and appropriate equipment, facilities and personnel to enable first aid to be given to employees if they are injured or become ill at work. These Regulations apply to all workplaces including those with five or fewer employees and to the self-employed.

Duty of employer to make first-aid provision

The Regulations state that there is a duty on employers to make provision for first aid at work by:

❑ Ensuring there is adequate and appropriate equipment and facilities to provide first aid to employees who become injured or ill at work.
❑ Ensuring that there are a sufficient number of 'suitable persons' able to administer first aid if employees become injured or ill at work.

The Regulations are supported by a detailed Approved Code of Practice (ACoP) and Guidance L74 First Aid at Work, and several leaflets, such as the INDG347 Basic Advice on First Aid at Work and INDG214 First Aid at Work – Your Questions Answered.

What is deemed 'adequate' will depend on the circumstances in the workplace. This includes whether trained first-aiders are needed, what should be included in a first-aid box and if a first-aid room is needed. Employers should carry out an assessment of first-aid needs to determine this.

The Regulations do not place a legal obligation on employers to make first-aid provision for non-employees such as the public. However, the HSE strongly recommends that non-employees are included in a first-aid needs assessment and that provision is made for them. However, the organisation's insurance may not cover the costs of claims or litigation as a result of first aid to non-employees.

Assessment of first-aid needs

Employers are required to carry out an assessment of first-aid needs. This involves consideration of workplace hazards and risks, the size of the organisation and other relevant factors, to determine what first-aid equipment, facilities and personnel should be provided.

The aspects to consider in the assessment include:

- ❑ The hazards and risks in the workplace.
- ❑ The number of people located in the premises.
- ❑ Previous accident/incident history.
- ❑ Nature and distribution of workforce – shift workers, young employees, trainees.
- ❑ Remoteness of the workplace in relation to the emergency medical services, hospitals, GP surgeries, etc.
- ❑ Needs of travelling, remote and lone workers.
- ❑ Employees working on shared or multi-occupancy sites.
- ❑ Annual leave and other absences of first-aiders and appointed persons.

Provision of first aid

To ensure the availability of appropriate first-aid provision those responsible in each workplace will have to assess their first-aid requirements, typically using a checklist. The assessment will ensure that appropriate first-aid personnel and equipment are available to:

- ❑ Give immediate attention to an employee suffering from common injuries and illness and those likely to arise from specific hazards at work.
- ❑ Call an ambulance or other professional help.

The amount of first-aid equipment and trained personnel necessary will depend on the circumstances of each workplace. No fixed level exists. Those responsible will estimate, using the assessment of first-aid needs checklist, the level of equipment and personnel necessary to their circumstances.

An organisation's health and safety policy and risk assessments will identify hazards in the workplace and will therefore be helpful to those assessing first-aid requirements. The information obtained from making an assessment will identify the most likely nature of an incident that may require first aid. Such assessments may also assist with estimating the most appropriate type, quantity and location of first-aid personnel and equipment.

In workplaces assessed as low risk, provision of a suitably stocked first-aid box and designating an Appointed Person to take charge of first-aid arrangements may be all that are required.

In the case of work activity with hazardous substances, dangerous machinery, etc., first-aid provision must be appropriate to the assessed risk. As work activities present a variety of risks throughout most organisations, separate first-aid needs assessment need to be undertaken in each work area and reassessed when there is any change in the working practice.

Table 20.1 gives suggestions as to the number of first-aid personnel required in differing workplaces.

Suitable person

A 'suitable person' is either:

(i) A First-Aider who has received training and a qualification in first aid at work from an organisation approved by the HSE. Some first-aiders will require particular first-aid training if their workplace has specific hazards associated with the work activity. The selection of first-aiders ought to take into consideration the individuals' ability to learn new skills and their capacity to cope with stressful and physically demanding emergency procedures. They should be able to go rapidly and immediately to an emergency.

Table 20.1   Determination of first-aid requirements in the workplace

Category of risk	Number of workers at any location	Suggested number of first-aid personnel
Low Risk (e.g. offices, libraries)	Fewer than 50 50–100 More than 100	At least one Appointed Person At least one First Aider One additional First-Aider for every 100 employed
Medium Risk (e.g. workshops, kitchens, grounds)	Fewer than 20 20–100 More than 100	At least one Appointed Person At least one First-Aider for every 50 employed One additional First-Aider for every 100 employed
High Risk (e.g. chemical exposure, dangerous machinery, sharp instruments)	Fewer than 5 5–80 More than 80	At least one Appointed Person At least one First-Aider One additional First-Aider for every 80 employed
Where there are specific hazards for which additional first-aid skills are necessary		In addition at least one First-Aider trained in the specific emergency action

The training of first-aiders lasts at least 24 contact hours, consisting of both teaching and practical sessions. At present this takes four consecutive days with an examination in the afternoon of the last day. Refresher courses lasting at least 12 contact hours are also provided and must be taken every 3 years to maintain a valid first aid at work certificate. It is important to inform all first-aiders of any changes in first-aid practice and to organise supplementary training sessions if the need arises.

The training will cover resuscitation, managing an unconscious casualty, bleeding control, various common medical conditions and legislation. Although a first-aider will be certified for 3 years, it is recommended that 1-day refresher training is offered every year.

or

(ii) An Appointed Person who has received training in the management of a first-aid situation, and who would take charge until more expert assistance becomes available, e.g. first-aider, paramedic or ambulance personnel.

The Appointed Person will have responsibility for the upkeep of first-aid equipment in workplaces, where the first-aid needs assessment indicates there is no need to provide a trained first-aider. All Appointed Persons will complete a course of 4 hours duration in emergency first aid. This course will need to be repeated annually to maintain skills.

Guidelines for first-aid equipment

The assessment of first-aid need, together with the health and safety risk assessment, will assist in the identification of the level of first-aid cover and first-aid equipment required.

❑   All first-aid equipment must be suitably marked, ideally a green box with a white cross, and easily accessible and available in places where working conditions require it.
❑   First-aid containers should protect first-aid items from dust and damp.
❑   First-aid boxes ought to contain only items for administering first aid and nothing else.
❑   There is no mandatory list of first-aid materials to be included in the first-aid box. The content selection of first-aid boxes will result from first-aid needs assessment.

Note: Medication, disinfectants, ointments, etc. are NOT to be held in a first-aid box under any circumstance.

In workplaces where there is a comparatively low risk to health and safety, a minimum level of first-aid equipment is required. For example, office type accommodation would normally only require:

❑   1 advisory leaflet giving advice on the prevention of infection.
❑   1 leaflet giving guidance on first aid.
❑   20 assorted adhesive plasters.
❑   3 triangular bandages.
❑   2 sterile eye pads.
❑   6 safety pins.
❑   2 small wound dressings.
❑   2 medium wound dressings.
❑   2 large dressings.
❑   1 pair disposable gloves.

❑   6 non-alcohol cleansing wipes.
❑   1 record sheet of any treatment given.

The assessment of first-aid needs may indicate that there ought to be additional requirements in certain workplaces, e.g. kitchens, workshops, laboratories and so on. Consideration should be given to providing scissors, cold packs, cling film, adhesive tape, aprons, and other specialist equipment. These can be stored in, or alongside, the first-aid container.

Where mains water is not readily available for eye irrigation, a litre of sterile water in sealed disposable containers should be provided. These containers must be replaced whenever the seal is broken or when past the expiry date.

First-aid rooms

These are only required where the risk assessment shows that the organisation is operating in a high risk industry. Many large premises may also have a room designated for first aid. The location of the room needs to be considered to allow easy access by the paramedics when moving patients to a nearby ambulance. Typically, the contents of a first-aid room would be:

❑   Bed or couch with waterproof covering.
❑   Clean pillows and blankets.
❑   Suitable heating, ventilation and lighting.
❑   A lockable storage area for first-aid supplies.
❑   Desk and chair.
❑   Telephone.
❑   Sink with hot and cold water, soap and towels.
❑   Drinking water and cups.
❑   Foot-operated waste bin for sharps and medical waste.
❑   A record book for treatments and incidents.

The facility must be regularly cleaned, and specifically after each use. The floor and wall surfaces need to be washable. The room needs to be available at all times that there are people at work and there needs to be sufficient space in the room to allow suitable access to the patient by the first-aider and also external paramedics.

Inspection of first-aid stocks

A designated staff member, either a First-Aider or an Appointed Person, ought to inspect the first-aid stocks on a regular basis and replace any stocks necessary. In some cases, this task could be part of the daily routine of checks conducted by the security teams during patrols.

Record keeping

Everyone using first-aid stocks should complete a First-Aid Record Form held within the first-aid box and also complete an Accident Report Form, a copy of which should be sent to the relevant person in the organisation. This reporting system will assist in the identification of any work activities which may be causing ill health or injury. Subsequent alterations to the work activity may then be required to prevent further ill health or injury.

Notification of first-aid arrangements

In order that first-aid arrangements operate effectively, it is important that they are known, understood and accepted by everyone at the workplace. The FM should be aware who and where the first-aiders are and the locations of all first-aid boxes. It is important to place first-aid notices in prominent positions and that there are sufficient displayed in each area. Staff who may have reading or language difficulties may require the provision of a relevant first-aid notice. All new members of staff, as part of their induction training, will need to be made aware of the first-aid provision and procedures in their work area.

Implementation of first-aid policy

In order that adequate and appropriate first-aid equipment and trained First-Aiders/ Appointed Persons are located in all workplaces throughout an organisation, it is recommended that the following activities are carried out:

❑   Undertake an assessment of first aid.
❑   Identify requirements to comply with the Regulations.
❑   Ensure that all members of staff are familiar with the first-aid arrangements in their area.
❑   Display first-aid notices.
❑   Review and update documents and notices as required.

20.3 Reporting of Injuries, Diseases and Dangerous Occurrences Regulations 1995

FMs who are in control of premises, have a duty to report to the HSE (or appropriate enforcing authority) some accidents and incidents at work under RIDDOR (the Reporting of Injuries, Diseases and Dangerous Occurrences Regulations 1995). There are various categories and types of incidents that have to be reported. These are:

❑   Death or major injury
   ○   These must be reported immediately without delay. Major injuries are likely to involve emergency services and hospital admissions. Injuries classified as major include: fractures (except toes, fingers and thumbs); amputation; dislocation of shoulder, knee, hip or spine; loss of sight (temporary or permanent); chemical or hot burn to eye or any penetrating injury to eye; injury from electrical shock or electrical burn; unconsciousness caused by asphyxia or harmful substance or biological agent; acute illness.
❑   Over 3-day injury
   ○   These must be reported within 10 days of the period of injury. The 3 days include weekends and holidays.
❑   Disease
   ○   There are several diseases that have to be reported via form F2508A. These include skin diseases, lung diseases, infections such as hepatitis, legionellosis, leptospirosis and some poisonings from heavy metals.
❑   Dangerous occurrence

o These are significant near-misses and must be reported immediately, followed up with the completed form within 10 days. Examples of occurrences are: collapse, overturning or failure of lifts and lifting equipment; collapse of building or structures under construction; explosion or fire; electrical short circuit or overload causing fire or explosion; accidental release of substance that could cause death, major injury or damage to a person's health.

Information about the incident must be reported using form F2508 and can be via telephone, fax, email, website or post. The report can be made to the UK national incident centre or to the local enforcing authority.

21 Asbestos

Asbestos is a natural mineral used primarily for insulation and fireproofing. There are three main types of asbestos:

(i)   chrysotile (white asbestos);
(ii) asbestos grunerite (brown asbestos);
(iii) crocidolite (blue asbestos).

Although the types of asbestos are listed by its colour, they cannot be identified purely by their colour. At one time, only blue asbestos was deemed to be dangerous, but today, all types are banned in the UK. Asbestos-containing materials (ACMs) may be found in buildings, machinery and equipment in many places and in many forms. It is now illegal in the UK to use asbestos in new buildings and refurbishment. The latest Regulations also state that second-hand asbestos materials are also banned. It will, however, be found in buildings that have been built or refurbished between 1945 and 1985. Asbestos was used extensively in buildings due to its thermal insulation properties. Asbestos is a problem when it becomes friable or damaged, releasing fibres to the air. When breathed in by people, these fibres damage the lung tissue.

Asbestos may be found in these materials:

❑ Sprayed asbestos and asbestos loose packing often found in fire breaks in ceiling voids or fire protection in ducts, panels, partitions, soffit boards, ceiling panels and around structural steel work.
❑ Moulded or preformed lagging often found around pipes and boilers.
❑ Asbestos insulating boards (AIBs) used for fire protection, thermal insulation, partitioning and ducts.
❑ Ceiling tiles.
❑ Millboard, paper and paper products used for insulation of electrical equipment, or facing on wood fibreboard.
❑ Asbestos cement products made into corrugated sheets or flat sheets used for roofing and wall cladding. Also these products can be used to make gutters, rainwater pipes and water tanks or cisterns.
❑ Certain texture coatings (such as artex).
❑ Bitumen roof material.
❑ Vinyl or thermoplastic floor tiles.

Due to the variety of products that asbestos has been incorporated into, it is best to presume that it may be present, unless there is strong evidence to the contrary. In addition, asbestos has been used in industrial manufacturing, such as aircraft and avionics, vehicles and car components and shipbuilding.

Disturbing asbestos can release small fibres into the air. Inhaling these fibres can cause fatal diseases. Tiny fibres can pass into the lower parts of the lung and may work their way through the lung lining, potentially causing: asbestosis or fibrosis (scarring) of the lungs, lung cancer or mesothelioma (a cancer of the inner lining of the chest wall or abdominal cavities). These diseases are characterised by long latency periods, i.e. 20–40 years from exposure to asbestos to the onset of disease.

Asbestos-related diseases are currently responsible for over 4000 deaths per year in Britain, and are likely to increase each year to 2015 and beyond. There are usually long delays between first exposure to asbestos and the onset of disease, which can vary between 15 and 60 years. Medical checks and surveillance of those likely to have been exposed to fibres is important.

FMs who own, occupy, manage or have responsibilities for non-domestic premises which may contain asbestos, will have to:

❏ Carry out the legal duty to manage the risk from this material.
❏ Co-operate with whoever manages that risk (such as a landlord).

21.1 Regulations

In recent years, the Regulations have been updated several times. The current Control of Asbestos at Work Regulations 2006 (CAWR) strengthen overall worker protection by reducing exposure limits and introducing mandatory training for those who manage, or work directly, with asbestos. The Regulations concern prohibition, control and licensing. The main parts are:

❏ Risk assessments.
❏ Licensed works and medical surveillance.
❏ Awareness training.
❏ Appropriate PPE.

The main purpose of the Regulations is to prevent and reduce asbestos exposure to building occupants, visitors, maintenance and construction workers. The single control limit is 0.1 fibres/cm^3. The short-term maximum limit is set at 0.6 fibres/cm^3 for 10 minutes. Licensed contractors may work 1 hour at a time up to a maximum of 2 hours to undertake short, non-continuous maintenance. Air monitoring and controls systems are required in the designated work area, with specific emergency procedures and notification to the HSE prior to the commencement of works. The licensed contractors will pay for medical surveillance of their employees.

Two Approved Codes of Practice (ACoPs) and several Guidance Notes support these Regulations.

❏ An ACoP has been introduced to support Regulation 4 of CAWR.
❏ The management of asbestos in non-domestic premises (L127) (revised) gives advice on how to comply with the new requirements.
❏ A guidance booklet 'A comprehensive guide to managing asbestos' (HSG227) is aimed at those duty holders in more complex organisations.
❏ A free leaflet 'A short guide to managing asbestos in premises' is aimed at those with smaller, less complex premises.

Regulation 4 imposes various practical duties on those who have control of buildings. The duty to manage requires those in control of premises to:

❑ Take reasonable steps to find asbestos in the premises and assess the condition of these materials.
❑ Presume that materials do contain asbestos, unless there is strong evidence that they do not.
❑ Prepare a record of the location and condition of these materials and assess the risk from them.
❑ Prepare and implement a plan to manage those risks.
❑ Provide in formation on the location and condition of the materials to anyone who is liable to work on or disturb them.

21.2 Asbestos management plan

The purpose of this plan is to aid the effective management of any known or presumed ACMs in order to minimise the risk of exposure to asbestos fibres. The Asbestos Management Plan recommends management actions based on the survey findings. These management actions may range from regular re-inspections, labelling confirmed/suspected asbestos products and training provision for building users to a complete asbestos removal programme. An Asbestos Management Plan typically includes asbestos assessment records, action plans, responsibilities, communication plan and emergency procedures. The asbestos register and survey documentation will form the basis of any good Asbestos Management Plan; however, the information contained within the survey documentation must be kept up to date and be made available to building users and contractors.

The plan should consist of:

❑ Details of each ACM and an explanation of the risk assessment.
❑ Tables of priorities and timescales.
❑ Personnel and responsibilities.
❑ Training for employees and contractors.
❑ Procedures for preventing uncontrolled maintenance and building work.
❑ Procedures for ensuring information on ACSM are made available to those who need it.
❑ Arrangements for monitoring ACM.
❑ Arrangements for updating and reviewing the management plan.

21.3 Management options

In terms of management duties, the FM has three main options:

(i) Undertake a comprehensive survey and removal programme. This is both expensive and disruptive. The HSE does not recommend this course of action.
(ii) Carry out a survey before any new building or maintenance work is required. This may be an expensive option, and also difficult to manage.
(iii) Review property and premises to identify where asbestos is more likely to be present. Surveys would be carried out on those buildings or areas identified, and risks would be assessed on a case-by-case basis.

In all the options above, the FM needs to appoint a specialist to conduct the surveys. It is also normal practice to have a retained specialist to deal with any incidents that may arise if ACMs are disturbed or become damaged by activities in the workplace.

21.4 Asbestos survey types

The key requirement of Regulation 4 is that duty holders must ensure that a suitable and sufficient assessment of whether asbestos is liable to be present is carried out. This will include the need for an inspection/survey of the premises.

The HSE have issued a new survey guide to replace the MDHS 100. This guide 'Asbestos: Survey Guide' is available as HSG264. This guide is available on the HSE website and is effective.

The three types of asbestos survey defined in the former MDHS are now replaced with two survey types. These are known as the management survey and the refurbishment and demolition survey.

The type of survey will vary during the lifespan of the premises and several may be needed over time. A Management Survey will be required during the normal occupation and use of the building to ensure continued management of the ACMs *in situ*. A Refurbishment or Demolition Survey will be necessary when the building (or part of it) is to be upgraded, refurbished or demolished. It is probable that at larger premises a mixture of survey types will be appropriate.

Management Survey

A Management Survey is the standard survey, and is used to locate, as far as reasonably practicable, the presence and extent of any suspect ACMs in the building which could be damaged or disturbed during normal occupancy. Management surveys will involve minor intrusive work and some disturbance. A management survey should include an assessment of the condition of the various ACMs and their ability to release fibres into the air if they are disturbed in some way. Management surveys should cover routine and simple maintenance work.

The survey will usually involve sampling and analysis to confirm the presence or absence of ACMs. A management survey can also involve presuming the presence or absence of asbestos. A management survey can be completed using a combination of sampling ACMs and presuming ACMs or, indeed, just presuming. Any materials presumed to contain asbestos must also have their condition assessed (i.e. a material assessment).

By presuming the presence of asbestos, the need for sampling and analysis can be deferred until a later time (e.g. before any work is carried out). However, this approach has implications for the management arrangements and the likely extra costs. Any work carried out on 'presumed' materials would need to involve appropriate contractors and work methods in compliance with CAR 2006 irrespective of whether the material was actually an ACM or not.

Alternatively, before any work starts, sampling and analysis can be undertaken to confirm or refute the presence of asbestos. The results will determine the work methods and contractors to be used. The 'presumption' approach also has several disadvantages: it is less rigorous, it can lead to constant obstructions and delays before work can start and can be more difficult to control.

Refurbishment and Demolition Surveys

A Refurbishment and Demolition Survey is needed before any refurbishment or demolition work is carried out. This type of survey is used to locate and describe, as far as reasonably practicable, all ACMs in the area where the refurbishment work will take place or in the whole building if demolition is planned. The survey will be fully intrusive and involve destructive inspection, as necessary, to gain access to all areas, including those that may be difficult to reach. A refurbishment and demolition survey may also be required in maintenance and repair work – such as plant removal or dismantling.

There is a specific requirement in the Regulations for all ACMs to be removed as far as reasonably practicable before major refurbishment or final demolition. Removing ACMs is also appropriate in other smaller refurbishment projects that involve structural or layout changes to buildings (e.g. removal of partitions, walls, units and so on).

Aggressive inspection techniques will be needed to lift carpets and tiles, break through walls, ceilings, cladding and partitions and open up floors. In these situations, controls should be put in place to prevent the spread of debris, which may include asbestos. Refurbishment and demolition surveys should only be conducted in unoccupied areas to minimise risks to the public or employees on the premises. Ideally, the building should not be in use and all furnishings removed.

For minor refurbishment projects, the survey may be applicable to a smaller area such as a single room or even a part of a room. In these situations, there should be effective isolation of the survey area (e.g. full floor to ceiling partition), and furnishings should be removed as far as possible or protected using sheeting. The 'surveyed' area must be safe for reoccupation before people move back in. This will require a thorough visual inspection and, if appropriate (e.g. where there has been significant destruction), reassurance air sampling. Under no circumstances should staff remain in rooms or areas of buildings when intrusive sampling is performed.

Issues to consider

❑ Check the scope of area to be surveyed.
❑ Materials may be obscured or hidden by other items or cover finishes (e.g. paint, over boarding and so on).
❑ Asbestos may be hidden as part of the structure of the building and may not be visible until the structure is dismantled at a later date.
❑ Debris from previous asbestos removal projects may be present in some areas, as the guidelines of former legislation were of a lower standard. The techniques for removal have improved over time.
❑ Full accessibility to areas may be limited due to occupants, location sensitivity, lack of access hatches, height or confined spaces.
❑ The need for air monitoring during the survey.

A risk assessment will include both a material assessment and a priority assessment. The risk assessments are carried out in two parts: the first is a material assessment which assesses the condition of the material and the likelihood of it releasing fibres if disturbed; the second part is a priority assessment which takes into account maintenance activities, likelihood of disturbance, human exposure potential, occupant activity or visitors. Algorithms are used to score each item which results in an overall risk assessment score.

Table 21.1   Asbestos material assessment

Score	Assessment
10 and above	High risk, with significant potential to release fibres
7–9	Medium risk
5–6	Low risk
4 and below	Very low risk

21.5 Asbestos material assessment algorithm

The material assessment looks at the type and condition of the ACM and the ease at which it will release fibres if disturbed. Asbestos surveys will present the results or data using an algorithm based on four parameters:

(i) product type;
(ii) extent of damage or deterioration;
(iii) surface treatment;
(iv) asbestos type.

Each of the parameters are scored and given a total from 2 to 12 as shown in Table 21.1.

21.6 Asbestos priority assessment

The management priority assessment looks at the likelihood of someone disturbing the ACM.

The management priority must be determined by carrying out a risk assessment, which is able to take into account factors such as:

❏ The location of the material and its extent.
❏ The use to which the location is put.
❏ The occupancy of the area.
❏ The activities carried out in the area.
❏ Maintenance activities and frequency.

Again scores are awarded in the same way as the material assessment as shown in Table 21.2.

Table 21.2   Management assessment

Score	Assessment
> 15	Very high priority
11–15	High priority
6–10	Medium priority
< 6	Low priority

21.7 Asbestos management strategies

Where ACMs have been found or presumed to be in premises during the asbestos survey and recorded in the asbestos register, asbestos management strategies have to be developed to ensure that any potential for damage or disturbance and the spread of fibres is minimised.

Generally it is better to leave ACMs in place, especially if they are in good condition, to avoid unnecessary disturbance of asbestos fibres. Therefore strategies to seal, encapsulate, repair, enclose and protect are preferred to the removal option.

Leaving an ACM in place

Asbestos products may be left in place provided it is:

❏   In good condition.
❏   Sealed or encapsulated if it is found slightly damaged or deteriorated, to prevent any asbestos fibre release.
❏   Repaired if the damage, or deterioration, found is more extensive, and it is very unlikely that the material will be disturbed by its position or location, or because measures have been taken to reduce its vulnerability to damage.

Management of contact with asbestos

Any potential contact with identified ACMs left in place must be managed by a robust management system so that damage or disturbance is avoided as far as reasonably practicable. This can be achieved by:

❏   Tight control of maintenance employees and maintenance contractors by ensuring that they know where asbestos can be found and to avoid disturbing it.
❏   Ensuring there is an up to date asbestos register or record to be able to give maintenance employees/contractors appropriate information.
❏   Use of permit-to-work systems to control the work in the vicinity of ACMs.
❏   The use of labelling and/or colour coding to indicate the locations where asbestos has been found.

Monitoring and re-inspections

Whenever an ACM is left in place it must be subject to a monitoring scheme to ensure that it has not been damaged or that its condition is not deteriorating. This should be in the form of a periodic visual inspection to check its condition and record the results. The frequency of the monitoring checks will vary and will depend on:

❏   The type and condition of the ACM and its location.
❏   The activities which generally occur in that location.

However, the frequency of inspection of ACMs should not normally be greater than 12 months. A useful method of comparing the condition of the ACMs with previous checks and to tell if it has deteriorated since the last check is by using photographs.

Remedial actions

Where an ACM is found to be damaged or deteriorating there are several options that need to be explored before its treatment or removal is considered. However, when exploring these options there are other certain factors which may affect the final decision, such as:

❑ Treatment work may require a certain amount of skill and on nearly every occasion it must be carried out by a licensed asbestos removal contractor, or by similarly trained people and work methods if using in house or external maintenance staff on own premises.

❑ Non-licensed removal contractors may only carry out the work if it is of a minor nature and of short duration.

❑ The fire resistance properties of the sealant, encapsulant or repair substance, if the original purpose of the ACM was to resist the spread of fire.

21.8 Managing an asbestos incident

If the FM has reason to believe that ACMs have been damaged or disturbed, they will need to consider these issues in the effective management of the incident:

❑ Stop work immediately.

❑ Get people in the area to remove clothing and personal effects that may be contaminated, leaving them in suitable bags or containers in the area for specialist examination.

❑ Close and secure area affected to prevent further damage and access.

❑ Close or switch off air conditioning systems to prevent spread of contaminated air to other areas.

❑ Advise workers affected to shower – especially washing hair and all contaminated skin with copious amounts of water (warm) and soap for at least 10–15 minutes.

❑ Draft written report on the incident, including a list of persons affected.

❑ Contact retained specialist for investigation and analysis to confirm nature of asbestos fibres exposed and level of contamination.

❑ Contact HSE or EHO.

❑ Contact insurance company.

❑ Complete a RIDDOR.

❑ Update the asbestos register.

❑ Ensure written note on the exposure is notified to all employees and contractors affected, ensuring appropriate records are placed in their personal files.

❑ Liaise with neighbouring departments or organisations that may be concerned or affected by the incident.

❑ Arrange decontamination works with specialist licensed or non-licensed contractor (depending on nature of ACMs to be removed).

❑ Ensure notice served to HSE prior to decontamination works (14 days) and plan of work is prepared if the works require a licensed contractor.

❑ Provide suitable space for establishment of decontamination cubicles, protected routes and storage areas. Showering facilities may be required.

21.9 Summary checklist

- ❏ Review all aspects of asbestos management.
- ❏ Confirm who has the specific responsibility for managing asbestos as the duty holder.
- ❏ Is there a management policy in place?
- ❏ Who is responsible for the policy?
- ❏ Conduct a survey to understand if and where there is asbestos in the premises.
- ❏ Implement an Asbestos Management System to enable the organisation to effectively meet the requirements of the new regulations and to have comprehensive information about asbestos in the premises.
- ❏ Carry out condition assessments to regularly check the condition of ACMs.
- ❏ Check the action plan for compliance.
  - o Assess the management plan.
  - o Does it reflect the findings of risk assessment?
  - o Is it up to date?
  - o What controls are in place to implement the plan?
  - o Are ACMs labelled or are there signs to help identify materials?
  - o Does the organisation have a permit-to-work system in place?
  - o What regular checks are in place to monitor the condition of ACMs?
  - o Is the asbestos register kept up to date?
- ❏ Provide training for personnel at all levels in asbestos awareness, from identification of ACMs to management of asbestos in the premises.
  - o Check that third-party suppliers and contractors have also been appropriately trained.
- ❏ Update the local Business Continuity Plan and Emergency or Disaster Recovery Plan with relevant information on management of an asbestos incident.

22 Water Supplies and Water Safety

22.1 Introduction

The Dublin Statement on Water and Sustainability in 1992 identified that water is a resource that is critical to the planet and human life. Just 1% of the water in the world is drinking water. Water is still consumed in developed countries with disregard to its unpredictable supply, despite its critical status.

❏ People use 70% more water as individuals than 30 years ago.
❏ Leaks in the distribution systems are significant and increasing.
❏ Rainfalls in the UK in recent years have been the lowest for 85 years.
❏ Water usage has doubled in the past 20 years.

The supply of water in the UK is the third most expensive in the world. Costs are expected to rise even more and therefore there is an increased focus and interest in water management in businesses. The average consumption in the UK is 150 litres per person per day, compared with 127 litres per person per day in Germany. It is predicted that demand for water will increase by 5% by 2020. The Government agency, Defra, have set targets to reduce water consumption by 20 litres per person per day by 2030. Other targets set by Government include a reduction in supply leakages of 36% and limits to the design capacity of new homes of 125 litres per person per day. The business sector accounts for one-third of the total water use within the UK. Therefore, it is essential that businesses develop their water conservation practices in order to achieve long-term sustainable supply and protect the environment. There are many simple and some more complex changes that businesses can make in order to reduce water consumption.

Water can cost a company around 1–2% of its turnover – so for a company with a turnover of £1 million, that is £10,000 to £20,000 a year on water costs. For a small company this is a considerable sum, which can be reduced relatively easily. Companies should start considering the management of water in the same way as other resources like gas or electricity. This can lead to considerable financial, social and environmental benefits.

22.2 Water systems

Water is found in many systems in buildings. These include:

❏ Hot and cold water supplies.
❏ Storage tanks.
❏ Cooling towers, humidifiers, showers and water features (e.g. fountains).
❏ Drinking water sources such as vending machines and water dispensers.

Water is required in buildings for both drinking and washing; and in some cases, for the heating and cooling systems in the building.

22.3 Water consumption

The increasing water use in the UK puts pressure on organisations to limit its use within buildings. For instance, when updating washroom facilities and toilets, the FM could replace regular taps in washbasins with sprinkler taps that use less water and adjust toilet cisterns to release less water when flushed. The introduction of recycling and reuse options such as grey water or the capture of rainwater for use around the premises can reduce water consumption. Smaller businesses can achieve realistic savings by using smart metering to detect water consumption targets and retrofitting or replacing old water appliances. Often the most cost effective and sustainable way to save water at the workplace is by raising staff awareness.

22.4 Benefits of water conservation

Studies have shown that businesses could save up to 30% of their water bill by reducing water consumption and using water wisely. Water conservation will have fringe benefits for a business. For example:

❑ Saving water will reduce energy bills associated with heating and pumping of the water around the building. In many cases, the financial savings on energy associated with the water supplies could be greater than the savings on water.
❑ There could also be savings in staff time and materials, as processes become more efficient.
❑ There will also be benefits to an organisation's reputation as a socially and environmentally responsible business, which will be appreciated by clients, investors, the public and employees.
❑ Conducting a water audit will help with compliance with current and future legislation. Businesses classified as large water users – this is using in excess of 50 million litres per annum – now have to comply with new legislation.

22.5 Water industry

The water industry in the UK is made up of regional monopolies. These organisations are responsible for:

❑ Collecting and abstracting raw water, storing and purifying it.
❑ Distributing water to customers.
❑ Collecting waste water.
❑ Treating waste water.
❑ Disposing or recycling the waste water.
❑ Metering and other ancillary operations.

The water industry market has been slow to respond to changes in the regulation of the industry. The pricing structure associated with the Water Supply Licensing (WSL) regime is complicated.

Substantial savings can be achieved for customers by the current water industry providers by:

- Improved customer service.
- Personal contacts or account managers.
- Accurate data.
- Billing to suit individual business requirements.
- Monitoring and targeting.

22.6 Compliance

The water industry has much current and future legislation to comply with. The current legislation includes:

- Environment Protection Act 1990.
- Water Resources Act 1991.
- Water Industries Acts 1991 and 1999.
- Groundwater Regulations 1998.
- Anti-Pollution Works Regulations 1999.
- The COSHH Regulations 1999.
- The Workplace (Health, Safety and Welfare) Regulations 1992.
- HSE L8 ACoP – Legionnaires' disease. The control of legionella bacteria in water systems.
- The Water Supply (Water Quality) Regulations 2000 and Water Byelaws.
- The Water Act 2003 increased the duties on water companies to promote water efficiency and placed a duty on public bodies to use water efficiently.
- The government Food Industry Sustainability Strategy aims to reduce water consumption in the food processing sector by 10–15% by 2010.
- The Pollution Prevention and Control Regulations 2002 has led to specific reporting and action on potentially polluting industries and includes specific water management targets in specific industries.
- The Code for Sustainable Homes will set benchmarks for water use in new homes and it will be compulsory to reach certain targets if any government land or funding is being used.
- Defra and DCLG are jointly looking at revising either the Water Fitting Regulations or the Building Regulations to mandate water efficiency in new and existing buildings (at time of refit).

22.7 Water pollution

Most of the concerns about water pollution relate to the contamination of inland and coastal waters. Pollutants include:

- Toxic materials such as pesticides and nitrates.
- Solid wastes and sewage which cause deoxygenation (arising from farm waste and sewage).

❏ Tipping of rubbish and other material that prevents water flow and often creates an eyesore.
❏ Nutrient enrichment such as fertilisers which encourage algae and plant growth.

In general, the UK rivers are the cleanest that they have been for many years; some speculate that could be as long ago as before the Industrial Revolution. However, water pollution continues to be one of the most common forms of pollution subject to court proceedings.

The Environment Agency (EA) in England and Wales, the Scottish Environment Protection Agency (SEPA) and the Department of Environment in Northern Ireland (DoE) are the public bodies responsible for dealing with water pollution and prosecuting offenders.

Water pollution from buildings will generally arise through the discharge of effluent into the sewage system and the surface water drains. It is vital to ensure that any discharges into drains are not unlawful. Checks that could be carried out by the FM and their team include:

❏ All cleaning fluids used within buildings are legal and have not been banned.
❏ People using the immediate area around the building should be aware of unlawful discharges.
❏ Activities such as repairing or cleaning a car next to a building must ensure that no oil, waste or otherwise is poured or leaks into the surface drains.

22.8 Drinking water

Wholesome potable water must be available at the place of work. FMs may choose to provide drinking water via the mains supply to either labelled, designated taps or to drinking fountains or to other water dispensers. In some cases, FMs may use bottled water supplies instead. This is sometimes the only option if there is no mains water supply available. All types of supply will have issues of hygiene, maintenance, contamination and availability.

The provision of drinking water is a legal requirement under the Workplace (Health, Safety and Welfare) Regulations 1992. This states that any drinking water should preferably be 'from the public source'. The regulations also state that a drinking vessel is to be provided.

Mains-fed or stand-alone dispenser

The FM needs to consider the advantages and disadvantages of supplying drinking water from a mains-fed system or from a portable stand alone bottle dispenser system. By taking water from the mains via a mains-fed dispenser there is no need for regular bottled water deliveries, resulting in a lower embodied CO_2 value, due to fewer delivery lorries on the road. There will also be fewer empty plastic bottles, which currently cannot be recycled in the UK, sent to landfill. Switching from a bottled water supply to a mains-fed drinking water dispenser will also free-up storage space that was once occupied by the plastic water bottles, and removes the health and safety risk of staff having to carry or lift heavy bottles.

A mains-fed water dispenser is more hygienic in managing risks of bacterial infection from legionella and other pathogens than the stand-alone plastic dispensers. Water in dispenser systems can be treated with UV technology, removing any harmful bacteria without adding chemicals or altering the taste of the water in any way. The dispenser's external surfaces can also be treated with anti-microbial protection, helping to minimise the risk of cross-workplace infection. Hygiene of all users and maintenance staff is important.

Health and productivity benefits

The consumer trend for bottled water is linked to the growth of awareness around the health benefits of drinking water. It has been scientifically proven that hydration aids performance: attention and concentration can decrease by 13% and short-term memory by 7% through not drinking enough water. The average adult should drink between six and eight glasses of water a day, with more in hot conditions. Encouraging staff to drink more water by raising awareness of the health benefits will result in a well-hydrated, and therefore happier and more productive workforce. Productivity and legality are not the only drivers in providing water for employees – there is also a level of perceived value in allowing staff access to free refreshments.

Hot water dispenser

There are a number of mains-fed water dispensers available on the market which provide both chilled water and hot water for tea, coffee and other hot drinks.

It has been estimated that in an office with 20 members of staff, as much as 2 hours a day will be taken up with waiting for the kettle to boil. Kettles also pose a potential health and safety risk; they can be knocked over, or steam can scald the unwary. Trailing cables can be easily damaged, allowing live conductors to be exposed. Every kettle in the work-place also has to be PAT tested annually. Replacing kettles with a mains-fed dispenser with a hot water function provides significant cost savings.

In offices where the demand for hot drinks such as tea and coffee is very high, a wall-mounted boiler may be the best option in terms of environmental sustainability, as well as health and safety. A mains-fed boiler with appropriate technology works by replacing the hot water that is drawn off immediately with cold water, carefully controlling the temperature and preventing excessive use of electricity. In addition, an in-built condensing chamber prevents steam escaping, which conserves heat and reduces energy use.

Plastic waste

Many organisations still find disposable plastic cups to be the best way of serving water. Partnering with a supplier with an environmental policy can help FMs to address this type of waste. Supporting initiatives such as the Save-a-Cup collection and recycling scheme enables organisations to reduce the environmental impact of using plastic cups, while staff are directly involved in implementing a green policy (see www.save-a-cup.co.uk). In addition, considering alternatives to disposable cups, such as reusable bottles or other vessels, can reduce the volume of plastic sent to recycling plants.

22.9 Washing and cleaning

Hot and cold water may be used for hand-washing, showers and general cleaning activities in a building. The number and location of these facilities will be a function of the needs of the business, the size of the premises and the number of users. Sanitisation of these facilities is required on a regular basis to ensure that the water is not contaminated.

22.10 Food preparation

Water will also be required to support catering and vending operations in buildings. Food safety legislation will dictate the requirements and locations of water supplies. Water not drawn down via the mains will be stored in cisterns or tanks until required. Maintenance and sanitisation of the storage vessels is essential to avoid contamination of the stored water.

22.11 Water pressure

In medium to high rise buildings, there will be inadequate mains pressure to supply water to the upper floors. Additional cisterns and tanks, together with pumps and other equipment, are installed to overcome this problem.

22.12 Drainage

Drainage of waste water may be in a combined or separate system. The systems are:

❑   Foul water sewer.
❑   Surface water sewer.

Grease traps and interceptors may be required in drainage systems to allow cleaning and removal of grease or other blockages. The drainage requirements will depend on the number of WCs, showers, urinals, basins, sinks and other equipment in the premises.

22.13 Specialist maintenance

Some maintenance activities may be outsourced to specialist contractors – such as rodding the drains, cleaning grease traps, chlorinating the water in tanks, water sampling and testing for bacteria presence.

22.14 Water design capacity

One issue facing FMs is the increased numbers of building occupants above the designed limit, giving rise to insufficient facilities to meet their needs. Over time, the 'as-built' capacity of water supplies and drainage will not support future growth, and systems will be at capacity. Water Regulations and Building Regulations must be observed with any changes in layout and installation of additional toilets and washing facilities.

22.15 Supply continuity

FMs should consider water supply in their business continuity planning. They need to ascertain how the business would cope if water supplies were interrupted or became unreliable. Some of the likely issues are the increased costs of water supplies, compromised health and safety compliance, or the failure of plant that requires a continuous water supply. In some cases, maintaining normal business operations may not be possible, and buildings may have to be closed until water supplies are resumed.

22.16 Management review

Consultants can provide an independent, accurate picture of the current water management regime. The results will ascertain whether current water management systems are adequate and, if not, will establish where improvements can be made and ensure that informed decisions based on practical information are made. A water management review will help FMs in four keys areas as shown in Table 22.1.

A review can help save money, maintain continuity, meet compliance and care for the organisation's reputation and the environment.

FMs can use external specialists independently to test and examine water systems including:

- ❑ Hot and cold water supplies.
- ❑ Storage tanks.
- ❑ Cooling towers, humidifiers, showers and water features.
- ❑ Drinking water sources such as vending machines and bottled water dispensers.
- ❑ Mains supplies.
- ❑ Legionella sampling and testing.
- ❑ Reviews of water services documentation.

Tests should be carried out on the domestic services following nationally recognised procedures for legionella and microbiological counts, pH, TDS (total dissolvable solids) and temperature to ascertain whether the water is of an acceptable or inferior quality.

Physical checks should also be conducted on the system to ascertain the condition of the plant, turnover of water (which should equal consumption in a 24-hour period) and the adequacy of any maintenance or treatment programme.

The results will ascertain whether the current maintenance and water management regimes are adequate and, if not, will establish where improvements need to be made.

Table 22.1   The four criteria of a Water Management Review

1	Costs	An in-depth review can help in finding ways to reduce consumption and identify tax-efficient options to make further sustainable savings in water usage and costs.
2	Continuity	Intermittent water supply as a result of rationing could cause problems with business critical water facilities. FMs need to develop plans to remain operational and mitigate associated business risks.
3	Compliance	FMs need advice on maintaining compliance with all safety, health, building and environmental requirements.
4	Care	Better water management is good for corporate responsibility, good for the corporate image and good for the environment.

22.17 Water management policy

In a review of the management of water, the following aspects need to be included in a water management policy:

❑ Identifying potential cost savings.
❑ Review of water services policy and documentation.
❑ Recommending better practices of both usage and risk management.
❑ Advice to allow premises to remain functional regardless of climatic conditions.
❑ Advice on management technologies – metering, controls, rainwater harvesting, etc.
❑ Identifying how to best meet corporate responsibility goals.
❑ Achieving legal requirements in normal and drought conditions, where required.

22.18 Water-saving technology

New technologies are being developed to reduce the water consumption in premises. One example is 'flush-wiser'. Flush-wiser is a new product that can be adapted to fit conventional WCs of varying size, performance and water pressure. Flush-wiser reduces the volume of water used per flush without harming the working parts of the WC and without loss of efficiency. Reduced water consumption means lower sewerage charges, saving organisations including schools, hospitals and other public sector organisations millions of pounds per year. Flush-wiser attaches to the siphon within the WC cistern and has six different volume settings. It works by allowing variable volumes of air into the siphon, which in turn reduces the amount of water used to flush. The more air that goes in, the less water is used per flush. Water is reduced by up to one-third – e.g. 3 litres on a 9-litre cistern. The average saving is likely to be around 2 litres.

The Water Supply (Water Fittings) Regulations 1999 require that all new WC suites installed after 1 January 2001 flush with no more than 6 litres of water. Flush-wiser provides a solution to reducing the flush for pre-2001 cisterns, typically 7 and 9 litres.

22.19 Grey water systems

Grey water is second hand water – that is, it has already been used for washing or another purpose. Grey water may also refer to collected rainwater or other spill-off water. Grey water systems can be used for a multitude of applications ranging from WC/urinal flushing, irrigation schemes, to full waste water recovery requiring sophisticated water treatment plant such as reverse osmosis. Much of the treated water supplied by the local mains is derived from 'dirty' sources such as rivers and waste recovery. The following factors need to be considered for water recycling schemes:

❑ Storage volumes.
❑ Demand.
❑ Availability.
❑ Cost.
❑ Plant/space requirement.

Despite the benefits of using once-used water, or collected rainwater, FMs must consider that:

❑ Grey water supply systems are increasingly expensive.
❑ It depletes the natural water courses and river ways.
❑ It requires both environmentally and commercially expensive treatment and distribution costs.
❑ The used grey water will need to be treated prior to discharge into the waterways and surrounding seas.

Rainwater recovery

Rainwater should be separated from foul waters to reduce the size of treatment plant, as rainwater volumes are considerably in excess of foul water volumes, making combined treatment costs uneconomic. Although storm water can be polluted, particularly in urban areas or during the beginning of a runoff event, it can generally be discharged to natural sources without treatment. Many older sewerage systems do not successfully separate rainwater from foul water, which swamps any foul water treatment plant, depleting its effectiveness.

Rainwater is particularly suitable for WC and urinal flush systems, which often consume 40–70% of total water consumption.

Rainwater recovery therefore has many environmental benefits and should be considered based upon the following:

❑ Treatment may be required depending upon the future use of the rainwater. Rainwater from roofs contains bird faeces, dust, dirt, bacteria and is mildly corrosive. If rainwater is used for WC/urinal flush applications, then cartridge or coarse sand filtration should be adequate.
❑ Storage will be required, which should be pre-filtered and fully accessible for maintenance.
❑ Temperatures should be maintained below 20°C and the tank should be screened with insect screens used to comply with L8 ACoP.
❑ Storage volumes should optimise rainfall prediction, cost and use.
❑ Mains supplied water top-up must be considered where necessary.
❑ Rainwater distribution pipework must not connect to any source of drinking water.

Waste water recovery

Waste water can be recovered from various sources including:

❑ Sinks.
❑ Wash hand basins.
❑ Showers.
❑ Dishwashing machines.
❑ Washing processes.
❑ Vehicle washing.

Certain processes will have contaminated the water with particular particles or chemicals and therefore the waste water will need pre-treatment, e.g. removal of detergents in vehicle washing and other wash processes or the removal of food products from commercial dishwashers.

Table 22.2   Building urinal control systems

1	Infrared controls	When selecting passive infrared controls ensure that the detecting head is correctly located to detect personnel presence.
2	Hydraulic (pressure) controls	Pressure-sensing valves can be used which sense the reduction in pressure experienced when taps, etc. are opened elsewhere in the system. This then allows flow to the urinal cistern. Hydraulic actuators should be selected to suit water pressures and be correctly located to detect pressure drop.
3	Electrical motorised controls	Simple time clock controls can be used to close supply during hours of non-occupation. More sophisticated versions are available linked with occupancy sensors and BMS systems.

22.20 Urinal controls

Urines have in the past been fitted with a continual flushing mechanism. The flushing continues whether the facility is used or not and therefore can be very wasteful of water supplies. Occupancy-based control of urinal flush systems is essential to minimise potentially huge losses of water. Controls, as shown in Table 22.2, can be either:

❑   Infrared.
❑   Hydraulic.
❑   Electrical.

22.21 Water-saving tips

(i)   Ensuring that water consumption is kept to the minimal reasonable level and publish targets, actuals and trends.
(ii)   Regular leakage tests should be undertaken on occupied buildings by shutting off all distribution points and observing the water meter flow rate.
(iii)   Meters should be installed to all buildings with sub-metering used to monitor high usage equipment such as dishwashers, vehicle washing plant, restaurants and large toilet facilities.
(iv)   Meter readings should be monitored by a computerised data monitoring system with high consumption plant monitored automatically.
(v)   No direct waste water cooling systems should be used.
(vi)   Toilets should have flush capacities less than 7.5 litres.
(vii)   Urinals should be fitted with automatic water supply regulation devices.
(viii) Storage cisterns (when required) should be sized to provide minimum storage relevant to demand and risk of mains supply breakdown.
(ix)   Service valves should be installed on all storage cisterns and on large diameter/long runs of distributing pipework to avoid unnecessary drain-downs to facilitate maintenance of taps, valves, etc.
(x)   Service valves should be installed on either side of pumps and equipment to allow removal for maintenance or replacement with minimal drain-down.
(xi)   Minimise dead legs on shower connections and include servicing valves.
(xii)   All power wash equipment should, where possible, be fitted with filtration and recirculation equipment.

(xiii) Reduce water wastage at the point of use including:
- spray taps;
- time controllers;
- PIR controls;
- electronic zone controls;
- foot-operated taps.
(xiv) Consider the use of timed controls on taps, showers, etc.
(xv) Leak detection exercises should be carried out on all supply pipes where demand readings change unexpectedly.
(xvi) Install overflows to discharge in conspicuous locations to suit water byelaws.
(xvii) Installation of trace heating and insulation on long dead leg runs of hot water distribution pipework.
(xviii) Backwash volumes should be minimised where practical.
(xix) Sprinkler test pipework should be configured where practical to return water to the storage vessel.
(xx) Shower heads should be compatible with the pressure available and volumes required.
(xxi) Replace built water macerators with bin and bag method of sanitary towel disposal.
(xxii) Grey water systems should be considered to recycle waste water or rainwater for use in non-potable water systems such as WC, urinal flushing and garden irrigation.

22.22 Leak detection

When connecting new supply pipes to incoming distribution mains, a leak detection exercise should be undertaken. This may take the form of a visual surface inspection or include specialist detection equipment.

Leak detection can be carried out by the following methods:

❑ Monitoring and assessment – water meters should be installed at principal usage points which can be regularly read/assessed to determine abnormal use. Pulse meter monitoring linked with computer software is ideal for this purpose.
❑ Total isolation – with all outlets isolated (or not in use, i.e. 2 a.m. in the morning). Indication of leakage can be assessed by inspecting the meter.
❑ Ultrasonic inspection – ultrasonic sensors can be strapped to pipelines to generate sound profiles along pipework systems. Analysis of the sound wave at various locations can pinpoint fairly accurately the location of a leak (not the quantity, however!).
❑ Ultrasonic flow measurement – can be used although it is only accurate to ± 15% and depends largely upon pipe material (PVC is ideal).
❑ Hot water can be pumped through a buried distribution system and sub-ground temperature plots taken to locate leaks. Thermal imaging may also produce an indication of the location of leaks.
❑ Water diviners, although controversial, can produce excellent results.

22.23 Water safety

There is much legislation and guidance concerning the safety of water systems in buildings. The Health and Safety commission have produced two important documents which offer essential practical advice on maintenance, water treatment and monitoring requirements – guidance document HS(G)70 and an approved code of practice (ACoP L8) – *Legionnaires' disease: The control of legionella bacteria in water systems*. These documents give advice on the competence and training for staff responsible for developing, managing and conducting the risk assessment and implementing the controls. It also emphasises the duties on suppliers of products and services to carry out work effectively and safely and to liaise with the client duty holders when deficiencies are identified. This is primarily aimed at water treatment contractors to help them improve their standards. The ACoP applies to any workplace or undertaking where water is used or stored and there is a reasonably foreseeable risk of legionellosis.

The compliance requirements will differ depending on the nature of the building and the water systems within it. For example, a building with cooling towers will require additional maintenance, water treatment and monitoring when compared with a building that uses an air-cooled dry system. Conversely, a building that uses borehole water supply will require additional monitoring to meet with the Private Water Supplies Regulations 1991.

Regular independent environmental auditing of the water systems within the building will help the FM demonstrate that they are meeting their legal obligations. It will also confirm that maintenance and water treatment regimes are effective and appropriate to the level of risk and ensure that the service providers are giving a good and cost-effective service.

22.24 L8 ACoP

The L8 ACoP and guidance covers five key areas of equal importance.

Identification and assessment of the risk

A suitable and sufficient assessment is required to establish what risks of exposure to legionella bacteria exist from both the water systems and work activities. It should identify the necessary measures to prevent, or adequately control, the risk from exposure to legionella bacteria.

The ACoP states that a risk assessment should be carried out by a competent person (i.e. someone who understands water systems and the risk from exposure to legionella bacteria associated with them).

The key to getting a risk assessment right is the competence of the assessor. Some of the questions to ask an assessor when judging their competence are:

❑ What experience of water systems do they have?
❑ What do they know about controlling the risks associated with exposure to legionella bacteria?
❑ Have they signed the Water Management Society and British Association of Chemical Specialties Code of Conduct on the control of legionellosis for service providers?
❑ What certificates of quality assurance do they hold?
❑ What training has the assessor successfully completed?

As part of the risk assessment, the guidance recommends that an asset register of all associated plant, pumps, strainers and other relevant items be provided along with a schematic diagram showing the layout of the plant or system.

Managing the risk: management responsibilities, training and competence

If the assessment shows that there is a risk from exposure to legionella bacteria, someone should be appointed to take responsibility for and supervise the implementation of the necessary precautions. This person should be a manager, director or have a similar status and sufficient authority. They should also be competent and have the knowledge of the system to ensure that all operational procedures are carried out in a timely and effective manner. This person may be appointed from a supplier if there is nobody in the organisation with the expertise.

Training should be provided for anyone carrying out the control measures (such as a maintenance engineer) to ensure the tasks are carried out in a safe and technically competent manner. Training records for the staff maintaining the water systems should be kept, including details of any refresher or top up training carried out since the first training given.

Staff responsibilities and lines of communication, both internally and between the various suppliers, should be properly defined and clearly documented.

Preventing or controlling the risk from exposure to legionella bacteria

Once the risk has been identified and assessed, a written scheme should be prepared for preventing or controlling it. This should include:

- An up-to-date schematic of the system.
- A description of the correct and safe operation of the system.
- The precautions to be taken.
- Checks to be carried out to ensure the scheme is successful and the frequency of such checks.
- Remedial action to be taken in the event that the scheme is shown not to be effective.

Conditions which allow legionella bacteria to proliferate should be avoided (e.g. water temperatures between 20°C and 45°C) including the creation of aerosols and sprays.

Record keeping

A record of the assessment, the precautionary measures and the treatments should be kept in a format that is accessible and retrievable. All records should be verified and signed by those people performing the various tasks assigned to them. This should ensure that precautions continue to be carried out and that adequate information is available at all times.

Responsibilities of manufacturers, importers, suppliers and installers

Designers, manufacturers, importers or suppliers of water systems have a legal obligation to ensure their systems can be operated, cleaned and maintained safely. The guidance provides a number of points to consider for the design and construction of water systems. These include fitting effective drift eliminators (cooling tower systems) and reducing stored cold water to a minimum required to meet peak periods (hot and cold water systems).

22.25 Code of Conduct

The WMS Code of Conduct was developed by various agents and organisations, including the Water Management Society, the HSE and BACS. The code is now promoted by the

Legionella Control Association and is designed to help building owner/operators select competent service providers by highlighting six critical areas:

❑   Allocation of responsibilities.
❑   Training and competence of personnel.
❑   Control measures.
❑   Communication and management.
❑   Record keeping.
❑   Reviews.

The Code specifies that there be a written agreement between the service provider and the client setting out the individual responsibilities of both parties. Adequate and up-to-date monitoring and treatment records should also be kept and retained for at least 5 years.

All competent service providers involved in the water management process will have signed up to the Code of Conduct and will be able to provide their client or FM with a copy of their certificate.

22.26 Risk assessment

The COSHH Regulations 1999, require the FM to carry out an assessment of the risks in the premises from exposure to legionella bacteria from all water systems. A written record of the findings of the risk assessment is required if the organisation employs five or more people. Failure to do so may lead to prosecution, especially if an incident has occurred that could have been reasonably anticipated if a formal risk assessment had been carried out.

If the occupant is a tenant in a managed building, it is the landlord's responsibility to ensure a risk assessment is carried out. However, the tenant and the landlord do have overlapping duties of care to the occupants. The FM should ask their landlord for written reassurance that a suitable risk assessment has been carried out and request a copy of the risk assessment report.

A thorough risk assessment will give the FM an action plan to help to eliminate or minimize the risks identified. The additional measures or controls required will protect the FM, work colleagues, all employees, staff, the public and the business.

Scope

The FM or duty holder is required to identify any significant risk presented by the workplace, working practices, products, etc. Therefore, all water systems (this includes showers, cooling towers, humidifiers and storage tanks) need to be assessed to judge:

❑   Whether legionella bacteria are liable to enter the system.
❑   Whether legionella bacteria grow in the system.
❑   Whether fine aerosols or water droplets are likely to be formed from the system.
❑   Who would be exposed to the droplets?
❑   Whether these people are in a susceptible group prone to contracting Legionnaires' disease?

In addition, the FM also needs to judge whether the current control measures are suitable and sufficient either to eliminate or control adequately the risks identified.

In order to identify the risks, the risk assessor will examine the maintenance documentation and water treatment records to ensure that the appropriate procedures are being followed and documented. The assessment should also incorporate:

❑   A detailed asset register of the water systems and the facilities they serve.
❑   A comprehensive schematic drawing or plan, to prove that all the systems that might present a risk in the premises have been identified and suitably assessed.

Ideally, someone with no vested interest in managing or servicing the water systems should carry out the risk assessment.

Frequency

The ACoP L8, Legionnaires' disease: 'the control of legionella bacteria in water systems', states that a risk assessment should be carried out every 24 months. However, if regular auditing identifies that significant control has been lost (such as repeatedly finding legionella in the water systems, such as cooling towers or showers), another risk assessment should be conducted. The same applies if any significant changes have occurred in the design and installation of building services.

22.27 Legionnaires' disease

Legionnaires' disease is a form of pneumonia which may affect other organs as well as the lungs. The disease was first identified when a number of ex-servicemen attending a 1976 convention in Philadelphia became sick with a pneumonia-like illness. The bacterium causing the illness was subsequently called *Legionella pneumophila*. Legionella causes both Legionnaires' disease and Pontiac fever. Pontiac fever is a milder disease with symptoms akin to acute influenza. No Pontiac fever fatalities have been reported.

The potential for an outbreak of Legionnaires' disease can arise in the pre-occupancy design, selection and construction processes, prior to any occupancy and building maintenance regimes. Legionella bacteria grow at temperatures between 20°C and 45°C. Water systems that generate droplets are those at risk, and include systems such as cooling towers, evaporative condensers, showers, humidifiers, spa baths and pools, and spray taps. If the droplets are contaminated with legionella bacteria and are inhaled, the person can potentially be infected with legionella. Legionella can be present in the water supplies of both new and old buildings.

Some facts about Legionnaires' disease

❑   It is caused by inhaling droplets that contain viable legionella bacteria that penetrate deep into the lungs.
❑   There is no evidence that it is transmitted by ingestion or from person to person.
❑   It has an incubation period that ranges between 2 and 10 days, usually 3–6 days.
❑   Males are more likely to be affected than females (ratio is about 3:1) and the age group between 40 and 70 years seems to be the most vulnerable.
❑   High risk individuals are smokers, alcoholics, cancer sufferers and those with respiratory or kidney diseases.
❑   The disease can be fatal but is treatable.
❑   Most outbreaks of Legionnaires' disease have been associated with poorly designed or maintained hot water services and recirculating cooling systems, such as those connected to air conditioning plant. (Cooling towers in industrial processes present the same hazards as those used in air conditioning systems.)

❑ Accumulations of sludge, scale, rust, algae and organic particulates are thought to provide an environment which favours growth of the bacterium.
❑ Man-made water systems with water temperatures in the region of 20–45°C also favour growth of the bacterium. However, it does not survive constant temperatures of 60°C or above and it is less common for it to multiply below 20°C.

22.28 The maintenance implications of Legionnaires' disease

These include:

(i) **Sampling** – Water systems may be colonised by legionella without being associated with infection. Sampling should be undertaken by a competent person (such a person has been defined elsewhere in the text). It should be understood that while sampling may yield positive results (the bacterium is so widespread in life), it is difficult to determine the risk solely on the results of a sample.

(ii) **Routine monitoring** – The maintenance programme should include the monitoring of cooling towers and associated water systems to control scaling, corrosion and fouling.

(iii) **Materials** – Some materials used in the construction of a system may encourage or support bacterial or fungal growth. Examples are some plastics, rubbers, jointing compounds or mastics. So as not to perpetuate their use, the advice of the local water supplier should be sought.

(iv) **System security** – The integrity of the following design features should be maintained:
  – Hot and cold water systems should be well enclosed to prevent the ingress of foreign matter. Supply tanks should have lids with overlapping edges and overflows should be protected with fine mesh screens.
  – Tanks and calorifiers should be readily accessible for cleaning.
  – Water should not stand undisturbed. (Beware oversized or underused tanks, calorifiers or pipes.) Two or more tanks in use should be in series.
  – Isolating valves and drain points for the removal of sludge should be incorporated in a system, or part of a system, that is only used intermittently.
  – Cold water tanks and pipes should not be located close to a heat source unless properly insulated.
  – Showers should be capable of being run below 20°C or above 50°C, without risk to users or be thermostatically controlled and mains fed or be automatically drained when the shower is shut off

22.29 Maintenance routines and operating procedures

Maintenance routines and operating procedures should be designed so as to minimise the risk to the individuals involved or affected. Water systems should be disinfected, drained, cleaned and then disinfected again:

❑ Before being taken into use.
❑ If they have been out of use for some time and not left dry.
❑ At regular intervals while the system is in use.

It is important that maintenance routines ensure that all parts of the system are disinfected, not just those parts readily accessible.

Where the throughput of water relative to the system volume can be low, legionella bacteria can become established and reach high concentrations, even where temperature regimes are followed. Legionella bacteria can survive for hours, even at 50°C.

It is not the absence (or presence) of legionella in a single sample that is significant. It is the existence of the circumstances that could lead to rapid growth of legionella to potentially hazardous levels. Ideally, these should be minimised by good design and operation but regular flushing may also be required where stagnation cannot be eliminated with certainty.

Air conditioning and industrial cooling systems should usually be scheduled for routine cleaning and disinfection each year in the early spring and autumn. More frequent cleaning may be necessary in a dusty atmosphere or for industrial applications. Systems in short seasonal use should be cleaned at the end of the season and then before being taken into use again, dealt with as a system that has been out of use for some time.

Maintenance routines should ensure that during cleaning, plant is inspected for damage or deterioration, with particular attention paid to cooling tower drift eliminators which minimise the escape of droplets. Regular discharging of water from cooling tower reservoirs helps to maintain water quality.

Water should be circulated at temperatures below 20°C or above 50°C. This may require the hot water to be stored above 60°C. As there is a real danger of scalding at 50°C, either safety notices must be posted alerting users to the dangers of hot water or fail safe devices must be incorporated in the system. In premises used by children, the elderly or disabled, the advantages of circulating hot water at 50°C may be outweighed by the risk of scalding.

Storage tanks and calorifiers should be inspected, cleaned and disinfected annually. It is good practice to discharge water from the bottom of the calorifier with sufficient frequency to prevent the build up of slime, scum or other deposits. Water treatment should be undertaken after expert advice from a competent person (consultant or water treatment company).

Building records should include precise details of systems that are susceptible to colonisation by legionella. There should be clear written testing, operation and maintenance procedures, and responsibility for the systems must be clearly defined.

22.30 Coliform bacteria

Coliform bacteria are a large group of various species of bacteria. They include both faecal coliform bacteria (bacteria that are found naturally in the intestines of warm-blooded animals) and non-faecal coliform bacteria. Coliform bacteria are indicator organisms. Their normal habitat is mammalian gut as well as soil and warm water. Many coliform bacteria do not cause disease and therefore do not pose any threat to human health. However, if coliforms are detected in drinking water it indicates that there may be more dangerous bacteria also present in the supply, such as Salmonella, and so on. One type of severe *Escherichia coli* (*E .coli*) poisoning can lead to abdominal cramps and watery diarrhoea. Fever and vomiting may also occur and most patients recover within 10 days.

Escherichia coli

Escherichia coli is a bacterium that is a common inhabitant of the gut of warm-blooded animals, including man. It is one species of faecal coliform bacteria and only grows in the mammalian gut. Therefore, its presence in drinking water is an indication of direct faecal contamination.

Contamination of the water supply can occur in the following ways:

❑ When there has been a leak of sewage into the drinking water source.
❑ Where staff or cleaners have employed poor hygiene practices, e.g. not washing one's hands after visiting the toilet then touching a water outlet, such as a tap.

22.31 *Pseudomonas aeruginosa*

This is another bacteria that may be found in water supplies. *Pseudomonas aeruginosa* is an opportunistic pathogen. The bacterium almost never infects healthy tissues, yet there is hardly any tissue that it cannot infect if the body's defences are compromised in some manner.

Pseudomonas aeruginosa is particularly good at forming biofilms. Its growth in drinking water can cause problems with colour, taste, odour and turbidity. Once established, biofilms can be difficult to eradicate from man-made water systems because they need a biodispersant (a chemical to breakdown the biofilm) and/or physical removal prior to disinfection.

Pseudomonas aeruginosa is very difficult to get rid of once established in a vending machine because of the inaccessibility of many of the components.

Contamination of vending machines and water coolers by *Pseudomonas aeruginosa* results from the bacteria either being introduced via the mains supply or through poor cleaning practices. Due to the often sporadic or low flow rates in the units, the bacteria can attach to the internal pipework surfaces and form a biofilm to protect themselves and start to multiply.

Pseudomonas aeruginosa can cause urinary tract infections, respiratory system infections, dermatitis, soft tissue infections and a variety of systemic infections, particularly in people with severe burns and cancer, or in HIV patients who are immunosuppressed. For 'healthy' people, it is more likely to cause problems with the taste and odour of drinking water and is not likely to have any dramatic effects on their health. However, the biofilms that *Pseudomonas aeruginosa* form could also be harbouring more dangerous bacteria such as coliform organisms and *E. coli*.

22.32 Water quality legislation

In the UK, the statutory instruments which apply to drinking water quality are the Water Supply (Water Quality) Regulations 1989 and the Water Supply (Water Quality) (Scotland) Regulations 1990. These regulations state that drinking water should have no unpleasant taste, colour, odour or turbidity. Nor should drinking water contain certain chemicals and microorganisms, such as coliform, *E. coli* or *Pseudomonas aeruginosa* bacteria.

This legislation is further enforced by the Workplace (Health, Safety and Welfare) Regulations 1992 which state that every employer has a duty to supply 'wholesome' drinking water. Furthermore, Report 71 (The Microbiology of Water 1994, Part 1 – Drinking Water) recommends that coliforms, *E. coli* or *Pseudomonas aeruginosa* are not present in a 100 ml sample of drinking water.

22.33 Water quality testing

Regular testing of drinking water supply by an independent company with no involvement in water treatment or maintenance of drinking water outlets, such as vending machine and water coolers, will ascertain whether coliforms or any other bacteria are present in the water system.

The microbiological quality of drinking water can be ascertained by using total viable bacteria counts to measure the effectiveness of water treatment and test samples for specific organisms to determine whether there has been any faecal contamination.

Drinking water supplied directly from the mains in the UK tends to be of an extremely high quality with over 99% of samples meeting the wholesome drinking water criteria. However, problems are frequently found with drinking water quality from vending machines and water coolers.

Detection

If coliforms are detected in a vending machine or water vending machine or water cooler, the following actions should be taken:

❑   Take the relevant machine out of service immediately.
❑   Disinfect the machine in accordance with the AVAB's (Automatic Vending Association of Britain) 'Code of Practice for Hygienic Machine Operation'.
❑   Review cleaning procedures to ensure that they comply with current recommended guidelines.
❑   Review and discuss procedures to minimise/remove contamination with vending contractor.
❑   A review of the location and usage of the machine(s).
❑   A regular review of water quality from the machines, ideally independent of the suppliers.

To avoid problems with cross-contamination of machines, it is extremely important to ensure that the staff responsible for the cleaning and sanitising of the vending machines or water coolers are correctly trained and aware of the potential for contamination during the cleaning process.

23 Construction Design and Management Regulations

23.1 Introduction

Poor management of construction projects is a major cause of accidents and of occupational health hazards in the building industry. In response to general concern over the level of avoidable illness and injury prevalent in construction, the Construction (Design and Management) Regulations 1994 came into force on 31 March 1995. The CDM Regulations were updated in 2007 to reduce the bureaucracy and put greater emphasis on management, planning, co-ordination and communication.

The CDM 2007 Regulations represent a step change in construction health and safety legislation. It brings the CDM 1994 Regulations and the Construction (Health, Safety and Welfare) Regulations 1996 into a single regulatory package providing a clearer focus on management, communication, co-operation and competence within the project team. The new CDM Regulations 2007 are published with an Approved Code of Practice.

The Management of Health and Safety at Work Regulations (1992) already requires employers and the self-employed to make effective requirements for managing health and safety in the work place. Employers must maintain a sufficient and appropriate risk assessment of all tasks they undertake. The CDM Regulations define these obligations with specific reference to the construction industry.

The CDM Regulations impose duties on all parties in a construction project to manage health, safety and welfare issues as part of a logical framework. Table 23.1 shows the duties of these parties. Clients – normally the person or representative of the commissioning firm, their agents, designers and contractors – must carefully consider their approach to health, safety and welfare when undertaking a construction project.

The Regulations cover the construction process from the design stage right through until the works are completed. A variety of personnel from different trade and professional backgrounds are involved in a construction project.

The aim of the new Regulations is to have the right people for the right job at the right time to manage risks on site. The amended Regulations are also supposed to reduce paperwork and encourage teamwork. The objectives of the new CDM 2007 regulations are to:

❑ Simplify the regulations and improve clarity.
❑ Focus on planning and management.
❑ Strengthen requirements on co-operation and co-ordination to encourage better integration of the duty holders.
❑ Simplify competence assessment, reduce bureaucracy and raise standards.

Table 23.1 Duty holders

Duty holder	Description
Clients	A 'client' is anyone having construction or building work carried out as part of their business. This could be an individual, partnership or company and includes property developers or management companies for domestic properties.
CDM co-ordinators	A 'CDM co-ordinator' has to be appointed to advise the client on projects that last more than 30 days or involve 500 person days of construction work. The CDM co-ordinator's role is to advise the client on health and safety issues during the design and planning phases of construction work.
Designers	The term 'designer' has a broad meaning and relates to the function performed, rather than the profession or job title. Designers are those who, as part of their work, prepare design drawings, specifications, bills of quantities and the specification of articles and substances. This could include architects, engineers and quantity surveyors.
Principal contractors	A 'principal contractor' (PC) has to be appointed for projects which last more than 30 days or involve 500 person days of construction work. The principal contractor's role is to plan, manage and co-ordinate health and safety while construction work is being undertaken. The PC is usually the main or managing contractor for the work.
Contractors	A 'contractor' is a business who is involved in construction, alteration, maintenance or demolition work. This could involve building, civil engineering, mechanical, electrical, demolition and maintenance companies, partnerships and the self-employed.

23.2 Notifiable works

The new Regulations apply to all construction work in the non-domestic sector. Notifiable work includes work lasting more than 30 days or involving 500 person days and all works involving demolition. Such works require the appointment of additional duty holders and duties in Part 3 of the Regulations and the statutory notification to the HSE (F10 Form) of the works. Most duties fall to the clients, designers and contractors. The former planning supervisor role under CDM 1994 has been removed and replaced with a new role entitled CDM co-ordinator.

One of the key changes is the clarified and enhanced client duty to ensure the adequacy of a construction project's health and safety management arrangements. The clients must now use their influence over the other project participants to ensure that things are done properly. Table 23.2 shows the client's duties. Where a project is notifiable to the HSE, the client is required to appoint a competent construction health and safety expert – the CDM co-ordinator – who must advise and assist the client with his/her duties. Because the client is liable for the adequacy of the management arrangements, there is a strong incentive to listen to the views of the CDM co-ordinator and ensure that everyone else does as well. The Regulations state that reaso-nable checks will suffice for non-notifiable projects. Non-notifiable works include any works to domestic premises, works that last less than 30 days or less than 500 person equivalent days.

Table 23.2   Client's duties

All projects	Notifiable projects
Check competence and resources of all appointees Ensure suitable management arrangements for the project Allow sufficient time and resources for all stages Provide pre-construction information to designers and contractors Appoint the right people Ensure client and the team communicate and co-operate	Appoint CDM co-ordinator Appoint PC Make sure that the construction phase does not start unless there are suitable welfare facilities and a construction phase plan is in place Advise contractors at tender stage how much time has been allowed for mobilisation Ensure the health and safety file is in place Retain the health and safety file

23.3 Changes to Regulations

There are a number of changes in the Regulations that the FM needs to be aware of. These are listed below:

❏ The new CDM co-ordinator will have more responsibilities for ensuring that all relevant project-specific information is compiled and included in the tender documents.
❏ The new Regulations have removed the Pre-tender Health and Safety Plan and replaced this statutory document with project-specific information being referred to as the 'pre-construction information pack'.
❏ The new ACoP provides advice on the content of this information pack in Appendix 2.
❏ The PC must produce the construction phase plan. Appendix 3 provides outline guidance on the contractor's 'construction phase plan' which remains in force and as before, must be considered 'adequate' by the client, prior to works commencing on site.
❏ The new competence criteria in the ACoP give greater clarity to the appointment and duties of the duty holders in Appendices 4 and 5.

A summary of the duties of the main duty holders in the Regulations is described in the following paragraphs.

23.4 CDM co-ordinator duties

❏ Advise client about selecting competent designers and contractors.
❏ Help identify what information will be needed by designers and contractors.
❏ Co-ordinate the arrangements for health and safety during the planning phase.
❏ Ensure that the HSE is notified of the project.
❏ Inform client if the initial construction phase plan is suitable.
❏ Prepare a health and safety file for the client.

23.5 Designer duties

❑ Make sure that they are competent and adequately resourced to address the health and safety issues likely to be involved in the design.
❑ Check that the client is aware of their duties.
❑ When carrying out design work, avoid foreseeable risks to those involved in the construction and future use of the structure, and in doing so, they should eliminate hazards (so far as is reasonably practicable, taking account of other design considerations) and reduce risk associated with those hazards which remain.
❑ Provide adequate information about any significant risks associated with the design.
❑ Co-ordinate their work with that of others in order to improve the way in which risks are managed and controlled.

23.6 PC duties

❑ Satisfy themselves that the client is aware of their duties (that a CDM co-ordinator has been appointed by the client and the HSE notified before they start work).
❑ Make sure that they are competent to address the health and safety issues likely to be involved in the management of the construction phase.
❑ Ensure that the construction phase is properly planned, managed and monitored, with adequately resourced, competent site management appropriate to the risk and activity.
❑ Ensure that every contractor who will work on the project is informed of the minimum amount of time which they will be allowed for planning and preparation before they begin work on site.
❑ Ensure that all contractors are provided with the information about the project that they need to enable them to carry out their work safely and without risk to health. Requests from contractors for information should be met promptly.
❑ Ensure safe working and co-ordination and co-operation between contractors.
❑ Ensure that a suitable construction phase plan ('the plan') is:
  o prepared before construction work begins;
  o developed in discussion with, and communicated to, contractors affected by it;
  o implemented;
  o kept up to date as the project progresses.
❑ Satisfy themselves that the designers and contractors they engage are competent and adequately resourced.
❑ Ensure suitable welfare facilities are provided from the start of the construction phase.
❑ Take reasonable steps to prevent unauthorised access to the site.
❑ Prepare and enforce any necessary site rules.
❑ Provide (copies of or access to) relevant parts of the plan and other information to contractors, including the self-employed, in time for them to plan their work.
❑ Liaise with the CDM co-ordinator on design carried out during the construction phase, including design by specialist contractors, and its implications for the plan.
❑ Provide the CDM co-ordinator promptly with any information relevant to the health and safety file.
❑ Ensure that all the workers have been provided with suitable health and safety induction, information and training.

❑   Ensure that the workforce is consulted about health and safety matters.
❑   Display the project notification.

23.7 Competence

In the past 'competence' has been open to interpretation. The new CDM 2007 Regulations put an end to this with clearer definitions and explanations as to the meaning and assessment of competence. According to the HSE, to be competent, an organisation or individual must have:

❑   Sufficient knowledge of the specific tasks to be undertaken and the risks which the work will entail.
❑   Sufficient experience and ability to carry out their duties in relation to the project; to recognise their limitations and take appropriate action in order to prevent harm to those carrying out construction work, or those affected by the work.

All persons who have duties under the CDM 2007 Regulations should:

❑   Take 'reasonable steps' to ensure persons who are appointed are competent.
❑   Not arrange for or instruct a worker to carry out or manage design or construction work unless the worker is competent.
❑   Not accept an appointment unless they are competent.

The above duties apply to both corporate and individual competence. The assessment of competence should focus on the needs of the particular project and be proportionate to the risk, size and complexity of the work.

CDM 2007 should streamline the competence assessment process. A key duty of the CDM co-ordinator is to advise the client about the competence of those employed by the client.

23.8 Corporate competency

Corporate competency should be assessed by a two-stage process:

Stage 1: An assessment of the company's organisation and arrangements for health and safety.
Stage 2: An assessment of the company's experience and track record.

Companies will be expected to reach the standards set out in the core criteria in CDM 2007 ACoP Appendix 4. The core criteria have been agreed between the construction industry and the HSE.

Duty holders can:

❑   Assess potential appointees against the core criteria or;
❑   Use independent accreditation schemes such as the Contractors Health and Safety Assessment Scheme (CHAS) or National Britannia Safe Contractor.

The agreed criteria will help prevent a diversity of demands from clients and others and reduce the amount of paperwork and bureaucracy.

23.9 Individual competency

Individual competency should be assessed by a two-stage process:

Stage 1: Assessment of knowledge, training records and qualifications, including basic understanding of site risks.
Stage 2: Past experience in the type of work the client is asking them to do.

Those new to construction work will need close supervision by a competent person until they can themselves demonstrate competence.

23.10 Designers' competency

When assessing the competence of individual designers, look for:

Stage 1: Membership of a professional institution, e.g. RIBA, CIAT, ICE, IStruct E, CIOB and so on.
Stage 2: Evidence of past experience in similar work.

The skills and knowledge of other designers must be taken into account if the work is to be carried out by a design team. Designers must be able to:

❏   Identify hazards, understand how they can be eliminated and address residual risk.
❏   Design in accordance with the Workplace (Health, Safety and Welfare) Regulations 1992.
❏   Identify significant remaining risks.
❏   Inform contractors.
❏   Co-operate and co-ordinate with the PC.

23.11 CDM co-ordinator

CDM co-ordinators play a key role in the CDM 2007 Regulations and need to:

❏   Have good interpersonal skills to encourage co-operation and co-ordination.
❏   Understand the design process and the need to co-ordinate designers' work.
❏   Have knowledge of health and safety in construction.
❏   Identify the key information others will need to know.

For smaller projects

Stage 1: Knowledge of the design process and health and safety in construction (e.g. qualification such as NEBOSH construction certificate, Membership of the Institute of Civil Engineers [ICE] health and safety register, Institute of Planning Supervisors [IPS], Association for Project Safety [APS] and so on).
Stage 2: Experience in applying the knowledge of construction.

For larger/higher risk projects

This person is likely to be a corporate CDM co-ordinator appointment. Appendix 5 of CDM 2007 ACoP provides detailed guidance on the competency required. The skills and knowledge of the CDM co-ordinator will need to reflect the complexity of the project and the specialist knowledge necessary to ensure that the risks are properly controlled.

23.12 Demolition

All forms of demolition are notifiable regardless of size, type or duration of project. This is due to the particular risks involved in this type of work – e.g. exposure of persons to hazardous materials and dust as well as more obvious risks such as falling masonry. In general, the Regulations imply that greater care must be taken in respect of the impact of building works upon the public. For example, problems that may arise around the perimeters of building sites and access points need to be carefully considered. These could include materials blowing or falling from a site, or equally by issues of unauthorised access. In addition, there are many risks encountered in excavations back filling, with potential problems from persons falling in.

23.13 Documents

(i) HSE F10 – Notification of Construction Project

This is the formal notice sent to the HSE regarding the nature of the project, dates, contractors, details of the local authority, client details, locations and nature of the project. The CDM co-ordinator completes the form. It must also be displayed at the site of the project. A copy of the form can be found under: https://www.hse.gov.uk/forms/notification/f10.pdf

(ii) Pre-construction Health and Safety Information Pack

This replaces the former health and safety plan. The pre-construction information provides information for those bidding or planning work, and for the development of the construction phase plan. Table 23.3 shows the contents of the information pack. The client, the designers and the CDM co-ordinator must work together to create the pack containing all the relevant project information.

(iii) Construction Phase Health and Safety Plan

The PC is responsible for production of this document. It will relate to the contractor's health and safety policy and assessments, together with that prepared by the CDM co-ordinator and details of potential risks that may arise as a result of work by subcontractors on the site. The plan may well evolve through the construction process, particularly if unforeseen issues arise out of the building process. Examples of this could be if ground conditions are affected during the process by bad weather or if dangerous or deleterious materials are found on site.

Sample contents

(i) General Project Information
(ii) Design Team

Table 23.3   Contents of the information pack

1 Description of project	Project description and programme details including:
	(i) key dates (including planned start and finish of the construction phase)
	(ii) the minimum time to be allowed between appointment of the PC and instruction to commence work on site
	Details of client, designers, CDM co-ordinator and other consultants
	Whether or not the structure will be used as a workplace (in which case, the finished design will need to take account of the relevant requirements of the Workplace [Health, Safety and Welfare] Regulations 1992)
	Extent and location of existing records and plans
2 Client's considerations and management requirements	Arrangements for:
	(i) planning for and managing the construction work, including any health and safety goals for the project
	(ii) communication and liaison between client and others
	(iii) security of the site
	(iv) welfare provision
	Requirements relating to the health and safety of the client's employees or customers or those involved in the project such as:
	(i) site hoarding requirements
	(ii) site transport arrangements or vehicle movement restrictions
	(iii) client permit-to-work systems
	(iv) fire precautions, emergency procedures and means of escape
	(v) 'no-go' areas or other authorisation requirements for those involved in the project
	(vi) any areas the client has designated as confined spaces
	(vii) smoking and parking restrictions
3 Environmental restrictions and existing on-site risks	(a) Safety hazards, including:
	(i) boundaries and access, including temporary access – e.g. narrow streets, lack of parking, turning or storage space
	(iii) any restrictions on deliveries or waste collection or storage
	(iv) adjacent land uses – e.g. schools, railway lines or busy roads
	(v) existing storage of hazardous materials
	(vi) location of existing services particularly those that are concealed – water, electricity, gas, etc.
	(vii) ground conditions, underground structures or water courses where this might affect the safe use of plant, for example cranes, or the safety of groundworks
	(viii) information about existing structures – stability, structural form, fragile or hazardous materials, anchorage points for fall arrest systems (particularly where demolition is involved)
	(ix) previous structural modifications, including weakening or strengthening of the structure (particularly where demolition is involved)
	(x) fire damage, ground shrinkage, movement or poor maintenance which may have adversely affected the structure

(Continued)

Table 23.3   (Continued)

	(xi) any difficulties relating to plant and equipment in the premises, such as overhead gantries whose height restricts access
	(xii) health and safety information contained in earlier design, construction or 'as-built' drawings, such as details of pre-stressed or post-tensioned structures
	(b) Health hazards, including:
	(i) asbestos, including results of surveys (particularly where demolition is involved)
	(ii) existing storage of hazardous materials
	(iii) contaminated land, including results of surveys
	(iv) existing structures containing hazardous materials
	(v) health risks arising from client's activities
4 Significant design and construction hazards	Significant design assumptions and suggested work methods, sequences or other control measures
	Arrangements for co-ordination of ongoing design work and handling design changes
	Information on significant risks identified during design
	Materials requiring particular precautions
5 The Health and Safety file	Description of its format and any conditions relating to its content

(iii)   Description and Nature of Work
(iv)   Organisation Responsibility
(v)   List of Responsible Persons
(vi)   Useful Contacts
(vii)   Training
(viii)   Setting Standards
(ix)   Information for Contractors
(x)   Selection Procedures
(xi)   Communications and Co-operation
(xii)   Activities with Risks to Health and Safety
(xiii)   Overlap with client's undertakings
(xiv)   Emergency Procedures
(xv)   Reporting of RIDDOR Information
(xvi)   Welfare
(xvii)   Information and Training for People on Site
(xviii)   Consultation with People on Site
(xix)   Site Rules
(xx)   Health and Safety File (see below)
(xxi)   Arrangements for Monitoring
(xxii)   Project Review

Health and safety file

This is similar to a normal maintenance manual but is specific for a CDM project. It will contain the information needed to allow future construction work, including cleaning, maintenance, alterations, refurbishment and demolition to be carried out safely. Information in the file should alert those carrying out such work to the potential risks, and should help them to decide how to work safely. It must be available to those who use the building following handover of the project. It is a record of information that will be referred to in future, when new works are undertaken to the building.

The file will contain information on the design of the structure and any additional information added during the construction phase by contractors. The client and the CDM co-ordinator will determine the format, scope and content of the file. The file should contain:

❑ A brief description of the work carried out.
❑ Any residual hazards which remain and how they have been dealt with (e.g. surveys or other information concerning asbestos, contaminated land, water-bearing strata, buried services and so on).
❑ Key structural principles (e.g. bracing, sources of substantial stored energy – including pre- or post-tensioned members) and safe working loads for floors and roofs, particularly where these may preclude placing scaffolding or heavy machinery there.
❑ Hazardous materials used (e.g. lead paint, pesticides and special coatings which should not be burnt off).
❑ Information regarding the removal or dismantling of installed plant and equipment (e.g. any special arrangements for lifting, order or other special instructions for dismantling and so on).
❑ Health and safety information about equipment provided for cleaning or maintaining the structure.
❑ The nature, location and markings of significant services, including underground cables, gas supply equipment, firefighting services, etc.
❑ Information and as-built drawings of the structure, its plant and equipment (e.g. the means of safe access to and from service voids, fire doors and compartmentalisation).

24 Business Continuity

24.1 Introduction

Business continuity management (BCM) can be defined as the ongoing process of ensuring the continual operation of critical business processes through the evaluation of risk and resilience and the implementation of mitigation measures. Plans should be subjected to comprehensive risk analysis.

The FM is usually expected to play a key role in emergency and disaster planning. They may have to develop business continuity plans that cover all aspects of the continuity cycle:

❑ Resilient design.
❑ Resilient operation.
❑ Service restoration.
❑ Salvage.
❑ Full recovery.

Business continuity management is a holistic management process that identifies potential impacts that threaten an organisation and provides a framework for building resilience and the capability for an effective response that safeguards the interests of its key stakeholders, reputation, brand and value creating activities.

Business continuity management comprises security, continuity and compliance. About 40% of businesses have no strategy for BCM in place. Continuous business success requires top management responsibility and commitment to a business continuity plan. Threats can be from man-made or natural disasters, from future terrorist attacks or environmental devastation. Risks faced by businesses include claims by employees or shareholders, oil price volatility, pension scheme legacies, terrorism, pandemics, climate change, political interventions and changes to financial systems. Losing access to business critical systems may put a business into jeopardy. Whilst complete protection from all threats and risks is impossible, successful businesses will have robust and well-rehearsed plans for business continuity.

Research shows that on average, a company will experience a major disruption about once every 4 years (see Table 24.1). Many of these companies will fail within another 2 years because they had no business continuity plan and were completely unprepared.

❑ Power failure – about 10% of business failures are due to power failures.
❑ IT failures – about 57% of business disasters are IT-related.

About 84% of companies do not identify risks in their supply chain, and 61% of companies do not publish their plans throughout the organisation.

Table 24.1   Average length of business interruptions and their cause

Fire	28 days
IT failure	10 days
Lightning	22 days
Flood	10 days
Theft	26 days
Power failure	1 day

24.2 Basic principles

FMs can follow some basic principles when establishing a business continuity ethos:

❏   Know your business.
❏   Know your location.
❏   Have a plan.
❏   Focus on communication.
❏   Practice.

24.3 Legislation

The Turnball Report by the Institute of Chartered Accountants (ICA) in 1999 raised the awareness of the consequences of not planning for future disruptions to business activities. Since this report, public listed companies and many others now have better processes in place to ensure their future. Legislation has also been developed as listed below:

❏   Basel II – affecting financial services sector.
❏   Sarbanes Oxley – affecting USA listed organisations.
❏   Companies Act 2006 – new requirements for enhanced corporate governance, directors to develop and test business continuity and emergency plans.
❏   Civil Contingencies Act 2004 – requiring government bodies and LAs to have plans in place to deal with various major incidents.

24.4 Standards

There are several sources of information on agreed standards in Business Continuity Planning.

❏   BS 25999.
❏   PAS 56 Guide to Business Continuity Management.
❏   BS ISO/IEC 7799.
❏   BS ISO/IEC 27001.

24.5 Impact on business

Organisations need business continuity plans to respond professionally to any incident that affects the business. It is important that the organisation's corporate reputation is safeguarded and customers, staff, shareholders and key stakeholders maintain that confidence in the organisation.

Plans should include identification of the key facilities and IT systems. It is important to apply the principles of business continuity to new development projects, such as new IT systems and buildings, in addition to the existing business activities.

24.6 Policy

An organisation should have a documented statement indicating the level of importance of BCM in the organisation. Table 24.2 shows the life cycle of BCP in an organisation. The policy statement should also outline the framework of BCM and will require commitment from the top of the organisation to get the support and resources to implement it.

A business continuity plan requires:

❑ Commitment from the highest and most senior managers in an organisation.
❑ Dedicated individuals in an organisation.
❑ Assistance from specialists.
❑ Informed staff to carry out the necessary procedures.
❑ Business units to undertake an assessment of their particular issues.
❑ Involvement from all levels.

An effective BCM will involve participation from all areas of an organisation.

❑ Managerial staff.
❑ Operational staff.

Table 24.2   Life cycle of BCM

1	Understanding the business	Organisation strategy Business impact analysis Risk assessment
2	BCM strategy	Corporate strategy Functional strategy Resource recovery strategy
3	Developing and implementing a BCM response	Crisis Management Plan Business Continuity Plan Business Unit Resumption Plans
4	Developing a BCM culture	Assessing awareness Developing culture Monitoring skills and culture
5	Exercise, maintenance and audit	Test and exercise Maintenance Audit

Table 24.3   BCP stages

1	Strategy	Determines the scope of the task and the resources required to complete it
2	Impact analysis	Examines the potential vulnerability of the business to unplanned interruption, the timescale over which the impact might be sustained and the financial consequences
3	Risk assessment	Assesses the likelihood of an event occurring and the degree of impact such an event might have on the business
4	Plan	Maps out the series of actions that may need to be taken to counter the identified threat to the business
5	Communication	Ensures that all who need to know the plan have effective knowledge of it and that it is tested and kept up to date

❑ Administrative staff.
❑ Technical staff.

24.7 Planning

There are five stages in business continuity planning as shown in Table 24.3.

24.8 Business impact analysis

Every organisation will have a unique threat and risk profile. The first step is to conduct an analysis of the potential risk. This will involve:

❑ A study of historical data – looking at previous emergencies in the neighbourhood, the company's premises and other businesses in the neighbourhood.
❑ An examination of the local environment – looking at the activities in the neighbourhood, such as transport routes and activities, manufacturing processes and storage of hazardous materials.
❑ An analysis of the technological risks – looking at both systems and human errors.

24.9 Corporate strategy

FMs should understand the key processes that their client's or employer's business need to function. FMs may also need to have a detailed understanding of existing IT business recovery plans: often business/disaster recovery is driven by the IT community. Business continuity, its importance and its focus will vary from business to business. However, for all key stakeholders – typically HR, finance, IT and communications, as well as the FM – working together is paramount.

A FM may wish to check their understanding of the organisation's corporate strategy by asking the following questions. This may help to focus the attention on the important business-critical aspects of the building and the FM services.

❑ What are the objectives of the organisation?
❑ How are the business objectives achieved?

Table 24.4 Examples of risks

Pure natural risks	Business commercial risks
Physical effects of nature, such as fire, storm, flood Technical events such as equipment failure Personal issues such as injury or disease Social impact such as theft, vandalism, violence and negligence	Impact of new technologies or changes in technology Impact of social change such as customer expectations or legal claims Economic impact such as inflation or funding constraints Political impact such as governmental legislation, policy and regulations

- ❑ What are the products/services of the organisation?
- ❑ Who is involved (internally and externally) to achieve these objectives?
- ❑ What are the time imperatives on the delivery of the products or services?

Knowing the premises and the business will help to identify the scope of the risks likely to be realised. Risks can be classified as pure natural risks or business commercial risks as shown in Table 24.4.

24.10 Critical assets

These can be defined as those assets which if lost, destroyed or malfunctioned would jeopardise the continuity of the business. They could be:

- ❑ Human.
- ❑ Physical.
- ❑ Intellectual property.

These assets will be affected by natural disasters, criminal activity, human error and terrorism, as shown in the list of risks earlier.

24.11 Hazards, consequences and impacts

On an organisation-wide basis, a three step analysis can be carried out. Firstly listing the hazards, then their consequence, and finally their impacts, as shown below. The following list of potential hazards and scenarios will be considered in the analysis:

- ❑ Fire.
- ❑ Flood.
- ❑ Terrorism.
- ❑ Lightning.
- ❑ Robbery.
- ❑ Riots.

- ❑ Activists.
- ❑ Storm damage.
- ❑ Exclusion zone.
- ❑ Transport accident (rail, road, air).
- ❑ Subsidence.
- ❑ Earthquake.
- ❑ Strike.
- ❑ Arrest (mistaken identity).
- ❑ Hostage/kidnap.
- ❑ Epidemic.
- ❑ Pollution.
- ❑ Loss of services.
- ❑ Equipment failure.
- ❑ Hackers.
- ❑ Virus.
- ❑ Product contamination.

In the analysis of each hazard above, the following consequences need to be worked through by the FM:

- ❑ Prohibited access to the premises.
- ❑ Loss of electrical power.
- ❑ Loss of communication lines.
- ❑ Ruptured gas mains.
- ❑ Water damage.
- ❑ Smoke damage.
- ❑ Structural damage.
- ❑ Air or water contamination.
- ❑ Explosion.
- ❑ Building collapse.
- ❑ Chemical release.

The impact on the actual core business must be then be considered, for example:

- ❑ Employees unable to work.
- ❑ Customers unable to get the services/products.
- ❑ Violation of contracts and contractual agreements.
- ❑ Fines or penalties.
- ❑ Legal costs.
- ❑ Cash flow.
- ❑ Loss of reputation and damage to image.
- ❑ Job losses.
- ❑ Failure of critical supplies being delivered.
- ❑ Distribution of goods to customers.
- ❑ Environmental damage.
- ❑ Shareholders loss of confidence and drop in share prices.
- ❑ Compliance with statutory obligations.

Table 24.5 Impact of risk to business

Criticality scales	Health and safety consequence	Staff reaction	Regulatory breach/legal enforcement	Loss of profit	Loss of goodwill	Management response
		Impact categories				
Very low	Minor injuries possibly	Dissatisfaction in one area				
Low	Minor injuries likely	Dissatisfaction in some areas				
Medium	More than minor injuries	Significant impact on performance				
High	Major injuries to limited numbers	General non-co-operation				
Very high	Likely to risk life with associated major injuries	Industrial action				

24.12 Benefits

A well-conducted business impact analysis will have a positive effect on the business by:

❑   Assuring employees that the matter is taken seriously by senior management.
❑   Involving suppliers in the process to ensure continuity of the supply chain.

24.13 Unavailability impact table

The results of the business impact analysis can be put into a table to show that the impact of business activities can be used to prioritise resources to restore key activities as illustrated in Table 24.5.

24.14 Risk assessment

The management of risks will require an assessment. This may be in the form of ranking and rating the likelihood and impact of various events. Multiplying 'likelihood' by 'impact' will provide an overall risk score. In the sample table (Table 24.6), the highest score is thus 25 and the lowest is 1. Once these assessments are made, risks can be ranked depending on their overall score as shown in Table 24.6.

Priorities in resources and training can then be determined to ensure readiness and preparedness to deal with the more likely and higher impact risks being realised.

Table 24.6   Worked risk assessment example

	Risk	Likelihood	Impact	Risk score (likelihood × impact)	Mitigation
1	Flood in computer room	3	5	15	High risk: consider relocating computer room; provide drip trays to pipe work
2	Fire in computer room	2	3	6	Lower risk on account of good housekeeping and fire suppression systems

24.15 Documents

Organisations may have two documents that make up their business continuity plan:

(i) Crisis Management or Emergency Plan.
(ii) Disaster Recovery Plan.

Smaller companies may have just one document combining the information of the two stages. The benefit of two documents is the separation of the two tasks involved in the management of the situation. When there are two teams involved in the situation each team will have their own process to follow. However, the downside is the need to keep both documents updated and consistent.

An emergency plan

An emergency plan is a policy document that gives guidelines on management of business continuity and all types of emergencies. This includes location of the emergency control centre, communication protocol, liaison with authorities and government agencies, roles and responsibilities of key personnel, details of fall back centres, alternative locations, control room or crisis centre procedures and media management details.

It may also include details on how staff and visitors will be identified and accounted for, general safety procedures and information to enable establishment of critical facilities.

Disaster recovery plan

The disaster recovery plan should help the person managing a major event and will help in the process of decision making and identify the appropriate course of action. It will include important information on dealing with particular disasters and an escalation process. Disasters are difficult to prevent or predict, but by anticipating their effects, it is hoped that the damage and disruption can be minimised. Typical major events include:

❑ Fire.
❑ Flood.
❑ Utility failure.
❑ Hazardous substances incident.

❑   Pollution.
❑   Storm damage.
❑   Terrorism (e.g. bomb threat, bio agents, hostage).
❑   Health incident (e.g. meningitis outbreak, legionella infection, asbestos contamination).

Ideally the disaster recovery plan will contain:

❑   An introduction.
❑   General administrative information, including addresses, telephone numbers and key facts about the organisation and staff.
❑   Escalation procedure, including command and control organisation.
❑   Contact information and processes.
❑   Response and recovery procedures, including list of questions regarding the incident such as:
    ○   Have there been any casualties?
    ○   What has happened and how serious is it?
    ○   What facilities have been affected and is their loss a short-, medium- or long-term prospect?
    ○   What access is there to the premises and if not, when will this be possible?
❑   Locations of specific contingency plans.
❑   Building information in both hard copy and CD-ROM format.
❑   Building floor plans.
❑   Location of fire isolation valves.
❑   Details of fire alarm panel location and zones.
❑   Location of flammable substances.
❑   Location of hazardous substances.
❑   Location of mains electricity isolation systems.
❑   Location of gas mains isolation valves.
❑   Location of water isolation mains valves.
❑   Review and audit process.

24.16 Implementation

The plan should be kept simple and concise as this will ensure it is actually read and kept up to date. It will need updating frequently with any changes in staff, buildings, procedures and technology A checklist is useful to ensure all areas are covered. See Figure 24.1.

24.17 Two-team approach

The majority of organisations will appoint two teams to manage business continuity. One team will focus on the actual event or disaster, whilst the other focuses on restoring operations. The issues these teams will have to deal with include:

❑   Damage assessment and salvage.
❑   Recovery of IT systems.

Chain of command	Management structure
	Depends on empowerment
	Crisis manager and support team
Communication	List of key personnel
	Cascade list of remaining staff contacts
	Customer contacts
Control centre	Safe, pre-identified location
	Control centre fully equipped
	Known to key personnel
Evacuation	Defined routes
	Muster points
	Named marshals and their duties
Important information	Emergency services details
	Organisation organograms
	Roles and responsibilities
	Key supplier details
Alternative sites	Pre-identified location
	Hot – fully equipped
	Warm – basic facilities
	Cold – building only
	Reciprocal arrangements
Key equipment needs	IT
	Building services
	Communications
	Stationery
	PPE
Vital records	Identification
	Storage
	Updates
	Reconstruction
Outline recovery strategy	Critical elements
	Reaction timescales
	Impact of work flows
	Alternative manual procedures
Media relations	One individual
	Authority
	Expertise
Transport	Staff
	Equipment
Protection and salvage	Damage limitation
	Security
	Identify contractors
Compliance	Protection of data
	Advise regulatory authorities
Staff	Medical facilities
	Counselling
	Catering
	Communication

Figure 24.1   BCP checklist

Table 24.7   BCP teams

Business continuity team	Personnel team	Communication/media team
Policy Strategic decisions Guidance to the crisis management team Update of policy, documents	Accounting for staff and visitors Providing a link between emergency services, company and relatives Company welfare policy Focal point in directing staff post-disaster	Managing and controlling the media and media activity Who speaks to and what is said to the media When it should be said and who deals with the questions What medium or format should be used

❑ Recovery of communications systems.
❑ Restoration of premises.
❑ Purchasing of salvage and recovery items.
❑ Public relations and media management.
❑ Recovery of operations and normal day-to-day core business activities.
❑ Welfare support to those directly affected.
❑ Insurance company liaison.
❑ Dealing with various agencies and enforcement authorities – depending on the nature of incident.

24.18 Crisis management team

A crisis management team will need to deal with the internal and external issues. It is best practice to set up a separate personnel response team and a communications response team. Each team has specific responsibilities as shown in Table 24.7.

24.19 Logistics

This aspect of business continuity planning deals with:

❑ Access to premises.
❑ Salvage, demolition and safety.
❑ Equipment substitution.
❑ Cessation of contracts and activation of others.
❑ Security of premises.
❑ Power supplies and regeneration of consumables.
❑ Relocation of premises.
❑ Transport and removal.

24.20 Telephony and data communications

The main issues to consider are:

❑ Quick access to telephones to continue business.
❑ Fax access.

❑ Pre-arranged recovery options and contracts with suppliers and providers.
❑ Managing the increased volume of telephone traffic during the incident.
❑ Allocating extra staff to deal with the extra workload.
❑ Control of the use of mobile phone traffic during and after the incident.
❑ Access to Internet, update of information.
❑ Access to intranet for internal communications.

24.21 Testing the plan

The final and most critical step is to test the plan and carry out regular rehearsals. It is vital to engage all senior management in testing the plans on a regular basis. Testing can take many different forms, from full computer simulation, role playing, to actual isolation of a building or an area. Desktop exercises and 'walking through' a plan are also well worth doing.

The benefits of a desktop or actual rehearsal is that the weaknesses in the plan are identified. It also identifies the roles that key staff have to perform to execute the plan. It is recommended that a rehearsal is done twice a year, and repeated if there are any major hiccups until it runs smoothly.

It is equally important to maintain records of plans and of all tests. Much will be learned and improvements identified which will need recording. Above all the organisation needs to ensure that the improvements are incorporated into the plan.

24.22 Upkeep of records

Simple things such as lists of key telephone contacts need to be maintained and reviewed on a regular basis. Remember that the contents of any disaster recovery files that are kept off site must also be updated.

24.23 Audit

Most disaster recovery plans will also benefit from regular review by a third party not connected to the business. For example, the insurance company may be able to review the plans in return for a lower premium. Alternatively, an external specialist could be used.

25 Maintenance – Definitions and Strategies

25.1 Introduction

Buildings could be said to be a nation's most valuable assets, providing people with shelter and facilities for work and leisure. The importance of maintenance can be judged from its relationship to the building industry and to the gross national product (GNP). Maintenance represents 40% of the output of the building industry, and in turn the building industry represents about 10% of the UK GNP. Maintenance is defined in several ways (see Table 25.1).

A prime aim of maintenance is to preserve a building in its initial state as far as practicable, so that it effectively serves its purpose. Essentially, maintenance is to:

❑ Retain the value of a building.
❑ Maintain full use of the building.
❑ Provide working/living environments that are safe.
❑ Reduce accidents and injuries arising from defects or deterioration of a building.
❑ Retain a good appearance or image.
❑ Meet contract obligations in a lease.
❑ Prolong the life of a building.
❑ Meet insurers requirements, reducing claims and costs.
❑ Meet guarantee and warranty obligations.

Table 25.1   Maintenance definitions

British Standard BS 3811	'The combination of all technical and associated administrative actions, including supervision actions, intended to retain an item in, or restore it to, a state in which it can perform its required function.'
Chartered Institute of Building (CIOB)	'Building maintenance work is undertaken to keep, restore or improve every facility, i.e. every part of a building, its services and surrounds to an agreed standard, determined by the balance between need and available resources.'

Every building faces deterioration over time. The process can be accelerated by neglect or delayed by proper care. Proper maintenance is cheaper, quicker and easier than resorting to major repairs or rebuilds. The principal criteria that influence the decision to carry out maintenance work are:

❑ Cost.
❑ Age.

❑   Condition of property.
❑   Availability of adequate resources.
❑   Urgency.
❑   Future use.
❑   Sociological considerations.

25.2 Maintenance priorities

It may be difficult to formulate a precise order of priorities of maintenance activities as they are so diverse. A possible order of priority is shown:

❑   Work required for health and safety, such as emergency exits and fire precautions.
❑   Work required to preserve the structure, such as essential roof repairs and external painting.
❑   Work required for occupational efficiency, such as increased lighting.
❑   Amenity work, mainly internal, such as interior decorations.

Classifications

There are a number of maintenance classifications defined in BS 3811 as shown in Table 25.2.

25.3 Maintenance policy

A fundamental tenet of a building's maintenance policy is that in addition to protecting the asset value, it should protect both the resource value of the premises concerned and the owner/occupier against breaches of statutory and legal obligations. It should:

❑   Define the organisation's view of the need to protect the value of its assets as represented by the premises.
❑   Demonstrate how premises and equipment are perceived to contribute to organisational image and the efficiency and effectiveness of staff.
❑   Reflect the criticality of maintainable elements and components to the performance of essential core functions.
❑   Reflect the organisational attitude to its statutory and legal obligations.

Factors to consider

The maintenance policy statement should cover anticipated future requirements for the use of the building. The following factors should be included in a maintenance policy:

❑   Physical performance and functional suitability of the building.
❑   Impact of any regeneration, adaptation or change of use on the life cycle of building elements or components.
❑   Statutory requirements and legal obligations.
❑   Cyclic maintenance work such as those defined by the statutory and legal obligations, building element or component maintenance profile, or manufacturers' warranties.
❑   Value for money.

Table 25.2   Maintenance classifications

Planned maintenance	'The maintenance organised and carried out with forethought, control and the use of records to a predetermined plan.'
Preventive maintenance	'The maintenance carried out at predetermined intervals, or to prescribed criteria and intended to reduce the probability of failure or degradation of the functioning of an item.' The terms *planned maintenance* and *preventive maintenance* are often heard used together as planned preventive maintenance. This is largely because preventive maintenance is always part of a planned maintenance programme. The concept is one of cyclical preventive action aimed at the avoidance of failure. It usually relates to items subject to mechanical or other wear and tear, or constant exposure to the elements.
Condition-based maintenance	'This is maintenance carried out according to the need indicated by condition monitoring.' The objective is to avoid unnecessary preventive maintenance and to reduce the failure rate. Initial costs of introducing condition-based maintenance are high and have to be weighed against the cost to the core operation in the event of equipment failure. High initial costs are attributable to the cost of the skilled labour required to set up the system, the sophisticated monitoring instrumentation necessary and the management techniques involved.
Running maintenance	'Maintenance that can be carried out whilst the item is in service.' In other words, the item can be maintained without being disabled and thus incurring down time/loss of service. Clearly, there will be occasions when it will be necessary for an item to be in a disabled state while it is maintained.
Corrective maintenance	'The maintenance carried out after a fault has been identified and is intended to put an item into a state in which it can perform its required function.'
Reliability centred maintenance	This is 'A systematic approach for identifying effective and efficient preventive maintenance tasks for equipment and items in accordance with a specific set of procedures and for establishing intervals between tasks.'
Emergency maintenance	'This is maintenance that it is necessary to put in hand immediately to avoid serious consequences.' Emergency maintenance is invariably disruptive and expensive. Contributing factors are: ❑ Accidental damage. ❑ Equipment defect. ❑ Fire, flood or storm damage. ❑ Lack of planned, preventive maintenance. ❑ Premature failure of an item or equipment. ❑ Sabotage. ❑ Terrorist activity. ❑ Vandalism.
Breakdown maintenance	BS 8210 adds the following definition to the above: 'Operation of restoring an item to fulfil its original function after a failure in its performance.'
Fixed cost maintenance	This is a relatively new variation on the theme of planned preventive maintenance which has not so far been defined by a BS. It includes responsibility for the capital cost of any replacement plant necessary. Its success depends on the sound application of financial and technical skills. Contracts are for 10 years and a significant attraction is that the building operator will not be faced with unbudgeted capital expenditure on contracted items over the term of the contract.

25.4 Computerised maintenance management systems (CMMS)

There are many computer systems available to help the FM develop a maintenance programme and manage the maintenance activities. Essentially, CMMS are databases which list all the assets of a building, the routines that must be carried out, the labour that can be used, the charge rates for the labour, and the materials required. These systems will generate the planned preventative jobs for work by the operatives. Most systems will be linked to a helpdesk or fault-reporting system so the ad hoc jobs can be recorded against each asset too.

The establishment of the asset inventory is the most challenging and time-consuming aspect. It will require an agreement on the level at which the work will be recorded. For example, are all the doors to be separately identified as individual assets, or are the doors to be listed under one generic asset – 'doors'? This is fundamental, as it will determine how future management reports are generated to aid decision making and asset tracking.

25.5 Maintenance programmes

An FM needs to devise and implement maintenance programmes for each element of building services, often in conjunction with other specialists. The benefits of a maintenance programme are numerous and include:

- ❑ Preserve installed services and value of the premises.
- ❑ Maintain optimum performance of the services.
- ❑ Comply with statutory and legal requirements.
- ❑ Ensure value for money – effective and efficient maintenance and repairs.
- ❑ Budget management to spread expenditure evenly over a period of years.
- ❑ Preserve warranties and guarantees following new installations.
- ❑ Create an effective and efficient working environment for occupants.
- ❑ Schedule of works for optimum use of workforce.
- ❑ Minimise disruption to occupants.

A maintenance programme is time based and allocates specific maintenance tasks to specific periods. Table 25.3 gives some examples of likely frequencies of maintenance.

In the case of a new building, maintenance programmes will be largely based on manufacturers' instructions and advice from the professional team. Maintenance programmes for second-hand stock are likely to be based on the outcome of a condition survey or an annual inspection of the estate.

25.6 Maintenance activities

The following examples of building maintenance can be found included in a planned preventive maintenance programme:

- ❑ Drainage.
- ❑ Guttering.
- ❑ Car park repairs.
- ❑ Curtain walling.

Table 25.3   Maintenance frequencies

Example of maintenance activity	
Daily	Fire doors – check closers and mechanisms Carpets – check no trip hazards
Weekly	Grass cutting in peak growing periods (intervals may be 9 or 10 days on either side of peak growing periods)
Monthly	Playground equipment – inspect, test and report
Quarterly	Clean/clear grease traps
Six monthly	Check gutters and drains – remove build up of debris and other rubbish
Annually	Double glazing – inspect sealant and replace defective
2 yearly	Kitchen redecoration Gulleys and drainage inspection and cleaning
5 yearly	External redecoration Re-mark car park Carpet renewal Playground equipment condition tests
10 yearly	Check flat roof Check and resurface car parks
25 yearly	Resurface roadways

❑ Doors.
❑ External decorations.
❑ External cleaning.
❑ Fenestration.
❑ Gardening, including grass cutting, litter and autumn leaves collection and disposal.
❑ Internal decoration.
❑ Road and path surfaces.
❑ Roofs.
❑ Snow and ice clearance.

25.7 Maintenance schedules

Maintenance schedule formats will vary from organisation to organisation and contractor to contractor. An example is shown in Table 25.4. All schedules will include the items listed below:

❑ The location of the item(s) to be maintained.
❑ An item description.
❑ The tasks to be performed and the frequency with which the maintenance work should be done.
❑ The quantity of like items to be maintained where there is more than one.
❑ The condition of the item at last inspection.

Table 25.4   Example maintenance schedule

Item	Sub-item	Frequency	Action	Notes
A brief and clear description of the main item	Each sub-item is listed	The frequency with which the sub-items should be maintained	Gives the maintenance action to be performed	Action to be taken by the maintenance operator in the event of failure or degradation
Hot water cylinders	Connections	Monthly	Check for leaks	If leaks found, drain down, clean and make good

Table 25.5   Maintenance scheduling issues

Safety	Safe operation of plant and the immediate environment. Adequate accessibility to items to be maintained, appropriate lighting and proper ventilation. Responsibility for safe access should be clearly defined.
Hygiene	Maintenance in food storage, food handling and food preparation areas must be carried out so as to avoid contamination. Maintenance operators working in these areas must wear appropriate protective clothing and maintain the highest standards of personal cleanliness. Maintenance operators must have a basic knowledge of food hygiene. They must be aware of accident-reporting procedures and if suffering from certain infectious diseases should know of the necessity for their exclusion from working in these areas. When maintenance work on dirty systems (e.g. WCs, sewage pipes) is carried out in food premises, maintenance operators should be aware of the need for cleaning and sanitising the area in order to avoid contamination with pathogenic organisms. Operators working in such areas should also understand the need to ensure that any contaminated clothing is washed before further use and that unprotected parts of the body should be thoroughly washed before continuing to work in food areas. These considerations should apply to operators working under dirty conditions which may affect the hygiene conditions of that area.
Electrical	Electrical equipment used for maintenance work must be capable of local isolation and be selected/erected in accordance with the Regulations of the Institution of Electrical Engineers (IEE Regulations).
Gas	The Gas Safety (Installation and Use) Regulations 1984 and amendments apply. Persons working on gas equipment should be registered with a body approved by the HSE. The Pressure Systems and Transportable Gas Regulations 1989 apply.

❏ The time it should take to perform the task.
❏ The person competent to perform the task (e.g. 'B' for bricklayer, 'C' for carpenter, 'E' for electrician, 'F' for fitter, 'M' for mechanical engineer, 'P' for plant attendant).

Other considerations in planning and scheduling the maintenance activities are shown in Table 25.5.

25.8 Controlling maintenance work

Figure 25.1 shows how maintenance work can be controlled at both strategic and operational levels with feed back and feed forward loops typical of most control systems.

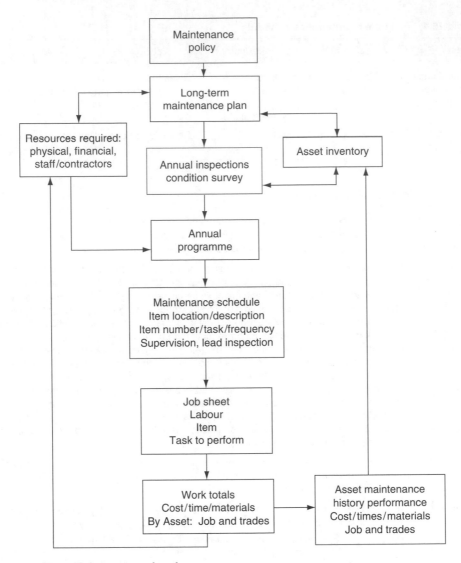

Figure 25.1   Maintenance planning

25.9 Building records

There are two types of building records. These are:

(i) The 'as built' records which should be handed over either before or when the post-occupancy phase begins. These records will include drawings, CDM files and the operation manuals.
(ii) The records which are kept during occupancy.

Table 25.6   Building records

General	Records should include location details, testing and commissioning data, appropriate test certificates, equipment type, model, serial number and manufacturer.
Premises	Block and site plans, general arrangements of floors and the roof with elevations and sections, foundation plans, structural plans and sections with details of permissible floor loadings, construction details of external elevations.
Mechanical	Fuel, gas, cold water, piped services and their associated apparatus, air ducts, silencers, grills and diffusers.
Electrical	Main and sub-main cables, lighting conduits, sub-circuit cables, switches, draw-in and point boxes. Lighting and emergency light fittings, single-phase and three-phase circuit details, lightning conductor details, earth tapes, electrodes and test points, smoke detectors and sprinklers, incoming supply details to include type of system, voltage, frequency and rated current. IEE Regulations completion certificate.
Communications	Floor plans of equipment rooms and operator rooms. Cabling details for exchange, private circuit, extension and coin box details, extension, etc., outlet drawings and pager information.

A significant problem for the FM team is getting the as-built drawings, building operating manuals and CDM documentation in sufficient time to enable a maintenance strategy and maintenance routines to be developed. Table 25.6 shows the scope of the records needed for effective maintenance planning. Without them there is a danger that manufacturers' warranties may be jeopardised by ill-advised fine tuning or tinkering which might result in premature failure or partial failure of equipment or services. The CDM documentation is that required under the Construction (Design and Management) Regulations 2007.

Having obtained the as-built records and operating manuals, it is essential that they are kept up to date. They provide the continuity that is necessary as the building evolves to meet the changes that will inevitably take place once it is in use. The up-to-date records are essential for the conduct of effective maintenance policy and are an important planning tool when building modifications, improvements or regeneration are being considered.

British Standard 8210 provides guidance for a systematic approach to building maintenance management which includes recommendations that records should contain information about legal obligations under leases (e.g. periodic external redecoration requirements relating to party or boundary walls, statutory and insurance inspections, any rights of way).

25.10 Annual inspections

Annual inspections are a visual examination which provide the latest check on the condition of the buildings, the building services and the surrounds. They:

❑ Confirm whether the work in the long-term plan actually needs to be done.
❑ Determine if there is work in the long-term plan that might need to be brought forward, due to unforeseen degradation or failure.
❑ Highlight items that were not previously included in the long-term plan.

❑ Provide a check that work previously carried out conforms to the specification and the required standard.
❑ Confirm whether the specification for work was appropriate.
❑ Provide indicators as to the performance of the maintenance system.

The annual inspection can be expected to be carried out by a competent person and follow the format of a condition survey.

25.11 Condition surveys

The condition survey is an important inspection and appraisal tool which contributes to effective building maintenance.

A condition survey is a periodic (usually five-yearly sounds) internal and external technical inspection and appraisal of a building carried out by a qualified professional (a surveyor for the building fabric and an appropriate engineer for the building services). The survey concentrates on the elements considered to be most at risk or likely to fail and on identifying repair or renewal requirements over an agreed time span. A checklist is used to grade the elements according to the severity of any defects found and thus the urgency of the requirement for maintenance work. A condition survey will establish whether essential maintenance is overdue. The information in the report will be used to establish short-, medium- and long-term maintenance costs and priorities, which will include deciding whether work can be deferred or whether it should be brought forward.

In some cases, a condition survey is required earlier than planned because:

❑ There is a perception that the building interior, its fabric and/or building services have deteriorated to an unacceptable degree. Indicators might be the image projected by a building, poor morale reflected by the extent of user dissatisfaction with the building and building services.
❑ Maintenance costs appear unacceptably high.
❑ The lack of a clear maintenance strategy.

25.12 Planning the survey

The essentials to organising a condition survey are:

❑ A list of elements to be surveyed must be drawn up by location and element.
❑ The property appraisal and recording procedures must be agreed. A consistent approach to the collection of necessary data to recognised criteria that will allow for benchmarking is essential, whether it be a manual one, using pre-formatted check sheets, or one conducted using hand-held computers.
❑ The suitability of any appraisal forms proposed by professional advisors must be verified or appropriate sheets created. These will be the basis of the surveyor's report and the maintenance plan. Headings could be:
  o Property and locational details.
  o The element/component – e.g. roof, structure, external staircase, fenestration.
  o Material – e.g. slate, brick, steel, hardwood, glazing.
  o Life expectancy as assessed by the surveyor.

o An assessment of approximate cost of work proposed.
o Condition as assessed by the surveyor or engineer with the grading clearly defined. Examples of gradings used in most surveys are:
A – Component is as good as new.
B – Some minor deterioration is evident. Requires maintenance to ensure a continued satisfactory state.
C – Is operational but in need of major repair.
D – Replacement is the only realistic option.
❏ The work required and its priority for action, as assessed by the surveyor or engineer. The first priority for maintenance is health and safety, closely followed by the avoidance of adverse effects on the business.
❏ The basis on which the assessment of approximate costs is made must be agreed. This will usually be one of the proprietary building maintenance costs (e.g. BMI Building Maintenance Price Book).
❏ Site plans and any previous survey reports, together with action taken, should be made available to the surveyors.
❏ Proper access arrangements for surveyors.

It is likely that the surveyors will have to carry out some of the work outside normal hours because to do so during normal hours might be unacceptably disruptive in some areas. They may require access to sensitive areas, or need to use a cradle to examine the outside of a building. It follows that the access arrangements must be made with building users as well as with the surveyors. The arrangements must also take account of any security requirements.

25.13 Component life cycles

There are some key terms to understand when considering the maintenance likely during the life cycle of a building. These are shown in Table 25.7. An anticipated post-occupancy life cycle of a building component may extend to 80 or more years, depending on the impact of obsolescence. The elements and components that make up the finished building are themselves subject to obsolescence.

In reliability terms, components can be expected to have a life cycle which follows the pattern shown in the bathtub curve in Figure 25.2.

Table 25.7   Definitions

Obsolescence	The process of becoming obsolete by way of reduced physical, functional or financial performance over time.
Obsolete	Disused, discarded, worthless, out of date.
Element	'The major parts of a building that are recognisable as performing a key function within the structure, services, finishes or surrounds into which they are built.'
Component	'A specific item within the fabric, services or finishes of a building whose breakdown or decay would lead to a failure or progressive deterioration in performance in the element of which it forms a part.'

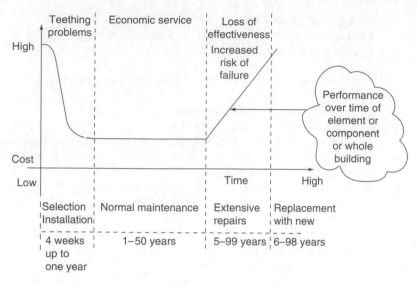

Figure 25.2   Bathtub curve of maintenance

25.14 Bathtub curve

From the bathtub curve (Figure 25.2) it can be seen that after the initial high costs connected with selection, installation and early teething troubles, there is a long period of economic service life, during which the component, or element, undergoes normal maintenance. This is followed by a period when the effectiveness of the item is reduced and there is an increased risk of failure. Costs during this period increase rapidly and there comes a point when it makes both financial and functional sense to replace the equipment before it fails.

The bathtub curve is a useful and valid generalisation which has its origins in the discipline of reliability engineering, the thrust of which is the prediction of performance with the aim of improving reliability over time.

25.15 Element and component life expectancies

A selection of target life expectancies for building elements and components is shown in Figure 25.3. This is not meant to be a definitive list. Its purpose is to give some relative examples of building components and elements.

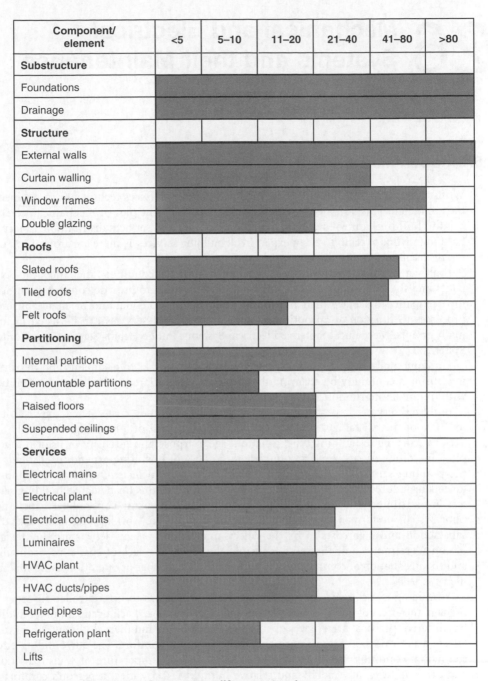

Component/element	<5	5–10	11–20	21–40	41–80	>80
Substructure						
Foundations						
Drainage						
Structure						
External walls						
Curtain walling						
Window frames						
Double glazing						
Roofs						
Slated roofs						
Tiled roofs						
Felt roofs						
Partitioning						
Internal partitions						
Demountable partitions						
Raised floors						
Suspended ceilings						
Services						
Electrical mains						
Electrical plant						
Electrical conduits						
Luminaires						
HVAC plant						
HVAC ducts/pipes						
Buried pipes						
Refrigeration plant						
Lifts						

Figure 25.3 Element and component life expectancies

26 Mechanical and Electrical Systems and their Maintenance

26.1 Introduction

Whilst it is not essential that FMs are qualified building services technicians or engineers, the competent FMs does need an understanding of the principles of mechanical, electrical and building control systems, structured cabling and services distribution. In fact it's hard for anyone to claim to be an expert in all building services as there are around 130 different disciplines involved!

Building services determine the internal environmental conditions that affect the occupants and the business processes. Maintenance is essential to provide comfort conditions for occupants to achieve their maximum performance potential and to enable business processes to function at an optimum level. The range of services can be listed in four main groups: Mechanical Systems, Electrical Systems, Public Health Services and Control Systems.

Fundamentally, maintenance is about minimising the risks to occupants and maximising business continuity by ensuring that building services are kept in a usable condition with minimal interruption of availability of the services.

Building services have a significant impact on facilities costs. They may account for 30% of the capital cost and 50% of the operating cost of a building. Obviously this varies according to building type, function, age, purpose and intensity of use (in a hospital, building services could account for up to 80% of operating expenditure). Many of the building service problems that FMs face arise from defects. Over 50% of building defects or failures are due to design errors and 45% of claims for defective building services are attributable to design. These defects give rise to many consequences including poor system performance, inability to commission, unsafe working, occupant/user dissatisfaction and high costs to fix the defects and failures. Many defects are due to lack of consideration to how the services fit into the space. The lack of spatial co-ordination and the installation of complex systems gives rise to a number of operational and maintenance issues.

A building is a climatic zone in its own right, which has to be controlled in order to manage the effect of pollution, heat gains and external noise. Each occupant in a building has different personal preferences due to their metabolism and their clothing. This in turn affects a person's skin temperature and their feeling of comfort. The surrounding environmental conditions, such as air temperature, surface temperature of walls, partitions and other fixtures, air velocity and relative humidity (RH), affect a person's comfort in their working space. The typical parameters in many offices are 22°C $\pm$ 2° with an RH of between 40% and 60%. It is also important to consider the person's age, activities and processes within the spaces, so parameters in residential or leisure spaces may be quite different to the traditional office.

26.2 HVAC

Heating systems may comprise radiators, convectors, underfloor systems, radiant systems, warm air units and boilers. Some organisations may use combined heat and power (CHP) systems. Air conditioning systems permit full control of air temperature, humidity, freshness and cleanliness of air in a building space. Typically they are expensive and complex with many controls. They require a large amount of space in a building and require maintenance specialists to ensure that they are running correctly. For effective air conditioning, a building is divided into zones or areas.

When installing and maintaining HVAC plant, the FM must consider:

❑   Acoustics – required temperatures have to be achieved within acceptable levels of noise. Fans and extraction equipment can generate noise in closed spaces.
❑   Thermal comfort – this has to be achieved by balancing the conflicting demands of statutory requirements, climatic conditions, the functions being performed and the need for energy conservation.
❑   Adequate natural or mechanical ventilation – Ventilation is provided so that the conditions in the building are conducive to safe working, comfort and efficiency.

26.3 Heating systems

Heating systems found in buildings include:

❑   Radiators.
❑   Convectors.
❑   Underfloor systems.
❑   Radiant systems.
❑   Warm air units.
❑   Boilers.

These work by generating heat in two ways:

(i)   direct heat output;
(ii) indirect heat output.

26.4 Direct heating systems

Direct heating systems are so called because they deliver heat directly from the source. Examples of direct systems are open fires, night storage heaters and radiant heaters.

Radiant heating systems work on the basis of warming people and not the air. They are good for high, tall industrial or sports spaces. They are ceiling mounted so this frees up floor and wall space. No circulation of warm air is needed and there are many different types available to suit the space. Radiant heating systems can be:

❑   Gas-fired.
❑   Electric.
❑   Hot water fed.

The disadvantages of radiant heating are the regular safety checks required, possible discolouring of materials stored in the space being heated, the compliance to statutory regulations and issues of access for maintenance staff.

26.5 Indirect heating systems

Indirect heating systems use a carrying medium such as air, water or steam and deliver heat via a heat exchanger such as a radiator or convector. Hot water systems are the most common and there are three types:

(i)	Low temperature systems	operating up to 1000°C.
(ii)	Medium temperature systems	operating between 1000°C and 1200°C.
(iii)	High temperature	operating over 1200°C.

Both the systems at (ii) and (iii) above require water to be circulated under pressure. Maintenance routines are required to ensure there are no leaks in the system and exposed pipework does not constitute a danger to anyone.

Fan heaters

Hot air delivered by fan heaters or from a central unit through ducts are other forms of indirect heating. Commercial fan heaters are used to provide the hot air curtains commonly found in shops. Large free-standing space heaters are often used in buildings or areas of buildings undergoing major regeneration work. They are also generally appropriate for heating large spaces, such as workshops or temporary work areas.

Radiators

The radiator is a common form of local heating. However, a radiator is very inefficient as it works by heating up the air around it by convection, not by radiation of heat. So the name 'radiator' is actually very misleading! For radiators to be effective, it is important to keep them clean and clear of items on them or near them. This is because the radiator needs to warm the air so that it rises to displace the colder air.

Radiators are still used in many domestic and office situations because they are simple and compact. They are a familiar technology with low maintenance and good temperature control and come in many colours and styles. The disadvantages of radiators are that they have a slow thermal response, they are often covered, placed too close to objects such as furniture and when under open windows, the hot air escapes too quickly to impact on the room being heated.

Convection heaters

Convectors are good alternatives to radiators as they are quick to warm up, have a high output and are safe because the heating element is enclosed. However, the disadvantages of convectors are that they need regular maintenance – cleaning out the dirt/dust in the casing, and they need local power supplies.

Underfloor heating

Underfloor heating is an option in large public spaces, as it is invisible and provides an even temperature. However, these systems are prone to leaks, have a limited heat output, are slow to respond to a demand for heat and the location of power/data in the same space is not compatible.

Warm air heaters

Warm air unit heaters are quick and simple with easy maintenance access and give an even heat distribution. However, the disadvantages are the high levels of noise emitted, the higher energy consumption compared with other systems, the floor space required, the need for good air circulation and the regular safety checks.

Boilers

Boilers can be of two main types – atmospheric or forced (induced) draught – and there is a huge range to choose from. They can be modular, condensing, dual-fuel systems or burn fossil fuels (e.g. gas or oil). They take up a lot of space and need specialist maintenance.

26.6 Ventilation

Ventilation works on the principle of air movement due to temperature differences and/or air pressure differences. Air will move from high temperatures, with cooler air replacing it. Air will move between areas of low and high pressure in an attempt to equalise the pressures – the basis of wind.

Ventilation is the process by which a proportion of the air in an enclosed space is withdrawn and replaced by air from outside the building in such a way as to maintain the required level of purity. Ventilation controls the extent to which the oxygen content of the air is depleted and prevents a build up of CO_2, moisture and other contaminants such as tobacco smoke, pollen or fumes.

Part F of the Building Regulations covers the methods of ventilation. The guidance is based on the principle of 'build tight ventilate right'. There is also an ACoP and a HSE Guidance Note accompanying the Workplace Regulations to support Regulation 6 Ventilation. The average air supply rate was set at 8 litres per second per person. However, the new Part L Regulations require this to be increased to 10 litres per second per person. There are specific higher rates for special rooms (e.g. food preparation, printing, toilets). Heavily contaminated spaces will require 32 litres per second per person. Low use and unoccupied areas in buildings will have lower rates – corridors 1.3 litres per second per m^2 and toilets 10 litres per second per m^2.

Offices	4–6 air changes per hour
Restaurant kitchens	20–60 air changes per hour
Banking halls	6 air changes per hour

26.7 Relative humidity (RH)

When managing the heating and ventilation systems in a building, it is also important to consider the relative humidity of the air within a building and also the external air too. The amount of heat the body can shed by evaporation is governed by the amount of water vapour in the surrounding air. Percentage saturation or RH is a measure of the water vapour in the air, compared with the greatest amount that could be held at the same temperature. Thus, when RH is 50% the air could hold twice as much moisture before it is saturated. On the other hand, for a given amount of water vapour, increasing the air temperature decreases the RH and *vice versa*. Thus, at low values of RH, the body can easily lose heat by evaporation, but this is restricted as the RH increases. Generally, so long as the air temperature is maintained at around 21°C, reasonable comfort is experienced by the occupants when the RH is between 40% and 65%.

Evaporation is also affected by air motion. When air moves across the surface of the body, saturated air is carried away to be replaced by unsaturated air, thus allowing more moisture to escape, taking body heat with it. Air motion also speeds up the convection process by removing the warm air close to the body and carrying away body heat along with it.

26.8 Natural ventilation

This is the provision of outdoor air into the building through openings within the building fabric. Table 26.1 shows types of natural ventilation systems. The air is driven into and around the building by a combination of wind and temperature differences. Openable windows and ventilators are the usual means of natural ventilation. Examples of natural ventilation include passive stack ventilation which utilises the combination of wind and temperature to drive a natural exhaust system. Draughts caused by gaps in the building envelope, or ill-fitting windows and doors, also contribute to natural ventilation.

Natural ventilation offers the advantage of a measure of local control not available in mechanical ventilation systems. However, it has the drawback that it is inherently unsuitable for maintaining a constant temperature and consistent air flow rates. In addition, filtration of the air is not possible. Even the use of simple direct local control such as opening a window can be controversial with occupants. Clearly there will be circumstances where those nearest to the windows may not be so keen to have them open as those further away. Externally generated noise or climatic conditions would also be examples of factors affecting the use or popularity of openable windows or other air intake features in naturally ventilated buildings.

Table 26.1   Natural ventilation systems

Cross-ventilation	This is cost effective to implement. It gives occupants some local control and is effective in deep plan spaces. It requires a wind to drive air in, and internal space must be kept clear of obstructions.
Stack ventilation	This method follows the simple principles of air flows – heat and hot air rises, displacing colder air.
Combined system	In this variation, there are no openable windows. Fresh air is obtained from a high level. The wind drives the air in and down, warm air is displaced and rises. This method only works when the outside air is cooler and there are no internal obstructions.

26.9 Mechanical ventilation

There are three methods of mechanical ventilation:

(i) Mechanical input, natural extraction – Fans draw air into the building, thus building up pressure, which forces used air out through windows, doors or other gaps in the building envelope.

(ii) Natural input, mechanical extraction – Fans mounted in the openings in the building fabric expel used air. Outside air is drawn in through other gaps in the envelope, such as the windows, doors or other gaps. A domestic kitchen extractor fan is a simple example of such a system.

(iii) A combined, balanced, mechanical input and extraction system – A tight building envelope is essential for satisfactory operation of combined systems. They allow for the inclusion of pre-heating devices, air cleaning and filtration.

26.10 Air conditioning

One limitation of mechanical ventilation is that even though a combined balanced, mechanical input and extraction system may include pre-heating, air cleaning and filtration, there is no provision for a cooling requirement or humidity control. If the building is to be a sealed unit, then air conditioning is the only way to achieve ventilation.

Heat recovery systems use the heat from air already circulated, thus conserving energy. These will save heating costs but high capital and maintenance costs may reduce the overall saving. All buildings must reduce the impact of solar gain which in turn reduces the demands on the air-handling system.

An air conditioning system is an arrangement of equipment used to achieve and maintain desired conditions of temperature, RH and cleanliness of the air in a given space.

26.11 Comfort control

The operation of an air conditioning system for comfort conditioning:

❑ Air from the conditioned space is drawn into the equipment and mixed with a proportion of fresh air as required.
❑ The mixed air passes through filters which remove particles of dirt and dust.
❑ The air then passes through a cooling coil which may:
  o Cool the air.
  o Extract moisture from it.
❑ If the system is to be used for heating as well as cooling, a heater battery or hot water coil is fitted.
❑ The air is circulated around the system with the assistance of one or more fans.

26.12 Selection of an appropriate system

The many air conditioning systems available have particular performance characteristics, which make them appropriate for different locations and types of building.

Factors that will influence the choice of air conditioning are similar to those for a mechanical ventilation system:

❑ The local external environment. The climate, noise levels internally and externally, and the extent of outside air pollution will determine the most appropriate design and system.

❑ The orientation of the building and its cladding. It is not unusual for some areas of a building to require cooling, at the same time that other areas require heating. For example, a glass fronted rectilinear building on a north–south orientation will suffer most solar gain on the east side in the morning, whereas the west side will suffer most solar gain during the afternoon. Windows facing south will be subjected to solar heat gain from sun up to sun down.

❑ Space management considerations. Firstly, the space required for a particular type of equipment is critical. The size of air conditioning will also depend on the occupation density, user comfort expectations, the heat gains likely from the use of lighting and small equipment (e.g. PCs) and the extent of partitioning.

❑ Building layout. Centrally controlled systems should be capable of delivering conditioned air to separate floors, or even part floors, of a building. The structure and accommodation layout of the building will determine the most appropriate type of air conditioning system.

❑ Specific areas. There will be occasions when the air conditioning can be restricted to particular areas within an otherwise non-air conditioned building – e.g. meeting rooms, high occupancy areas, server rooms or IT equipment rooms.

❑ Flexibility. The system must be sufficiently flexible to enable expansion or contraction to cope with changing operational activities and processes and other organisational requirements.

❑ Costs and energy consumption. Due attention must be given to life cycle costs, operating costs, energy consumption and ease of maintenance.

❑ Legislation. Compliance to the Energy Performance Regulations require that air conditioning systems are inspected and checked. The F Gas Regulations determine the types of refrigerants used in air conditioning systems. Virgin HCFC and R22 gases are banned from December 2009.

26.13 Air conditioning systems

A full air conditioning system will offer full control of air temperature, humidity, freshness and cleanliness of the air within any given space. They are complex engineering systems with many controls, that are costly to install and maintain. They require varying amounts of space and specialist maintenance. Air conditioning systems are made up of two main components – the air conditioning plant and a thermal distribution system. Air, water or refrigerants are the media used in the distribution system to transfer the energy from the air conditioning plant to the areas of the building that need the conditioned air. Systems can either be described as all-air systems, all-water systems or a combination of both air and water. In addition, there are unitary or packaged systems. The main types are:

❑ Centralised air systems, either:
  o constant volume (CV);
  o variable air volume (VAV) or;
  o displacement ventilation.

❑ Partially centralised air/water systems with either:
- o fan coils;
- o chilled beams;
- o chilled ceilings or;
- o room-based heat pumps.

❑ Local systems such as:
- o split units;
- o variable refrigerant flow.

Zoning

Air conditioning systems require the building to be divided into spaces or areas to create zones. These may have different conditions due to activity, type of fire alarm, processes, etc. The size of the zones will depend on the heat gains in the different areas. Zoning must take into account solar gain, internal conditions and internal partitions.

In a **centralised air system**, the plant is in one area, normally the roof. There will be several air handling units (AHU) that condition air and distribute it via ductwork. Chillers and boilers adjust air temperature through coils. This type of system only works very well in single occupancy buildings. It needs thermostats throughout the building which in turn send the message back to the central plant for cooler conditions or hotter conditions.

Single duct systems. These systems are suitable for large areas such as atria, banking halls, a large auditorium or an open plan office area. They can also be used in groups of rooms with similar air conditioning requirements. Supply and return ducts provide input and extraction from a central source at a constant temperature determined by the ambient outside temperature. With these systems, there can either be cooling or heating, not both, as there is only a single duct.

A variable air volume (VAV) system may have a temperature sensor and either an air volume control damper or a fan in the terminal unit in the room. The room sensor detects temperature fluctuations which cause the fan or damper to be activated until the temperature stabilises or the minimum air flow setting is reached.

Dual duct systems. These systems are intended to meet wide ranging demands for heating and cooling in large multi-roomed buildings. Because there are two ducts, it is possible to provide both heating and cooling simultaneously – hence they are suitable for multi room zones which may need these contrasting conditions. Air flow may be of high velocity, which will necessitate the use of acoustic silencers to limit air noise and turbulence.

Induction systems. These are an alternative to the single and dual duct systems. They require that the central air conditioning plant handles about a quarter of the fresh air handled by a single duct system, carries out all of the humidity control and some of the air heating/cooling. Induction units may be located in the floor, under a window sill or in the ceiling void. Fresh air from the central system is injected into the induction unit and mixes with air induced into the unit from within the room via a filter. The air then passes over cooling or heating fins. The air mixture is then delivered back into the room in a continuing process of recirculation. The air flow into the room can be adjusted by the use of local damper controls. Hot or chilled water provides the heating/cooling medium and may be delivered by a two-, three- or four-pipe system.

With a **partially centralised air conditioning system**, there will be fan coil units in local areas, which allow local controls as each area has its own controller. The actual air flow can be altered by engineers for larger rooms/higher occupancy rooms, etc.

Constant volume (CV) systems operate in a single zone and are typically found in hospital operating theatres, IT clean rooms or laboratories. They are simple, and relatively easy to maintain. They are not suitable for multiple zones.

Variable air volume (VAV) systems operate across multiple zones in a building. They must be designed and commissioned to a high standard. They are energy efficient as local VAV units adjust speed/volume of air at local points.

26.14 Dampers

Dampers are used to regulate the amount of air flowing through each branch of the system. They may be used for control, where they move continuously, or may be set in a fixed position during the commissioning of the plant to balance the overall distribution of air. Some systems incorporate fire dampers that can be used in the event of a fire to exhaust smoke or control the spread of smoke from one area to another.

26.15 Fans

There are two main types of fans used in air conditioning, centrifugal and axial. Each type has its own benefits for particular applications. The fan's purpose is to circulate the air around the ductwork, and must be sized correctly to produce sufficient pressure, and move the required volume. In large systems, there may be more than one fan.

26.16 Filters

The filters in air conditioning systems clean the air before it is delivered to areas where people are working.

There are various methods of filtering the air, each of which is designed to extract dust particles of a certain size. The coarsest type of filter is the bag filter, usually made of a cloth material designed to remove the large pieces of debris. General-purpose filters are usually a cartridge type with a loosely woven material between a cardboard outer case. Filters to remove the small particles are often made from compressed paper or similar material. Carbon filters are sometimes used in specialist applications, for instance, in clean rooms where computer components are manufactured. The finest is the absolute filter which as its name suggests, takes out absolutely every particle of dust down to $0.10\,\mu$ ($1\,\mu{:}0.001$ mm).

26.17 Displacement ventilation systems

Displacement ventilation systems are a recent development and need open spaces to function; this means no obstructions in the air flow from equipment/furniture. They are quiet, energy efficient and work on the principle of natural convection. People and/or equipment heats up the cool air.

26.18 Fan coil units

These are separate units that can be fitted into each room. They offer better air filtration than induction units; however, they can be quite noisy. They work as a convector cooler or heater to provide heating and cooling to a localised area. This system is good for multiple zones because they enhance the flexibility of options in a building. There are two types – either under a window or in the ceiling. There is a need to ensure good access for maintenance of controls and filters, and the installation and maintenance of condensation trays to collect the drips/leaks. This is particularly an issue for the units mounted in the ceiling.

Perimeter fan coil units discharge directly into the occupied space and take up floor space in the occupied area too. The advantages of these when compared with the ceiling mounted units are that they provide easier access for maintenance (provided they are not obstructed!) and they counter the effects of cold downdraughts from glazing.

26.19 Chilled beam

Chilled beams are simple devices, offering quiet, draught-free air conditioning with minimal maintenance. They require less ceiling void space than other systems, and function like a cold radiator. There is a potential for condensation to form (arising from the differential between room dew point temperature and beam water temperature).

26.20 Diffusers

Diffusers provide an even distribution of conditioned air within an occupied space. To be effective, diffusers allow control of the flow of air and the direction of flow. They can be linear, cones, jets or incorporated into luminaires (light fittings).

26.21 Heat pumps

Room-based heat pumps are independent units which heat or cool air in the immediate area. They are all linked by a piped water circuit around the building and can save energy by transfer of heating or cooling via the piped circuit. They offer a quick response to calls for heating or cooling, and more local occupant control. They require specialist maintenance but local failures don't impact on the whole building.

26.22 Packaged air conditioning units

These come in two types – either self-contained or connected to central heating and cooling condensers. Self-contained units have their own sealed refrigerant compressor, an evaporator coil to cool the room air, heater, filter, condenser, controls and electricity supply. The self-contained units are frequently seen fixed on the outside of buildings protruding through walls or windows in non-air conditioned buildings. The packaged units can combine a heating and cooling function. Maintenance consists of lubrication of moving parts, filter cleaning or replacement, and parts replacement. Units in which the compressor is separated from the internal unit are called 'split' systems. They offer the opportunity to site the noisy compressor outside the space being cooled or heated. Split systems are quick and easy to install, and require no central plant room. They offer simple controls for local occupant use and are suitable for small spaces and single zones. They can, however, look very unsightly on the exterior of the premises.

26.23 Refrigeration

Chillers are the refrigeration equipment at the heart of any air conditioning system. All air conditioning systems need chilled water. Heat is extracted from water and dispersed. When a system combines extraction of heat with the chilling of water (the simplest method), it is known as a 'packaged system'.

26.24 Humidification

Humidification means adding water to the air to give comfort conditions. To do this, the currently preferred method is to inject steam into the path of the air. This is absorbed into the air and increases the moisture content. Another method is to heat up water in a pan situated in the bottom of the duct; as the air passes over the heated water, it absorbs water vapour and adds to the moisture content.

26.25 Cooling systems

Cooling towers are an efficient heat rejection system and work on the principle of the cooling effect of evaporating water. Warm air is exhausted to the atmosphere. They require a small amount of floor space on a roof and need a rigorous maintenance regime to conform to the L8 ACoP to minimise risks of Legionella outbreaks. It is possible to track the dispersal of water droplets in warm air in the prevailing winds. The dangers of Legionella increase when there is local temperature inversion in certain weather conditions, and the warm air is trapped and descends rather than blowing away. The legislation – The Notification of Cooling Towers and Evaporative Condenser Regulations 1992 – requires a building with cooling towers to register all equipment with the local authority.

Dry coolers are safer than cooling towers, but can take up more floor space on the roof. They consist of a low profile unit, which can be more suitable in sensitive areas, with fans driving fresh air across coils. The hot water in the coils from the chiller is cooled, then pumped back to the chiller.

26.26 Fire safety

Smoke is a killer and can cause extensive damage to assets and premises. The design of the air-handling system can help with the control of smoke in the event of fire. For example, a mechanical ventilating system can be designed so that a positive pressure, relative to the rest of the building, is maintained in areas such as lobbies and staircases. By minimising the ingress of smoke, this will help to maintain a safe escape route.

Another important feature is that the controls of a mechanical ventilation system should be clearly marked so that firemen can operate them. The off position should be marked so as to be clearly visible and a notice 'Ventilation Emergency Control' should be prominently displayed in the plant room.

Other important design considerations in air conditioning installations include:

❑ The system must automatically shut down in the event of fire so as to prevent the discharge or re-circulation of smoke-laden air.
❑ There should be adequate access to enable thorough duct and filter cleaning to avoid the build up of dust or inflammable materials.
❑ Ductwork should be non-combustible and flexible connections should be avoided.

26.27 British Standard Code of Practice

For detailed information on the design, installation, commissioning, operation and maintenance of mechanical ventilation and air conditioning systems in buildings, FMs could consult BS 5720:1979 'Code of Practice for mechanical ventilation and air conditioning in buildings'.

26.28 Lifts

Lifts are needed in buildings to provide easy access to upper floors. They are usually located centrally in a building to minimise horizontal travel distances to a lift. They are often grouped together if the building is large enough to warrant several passenger lifts. Buildings that are taller than 15 storeys will have high-speed lifts which may bypass lower floors. Table 26.2 shows the types of lifts and their speeds.

Since 2005 building owners and occupiers have had to meet the requirements of the DDA to ensure equality of access for the disabled at work. Lifts are essential:

❑ In all buildings of three storeys or more.
❑ For all buildings over one storey for disabled access.

The minimum standards for providing lifts in a building are:

❑ One lift per four storeys.
❑ 45 m walk distance to access a lift.
❑ Lift car capacity of 0.2 m^2 per person.

Table 26.2   Typical speeds of lifts

Type		Speed (m/s)
Goods		0.2–1
Passenger	< 4 floors	0.3–0.8
	4–6 floors	0.8–1.2
	6–9 floors	1.2–1.5
	9–15 floors	5–7
Paternoster		<0.4

In addition to the actual lift car, other equipment associated with each lift that has to be maintained includes the:

- ❑ Electric motor.
- ❑ High tensile steel ropes.
- ❑ Counterweight.
- ❑ Traction gear.

The lift plantroom is usually sited above the lift shaft. FMs should ensure:

- ❑ The room is well ventilated.
- ❑ The room is secure and access is controlled via a permit to work system.
- ❑ The room is well lit.
- ❑ The machinery is secured to a concrete base.
- ❑ A steel lifting beam is incorporated into the room to allow easier removal of equipment for maintenance and repair.
- ❑ A temperature of 10–40 °C is maintained.
- ❑ The room is regularly cleaned to avoid dust build-up.
- ❑ Walls, ceiling and floor should be smooth finished and painted.

The performance of a lift depends on a number of attributes, listed below:

- ❑ Acceleration speeds.
- ❑ Retardation rate or stopping speed.
- ❑ Car speed.
- ❑ Speed of door operation.
- ❑ Stability of speed and performance with variations of car load.

Other factors affecting the performance of the lifts in a building include:

- ❑ Signage and display information that shows the direction of lift travel and location of the lift at any one moment in time.
- ❑ Ability to locate and easily reach the call buttons in landings and inside cars.
- ❑ Good line of sight of the call display.
- ❑ Audible facility to indicate the first lift car available, direction it is travelling and 'in-car' information.
- ❑ Lobby space to ease congestion by lift users and others.
- ❑ Emergency telephone system to allow contact and communication between the occupants of a lift and the emergency response team. This team could be the onsite maintenance team, the lift installer, the security control team or an other designated service centre.
- ❑ Type of maintenance contract. Age of the lifts.
- ❑ Availability of replacement parts.
- ❑ Volume of users.
- ❑ Extent of abuse or vandalism of lifts.

Fireman's lift

The special provisions for a fireman's lift include:

- ❑ Duty load of 630 kg.
- ❑ Dimensions of 1.1 m wide × 12.4 m deep × 2.0 m high.

❑ Escape hatch in car roof.
❑ Access to top floor within 60 seconds.
❑ Made from non-combustible material.
❑ Two-way telecommunication system.
❑ Opening doors of 0.8 m wide $\times$ 2.0 m high.
❑ Two power supplies (mains and generator).

26.29 Lighting

Light is a form of electromagnetic radiation. The FM needs to be aware of the key terms used in lighting, as shown in Table 26.3, and the types of lamps used (as listed in Table 26.4).

Examples of illumination levels and limiting glare indices for different activities are shown in Table 26.5.

Table 26.3   Lighting terminology

Term	Explanation
Luminous intensity	Candela (cd), a measurement of the magnitude of luminance or light reflected from a surface, i.e. cd/m^2
Luminous flux	Lumen (lm), a measurement of the visible light energy emitted
Illuminance	Lumens per square metre (lm/m^2) or lux (lx), a measure of the light falling on a surface
Efficacy	Efficiency of lamps in lumens per watt (lm/W)
Luminous efficacy	Luminous flux output divided by electrical power input
Glare index	A numerical comparison ranging from about 10 for shaded light to about 30 for an exposed lamp. Calculated by considering the light source size, location, luminance and effect of its surroundings

Table 26.4   Types of lamps

Filament lamps	The tungsten iodine lamp is used for floodlighting. Evaporation from the filament is controlled by the presence of iodine vapour. The gas-filled, general-purpose filament lamp has a fine tungsten wire sealed within a glass bulb. The wire is heated to incandescence (white heat) by the passage of an electric current.
Discharge lamps	These do not have a filament, but produce light by excitation of a gas. When voltage is applied to the two electrodes, ionisation occurs until a critical value is reached and then current flows between them. As the temperature rises, the mercury vaporises and electrical discharge between the main electrodes causes light to be emitted.
Fluorescent tube	This is a low pressure variation of the mercury discharge lamp. Energised mercury atoms emit ultraviolet radiation and a blue/green light. The tube is coated internally with a fluorescent powder which absorbs the ultraviolet light and re-radiates a visible light.

Table 26.5   Light levels (lux) in different settings

Activity/location	Illuminance (lux)	Limited glare index
Assembly work (general)	250	25
Assembly work (fine)	1000	22
Computer room	300	16
Laboratory	500	16
Lecture/classroom	300	16
Offices (general)	500	19
Offices (drawing)	750	16
Public house bar	150	22
Shops/supermarkets	500	22
Restaurant	100	22
House	*50–300	n/a

* Varies from 50 in bedrooms to 300 in kitchen and study.

26.30 Lighting requirements

The Building Regulations, Approved Document L2 requires that non-domestic buildings have reasonably efficient lighting systems and make use of daylight where appropriate. There are two main types used in the workplace to comply with the Regulations – the fluorescent strip lamp or the high pressure sodium lamp – described below in more detail.

Fluorescent strip lamps

The fittings and reflectors are appropriate for use in industrial locations, with a variation which creates an illuminated ceiling more suited to shops and offices. A false ceiling of thermolucent panels provide well-diffused illumination without glare and contribute to the insulation of the ceiling. Other services should not be installed in the void as they will cast shadows onto the ceiling. Tubes are mounted on batten fittings and the inside of the void should be painted white to maximise effect.

High pressure sodium discharge lamps

These produce a consistent golden white light in which it is possible to distinguish colours. They are suitable for floodlighting, commercial and industrial lighting and illumination of highways. The low pressure variant produces light that is virtually monochromatic. The colour rendering is poor when compared with the high pressure lamp. Sodium vapour pressure for high and low pressure lamps is 0.5 Pa and 33 kPa, and typical efficacy is 125 and 180 lm/W respectively.

26.31 Light fittings

Fittings for lighting may be considered in three categories:

(i) **General utility** – Designed to be effective, functional and economic.
(ii) **Special** – Usually provided with optical arrangement such as lenses or reflectors to give directional lighting.

(iii) **Decorative** – Designed to be aesthetically pleasing or to provide a feature, rather than to be functional.

26.32 Lighting efficiency

Lighting efficiency is expressed as the initial (100 hour) efficacy averaged over the whole building as shown in Table 26.6.

The formula and tables for establishing conformity with these criteria are provided in the Building Regulations Approved Document L2.

Table 26.6   Light efficiency

Offices, industrial and storage buildings	Not less than 40 luminaire-lumens per circuit-watt
Other buildings	Not less than 50 lamp-lumens per circuit-watt
Display lighting	Not less than 15 lamp-lumens per circuit-watt

26.33 Lighting controls

The purposes of lighting controls are to:

❑ Maximise daylight.
❑ Avoid unnecessary use of artificial lighting when spaces are unoccupied.

To achieve these objectives, the controls need to have the following features:

❑ Local, easily accessible manual switches or remote devices including infrared transmitters.
❑ Sonic, ultrasonic and telecommunication controls.
❑ Reasonable walk distances from the switch to luminaire, up to a maximum 8 m or 3 times fitting height above floor (take greater).
❑ Time switches as appropriate to occupancy.
❑ Photoelectric light metering switches.
❑ Automatic infrared sensor switches which detect the absence or presence of occupants.

A luminaire describes the complete lighting unit, including the lamp, and it has several functions:

❑ It defines the position of the lamp.
❑ It protects the lamp.
❑ It contains the lamp control mechanism (usually).
❑ It is well insulated (for safety).
❑ It should be resistant to water and moisture.
❑ It should be of suitable appearance, purpose and strength.

26.34 BMS

Controlling or managing building services is typically carried out via a building management system (BMS), as well as other information management technologies. The basic functions of building controls are the switching on or off of equipment and adjusting equipment output to maintain the required operating conditions.

Controls can be manual, analogue, pneumatic, mechanical, electrical, computerised and integrated. Examples of controls are time switches, room thermostats and optimisers (which set equipment for start and end times to ensure a specific temperature), compensators (which sample the outside weather conditions and compensate for temperature or RH), sensors, actuators (which operate valves and dampers) and controllers.

Building management systems can provide comfort control, energy monitoring and management and integrated services management. A BMS can be defined as a microprocessor system that can monitor and control one or more services in a building or a complex of buildings. It is an expert computer system that monitors, controls and adjusts the environmental performance of the building's mechanical and electrical services (HVAC, lighting, power, lifts, security and fire protections systems). The operator terminal controls all elements of the systems in a building and may be located in a security control room, plant room or the FM office. BMS systems are often over-specified, resulting in the building services fighting against one another in a complex design. Building control systems must be recognised as a specialist function requiring competence in design, installation, commissioning and trained operators.

A BMS can be used for room temperature adjustments, local occupancy records, occupancy detection, demand control ventilation, fan control, window daylight sensors, solar gain, window blind operation switching, telephony interface, occupant user interface, condition-based maintenance, integration with fire systems and monitoring of comfort conditions. The benefits are reduced operating costs, security of production/function/ access of building (failures can be predicted), improved working environment, increased flexibility of building use and better management information (to inform decisions). A BMS is said to be the equivalent of a trained and competent engineer. Systems are described as either open or closed loops. The open systems permit various manufacturers' equipment to be interfaced, whereas a closed system will only permit that supplier's technologies and protocols to be recognised, thus limiting the scope and expansion of the system.

26.35 Intelligent buildings

As technologies are improved and developed, there is real prospect of an intelligent building in which the various systems communicate and share information. Different types of information can be carried over common physical connections enabling voice, data and building management connections to be simply made and maintained. All data traffic can use one network system or if this is not possible (e.g. for business, security or safety reasons), then separate systems can be used. Cabling systems can be distributed in floor and ceiling voids thus providing a matrix to which easy connection points are accessed for all types of services. Such buildings can be described as intelligent, and offer their occupants high utilisation of the space, fine tuning of the services to suit their occupation and operational needs, and this in turn, may reduce occupancy costs. Such buildings require expert and technically competent FMs to operate the built-in systems, as well as educated occupants who appreciate the limits on the parameters, such as lighting levels, temperature or RH, set for the building.

Internet

Internet-enabled building automation and energy management software systems now allow access and control of energy-intensive devices and systems in real time using standard web browsers. These products are giving companies and organisations the ability to obtain critical energy data from existing buildings systems and analyse the information to make intelligent procurement decisions and improve the overall performance of the building's mechanical and electrical systems.

27 Telecommunications and Networks

27.1 Introduction

Telecommunication is the transmission of signals over a distance for the purpose of communication. This process involves the sending of electromagnetic waves by electronic transmitters. Television, radio and telephone are all devices in telecommunications. The networks that connect the devices include computer networks, public telephone networks, radio networks and television networks.

Things to consider in the selection of a supplier and a system are shown in Table 27.1.

27.2 Ownership options

As with most equipment, an organisation can choose to either buy the system outright, or to lease the system. FMs may have to do a cost benefit analysis, weighing up the advantages and disadvantages of leasing or owning the telephone system.

Advantages of lease arrangements

❏ Costs for the telephone system are certain and are known in advance.
❏ The telephone system cannot be withdrawn once the contract is signed and its conditions complied with.
❏ No need to tie up capital in fixed assets such as a telephone system.
❏ Allowances, depreciation and other calculations are not needed, since leasing is concerned only with rentals.
❏ Leasing provides a medium-term source of capital which may not be available elsewhere.

Table 27.1 Selection of IT systems

Initial advice	Does the FM need help identifying appropriate systems and functions?
Installation	Will the supplier install the system?
Maintenance	What happens if there's a problem? Will there be a charge for maintenance?
Training	Is training needed to use the new system and conduct day-to-day maintenance?
Scalability	Can the system accommodate extra users or enhanced functions if the business grows or its needs become more complicated?
After-sales service	Will there be ongoing telephone or online support? Using a local dealer may give easier after-sales access to the supplier.

❑ Leasing provides a hedge against inflation as the use of the asset is obtained immediately – payments are made out of future funds and are made in fixed money terms, with real costs falling as inflation increases.
❑ Possibility of immediate acquisition of cost-saving telephone system equipment.

Disadvantages of leasing

❑ It is generally not possible to dispose of the telephone system before the end of the lease.
❑ The telephone system is not owned.
❑ Funds must be found to pay the lease throughout its duration.

27.3 Telephone systems installation and maintenance

Telephone system service contracts are separate agreements independent of whether an organisation owns or leases the system.

Components

The basic elements of a telecommunication system are:

❑ A **transmitter** that takes information and converts it to a signal for transmission.
❑ A **transmission medium** over which the signal is transmitted.
❑ A **receiver** that receives and converts the signal back into usable information.

Often telecommunication systems are two-way and devices act as both a transmitter and receiver or transceiver.

In a conventional telephone system, the caller is connected to the person they want to talk to by the switches at various exchanges. The switches form an electrical connection between the two users and the setting of these switches is determined electronically when the caller dials the number based upon either pulses or tones made by the caller's telephone. Once the connection is made, the caller's voice is transformed to an electrical signal using a small microphone in the telephone's receiver. This electrical signal is then sent through various switches in the network to the user at the other end where it is transformed back into sound waves by a speaker for that person to hear. This person also has a separate electrical connection between him and the caller, which allows him to talk back.

The fixed-line telephone system in most residential homes are analogue – that is the speaker's voice directly determines the amplitude of the signal's voltage. However, although short-distance calls may be handled from end-to-end as analogue signals, increasingly telephone service providers are converting signals to digital before converting them back to analogue for reception. The advantage is that digitised voice data can travel side-by-side with data from the Internet and that digital signals can be perfectly reproduced in long-distance communication as opposed to analogue signals which are inevitably affected by noise.

27.4 Telephony services

Traditional telephone services connect homes or small businesses over copper wires that are wound around each other and called twisted pair. Traditional 'telephone services' were created to allow communication via an analogue signal – voice information is transmitted with other telephone users. An input device such as a telephone handset takes an acoustic signal (which is a natural analogue signal) and converts it into an electrical equivalent in terms of volume (signal amplitude) and pitch (frequency of wave change).

There are two types of telephone service infrastructure:

❑ Fixed – wire (standard telephones using copper or fibre cables) and wireless (cordless analogue and DECT digital).
❑ Mobile – cellular analogue and digital global system for communication (GSM), and satellite (Inmarsat and the new low earth orbit [LEO] services).

The technologies used by these services may be analogue, or in the case of newer technologies, digital. Most can be used for more than simple voice telephony, e.g. to transmit faxes and to transfer files including data, audio and video.

27.5 Integrated services digital network (ISDN)

ISDN is a high-speed, fully digital telephone service. ISDN upgrades the analogue telephone network to a digital system. ISDN can operate at speeds up to 128 kilobits/second, which is five or more times faster than an analogue modem.

ISDN can dramatically speed up transfer of information over the Internet or over a remote local area network (LAN) connection, especially for rich media like graphics, audio or video or applications that normally run at LAN speeds.

Basic rate ISDN divides the telephone line into three digital channels: two 'B' channels and one 'D' channel, each of which can be used simultaneously:

❑ The B channels are used to transmit data, at rates of 64 kilobits/second or 56 kilobits/second (depending on the telephone company). With two B channels, two calls can be made simultaneously.
❑ The D channel does the administrative work, such as setting up and tearing down the call and communicating with the telephone network.

27.6 Basic telephony functions

Most business telephone systems offer functions that give flexibility in making and receiving telephone calls. These functions can help improve communication within an organisation. The FM needs an understanding of the terminology used – as shown in Table 27.2.

In countries where the telephone system has been deregulated, it is possible for subscribers to choose from a variety of carriers for long-distance calls. The choice of carrier, is based on cost of calls and the quality of lines offered. The subscriber opens an account with the carrier, who will provide an access code. The subscriber will dial this access code before dialling the telephone number they wish to call. The carrier market is very competitive and it is possible to make significant cost savings. Normally, the subscriber does not have to change his/her telephone line to be able to access cheap long-distance calls. Many companies use special hardware in conjunction with their telephony equipment to access least cost routing (LCR) calls by the cheapest carrier.

Table 27.2   Telephony terminology

Voicemail	One of the simplest telephone functions is voicemail, which allows callers to leave messages. Voicemails can be stored, redirected and accessed remotely.
Redirection of calls	Call redirection automatically re-routes calls received from the usual phone to another phone.
Conference calls	Connects telephone calls involving more than two people – a useful way of co-ordinating work on projects involving different teams or businesses.
Call logging	Records the number, timing and duration of calls made from each extension. Ensures the telephone system is used appropriately. Also can monitor productivity in departments where telephone activity is a core business activity, such as customer service or sales departments.
Call barring	Using call barring restricts access to certain numbers, to enforce limits on the use of the telephone system. For instance, some businesses use call barring to prevent employees from dialling numbers with prefixes indicating overseas or premium-rate numbers, thus preventing costly private calls.
Least cost routing (LCR)	Automatic selection of the least costly facility for transmission of a call. This is also referred to as: • Most economical route selection (MERS) • Route optimisation • Automatic route selection • Flexible route selection

27.7 Typical telephone services

A wide range of various telephone services may be provided via the FM department or the IT department – this depends on the structure of the organisation.

❑ Telephone lines.
❑ Call logging and call charging.
❑ Conference services.
❑ Equipment purchasing.
❑ Emergency calls.
❑ Extension moves and changes.
❑ Fault reporting.
❑ IP telephony.
❑ Mobile phones or connect cards.
❑ New extensions and engineering work.
❑ Operator assistance.
❑ Pagers.
❑ Short messaging service (SMS) messaging.
❑ Customer (student/patient/resident) telephony service (STS).
❑ Telephone directories.
❑ Organisation or business telephone directory.
❑ Video conferencing.
❑ Voicemail service.

27.8 Telephone handset or extension facilities

An individual telephone handset may have the facilities listed below programmed into the equipment, or available via the telephone system.

- ❑ Abbreviated dialling.
- ❑ Account codes.
- ❑ Audio conference calls.
- ❑ Call diversion.
- ❑ Call forwarding.
- ❑ Call hold.
- ❑ Call offer.
- ❑ Call pick-up.
- ❑ Call transfer.
- ❑ Do not disturb.
- ❑ Enquiry call.
- ❑ Groups.
- ❑ Intrusion.
- ❑ Lock/unlock extension.
- ❑ Override a diversion.
- ❑ Park call.
- ❑ PIN access.
- ❑ Private call.
- ❑ Reminder calls.
- ❑ Ring back when busy or on return.
- ❑ Save number dialled.
- ❑ Trunk access class (TAC).

27.9 Information to management and users

A good telephone system will be able to generate a variety of management reports on the use and cost of the telephone services in an organisation. Information often required by both users and the management include the following

- ❑ Call costs.
- ❑ Dialling codes (national).
- ❑ Dialling codes (international).
- ❑ Dialling codes charge bands (international).
- ❑ Directory enquiries.
- ❑ Departmental telephone contacts.
- ❑ Frequently asked questions (FAQs).
- ❑ Good practice guides.
- ❑ Handbooks.
- ❑ Guidance on handling malicious phone calls.
- ❑ Costs and revenues from payphones on premises.

- ❏ Details of personal calls.
- ❏ Security telephones on premises.
- ❏ Service level agreements (SLAs).
- ❏ SLA key performance indicators (KPIs).
- ❏ Telephone exchange details.
- ❏ Switchboard and telephonist answering statistics.
- ❏ Telephone/fax preference service (TPS/FPS).
- ❏ Telephone policy.
- ❏ Wiring specifications.

27.10 Telephone policy

Organisations should have a telephone policy in place to ensure that high standards of customer service are maintained. This applies to both internal calls and external calls. A telephone call is often the customer's first point of contact with the organisation and therefore first impressions count.

A telephone policy could include a wide range of issues as shown in Table 27.3

Table 27.3   Management control features

Standard greetings	A consistent approach to responding to calls is an important part of customer service. Employees might greet callers with the business name, their own name and then ask: 'how may I help you?'
Message quality	Make sure that the quality and content of any automatic messages or recorded guidance are supervised and approved at management level. Regular reviews should be carried out to ensure that the recorded information is still appropriate.
Transferring calls	Employees in all areas should be aware of the names, roles and responsibilities of people across the business, so calls can be transferred swiftly and accurately.
Call scripts	Businesses conducting large numbers of similar calls might use manuals, checklists or prompt cards providing lists of standardised responses to frequently received queries.
Private use	Limits on personal calls being made at work may be required, including a restriction on the use of private mobile phones.
Quality control	To ensure appropriate standards are maintained, organisations may want to record calls that employees make and receive.
Training	All new staff should receive training on the actual telephone system used, as well as guidance on the telephone policy and any restrictions in place.
Privacy	Monitoring calls at work has privacy and data-protection legislation implications. Clear business benefits must be identified if calls are monitored. Employers must weigh these against any adverse impact on employees and customers. Both employees and customers must know that their calls may be recorded.

27.11 Video conferencing

Video conferencing allows two or more people to communicate with both sound and vision. A significant proportion of communication in face-to-face meetings is visual rather than auditory – 'body language' communication can be more informative than the words spoken. For critical business deals where a face-to-face meeting is not possible, a video conference might offer a useful alternative. Technologies are improving and developing in the field of video-conferencing, and the FM needs to keep up to date with new systems being made available. Videophones offer an entry point into this technology.

The main drawbacks are:

❑ The bandwidth, or data transmission rate, needed to transmit high-quality images can be high and therefore expensive.
❑ Video conferencing is not a perfect substitute for meeting face-to-face.

27.12 Voice over Internet Protocol (VoIP)

Voice over Internet Protocol (VoIP) allows a person to make telephone calls over a computer network. A voice message is delivered using the Internet Protocol. VoIP is a term used in IP telephony for a set of facilities for managing the delivery of voice information using the Internet Protocol. In general, this means sending voice information in digital form in discrete packets rather than in the traditional circuit protocols of the public switched telephone network (PSTN).

This could allow a company to make enormous savings on telecommunication costs by sending voice traffic anywhere around the world via an Internet connection.

The practice of using an Internet connection to pass voice data using IP instead of using the standard PSTN can allow a remote worker, for instance, to function as if directly connected to a PBX even while at home or in a remote office.

VoIP offers significant potential savings. An always-on broadband connection to the Internet will allow free calls between individuals with VoIP equipment – even international calls. The only costs are Internet connection and the appropriate handsets. In bypassing the public network, it also avoids standard long-distance charges, as the only connection is through an Internet Service Provider (ISP). VoIP is being used more and more to keep corporate telephony costs down.

There are, however, a number of drawbacks:

❑ Potential savings have to be weighed against the quality and reliability of VoIP connections, which are not as good as standard telephone connections.
❑ Additional costs are incurred if VoIP is used to telephone someone without VoIP capabilities.

27.13 Digital subscriber line (DSL)

DSL (digital subscriber line) is a technology for bringing high-bandwidth information to homes and small businesses over ordinary copper telephone lines. A DSL line can carry both data and voice signals. The data part of the line is continuously connected. DSL is expected to replace ISDN in many areas.

Table 27.4   The pros and cons of ADSL

Advantages	Disadvantages
High speed 'always on' connection	Not available to everybody (approximately 81% household coverage – October 2003).
Fixed monthly cost	Contended service could result in variable speeds depending upon time of day.
Great value for money	Possible teething troubles for new or inexperienced customers.
Competitive modem and router prices	

DSL is a technology that assumes digital data does not require change into analogue form and back. Digital data is transmitted to a computer directly as digital data and this allows the telephone service provider to use a much wider bandwidth for transmission.

27.14 Asymmetric digital subscriber line (ADSL)

Asymmetric digital subscriber line (ADSL) is a type of DSL. It works by splitting the existing telephone line signal into two, one for voice and the other for data. ADSL technology can work at up to 8 Mbps download. Table 27.4 shows the various advantages and disadvantages. The most popular services in the UK are running at speeds of 512 Kbps (approximately nine times faster than a modem), although speeds of up to 2 Mbps can be obtained. Upload speeds are 256 Kbps on all products and hence this is why it is 'asymmetric', because the download speed is different to the upload speed.

27.15 Wireless networks (WLANs)

Wireless networking technology is being used as an alternative to cable and fibre optic networks. The aim of wireless technology is to remove the restrictions of being attached to expensive and messy wires and cables, both inside the office and out. Wireless technology carries the capability of wired networks to areas that cables cannot reach. It can therefore offer many advantages in older buildings, buildings with limited capacity for additional wiring and communal areas such as coffee shops, hotel lobbies, corporate receptions, libraries, trains and airport lounges. Table 27.5 shows the advantages of enabling wireless working for the organisation and the individual.

A wireless local area network (WLAN) allows connections to be made using radio waves instead of wiring.

A WLAN is often combined with a wired LAN in a business environment. It is sensible to combine wired and wireless technologies to get the best mix of facilities and also a standby should there be a fault or failure in either of the services.

The components that make up a WLAN are:

❑   **A wireless access point:** This is a small box with one or more aerials. It has a connector to attach it to the rest of the wired LAN. More than one access point may

Table 27.5   The benefits of wireless working

Increased efficiency	Improved data communications will lead to faster transfer of information within businesses and between organisations and their customers.
Better coverage	Because wireless technology enables the user to communicate whilst away from the office, employees can keep in touch with their work colleagues and customers.
Flexibility	Office-based wireless workers can be networked without sitting at dedicated computers, and can continue to do productive work while away from the office. This can lead to new styles of working, such as home working, direct access to corporate data while on customer sites, or travelling.
Cost savings	Wireless networks can be easier and cheaper to install, especially in listed buildings or where the landlord will not permit the installation of cables.
New opportunities	Wireless working could allow organisations to offer new products or services. For example, many corporate reception spaces, meeting rooms, cafes and restaurants have installed 'hot spot' wireless networking services to allow mobile users to connect their equipment to their 'home' offices while travelling and visiting other organisations. This can be considered as an added value service to their visitors, clients and customers.

be needed to cover a building. Access points handle the receiving and transmitting of data to all the wireless devices in their area. They can handle many different connections between different devices all talking to each other simultaneously. The more devices using a particular access point, then the slower they will operate. This may be a factor to consider when providing WiFi zones as an added value service (e.g. premium airport lounges).

❑ **A wireless network card:** This card acts as the radio receiver/transmitter for a specific computer. Modern laptops have this built-in, but with desktop PCs, the card will need to be installed.

These components (the access point and the card) need to work together. This is made possible because they will comply with a set of standards intended to enable devices from different manufacturers to inter-operate.

The standards have changed and improved significantly since the advent of the first WLANs. Two factors have driven this, namely:

❑   Speed – getting data transmitted faster between PCs and access points.
❑   Security – making sure that the wireless capability is not abused by unauthorised people and organisations.

There are also certain drawbacks associated with the use of wireless networks which need to be carefully considered and managed as shown in Table 27.6.

Table 27.6   The drawbacks of wireless working

Security	Wireless transmission is more vulnerable to attack by unauthorised users, so particular attention has to be paid to security. Firewalls, passwords, encryption and training are all ways of improving the security of wireless working.
Connection	Users may suffer interference when others in the same building also use wireless technology or where other sources of radio signals are present. This could lead to poor communication or, in extreme cases, loss of wireless communication altogether.
Installation	In some buildings, getting consistent network coverage can be difficult, leading to 'black spots' where no signal is available. For example, in structures built using steel reinforcing materials, it may be difficult to pick up the radio frequencies used. Signal boosters may be needed, or just an acceptance by the users that the WiFi is not universally provided in a particular building or site.
Transmission speeds	Wireless transmission can be slower and less efficient than 'wired' networks. In larger wireless networks, the 'backbone' network will usually be wired rather than wireless.

Purpose of a WLAN

WLANs can broadly do anything that a 'wired' LAN can do, without the encumbrance of cables between the user device and the network. This enables workers to share a network and hardware. It also allows workers to remain online if they move their laptop or PDA around the wireless-enabled space, known as 'hot desking', which can allow for a more flexible use of space.

WLANs can extend network access to areas where cabling might not be cost-effective or practical, e.g. from an office to its adjacent warehouse or storeroom, or across retail outlets, hotels or public spaces such as universities, schools, health centres and job centres.

WLAN 'hotspots' are wireless-enabled areas offering customers access to a broadband Internet connection, usually for a usage fee. Such services are becoming common in public areas such as airports, stations, trains, cafes and hotels, so that workers can be in regular communication with their business while travelling.

WLANs are particularly suited to businesses that have staff working away from the office where flexible working styles such as 'home working' have been implemented, or where the use of wireless is desirable to avoid damage to the fabric of a building.

27.16 Cellular networks

Cellular networks are increasingly used for more than just voice calls. Improved handsets and the networks' increased data transfer speeds have resulted in the development of a range of sophisticated mobile phones and handheld PCs/PDAs.

Technologies connected with cellular phone services include:

❑ Global positioning system (GPS) – allows the position of a device to be precisely located.
❑ SMS – text messaging.

❑　Multimedia services (MMS).
❑　Wireless application protocol (WAP) – the collection of services that allow web access on mobile phone devices.
❑　GSM/general packet radio service (GPRS) – data transmission services carried over cellular networks.
❑　3G – third-generation data transmission services that promise higher data rates equivalent to broadband networks.

Greater access

These technologies offer additional ways for mobile devices to be networked. The worldwide coverage of cellular networks means that such facilities are often available in places where other types of networking (LANs, WLANs) cannot reach. Consequently, these technologies can be used in addition to WLANs as a means of 'roaming' – maintaining contact while travelling.

Mobile phone handsets can offer access to email, SMS, GPS, MMS and WAP. Smart handsets can offer remote workers access to mobile business applications and wireless Internet services. For example, combining MMS with Internet technology enables staff to take, record and show images in real time.

Using web-service technology, organisations can create new applications for mobile phone business use, e.g. enabling mobile service engineers using mobiles or PDAs to access wireless job sheets, fault reporting, time sheets, checklists, etc.

Third-generation networks offer faster data transfer and allow the development of more handset-based real-time business applications. Although GSM and GPRS data services will still be available for many years, the faster data rates available with 3G mean that it offers a more attractive service, and over time it will replace the other two services.

Disadvantages

It is important to consider the possible drawbacks of these cellular networks and equipment. In particular the FM must consider:

❑　Costs for handsets and network operators' packages vary enormously.
❑　Data services may initially be expensive to use.
❑　Mobile network speeds have not increased as quickly as predicted.

27.17 Personal area networks

Personal area networks (PANs) are short-range wireless networks that operate over a range of tens of metres. The main application of PANs is as a means of eliminating cables connecting devices to equipment peripherals.

Typical PAN technologies include the following:

❑　Cordless products, such as mice and keyboards, that use radio or infrared. These are inexpensive and easy to install and use. Certain products, such as the cordless phone, can have a considerably wider range.
❑　Bluetooth, which allows enabled devices such as phones, mobiles, mice, headsets, PCs, printers and keyboards to connect wirelessly within a range of 10 m. Bluetooth technology is built into some devices, while other models can be upgraded with a Bluetooth card.

Use of wireless

Wireless connections between PCs and peripherals can free up desk space, floor space, remove unwanted cables and change the way space can be planned and used. Connected Bluetooth devices can automatically synchronise data downloads and uploads, and exchange information. Mobile employees can use Bluetooth-equipped devices to access enabled office-based peripherals such as printers. Bluetooth can be used to wirelessly control equipment and machinery. For example, the building management system could be Bluetooth-enabled, allowing the service engineer to diagnose and fix faults.

Personal area networks can have more interesting applications, e.g. attendees at an exhibition could be given PAN-enabled 'smart' badges that could be read wirelessly to control access to the venue and to allow an attendee to pass contact information to exhibitors.

Pros and cons of PANS

❑ PANs are efficient, cost-effective and convenient.
❑ Some PANs can interact with other wireless networking technologies using the same radio bands, resulting in interference and loss of data integrity.
❑ Bluetooth networks are relatively secure, but have slow data transmission rates.
❑ Bluetooth is a short-range solution – tens of metres – and is not suitable for wireless connection over larger distances.

27.18 Personal digital assistant (PDA)

These devices are small palm-sized computers and they give the user access to their personal information, such as addresses, diary, email, notes and tasks. There are a number of different makes available.

They have a touch screen LCD that responds to a finger or stylus. They have ROM and RAM, but no hard drive. The common uses of PDAs are:

❑ A business diary.
❑ A business names and address index.
❑ A personal names and address index.
❑ A record of important information such as PINs, bank account details, birthdays, expenses, etc.
❑ To receive and view emails.
❑ To create documents and spreadsheets.
❑ To provide entertainment – games and music.

Some organisations issue PDAs to employees as standard office equipment.

27.19 Security

WLANs are convenient, cheap and easy to install. They allow for mobility around the office and deliver great flexibility. Unfortunately, they can also be insecure unless appropriate precautions are taken.

It is important to ensure that wireless working is secure and safe. Risks may include unauthorised people being able to eavesdrop on business activities and use any information gained to undermine the business. Furthermore, a hacker could use a wireless connection to change the data in key business systems for fun or for fraud.

Challenges for FMs

The challenge to estates and FMs will be to provide a safe, secure and efficient wireless system and network that does not interfere with neighbouring systems. A policy of managing the building or site airspace will ensure that interference is reduced, performance is monitored and upgrades are managed. This is particularly important in a multi-tenanted space where they may be many occupants with their own individual networks.

WLAN security

The early WLAN security methods proved easy to break into, so the WLAN industry has produced a better method called WiFi protected access (WPA).WPA uses a different method of encryption that is stronger and better designed than wired equivalent privacy, an older form of security. Products that use this method will state 'Wi-Fi WPA' in their specifications. The WiFi Alliance ensures that products that comply with WPA will work together – a critically important requirement.

WiFi protected access is a major step forward but a newer technique, WPA2, using another encryption standard, has been released. It is better to use WPA2 rather than WPA where possible.

Both WPA and WPA2 can operate in two modes:

(i) Personal mode is a pre-shared password or pass phrase used for authentication. This is a simple approach that ensures a computer can only get access to the WLAN if the password matches the access point's password.
(ii) Enterprise mode is a more sophisticated method and is more suited to larger organisations needing stronger protection.

When choosing WLAN components, it is a good idea to look for a combination of IEEE standard 802.11g and WPA or WPA2.

27.20 Virtual private networks (VPNs)

With a VPN, a secure network can be created even with an insecure system such as an early WLAN. This is achieved by encrypting all of the data that passes over the insecure network so that it cannot be read by an eavesdropper.

This might seem like an ideal solution, but there are some limitations. For example, VPNs may:

❑ Make it more difficult for users with laptops to roam around the building, particularly if it is a large building with several access points, which transfer data between devices – this is due to the need to hand over from one access point to another.
❑ Be too complex to set up internally – a dedicated expert may be required to design and implement an effective VPN system.

27.21 Firewalls

A firewall is a device or piece of software that controls what data is allowed to pass through it. A firewall can be used in a network to separate an insecure part of the network from the secure area where the most critical data is managed. A firewall can be used to separate all the wireless data traffic from the rest of the wired network.

27.22 Origins of digital communication

In 1844 Samuel Morse sent a message using his new invention 'the telegraph'. Morse code is a type of binary system which uses dots and dashes in different sequences to represent letters and numbers. Modern data networks use 1's and 0's to achieve the same result. Emile Baudot developed a printing telegraph machine which used a typewriter style keyboard with a different 5-number code. The speed of serial communications is still measured in Baud rate.

ASCII code

The Baudot 5-bit code had limited application, so in 1966, a group of American communications companies got together to devise a new code. They used 7 bits which could represent 128 characters. This is known as the American Standard Code for Information Interchange or the ASCII code. It was immediately accepted by nearly all of the world's computer and communications companies.

Although the telegraph and the teletypewriter were the forerunners of data communications, it has only been in the last 30 years that things have really started to speed up. This was born out of necessity, as the need to communicate between computers at ever-increasing speeds has driven the development of faster and faster networking equipment and higher and higher specification cables and connecting hardware.

Ethernet

Ethernet was developed in the mid-1970s by the Xerox Corporation. In 1979 DEC and Intel joined forces with Xerox to standardise the Ethernet system for everyone to use. The first specification by the three companies called the 'Ethernet Blue Book' was released in 1980; it was also known as the 'DIX standard' after their initials. It was a 10 mega bits per second system (10 Mbps or 10 million 1's and 0's per second) and used large coaxial backbone cable running throughout the building with smaller coaxial cables tapped off at 2.5 m intervals to connect to the workstations. The large coaxial cables which are usually yellow became known as 'Thick Ethernet' or **10Base5**. The '10' refers to the speed (10 Mbps); the 'Base' because it is a base band system (base band uses all of its bandwidth for each transmission as opposed to broad band which splits the bandwidth into separate channels to use concurrently) and the '5' is short for the systems maximum cable length, in this case 500 m.

The Institute of Electrical and Electronic Engineers (IEEE) released the official Ethernet standard in 1983 called the IEEE 802.3 after the name of the working group responsible for its development, and in 1985 version 2 (IEEE 802.3a) was released. This second version is commonly known as the 'Thin Ethernet' or **10Base2**. (In this case, the maximum length is 195 m even though the '2' suggests that it should be 200 m.)

Token ring

In 1984, IBM introduced Token Ring which was able to transmit data at 4 Mbps, this system uses a thick black two-pair shielded cable with large four pole connectors. The IBM data connector, or IDC as it is sometimes called, was an engineering masterpiece. Instead of the normal plug and socket arrangement of male and female gendered connectors, the data connector was designed to mate with itself, a sort of hermaphrodite. Although the IBM cabling system is to this day a very high quality and robust data communication media, it has lost favour with a lot of customers. This is partly due to its large size and cost and partly because it only has four cores and therefore is not as versatile as an eight core unshielded twisted pair (UTP) cable.

There were many other types of network at that time which used different types of cables and connectors, so it soon became clear that a standard for telecommunications wiring was needed.

In 1985, the Computer Communications Industry Association (CCIA) asked the Electronic Industries Association (EIA) to develop a cabling standard which would define a generic telecommunications wiring system for commercial buildings that would support a multi-product, multi-supplier environment. In essence, this was a cabling system which would run all current and future networking systems over a common topology using a common media and common connectors.

Structured cabling system

By 1987 several manufacturers had developed Ethernet equipment which could utilise twisted pair telephone cable, and in 1990 the IEEE released the 802.31 Ethernet Standard 10BaseT (the 'T' refers to twisted pair cable). In 1991 the EIA together with the Telecommunications Industry Association (TIA) eventually published the first telecommunications cabling standard called EIA/TIA 568 and the structured cabling system was born. It was based on a Category 3 Unshielded Twisted Pair (UTP) cable, and was closely followed 1 month later by a Technical Systems Bulletin (TSB-36) which specified higher grades of UTP cable, Category 4 and 5 (Cat 4 and Cat 5). Cat 4 specified data rates of up to 20 MHz and Cat 5 up to 100 MHz, which at the time must have seemed like ample bandwidth for future development. However, even Cat 5 is being pushed to its limits by new networking technologies. Recent developments have been Cat 5e, Cat 6, Cat 7 and Cat 8 standards.

27.23 Cabling standards

The reason for having a 'standard' is to define a method of connecting all types of suppliers voice and data equipment over a cabling system that uses a **common media**, **common connectors** and a **common topology**. This means that a building can be cabled for all its communication needs without the planner or architect ever having to know what type of equipment will be used by future occupants.

There are three main cabling standards:

(i) **EIA/TIA 568A** – This is the American standard and was the first to be published (1991).
(ii) **ISO/IEC 11801** – The International standard for structured cabling systems.
(iii) **CENELEC EN 50173** – the European Cabling standard (the British version is BS EN 50173).

27.24 Use of structured cables

The rules of cabling and wiring are changing rapidly, creating a series of issues that engineering and maintenance managers are having to address to keep their facilities operating smoothly.

With the advent of technology such as Internet/intranet and the rapid proliferation of e-commerce, higher bandwidth and faster communication have become basic requirements for a growing number of building IT facilities. Therefore, cabling and wiring systems with greater capacities are an essential element in the viability of any building.

As the cost of hardware continues to drop, the idea of more powerful communication backbones is becoming economically viable. With these expanding capabilities and growing expectations, however, come greater expectations for system flexibility and reliability.

27.25 Power and communication wiring

Most commercial and institutional buildings use standard wiring for electrical systems. An electrical cable consists of one or more conductors – copper or aluminium – covered with insulation and a protective sheath. Electronic cables are now predominantly copper due the the the metal's lower price.

Electrical cables commonly run inside conduits or in cable trays. Fire-rated cables, however, can be used in plenum areas without a conduit or cable tray.

Communication cabling consists of a number of twisted wires, which can be shielded, unshielded, coaxial cable or fibre optic. Wire pairs are twisted to minimise interference with the other circuits in the cable. To eliminate electrical interference, the cable is shielded using a grounded metal braid.

Coaxial cable consists of a conductor at the centre of the cable surrounded by a cylindrical copper tube. The two conductors are separated by insulation. The outside of the cable is sheathed with a shield, as well as insulation to provide physical protection for the cable.

Coaxial cable generally can accommodate longer distances and greater bandwidth, so it is used largely for video and Ethernet applications. One advantage of coaxial cable is its lack of susceptibility to radio frequency interference. The main disadvantage of coaxial cable is the higher cost of terminations and splicing.

The use of twisted pair cable has increased. Shielded twisted pair (STP) cables can support higher transmission rates than those of UTP cables. Originally, it was believed that UTP had a limited application in data transmission.

The UTP data transmission rate is 155 Mbps for Category 5 wiring. So UTP can be used for data transmissions that until recently were reserved for fibre optic wiring. For most local area network applications, UTP is preferred over fibre because of its lower installation cost.

27.26 Fibre optics

Fibre construction

There are many different types of fibre optic cable, labelled with numbers. The numbers represent the diameters of the fibre core and cladding and are measured in microns (a millionth of a metre). Loose tube fibre cable can be indoor or outdoor or both; the outdoor cables usually have the tube filled with gel to act as a moisture barrier which stops the ingress of water. The number of cores in one cable can be anywhere from 4 to 144.

Over the years, a variety of core sizes have been produced, but these days there are only three main sizes that are used in data communications. These are **50/125**, **62.5/125** and **8.3/125**. The 50/125 and 62.5/125 micron multi-mode cables are the most widely used in data networks, although recently the 62.5 has become the more popular choice.

Advantages and disadvantages

Fibre optic wiring has a number of advantages over copper and these are:

❏ They give superior speed and greater bandwidth. The low loss, high-bandwidth properties of fibre cable means they can be used over greater distances than copper cables; in data networks this can be as much as 2 km without the use of repeaters.
❏ They are smaller and lighter. Their light weight and small size make them ideal for applications where running copper cables would be impractical, and by using multiplexers, one fibre could replace hundreds of copper cables.
❏ As the medium for transmission is light and not electricity, it is not susceptible to radio interference. Fibre optics are immune to electromagnetic interference (EMI). Because fibre is non-conductive, it can be used were electrical isolation is needed, for instance between buildings where copper cables would require cross-bonding to eliminate difference in earth potentials.
❏ It is safe to use in dangerous environments. Fibres also pose no threat in dangerous environments such as chemical plants where a spark could trigger an explosion.
❏ It is more secure than copper, as it is very, very difficult to tap into a fibre cable to read the data signals.

The major disadvantage of fibre optics is the associated electronics required at each end of the line to convert electronic signals to light and *vice versa*.

27.27 Cabling distribution

A cable distribution system can be divided into two major areas:

(i) **Inter-building cabling** is achieved using underground duct banks, conduits or tunnels. When installing a new conduit or duct bank, managers should ensure there is spare capacity for future use because when a trench is opened to add conduits, it increases the project's material cost. So even if the facility uses only a small percentage of built-in spare capacity, it still is money well spent.

(ii) For **intra-building cabling**, the most critical step is identifying the location of communications closets. They should be located to minimise individual cable runs to every location. FMs should ensure that closets are not near any EMI source, such as power transformers or copying centres. Ceiling distribution or floor distribution systems are the two most common approaches for intra-building cabling. The inclusion of cabling in the structure of a building at construction phase gives rise to the term 'structured cabling'.

The ceiling distribution approach uses space between the structural floor and the suspended ceiling. Cables run down along the walls or wire poles and terminate at the power or communication outlet. Ceiling distribution offers a high degree of flexibility for future additions and changes and allows easier access to a large portion of the service area.

Floor distribution systems use conduits or channels under floors and can be used with raised or cellular floors. Under-floor systems can have separate channels to accommodate both power and communication systems in the same assembly, reducing the overall cost. They can be encased in concrete and accessible through junction boxes, and they provide a high degree of security.

An integrated system

Using a consolidated approach in designing common cable pathways can reduce initial construction costs by 10–30%. The cost of future renovations and modification attributed to cable changes also can be reduced by 25–40%.

Using structured connectivity solutions (SCS) creates a framework for integrating building automation needs and telecommunication requirements. Much of the cost reduction stems from the fact that SCS enables facilities to avoid traditional construction practices, where each part is specified and installed separately without any regard to others. Moreover, telecommunication requirements are typically addressed as one of the last tasks before occupancy.

Common distribution benefits

The standard medium used for telecommunication networks is the 24-gauge UTP cable. This type of wire is more than adequate for most signal applications. Besides creating significant cost savings by lowering the cost for modifications, specifying a common cable infrastructure for telecommunication and data can ensure greater system flexibility.

Standards from two organisations – the Electronic Industry Association/Telecommunications Industry Association (EIA/TIA) and the International Organisation for Standardisation/International Electrotechnical Commission (ISO/IEC) – have given rise to cabling architecture in which horizontal pathways terminate at telecommunication closets. This structure allows facilities to consolidate services in one location.

28 Grounds and External Areas

28.1 External areas

Visually attractive external areas present a good image to employees, visitors and clients on the premises. It is also a great source of pride for the staff by giving the impression that they are working for a caring and considerate employer.

By the same token, the standing of the company in the community can be enhanced if the external areas are neat and tidy, with well-tended trees and gardens.

Soft landscaping refers to the vegetation and hard landscaping refers to the pavements, patios, walkways and other structures surrounding the external parts of premises.

28.2 In-house or contract-out landscaping maintenance

As in common with most services, gardening and maintenance of external areas can be done in house or via a specialist contractor. Some buildings will have a large enough area of external areas and gardens sufficient to justify the employment of a full time gardening team. Smaller sites may only need the services of a gardener once a week, with flexibility due to the weather and the time of the year. Maintenance of the hard landscaping areas will often come under the remit of the fabric maintenance contractor. Snow clearance and grit application tasks may also come under this service contract.

Apart from arranging remedial works to be carried out to diseased or dangerous trees, the FM may decide to undertake landscape improvements to enhance the visual impact of the immediate environs of the building. An example of a maintenance schedule and checklist is shown in Box 28.1 and Figure 28.1 respectively.

28.3 Landscaping standards

There are a number of British Standards pertaining to landscaping operations:

- ❑ BS5837 (1980)
- ❑ BS4428 (1989)
- ❑ BS3975 (1974)
- ❑ BS 3998 (1989)
- ❑ BS 5837 (2005)
- ❑ BS 4043 (1989)
- ❑ BS 7370 (1993)

Box 28.1   Example of an external areas maintenance schedule

The provision of grounds maintenance services that encompass, but are not limited to, all accepted practices and methods used in undertaking good horticultural and grounds maintenance to keep all sites in a neat and tidy state. This service includes litter removal and disposal.

Inspect and perform grass cutting to maintain a maximum grass height of 40 mm unless otherwise agreed with the client representative.

Remove fallen leaves when necessary.

Inspection and maintenance of all trees, hedges, herbaceous shrubs and planted areas to retain shape and site-lines; removal of overhanging growths from footways and carriageways and weed control.

The provisioning of new trees, shrubs and plants and the re-provisioning of the same that have expired due to natural causes is to be billed as a demand service. Any re-provisioning necessary due to negligence will be the contractor's responsibility.

In addition, maintain the area extending to 1 m on either side of the perimeter fence, unless otherwise agreed with by the client manager. Keep the area free from weeds, shrubs and other visual impairments.

Sweep the roads and clear road gullies when necessary.

Upon request, make available to the client management for approval, lists and COSHH assessments of all chemicals, hazardous materials and poisons required for the execution of these works. Requests will be made with reasonable notice.

Gritting and clearance of snow and ice from paths, roads and car parks as dictated by weather conditions to assist with the safe movement of people and vehicles around the site.

Provision of all vehicles, machinery and hand tools required for the delivery of this service is the responsibility of the contractor.

The costs of consumables, for example grit and sand and so on, are charged as required.

There are other standards that the FM could request or check when appointing a landscape contractor (The British Association of Landscape Industries (BALI) can provide further information):

(i) ROLO Scheme (Registration of Land based Operatives)
(ii) NHSS (National Highways Sector Scheme 18)

28.4 Landscape architects

In order to obtain expert help in landscaping operations, a landscape architect should be consulted. They can be commissioned for all sorts of tasks from the total redesign to footpaths, fencing, turfing, planting of trees and shrubs, hedges and bulbs. The Landscape Institute can provide a list of their members and give advice on which one would suit the particular type of work. The Institute can also advise on conditions of contract and scale of charges. Standard forms of contract for landscaping works can also be obtained from the Landscape Institute.

28.5 Decay of trees

It is difficult to assess the extent of the danger presented by a decaying tree. Several different types of fungi exist and little is known about many of them. If unusual symptoms are evident,

Grounds Maintenance KPM, Record Sheet and Check List Site:.................................							
Specific location(s) Assessed:................. .... (e.g. area, zone, etc.)	Grounds maintenance activity performance: Score 1 to 5 (or N/A - Not Applicable) 5 = Perfect, excellent 4 = Very good 3 = Acceptable 2 = Could do better						
Date of assessment:	1 = Neglected (significant failure of service)						
Grounds maintenance-related activities requiring check against agreed standards:	Circle appropriate score, i.e. 1-5 or N/A						Comments/action taken on scores 1 or 2 (details on separate sheet if necessary)
Grassed areas are well maintained	N/A	1	2	3	4	5	
Shrubs are pruned and are neat and tidy	N/A	1	2	3	4	5	
Weed control measures are in force	N/A	1	2	3	4	5	
Area is free of any accumulation of litter	N/A	1	2	3	4	5	
Trees are appropriately trimmed	N/A	1	2	3	4	5	
Leaf, pine needles and cone accumulations are collected up	N/A	1	2	3	4	5	
Roads are kept clean and tidy and free from accumulations of dust/clippings and the like	N/A	1	2	3	4	5	
Road gullies are free from blockages	N/A	1	2	3	4	5	
Site lines are maintained	N/A	1	2	3	4	5	
	N/A	1	2	3	4	5	
	N/A	1	2	3	4	5	
**Customer satisfaction: Are you generally satisfied that the grounds maintenance service is to an acceptable standard? (dependent on customer availability, or subject to prior agreement, the customer may choose not to participate in these checks. In this instance, score should be N/A)	N/A	1	2	3	4	5	Customer comments:
	(** This score not to be included in the KPM calculation) Customer signature						
Total number of activities scoring 1 _____ At this location	Total number of activities scoring 2 _____ At this location						
Contractor's signature (wherever possible the contractor's representative should sign to acknowledge these results)					Date: _____		
Contractor signature					Date: _____		
Client signature					Date: _____		

Figure 28.1   Grounds maintenance audit tick list

expert advice should be sought as to the best method of treating the decay. Failure to get expert advice or to act upon such advice could lead to allegations of negligence if the tree then presents a danger.

Many fungi invade a tree through wounds – areas where wood has been exposed by breaking, loss of bark, pruning or lopping. It is worthwhile paying particular attention to such areas when checking for symptoms of decay. The way a tree is pruned and the time of the year that it is carried out will affect decay and thus this sort of work is best left to the experts.

28.6 Damage to trees

Unhealthy trees could present a danger to the public. The FM should initiate a regular inspection of trees so that timely remedial action can be taken.

Damage may be caused to a tree because it is close to a building when, in high winds and storms, it is damaged by striking the building or continually rubbing against it.

Further sources of damage may be caused by insufficient water to feed the tree because it is situated near paved areas and insufficient ground is left uncovered to allow water to penetrate to the roots. Its proximity to a source of heat or pollution such as an exhaust air outlet or fumes may cause the tree great distress. Another cause of decay is when the earth surrounding the tree is compacted by constant heavy vehicles which in turn will limit the penetration of water and the free movement of oxygen and carbon dioxide.

Tree roots may also be damaged by any underground work on sewers, pipes cables and foundations and also nearby kerbs and roadways. Box 28.1 shows some of the factors affecting tree root growth.

A specialist will be able to warn the FM of potential dangers and advise on the corrective action required. Pruning of branches too close to a building or the erection of fences around trees to protect them from damage by vandals or vehicles may be all that is required. More serious problems could require the tree to be felled.

However, felling a tree on clay soil may be potentially dangerous as the ground may swell causing surface heave – which is as destructive as shrinkage or subsidence.

28.7 Removal of trees and tree stumps

If a tree stump is situated on a boundary, the ownership must first be established before any action is taken to remove it. It may require the negotiation of a wayleave (rented right of way) if access to the adjoining property is required. If the removal work will affect the use of a public highway or footpath, the local highway authority should be informed of the intended works so that measures can be taken to protect the safety of the public.

If a tree surgeon is contracted for the work, the contract should clearly indicate whether or not provision is made for the removal of a stump from the premises and whether the tree surgeon will clear away all debris. Terms can vary between different contractors. Alternatively, the stump could be taken to a nearby waste tip, but first it is sensible to check with the local authority, as some do not permit this form of waste disposal. If no suitable tip can be found, the stump may be burned but due consideration must be given to local smoke control requirements under the Environmental Health Regulations.

28.8 Ownership of trees

The law regards all trees as permanent assets attached to the land. However, this does not apply to the crops from trees such as fruit which can easily be removed. Unless there is a written agreement to the contrary, the trees belong to the freeholder. Thus any tenant must obtain the consent of the landlord to fell or lop any tree. The lease should always be consulted, as there may be a requirement for the tenant to be responsible for their upkeep.

Ornamental trees and shrubs are not regarded in law as 'timber or timber-like trees'. These would be regarded as the tenant's property to do with as he pleases. If on the other hand, a tenant plants a timber tree, the landlord can claim possession at the expiry of the lease without necessarily paying any compensation. If a timber tree is felled and the timber sold, the landlord is entitled to the proceeds.

Problems may arise with the ownership of trees when situated on the boundary of adjoining properties. Normally, the trees will be deemed in law to belong to the landowner on whose land it was planted, not withstanding the fact that its trunk, roots and branches encroach onto the neighbouring property. If the persons who planted the tree or his descendants in law cannot easily be traced, ownership may be inferred by such actions as regular pruning and general husbandry of the tree. If ownership is still in doubt, the position of the trunk is the decisive factor. Where ownership is in doubt and the tree stands fairly equally on both sides of the boundary, the tree will be considered to be in joint ownership.

28.9 Spreading of roots and branches

Spreading roots and branches can cause disputes with neighbours.

Branches

It is rare that the owner of the tree is required to remove branches except in the case where they present a danger or create a nuisance to neighbours or their property. The usual practice is for the neighbour(s) to prune any branches overhanging their property. They do not need to give notice to the tree owner but common courtesy would expect them to do so. The branches removed are still property of the tree owner and they must be offered to the neighbour, who is not obliged to accept them.

Roots

The tree roots are designed to extract moisture from the ground to sustain the tree. This extraction from the soil and subsoil, in turn, can cause movement of nearby walls and foundations. Compensation by the tree owner may be payable to a neighbour if spreading roots affect the stability of a neighbouring wall or building. The neighbour is entitled to prevent the roots spreading onto his/her property by such methods as digging a ditch. The effect of roots on buildings and foundations is difficult to predict. It is important to consider a number of factors which can help determine likely risk – these are shown in Table 28.1 below.

28.10 Dangerous trees

There is a duty of care on every tree owner to make regular inspections of their trees to check for disease and decay. Bearing in mind the tree owner's responsibility for any damage

Table 28.1   Risk factors affecting root growth and damage

The tree species	Some species such as poplar, elm and willow have a high moisture requirement.
The soil type	Clay, found in large areas of south east England, contains large amounts of water and thus shrinkage will occur if there is a great demand for moisture by trees. This in turn can lead to movement of foundations.
Building structure	Building design, materials used and construction techniques will affect the buildings tolerance to movement. Single storey buildings, extensions, additional porches and bay windows are particularly vulnerable.
Tree age	In the case of a mature tree, there is little likelihood of foundation movement except in extreme dry weather conditions.

the tree causes if it breaks or falls, then this is a prudent act. If the tree had previously shown signs of decay externally, it is more than likely the tree owner is responsible. Other indirect evidence is difficult to come by, but light foliage and dieback could also be an indication of future trouble.

If animals were affected by the ingestion of poisonous parts of the tree such as berries, fruits or fronds, the tree owner would not be liable if it is demonstrated that the animals were trespassing. However, foliage or fruit which were thrown onto a neighbour's property with adverse results could mean that the tree owner was liable.

28.11 Licence to plant

The Highways Act 1980 – S 142 – gives the highway authorities the power to grant licences to owners or occupiers of premises adjacent to a highway to permit them to plant and maintain trees, shrubs, plants or grass in specific parts of the highway as shown in the licence. There will be conditions attached to ensure safety for the users of the highway.

Application for such a licence is free but reasonable costs and other expenses occurred in connection with the granting of the licence and a reasonable annual charge to cover administration are both recoverable from the licence.

28.12 Tree preservation orders (TPOs)

Planning legislation recognises the importance of trees to the beauty of the countryside and the need to preserve and enhance the proper management of trees and woodlands. Thus a tree preservation order can be obtained by the local planning authority or from the courts to prevent the felling, topping, lopping or wilful destruction of any trees included in the order.

The consent of the authority has to be sought before tree felling or surgery can be carried out on such a tree. This application is free.

However, in an emergency, where a tree is dying or dead or becomes dangerous or is a nuisance, the prevention to fell, lop or prune the tree does not apply. Part of the terms of such an order may stipulate that if consent is given for the felling of a tree, a replacement tree of an approved species and size is planted in its place.

Consideration must also be given to the fact that the tree roots can disturb or fracture drains and sewers and water mains especially if they are old and leaking.

28.13 Conservation areas

In the case where premises are situated in an area which has been designated a conservation area by the local authorities, then 6 weeks' notice is to be given to the authority of any work to be carried out on any tree in the area. This has no fee attached. This is to give the authority the opportunity to decide whether to place a tree preservation order on the tree in question.

28.14 Internal planting

Internal planting has to be selected to thrive in an unnatural indoor environment. Internal planting will require special maintenance, watering and feeding regimes.

Environmental considerations

There are four aspects of environmental conditions to be considered as shown in Table 28.2.

Maintenance

The maintenance regime could well include watering, feeding, cleaning, pruning and staking. Time during daylight hours will need to be spent by the maintenance contractor to carry out tasks. The maintenance programme needs to take into account the requirements of the personnel in the area and the areas in which the plants are living. Great care must be taken to ensure that they are not over or under watered and that there is not a great deal of mess and water spread about the area. Vandalism and deposits of coffee and tea dregs should be actively discouraged.

Disease

There is a need to regularly examine and protect the plants against damage, disease and pests. Sometimes this may require fumigation, which will need the areas to be evacuated.

Table 28.2   Environmental factors affecting landscaping

Light	Light within a building, both in intensity and duration, can be vastly different to that which the plants would expect in their normal environment. Higher light levels than those usually found in an office area will be required. Normally, plants require light levels of the order of 750–5000 lux but an office may need only 200–1000 lux. Although plants will survive in less light, their health and general appearance will suffer. By the same token, plants do require at least a 6-hour period of darkness for recovery and regeneration.
Temperature	Most interior plants will survive in temperatures during the daylight period between 21°C and 24°C which is the normal occupation comfort zone. During darkness, the temperature should fall approximately 10°C. Sudden temperature changes should be avoided at all costs as this will severely damage or kill the plants. The temperature should not be allowed to fall below 0°C.
Ventilation	So that plants can replenish their carbon dioxide used during photosynthesis, they need proper ventilation. However, plants should not be placed near ventilation grilles where they may be in a draught and subject to rapid changes.
Humidity	Most interior plants appreciate the same RH as humans – about 30–50% RH. Some plants may require a higher humidity such as tropical and succulent plants. A lower RH should be avoided as this can lead to dehydration.

This sort of treatment is best done during weekends or national holidays. The extra cost of this needs to be covered in the maintenance contract.

28.15 Artificial plants

As an alternative to real plants in internal planting schemes, plastic or silk artificial planting may be an answer especially where there are low light levels or the lighting is kept on for more than 20 hours per day. However, there are certain points that need to be considered.

Budget and costs

There will be the requirement for regular dusting, washing and cleaning to give the overall desired effect. They are not a cheap alternative to real plants. Artificial plants are made of plastic, polyester or artificial silk. Problems of light levels and temperature do not arise and thus they may be sited where real plants would die. Their colour will fade over time and they will need to be replaced. A full cost analysis is needed when comparing with the real plant option.

Fire hazards

As some of the types of artificial plants constitute fire risks, specialist fire protection advice should be sought prior to purchase.

28.16 Maintenance of hardstandings and external areas

Gravel and hoggin

Gravel and hoggin areas are believed to be relatively maintenance free. However, if they are to be looked after properly there is some maintenance required to keep them looking presentable.

Where gravel or hoggin is to be used as a drive or footpath, it is necessary to ensure that edges have a kerb to prevent the material from spreading, thus forming depressions. The gravel will require raking and rolling as well as the refilling of depressions with new material.

Periodic weed killing or defoliation is also necessary to keep the material looking clean and well kept. The initial laying of this type of material may be of low cost in comparison with others but the ongoing maintenance can be expensive.

Paving stones and slabs

Stones and slabs are popular materials for footpaths and forecourts, as they are easy to repair or reinstate. There is a large selection of colours, shapes and sizes available. Common faults are depressions where the bedding materials have compressed or washed away or have just settled over time.

Uneven bedding material can cause slabs to rock and protrude, forming a trip hazard. The recognised limit for such a protrusion is 20 mm. One of the most obvious causes of defects in paved areas are when vehicles mount or park on them. Most paved areas are designed for pedestrian use not vehicles. If the area is subject to authorised vehicle parking then it should be redesigned to accommodate it with more suitable hardstanding substrate.

Other problems are tree and shrub roots growing under the slabs causing rocking, unevenness or even cracking. Correct selection of shrubs or trees should be made to take account of the spread of roots in search of food and stability.

With all paved areas, the drainage and gully channels need to be kept free from obstructions.

28.17 Vegetation and planted areas

Grass cutting

Grassed areas will need a maintenance schedule. It needs to be cut during the growing season. The frequency will depend on:

❑   The chosen standard expected.
❑   The intended use – such as playing fields, sports activities, ornamental features and so on.
❑   The weather conditions.
❑   The season (more cuts are required in summer than winter).
❑   Its location (such as out of sight of the public, or in main entrance areas to corporate HQ).
❑   Fire risk.

Cutting frequencies can be as low as four cuts per month or up to ten per month depending on the standard set by the requirements of the corporate image, use of the grassed areas, or finances available.

Grassed areas up to the edge of the building or other obstructions may increase the cost of cutting, due to the care required by the operatives to avoid damage to the building or other structures.

A stone edge or apron around the building may prevent such damage. It will also allow machinery to cut to an edge and therefore reduce time and cost of edge strimming.

Another issue with grass cutting operations is the loose stones and other sharp objects striking the building and cladding causing damage.

Grass treatments may include overseeding to fill in any patches, aeration to improve growth, demossing to remove moss, fertiliser and weed killing treatments.

Shrubs and borders

Obviously if shrubs and flowers are incorporated into external areas, they require considerable attention to maintain a pleasant state. If the right choice of shrub is made for its location, it may be self-regulating in size and shape. If not, time will need to be spent maintaining the desired effect.

Flower borders

Generally these need attention all year round. If it is the corporate image to have colour throughout the year then a continual change of plants will be necessary.

Employing a permanent gardener with greenhouse facilities to produce his own plants or a contracted landscape gardener is costly.

Large trees and shrubs

Large trees and shrubs should be carefully considered when planting in close proximity to buildings. The roots have a tendency to find their way into surface and foul drains and cause blockages as well as cause damage to building foundations.

28.18 Boundary fencing

If timber fencing posts and panels are used then they need to be correctly constructed with sufficient depth into the ground to withstand wind pressures blowing them over. The lighter interwoven slatted panels are more susceptible to damage from the elements and slight impact. Though most timber fencing posts and panels are manufactured and supplied with treated timber, periodic re-treatments are recommended which will prolong the life and enhance the colour.

Chain link fencing is supported by concrete, steel or timber posts with three or four strands of straining wire between each post. Bracing legs are positioned at intervals to give additional strength. If not coated with plastic, the wires and fencing are susceptible to rust, even if the wire has been factory coated with a galvanise protection. The galvanise layer is very thin and after a few years corrosion and rusting takes place.

28.19 Brickwork walls

If the correct specification of bricks are chosen the 'elements' have little effect on this material. If a lesser specification is chosen then deterioration will be evident.

Faults such as spalling, cracks in the mortar joints, effluorescence, loose coping stones or continually damp bricks (caused by rising ground water or rain on the coping details saturating the brickwork) make the structure of brickwork walls susceptible to frost damage.

28.20 Grounds maintenance contract

This may include the following elements:

❑ Comply with legal and company standards including Health and Safety, Hygiene and Fire Regulations.
❑ Comply with COSHH when handling chemicals, fertilisers or hazardous substances.
❑ Maintain the herbaceous, rose and shrub borders and ensure they are kept free from weeds.
❑ Ensure they are pruned, watered, deadheaded and supported when necessary.
❑ Provide a spring and summer bedding scheme and maintain it as required.
❑ Maintain all flowering tubs, troughs and hanging baskets.
❑ Detect any common pests and diseases and take the necessary appropriate action.
❑ Clear weeds from paths, paved areas, car parks, shrub beds, etc. and apply a suitable herbicide.
❑ Competently use and care for all tools and gardening equipment, ensuring the security of these items.
❑ Operate and maintain the motor mowers and attachments as necessary ensuring that regular servicing occurs.

❑   Cut grassed areas to accommodate specification standard and frequencies.
❑   Trim hedges as required, but at least twice a year.
❑   Regularly inspect trees for storm damage and signs of decay and instigate action to maintain their condition and safety.
❑   Ensure ponds are kept free of obstruction and weeds are kept in an algae-free condition.
❑   Keep grounds and gutters free from leaves, debris and general rubbish.
❑   Dispose off all arisings safely, burn only when safe to do so and when neighbours will be least affected.

28.21 Site footpaths and roads

The FM team will need to give particular attention to the maintenance of steps, ramps and associated hand rails. Changes of level, wet and slippery surfaces and areas where people walk to and from the premises must be kept safe.

Concrete paving slabs

Slabs are normally bedded on sand or gauged mortar bed. To repair any broken, missing, uneven and rocking slabs, the FM team will need to remove affected slabs, and then replace the foundation bed and relay the slabs.

Gravelled areas

The only maintenance required will be the removal of debris and weeds. Gravel may occasionally require some replenishment.

Concrete

Maintenance requires regular inspection for cracks, crumbing and missing pieces. If only minor defects are found, then it is acceptable to remove loose material and then replace with new concrete. Cracks can be filled with proprietary filler. If major defects are found, then a competent consultant should be used to give advice.

Bituminous surfaces (black top)

Many roads and footways are constructed using bituminous materials (black top). Most maintenance to these surfaces will be in the top layers, i.e. the wearing course. Minor deterioration can be repaired by the application of a bituminous emulsion and 3–6 mm chippings. Any depression over 25 mm should be filled and levelled. Materials for this will be mainly patching Macadams such as Fine Cold Asphalt or other proprietary material, such as Rapid Road Repairs by Ermcol.

   Major failures should be investigated by highways engineers as more major resurfacing and repair may be necessary.

Manholes

Maintenance checks involve visual inspections to make sure that the covers are sound. Particularly in footpaths, check that they are not rocking or causing a hazard. If the manholes are uneven, then they must be removed, cleaned off and re-bedded using cement and sand.

Pooling

Pooling of water on pavements or roads is an indicator of other problems. A maintenance regime could log where puddles naturally occur, so if a puddle appears in an unexpected place investigation may be necessary.

Road and car park markings

These markings wear out and require renewing to comply with the Highways Code and also to ensure any local rules on use of parking. Legislation governs the wording, size, colour and positioning of road signs.

28.22 Workplace parking

The management of parking in the workplace often falls into the FM remit. As an area of much contention and emotion, it is not always an easy task, often taking a disproportionate amount of time to effectively manage a relatively low priority service within the overall FM span of responsibilities.

Benefits

The benefits of strict parking management include:

❑ A reduction in the number of cars on site may offer both financial and environmental benefits.
❑ Land and space previously allocated to parking can be used to create more offices or green space for landscaping.
❑ A balance between parking for employees and visitors may result in more spaces for clients, customers and visitors.
❑ If charging is introduced then this can produce revenue for investment to support other initiatives in the travel plan and contribute towards the maintenance costs too.
❑ An allocation of spaces on the basis of need will ensure those who can only use a car to travel to and from work are able to park on arrival.

28.23 Parking policy

There are a number of issues to consider in determining the parking policy.

❑ Availability of transport alternatives, such as rail and bus.
❑ The ability and confidence of staff to walk or cycle if the routes are safe and well signposted.
❑ Motivation of employees to try alternatives to their car.
❑ Travel distances of employees and visitors.
❑ Location and access to the site or premises.
❑ Security risk profile of the organisation.
❑ Type of business and activities undertaken at the premises.

❑   Demographics of the workforce.
❑   Company culture and work ethos.

Implementation

Implementation of a new parking policy will depend on a number of issues.

❑   Research into current use, costs, options and impact of the proposed arrangements.
❑   Consultation with various staff groups prior to implementation
❑   Senior managers must be willing to lead by example.
❑   Offer incentives to people who reduce the use of their cars. For example, prime parking spots for car sharers.
❑   Zones of space for specific use and users.
❑   Visitors.
❑   Disabled.
❑   Short-term parking.
❑   Company or pool car.
❑   Car sharers.
❑   Motorbikes.
❑   Bicycles.
❑   Deliveries.

The travel plan should offer viable alternatives and incentives to people if the number of parking spaces is to be reduced. The travel plan and parking policy needs to be linked to the allocation of employee company cars and company vehicles.

Soft issues

The softer issues involved in management of parking will include:

❑   Crime recording and statistics.
❑   Management practice.
❑   Travel plan.
❑   Employee expectations, custom and practice.
❑   Use of permits, passes or tokens to control use of spaces.

Permits

Depending on the number of spaces that need to be managed, consideration must be given to the type of permit system to be used. Examples include a simple permit, security pass, proximity token or radio frequency identification (RFID) system.

The administration of permits of any type is not to be underestimated. Staff may have more than one car, lose their passes, have their car vandalised or broken into and so on. Passes can be copied, forged or borrowed. Linking access control of the car park to the other systems in the buildings is often the easiest and quickest system of control.

However, there may still be a requirement for short-term parking for visitors, contractors and others who do not possess the access control device or other system that is used to manage the allocation of parking spaces.

28.24 Car park categories

Parking can be in many locations, and take many forms. It may be appropriate to consider parking facilities in the following categories:

❑   Surface parking facilities – urban areas.
❑   Surface parking facilities – rural areas.
❑   Multi-storey parking facilities.
❑   Basement or underground parking facilities.
❑   Roof top parking facilities.
❑   Lift-operated parking facilities.

Physical attributes

The physical features of parking areas that should be considered by the FM when reviewing existing or new car park designs include:

❑   Boundaries and perimeters.
❑   Access control.
❑   Lighting.
❑   Parking areas or zones.
❑   Pedestrian access.
❑   Signage.
❑   Surveillance.
❑   Vehicular access.
❑   Facilities for cycles and motorbikes.
❑   Facilities for oversized vehicles.

28.25 Car park design

Ideally an existing or new car park should meet the criteria outlined in the 'Secured by Design' guidance document issued by the Association of Chief Police Officers (ACPO). There are seven attributes that are particularly relevant to crime prevention as shown in Table 28.3. The attributes have emerged from in-depth research into crime prevention and urban design practice and theory. The implementation of these design principles requires a sound appreciation of both crime prevention and urban design. It also requires planners, designers, operators and crime prevention practitioners to work closely together in a pragmatic way.

Security issues

Parked cars, motorbikes and bicycles can be particularly vulnerable to crime and, unless they are in a private garage, must be overlooked. The most secure place to park is in an enclosed space such as a garage. However, workplace and public parking is more usually in an open space with barriers or gates.

Ideally, areas used for parking should be seen or visible to others either directly or via closed circuit television (CCTV). In addition, a single, gated narrow entrance will make crime more difficult. Larger, typically non-residential car parks should comply with the specification set out in the Association of Chief Police Officers' (ACPO) Secured Car Parks Award Scheme.

Table 28.3   The key attributes of car park designs

Access and movement	Places with well-defined routes, spaces and entrances that provide for convenient movement without compromising security.
Structure	Places that are structured so that different uses do not cause conflict.
Surveillance	Places where all publicly accessible spaces are overlooked.
Ownership	Places that promote a sense of ownership, respect, territorial responsibility and community.
Physical protection	Places that include necessary, well-designed security features.
Activity	Places where the level of human activity is appropriate to the location and creates a reduced risk of crime and a sense of safety at all times.
Management and maintenance	Places that are designed with management and maintenance in mind, to discourage crime in the present and the future.

Car parks can also pose particular threats to an organisation as they provide locations for others to leave explosives or dangerous chemicals in close proximity to their intended targets. The damage caused by explosions in car parks is considerable. FMs should undertake a threat and risk assessment for the locality of their parking areas. Depending on the outcome, a higher level of monitoring and control of parking may be required.

Risk assessment

The assessment should take into account:

❑   Buildings used by the organisation.
❑   Vehicles owned by both employees, third parties and the company.
❑   Neighbouring premises, buildings and assets belonging to others.
❑   People including staff, customers, visitors, and members of the public.

It may be useful to adopt a five-step approach, as outlined below:
   (i) **Identify** any issues. In particular look at the temptations on offer, look at the surroundings and the occupancy of the building.
  (ii) **Identify** potential victims. A car park that is used over a 24-hour period will mean workers making their way across the car park when it is dark. The organisation could be held liable for any injury or the mugging of a staff member if a safe and secure environment, including car parks, has not been provided.
 (iii) **Assess** existing measures, such as perimeter fences and access controls. Will they meet the challenge of the risks identified?
  (iv) **Record** findings and details of any actions taken. This is a requirement under the Health and Safety at Work Act 1974 and may be necessary for insurance purposes.
   (v) **Review** and amend accordingly. Make sure that any new circumstances, such as change of occupancy levels or closure of neighbouring premises, are factored into any new risk assessments.

Securing the perimeter

Wherever possible, it is important to define the car park as company territory. As a very basic security measure, FMs need to ensure that there is a robust physical barrier to keep out intruders. Perimeter boundaries can consist of walls, hedges or fences.

Walls are not necessarily the best perimeter boundary because they:

❑ Are a graffiti target.
❑ May require anti-climbing measures.
❑ Can muffle sound.
❑ Will restrict visibility.
❑ Can present an unwelcoming picture to visitors and customers.
❑ Can fall into disrepair, causing damage to nearby objects.
❑ Are easily damaged intentionally or otherwise.

Hedges are environmentally sound and aesthetically pleasant. Low level defensive planting can be a real deterrent, especially for denying burglary attempts or stopping people taking short cuts. For maximum effect, use thorny bushes such as pyracantha, berberis, gorse or holly.

The disadvantages of hedges include:

❑ They require regular maintenance to cut back growth.
❑ They have a larger footprint than a fence which may result in the loss of valuable parking space.
❑ They could be a concealment place for intruders.

Fences allow for natural surveillance of the surrounding area and used in conjunction with low level planting can pass the aesthetics test. To be fully effective fencing must:

❑ Have a minimum recommended height of 2.4 m, although planning permission will be required for a fence of this height. A compromise fence height of 1.8 m, plus an additional anti-climb barrier of 0.2 m (total height 2 m) is unlikely to require planning permission.
❑ Feature railings, expanded metal or wire mesh, professionally installed to BS 1722-10-14.
❑ Be grounded in a hard surface.
❑ Be inspected regularly.

Controlling access

A gate house, with an attendant on duty, may only be cost effective for large sites with constant traffic over a 24-hour period. However, there are a number of different types of vehicle-restricting systems available, ideally with pedestrians and cyclists having separate entrances.

Gates for both pedestrians and vehicles can be controlled by swipe card, hands-free controls and biometrics, while vehicle-only entrances can also be controlled by systems such as RFID tags or number plate recognition technology. Gates should have anti-lift hinges, be well lit at night and be covered by any monitoring system in use.

To facilitate any control system, it is necessary to register all car park users on a central database to enable use of number plate recognition technology. Issuing windscreen display permits will allow for an easy check by car park patrols on who should and should not be in the car park.

Access for visitors

The organisation owes a duty of care to visitors and so must ensure that any security arrangements are inclusive. Visitors' vehicles may not be registered on any access control database unless the visit has been pre-booked and vehicle details logged in advance. Ensure that visitors' car parking areas are well defined, accessible, secure and are offered the same level of security as the staff car park, even if they are not sited in the main car park.

Lighting

Car parks that are used during any period of darkness should be lit. Dark places and strong shadows provide hiding places for criminals and any lighting systems should be designed to eliminate these. It is good practice to install low level dusk-to-dawn lighting as opposed to harsh, sensor-activated spotlights. This can be very cheap to run using 9–11 W fluorescent tubes and does not cause harsh shadows.

In addition, FMs may wish to consider the following best practice:

❑ Get expert advice from an accredited body such as the Institute of Lighting Engineers.
❑ Conduct patrols and surveys at night time to check on lighting levels.
❑ Replace defective bulbs promptly.
❑ Do not over light – it is expensive and can cause dark shadows.
❑ Mount the lighting out of reach of criminals and vandals, but avoid 'light trespass' on to neighbouring properties, into the road or upwards.

Closed circuit television

Use of CCTV is growing and many business premises now display warning signs and prominent cameras to advertise its presence.

In a basic system, cameras may be viewed via a central monitor in rotation, so if there are five cameras, each one may only be viewed for 12 minutes in each hour – unless a split screen monitor is used. A basic system may record the images, but it is unlikely that it will capture images that are good enough to offer positive identification of a criminal. The best use of such a system is as a deterrent.

Operator-driven systems can be used to target areas of risk or individuals thought to be a threat. If high quality equipment is used, this can be a major deterrent. However, watching TV monitors can be very tedious and requires a high level of concentration to identify events out of the ordinary. Operators are said to be able to concentrate for only 20-minute spans.

Latest developments include linking CCTV to behaviour recognition software. All cameras connected to a behaviour recognition system become proactive, alerting the operator when unusual or predetermined behaviour occurs. In partnership with Intelligent Pedestrian Observation Technologies (IPSOTEK), software systems can automatically detect commonly occurring security and safety incidents such as abandoned packages, vandalism, loitering, fighting and so on. The system will not make the decisions as to what is going on; however, it will alert the operator who can interpret the information and then rapidly attend to the situation.

To get best value from CCTV, place cameras:

❑ Where they are easy to spot.
❑ Where they can protect items that are vulnerable or quiet areas.
❑ Where they cannot be tampered with.

Patrols

Random foot patrols will be a deterrent to would-be criminals and a comforter to those using the car park, especially if the patrols are highly visible after dark. The patrol can have many roles:

❏ Checking that only authorised vehicles are in the car park (if wheel clamps are used, a licence from the Security Industry Association is needed).
❏ Alerting the FM to damage or problems on site.
❏ Alerting car owners to windows left open, lights left on, etc.
❏ Checking suspicious packages.

28.26 Bicycle parking

The main points to consider when planning cycle parking areas and facilities are:

❏ Location.
❏ Design and installation.
❏ How many cyclists there are, and how many potential users would use the facilities?
❏ How much parking space is needed?
❏ Cost and source of funding.

Design of cycle parking areas

The design of areas for safe and secure parking of cycles will need to satisfy a number of requirements including:

❏ Conveniently located.
❏ Secure.
❏ Easy to use.
❏ Well signed.
❏ Sheltered.
❏ Vandal-proof.
❏ Well lit.
❏ Accessible.

When providing medium-term parking facilities, the following additional criteria must be considered in the design:

❏ Higher level of security.
❏ Weather protection.
❏ Storage areas.

Cycle lockers, cycle shelters or supervised areas within car parks are likely to be more appropriate than unsupervised Sheffield stands (see page 380) as they provide increased security and storage facilities. Where necessary, location of Sheffield stands near to luggage lockers may be used.

The cost of cycle storage varies between products, design and site conditions. A basic stand to accommodate two cycles will cost around £100 to supply and install. A quality cycle locker costs around £500 per cycle installed. A shelter for 20 cycles can range from £1000 to £5000 upwards.

Cycle stands

Ideally, a cycle parking facility should allow for the frame and both wheels to be locked to the fixture. Cycle stands which only grip the cycle by a wheel (these include concrete slots) are not recommended as they offer only limited security and can result in damage to wheel rims. Cyclists will be reluctant to use them and will instead lock their bike to other fixtures and fittings they see around the site.

Sheffield stands and wall loops are recommended, preferably situated as close to the destination point as possible, in frequent well-signed small groups within appropriately illuminated areas.

When designing parking facilities, the space required for a parked cycle should be 1800 mm (length) by 600 mm (width) to allow access to secure the bike.

Sheffield stand

The stand provides good support to the cycle and allows the cyclist to secure both the frame and wheels without risk of damage.

Stands should be 750 mm high and a minimum of 700 mm long. A desirable minimum distance of 1000 mm should be provided between stands to accommodate two cycles per stand. Stand ends should either be embedded in concrete, bolted to the ground or welded to parallel bars at ground level to form a 'toast rack' system. Adequate space should be provided at either end of the stand to enable cycles to be easily removed.

Wall loops

Wall loops (or locking rings) are simple, relatively inexpensive and may be more appropriate than Sheffield stands in areas where pavement widths are restricted. They may also be less environmentally intrusive than Sheffield stands in certain circumstances. The disadvantage with wall loops is that an excessively long chain is required to secure both the cycle wheels and the frame. Therefore, in the majority of circumstances wall loops are likely to only offer a limited level of security.

Loops should be 750 mm from the ground, project no more than 50 mm from the wall and be a minimum of 1800 mm apart.

Location

It is recommended that parking facilities should be located as close as possible to the entrance of the building they are intended to serve in order that convenience and security may be maximised. Where possible they should be placed so that they may be overlooked by occupiers of the buildings or be in clear view of pedestrians. Consideration may be required for visitor's cycle parking if the area for staff is within an enclosed secure area.

Stands placed in dark recesses or at the rear of car parks will not be attractive in terms of security and are therefore unlikely to be used.

Cycle stands should be placed carefully in relation to their surroundings. The appearance of cycle stands may be enhanced by incorporating them into wider environmental improvement schemes. Care should be taken to ensure that any stand provided does not obstruct pedestrians or incorporate dangerous projections.

Availability

Cycle parking is generally required for one of three possible time periods as listed below:

❑   Short-term is a period less than 2 hours.
❑   Medium-term is a period from 2 to 12 hours.
❑   Long-term is a period of 12 hours or more.

If the company has many locations within easy cycling distance, then all three categories may be required. Some companies will also pay a cycle mileage allowance for use of bicycles on company business, so this would encourage the keen cyclists to use their bikes between locations on a campus or within an area. However, for the majority of organisations, medium-term parking for bikes is required as the user will simply leave their bike for the duration of the working day.

28.27 Motorcycle parking

A number of secure parking schemes for motorbikes are in use across the UK. Motorcycles can be locked when parked by using an integral steering lock or a secondary device such as a chain and padlock. However, this does not prevent the locked machine from being removed by thieves. Anchor points may be set into the roadways near to the kerb-edge or into the wall or floor of off-road parking places.

Anchor points can be provided quite easily and cheaply, allowing riders to secure their bikes when parked. Such designs are generally easy to use, although a few basic considerations should be addressed to avoid potential problems.

The most successful designs are often the most simple. These are often based on simple steel rails or loops of various sizes especially in outdoor locations. Devices with moving parts that lie flat on the carriageway may present problems in use, and present a greater need for maintenance; hinges may be subject to wear and tear, distortion or interference from foreign bodies. There is the potential for pedestrians to trip or fall over them and the possibility that riders' feet or motorcycle wheels may slip on smooth metal when wet. Additional non-slip surfacing may be required to reduce the risks of slips. Ideally, secure motorcycle parking facilities should be designed with the following points in mind.

Location

They should be provided at appropriate sites at workplaces and should be well signposted from the arrival points. Locations should ideally have the following aspects:

❑   Well lit.
❑   In a busy well-used area that has many passers-by who will deter thieves who might otherwise be able to breach the security device undisturbed.
❑   Viewed by CCTV if not in the public domain.
❑   Not be affected by flooding, falling tree sap, bird droppings, etc.
❑   The anchor points must not be placed over gully gratings, where keys to locks and vehicles are easily dropped.
❑   Protection from encroachment or obstruction by other vehicles.

Manoeuvring space

Care should be taken to allow reasonable manoeuvring space by placing the anchor points away from obstructions. Where anchor points are installed along more than one side of the parking bay, care should be taken to ensure that enough space is allowed for larger machines without obstructing access to anchor points on another side. Motorbikes can be very heavy to move.

Construction

The anchor point should offer a useful degree of protection from theft and interference. At the very least, the anchorages should be able to defeat attempts to lift them out of the ground or breach them with hand tools, and withstand reasonable wear, tear and abuse.

The anchor point must be easy to use yet be compatible with a wide range of motorcycles and the locking devices commonly used by their riders. In particular, consideration should be given to the height at which anchor points are set – a height of about 60 cm will accommodate a wide range of wheel sizes but hinder thieves using the floor or carriageway as leverage for bolt-cutters and jacks.

Other road users

The design of the anchor point(s) and layout of the site should not present additional hazards to or from other road users and vehicles. Pedestrians, especially those with visual or mobility impairment, can be especially vulnerable – a rail set at shin height may be acceptable when mounted on a wall at the rear of an off-road parking bay.

Costs

The costs of design, construction, installation and maintenance need to be kept low whilst still achieving the required level of performance. This will allow the number of anchorage points and sites to be maximised. Designs based on familiar materials, methods of construction and installation are likely to be the least costly, yet are often the most successful.

Environmental impact

In some locations, such as listed buildings, historic town centres, conservation areas, sensitive design of secure parking facilities for cycles and motorbikes is recommended. Choice of size, shape, colour and location must be appropriate to the surroundings, perhaps featuring architectural bollards or rails in the design. This can be achieved without compromising security or safety. Providing it is well thought out, formal parking places can reduce the frequency of illegal and inappropriate parking in sensitive areas dramatically.

28.28 Car parking standards

The highest standard of car park management can be achieved through participation in the national Safer Parking Scheme (SPS), jointly run by the British Parking Association (BPA) and the ACPO. The Park Mark® Safer Parking award is granted to parking areas that have achieved the requirements of a risk assessment as conducted by the Police. These requirements mean the parking operator has put in place measures that help to deter criminal activity and anti-social behaviour, thereby doing everything they can to prevent crime and reduce the fear of crime in their parking area.

For staff and visitors, using a Park Mark® Safer Parking area means that the area has been vetted by the Police and has measures in place in order to create a safe environment. Institution of Civil Engineers (ICE) issue guidance in – 'Recommendations for the Inspection, Maintenance and Management of Car Park Structures' (published by ICE in December 2002).

Safer Parking Scheme: The award the SPS bestows on parking facilities that meet the required standards of the scheme is called the Park Mark Safer Parking Award (PMSPA).

The initiative is primarily aimed at the management of criminal behaviour within the parking environment, and hence requires owners/operators to adopt an active management strategy to ensure that there is minimal occurrence of crime.

The standard is owned by ACPO and ACPOS (Association of Chief Police Officers Scotland); it is managed by the BPA through Development Managers (DMs), and the scheme is supported by the Home Office, the Scottish Executive and all Police Forces in England, Scotland, Wales and Northern Ireland.

The purpose of the SPS is to:

❑ Reduce crime and the fear of crime within parking facilities.
❑ Provide guidance to owners, operators and developers of parking facilities, both new and existing, on how to establish and maintain a safe and secure environment through the introduction of proven management processes, physical measures and site security systems, having considered the local crime and disorder within the immediate location.
❑ Raise awareness to the general public, when parking their car, motorcycle, bicycle, etc. that the owner/operator has considered, and where appropriate taken action, to reduce crime and the fear of crime within the parking facility that they have chosen to use.
❑ Provide a design framework for architects and developers of new parking facilities.

Legislation affecting car parking

The FM needs to consult a number of laws to ensure that the parking facilities are compliant. In particular the legislation that affects parking includes:

❑ Health and Safety at Work Act.
❑ Occupiers Liability Act 1984.
❑ Data Protection Act 1998.
❑ Clean Neighbourhood and Environment Act 2005.
❑ Road Traffic Regulations 1984.
❑ Private Security Industry Act 2001.

28.29 Travel planning

A travel plan is a package of measures designed to promote greener, cleaner travel choices within organisations and encourage the use of travel alternatives such as car sharing, public transport, walking and cycling. A travel plan should be tailored to the specific circumstances of the organisation.

It should take into account a wide array of factors including: the size and location of the organisation or building; the number of staff employed; the number of visitors and deliveries expected; and also the number of contractors servicing the building.

Often organisations are obliged to introduce travel plans for reasons such as:

❑ Planning conditions attached to new sites or site expansion (section 106 agreements).
❑ Parking shortages.
❑ Congestion problems.

Some organisations want to be able to:

❑ Recruit and retain staff more effectively.
❑ Save money on car parking spaces and business travel.
❑ Become more accessible to the local community.
❑ Simply promote a more environmentally friendly corporate image.

Benefits of a travel plan

A travel plan can bring a wide variety of benefits to the organisation, the local community and the environment (see Table 28.4).

Traffic management

There are many financial and environmental incentives to implement better management of traffic to the workplace. The two main ways are car sharing and car park management.

Car sharing

Car sharing can be a very effective way of reducing peak hour congestion and easing parking problems in the car park. With car sharing, a problem shared really can be a problem halved (and maybe even quartered)! Basically, car sharing involves two or more people sharing a car for their journey to and from work.

Benefits
The benefits of car sharing include:

❑ Reduces traffic which in turn reduces pollution and also shortens journey times.
❑ Less cars mean less need for car parking so saving both space needs and its associated costs.

Table 28.4   Travel plan contents

1	Organisation	Increased productivity generated by a healthier, more motivated workforce. Cost savings, reduced congestion, reduced demand for car parking. Improved access for employees, visitors and deliveries.
2	Staff	Improved health, cost and time savings, reduced stress, a general improvement in quality of life.
3	Local community	Reduced congestion, reduced journey times, improved public transport services, energy savings. Reduced overspill parking in residential areas.
4	Environment	Improved air quality, less noise and dirt. Reduced impact on other national and global environmental problems such as climate change.

- Sharing a car will save employees money, because they'll also be sharing the costs of their petrol.
- Increased socialising amongst employees.
- In a more global context, less cars on the road means that fuel supplies will last longer.
- Less cars also reduces carbon emissions.

However, car sharing schemes are often difficult to implement. The key barriers are:

- Employees may not know which other employees they live close to.
- Fears about becoming stranded at work.
- Fears about others knowing employees' home address.
- Abundance of car parking.
- Flexible working so that employees start and finish at differing times.
- Child care duties such as taking children to nursery or school.
- Healthcare appointments.

There are a number of initiatives that FMs can undertake to facilitate car sharing in the organisation:

- Identify potential car sharing partners. Depending on the size of the organisation, this can be done by word of mouth, through a simple database or through specialist car sharing software.
- Offer car sharers prime car parking spots.
- Point out the potential cost savings to the employees.
- Make registering for the scheme as easy as possible for the staff. Possibly, even include an incentive to register.
- Make sure any data collected is carefully and securely managed.
- Liaise with other organisations in the local community to expand the scheme.

29 Fabric Maintenance

The fabric of buildings comprises both the external envelope and the internal structures, such as the floors, partitions, doors, ceilings and other fixtures, fittings and equipment (FF&E) components. Depending on the premises it may also include guttering, drainage, shelters and canopies. Fabric accounts for about one-third of the annual maintenance budget.

The maintenance of premises includes buildings, the building's mechanical and electrical services and the building surrounds. This chapter focuses only on the structures and fabric of a building.

29.1 Maintenance implications of building structures

Buildings comprise various structural elements such as roofs, framework, floors and fenestration. Maintenance has to take into account the number of floors, the height of the building, the roof type, special features such as canopies, external lift shafts and balconies, and drainage.

There are many materials used in construction, from timber, stone, concrete, cladding and curtain walling systems, brick, PVC and plastics to metal (steel/aluminium). Each will have their particular maintenance requirements. Some materials will be deleterious and may pose health hazards to both occupants and the maintenance staff. Examples include lead, foam and asbestos.

An understanding of building components and typical building defects related to the age of the building and types of materials, such as concrete cancer, is useful in planning maintenance activities.

29.2 Fabric maintenance programmes

Maintaining the fabric keeps buildings safe and usable, and also helps retain the value. The programme will depend on relevant legislation, resources (skills, budget and time), accessibility to the fabric components, importance of the building to the business, complexity of materials used in the building, age of the building and intensity of use. In addition, the programme of maintenance will ensure that the leasehold requirements are adhered to, that re-occurrence of accidents/near-misses are prevented, and that the risk of failures of fabric components is reduced. Detailed maintenance programmes may be drawn up to show daily, weekly, quarterly and annual tasks. The performance of fabric components will be affected by many conditions including:

❑   Weather – rain, wind, temperature fluctuations, salt and pollution.
❑   Orientation – prevailing winds, sheltered location, north/south aspect, solar gain.

❑   Building assembly – original design, setting out, quality of individual components and integration of all parts to create whole building, ability and skills of original workforce.
❑   Maintenance approach – planned or reactive.

29.3 Internal and external finishes

The word finishes can be used to describe a whole host of materials, surfaces and textures that can be used for decorative and protective effects in buildings. The type of finish will depend on its location, its hygienic requirements and decorative effect. Each finish will have differing maintenance issues.

❑   Floor finishes – linoleum sheet or tiles, PVC sheet or tiles, rubber sheet or tiles, quarry tiles, carpet sheet or tiles, terrazzo, stone, paint, resin, etc.
❑   Ceiling and wall finishes – plaster, cement render, paint, laminates, paper, board with decorative effect, plasterboard, mirrors, ceramic wall tiling, hardwood panelling, etc.

Renders

Render is a wet system of application and is generally applied in several coats, i.e. two or three. The thickness will depend on the location, its final finish and the backing base material.

If rendering is required on the outside then careful selection is needed – based on the material it will cover, the severity of exposure to the elements and the decorative finish.

The types of finish available are:

❑   Smooth finish, wood float.
❑   Scraping.
❑   Pebble dash.
❑   Rough cast.
❑   Tyrolean.

The main maintenance problem with rendering is potential debonding from the backing, forming hollows behind the plaster, which will allow moisture to gather which can then freeze. Cracking both on the surface and through the thickness will also allow moisture to pass through.

The roughcast surfaces and scraped finishes trap dirt, whereas pebble dash finishes are allegedly self-cleaning, but they tend to lose the pebbles over time.

Rendering is often used to cover over a wall finish that has been severely damaged and is uneconomic to renew. Rendering is also used to protect materials that may be damaged by the elements, such as frost damage to the external bricks.

Plaster

Plaster is another wet material used for internal surfaces to give a smooth hard surface which can receive decoration in the form of paint or wallpaper.

Plaster is used as a wall and ceiling finish. On wall surfaces constructed of brick or block, a two-coat application is provided. The first coat is a levelling coat of about 10–15 mm thick. The final coat is a skim coat of about 3–5 mm thick and it is this that gives the hard smooth finish.

When plasterboard is used as a wall material or ceiling board, a thin skim is applied to give it a dense hard finish. The skim plaster is approximately 3 mm thick.

Plaster finishes are used especially where hygiene is important, because plaster is a smooth, jointless material and it is easier to keep such surfaces clean.

Board finishes

Sheet board can be a decorative wall finish fixed to the walls either by adhesive, nail, or screw fixings.

With decorative panelling, the joints can be either butt jointed or covered by a cover strip. Laminated wall finishes are usually sealed so that insects, fungi and rodents cannot get behind the boarding to breed and cause infestation.

These laminated wall surfaces are generally used in areas where hygiene is to be of a high standard, i.e. food preparation, toilets, hospital areas and so on.

Ceramic wall finishes

Ceramic wall tiles are also used in areas where hygiene is important. One of the reasons for affixing tiles to walls are due to the location and purpose of the space, and this in turn will dictate the type of adhesive used and the grouting for joints.

If the wall tiling is to be subjected to continual moisture, that is showers, baths, wash areas, then a waterproof adhesive and grout should be specified.

In other areas such as sink splash backs and general wall areas, a waterproof-resistant tile adhesive and grout can be used.

If a wall area exceeds 4.5 m in length or at any internal angle, then wall tiling should have movement joints.

Floor tiling

There are three main types of floor tiling used in commercial premises: quarry, ceramic and stone. Both tiles have good resistance to chemical attack. Tiles are laid on to either a bed of cement mortar or a tile adhesive. The cement mortar bed can vary between 12 and 19 mm thick.

Movement joints should be built in at intervals of between 3 and 4.5 m and around all perimeter walls and any structural supports which it will surround. The movement joint should be at least 13 mm and pass through to the structural floor.

The joints should then be filled with a filling strip and sealant. The sealant should be chosen to resist any acids or contaminants likely to be in contact with it.

Sheet flooring

Sheet flooring can be used in areas of heavy wear or where an impervious surface is required. There are many choices of colours available to enhance any decor that may be required to project company image.

For large buildings used by the general public, sheet flooring in corridors is used to indicate routes around the buildings. Hospitals are a good example where different colours inlaid into the sheet indicate the routes to the wards and therapy areas, etc. Large building complexes sometimes use this system to show alternative exits.

The sheet can be turned up the walls to form a skirting. All joints and seams are heat welded. This type of covering will always be fixed with an adhesive. If not fully bonded ripples and bubbles occur.

PVC tiling

Tile styles vary from 300 mm × 300 mm to 900 mm × 900 mm. There is a large variety of colour choice and patterns available for selection. This type of finish will always be fixed by adhesive. Adhesives can be water based or spirit based. Water-based products should not be used if spillages are likely to occur.

When using spirit, it is necessary to be aware of the requirements of COSHH Regulations.

Paint and resin floor finishes

In industrial areas, paint is often used to colour and seal the concrete floor which makes it easier to keep clean. If the paint is not correctly applied, then during use the paint surface will crack and flake off.

This type of finish is often used in store rooms, plant rooms, boiler houses and workshops. It has the disadvantage of slipperiness when wet. It is also necessary to repaint at regular intervals – these intervals will depend on wear and tear.

Continual repainting will eventually result in a thick build up of paint film which may break off. When this happens, it will be necessary to remove the paint build up to a clean sound surface for re-treatment.

Resin paint

This is an alternative floor finish, but is a more expensive product and known as resin scrim. A resin liquid is spread over the floor to form a hard durable surface; it is especially good in areas where there is vehicle traffic or heavy wheeled trolleys. It is common in buildings such as hangars and small warehouses. Fine grains of aggregate can be sprinkled into the wet material to provide a slip-resistant finish.

Carpet

Carpet is often chosen in offices because of its pleasing appearance and its comfort level. Varying qualities can be introduced throughout the building to vary the cost and to suit the working practice. The choices of carpet are considerable, in both tile formats or in broadloom. The method of laying can be:

❑   Loose laid onto a separating sheet.
❑   Loose laid onto a thick underfelt.
❑   Fixed with an adhesive.

It may be necessary to take advice from a local fire advisor before laying carpet into areas designated as escape routes. Carpet laid in such areas should satisfy a basic flame resistance test before being considered for escape routes.

Carpets generate dust, and consideration should be given to this when installing into areas that need dust-free criteria, such as computer suites, food areas such as restaurants, vending areas and hygiene areas such as first aid and medical centres. Carpets can also be a source of static electricity, which may cause problems if computers are installed or there are partitions with metal framework and ironmongery.

29.4 External walls and building envelope

Parapets

Walls need to be inspected for any signs of cracking, movement on the damp proof course (DPC) and for loose copings. The external walls are in a very exposed position and are prone to defects. If there is no parapet, then (particularly on flat roofs) there will be safety rails or balustrades, and these fixings need to be checked on a regular basis.

Wall cracks

Hairline cracking that follows the mortar joints is generally of no structural significance and normally just requires chopping out and re-pointing. Simple cracks require attention, otherwise water and frost will penetrate and expand the crack. A competent engineer should check defects such as cracks passing through the bricks themselves, any signs of bowing or distortion, or cracks that suddenly appear. Appearance of white powdery patches will generally be effluorescence and this only requires soft brushing to remove, not water. Any air bricks or weep holes should be checked to make sure they are not obstructed.

Dampness

If the source of dampness in walls cannot be traced easily, for example leaking gutters, downpipes or other service pipes, then the FM will need to check for other sources such as flower beds and paving which may be above the DPC.

Cladding, rendering and mosaics

The FM needs to inspect these structures for signs of cracking, crazing and looseness. Small isolated areas of rendering are easily repaired by removing the unsound area and replacing with render of the same mix proportions as the existing. If the problem is extensive or there is damage with claddings and mosaics, then specialist advice should be sought.

Concrete frame construction

These kind of buildings rely on the integrity of the concrete for their strength. Any signs of concrete cancer, spalling or cracking of these columns/beams should be checked by a structural engineer.

Timber fences

Wooden fences must be checked for soundness, i.e. broken or loose panels/posts and rot, particularly at ground level. These faults may only require re-fixing or removal and replacing. Fences with painted/creosote surfaces have to be checked for signs of deterioration and retreated as necessary. Before carrying out the maintenance work, it is recommended that the FM checks the ownership of the fence and the boundary lines of the premises.

Doors and windows

Wooden door and window frames must be inspected for signs of flaking paint, splitting, and wood rot. Painted frames need to be maintained in good condition to prevent moisture entering and causing decay. UPVC frames need regular cleaning and checking to ensure that there is no damage or movement. Glass needs checking for cracks, loose and missing putties and beads which will need replacing particularly before being repainted. Window latches and catches should be checked. All door closer and other mechanisms must be regularly checked, especially those fitted to fire doors and fire exit doors.

29.5 Guttering and rain downpipes

Roof structure

Pitched roofs are normally provided with eaves, gutters and with downpipes to carry the water to the ground. Flat roofs are usually provided with a slight fall to carry rain water directly to a roof outlet or to a channel formed in the roof leading to an outlet or to an eaves gutter.

Guttering options

Guttering can be applied in two ways:

 (i) Fixed to the external face of the building and therefore visible.
 (ii) Concealed behind the external walls or the extensions of the walls (called parapets) and are therefore not visible.

All guttering in turn is connected to downpipes which convey the water away via the drainage. Most downpipes are fixed externally, but particularly with flat roofs they can be sited within the building.

Materials

Gutters and downpipes are normally of the same material. The range of materials being:

  (i) Cast iron.
 (ii) Plastic (usually UPVC).
(iii) Asbestos cement.
 (iv) Aluminium.
  (v) Lead, copper and zinc.
 (vi) Timber – rather outdated and usually have an inner lining of precast concrete units.
(vii) Asphalt and bituminous felts.

Materials (i) to (iv) above are usually used for the eaves exposed type of gutters.
   Materials (v) to (viii) are usually found in the concealed parapet box/channel type gutters. All guttering is installed so that it is inclined towards the downpipes.

Maintenance

Ideally, an inspection should be carried out during a period of rain. This will obviously reveal any leaks that would not otherwise be seen. The soundness of fixings to the building should be checked to make sure it is fixed securely in place and is in no danger of falling.

Guttering will accumulate debris and particularly leaves. This could lead to an eventual blockage and therefore it is advisable at least once a year to have the gutters cleaned out. At the connection of the guttering to a downpipe, a wire cage is inserted to prevent birds nesting – these cages should be checked too. Some of the materials will require painting at frequent intervals to prevent corrosion. Joints in both guttering and downpipes are susceptible to leakage and may require taking apart and remaking with a jointing compound (depending upon material). Plastic guttering does not require painting and is therefore virtually maintenance-free, but is easily damaged by ladders being leant against them. The base of the downpipe discharges into the drainage system by either being directly connected to the drainpipe or discharging into or over a gulley. These gulleys may require cleaning to remove obstacles.

30 Energy Management

30.1 Introduction

FMs often have responsibility for energy management. Energy efficiency is no longer an optional extra; 'green' issues are now both political and global, affecting organisations via taxes and legislation. The drivers for energy management include legislation, taxes, price increases, and climate change impacts. Employees too are putting pressure on their employing organisations to be more efficient and sustainable in their procedures and policies.

Energy is crucial to everyday existence and its use results in:

- Costs to an organisation.
- Environmental pollution arising from the emission of CO_2, SO_2, NO, NO_2 and certain other 'greenhouse' gases.
- Reduction in the world's natural resources.

30.2 Energy consumption

Energy consumption is affected by many factors – building management, equipment and processes, maintenance of systems, building fabric thermal qualities and operating hours of the premises. It is claimed that 40% of energy consumption in the UK is attributable to buildings. This is due to the need to provide and manage a comfortable climate inside a building – providing heating and/or cooling; providing hot water; offsetting the effects of solar heat gain or losses via the building fabric.

Energy consumption can be significantly reduced through good building design, and management of buildings and systems. Energy can be easily wasted through lack of consideration of the consequences of poor management procedures, and lack of insight into the opportunities to reduce energy consumption.

Many energy-conserving schemes have real financial justification, and should be considered as appropriate for incorporation into a wide range of projects.

Energy consumption targets exist for a variety of building types, and these should be used as benchmarks to identify how a particular building is performing. Energy targets should be set for all buildings, using CIBSE guidance documents:

- Fresh air quantities should be commensurate with the operational/occupational requirements, and in accordance with the relevant standards and regulations.
- Plant operational periods should be restricted to the operational/occupational requirements. Building management systems (BMS) should be used to optimise the

operation of the building services installation, minimising the start-up time and uti-lising the thermal mass of the buildings to enable early shut down of plant.

❏ All energy sources should be metered, with submetering installed as appropriate where a single source serves a number of different buildings or applications. All data should be entered into a monitoring system which should be regularly reviewed and benchmarked against previous usage and energy trends.

❏ Building Regulation requirements should be compiled with. These regulations specifi-cally require the following areas of energy consumption to be addressed:

o Limit the heat loss through the roof, wall, floor, windows and doors, etc. and where appropriate, permit the benefits of solar heat gains and more efficient heating systems to be taken into account.

o Limit unnecessary ventilation heat loss by reducing air leakage around openings and through the building fabric.

o Enable effective control of space heating and hot water systems by controlling tem-peratures and duration of system operation.

o Limit the heat loss from hot water vessels and hot water pipes and ducts where such heat does not make an efficient contribution to the space heating.

30.3 Energy efficient building designs

Building design affects the energy profile due to its site, location, shape and form. The materials used will have embodied energy. Materials will affect the thermal capacity – in particular, the insulation and air tightness of the building. Ventilation via windows and the impact of shading must also be considered. The types of building services installed will also affect the energy performance of the building design.

Provision should be made to limit the thermal bridging which occurs around windows, doors and openings and where fixings penetrate insulation. Minimising the risk of condensation should also be addressed when designing the structure of the building. Care should be taken to avoid heat loss due to stack effects within cavity walls.

Due consideration should be given to the embodied energy incorporated within the materials used in all new construction projects. Embodied energy is the energy required to produce a particular product, from extracting raw materials, manufacturing, through to installation. Embodied energy calculations should be made for all new construction projects with the best information available at the time.

Energy conservation should not be achieved through non-compliance with Health and Safety requirements, British Standards or European Regulations. New building construction should have air infiltration properties below 5 m^3/hour per m^2 envelope area at 25 Pa static pressure difference across the structure. Thermal properties of buildings should comply with Building Regulations. Consideration should also be given to the use of high efficiency electric motors.

30.4 Energy management

Energy management may be defined as the application of business management and industrial organisation methods to aid the optimal use of energy resources. Many savings can be achieved by adopting an energy management strategy. Good energy management is essential to realise all energy initiatives and policies. Some examples of good practice initiatives are shown below:

❑ Staff education and training is important – energy efficiency awareness should be communicated at all levels using methods such as journals, bulletins, posters, training films, case studies, feedback on achievements against targets and so on.

❑ Establish a site energy management organisational structure and integrate its function with the general management of facilities and other business operations.

❑ Targets should be developed for improvement of energy conservation and energy performance, and a reporting system should be developed so that achievements or shortfalls are clearly visible to all concerned.

❑ All plant and equipment must be optimised to improve efficiency/reduce energy consumption.

❑ An energy efficiency audit should be undertaken to determine the correct energy expenditure on an asset-by-asset basis. This will enable the organisation to identify potential improvements.

❑ A significant part of the total cost of energy in an organisation is its actual purchase net cost. A continuing audit of energy purchases and contracts of supply will enable prices to be optimised.

❑ Space temperatures should be controlled to ensure optimum working conditions, and so in turn reducing energy consumption.

❑ Building services systems and plant and equipment should be operated only within the occupied periods – all systems should be switched off beyond normal working hours.

The FM can carry out simple checks on the operational activities in buildings, as shown in Figure 30.1.

Where appropriate, the building's mechanical and electrical services will be monitored to minimise energy consumption, e.g. night-time natural ventilation should be used to sub-cool buildings where there is a high day-time cooling load. Building users should be encouraged to close doors and windows to minimise heat loss in winter, and in cooled areas to minimise heat gain in summer.

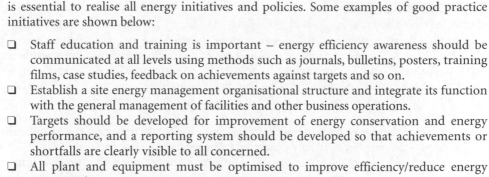

Thermostat settings
Chiller operation during winter periods
AHU damper controls
The use of portable electric heaters
Unnecessary opening of windows during cold weather
Flue gas emissions
Refrigerant leaks
Excessive dehumidification (condensate) from cooling coils
Doors left open
Cleaning operations
Lighting, in areas of good daylight
Steam humidifiers
Reheater batteries
The correct use of solar blinds
Boiler start and stop times
Plant operating periods

Figure 30.1 Operational check list for FMs

30.5 Choice of fuel

In the UK, there are over 2000 power stations (powered by gas, coal and nuclear energy) that generate the energy required. Around 4% of electricity comes from renewable energy installations including hydropower schemes and wind farms. The six largest energy suppliers control 99% of the market in Britain. It is predicted that in a few years, the UK will need to import energy, as there will not be enough generated in the UK to satisfy demand.

Most of the energy used in buildings and industry comes from non-renewable primary sources – gas, oil, and electricity generated from fossil or nuclear fuels.

The choice of fuel used is governed mainly by its price, unless the choice is limited by the application (e.g. lighting and motor drives). Where there is a choice of available energy sources, the following factors should be considered:

❑ The efficiency of the source fuel generation: a global viewpoint is required since certain fuels (such as electricity provided by electricity generating companies) are generated from fossil fuels very inefficiently, which makes their use less environmentally viable on a global scale, although their use in-house may be very efficient. It may be more acceptable to install a local generating plant.
❑ The efficiency of the appliance.
❑ Available storage and ancillary equipment required.
❑ Availability of supply.
❑ Maintenance.

30.6 Electricity

There are four distinct phases to the process of making electricity and supplying it to consumers. These are:

(i)   Generation – where the electricity is first made, either by the consumption of fuels (gas, coal, etc.) or harnessing natural resources (wind, wave, etc.).
(ii) Transmission – a high voltage network running along the length of the country. This is the means by which large quantities of electricity can be transported from generators to the areas of the country where electricity is consumed.
(iii) Distribution – electricity is taken off the high voltage transmission system and distributed over low voltage networks to industrial complexes, offices and homes. This is done by 14 distribution companies, each covering a discrete geographical region of Britain.
(iv) Supply – this is the business of supplying end-users and billing them appropriately for their electricity consumption.

In order to be able to distribute electricity on the distribution systems in the UK, a Distribution Network Operator (DNO) must hold a licence. Following a number of corporate mergers and acquisitions since privatisation (in 1990), seven different companies now hold the licences for 14 areas.

The National Grid Company operates the high voltage transmission network, which feeds the regional electricity companies. Power stations are usually connected directly to the transmission grid. There are also interconnectors with France and Scotland.

Electricity tariffs

The cost of electricity is made up of charges from:

❑   Generators.
❑   Suppliers.
❑   Grid operators.
❑   Regional electricity distribution companies.
❑   Meter operators.
❑   VAT taxes levied by government.

Traditionally, tariffs have been of two basic types; the flat rate price and the block tariff. The most complex tariffs are those that have price bands across the day and time of year. Additional factors making up the price charged to consumers are:

❑   Transmission charges.
❑   Distribution charges.
❑   Administration charges.
❑   Meter operation costs.
❑   Meter communication charges.
❑   Data aggregation charges.
❑   Settlement charges.
❑   Taxes and levies.

The installed load and the peak rate of use by a premises will determine the size or category of the block tariff. There are a few special categories such as catering, restricted hours, off-peak, evening and weekend, and seasonal time of day. The most complex is the maximum demand tariff with charges based on units consumed, maximum demand, supply capacity and power factor.

The load factor is a measure of the extent to which the available supply has been used. FMs should have a broad understanding of their demand profile over a 24-hour period. Peaks of demand impose costs on the electrical industry, and so tariffs reflect this. Maximum demand is the measure of the peak rate of electricity usage by a consumer. In the UK, the maximum demand is defined as the highest average rate of consumption in any half-hour period. It can be determined by doubling the highest number of units recorded in any half-hour period.

Supply capacity or availability relates to certain aspects of the supply of electricity, such as the cabling and switchgear. These have to be suitably sized for the current and future levels of electricity required. Certain types of electrical equipment, such as electric motors, will adversely affect the load profile of a building. They will draw a higher current than necessary to generate the power needed. Power factor is the ratio of useful power relative to apparent power and ideally this should be 1.0.

Electricity procurement

Contracts are required with a supplier, a meter operator and a regional distribution company. Procurement effort should be focused on the selection of an electricity supplier. Ideally, all bids to supply electricity should be presented in a common way to allow comparison. Tenders for electricity purchase can be managed via an electronic auction. Some organisations will join a purchase consortium to increase their buying power. Electricity contracts can be relatively short term, to benefit from the volatile peaks and troughs in supply prices. Bids from suppliers will need to be checked for:

- ❑ Inclusions and exclusions.
- ❑ Transmission charges.
- ❑ Distribution charges.
- ❑ Distribution and transmission losses.
- ❑ Administration charges.
- ❑ Metering and metering communication.
- ❑ Aggregation and settlement charges.
- ❑ Levies and taxes.

30.7 Combined heat and power (CHP) systems

A CHP system may be used to generate all or part of the building's energy requirement, either on a multi-building site or locally. The plant 'waste' heat can be utilised for space or water heating, for process use or for amenity heating, and this will greatly increase the overall fuel efficiency.

The 'waste' heat rejected from the CHP plant provides an ideal source to supply hot water to absorption chillers, where cooling is required. This increases the overall annual energy efficiency of the CHP plant, as both a winter load (heating) and summer load (cooling) are available, and it is unlikely that heat will be 'dumped'.

Combined heat and power plant must be carefully selected to closely match the energy demand, and large plant may not operate satisfactorily below a certain figure. Base load CHP with peak loads from conventional sources should also be considered.

30.8 Renewable energy sources

Renewable energy is that generated from natural resources that are replenishable. The market for renewable energy (such as ground or heat pumps, biomass, wind power or hydroelectric power) is growing all the time. The big six energy suppliers have introduced a variety of green tariffs. New companies such as Ecotricity and Good Energy have been set up specifically to help combat climate change. FMs can specify a percentage of renewable energy in a supply contract. They can choose a supplier that provides renewable electricity or select a scheme that supplies an equivalent amount of renewable energy into the national grid for the amount that the organisation consumes (although the energy used may come from a traditional energy source). They could also choose a supplier that makes contributions to environmental projects on a regular basis.

Wind farms

The energy used in manufacturing and erecting a wind turbine is paid back in 3–6 months of operation. With a 1000-mile coastline, the UK (especially Scotland) has a high potential for wind energy generation.

Hydroelectricity

Hydroelectricity is a generic term for energy created by falling water. In Scotland and Wales, there are several hydroelectric power stations. Large water reservoirs are managed via hydroelectric dams that hold back water, creating a store of potential power. A water gate lets it surge through a tunnel leading to turbines. The water turns the turbines, which in turn spin electricity generators. An example of the power of water is the Electric Mountain in Snowdonia, Wales. It creates 1320 megawatts of power in 12 seconds when there is a sudden surge in demand that cannot be met by power stations already connected to the national grid.

Solar power

Harnessed by solar panels, the sun's energy can be converted to electricity or used to heat water. A single photovoltaic (PV) solar panel can provide enough electricity to power a TV.

Solar panels are provided as stand-alone units on the roof of a building, in an external ground level compound, or alternatively integrated into the building facade, where the panels can also be used to act as a solar shading system (thus providing twofold benefits). There are two main types of system:

❑ Solar thermal – Concentrates the solar energy to affect the water in tubes. This energy is then used to indirectly preheat water serving a DHWS or process system, or alternatively to offset local heat losses through the building fabric. The heat generated, however, is low grade, and therefore is not viable to displace primary heating systems.
❑ Solar electric – Uses PV cells to generate electricity directly. The electricity can then be supplied into the building power system, offsetting a small proportion of the total building demand from the primary electrical supply. These solar panel systems are quite expensive; however, as technology progresses, the manufacturing costs are reducing and this renewable energy source is likely to become a real financially viable alternative in the future.

Biomass or refuse-derived fuel

Biomass or refuse-derived fuel is burnt to provide electricity generating steam. Biomass materials are usually fast growing soft woods, which can be coppiced on a regular basis, such as willow, and are grown specifically for this purpose. There are obvious environmental benefits in promoting tree growth as part of this process.

Refuse-derived fuel is usually methane, which is captured from refuse tips or sewage farms. This methane is then used to fire incinerators/boilers. In addition to offsetting the need to use non-renewable fuels, these methods also reduce the amount of methane being released into the atmosphere.

It is also possible to incinerate waste products, and use the heat from the process to offset the need to use non-renewable fuels. These systems are often found in hospitals, although they are becoming more widespread due to the Environment Act 1995 which legislates on the reduction of land fill waste disposal.

Wave and tidal energy

Lines of floating power generators offshore or on the shoreline capture wave energy and turn it into electricity. Tidal barrages trap the predictable energy in tides, exploiting the natural rise and fall of the sea level. Despite its potential and efficiency (80% conversion rate), tidal energy is not used widely due to the high initial costs of equipment installation.

Heat pumps

Heat pumps work on the basis of extracting the heat from a variety of sources – such as ambient air, ground water, the ground itself, and waste heat from other processes. Heat pumps have been used for many years in buildings, but they are now becoming more important as organisations search for low carbon and energy efficient sources of heating. The capital cost of heat pumps is higher than conventional heating systems, but they have a lower operating cost. Heat pumps are classified by their heat source and means of delivery. The main types are:

❑ Air to air.
❑ Air to water.
❑ Water to air.
❑ Water to water.
❑ Ground to air.
❑ Ground to water.

Heat pumps may be a single packaged unit, part of a split system, part of a ducting system, installed on rooftops or in the ground, part of central system or a zoned system or they may be stand-alone.

Landfill gas

There is huge untapped potential in landfill gas energy. The waste in landfill depots degrades over time and generates methane gas. This can be recovered and converted to a source of energy, for example to drive generators.

30.9 Gas

Gas consumption in the UK has risen by 66% since 1992. The UK will become a net importer of gas as the North Sea and Irish Sea supplies are depleted. It is predicted that 90% of gas consumption in the future will be from imported gas. Gas can be imported through the existing interconnector from Europe and as shipments of liquefied natural gas (LNG). It is therefore becoming increasingly important to use gas efficiently. Ways to achieve greater efficiency range from the use of combined heat and power stations to metering at the point of consumption.

There are four main categories of organisations operating in the gas market and these are:

❑ Producers.
❑ Shippers – these procure gas and sell in bulk to suppliers.

❑ Suppliers.
❑ Network and storage operators.

In the UK, the transmission and distribution system for gas supplies is operated by Transco. There has been major investment in the gas infrastructure in recent years, with more planned.

Gas safety

FMs and others in control of premises, such as landlords or managing agents, have a duty to ensure that the installation, servicing, repair and maintenance of gas appliances, fittings and flues are carried out to a standard that ensures they operate in a safe condition.

The watchdog for gas safety in the UK is the Gas Safety Register (replacing Corgi in April 2009) and it operates a register of competent persons. Checks can be made to verify an operator's competency to work on particular gas installations.

FMs need to ensure:

❑ New installations have a safety or emergency valve to isolate the supply.
❑ Access to up-to-date drawings of the locations of:
    o meters;
    o valves;
    o risers;
    o gas appliances;
    o isolating valves.
❑ FM staff know what to do if a gas leak is suspected – calling the Transco emergency number 0800 111999.
❑ Adequate records of safety checks for at least 2 years are kept.
❑ Tenants are given copies of safety checks.
❑ Gas appliances in residential accommodation (such as student halls of residence) are checked annually, with certificates issued to each dwelling and records kept.

Gas procurement

The UK gas market is affected by North Sea production levels, unpredicted weather, the seasons and the perception of security and environmental constraints on the supply of gas. It is a complex market which is also affected by gas storage levels, the operation of the interconnector pipe between Bacton and Zeebrugge and the import of LNG. The UK is now becoming an importer of gas.

The complexities of political, industrial, economic and environmental drivers affect the purchase decision. Traditionally buyers would fix the price for a year; however, the timing of this decision may result in paying too high a price. A more flexible purchasing arrangement is required, but this means that the users need to appreciate and understand this sophisticated market so that good decisions are made.

Some purchasers may index their options to demand and supply. Financial tools such as hedging, swaps and shared risk agreements may give buyers good deals. Other options may include monthly or quarterly purchasing. Smaller users may not be able to use these tools as their demand is insufficient, having to use fixed-price contracts instead. The checklist shown in Figure 30.2 can help the FM in gas purchase and utilisation.

Check and scrutinise bills thoroughly

Read meters regularly, identify trends

Allow 13 weeks notice to current supplier

Allow plenty of time to tender next supply deal

Ensure a fair tender process is followed

Use market intelligence consultants

Find out which suppliers have excess gas

Buy on an energy-only basis, excluding the transport and risk costs

Consider longer-term contracts

Get prices on a site-by-site basis

Figure 30.2   Checklist to ensure efficient use and procurement of gas

Tariffs

The cost of gas is determined by the charges levied by:

❑   Exploration companies.
❑   Production companies.
❑   Shippers.
❑   Suppliers.
❑   Network distributors, such as Transco (costs of storage, transmission, distribution and metering).
❑   Government (VAT).

In effect the price paid for gas covers the three elements of its production, transport and tax. The cost of transport can be a high proportion of the whole cost. This cost will vary according to:

❑   The location to where the supply is delivered.
❑   The annual quantity.
❑   Peak day demand.
❑   The ratio between winter and summer.
❑   Number and type of meters and who reads them.
❑   Type of supply – interruptible or guaranteed.

30.10 Energy monitoring

The monitoring of actual energy consumed is probably the single most important factor in any energy conservation management system. Rogue energy use and unexplained energy trends can easily go unnoticed unless regular monitoring is undertaken. The consequences in a large property portfolio can result in excessive energy costs and large global CO_2 emissions.

All sources of energy must be monitored including water, gas, electricity, oil and waste. This is best achieved with computerised systems which can automatically log and trend yearly differences and flag up specific areas of concern.

All buildings will benefit even from a simple monitoring programme/register of actual figures consumed, provided that the readings are taken regularly and reviewed accordingly.

Careful energy monitoring will, for example, detect where overheating occurs due to a maintenance contractor increasing unnecessarily the building set-point control rather than addressing a fault in the building system performance.

30.11 Metering

The meter is the point of contact between the energy supplier and the consumer. Historically, meters were inaccessible, buried or hidden away. Many consumers paid for their utilities on estimated bills, and without meter reading on a regular basis, they would have no means of checking or reconciling invoices. The Energy White Paper calls for a more proactive use of meters, submeters and the use of smart technology. There are two types of meters that can be used – the smart meter or automatic meter reader (AMR).

Smart technology refers to real-time monitoring equipment that gives a graphical representation of the actual consumption of energy. Smart meters will become increasingly important to reduce energy consumption in small to medium size enterprises and the domestic market.

In the future, smart meters will be able to control the use of equipment – for example switching off equipment when the tariff is high. Integration with other technologies, e.g. Zigbee, will allow communication with other devices such as thermostats and health monitors, via an open protocol standard. This may also help industry and other users to benefit from the spare capacity in energy supply at off-peak times.

Automated monitoring and targeting via smart metering technology, which reads consumption at ½ hourly intervals, will help to keep track of energy use in a more dynamic way. The return on investment of the smart technology can be achieved within a relatively short period. Sites with utility bills of £10,000 will achieve significant savings.

Commercial premises will normally use automatic meter reading (AMR) technology. This enables the suppliers to get accurate readings of consumption, and the users to also get more accurate bills. It saves the time and effort of physical checks and record keeping of the many meters that an organisation could have in their property portfolio.

The data generated can be quite complex and it is beneficial to include software that will present the information in a usable format. The most advanced metering, monitoring and targeting equipment will activate alarms for out-of-range values, and alert managers for equipment breakdown and set-point drifts. They will alert users when consumption is excessive, provide waste analysis and attribute consumption to particular categories or uses. The CIBSE Technical Memorandum 39 (TM39) is a useful source of further information.

Utility monitoring and targeting

Effective monitoring of utilities is needed to overcome:

❏   Leaks in the systems.
❏   Excessive frost protection systems (i.e. keeping a building warmer than really necessary).
❏   Continuous operation of heating or ventilation systems.
❏   Simultaneous operation of heating and cooling.
❏   Excessive supply of fresh ventilation air.
❏   Humidity control systems operating when the ambient RH is already acceptable.

The benefits of the operation of a systematic monitoring and targeting regime are to:

- Highlight inefficiencies.
- Identify anomalous patterns of consumption.
- Avoid waste.
- Identify faults in the plant and system.
- Track changes in occupant and consumer behaviour.
- Identify maintenance errors.
- Benchmark with other sites and processes.
- Provide information for budgeting estimates.
- Track consumption against budget.
- Allocate accurate energy charges to individual business units or sites within an organisation.
- Target areas of excessive consumption.
- Use data to support energy awareness campaigns and the organisation's environmental policy.

30.12 Investment

Some energy managers have found it difficult to gain the support of senior colleagues to invest in energy initiatives or reinvest any savings achieved into further energy conservation measures. For example, this may be because the implementation of energy-saving measures is part of a larger capital project, and it is difficult to identify the energy cost and savings elements within such new-build or refurbishment projects. The multi-occupancy of buildings and the absence of submetering data for such buildings have also contributed to a lack of management information and the lack of investment regarding operation of these facilities.

Capital allowances

Capital allowances provide tax relief on certain building fixtures and equipment costs at specific rates. These allowances are offset against taxable profits. It is a complex aspect of accountancy, taxation and financial management. FMs are advised to consult knowledgeable experts in their organisation or external specialists for further information. As part of the government's drive to improve the energy performance of buildings and reduce carbon emissions, there are incentives and an enhanced capital allowance (ECA) of 6–15% available for energy efficient plant, such as energy efficient motors.

Grants

Some sectors are able to qualify and obtain government funded grants for use in energy efficiency projects. There are also interest-free loans available too. Information on the current schemes can be found via the Department of Business Enterprise and Regulatory Reform (BRERR). The Carbon Trust is the government agency who administer some of these schemes. The Carbon Trust also provide training courses, seminars and free consultancy to advise FMs on ways to reduce energy consumption and reduce carbon emissions.

30.13 Energy policy

An energy policy must be agreed at the organisational level – it requires commitment and top-level support. It is best to have an energy champion at a senior level, and there should be a link to the organisation's corporate social responsibility (CSR) agenda and over-all business performance. An effective policy requires motivation and involvement from everyone in the business – not just the FM team and their contractors. It requires good information systems, marketing, investment plans and an effective matrix measurement to show achievement and progress against agreed targets.

An effective energy policy will include a wide range of information – perhaps under these example headings:

❑ Declaration of commitment.
❑ Purpose.
❑ Objectives.
❑ Immediate aims.
❑ Responsibilities.
❑ Structure.
❑ Lines of communication.
❑ Action plan.
❑ Resources.
❑ Review.

The UK Government energy policy has set out targets and practical measures to reduce carbon emissions, and manage energy utilisation over the coming 50 years. One of the outcomes of the new Government policy is the new carbon trading system, Carbon Reduction Committment (CRC), that begins in 2010.

30.14 CRC Energy Efficiency Scheme

This UK initiative is a new approach to carbon management. It is a mandatory cap and trade scheme intended to impact on at least 10% of all energy users in the UK. The Government have set thresholds which determine if an organisation needs to register and participate in the scheme. Organisations must register on the CRC scheme by April 2010 if they have:

❑ Half-hourly meters.
❑ An annual spend of approximately £500,000 in 2008.
❑ Consumption of more than 6000 megawatts of electricity.

It is likely that a dedicated energy manager is required to ensure that the organisation complies with the new CRC requirements. The organisation will need to measure its consumption in absolute and real terms. For companies that are growing and expanding, then there will have to be a calculation of energy consumed linked to the turnover or headcount.

Organisations will have to submit a report of carbon emissions each year. The first report is due on 30 September 2010. Fines of £1000 will be levied if an organisation is not registered, or if savings are not achieved on a year on year basis. Organisations in the scheme will have to purchase a carbon allowance for their predicted consumption. The

2011 carbon allowance price is set at £12 per tonne for the first purchases of allowances. Organisations will need to budget in advance for this purchase. FMs, energy managers and finance departments will need to work together to ensure compliance.

A league table will establish if organisations have managed their energy efficiently, and those in the top quartile of the table will be rewarded, whilst those at the bottom of the table will have to pay more for their energy consumption. Organisations can improve their performance by obtaining early action metrics, such as the Carbon Trust Standard.

Phased approach

The Scheme is divided into phases. The introductory phase runs for 3 years. Subsequent phases will each last 7 years. Each phase includes a number of consecutive compliance years, which run from April to March, like financial years. There are no gaps or breaks between phases or compliance years.

Before each phase starts there is:

❏ A qualification period when organisations must determine whether they meet the qualification criteria to take part in the scheme, or make an information disclosure to the scheme administrator.
❏ A registration period when organisations must register as a participant in the scheme or submit an information disclosure.
❏ A footprint year when participants must work out their carbon emissions responsibility under the CRC.

Process

In each compliance year, an organisation must complete four steps:

 (i) At the beginning and during each compliance year, the organisation will buy allowances based on expected energy use emissions, taking into account energy efficiency efforts planned for that year.
 (ii) The organisation must monitor energy use during each scheme year and by the end of July, after the end of the scheme year, they report emissions to the scheme administrator.
(iii) The organisation will hold or cancel allowances equal to their emissions during that year, also by the end of July.
(iv) The organisation will receive a revenue recycling payment from the government in the October after reporting their energy use, based on their relative performance in the scheme, which will be published in a performance league table. If they are not performing well, then it is predicted that they will have to pay a penalty.

Incentives

The rewards and penalties in the scheme are set as follows:

2011 plus or minus 10%
2012 plus or minus 20%
2013 plus or minus 30%
2014 plus or minus 40%

30.15 Carbon Trust Standard

This is an example of an early action metric in the new CRC scheme. The standard is awarded to organisations that can demonstrate a reducing of carbon emissions year on year. It is only valid for 2 years, requiring regular recertification by the Carbon Trust. To obtain this standard, an organisation will need to have at least 3 years of energy management data. The pass mark is 60% and the process of assessment includes both a site visit, data interrogation and interviews with senior managers, users and the FM team. A standard issued and dated before 31 March 2011 will qualify as the early action metric for CRC purposes. The fees to register and obtain this standard are based on the energy consumption of an organisation. It is recommended that a timescale of 9 months is allocated to complete the process of certification.

30.16 Legislation and standards

There are many laws and regulations to consider in the management of energy, as shown in the list below.

- Gas Act 1986
- Utilities Act 2000
- Electricity Act 1989
- Fuel and Electricity (Heating Control) Order 1974
- Energy Conservation Act 1981
- Building Regulations 2000
- Boiler (Efficiency) Regulations 1993
- Meters (Certification) Regulations 1998
- Gas (Meters) Regulations 1983
- Health and Safety at Work Act 1974
- Electricity at Work Regulations 1989
- Gas Safety (Installation and Use) Regulations 1998
- Environment Protection Act 1990
- Energy Act 2004
- The Energy Performance of Buildings (Certificates and Inspections) (England and Wales) Regulations 2007
- Climate Change Act 2008
- BS EN 16001 – this is a new European Standard for Energy Management Systems
- Climate Change Levy Regulations 2001
- European Union Emission Trading System (EU ETS)
- Carbon Reduction Energy Efficiency Scheme (CRC)

30.17 Building Regulations

The new Building Regulations Thermal Standards – Part L in England and Wales, Part J in Scotland – require the following in new buildings:

- Improved μ-values.
- Limit exposure to solar overheating especially naturally ventilated buildings.

❑ Measures to improve as-built and in use efficiency of air conditioning, mechanical ventilation and lighting.
❑ Provision to improve air tightness of buildings.
❑ Fitting of energy meters for mandatory metering.
❑ Setting CO_2 emission standard.
❑ Building log book.
❑ Utilities Act compliance.

Building Regulations Part L

These regulations require an improved μ–value in building components. There is a need to limit exposure to solar overheating especially naturally ventilated buildings. The regulations require the industry to improve the efficiency of existing and new A/C systems, mechanical ventilation and lighting systems. Organisations must also improve air tightness of buildings and new buildings require the fitting of energy meters to comply with future mandatory metering. The Regulations set CO_2 emission standards, and require each new premises to have a building log book.

30.18 Building Energy Performance Directive (EPBD)

Under the law, EU member states were compelled to set up, by 4 January 2006, a scheme to certify the energy performance of all buildings and carry out regular inspections of boilers and air conditioning systems. By the same deadline, all building construction, sale and rental transactions had to be accompanied by an energy performance certificate no more than 10 years old, allowing potential occupants to compare building energy efficiency of buildings. For large public service buildings, the certificate has to be on public view, normally in the lobby or reception area. The certification requirement formed the main driver of greater energy efficiency in buildings, but the directive also required member states to lay down their own national minimum energy efficiency standards. No EU minimum standard has been set. Religious buildings, temporary buildings, protected historic buildings and holiday homes are exempt. The UK timetable for compliance is shown in Table 30.1 Updates to the initial EPBD are ongoing with new standards and requirements likely in 2010.

Table 30.1 Implementation timetable

6 April 2008	Energy Performance Certificates (EPCs) were required for the construction of all dwellings and residential property. EPCs were also required for the construction, sale or rent of commercial buildings with a floor area over 10 000 m².
1 July 2008	EPCs were required for the construction, sale or rent of commercial buildings with a floor area over 2500 m².
1 October 2008	EPCs were required on the sale or rent of residential properties and dwellings. EPCs were required on the construction, sale or rent of all remaining commercial buildings. Display Energy Certificates were required for all public buildings >1000 m²
4 January 2009	First inspection of all existing air-conditioning systems over 250 kW capacity was required.
4 January 2011	First inspection of all remaining air-conditioning systems over 12 kW capacity is required. Data centre air conditioning systems are not covered in this legislation.

30.19 Energy Performance Certificates

These are required when there is a change of ownership of a building. They give a rating or relative measure of the energy performance when compared to other buildings of similar size and type. The enforcement authority is the local weights and measures department and local trading standards officers. It is anticipated that more fines will be levied, due to the lack of compliance. Fines will be 12.5% of the rateable value of a property for failure to comply. A £300 fixed fine will also be levied for failure to produce a valid air conditioning report.

Air conditioning inspections

These need to be carried out by a competent person, as instructed by the responsible person described in the legislation. A central database of accredited Energy Assessors has been created, to help organisations to appoint suitable specialists to undertake this work. It is important to check the level of qualification of an assessor, as there are 5 levels, and only those who have achieved levels 1 and 2 are able to assess conditioning systems. The assessor will provide a report on the air conditioning system, measurements on its performance and recommendations to improve its performance. The CIBSE technical memorandum 44 is a guidance document published covering these inspections.

30.20 Display Energy Certificates (DEC)

A DEC contains three main charts of information. These are the operational rating, carbon dioxide emissions and previous operational ratings from the last 3 years.

The DEC must be updated every year. There are fines for non display of the DEC and also fines for a non valid advisory report. There are two aspects to the certificate:

(i) asset rating;
(ii) operational rating.

The ratings will use a visual indicator rating – A to G. The asset rating will be a measure of the energy efficiency of the 'as-built' building and it will take into account the type of construction materials, the type of building services and the methods and systems of operation as intended in the design. The operational rating will be a measure of how well the building is actually operated. This measure will be a key indicator of an organisation's performance as well as the FM, contractors and specialists employed in management of the building. Both measures may impact on the value of a property and its attractiveness to potential tenants. Energy conservation and energy-saving measures will become more important in the effort to ensure the best rating. An advisory report with recommendations on how to improve the rating is issued to the building owner or occupier and is valid for only 7 years maximum. Whilst these certificates are only required in buildings over 1000 m² in the public sector, it is expected that the government will be looking to introduce the same requirement into the private sector in future years.

31 Front of House

31.1 Reception services

The purpose of reception services can vary from company to company, depending on size, culture and security needs. However, typical functions will include the following:

- ❑ Entry and welcome.
- ❑ Protection of staff, assets and visitors.
- ❑ Information and direction.
- ❑ Waiting and meeting area.

The reception can also be managed alongside a wide range of other functions in the FM department. In smaller organisations, reception can play a key part in general office management or, in a larger organisation, part of a dedicated front-of-house operations department.

31.2 The first impression

Most reception areas form the entry point for both staff and visitors. As such, the reception will have a fundamental role on how an organisation is viewed and will provide the first, and often lasting, impression of a company and its FM provision. First impressions are formed within seconds, and there is never a second chance to form a first impression.

Consider the reception as part of a stage set, with the receptionists playing the lead roles and the visitors as the audience. After the visitor has absorbed the physical setting, the next major influence will be the nature of the personal greeting given by reception staff. Thought should also be given to the impression on visitors as they leave. The overall impression needs to be lasting, memorable and, above all, positive.

31.3 The welcome process

A good welcome from reception should aim to do the following:

- ❑ Confirm that the visitor has come to the right place.
- ❑ Confirm whether the visitor is expected.
- ❑ Show that the receptionist has a genuine interest in the visitor.
- ❑ Put an anxious visitor at ease with casual small talk.

❑ Offer refreshments, such as a glass of water, a cup of coffee or tea.
❑ Invite the visitor to take a seat, read magazines/newspapers whilst waiting.

It is not recommended to use standard phrases and procedures to greet visitors – this can make the interaction appear insincere. However, it is important to maintain standards and offer a consistent service. A typical welcome could begin with the following:

❑ Good morning/afternoon.
❑ Welcome to [name of organisation].

The use of open questions such as those beginning with what, who, when, where, why, which and how can help obtain appropriate information, initiate a conversation and complete the task of greeting a visitor. If reception staff are encouraged to use their initiative and natural style, then the visitor will receive a warmer, more natural welcome. It is important that individual visitors receive the same standard of service, however difficult the interaction between reception and visitor may be.

The requirements of the visitor should be dealt with as efficiently as possible. A good welcoming process for visitors could include the following steps:

❑ Read the body language of the visitor(s) – do they look lost, happy, annoyed, familiar?
❑ Greet – with names if known.
❑ Find out who they have come to see, the purpose of their visit and any other information that is required.
❑ Advise what happens next – are they to take a seat, wait for collection, any delays expected?

31.4 Welcome formalities

During the welcome, reception will also have to conduct a number of formalities depending on an organisations' particular procedures and policies. These may include the following:

❑ Verification of visitor details.
❑ Contact with host to confirm arrival of visitor.
❑ Visitor sign-in books or logs.
❑ Issue and collection of passes or badges.
❑ Details of car registrations.
❑ Issue of copies of health and safety regulations.
❑ Details of local security regulations.
❑ Bag and person security searches.
❑ Completion of forms or questionnaires.
❑ Collection of money and issue of receipts.
❑ Goods-in/-out logs for receipt and issue of goods and packages.
❑ Issue and receipt of bag tags for left luggage facilities.
❑ Issue and receipt of room keys.
❑ Issue and receipt of locker room keys.
❑ Hotdesk allocations and issue and receipt of secure pedestal/locker keys.
❑ Issue of visitor guides.

31.5 Managing visitor expectations

A good receptionist is able to make and use opportunities to exceed the visitor's expectations. Good customer service is about delighting the customer, giving them an experience over and above their expectation. Front-of-house operations can therefore provide an excellent opportunity to add value to an organisation. The professionalism and the service standards of reception staff will have both a direct and indirect effect on the organisations' staff, visitors and assets.

For example, if a visitor is very late due to poor weather conditions, road conditions or problems with public transport, it may be an opportunity to ask whether they would like to call anyone as reassurance of their safe arrival.

The management of queuing is essential for good customer service. It must be obvious to the visitor where to queue and that the queuing system is fair. When queues do arise, the receptionist should be able to identify the next person and offer apologies for any delays. If a designated meet and greet person is employed in addition to the static reception staff, then this person has a clear duty to approach visitors and guide them to the next available reception service point.

31.6 Best practice

Receptionists can give a more professional, knowledgeable and welcoming acknowledgement to a visitor when they know who is expected and whom they are visiting. Good performance as a front-of-house employee can be likened to being a good performer, knowing the script and acting the part as a true professional. To help receptionists give a good performance, it is good practice to encourage hosts to supply the following details prior to the visitor's arrival:

- ❑ Name of visitor(s).
- ❑ Company.
- ❑ Date.
- ❑ Time.
- ❑ Mode of travel.
- ❑ Parking requirements (if appropriate).
- ❑ Name of host and department.
- ❑ Contact number for host and an alternative contact number if engaged or voicemail activated.
- ❑ Special needs of visitors (if known).
- ❑ Nationality (if not British).

31.7 Customer service

Customers of the reception services in an organisation can be both external and internal:

- ❑ The external customer – visitors, clients and customers, whose first contact with the business will most often be the reception desk.
- ❑ The internal customer – employees within the company who need to be provided with a service or information.

Ensuring that external customers are welcomed and attended to, and that internal customers are adequately provisioned so that they can work to their fullest potential, is therefore a crucial part of a FM's role.

Service needs and expectations of visitors may vary but essentially will encompass help and assistance, care and attention, availability of suitable services and facilities and an efficient, sincere service.

31.8 Customer satisfaction

Customer satisfaction arises from matching service delivery to service expectation. For example, visitors will form service expectations from the quality and accuracy of the information received prior to arrival. If the expectations and delivery do not match, visitors will be dissatisfied. Examples could include the following:

❏   Despite a promise of parking, the visitor cannot find a parking place on arrival.
❏   The visitor gets lost as a result of inaccurate directions.
❏   The visitor arrives too late or too early because of inaccurate estimated journey times, or inadequate directions and instructions.
❏   Despite making prior arrangements with their host, the visitor is not expected.
❏   A cluttered and disorganised reception contrasts with the good quality of information provided prior to arrival.
❏   A bland reception fails to reflect the organisation, its products, service or success.

An encounter that fails to meet expectations will always be remembered and it can be hard work to 'recover' that customer's perception. Service recovery at the point and time of service failure will achieve better and longer-lasting results than if recovery is left until much later. It is worth noting that word-of-mouth experiences of poor service spread quickly to colleagues and friends and can do much to discredit an organisation.

Visitor expectations therefore affect perceptions of service quality. The expectations and needs of visitors and users of front-of-house services should therefore be understood and measured by the providers of the service.

31.9 Visiting groups

Some organisations may on occasion have to deal with large groups of visitors, which may include the following:

❏   Delegates attending training courses.
❏   Delegates attending conferences or events.
❏   Visitors arriving by public transport or company shuttle buses.
❏   Candidates arriving for auditions, interviews or selection tests.
❏   Contractors invited to tender for supply of services or goods.
❏   Visitors attending building tours.
❏   Public relations events.
❏   Marketing and product launch events.

Receptions should be informed of any large groups expected, particularly from the point of view of capacity management. If high volumes of visitors are expected on a regular basis, then it may be appropriate to use either a dedicated 'group' desk, a number of individual separate desks in an echelon arrangement or a meet and greet service.

31.10 Meet and greet service

Some organisations provide a 'meet and greet' service for visitors as part of their drive for competitive advantage and excellent customer care standards. A member of the reception team is located in front of the reception desk to approach visitors and engage them in dialogue as soon as they enter the building.

This meet and greet approach aims to break down the barrier created by a reception desk and offer a genuine welcome to the visitor. The procedure can also be used effectively in queue management to ensure that the next visitor is dealt with promptly by the next available person, or is directed to another facility as appropriate.

This is a high level of service, and requires both high standards in customer care and high staffing levels. Staff employed in this role must be fully aware of their own body language, its impact on others and ensure that they adapt it to suit the visitors' needs.

Advantages and disadvantages of a 'meet and greet' service

The advantages and disadvantages of a meet and greet service are set out in Table 31.1.

Table 31.1   Pros and cons of a meet and greet service

Advantages	Disadvantages
The organisation has greater control of the visitor experience.	Some visitors may feel intimidated by this direct approach.
The visitor is not left unattended. 'Meet and greet' can also be used effectively in queue management to ensure the next visitor is dealt with promptly or redirected elsewhere.	The visitor may have to repeat information. Could lead to a duplication of effort by both parties – the visitor and the front-of-house staff. When there are no visitors, this resource is excess to requirements.
The 'meet and greet' resource could retreat behind the desk if short staffed.	It is difficult to justify and quantify the benefits. Consequently, it can be seen as an excessive and wasteful use of resources, and raise suspicions that this will be reflected in the price of products and services.
Provides a high level of customer care and added value to the visitor's experience.	
Removes the physical barrier created by the reception desk and gives a more open welcome to visitors. Can be useful to overcome issues in services provided to disabled visitors.	Removal of the reception desk could have security implications. Staff need to be comfortable working 'in the open' and trained to operate without the protection of a desk.
Staff feel more ownership of the whole reception space – not just the workstation and desk area.	Presentation and appearance is absolutely critical at all times – both staff and their clutter will be on full view.

Table 31.2   Style of service offered to different visitors

Type of visitor	Style of reception service
VIP	Discreet
Official/enforcement officer	Knowledgeable, calm, professional
Customer	Helpful
Supplier	Confident, knowledgeable
Job candidate	Reassuring, sympathetic
Member of staff	Friendly, helpful
Couriers	Diplomatic, resourceful
Taxi drivers	Firm, cautious
Unexpected	Inquisitive, helpful, security focused

31.11 Styles of welcome and reception service

The style of welcome offered by reception staff may be affected by the state of both the visitor and the host, and these may be specific to a particular service encounter. For example, a receptionist may need to keep an angry or nervous visitor calm, and an impatient or tardy host informed.

It is also possible to determine particular styles of reception service depending on the type of visitor and nature of their visit as shown in Table 31.2.

31.12 Welcome boards

Some organisations use welcome boards and electronic notice boards to welcome known visitors. Typically, such boards are used in hotels, conference centres, training establishments and in large corporate headquarters.

Welcome boards can be very effective if used accurately and efficiently. Names must be spelt correctly and, if a number of delegates are expected, these names should be listed in alphabetical order. This will make visitors feel that their visits are valued and important to the organisation. If, however, some visitors are not listed or names are spelt incorrectly, this will have a detrimental effect. It is also important to update welcome boards frequently to ensure currency of information.

Information on the location of events can also be provided. This is useful in large buildings where there may be a number of different events taking place.

31.13 Remote entry points

Some organisations may decide to use remote or adjacent locations to accommodate large numbers of visitors. This may be appropriate if car parking is limited or security clearance procedures are detailed and time consuming. Frequent shuttle bus services connecting locations can bring visitors to their final destination, with the necessary security checks and issuing of identity passes completed elsewhere.

If such a procedure is put in place, the visitors' expectations must be managed carefully. Adequate time should be allowed and appropriate instructions, such as presentation of photographic identification evidence, issued well in advance.

31.14 The goodbye

The last impression a visitor may have is equally as important as the first; the departure of a guest can confirm or alter their impressions. A good receptionist will employ active customer care skills to ensure that visitors leave the organisation feeling well treated and respected. It is courteous to thank the visitor(s) for their visit.

For example, receptionists can inform the departing visitor of any known transport delays, offer updates on the local weather conditions and even give souvenirs such as company samples or marketing material.

31.15 Reception service standards

Appropriate service delivery standards can be developed and recorded in a service level agreement (SLA). An example of a reception SLA is shown in Table 31.3. Daily checklists are also useful to provide a measurement structure to the workload and performance of the staff in achieving a given standard stated in the SLA.

31.16 Corporate duty of care

The reception area – as the entry and exit point for staff and visitors – will play an important part in corporate health and safety management as well as security. An organisation has a duty of care towards its employees and the public. Security procedures and considerations distinct to the reception area are described later.

Health and safety information

The Health and Safety (Information for Employees) Regulations 1989 require employers to provide employees with certain basic information concerning their health, safety and welfare at work. This information is contained in both a health and safety law poster and a leaflet approved by the HSE. Employers can comply with their duty by either displaying

Table 31.3   Example service level agreement for a reception service

Greeting of guests	All guests must be acknowledged immediately and dealt with within 2 minutes of entering reception.	Measured by mystery guest	100%
Processing of guests	All hosts must be contacted within 1 minute of the receptionist greeting the guest. (If the host is not available or not contactable, then every effort should be made to contact the host on a regular basis; if we have alternative number use this.)	Measured by mystery guest	100%
Reception areas	All areas must be kept clean, tidy and organised at all times.	Daily checklist completed	100%
Telephone greeting	All telephones must be answered within three rings in a courteous and professional manner, using the agreed telephone answering response.	Measured by mystery caller	95%

the poster or providing employees with a copy of the leaflet. The poster is most often displayed in reception areas and should be personalised to include all of the following information:

❑ The names and locations of trade union or other safety representatives and the groups they represent.
❑ Name of appointed person with health and safety responsibilities.
❑ The name and address of the local enforcing authority whose health and safety inspectors cover the particular workplace.

Visitor guides

Visitor guides can also be used as a means of discharging the duties in the Management of Health and Safety at Work Regulations 1999 (to inform visitors of the local arrangements for their health and safety). Typically, such guides need to be simple, easy-to-read and in a format for easy reference. Ideally, the visitor should keep the guide handy for the duration of their visit.

The minimum requirement could be met in two ways:

(i) A simple set of instructions printed on the reverse of a visitor pass.
(ii) A statement of instructions displayed adjacent to the signing in book which visitors are asked to read.

The guide should include the following details:

❑ Emergency procedures at the premises.
❑ Appointed persons to deal with specific tasks.
❑ Potential risks.

Additional information

It is common practice, however, to use the opportunity to give more details than just the health and safety information. Maps with location details, photographs and opening times of key services, details of other company rules (such as no smoking) and contact numbers are often included in visitor guides. Suggested headings include the following:

❑ Accident reporting.
❑ Smoking policy.
❑ Use of mobile telephones and personal laptops on the premises.
❑ Protective clothing.
❑ Restricted areas.
❑ Stop and search policy.
❑ Prosecution for thefts.
❑ Permits to work.
❑ Use of catering/vending facilities.
❑ Responsibility for personal possessions.
❑ Lost property.

Guides may also serve as souvenirs of a visit and act as good publicity for the organisation.

The size and weight of the guide also needs to be considered: these may need to be sent out in advance with a confirmation letter of a future meeting. An alternative may be to direct visitors to a website, where details can be downloaded and printed by the visitors. This assumes that the visitor has access to, and is comfortable, with this technology.

31.17 Recording visitor information

To keep accurate information of visits by non-employees, records of arrival and departure are required. Whilst not a particular legal requirement, it is considered best practice to keep visitor records to assist an organisation in meeting its statutory obligations towards visitors on its premises. Care must be taken to comply with the Data Protection Act – visitors' personal details must be kept secure and not kept longer than is justifiable.

Records are important for a number of reasons:

❑ Evacuation role calls.
❑ Investigations arising from claims due to injury on the premises.
❑ Investigations into missing property or alleged theft of property from the premises.
❑ Statistics on visitor numbers for future planning.
❑ Marketing and communication.
❑ Daily management of visitors' whereabouts on site.

Typical information

Records of visitors will typically include a range of information:

❑ Name of visitor.
❑ Name and address of their employer.
❑ Contact point in case of emergency.
❑ Vehicle registration.
❑ Date and time of arrival.
❑ Predicted length of stay.
❑ Name of host and department.
❑ Details of higher-risk visitors such as disabled persons or children.
❑ Details of equipment, substances or articles being brought to site.
❑ Date and time of departure.

In addition, it may be useful to record the following details:

❑ Have the relevant emergency procedures been explained to the visitor?
❑ Has PPE been issued?
❑ Are permits to work required?
❑ Have permits or hot work permits been issued?

Visitors to particularly sensitive or high-risk areas may also have other restrictions imposed or records kept, e.g. dose monitoring in X-ray, ionisation or radiation areas. In obtaining the above details about the visitor, the FM should consider whether the visitor completes a form or if the receptionist does this on behalf of the visitor. This has implications later when considering access to a visitor book, a computer, or system of recording the information.

Methods of record keeping

Records may be kept manually in a loose-leaf register, a standard pre-printed visitor book or they could be computerised. If a computer-based system is used, the data may either be entered by the visitors themselves, or by the host or receptionist. The ability to choose the most appropriate method of record keeping can be beneficial in managing specific needs of disabled visitors. If the receptionist, rather than visitors, handles visitors' details, then the need to make physical alterations to reception desks may be overcome with a simple change in procedure and process. The location and speed of data entry are also important aspects to consider. If the data entry takes too long, and the printing of badges or passes is also a lengthy process, then the performance standards of visitor processing will be affected.

In some instances, if visitor details are known in advance, then the records can be completed either fully or partially and then confirmed on arrival. This can benefit the efficiency of the process – reducing overall times taken to complete the transaction. If the host does data entry in advance, and the electronic form is linked to a central visitor database, then the receptionist can be automatically advised of expected visitors.

The length of time that records are kept, together with the security of personal data, is important when considering the legal duties under the Data Protection Act.

31.18 Display of company signage

The reception is most often the best place to display company information. This may include names of businesses, official addresses, national and international awards, brochures and so on.

Company administration

Under the Business Names Act 1985 and the Companies Act 1985, all organisations trading from a place of business in the UK are required to display certain information about their business.

Both Acts require the names and contact addresses of the owners of the business to be prominently and legibly displayed in a place visible to customers and suppliers. If it is not displayed, visitors can demand a name and address, a request which must be responded to immediately and in writing.

Depending on the size of organisation, the following information should be displayed:

❏ Name of the owner(s), e.g. Keith Jones or K Jones.
❏ Contact address of the owner(s).
❏ Names of all partners.
❏ Full corporate name of the company including limited status where applicable, e.g. AB & CD Brown Ltd (this applies only where the trading name is something other than the full corporate name).

Company insurance

In accordance with the Employers' Liability (Compulsory Insurance) Regulations 1998 regulation 5, one or more copies of an employer's liability insurance certificate must be displayed at each place of business at which the policy holder employs persons covered by the policy. Such certificates must be valid. Too often, the updated copy stays in the file, and does not reach the official notice boards where it must be displayed.

31.19 Visitor risk assessments

The Management of Health and Safety at Work Regulations 1999 regulation 3 requires risk assessments to be carried out to identify the measures required to safeguard the safety of visitors.

Whilst carrying out such an assessment, it is important to consider both the risk caused by the visitor to the site and that to which the visitor may be exposed. It is also important to take into account that most visitors will be unfamiliar with the premises and local procedures.

The role of reception staff in risk assessments

Reception staff have a duty of care to the health and safety of visitors and should be encouraged to adopt a responsible attitude for the whole reception space, not just their workstation or desk. It may be appropriate to set specific risk assessment tasks on a daily or weekly basis.

Assessment checklist

A risk assessment checklist could include the following tasks:

❑ Remove all trip hazards.
❑ Assess the cleanliness (floors, work surfaces, bins, glass, toilets) and take corrective action if required.
❑ Check that fire extinguishers are in place and checked for validity.
❑ Test the correct operation of the panic alarm.
❑ Review the display screen equipment risk assessment on a periodic basis, and for each new member of staff who may use the equipment.
❑ Make test calls on the public address system.
❑ Test the remote access controls for doors and gates.
❑ Confirm visibility and quality of pictures on the CCTV system.
❑ Check accurate signage is in place – mandatory, directional and information.
❑ Make emergency telephone line tests.
❑ Check emergency exits are clear and accessible.
❑ Organise the removal of obstacles that may be hazardous for disabled visitors.
❑ Confirm location of accident book.
❑ Check location of first-aiders and first-aid box.
❑ Check adequate stock of health and safety guidelines for visitors.

31.20 Fire precautions in the reception area

A reception area will need to comply with Regulatory Reform Order (Fire Safety) 2006. The fire risk assessment will require that adequate fire protection must be installed and provided and may include the following:

❑ Call points.
❑ Fire extinguishers.

- Fire action signs.
- Fire doors.
- Fire escape routes.
- Fire exits.
- Emergency lighting.
- Sprinklers.
- Smoke and/or heat detectors.

In addition, the fire alarm panel for the whole building or office may be located in the reception space. Copies of the plans of the building, the zoning of the fire alarm installation, fire alarm system commissioning and maintenance records, fire risk assessment and records of training may also be kept at the reception. This information will be required in routine checks and inspections by FM staff and external enforcing authorities. Reception may also be the location for giving information to staff and visitors that a routine test or evacuation drill may take place. In some buildings, this may be a simple sign or notice board put in place on the day of the test or drill.

Staff training

Staff working at the reception desk will need to be fully trained in what to do in an emergency, and what action to take if a fire starts in reception. Their responsibilities will include ensuring the health and safety of visitors in the reception area during a fire evacuation.

Fire exits

The Health and Safety at Work Act 1974 requires that fire exits are maintained as sterile areas to allow the safe move of people in an emergency. This is critical for the staff to exit the space and also for the fire brigade officers entering a building. Fire exits near reception areas may sometimes be used to store items awaiting collection, cleaners' trolleys, bags of rubbish, overgrown plants, unwanted items of furniture or other fixtures and fittings of a building. It is essential that the reception staff do not allow fire exits to be obstructed with such items and should ensure that the routes are kept clean and tidy at all times. It is important that others in the building are not permitted to leave unattended items in reception for both security and safety reasons.

31.21 CCTV surveillance

Front-of-house operations could be monitored by CCTV surveillance. The Data Protection Act 1998 covers the processing of images of individuals recorded by CCTV cameras. The same legally enforceable information-handling standards, which apply to the processing of personal data on computers, now cover CCTV. It is important that staff working in these areas are aware of the presence of cameras. In some public spaces, CCTV can be a useful deterrent to abuse and threatening behaviour, giving the front-of-house staff a sense of protection when located in a vulnerable area. The use of CCTV can also enable blind spots in large reception areas to be checked.

31.22 Trespassing and theft

FMs and reception managers will also need to be aware of other legislation related to security and conduct of visitors including:

❑ Law relating to theft and trespassers.
❑ Powers of arrest.
❑ Powers of search.

31.23 Switchboard services

It is often practical to combine switchboard and reception functions in small- to medium-sized organisations to optimise efficiency. The need for extensive switchboard services in many organisations has diminished in recent years due to the increasing use of 'direct dial' and mobiles in many organisations. This has resulted in fewer requests by incoming callers to connect calls to known extensions. There is, however, still a need for a limited switchboard service for general enquiries and to connect callers who do not know an extension or direct dial number.

Management issues

Operational issues to consider include the following:

❑ Immediate access to up-to-date contact information.
❑ Management of callers waiting for connections to engaged extensions.
❑ Unknown callers who could be making threats, giving verbal abuse or generally being unpleasant.
❑ Callers who need a lot of information, such as names of senior staff, address and website details.
❑ International callers whose command of English may be limited.
❑ Mystery shoppers calling to test the organisation and its services.
❑ Market researchers doing telephone surveys.
❑ Similarity to other numbers in the neighbourhood.
❑ Level of wrong numbers or misdialled calls.
❑ Effect of marketing/advertising/recruitment campaigns when higher volumes of enquiries may be expected.
❑ Effect of good or bad publicity in various media and increased number of enquiry calls.
❑ Known high peaks in number of incoming calls such as to obtain or query examination results, applications to university, special offers, job advertisements, etc.

Assessing priorities

Combining reception and switchboard duties may create some operational dilemmas, which also need to be managed.

The most obvious difficulty will be when the reception is faced with simultaneous customer requests – e.g. should they deal with an incoming telephone call or the visitor standing at the desk? It is often the case that a ringing telephone will take priority, as this can be distracting to a conversation with a visitor. However, answering the telephone can also be annoying to a visitor who has queued for some time. Another issue is the need to look at a screen or console to enter data, resulting in 'heads down' behaviour by the reception staff. This is not conducive to welcoming and acknowledging the visitors.

A receptionist carrying out both functions will need to be confident in both tasks, adept at multi-skilling and capable of using body language in the form of eye contact and offering suitable gestures to assure the visitor that they have been acknowledged and will be dealt with as soon as possible.

It is normally only recommended to combine these functions in small organisations where the number of visitors and telephone callers is relatively low. If there are two staff manning a reception desk, then one person can deal with the switchboard functions, leaving the other to concentrate on the visitors. If the staff member dealing with telephone calls is on view to the waiting visitors, then they must pay particular attention to their body language, particularly facial expressions, so as not to give an unprofessional impression to visitors.

31.24 Room booking services

Reception may be required to deal with a variety of room bookings for internal staff and external customers and staff:

❑   Meeting rooms.
❑   Conference rooms.
❑   Teaching or training rooms.
❑   Hotdesks.
❑   Designated areas within open-plan space for particular events.

A room booking service can be manual or computerised. If using a computerised system, then it is important to determine who is eligible to view only, and who has access to view and book. An audit trail may be required to support changes and cancellations. If the internal staff can have access to view only, then it will reduce the number of internal telephone enquiries. The system can be set up so that the user can send an email with a specific request for a booking, having first checked availability, or an electronic request sent to the database for subsequent confirmation by reception. There are many proprietary room booking software packages now available on the market for the FM to select from.

Another issue which sometimes arises is the pulling of rank by senior staff to obtain the room they need for a particular meeting or event. This can put the reception staff or room booking staff in a very difficult position if they are the ones left to deal with reorganising alternative space for others, and advising all concerned. To avoid embarrassment and conflict, it is best to establish an agreed policy and set of guidelines in advance.

Booking parameters

It is essential to determine what maximum length of time is permitted for pre-booking of rooms. Depending on the volume of bookings, the number of rooms and the frequency of change/cancellation, the limit could be as short as 3 weeks or as long as 3 months. This will ensure that there is no block booking of rooms, preventing others from access, and the need is continually reassessed. Another aspect of room booking confirmation is the need to match requirements to availability; that is, ensuring that the number of expected users of a particular space is suited to the capacity of that room. Without central control by an independent function, it would be too easy for staff to book their preferred rooms, and not maximise the space utilisation. It is also recommended to keep records of cancellations – this may assist in the settlement of disputes and the production of statistics.

Booking requirements

Additional information that may be required to complete the booking for the user could include the following:

- ❑ Set-up and layout.
- ❑ Audio visual equipment requirements.
- ❑ Is a technician required?
- ❑ Name of host and contact details.
- ❑ Department details.
- ❑ Budget or charge code details.
- ❑ Hospitality or catering requirements.
- ❑ Special needs for the disabled.
- ❑ Directional signage.
- ❑ Flowers.
- ❑ Data and voice requirements.
- ❑ Video conferencing.
- ❑ Stationery – name cards, note pads, pens.
- ❑ Length of time room required.
- ❑ Escort of external visitors to room by host, reception or security.

Utilisation statistics

To ensure that the room booking function is achieving best value for an organisation, statistics on room utilisation are required. The reception or room booking team can compile a list of rooms booked, showing the percentage of utilisation, percentage availability/unavailability, cancellation, demand peaks and no shows. The recording of information at the time of booking is key to the compilation of data, and it should be agreed at the outset what management information will be required. To ensure that a rigorous analysis of the room utilisation is undertaken, it is good practice to employ 'room checkers' once a year to undertake a visual check of room utilisation. If the same time period every year is surveyed, then a year-on-year analysis of room utilisation is then possible. The analysis can then reveal numbers of rooms used and not booked, the numbers of rooms booked and not used, actual occupancy of rooms against the theoretical capacity of the room. Such information can be used for management decisions on the future viability of bookable meeting and training rooms for the organisation. Rooms not achieving the agreed minimum utilisation percentage can then be redesignated for alternative uses if required. New technologies and systems are now available to give real time room booking information outside each bookable room. This gives users the opportunity to sign out of a room earlier or allow users to gain access to an unbooked room, etc.

32 Housekeeping and Cleaning Services

32.1 Cleaning services

Cleaning is defined by the British Institute of Cleaning Science (BICS) as the removal of dirt, soil or unwanted matter from any surface. Cleaning services are required to provide a safe, hygienic and comfortable working environment. The organisation has a duty to ensure that cleaning takes place to the required standards and to meet statutory obligations. The standard of cleaning indicates a great deal about the values held by an organisation and their FM function. Clean buildings show to both the employees and the customers that the organisation is able to provide a suitable working environment. A clean workplace will directly and indirectly impact on the productivity and well-being of employees. The main reasons for cleaning are to:

- ❏ Promote health and safety.
- ❏ Prolong the life of fixtures, fittings and surfaces.
- ❏ Improve the appearance of the establishment.

The duty to provide a clean working environment comes from the Health and Safety at Work Act which states that the employer has a general duty to provide a safe place of work and not expose their employees to any risks to health and safety. There are also specific cleaning duties under the Workplace (Health and Safety and Welfare) Regulations. These duties include:

- ❏ All workplaces, furniture, furnishings and fittings should be kept sufficiently clean.
- ❏ Surfaces of the floors, walls and ceilings of all workplaces inside buildings should be capable of being kept sufficiently clean.
- ❏ Waste materials should not be allowed to accumulate in a workplace except in suitable receptacles.
- ❏ All windows and skylights should be of a design or constructed to allow them to be cleaned safely.
- ❏ Sanitary conveniences and washing facilities should be kept in a clean and orderly condition.
- ❏ Every floor in a workplace and the surface of every traffic route in a workplace should be kept free from obstructions and from any article or substance that may cause a person to slip, trip or fall.

Cleaning is one of the most outsourced services in FM. It is a thankless task, as it is only noticed when not done or not done well. As soon as an area or surface is clean, it deteriorates and will need to be done again – it is a repetitive task. It has historically been carried out in out-of-office hours to avoid disruption, leading to many operatives working in shifts

Table 32.1   Range of cleaning activities

Routine cleaning tasks	Specialist cleaning tasks	Supplementary services
Removal of loose and impacted debris	Washing both exterior and interior glazing	Personal hygiene services (sanitary disposal bins, vending machines)
Vacuuming soft floors	Pressure washing of external paved areas	
Sweeping, mopping or polishing of hard floors		Recycling and waste management
	Graffiti removal and prevention	
Dusting and damp wiping vertical surfaces	Deep cleans of catering equipment and kitchens	Linen services (roller towels, tea towels, shower towels)
Dusting and damping, wiping furniture, fixtures and fittings	Dusting ceilings and light fixtures	Consumable supplies (toilet paper, hand towels, hand soap)
Disposing of rubbish and other waste	Carpet deep cleans	Pest control, including pigeon spiking and hawk flying
Washroom cleaning and maintenance	Cleaning upholstery, curtains, blinds	Eye bolt and latchway testing (for window and cladding cleaning)
Cleaning of kitchen, dining area, canteen, vending areas, rest areas	Supply and exchange of entrance door mats	IT equipment sanitation

around the normal working day. There have been changes to this in more recent times, with the introduction of day-time cleaning contracts. Cleaning contracts are usually let on a 3–5 year basis. There are many cleaning contractors to choose from – local, regional or national. There are five typical components of housekeeping or cleaning services:

(i)   general;
(ii) waste disposal;
(iii) janitorial;
(iv) windows;
(v)   deep cleaning.

Cleaning activities should remove all surface soil and obstructions from surfaces, fixtures and fittings. The range of activities is shown in Table 32.1. Ideally, the least obstructive and disturbing methods of cleaning should be used. The aim is to restore all surfaces to as near perfect condition as possible and to remove all dust and dirt without transferring to other areas. Cleaning tasks can be categorised into either routines or specials. The specials are also known as periodics, and will typically take place at less frequent intervals, and need specialist equipment or trained operatives.

32.2 Cleaning methods

As a general principle, the simplest methods of cleaning with the mildest and safest cleaning agents should be used. Cleaners and their supervisors must be aware of the safety

Table 32.2   Ways to clean

Physically clean	The surface is apparently free from dust and dirt when the hand is wiped over the surface
Chemically clean	Free from harmful chemicals on the surface and floating in the air
Bacteriologically clean	Free from harmful bacteria which must be removed to prevent infection
Entomologically clean	Free from harmful insects, surface dust and dirt
Osmologically clean	Normally in hospitals, operating theatres, intensive care and can also be in high-tech food factories

hazards of the substances, the equipment and methods used. Each cleaning process should be carried out in the quickest time possible, to the highest standard, with due regard and consideration to occupier.

Cleaning can occur in many ways – by heat, by chemicals and by friction as shown in Table 32.2.

32.3 Cleaning standards

The British Institute of Cleaning Science has produced standards for the main activities to show what is expected when a task is completed, what is unacceptable and what is permitted between each clean. Standards have been produced for hard floors, soft floors, vertical surfaces, high level surfaces, furniture, fixtures and fittings, and sanitary fittings. An extract of the general standard is shown in Table 32.3.

It is important at a very early stage to establish a regular monitoring regime for the checks by the appointed supervisor or manager. By using a checklist, cleaning standards can be more easily verified. Here is a list of some checks that could be done.

❏ Bang cushions and fabric furnishings to see if dust is present – if so, not adequately cleaned.
❏ Venetian blinds – are the slats clean?
❏ Have hands and finger marks been removed from doors, glass and light switches?
❏ Are metal surfaces free from water marks?
❏ Are wet wipe areas free from streak marks?

Table 32.3   Example of a BICS general cleaning standard

Task	Acceptable on completion of task	Unacceptable	Acceptable between cleaning tasks
Removal of loose debris	Free of litter, debris, dust and loose foreign matter	Build-up of litter, debris, dust and loose foreign matter	Debris arising from usage between cleans
Removal of impacted debris	Free from impacted debris, e.g. chewing gum, labels	Build-up of impacted debris	Debris arising from usage between cleans

❑   Have the cleaning operations been carried out? If not, why?
❑   Make note of tasks not carried out.
❑   Consider descaling toilets out of hours.
❑   Consider cleaning tea points and fridges out of hours.
❑   Check what frequency tasks should be done. Note those not done.
❑   Check that the right materials are being used for the appropriate surfaces.
❑   Check materials for COSHH assessments.
❑   Has the contractor adequate safety notices if they are required?
❑   Check the areas not immediately in sight, that is:
   o   backs of toilet pans;
   o   under taps;
   o   plug holes;
   o   behind pipes;
   o   below toilet seats.
   o   Check whole area of mirrors – all four corners.

A more indepth audit checklist is shown in Figure 32.1.

32.4 Cleaning specifications

The factors that affect preparation of cleaning specifications include:

❑   Type, size and layout of building.
❑   Time allocated for cleaning.
❑   Number of people using building.
❑   Amount of work to be done.
❑   Type and degree of soil and debris.
❑   Type of surfaces, furniture, fixtures and fittings.
❑   Accessibility to all areas.
❑   Standard of finish required.
❑   Budget available.
❑   Experience and quality of workforce.
❑   Quality of supervision.
❑   Age, physical build, general ability (intelligence and literacy) of cleaning operatives.
❑   General attitudes of cleaning operatives.
❑   Motivation and incentive schemes.

Specifications can be output or input. The difference is the level of detail shown – the input specification has far greater detail of the work required, the methods to be used, hours of work and equipment to be used. Another fundamental difference is that the input specification gives details of the cleaning frequencies, whereas the output specification is focused on performance. An output specification will require an SLA so that a mutual understanding of the standards and measurements is agreed. A sample specification is shown in section 32.17 on page 441. Cleaning can be done by a directly employed or 'in-house' team or via a cleaning service contractor.

Contractor Cleaning KPM Record, Cleaning Record and Check List
Customer's Site:...

Specific location(s)	Cleaning activity performance:
Assessed:.................……………...........	Score 1 to 5 (or N/A – not applicable)
....	5= Perfect, excellent
....	4= Very Good
(e.g. room number, toilets location, etc.)	3= Acceptable
	2= Could do better
	1= Neglected (significant failure of service)

Date of assessment: Cleaning related activities requiring check against agreed standards: (cleaning as applied to accessible areas)	Circle appropriate score, i.e. 1–5 or N/A	Comments/action taken on scores 1 or 2 (details on separate sheet if necessary)
Bins emptied	N/A 1 2 3 4 5	
Floors/carpets free from dirt, debris and spills	N/A 1 2 3 4 5	
Hard or polished floors maintained and clean	N/A 1 2 3 4 5	
Relevant furniture, surfaces and fittings dusted	N/A 1 2 3 4 5	
Stair wells free from dirt, debris and spills	N/A 1 2 3 4 5	
Radiators and pipe work wipe/dusted clean	N/A 1 2 3 4 5	
Waste collection requests satisfied	N/A 1 2 3 4 5	
Sinks, showers, WCs and urinals clean	N/A 1 2 3 4 5	
Walls and surfaces including ledges wiped down	N/A 1 2 3 4 5	
Toilet rolls are fully stocked	N/A 1 2 3 4 5	
Soap dispensers stocked adequately	N/A 1 2 3 4 5	
Paper towels fully stocked	N/A 1 2 3 4 5	
Ashtrays emptied	N/A 1 2 3 4 5	
**Customer satisfaction: Are you generally satisfied that the cleaning service is to an acceptable standard? *(dependent on customer availability, or subject to prior agreement, the customer may choose not to participate in these checks. In this instance, score should be N/A)*	N/A 1 2 3 4 5 *(** This score not to be included in the KPM calculation)* Customer signature	Customer comments:

Total number of activities scoring 1 _____   Total number of activities scoring 2 _____
At this location   At this location

Contractor's signature (wherever possible the contractor's representative should sign to acknowledge these results)	Date: _____
Contractor signature	Date: _____
Contractor signature	Date: _____

Figure 32.1   Cleaning audit tick list

32.5 Cleaning costs

The elements that make up the cost of cleaning include:

❑ Labour.
❑ National insurance.
❑ Holidays.
❑ Supervision.
❑ Training.
❑ Uniforms.
❑ Materials.
❑ Equipment.

Costs can be obtained from contractors using a number of proformas as shown in Table 32.4.

32.6 Advantages and disadvantages of contract cleaning

Advantages

❑ A known budget over a given period.
❑ Contractor responsible for employing, training, paying and dismissing staff.
❑ Contract services may alleviate many industrial relation and staff problems.
❑ Alleviate the necessity to buy or hire specialist equipment.
❑ Specialist services may be more readily available.
❑ Risk of cleaning is shared with expert contractor.
❑ Innovation and new methods introduced by contractor.
❑ Management of consumables, waste and other allied services outsourced to gain economies of scale and better costs.

Disadvantages

❑ Cost may be too high for standard of services offered.
❑ VAT added to the cost of labour, materials, equipment and overhead.
❑ Client may lose control over the cleaning operation.
❑ Poor supervision may lower work quality.
❑ Tendency for contractors to use poorer quality products which could cause damage to surfaces being cleaned.
❑ The specification is open to interpretation.
❑ High turnover of staff.
❑ Breach of security due to poor supervision.

32.7 Staff

About 80% of the costs of cleaning are in the labour element. The majority of cleaning contracts use part-time staff to carry out the work. Part-time cleaners work on an average of 12–14 hours a week – either early morning or evening shifts. Many of these workers will be paid the national minimum wage.

Table 32.4   Cost proformas

Labour costs

Grade of staff	No. of personnel	Shift	Hourly rate of pay	Total weekly hours per grade	Holiday pay per week	NI per week	Total weekly cost	Total charge per month

Equipment costs

Type of equipment	Specification	Weekly charge	Quantity required	Charge per week	Charge per month

Window cleaning costs

Task	Frequency	Price per clean	Charge per month
Outside glass to external windows			
Internal glass to external windows			
Internal glass partitioning			
External cladding/metal framework			
Glazing at ground floor, staircases, balustrades, lobbies and mirrors			

Periodic cleaning costs

Task	Proposed frequency per annum	Hours per clean	Charge per clean	Charge per month
Shampoo upholstered chairs				
Wash vinyl chairs				
Carpet cleaning				
Scrub toilet floors				
Wash toilet walls				
Wash ceilings				
Clean computer equipment in IT room				
Damp wipe venetian blinds to 2 m				
Damp wipe venetian blinds above 2 m				
Clean exterior fencing and external lights and signs				
Scrub staircases				

Site management fees

Description	Charge per month	Charge per annum
Administration and overheads		
Training		
Quality control		
Uniforms		
Cleaning materials		
First-aid allowance		
Staff vetting procedures		
Profit from site operation		

There are national occupational standards (agreed statements of skills, knowledge and understanding required of individuals at work) at levels 1 and 2 for the cleaning industry. BICS also offers national vocational qualifications (NVQs) at levels 1 and 2. It is becoming more common to state the BICS NVQ 2 qualification as a minimum standard in a cleaning specification or tender.

Section 8 of the Asylum and Immigration Act 1996 requires that employers of staff conduct the necessary background checks of new recruits. Employers must also retain records of these checks. The checks must be applied to all staff to avoid any discrimination claims and will include verification of identity, permit to work, national insurance number (NI), age, passport and prior training records (using the Pathway Card scheme). If the cleaning contractor uses illegal staff, the client may be liable to prosecution and his reputation may be at risk. Some clients may also wish to include indemnities for losses such as fines imposed as a result of prosecution, inconvenience, training costs or other expenses as a result of illegal staff working on the premises.

32.8 Daytime cleaning

This mode of cleaning offers many benefits. It requires careful consultation and planning when changing from night-time to part-time shift patterns. Some noisy and specialist work will still have to be planned outside normal working hours to minimise disruption; however, there is still much cleaning that can be done in the occupied areas and communal areas in the daytime.

❑ Full time roles can be created.
❑ Closer working with the client and employees to understand the needs and requirements.
❑ More co-operation by client's employees to keep workplace tidy.
❑ Flexibility to deal with 'on the day' issues.
❑ Ability to clean according to actual need.
❑ Easier to recruit and retain cleaning operatives.
❑ Ability to offer formal training programmes to cleaning staff.
❑ Better rates of pay.
❑ More productive cleaning regimes as less time is spent on getting areas and equipment ready and then putting equipment away again.
❑ Reduced energy consumption.
❑ Healthier staff by reducing health risks of night-time shift work.
❑ Involvement in general FM functions.
❑ Improved security.

32.9 Equipment

The equipment used by the cleaning operatives must comply with various regulations (described in Chapter 16) including PUWER, LOLER, PPE, Electricity at Work Regulations, Working at Height, etc. Cleaning equipment covers a wide range of powered and manual tools. Whilst there has been little innovation in cleaning equipment, the introduction of battery operated, backpack vacuum cleaners and quieter machines have created new methods and opportunities in cleaning operations. Other equipment commonly used are floor buffers and floor scrubbing machines.

32.10 Microfibre materials

Microfibre mops and cloths are made of composite synthetic fibres which are extremely fine, and which are engineered to have a large surface area. This gives a much greater effective cleaning capacity, and enables the extremely efficient removal of microscopic particles. The small size of the microfibres enables them to reach into microscopic crevices in surfaces. Additionally, the microfibres are naturally statically charged. This combination of electrostatic attraction and capillary action allows the removal of a far greater number of contaminant particles than conventional mops and cloths.

Many organisations using microfibre cloths have reported that the time taken to perform cleaning tasks has reduced, and that the introduction of microfibre has been followed by improvements in measured cleaning scores.

There are limitations on the use of microfibre cloths. They are designed to be used dampened only with water, and therefore should not be used in conjunction with chlorine-based disinfectant cleaners or other biocides. Used cloths will contain potentially harmful contaminants. A separate cloth should be used for each area and cloths must be thermally disinfected to prevent cross-contamination. Microfibre cloths are less effective when used on old and damaged surfaces because of repeated snagging and perform best in the routine maintenance of surfaces which are not heavily soiled.

There are now many commercially available microfibre products. Not all of these are of the highest grade and careful consideration should be given to the relative merits of products on the market. Once a product is chosen, a detailed implementation plan should be created, including thorough training for supervisors and staff with cleaning responsibilities. The method statement provided below is given as an example. It should be noted that different manufacturers may make different recommendations for how their products should be used. Organisations should ensure that practice is consistent with the manufacturer's recommendations.

Microfibre cloths are designed to be used as part of a well-coordinated and tightly controlled cleaning system. Equipment and materials required:

❑   Colour-coded domestic gloves.
❑   Cleaning trolley designed for use with microfibre cleaning system.
❑   Dust-control mop and handle.
❑   Damp-mopping mop and handle.
❑   Colour-coded labelled net bag containing clean microfibre flat mops.
❑   Colour-coded labelled net bag containing clean microfibre cloths.
❑   High-dusting tool, with telescopic attachment if required.
❑   Microfibre sleeve for high-dusting tool.
❑   Colour-coded dustpan and brush.
❑   Laundry bag for used microfibre cloths.
❑   Laundry bag for used microfibre flat mops.
❑   Labelled spray gun containing general purpose detergent or other compatible cleaning product.
❑   Labelled spray gun containing cold water.
❑   Warning signs.

Table 32.5   Range of chemicals used in cleaning activities

Alcohols	Used to disinfect working surfaces. Not suitable for dirty surfaces, often used in conjunction with iodine for general purpose use.
Aldehydes	May be used in the form of colourless gas with an irritating smell, main type is formalin. Used for large-scale fumigation.
Halogens	Include chlorine and iodine, used to disinfect a variety of surfaces, can be used in conjunction with detergents for greater efficiency.
Phenolics	Are widely used as disinfectants (i.e. dettol, izal, clearasol, etc.).
Pine fluids	Have very pleasant smells, but not very efficient for industrial use, more for home use.
QACs (quaternary ammonium compounds)	More suitable as detergents with germicidal properties than as disinfectants because they are inactivated by a wide range of materials.

32.11 Cleaning chemicals

There are many cleaning products available, see Table 32.5. It is good practice to always use the least harmful agent first before resorting to harsher products. Products must never be mixed together. The dilution rate and the working strength should be checked. Cleaning products come in a variety of pH strengths going from strong acids to strong alkalinity. The scale is on a range of 0–14. As an example, toilet cleaners are acidic and heavy duty floor cleaners are alkaline. The further away from pH 7, the more aggressive the material. The more aggressive a cleaning substance, then the more hazardous and more damaging it is to items that are not suitable for that treatment. Containers of cleaning substances may have the pH shown. This information will also be shown on the manufacturer's or supplier's Manufacturer's Safety Data Sheet. They must provide such information by law. The safe storage and use of all chemicals is covered by COSHH Regulations.

32.12 Detergents

A detergent is a substance which detaches particles of foreign matter (dirt) from the article, thus cleaning it. Its efficiency depends on some mechanical action such as mopping, scrubbing or agitation. Detergents are available in liquid, cake or powder form.

There are many types of detergent:

❑ Soap.
❑ Synthetic detergents.
❑ Neutral or non-alkaline or anionic detergent.
❑ Cationic or germicidal detergents.
❑ Amphoteric detergents.
❑ Alkaline detergents.
❑ Caustic detergents.
❑ Detergent crystals and alkaline degreasing agents.
❑ Solvent-based detergent wax removers.
❑ Window cleaning agent.

❑   Metal cleaners.
❑   Toilet cleaners.
❑   Furniture polish.

32.13 Properties of detergents

A detergent should:

❑   Be readily soluble in water.
❑   Be effective in all types of water and act as a softener (no scum).
❑   Have good wetting powers, so that the solution penetrates between surfaces and dirt particles.
❑   Have good emulsifying powers, so that grease and oil are broken up and to some extent dissolved.
❑   Have good suspension powers, so that the dirt particles when removed are suspended in solution and not re-deposited onto the article.
❑   Be effective over a wide range of temperatures.
❑   Be harmless to surfaces, articles or skin.
❑   Clean reasonably quickly with minimum agitation.
❑   Be easily rinsed away.
❑   Be biodegradable.

Not all detergents will have all of the above properties. It will depend on types, quality and strength of detergent.

32.14 Types of detergent

Soap

These are manufactured from fats or fatty acids and alkali and are not used a great deal as general cleaners. They are not effective in hard or cold water. They tend to scum and leave film on a surface.

Synthetic detergents

These are made up of:

❑   Surfactants (Surface Active Agents) – inorganic builders or alkaline salts (i.e. soda, phosphates, sodium silicate) to assist in soft water.
❑   A synthetic gum to help suspending powers, sodium perborate (an oxidising bleach), foam boosters to increase and stabilise suds, brightening agents and perfumes, enzymes to remove protein stains (e.g. egg, blood), germicides and solvents to help the removal of surface grease.

Neutral or non-alkaline or anionic detergent

These are manufactured from strong alkalis and weak acids with a pH of 7–9. They are general purpose detergents, not harmful to skin or materials and represent 80% of total usage of all detergents. They are available as general purpose cleaners, washing up liquids, carpet shampoos and window cleaners. They have high foaming power and could produce rinsing problems. They can be effective in extremely hard water.

Cationic or germicidal detergents

These are manufactured from alkalis and acid with a pH of 6. They contain ammonia compounds and possess good germicidal and antistatic properties. The main cationic detergents are quaternary ammonium compounds (Quats and Quacs). These are used where hygiene is of paramount importance (i.e. hospitals, food factories). They are mild in their actions and have indifferent foaming powers (deodorants, aerosols, i.e. air fresheners, fabric softeners).

Amphoteric detergents

These are basically neutral with a pH of 6–8 and have some germicidal properties. These are specialised products and tend to be very expensive compared with other detergents. They include medicated liquid detergents, aerosol shampoos and metal cleaners.

Alkaline detergents

These are manufactured from alkalis with a pH of 9–12.5. They are used for heavy cleaning jobs to remove grease, heavy dirt accumulation, carbon black marks and build-up of emulsion floor wax. Care should be taken when used as they could cause damage to surfaces. They should be rinsed well and neutralised with vinegar in the final rinse water. These detergents should not remain in contact with skin for long periods. If a very concentrated solution is used, then full protective clothing may be required.

Caustic detergents

These are manufactured from caustic soda in either flake or liquid form, with a pH of between 12 and 14 depending on concentration. They can be used for blocked drains and very dirty ovens. They should not be used on flooring as they may have damaging effects.

Detergent crystals and alkaline degreasing

These are manufactured from sodium metasilicate and blended with other surface active agents to give an alkaline solution with a pH of 11–13 depending on dilution. They can be used for removing accumulated oils and grease from floors, especially concrete. They can also be used to remove heavy build-up of emulsion floor wax where other detergents have failed. It is important to protect skin and eyes.

Solvent-based detergent wax removers

These are not strictly detergents, but are manufactured from a solvent (often white spirit type), water, a wetting agent and other additives. They are used to remove solvent-based waxes and oils from floors, and oil and grease from equipment and machines. They are used by applying to the surface and then left for approximately 2 hours to loosen grease and hold in suspension. The area is then scrubbed, rinsed and dried. They must not be used on PVC, rubber, or linoleum surfaces, which may be affected.

Window cleaning agents

These are made from water-miscible solvents (e.g. isopropyl alcohol, detergent and alkali). A fine abrasive may also be added. They are applied with a cloth and then rubbed off with a clean cloth to remove product. Water and methylated spirit can also be used. These may be cheaper but require more effort.

Metal cleaners

These are made from fine abrasive grease solvents, and in some cases mild acid. Some proprietary brands may have 'long life' elements to help prevent re-tarnishing quickly.

Hard metals (copper, brass) can be cleaned with compounds based on acid, generally vinegar or lemon mixed with fine abrasive such as pumice or salt. The acid should be washed off quickly to prevent further staining. This will remove stains but will not produce a shine.

Soft metals, for example silver and silver plate, require the use of a propriety brand or product or impregnated cloth. Large quantities of silver can be cleaned using either:

❑ A hot solution of soda, water and aluminium strip or plate or;
❑ A burnishing machine, by using highly polished steel balls immersed in hot water and a detergent in a special container. The steel balls roll against the surface of the silver, remove tarnish and restore shine; silver should be rinsed and dried after burnishing.

Toilet cleaners

These are available in crystalline form or liquid.

❑ Crystalline form is manufactured from sodium acid sulphate (and a detergent to prevent corrosion of the surface).
❑ Liquid form contains hydrochloric acid. They should be sprinkled on the surface of the pan and in water. They need to be left as long as possible before cleaning the toilet.

These products must never be used for any other area and should not be mixed with other cleaning agents as they are harmful, and gas may be produced from the mixing of chemicals.

Furniture polish

These are made from special blend of waxes and spirit solvents; often a silicone is added which makes the polish easier to apply. This reduces the amount of buffing and gives added protection from heat and moisture.

❑ Paste wax contains a high proportion of wax to solvent and may include silicones. This is applied sparingly with a soft cloth and rubbed up with a clean duster. This product has generally been superseded by spray polish.
❑ Cream wax contains higher amounts of wax and higher proportions of solvent and silicones than paste wax. It is applied as earlier, but has some cleaning action as well.
❑ Liquid or spray polish contains more solvent and silicone and less wax than cream or paste wax. The polish is sprayed on and immediately wiped off to remove dust and

marks and provide a shine. It is expensive and can be wasteful; it is more economic to spray onto the cloth than onto the surface.

32.15 Sealants

A floor seal can be described as a 'semi permanent' material which is applied to prevent the penetration of dirt, stains, liquids and foreign matter. The aim is to make a porous material – the floor surface – non-porous. Before the seal is applied, it is essential that the surface is clean and dry, otherwise the seal will not 'key' to it and it will have to be removed and re-applied. There are many products and speciality products as shown in Table 32.6.

Properties of a sealant

❑ Prevent dirt penetrating the surface.
❑ Provide good appearance.
❑ Protect surface from spillages.
❑ Have good anti-slip qualities.
❑ Durable.
❑ Have good adhesion.
❑ Resist scuffing.
❑ Easy to apply, remove and re-coat.
❑ Have sound colour pigment.
❑ Quick drying.

Table 32.6   Speciality products

Type	Features
High solids emulsion floor waxes	Used where good durability is required because of heavy traffic in main corridors, etc. They have excellent dry-bright properties, with only one coat required, instead of two or three of water-based waxes to give same results. They can be buffed and have good slip-resistant properties. They can be removed using an alkaline or fortified alkaline detergent.
Wash and wax emulsions (clean and shine)	Consists of wax and detergent combination. Used to clean and wax in one operation. Not suitable to remove heavy soilage, but to maintain light normal traffic areas. Sensitive to water and tend to water spot. Easy to remove because of little build-up.
Acid-sensitive emulsion floor waxes	Not greatly used. Resistant to detergents, so heavy dirt deposits can be cleaned without detergent affecting wax. Special acid stripper must be used to remove wax.
Detergent-resistant emulsion floor wax	Consists of metal-containing polymers – metal component is usually zinc. Hard wearing and contains dry-bright buffable properties. Resistant to detergents and therefore a stripper containing ammonia should be used to remove. Sometimes surfaces become too hard to be removed by a stripper and an abrasive method must then be used.

❑ Realistically priced.
❑ Have low or no odour.

No one seal will provide all these properties; however, most of them will be in a majority of seals. The purchaser will have to decide which qualities have the greatest priority.
   Selection of sealant is determined by consideration of these factors:

❑ The type of surface (e.g. wood, PVC or concrete).
❑ Reason for sealing.
❑ Existing finish.
❑ Amount of and type of traffic (i.e. pedestrian, wheeled).
❑ The availability of the surface to be retreated on maintenance.
❑ Existing maintenance.
❑ Initial and long-term cost.
❑ Speed of operation.
❑ Location – internal or external.

Application

The surface should be clean, chemically neutral and dry. The activity must be carried out at room temperature, normally 18.3°C. Any lower may inhibit drying. There must be good ventilation in the location and all materials and surfaces must be prepared prior to applications. The sealant must be applied in thin even coats rather than one thick coat. It is important to cordon off the area and not allow traffic until fully dry. Notices should be displayed to this effect. There are various types of applicators in use as shown in Table 32.7.

Floor waxes

The application of a floor wax improves appearance and also facilitates maintenance by protecting the surface from wear, prolonging the floor life. There are two main types of floor wax in use:

❑ Solvent-based waxes made from natural or synthetic waxes, synthetic resins, colouring, perfume and silicones. Available in paste and liquid form.
❑ Paste waxes contain a higher proportion of wax than liquid and are more expensive.

Table 32.7   Applicator types and features

Applicator	Features
Brush	Useful for small areas and for ledges and difficult details.
Mops	Should be good quality cotton.
Lambswool/bonnets	Large areas – seal poured onto floor and spread. Not suitable for two pack plastic seals. Use rollers.
Roller applicators	Large areas. Usually made of mohair with an applicator tray. Not suitable for water-based seals.
Turkshead brush	Used to work seal into uneven or pitted surfaces especially with pigmented seals. Can be initially applied with roller or bonnet and worked in with turkshead.

Table 32.8   Types of water-based waxes

Fully buffable	Normally dries with low shine that can increase to high shine with buffing. They contain approximately 50% wax; buff not only gives high gloss but also hardens wax film which increases durability. Needs to be buffed up regularly to renew gloss and remove marks.
Semi-buffable	Dries to a subdued gloss but can be improved by buffing – contains approximately 30% wax. Buffing will harden wax and increase durability. This wax is more resistant to water than the fully buffable wax.
Dry bright	Dries to high initial gloss and will not be improved by buffing. Contains approximately 10–15% wax and more additives. Gives good initial appearance and durability but will deteriorate under heavy traffic.

Waxes are used to form a protective layer on the floor. Waxes should not be used on PVC, thermoplastic or rubber surfaces as they may be damaged by the solvents. Waxes should be applied in thin coats. If too thick a coat is applied, slippery surfaces may occur. A heavy build-up of wax requires a great deal of buffing. Floors can be buffed up between applications of wax.

Solvent paste waxes can be removed by using a solvent-based detergent. After the detergent has penetrated into the wax, it can be rinsed off without the use of too much water. The floor surface must be allowed to dry before applying new coats.

Water-based waxes

These are made from synthetic waxes, alkali-soluble resins, polymer resins and additives. Water-based waxes are widely used because they can be used on a variety of surfaces including PVC, thermoplastic and rubber, asphalt terrazzo and marble, sealed wood, cork and linoleum. There are three types of water-based waxes as shown in Table 32.8.

Most water-based waxes on the market are a combination of more than one type so that the surface can be buffed to renew appearance without applying more wax. These waxes can be removed using an alkaline detergent.

Benefits of wax applications on floor surfaces

❑   Protect the surface.
❑   Improve safety.
❑   Improve surface appearance.
❑   Assist cleaning process.
❑   Improve hygiene.

32.16 Solvents

For some cleaning purposes, detergents and water alone may not be sufficient. Solvents have been included with detergents to aid cleaning and remove fats, oils and grease, etc. When these are not effective, solvents alone may be used, but with care under strict conditions. They may have an adverse effect on the surface and on contact with skin.

Remember solvents are a fire hazard and good ventilation is required

Typical solvents

Typical solvents are ethyl/alcohol and methylated spirits. They are used to dissolve resins, waterproof inks, biro, iodine and the colouring matters of many plants and fruits. They are reasonably mild to the skin, but give off intoxicating vapours and can be very dangerous.

Chemical disinfection

The range of chemicals used in cleaning can be extensive. A chemical disinfectant should never be used to mask unpleasant smells. The source and cause of smells should be found and removed. All chemical disinfectants are inactivated by certain materials, for example soap, detergents, hard water and synthetic products (plastic, sponges, mops, brushes, etc.), and some are activated by several materials. This reduces the effectiveness of the disinfectant. They should not be mixed together as they may inactivate each other.

Correct use of disinfectants

❑ Measure the disinfectant for the correct dilution rate.
❑ A disinfectant is ineffective if it is not able to come into contact with the organism/bacteria. This is the main reason why aerosol disinfectants are not very effective.
❑ It must remain in contact with the organism long enough to destroy it or render it harmless.
❑ Clean the surface before disinfection.
❑ Always dispose of disinfectant solutions when they have been finished.
❑ Never top-up solutions.
❑ Do not leave cleaning equipment (e.g. mops) immersed in solutions overnight.
❑ Always be aware that disinfectant may be inactivated by other materials.

32.17 Example contract cleaning specification

The management and provision of cleaning services are to be within normal working hours unless otherwise specified. The checklist shown in Figure 32.1 can be used to monitor the cleaning service.

The contractor will supply the necessary equipment and cleaning materials to execute all internal accommodation cleaning tasks.

The following consumables are to be provided by the contractor as part of the baseline service:

❑ Refuse sacks.
❑ Waste bin liners.
❑ Soap.
❑ Paper hand towels.
❑ Toilet rolls.

These consumables shall be replenished regularly to ensure constant availability. In the event of an availability failure, they shall be replenished upon customer request during normal working hours.

All cleaning shall be executed to the standards defined in the following paragraphs.

All cleaning must comply with the statutory requirements.

Signs to warn of hazards must be displayed whenever appropriate.

Provision of an on-call janitorial service within normal working hours to remove and safely dispose of debris resulting from accidents (including but not limited to bodily fluids and other personal detritus) and to return the premises to the normal clean state.

Offices, stairs, corridors and building entrance areas

- ❏ All floors (regardless of type) to be kept clean, free of debris, scuffs and stains (unless of a permanent nature). Additionally, the surface of all polished floors is to be maintained shiny.
- ❏ All other flat surfaces (desks, windowsills, etc.) are to be kept clean and dust free provided that they are clear of papers and objects.
- ❏ No visible build-up of dust, marks or cobwebs is permitted.
- ❏ Ceilings to be free from visible cobwebs and ceiling lights including, but not limited to, fluorescent lights to be kept clean, provided that ladders or other climbing apparatus is not needed.
- ❏ Doors (including glazed and polished panels) and walls to be kept clean and free of finger and feet marks and soiling (unless of a permanent nature), provided that ladders or other climbing apparatus is not needed. Spot cleaning is to be conducted as required.
- ❏ Handrails and balustrades to be free of dust, dirt and finger marks.
- ❏ Polished surfaces not dulled nor tarnished.
- ❏ Carpets, soft furnishings and fabrics free of dust, debris and stains. Spot cleaning is to be conducted as required.
- ❏ No surface scuffing or soiling of commonly accessed surfaces.
- ❏ All blinds (including, but not limited to, venetian blinds) to be free of cobwebs, dust, grease and contaminants.
- ❏ No immediately visible litter.
- ❏ Telephones free from dust.
- ❏ Bins to be emptied on each working day.
- ❏ Cigarette butt receptacles (inside and outside buildings) are to be emptied regularly so that they are never full and do not represent a fire hazard.
- ❏ Carpets to be deep (shampoo) cleaned at an agreed period to reflect the amount of use. Should this result in the cleaning of office carpets more than once and stair/corridor/entrance carpets more than twice in one year, then the additional cleans shall be tasked and executed as optional services.
- ❏ Computer and equipment cleaning is specifically excluded.

Note: Building entrance areas are defined to be both the internal and external areas within the building footprint including, but not limited to, porches.

Laboratory and store/plant rooms

Cleaning of these areas is a demand service from the relevant department.

Kitchen/tea points

❑ Kitchens and tea points should be thoroughly cleaned and disinfected, in order to maintain them clean, hygienic and tidy at all times.

❑ No build-up of limescale or evidence of hard water is permitted.

Toilets and showers

❑ Toilets and showers should be thoroughly cleaned and the sanitary ware disinfected, in order to maintain them clean, hygienic and tidy at all times.

❑ No build-up of limescale or evidence of hard water.

❑ Doors, walls, floors and other flat surfaces plus mirrors to be left without marks.

In some areas, the toilets and showers receive very heavy use and more frequent cleaning is necessary and included within the baseline.

Cleaning of windows internally and externally every 4 months

❑ The windows of all occupied buildings are to be cleaned inside and outside every 4 months. The exact cleaning dates are to be agreed with the client manager within normal working hours. For inside window cleaning, building occupants are to be notified at least one working week in advance and, whenever possible, arrangements are to be made to ensure that the cleaning is undertaken at convenient times to the occupants.

❑ The necessary equipment and cleaning materials to execute all window cleaning tasks will be supplied by the contractor.

❑ Windows to be smear free upon completion of cleaning.

❑ Windows are defined to be glass and sills (if any).

Management and disposal of general office and domestic site waste

❑ Management of controlled waste disposal services is to be executed in accordance with the client's environmental policies. Disposal of controlled waste is a demand service.

❑ Provision of management and advice in matters pertaining to waste, handling and disposal issues and the management of associated records, including but not limited, to compliance with statute, notification of changes of statute and notification of breaches.

❑ Management of an analytical and cataloguing service for identification and subsequent classification of unidentified waste. Analysis, cataloguing and, if required, disposal of any controlled waste is a demand service.

❑ All glass disposal is included within the baseline and is undertaken separately from domestic waste disposal. Glass must be clearly separated from domestic waste.

❑ Domestic waste is defined as waste disposed of in standard office waste bins, recycling bins in central collection points, toilet, shower, kitchen and tea-point bins plus all cardboard and packaging materials.

❑ All waste should be handled and disposed off in accordance with appropriate guidelines and should not present a health and safety hazard.

❑ For all baseline and demand waste services (regardless of waste type or classification), fully auditable records must be maintained and available to the client upon request.

❑ Processes for the following waste must be provided:
   o Waste covered by a classified or hazardous waste service
   o Electrical or electronic equipment – removal/disposal

- o Furniture (or parts) – removal/disposal
- o Fixtures and fittings – removal/disposal
- o Recycling – paper, timber, cardboard, glass, metal, etc.

Feminine hygiene services

❑ To manage and arrange the removal of feminine waste in a timely and hygienic manner such that the waste does not create a health, safety or environmental hazard.

❑ Emptying of waste receptacles as appropriate dependent on usage such that they are never full.

Pest control

Provide and manage pest control services to discourage and control infestations of pests internally and externally within the estate. The service is to include the provision of poisons, treatments, deterrent agents and devices plus the removal of dead pests and the implementation of practices to deter pests. The requirements of conservation plans are to be taken into consideration where such plans exist. Identified pests include, but are not limited to, rabbits, rats, pigeons, mice, foxes, squirrels, bees, wasps, ants and other insects.

Upon request, make available to client for approval, lists and COSHH assessments of all chemicals, hazardous materials and poisons required for the execution of these works. Requests will be made with reasonable notice.

32.18 Summary action plan

❑ Different building types will require specific cleaning specifications.

❑ Specialist contractors may be required for certain buildings and cleaning services.

❑ Select a local cleaning company, or one that is no more than 2 hours travelling time away.

❑ Consider the pros and cons of input versus output specification.

❑ Consider the pros and cons of in-house versus outsourced cleaning services.

❑ Ensure cleaning supervisor is qualified, trained, supported and proactive.

❑ Link the cleaning specification to the environmental policy in terms of waste and use of materials.

❑ Specify clearly the areas to be cleaned.

❑ Agree methods of cleaning and equipment to be used.

❑ Specify the supplementary services.

❑ Specify the types of waste.

❑ Indicate recycling schemes.

❑ Confirm responsibility for transfer note management.

❑ Specify maintenance and cleanliness of waste containers.

❑ Know the local pay rates for cleaners.

❑ Consider the working hours, and consider daytime cleaning shifts.

❑ Investigate levels of management support for the onsite cleaning team.

❑ Check emergency call-out procedures for the events such as flooding.

❑ Establish regular meetings to review performance levels.

❑ Conduct customer satisfaction surveys.

❑ Conduct annual contract reviews.

33 Security Management

33.1 Introduction

Security is about prevention. It can be defined as 'preventing adverse consequences from the intentional and unwanted actions of others'. Because both society and organisations want people to behave in a certain way, and often they don't, security management is used to mitigate the effects of this behaviour. The impact of security management and security systems includes cost, time, convenience, flexibility and the loss of privacy.

Most intentional and unwarranted actions, or attacks, are on assets belonging to people and organisations. Security systems are set up as countermeasures to protect these assets.

33.2 Security strategy

Before embarking on any security programme, such as installing or upgrading devices or systems, employing security personnel or engaging a contractor, the FM needs to carry out a security audit and determine an overall security strategy. This should have full involvement and support at board level, since security is crucial to the organisation's continued existence and success. It may be beneficial at this stage to engage the services of a security consultant, and the local Police crime reduction or crime prevention officer will be able to provide advice.

The audit should look at the geographic environment within which the organisation operates, and every physical aspect of the site and all it contains, with reference to the aforementioned hazards, and identify and analyse the risks. The risk analysis will enable a strategy to be defined and this can be further developed into a list of the measures required to eliminate or manage the risks.

In-house security staff

Having agreed the security strategy, and studied the risk assessment, the board may decide that security personnel need to be employed in-house. The main advantage over contract security is the low turnover of staff and the fact that in-house staff can 'identify' more with the organisation they protect.

It may be appropriate to employ security officers who have backgrounds in:

❑ The Fire Service.
❑ Safety.
❑ Military operations.
❑ The Police.

❑   Customer services.
❑   The hotel industry.

However, this type of background alone will be insufficient unless special training is given in all aspects of security, the site and premises, and customer service skills too.

There are various training courses available for security staff at all levels – including residential and in-house training on the premises. Much of the industry training has been developed by Skills for Security – the specific sector skills agency (website: http://www .skillsforsecurity.org.uk/).

When employing in-house security staff, the FM should check that they have sound and stable employment histories. It may be prudent to require the applicants to account for every period in their employment histories in excess of 30 days. References should be taken up even if the applicant has been self-employed at some stage and the references should always be verified with the referee. Military personnel would have a 'release' book outlining their time in the army, etc., any charges made against them and the commanding officer's comments. More guidance on the screening or vetting of security staff may be found in BS 7858: 1996, Code of Practice for the Security Screening of Personnel Employed in a Security Environment. In-house security staff may also need an individual license as part of the compliance, the Private Security Industry Act 2001, if the premises are licensed.

33.3 Contract security services

Historically, contract security service providers have not been regulated by law. This has sometimes resulted in inappropriate people setting up, running and being employed in security services, and as a result some security contractors have provided sub-standard service. However, the Private Security Industry Regulations have changed this situation. The legislation is intended to protect and reassure the public by preventing unsuitable people getting into positions of trust in designated sectors of the private security industry including manned guarding, door supervisors, security consultants and keyholders, and to raise industry standards generally.

One of the main outcomes of the legislation has been the establishment of the Security Industry Authority (SIA) (http://www.the-sia.org.uk/home). The SIA manage the licensing of the private security industry as set out in the Private Security Industry Act 2001. They also aim to raise standards of professionalism and skills within the private security industry and to promote and spread best practice. An approved contractor scheme enables security companies to seek approved status. The Authority can inspect companies and control standards of conduct, training and supervision. The SIA has investigating and prosecuting powers under the regulations. Breaches of the Act may result in fines and/or prison sentences. The estimated annual revenue of the UK's private security industry is between £3 billion and £4 billion, and there are around half a million security operatives working within the industry.

33.4 Licensed security roles

Licensing of personnel has been introduced in various security roles, such as Door Supervisors and Clampers. The licence is obtained by the individual, and is valid for

3 years. Operatives undertake training to a level 2 standard to obtain the relevant licence. The current designated sectors or activities that must be covered by a licence are as follows:

- ❏ Door supervisors both in-house and supplied under contract.
- ❏ Vehicle immobilisers on private land both in-house and supplied under contract.
- ❏ Security guards supplied under contract.
- ❏ Key holders supplied under contract.
- ❏ Close protection operatives supplied under contract.
- ❏ Cash and valuables in transit operatives supplied under contract.
- ❏ CCTV (public space surveillance) operatives supplied under contract.
- ❏ Private investigators supplied under contract.

33.5 Increased importance

A MORI business security survey 2004 showed that security is a great concern for UK businesses today, with over 80% of CBI members having discussed an overhaul of their security arrangements at board level. Two in three companies now have a chief security officer, with one in five being a board member. Over 80% of companies said they now spend more on security than they did 5 years ago.

33.6 Contractor selection

Notwithstanding the impact of the Private Security Industry Act 2001, when selecting and engaging a security contractor, the FM should ascertain the following:

- ❏ Is the security company in question properly incorporated? Enquiries can be made at Companies House (www.companieshouse.gov.uk).
- ❏ What is the age of the company? Ask the company directly or check with Companies House.
- ❏ Is it financially sound? Check its credit rating with the bank.
- ❏ Who are the directors? Check with Companies House.
- ❏ Are there any outstanding court actions against that company or any of its principals, e.g. for negligence? Check with the courts.
- ❏ Is the company known to the police and are they satisfied with its operation? The police keep a file on all registered security companies – contact the crime prevention officer for this information.
- ❏ Who else do they provide a security service for and can they be contacted for reference purposes? In the preamble to a tender bid, a security firm will normally give a list of their clients – ask if they have not.
- ❏ What contracts or customers, if any, have they lost through poor performance? Ask the security company this question directly.
- ❏ Do they have adequate insurance? This should be specified in the contract.
- ❏ How much do they pay their security officers? If the pay is poor, it normally follows that the service will be poor. Apart from basic pay, what do their employees earn for nights, weekends, bank holidays and other special duties?

❏ What, if any, provisions are made for their staff with respect to holidays, sickness and pensions?

❏ What precautions and checks do they make when employing staff?

❏ What training do they give their staff and how often?

❏ What equipment do they provide?

❏ What is the structure of the company? What is the ratio of supervisors to staff?

❏ What backup, holiday and out of hours coverage arrangements do they provide? How do they define day/night shifts? What is the maximum number of hours per shift? What is the maximum number of consecutive duties?

❏ Has the company been inspected by an accredited regulatory body, such as The National Security Inspectorate (NSI). This is an independent, not-for-profit approvals body providing inspection services for the security and fire industries. Companies are inspected regularly by highly qualified, full-time inspectors to prove their ongoing competence. All NSI schemes meet or exceed the appropriate requirements of the police, fire service and insurers.

❏ Does the company comply with:

   o BS7499 – 1998 'Code of Practice for Static Guarding, Mobile Patrol and Key Holding Services'.

   o BS7858 – 1996 'Code of Practice for Security Screening of Personnel Involved in a Security Environment'.

❏ Does the company have a quality manual in accordance with BS EN ISO9002: 1994?

33.7 Service standards

Once a particular security company has been chosen, it is essential that the FM lays down strict guidelines as to the service expected and the quality of the security officers required on the premises. It is recommended that a probationary period of 90 days be stipulated in the contract to enable management to assess the quality of the security company, especially in the area of staff turnover. If unscheduled or high levels of staff turnover is experienced, it could be assumed that the contractor is not able to provide a satisfactory service.

Security associations such as the British Security Industry Association Ltd (BSIA) and the International Professional Security Association (IPSA) may be able to provide names of reputable firms. The BSIA is the professional trade association for the security industry in the UK. Its aim is to help its member companies succeed in an ever-changing and highly competitive business environment. A vitally important element of this is ensuring its members provide the highest possible standard of products and service to their customers. Its 500 members are responsible for more than 70% of UK security business, including CCTV, access control, manned security, information destruction, physical security, cash-in-transit and alarm manufacture, distribution and installation.

The British Security Industry Association Ltd lays down rules and conditions which must be satisfied before a security firm can be accepted as a member. These include evidence of adequate liability insurance cover, evidence of sound management, i.e. the company's financial backing and directors' reputation, screening of employees, adequate remuneration, etc. It has sections covering guards and patrols, alarm manufacturers, safes and locks, and a security transport section.

The IPSA was formed 46 years ago to ensure professionalism in the management of security operations. IPSA as an established and recognised worldwide professional organisation provides a specialised service to industry and commerce. The Association operates within the framework of 14 regions which includes many overseas countries. The IPSA runs seminars, conferences and training courses and seeks to foster ethical and professional standards amongst its members.

Standards for intruder alarm systems are set by the National Approval Council for Security Systems (NACOSS). This organisation is part of the Loss Prevention Council and will supply the names of approved installers of intruder alarm systems; most insurers specify membership of the NACOSS as mandatory when an electronic alarm system is to be installed. The police can usually provide names of security firms to the FM so that they can check them out personally.

33.8 Site survey and analysis

Before finalising security arrangements, it is advisable for the FM to conduct a very detailed physical survey of the premises to assess the building 'personality'. This is not a job that should be left to the security contractor, not even on an output specification basis. Many contractors are simply not qualified (or do not employ suitably qualified staff) to carry out site surveys. If necessary, it is preferable for the FM to call in the services of an independent security consultant.

Some of the features that make up the building personality and which should be identified in the site survey are:

❑   The location of the premises.
❑   The general use of the premises.
❑   The physical size of the premises.
❑   The types of people who use the premises.
❑   The management of the premises, i.e. who prepares security policy, e.g. in multi-tenanted premises is it the managing agent's or tenant's responsibility?
❑   Vehicle and human traffic patterns.
❑   Attitudes towards security.
❑   Sensitive and confidential areas.

An analysis of the survey findings will determine the types and frequency of patrols to be made on the premises, the type of access control, emergency procedures, standard opening hours of the premises, equipment shut-downs, etc. These can then be discussed with the in-house security staff or security contractor, whichever is the case.

33.9 Assignment instructions

A security officer, no matter how well-trained, cannot function effectively unless a set of written instructions is available, tailored to the specific location. These instructions, known in the security industry as assignment instructions, are derived from an analysis of the site survey and represent an agreement between the FM and the security contractor as to what systems and procedures are necessary.

Assignment instructions for most locations follow the same basic format and include the following:

❏ General information about the premises and security coverage.
❏ Details of breaks and meals for security staff and where they may be taken.
❏ Procedures for reporting for duty.
❏ The locations of keys, reports and other essential equipment.
❏ Access control procedures and times applied (see later).
❏ Property removal procedures and times applied (see later).
❏ Lost property procedures.
❏ Theft procedures.
❏ Accident procedures.
❏ Intruder procedures.
❏ Patrols – which types, covering which areas, frequencies and limitations.
❏ Specific duties and times.
❏ Details relating to clear desk policies in occupied client areas.
❏ Details about the site equipment and any basic checks that need to be undertaken, e.g. shut-off valves.
❏ Details about the fire systems and equipment.
❏ Emergency procedures – lifts, fire alarms, bomb threats, etc.
❏ Emergency telephone and contacts listings.
❏ Reference material, e.g. literature provided by the police on bomb evacuation.
❏ Procedures for dealing with statutory authorities and enforcement agents.

33.10 Access control

Access control is just one example of a security countermeasure. Door locks, guards and identity cards are all components of an access control system.

In assessing the appropriate access control system for the organisation and its assets, it is useful to consider the following questions:

❏ What assets need protection?
❏ What are the risks to those assets?
❏ How well does the security solution mitigate those risks?
❏ What other risks does the security solution cause?
❏ What trade-offs does the security solution require?

In this context trade-offs in the cost-benefit analysis may include:

❏ Costs and funds to purchase the equipment.
❏ Employment of trained staff to administer and manage the equipment and procedures.
❏ Impact of the inconvenience to people and their perception of the invasion of their privacy.
❏ Potential claims and grievances from staff and others when using the security system.

33.11 Structure of buildings

The weakest links in the security of a building are the doors and windows. These 'holes' permit entry and egress and will need to be controlled if access and egress is to be controlled. The main concern is unauthorised entry. In an ideal world, access is easier to manage with just one door. Many organisations implement a 'one-door' status in times of heightened security status to improve the control of movements in and out of premises, ensuring that all other doors are closed. One task for FMs is therefore to consider how this can be achieved and by whom.

33.12 Control concepts

There are three basic concepts in access control. These are:

(i)   Identification – a means of identifying who a person is.
(ii) Verification or authentication – a means of confirming or proving who the person is.
(iii) Authorisation – a means of confirming what the person is allowed to do.

Many access control systems integrate these three steps so that it is difficult to separate them. It is important to remember that knowing who someone is will not be the same as knowing what they are permitted to do. For example, asking to see a copy of a driving licence may confirm an address or an age, but unless there is a photograph to match with the person in front of the checker, how does the checker know it is still valid and it relates to that particular person.
   Examples of means of identification of a person include:

❑   Account number.
❑   Staff number.
❑   Customer number.
❑   Order number.
❑   Transaction number.
❑   National Insurance number.
❑   Driving licence number.
❑   Passport number.

The next stage is to verify or authenticate the identity using one of the three methods. These are:

(i)   By someone who knows the person.
(ii) By something that the person has or possesses.
(iii) By something that the person is.

Examples include:

(i)   Line manager, work colleague, family member.
(ii) Passwords, PIN codes, secret handshakes, lock combination numbers, photograph, key, membership card, SIM card.
(iii) Signature, biometric feature (iris or retina scan; earshape, voice or fingerprint; hand geometry).

In most cases, the better access control systems will use a combination of two of the above methods of verification. Examples include a passport with a photograph or an ATM card with a PIN.

33.13 Access control system design

There a number of issues which must be considered in designing an access control system and these include:

- **Data storage** – The authentication information must be securely stored to prevent inappropriate use or theft. Examples of vunerable information includes the central database of PIN in a bank, or an organisation's database of employee photographs. With increasing threat of identity thefts, this is an important consideration.
- **Decision-making** – Who actually decides who is authorised and is this one or more people? What checks and balances are in place to verify the decision-makers' decisions?
- **Time period** – Expiry dates are useful to limit the impact of forgeries as it limits the period of authentication. Examples include visitor passes, car park tickets.
- **Security of blank tokens/permits/passes** – The blank cards or tokens must be kept secure to limit the opportunity of forgeries and counterfeits being made.
- **Familiarity** of the authentication system – Those employed to verify identity must be able to spot the real thing, and differentiate it from fakes or substitutes. For example, without experience would the checker know how to spot a genuine EHO's warrant from a fake? If a person had rarely seen the real thing, then it will be very difficult to judge a good fake from the bona fide identity card.

The simplest forms of access control are tickets, vouchers and tokens. These are issued to permit one-time access to locations such as theatres, buses and car parks. The possession of these gives authorisation of what is permitted. There is no verification of identity or proof of identity. If the organisation is not concerned about who is given the authorisation to access the facility, then this level of access control is simple and cost effective. Ownership of the means of access may change, as people sell and buy the 'tokens' before they are exchanged for permitted access or use of the facility.

33.14 Manned access control

The use of security personnel or guards is the most common method of access control. The ability to recognise people from their facial characteristics is the oldest form of identification. In some cases, security personnel have to memorise faces as part of their training. The lighting and setting in which the identification is verified may affect the performance of this method. Ability to check a person in gloomy lighting conditions via car windows or layers of outer clothing may present difficulties to the security personnel. FMs may need to consider their procedures to ensure that helmets, hoods and hats are removed, car windows lowered and sufficient ambient lighting is provided.

As mentioned earlier, ideally there should be only one point of entry. All people desiring access to a location should be able to enter through only one point, at which the security officer is positioned. If there is more than one point of entry to a location, then each access point may have to be manned by security personnel. This is more costly, and may be inappropriate use of valuable staffing resources. The fundamental issue of a manned access control is the type of identification and verification that is being used and the integrity of the security officer carrying out these checks. The simplest manned access control will use a list of those authorised with a simple form of identity check. A register of people entering and leaving the premises may be kept for reference and monitoring.

☐ Authorised access list – The security officer controlling access may have a list of people who are authorised to enter the premises. The access list may also specify the specific areas to which a person may be admitted. This list would need constant updating and reissue from the authorising manager.

☐ Identification – Proper identification of all personnel (such as employees, contractors and visitors) must be carried out to confirm that the person with the authority to enter is indeed that same person requiring access. This may be via identity badges or some other form of authentication, such as staff number, PIN, password, etc.

33.15 Access log or register

A register or access log will provide a manual record of movements in and out of premises. All persons allowed entry are required to sign an access register indicating the time of entry and the area to which they are going. This procedure serves several purposes:

☐ It provides a permanent record for reference.
☐ The access register can be analysed to make recommendations to management concerning hours of activity in the premises (e.g. it may be established that no one enters a building between 0100 hours and 0700 hours; and therefore the building could be locked shut and alarmed).
☐ In the event of an emergency, a record exists of where people are in the building.

In most cases, persons leaving are required to sign out, although because there are normally alternative exits (usually fire exits), it is generally more difficult to control egress than access.

33.16 Entry to interior or restricted areas

In some cases, there will be an additional level of checking for access to internal or restricted areas. In such cases, a restricted access list will specify the area to which the person may be admitted, and the identification that must be produced indicating that the person works in the area to which entry is required. Often, security guards will escort people to internal office areas after he has checked them into the building. This may include VIP visitors and guests. In many organisations, visitors are not permitted to enter the internal areas of a building unless escorted by their hosts. It is often a requirement that visitors are to be collected, accompanied by them at all times and taken back to reception by their host.

33.17 Vehicle control

In addition to controlling people, access control systems are also designed for control of vehicles in and out of premises. There may be restricted areas that require permission for access. These may include delivery or loading areas, specially designated areas such as drop off zones, airside zones, visitor or disabled parking areas. The simplest method is via a token or pass for the permitted driver to display in their vehicle. To ensure this token or pass is only used by the permitted driver in the permitted vehicle, additional details need to be recorded on the 'pass'. These details may include name, licence number of vehicle, valid from/to, date of issue, etc. This will ensure that only particular pre-authorised vehicles can be admitted. In some restricted areas, special driving licences are required by drivers. In such cases, the security checks may include presentation of a valid driving licence too.

Departure of vehicles from a site may also be subject to a variety of measures in an access control system. Passes may have to be surrendered to a gatehouse, a token entered into a barrier system, a 'stop-and-search' exercise may be carried out or a form of identity collected on departure.

33.18 Equipment control

In addition to people and vehicles, general assets of an organisation and personal belongings will be subjected to some aspect of access control. The stop-and-search process will identify items that are being removed without the appropriate authority. Employees with permission to remove company equipment should have the appropriate documents that verify that they are permitted to transport and use the listed equipment (with its serial number) off-site. All items of value should be permanently and prominently marked with the company name and postcode. This will aid recovery of lost or stolen items found by the police. A register of company assets should be kept up to date.

Visitors may not be permitted to bring certain electronic equipment into the premises, such as mobile phones, laptops, cameras, video-recorders, or food, alcohol and drugs. Depending on the organisation, these restrictions may also apply to the employees, and therefore the access control measures will need to take this into account.

33.19 Asset tagging

Visual checking of removable assets by security staff can be supplemented by tagging the items in some way. Electronic ID tags can be stuck onto or inside items such as portable tools or laptops and the codes incorporated into the electronic access control system. An alarm can be programmed to alert staff when the item is carried through a door, and over-ridden if the item is linked to the 'owner's' access control card.

Where items should not be removed, for example desktop computers, they can be fitted with tilt or lift alarms which sound when the unit is moved. Smoke or dye alarms can be fitted inside computers to protect RAM chips which contain valuable data. It may be appropriate to bolt equipment such as network servers to the desk or floor by means of custom-made or adjustable steel cages.

33.20 Door security

Doors can be considered as 'holes' in the security of a building. However, doors are required for many reasons, such as to provide privacy, provide access, prevent the spread of fire, for decorative purposes and to prevent draughts. Therefore not all doors will create security risks, and may not require locks or other devices to ensure access is controlled.

As a general rule, any door that requires a lock or similar mechanism installed to control access should be constructed of solid wood or metal. Hardwood doors are stronger than softwood. In addition, the door frame will need to be considered in terms of its strength and integrity. The vision panel or glass in such a door must be positioned to preclude access to the lock and should be mesh-reinforced tempered glass.

33.21 Door furniture

The door furniture includes the locks, door handles, hinges, closers and signage. In access control systems, the locks and their keys are the most important components. Door security chains, door check restraints, door viewers and hinge bolts are supplementary protective devices that may be used effectively in certain situations. How these are fitted or installed may impact on the effectiveness of the door in an access control system:

- ❑ Hinges should be installed so that pins are not exposed, i.e. all high security doors must open inward.
- ❑ Failing the above, the hinges should be equipped with screw-in pins and positioned to prevent the pins being removed (i.e. so that a screwdriver cannot be used).
- ❑ Door-closers of self-locking doors must be adjusted and inspected regularly so those doors will continue to close automatically.
- ❑ Locks can be right or left handed. Some manufacturers' locks allow adaptation to suit the particular need.

Locks

A locked door is the most common form of access control. However, no matter how good locks are, they are only deterrents; a good quality lock makes it harder to get in, but not impossible. The better the lock, the harder it is to pick or force it open and the more noisy and obvious will be the illegal entry.

The workings of a lock

When a door is locked, the strike is immobile in the strike channel. To unlock the door, a key is slipped into the keyway, which engages pins in the cylinder allowing the key to be turned and the strike to be withdrawn from the strike channel. From a security standpoint, the two limiting factors are the keyway and the strikes or bolt. To provide a high level of security, a locking system should feature:

- ❑ A restricted keyway.
- ❑ A dead bolt strike.

Locks with these two features will have several benefits for access control.

❑ Keys cannot be readily duplicated.
❑ The locks cannot be easily picked.
❑ The strike cannot be slipped.

The following are examples of lock types available for fitting to external doors.

❑ **Rim cylinder nightlatch** – These are commonly used and provide a low level of security by means of a key-operated latch that sits on the inside surface of the door and automatically clicks shut as the door closes. It is very convenient but a thief can open it in many ways. A solution is to replace the nightlatch with a rim automatic deadlock which offers the same operational convenience, combined with high security. A security mortise deadlock should also be fitted.
❑ **Rim cylinder automatic deadlock** –This is a lock with a bolt which, when in the locked position, cannot be pushed back into the case except with the use of a key. The inside handle is also lockable from inside the premises. An attempt by an intruder to gain entry from outside the premises therefore becomes more difficult and time consuming.
❑ **Mortise deadlock** – This differs from a rim cylinder deadlock in that it is 'mortised' into the edge of the door rather than being fixed to its surface. A mortise deadlock can be most effectively used on a front door to supplement an existing nightlatch for improved security. The specification for a mortise deadlock is to have at least five levers and conform to BS 3621:1980. This is the specification for thief-resistant locks as a minimum standard, which ensures that there are at least 1000 possible key combinations. The greater the number of levers a lock has, the greater the protection provided against it being picked by a variety of tools. The levers are ridges and hollows that can be seen on a normal mortise lock.
❑ **Sashlock** – Automatic rimlocks or mortise deadlocks are not always the most convenient protection for back and side doors, which are more usually fitted with a sashlock. This is a lock which incorporates a mortise deadlock and a latch; the latter is operated by knobs or lever handles at either side of the door. The latch is normally used during the day and the deadlock at night or when the premises are unoccupied.

Where an external door is also designed as a means of escape in an emergency, the above-mentioned locks may be fitted with fire safety options.

Keys

The number of keys issued against a lock will be a limiting factor of the effectiveness of the lock. Some manufacturers operate a scheme for registering the keys of their locks. Extra keys can usually be obtained only from the manufacturer, using appropriate paperwork and authorising signature. Key blanks are not issued to key cutting companies. There are various categories of keys:

❑ Grand master.
❑ Masters.

(iii) Submaster.
(iv) Room keys.

The use of masters and submasters will enable suites of rooms to be controlled by one key. This is especially important for cleaning and security patrolling, so that bulky and heavy collections of keys are not needed to open and lock each door. Access is quicker and the work of cleaners or security patrols is done more efficiently.

It is good practice to attach large, bulky key fobs to the masters and submasters, so that they can be easily found, and not so easy to take home by mistake. The use of labels is another issue – the label needs to be of value only to security and authorised users only. Specific information on the address of the building and organisation should be avoided, so that if it falls into the wrong hands, a breach of security is minimised.

A key register to record each key issue is essential, and this may be kept at a reception desk, or in a security control room, with a back-up copy in the safe.

Typically, each door in an office or non-domestic premises will have three identical keys for each door lock. This allows the occupant, security and building maintenance to each have a copy. In most cases, this is sufficient for the majority of occasions. In an office environment, the occupant of an office will be issued the key on arrival or start of occupation. They will be expected to surrender the key on departure or vacation of the office. However, in multiple occupied rooms, it may be more efficient for the key to be kept in reception, and signed out by the first to arrive and returned by the last to leave. This system avoids the need and the expense of cutting many copies, which reduces the effectiveness of security. A system of authorised signatories to draw a key is set up, with a key log to record the date and time of each key issue. Lists of authorising staff need to be checked on a regular basis – quarterly is recommended.

Other aspects of key management include procedures for lost or broken keys and the issue of replacements. In some organisations, a fine or charge is levied to act as a deterrent and motivate the staff to keep keys safe and secure.

Lock maintenance

Locks will require lubrication and maintenance about every 6 months. In addition, it is wise to check the door and the doorframe for integrity too.

33.22 Windows

Windows are another 'hole' or weakness in the premises that needs control to prevent unauthorised access. They are the most popular routes for illegal entry to buildings. The amount of protection and control of access will depend on the height of the window from the ground floor. As intruders are often reluctant to break glass for fear of noise and the possibility of injury, all ground floor windows which are capable of giving access may be alarmed, locked or fitted with inhibitors, as all these devices will make intrusion more difficult. It is recommended that ground floor windows be fitted with two locks. Procedures are needed to ensure that windows are locked, with keys removed from sight at the end of each day. It is best practice to ensure that window blinds are fully down or closed at the end of the day to reduce temptation and a view of the contents from the outside.

Window locks

The type of window lock will depend on the window design. Many products are commercially available and they fall into a number of groups:

❑   Locks with conventional lever and pin tumbler mechanisms (suitable for casement and sash windows).
❑   Locks with screw-up action operated by a special key (suitable for casement and sash windows).
❑   Locks which secure the opening frame to the fixed frame.
❑   Locks which prevent the window catch from being moved or a lock the stay onto its pin.
❑   Locks incorporated into the window latch (suitable for casement windows).
❑   Locks which block the channel of sliding windows.

Inhibitors, as their name suggests, allow windows to be secured in an open position to allow ventilation but not so wide as to allow access. Inhibitors save staff the chore of remembering to lock windows each evening; they are also fairly inexpensive to buy and fit. Width should be severely restricted to prevent the smallest child from gaining access. If it is necessary to have a window capable of being opened allowing free access, it should be connected to the alarm system.

Window glass

There are several types of glazing used in windows, including:

❑   Clear float glass.
❑   Double glazing.
❑   Wired glass.
❑   Toughened glass.
❑   Laminated glass.
❑   Glass blocks.
❑   Plastics.

Protection

A risk assessment will determine if additional protection of the window is required to protect the glass from breakage. Options include:

❑   Internal roller shutter.
❑   Internal grille.
❑   Anti-shatter film.
❑   Bomb blast net curtains.

33.23 Electronic access control systems

Controlling access and egress of the premises by means of electronic devices and systems may provide a balance between convenience, cost and control. There are various electronic systems available that can identify people and allow them entry and egress through the appropriate points. Electronic access control systems work on the basis of identifying an individual and then refer to a database to check the times and doors through which that individual is allowed entry.

Options range from simple, single door devices or stand-alone systems, to multi-user, multi-site systems controlled and monitored via computers. The data can be viewed and managed via PCs, or LAN, WAN or Internet. In addition, security access systems can be integrated with other security or building management systems.

The process of all these systems is essentially the same, as shown below:

❑ An individual uses some means to identify himself.
❑ The device enables staff to check the ID, compares the ID data to data already held, or passes the data to a centrally held database for comparison.
❑ If the individual is to be allowed entry at that point, and at that time, a magnetic lock is released remotely.
❑ The more complex systems retain the fact that the individual is on site until his ID is registered at time of egress, and may be able to track them through the premises and locate them in case of emergency.

33.24 Components in electronic systems

Various technologies are used in electronic systems

❑ **Voice entry** – Visitors communicate with a receptionist or security officer via a microphone and loudspeaker. These can be combined with CCTV surveillance to give a visual check via a video image. Once verification and validation is complete, the door can be unlocked remotely.
❑ **Pin pads** – Pin pads are perhaps the simplest automatic system, whereby a pre-programmed number combination is keyed into a pad at the door. These are only as secure as the practice and discipline of the authorised users. These devices may be just numbers or they may include alphabetic letters too. The sequences should be changed regularly and not written down where they can be seen. Another problem is that it is easy for non-authorised individuals to watch the numbers being keyed. The area around the pin pad should be checked frequently to remove graffiti or notes left fixed to doors, panels and adjacent notice boards which display the access code for all to see. If these devices are electronically linked to a control room, then pin pads can be used to detect duress situations where an intruder forces an individual to enter their code to enable unauthorised access. The victim can enter a preset duress number which allows access, thus avoiding violence, but alerting security personnel remotely.
❑ **Contact card systems** – More complex systems use tags or cards pre-programmed with unique codes to identify users. Technologies include magnetic strips or Wiegand where cards are swiped through or in and out of a reader. The replacement cost of cards due to wear and tear, losses and volume of authorised users should be considered in this type of access control system.
❑ **Non-contact card systems** – Proximity or hands-free cards work with a short distance of a reader. These may or may not contain a battery – they tend to be expensive but have a long life.
❑ **Biometrics** – Verification of identity and authority to enter can now be achieved via biometrics. The use of measurable physical characteristics is the fastest growing access

control technology. There are a range of systems available giving the FM many choices including fingerprinting, hand geometry, face recognition, voice verification, retinal scan and signature. The most popular is fingerprinting. The downside of the technology is the deterioration of a person's physical characteristic with age, disease or injury. In addition, it is easy to copy the characteristics in a photograph, photocopy or by the creation of a dummy finger. As well as physical access control, biometric identification is being applied to IT access control, cheque and credit card fraud and ATM fraud.

Smart cards

A smart card is a plastic card resembling a traditional credit or debit card that contains a built-in integrated circuit chip used for identification and authentication purposes. There are several types of smart cards.

❑ Memory.
❑ CPU.
❑ Contact.
❑ Contactless (proximity and vicinity).
❑ Hybrid (twin).
❑ Combi (dual interface).

Smart cards use a serial interface and receive their power from external sources like a card reader.

Biometrics

Biometrics can be defined as 'the science and technology of authentication (i.e. establishing the identity of an individual) by measuring the person's physiological or behavioural features'. The term is derived from the Greek words 'bios' for life and 'metron' for measure or degree. Biometrics usually refers to technologies for measuring and analysing human physiological characteristics such as fingerprints, eye retinas and irises, voice patterns, facial patterns and hand measurements, especially for authentication purposes.

In terms of security management systems, biometric security systems provide automated methods for uniquely recognising humans based upon one or more intrinsic physical or behavioural traits. These systems will use information technologies that measure and analyse human physical and behavioural characteristics for authentication purposes. Examples of behavioural characteristics which can be measured include signature recognition, gait recognition, speaker recognition and typing recognition. Biometric technologies are becoming the foundation of an extensive array of highly secure identification and personal verification solutions.

The cost of biometric technologies is decreasing and they are increasingly used in a variety of organisations such as governments, military and the commercial sector. In a typical biometric system, a person registers with the system when one or more of their physiological characteristics are obtained and processed by a numerical algorithm, from which the resulting template is entered into a database. Ideally, the measured features can be compared to the stored template with an adequate confidence level; then when someone else tries to log in, their information should not fully match, so the system will not allow them to log in.

British Standards have developed four new standards in biometric security systems. BS ISO/IEC 19794 is the new standard in access control and identification systems, such as those based on smart cards or other recognition tools, and also applies to the storage of biometric identification data in corporate databases. The BS ISO/IEC 19794 is applicable to UK ID cards, and access management systems

Radio frequency identification (RFID)

This is a method of access control that uses RFID tags to remotely store and retrieve data. These tags can be used for building access control. An RFID tag is a small object, such as an adhesive sticker, that can be attached to or incorporated into a product. A RFID tag contains an antenna to enable it to receive and respond to radiofrequency queries from an RFID transceiver. There are four different kinds of tags commonly in use. They are categorised by their radio frequency:

❑   Low frequency tags (between 125 kHz and 134 kHz).
❑   High frequency tags (13.56 mHz).
❑   UHF tags (868–95656 mHz).
❑   Microwave tags (2.45 gHz).

33.25 Advantages and disadvantages of electronic systems

Electronic access control systems have the following advantages over manual access systems:

❑   Removal of human error allowing unauthorised entry.
❑   Access can be cancelled when staff leave the organisation (whether or not an ID pass has been retrieved).
❑   Access to highly sensitive areas can be restricted to certain nominated staff.
❑   Staff may have to carry their ID card or proximity token with them enabling more effective challenges of unrecognised individuals.
❑   Authorised access can be restricted to a certain time of day or days of the week.
❑   Staff may find an electronic system quicker, easier and more convenient.
❑   Staff may find this approach less intrusive.
❑   Time and attendance can be recorded.
❑   Reports may be generated to show trends and irregularities for investigation.
❑   Evidence for investigations may be easier to produce.
❑   Complex systems can be configured to allow users multiple levels of entry with regards to time and place.
❑   Systems can be linked to other systems such as time and attendance for payroll purposes.
❑   Cards can be multi-functional to allow other services to be used by the authorised user. The range of services is vast and will depend on the organisation and its business. Typical services include vending, photocopying, cashless catering services, lockers, fitness centres, library services, pool cars, intranet and Internet access.
❑   Cards can also be linked to building and energy management systems to enable better management of the building.

Advantages of electronic systems over keys include:

❑   Easier control.
❑   Reduce need for extra and duplicate copies.
❑   Unlikely to be left in the lock or locking device.
❑   When lost, easier to remove, replace and reissue than complete replacement of lock and set of keys.
❑   Removes need for secure storage of keys, masters and records of issue.

Disadvantages of electronic systems include:

❑   Good management controls are required to purge the database of expired or unauthorised people.
❑   Management procedures must be in place when the card, token or other device is lost, forgotten or stolen.
❑   Back-up procedures will be required when the electronic systems fail.
❑   It is a less friendly, personable way of dealing with staff. It may limit the ability of the operatives of the system to build up good working relationships with users.
❑   Complacency by management in the belief that the system will always prevent unauthorised access.
❑   Expense of consumables, such as cards and tokens.
❑   Trouble shooting when the system fails to allow authorised access.
❑   Withdrawal of product from the market place by suppliers.
❑   High cost of maintenance contracts with installers or suppliers.
❑   Need to have more than one device to prevent fraud and unauthorised access, e.g. swipe and pin or swipe and biometric.
❑   Tailgating is not as easy to control, as unauthorised people may follow on behind.
❑   All systems need to fail safe open in event of fire and other emergencies.

33.26 Training

Employees must be trained in how to use the access control means they are given. They should know what is expected of them in terms of safe keeping of the keys, cards, tokens or codes they are given. They should know to whom to report missing cards/keys and potential breaches of access control.

Such training may take the form of awareness sessions at induction training, or specific security training events. Employees may access information on a company intranet, or in staff handbooks. It is important to keep the training and information up to date and relevant with continual evaluation and review.

33.27 Special considerations

If turnstiles, gates, barriers, sliding or revolving doors are used to control access, then consideration must be given to particular categories of staff and visitors who may have difficulty with access, such as disabled people, people carrying goods, pregnant women and children. In many cases, the application of inclusive design principles will ensure that everyone benefits from simple adaptations to access control systems.

33.28 Disability discrimination

Access control measures implemented by an employer or organisation providing a service to the public will need to consider if there is a potential case for discrimination against disabled persons. FMs should check the following:

❑   Height of controls, readers, PIN pads, scanners and other devices to check identity of people.
❑   Width of gates, doors, turnstiles and barriers.
❑   Automatic doors, gates, turnstiles and barriers.
❑   Time delays to allow safe passage through.
❑   Use of audible or visual alarms to signal verification of identification.
❑   Use of proximity devices in preference to contact systems.
❑   Colour contrast of devices against background decoration.
❑   Clear instructions on operation of devices.
❑   Registers and logs requiring user completion and/or signatures.
❑   Awareness training for security and reception staff.

34 Customer Relations

34.1 The importance of good service delivery

FM is the provision and management of services to both internal and external customers. Service delivery performance against agreed standards will therefore highlight the efficiency, or otherwise, of an FM department.

The future of many businesses and organisations depends on current and potential customers and how they are treated. Customers are people, and so the skills of customer service-focused activities, such as the helpdesk or FM Service Centre, are people management skills. There are many definitions or expressions of good customer service:

❑ Putting the customer first and at the centre of everything we do.
❑ Finding out what customers want and making sure it is delivered.
❑ Making sure that every customer recommends the service provided.
❑ Getting the details right first time and every time.
❑ Exceeding the customers' expectations.

Excellent customer service therefore depends on the people management skills of the team and:

❑ Their attitudes.
❑ Their interactive listening skills.
❑ Their ability to build emotional relationships that encourage customers to return.
❑ Their willingness to go the extra mile.

34.2 Customer care

FMs need to adopt excellent customer service and customer care skills across all the services provided to the occupants of their buildings and their immediate community.

Customer care is about looking after your customers to ensure that their wants, needs and expectations are met or exceeded, to create customer satisfaction and loyalty. The aims of good customer care are:

❑ To improve customer service by managing all customer contacts to the mutual benefit of provider and receiver.
❑ To persuade customers to purchase or request the service again – not going elsewhere the next time.
❑ To increase the profitability or cost effectiveness of the services provided.

Customer care skills

FMs need to have good customer care skills whether they work in-house or for the outsourced service provider. FMs need to:

❏ Use highly developed communication skills (listening, presenting, giving feedback).
❏ Use observation techniques to anticipate a customer's needs.
❏ Use an empathetic approach to understand a situation from a customer's point of view.
❏ Be approachable and available.
❏ Be accountable and take ownership of a customer service issue.
❏ Be confident and empowered to act.
❏ Use common sense to deal with emergencies.
❏ Have a natural ability to give good customer service.
❏ Manage the 'moments of truth' with care and concern, spontaneity and ability to recover the situation if necessary.

34.3 Customer service

In general terms, good customer service is about:

❏ Knowing who the customers are and what the customers want.
❏ Knowing the service journey (and the moments of truth) that the customer experiences.
❏ Building excellent customer relationships.
❏ Developing relationships with more than one contact in the customer base.
❏ Always adding value to the service experienced by the customer.
❏ Asking customers for their opinion.
❏ Making customers feel special and valued.
❏ Being able to deal with awkward and difficult customers in an appropriate way.
❏ Being able to use complaints as an opportunity to put things right.

34.4 Communication

Communication can be defined as the transmission of a message that can be understood in order to cause an action or reaction and involves both verbal and non-verbal signals. A good communicator will be aware of the impact of their body language, and the non-verbal signals they give in voice tone, style of writing and the appropriateness of their chosen communication medium for that situation. There are three opportunities to communicate effectively. These are verbal or oral, visual or body language, and written formats.

FMs need to use a variety of ways to engage with their customers and choose the most appropriate for the situation. These may include:

❏ Written formats, such as a letter, memorandum or SLA.
❏ Presentations, such as awards ceremonies, business updates and training events.
❏ Newsletters.
❏ Telephone calls.
❏ Face-to-face meetings.
❏ Electronic formats such as email, intranet and website.

- ❑ Group meetings, such as monthly user group meetings.
- ❑ Events, such as social gatherings and excursions.
- ❑ Activities, such as teambuilding.

34.5 Service delivery requirements

Before any measurement, it is important to establish the priorities of the customer – those aspects of the service that are most important. It is also important to establish what the customer expects in terms of the 'deliverables', which can include:

- ❑ Conformity to specifications.
- ❑ Quality.
- ❑ Price.
- ❑ Reliability of service in terms of delivery dates, price and after-sales service.

Service delivery needs to be continually monitored and improved so that service delivery in the next encounter with the customer exceeds their expectations. Adequate resources will be required for such continual improvement. Most services provided to customers are made up of many transactions, encounters or 'moments of truth'. At each of these encounters, the customer is forming opinions about their experience, with reference to the last encounter and their expectation. Services that have many moments of truth may be more difficult to manage consistently. Each encounter is only as good as the last experience.

Measuring and improving the quality of service delivery will require the answers to several key questions, as shown below:

- ❑ Do the customers perceive your offerings as meeting or exceeding their expectations?
- ❑ Does the organisation have an accurate understanding of customers' expectations?
- ❑ Are there any specific standards in place to meet customers' expectations?
- ❑ Do the services offered to customers meet or exceed the standards?
- ❑ Is the information communicated to customers about the services offered accurate?

34.6 Analysis tools

FMs may use a variety of tools to identify and gauge customer satisfaction, including:

- ❑ Customer surveys.
- ❑ Customer questionnaires.
- ❑ Focus groups.
- ❑ Benchmarking.
- ❑ Mystery shopper.
- ❑ Independent audits.
- ❑ Peer reviews.
- ❑ Supervisor observations.
- ❑ Company analysis.

Each tool will have their advantages and disadvantages, and will depend on the resources such as time and effort available.

34.7 Questionnaires

Customer questionnaires need particular care in their design, as they may lead to unexpected answers. It is recommended that an even scale is used for response scores, as this will force the respondent to choose between higher or lower scores, and not opt for the easy middle option. (For example – poor, not met, met, exceeded) It is also important to know if the customers have been surveyed by another department or organisation recently, as this will affect the response rate and its accuracy. The use of incentives to coerce customers into a response can be useful, but be wary of using prizes or incentives if the survey is confidential or anonymous. Analytical skills to compute the results are required, and this must be rigorous and thorough to withstand questioning from the respondents or others in the organisation. FMs will need to consider if the questionnaire is to be on-line or a hard copy delivered via post. A pilot scheme may be useful to gauge initial reaction. Another issue is whether to survey every customer, or occupant in the building, or whether to sample a selection. The sample size must be determined to give statistical validation to the results. Surveys carried out each year reveal trends and can be useful to see how customers' expectations may be changing over time.

34.8 User groups

User groups or focus groups are excellent ways of collecting information about the services from the customers. However, these groups do need an expert facilitator present, and ideally this person should be outside the organisation. Members of a focus group can be mixed across the customer base, or they could be selected from a particular group of customers to get more in-depth investigation of their particular needs. Focus groups are also excellent ways to test out new services, to sound out some sensitive issues that may be limiting the customer service standards or to probe deeper into issues revealed in a questionnaire survey.

34.9 Mystery shopping

Mystery shopping can take the form of an unannounced visit, or a telephone call. Organisations can appoint external consultants to do this task, or use senior staff relatively unknown to most of the customers and customer facing staff. The mystery shopper will record their observations of how well or badly they were handled against a set of basic standards. This may seem an underhand way of measuring service delivery standards and customer care skills. The best way of implementing such a tool is to ensure that all the staff are aware of the scheme, and to ensure that the reports focus on strengths and weaknesses with particular emphasis on identifying customer needs. An ethical approach to this would also ensure that no references to particular individuals are made. It is essential that the consultant is fully briefed by the organisation and that their feedback is not ignored.

34.10 Critical service features

One of the benefits of using tools to measure customer satisfaction is the identification of the critical success factors. These may include speed of response, quality of response, complaint handling and knowledge of the team. As in all management systems, it is important to review the results of performance measurement systems, so that the feedback can be acted on and changes incorporated into the design and delivery of existing and new services to meet customers' needs.

34.11 Gap analysis

It is also equally important to establish what the customer actually gets. If the service delivery level falls below the customer's expectations then dissatisfaction will occur. This may be expressed as a gap between the customer expectation and the service actually received, and it must be remedied. One way to identify the gaps is using mystery shopping as this enables the quality of customer service to be assessed at the critical point at which customers receive the service. An alternative more complex tool is the SERVQUAL methodology described below.

34.12 Service quality (SERVQUAL)

This is a complex method for assessing customer satisfaction or service quality – known as the PZB or the SERVQUAL instrument. The model is based on finding out what are the most important needs your customers have. The perceived value of what the customer values is a measure of service quality. The gap between expectation and perception of service is the service quality gap. There are five gaps as shown in Table 34.1. If perception exceeds expectation, then the customer is delighted; if perception equals or meets expectation, then the customer is satisfied; if perception is less than expectation, the customer is dissatisfied as their expectations have not been met.

The use of this particular customer satisfaction methodology is very time consuming. There are five dimensions of quality to be evaluated:

(i) Tangibles – The appearance of physical facilities, equipment, personnel and communication materials.
(ii) Reliability – The ability to perform the promised service dependably and accurately.

Table 34.1   The gaps in service quality

Gap 1	What is expected	Gap 1 is the difference between what customers expect and what the service provider thinks they expect.
Gap 2	Incorrect standards	This is the gap between the service provider's perception of customer expectations and the specifications set in order to achieve the perceived level of service quality. Gap 2 means that the service quality specifications are wrong.
Gap 3	Service performance	This gap occurs when the service delivery system simply fails to perform to the specifications which have been set.
Gap 4	Delivering the promise	Gap 4 exists when customers are led to expect a level of service, through promotional material or other communications from the service provider, which cannot be delivered.
Gap 5	Customer satisfaction	Gap 5 determines the level of customer satisfaction. The way to close gap 5 is to close the other four gaps.

 (iii) Responsiveness – The willingness to help customers and provide a prompt service.
 (iv) Assurance – The knowledge of employees and how much they inspire trust and confidence in the customer.
 (v) Empathy – Caring, individualised attention provided to customers.

An exhaustive set of 22 paired questions are asked of all parties involved in the service encounter. In the case of the FM services, this would include all the staff, contractors, suppliers, end-users, client users, colleagues, supervisors and managers of the service.

Customer satisfaction is defined as the result of a customer's assessment of a service based on a comparison of their perceptions of the service delivered against their prior expectations.

Using the five dimensions, customer research typically shows that most customers will rate reliability as the most important, followed by responsiveness, empathy, assurance and tangibility in descending order of importance.

Service quality is a long-term process, and critics of the SERVQUAL methodology suggest that the use of questionnaires simply measures customers' experiences at a single point in time. SERVQUAL can only be used on existing or lost customers. Some of the questions are vague, and the participants need to fully understand the process to administer it correctly. In addition, it cannot be used to understand future or potential customers. It may be useful therefore to distinguish between customer satisfaction based on a specific service encounter and service quality in a general context.

Other points that must be borne in mind when measuring customer service quality include:

❑ Service can be perceived as good when it is in reality bad.
❑ Service can be perceived as bad when it is in reality good.
❑ Service can be perceived as good last time, but the next time is perceived as bad although there has been no change in service delivery.
❑ Satisfied customers may switch service providers anyway if given a choice.

34.13 Internal customer service

Every member of staff within an organisation will be an internal customer; whether they are based in the same building or in a remote location. Customers can therefore be from all levels within an organisation – from porters and cleaners to senior managers and directors. It is important not to forget to treat one's close work colleagues as customers too. These groups may include members of the FM department, security and members of the reception team.

Internal customers may also include other types of staff who are based in the organisation but are not direct employees:

❑ Contractors and subcontractors.
❑ Consultants.
❑ Trainees.
❑ Work experience placements.
❑ People on secondments from other companies or organisations.

Table 34.2 Benefits of excellent customer service

To FM staff	To the internal customer or client
Job satisfaction	Needs are met
Easier job	Fewer errors, transactions more efficient and
Involvement in the business	quicker
Co-operation from others in future transactions	Needs are anticipated, fewer explanations required
Praise and compliments received	Obligation to return good service to others
Pride in job well done	Tells others
Reputation of good service	Customer feels special and valued
Control of transaction	Exceeds expectations
Rapport with customers	Better informed
Recognition of value and worth to organisation	More likely to accept delays or mistakes on
Supportive environment	another occasions
Motivated employees	Will repeat the transaction or request for service
	No complaints or allegations of wrongdoings –
	deters a blame culture
	Reassurance that their request is being dealt
	with efficiently

There are many benefits to both parties in promoting a high standard of customer care in the internal customer service transactions, many of which are equally valid for external customer service. These are summarised in Table 34.2.

34.14 The FM Helpdesk

The FM helpdesk is a customer relation tool. The helpdesk has two main functions:

(i) Serve the internal customer.
(ii) Serve the company or business.

A helpdesk is essentially an organised resource to answer questions, and to solve or manage the resolution of problems and requests for additional services that staff encounter in their use of corporate technology or facilities in the course of their normal daily work. Some organisations will have one central helpdesk for both FM, HR and IT departments – whilst other organisations will have separate helpdesk operations for each function.

The fundamental purpose of any helpdesk is the speedy restoration of a user to full productivity in their core role. The occupant of a building may be less productive if a facility in the building has failed or a service has not been delivered to the agreed standard. The impact of an efficient helpdesk can therefore be measured against productivity of both employees and the technology they use, i.e. maximising the corporate return on investment in both human and physical assets.

The helpdesk should be an integral part of the FM strategy and should be incorporated into the company's business processes. A good helpdesk will be key to the success of the FM department, helping to process the workload, keep track of resources and monitor customers' needs and issues. Whilst a manual system can be used for smaller organisations, many FM contractors use bespoke computer systems for helpdesk operations.

A helpdesk computer system can be used as a key tool to improve facilities services: it provides the most accurate, current (and free) feedback on what is working, and what is not, in the business. The helpdesk can provide a unique record of how user productivity is impeded by the behaviour of the technology or shortfalls in user competence. The database of logged enquiries can be queried to show patterns in these areas, e.g. disproportionately high numbers of enquiries from certain departments regarding air conditioning. Such reports can be used to create reports on services delivered, achievement of SLAs, response times and other measures of performance. Such reports may generate work to investigate the mechanical and electrical services, the control systems, the local air conditioning units and associated equipment.

A FM helpdesk can provide data and information on recurrent failures in heating, ventilation, lifts, cleaning and a range of services. This will be valuable in tracking performance of building assets, contractors' response to defects and outstanding defects in the building infrastructure.

Typically, a helpdesk may deal with a large variety of calls and requests:

- Fault reporting.
- Room booking.
- General enquiries about service standards.
- Complaints regarding services received.
- Requests for new services.
- Office moves.
- Audio visual aids.
- Office stationery.
- Office consumables.
- Porterage requests.
- Office decoration.
- Presence of pests, rodents, vermin, etc.

The helpdesk function can be assisted by a computerised database, giving each request a unique reference number against the asset description. Job sheets are generated for the appropriate maintenance team to carry out the work according to agreed priorities and SLAs.

Staffing the helpdesk

The FM helpdesk service is a function that can be combined with other roles and duties in the FM team, such as reception, switchboard, general administration and back of office tasks. The advantage of combining this function with reception is that the skills required by the staff are similar, and the hours of operation tend to be similar. Furthermore, if the reception is manned 24 hours a day, then the helpdesk function can also be covered within the same rostering arrangements. Job swaps between reception and helpdesk can also offer variety and staff development opportunities.

The traditional way of staffing is to employ low-skilled and low-paid people on the first line of enquiry and more highly skilled and better-paid people further up – sometimes referred to as the second line. This is due to the traditional view that people are remunerated according to their level of technical knowledge. This model is ubiquitous, but in fact it is one of the most expensive and least effective ways of staffing a helpdesk.

Second-line resolutions cost much more to organise than first-line resolutions. FMs should always look to increasing the proportion of first-line fixes by the help desk staff: not only is it cheaper in terms of helpdesk staff productivity, but it is what the users want and it minimises employee downtime – a first-line fix is faster than a second-line fix. So here, the higher quality service is actually the cheaper option. There are, however, a number of tasks that will have to be done by qualified engineers, technicians and others, so the skill of the helpdesk team is to ensure that the jobs are accurately given to the correct staff member or contractor promptly. Much downtime and frustration can arise if there are errors in allocation of jobs by the FM team of specialists.

Managing the helpdesk

The FM may need to consider a number of issues when establishing and managing the helpdesk function. These are described below:

❑ **Workload measurement** – Accurate staffing levels are impossible without measurement of the workload. Most helpdesks never actually measure their work flow and load, and tend to hire too few or too many staff. It is impossible to predict exactly when that demand crisis point will be, but if there have been problems with the heating system, for example, it makes sense to ensure there are enough helpdesk operators on hand to answer an expected surge of complaints about the cold. The astute helpdesk supervisor will be ready for these occasions with a fully briefed team.
❑ **Skills management** – The helpdesk supervisor needs to ensure that there are sufficient helpdesk operator resources available at the relevant times to deal with common enquiries the first time, as passing queries to experts further up the management chain will be costly in time and expense.
❑ **Problem identification** – Agreement is essential between the first-line and second-line groups (such as maintenance, security, housekeeping, catering, procurement and service contractors) on the nature, method and mutual responsibilities of call escalation. Where the query cannot be answered by the helpdesk operator who takes the initial call, the problem has to be passed to someone else in the organisation to handle. The ownership of the problem changes, and this must be tracked and monitored to 'close' each job or request correctly.
❑ **User expectation** – SLAs (service level agreements) are one way to manage customer expectations. However, many staff are not given this detailed information or if they are, they do not read them, so something more practical is needed like a service statement posted in strategic areas or a regular newsletter. Expectations that get out of control can destroy the viability of, and user confidence in, the whole service.
❑ **Tools** – Automatic call logging, enquiry handling and reporting are all needed for a viable helpdesk.

Contacting the helpdesk

Contact with the helpdesk needs to be made as easy and convenient as possible for the occupants, customers and users of the helpdesk. There is a wide range of methods – such as telephone, fax, email, and SMS text messaging. Offering the customer direct access to self-report and track their requests is now becoming more common. By using web technology, organisations can provide intranet or extranet sites for internal and external customers to log service requests, obtain status updates and generally communicate more informatively with the helpdesk team.

Helpdesk software

There are many helpdesk software packages, ranging from enterprise-scale (such as customer relationship management [CRM] systems), through mainstream packages, to cheap entry-level options that can be downloaded from shareware sites. The ideal way is to decide on what processes are required first and turn that into a 'statement of requirements' (SOR) and approach vendors to judge how they can meet the terms of the SOR. It is also a good idea to acquire half a dozen demonstration versions and choose the one with the most attractive or appropriate features.

34.15 Service level agreements (SLAs)

Service level agreements are useful tools in the provision of customer-focused FM services for the following reasons:

- ❑ The process of developing an SLA ensures the customer's voice is heard.
- ❑ They enable the customer and the provider to negotiate what it is sensible to expect and reasonable to deliver.
- ❑ They are negotiated and so avoid imposed solutions on either party.
- ❑ They can form a contract between customer and supplier.
- ❑ They help to prevent disappointment through unrealistically raised expectations.
- ❑ They are unambiguous.
- ❑ They can be widely disseminated to customers and staff.
- ❑ They provide an auditable reference in the event of a dispute.
- ❑ Outcomes should be quantifiable so that success (or failure) is easily measured.

34.16 Service standards

Standards serve three main functions in helping to provide an effective customer service:

- ❑ They are a guide to help staff do their job.
- ❑ They help to ensure consistency in the level of service.
- ❑ They are a benchmark against which customer service can be measured.

Quality standards should begin with the customer. Service standards are tools to express quality and are important for customers, potential customers, employees and management of an organisation. They help to define what a customer can expect and to remind management and employees of the challenges and obligations that they face. A service standard needs to include three fundamental aspects of the service:

- ❑ Timeliness.
- ❑ Accuracy.
- ❑ Appropriateness.

Service standards can be defined in the following aspects of a service encounter:

- ❑ Service experience.
- ❑ Service outcome.
- ❑ Tangible factors (e.g. functionality, reliability, availability).
- ❑ Staff.
- ❑ Facilities.

There are many sources of information used to create appropriate service standards. Examples include:

- ❑ Contract documents.
- ❑ Consultation with management, employees, suppliers.
- ❑ Consultation with existing and potential customers.
- ❑ Review of competitors' services.
- ❑ Consultation with regulatory and enforcement authorities.

35 Waste Management

35.1 Introduction

Waste is a man-made problem! Waste can be defined as any substance or object discarded for which the owner has no further use or need. It applies to materials, services and products. Waste is classified by the harm it can do and its origin. It can be controlled (e.g. household/industrial/commercial) or special (e.g. dangerous, toxic, flammable, irritant, carcinogenic, radioactive, chemical, clinical).

An effective waste management structure is essential to comply with ever-strengthening legislation and environmental concerns. The 'producer pays and the polluter pays' principle underpins the legislation in Europe. There is a requirement for an organisation to consider all areas of their operation from specification and procurement to demolition and disposal (the life cycle of products and services).

A waste management strategy should be set up for all products and processes aimed to:

❏ Reduce the amount of waste produced.
❏ Recycle the product wherever feasible.
❏ Reuse products and equipment where practical.
❏ Responsibly dispose of waste products at all times.

The UK government has introduced targets on recovery and recycling of waste to minimise waste to landfill. The cost of waste management has risen steeply in recent years, partly due to the cost of treatment and also due to the limited number of registered sites that can now be used for commercial or industrial waste. Organisations are expected to exercise a duty of care to keep waste safe at all stages by adopting a 'cradle to grave' approach – known as the waste hierarchy. The use of transfer notes and due diligence checks on appointed waste contractors is essential to show accountability for correct handling and disposal of waste.

35.2 Waste management policy

A robust waste management policy is important for two reasons:

(i) The business must utilise its resources efficiently.
(ii) There is increasing focus through legislation and from pressure groups on environmental issues, especially pertaining to waste.

Senior management within any organisation should recognise the importance of these issues. It may be appropriate for an organisation to develop a series of initiatives to promote good waste management as an issue within the company.

35.3 Waste management structure

It is essential to centrally co-ordinate waste activities, although responsibility for the proper disposal of waste and the duty or care must remain with the user.

Waste data collation and management co-ordination activities are carried out by FM departments. In some organisations, the FM may also have to liaise with other departments such as safety, corporate social responsibility or environment, or the manufacturing and/or production departments concerning all aspects of waste minimisation and disposal. Some organisations are large enough to warrant a dedicated member of staff responsible for waste management.

35.4 Waste management procedures

An organisation will need to document its procedures for handling and controlling waste. It should cover the following:

❑   Production.
❑   Classification.
❑   Handling.
❑   Storage.
❑   Packaging.
❑   Labelling.
❑   Transference.
❑   Disposal.

A procedure will need regular reviews to test its appropriateness and validity, and to incorporate variations and improvements.

35.5 Duty of care

Under the Environment Protection Act Section 34, a waste producer has a responsibility for waste from cradle to grave. This in effect means that an organisation is responsible for the waste it produces until that 'waste' is deemed not to be 'waste'. The process of degradation especially in landfill sites can take many years. Everybody involved in waste has a 'duty of care' to ensure that each step in the waste chain is undertaken in compliance with current legislation as shown in Table 35.1.

FM or the dedicated manager responsible for waste management should undertake regular audits to check compliance with each stage of the waste chain. The duty of care requires the organisation to ensure that:

❑   Waste is disposed of in a safe and secure manner.
❑   Only authorised contractors are used to transport the waste.
❑   The disposal site is licensed for that waste.
❑   Documents are correctly completed and retained for the statutory period.
❑   Waste is correctly described, labelled and contained in suitable vessels.

Table 35.1   Responsibilities in the waste chain

Waste producer	Waste importer	Waste carrier	Waste manager
Store waste safely on site	Responsibilities are similar to those of producers	Ensure adequacy of packaging while waste is in their control	Be well informed about nature of waste streams
Pack waste securely	Make a quick visual inspection to check accuracy of description	Repack waste if necessary	Maintain central register of documentation
Ensure waste does not escape	Check description, e.g. by sampling	Ensure correct and adequate description is transferred	Ensure disposal site licence is valid
Describe waste fully and accurately	Ensure waste does not escape	Check description, e.g. by sampling	Select an appropriate treatment/disposal method
Label waste correctly	Re-describe waste if necessary	Issue full compliance documentation, e.g. waste transfer notes	Make reasonable checks on the carrier/waste manager
Ensure documentation is correct	Check the carriers registration	Act on causes for suspicion	Ensure carrier is registered
Maintain local register of copies of documentation	Check documentation	Report offences to the WRA	Ensure waste falls within the terms of the contractors waste management licence

35.6 Waste minimisation

Waste minimisation strategies should be implemented to determine where improvements could be made. The benefits of such a policy include:

❑ Reduced procurement costs.
❑ Reduced waste disposal costs.
❑ Improvement in the company's environmental image.
❑ Reduction in long-term environmental liability and insurance costs.

A typical minimisation policy could be implemented using the waste management hierarchy of the 4 'R's:

Reduce
Reuse
Recycle
Responsible disposal

Waste minimisation strategies should be implemented to determine where improvements could be made. For example:

❑ At least 50% by weight of all packing material should use recycled products by an agreed date.

❑   At least 70–85% of all packaging waste should be recovered by agreed date.
❑   At least 70–85% of all packaging waste should be recycled by agreed date.

35.7 Building design

Another effective way to minimise future waste from a building is to implement a waste minimisation strategy in the pre-occupancy phase throughout the concept, design, construction and installation stages of a building. Consideration should be given to the design solutions that are:

❑   Adaptable to allow for changes of use during the lifetime of the building with the minimum production of waste.
❑   Simple construction types so as to minimise waste during construction.
❑   Logical so as to minimise material usage during construction, i.e. locate plant locally to point of use.
❑   Able to meet energy targets so as to minimise gaseous and effluent waste.
❑   Made of materials that are capable of being recycled or reused whilst remaining compatible with performance requirements.
❑   Made of materials with minimal waste by-products and low comparative embodied energy contents.
❑   Made of materials with a high percentage of recycled material.
❑   Subject to environmental impact audit procedures.
❑   Enable safe removal/demolition of systems with controlled collection of liquid/gaseous process fluids, i.e. refrigerant gases.
❑   Not incorporating extensive usage of refrigerant pipework which only serves to increase the potential volumetric discharge of refrigerant gases in the event of failure of the system.

35.8 Operational buildings

In occupied operational buildings, waste is produced by the occupants. Mostly this waste arises from the process of maintaining satisfactory internal environmental conditions. It will also arise during the lifetime of the building because of changing building usage. All aspects of managing a building should be subject to a waste minimisation exercise. Consideration should be given to the following:

❑   Items suitable for recycling should be identified and collected, sorted and stored in an organised manner. Specialist recycling companies should be identified who will help the organisation to meet its waste management targets.
❑   Partnering arrangements with suppliers and waste disposal/recycling companies to enable development of new recycling techniques.
❑   Identification of equipment where life expectancy can be significantly extended by mid-life refurbishment.
❑   Establishment of water, power and fuel metering and monitoring programmes to identify resource flows and wastage.
❑   Materials/systems that are not suitable for reuse, recycling or not economically suitable for sorting into constituent parts should be disposed of, preferably by incineration

in a plant with waste heat recovery. If items cannot be incinerated, then they could be sent to a reputable landfill disposal company, preferably one with a methane gas recovery system.

35.9 Business activities and business processes

Depending on the nature of the business activities, there may be opportunities to minimise the waste output by review of each process or operation in the organisation. Environmental impact of the waste outputs should be conducted and reviewed in light of local authority guidelines and the changing legislation. FMs may contribute to a review of alternative process procedures and identify changes in current processes that may reduce waste/environmental impact. It is important to understand the organisation's core activities so that appropriate waste management strategies can be put in place. Businesses that produce more than 50 tonnes of packing must comply with the Producer Responsibility Obligations (Packaging Waste) Regulations. This legislation aims to reduce the packaging used in supply of goods, and to recover and recycle packaging waste.

35.10 Product labelling

Adequate product labelling is the key to environmentally conscious waste disposal. Without sufficient and consistent labelling, the users or disposers of products will have greater difficulties in safe waste disposal. Information should clearly identify potential recycling options and waste disposal methodologies, such as:

❑   Waste relevance.
❑   Soil pollution and degradation effects.
❑   Potential water contamination.
❑   Potential air contamination.
❑   Noise contamination.
❑   Energy consumption.
❑   Consumption of natural resources.
❑   Effects on ecosystems.

This information is required so that potential recycling options and the required disposal routes and methodology can be assessed. All items and component parts must be labelled to clearly identify recycling capabilities and waste disposal options. All items and components must be assembled to facilitate simple dismantling for possible future recycling/re-use. Product life spans must be maximised to minimise the waste quantities produced over long periods of time.

35.11 Recycling

Recycling of products is an integral part of the waste management strategy. Typical waste products that can be managed in recycling activities include:

❑   Paper.
❑   Textiles.

❑   Polythene.
❑   Metals.
❑   Printer circuit boards.
❑   Toner cartridges.
❑   Waste oil and fuel.
❑   Cooking oils.
❑   Furniture.
❑   Computers.
❑   Plastic cups.
❑   Drink cans.

Further opportunities for recycling need to be constantly reviewed as technologies and processes change.

35.12 Waste product database

A waste product database should be used to log and monitor the various waste streams, the disposal quantities and locations of each waste product in an organisation. All waste can be registered on an organisation's database using the following criteria:

❑   Date.
❑   Quantity – mass or volume.
❑   Location.
❑   Classification.
❑   Reason for waste.
❑   Waste minimisation assessment.
❑   Disposal details.
❑   Documentation number.

It may not be practical to classify each source of waste on an 'item by item' basis . In such cases, a split apportionment is used – based upon an approximate percentage distribution of the various types of waste within the product being discarded. Where specific details are known, the information is included as appropriate.

The database provides the following information:

❑   Quantities per classification.
❑   Source of waste.
❑   Waste minimisation assessment.
❑   Disposal route.
❑   Disposal costs.
❑   Type/classification of waste.
❑   Dates of disposal/collection.
❑   Reason for waste.
❑   Document number.

Management reports can then be created by searches for information on the database.

❑   Per waste classification.
❑   Per site area, function or department.

❏   Per disposal rate.
❏   Per building.

35.13 Waste classification

The majority of an organisation's waste is either commercial or industrial as controlled by the Controlled Waste Regulations 1992. There are two classification schedules to consider as described below.

Classification of dangerous substances during transportation

Where products are transported by road and rail, suitable identification must be used in accordance with CDG – CPL (Carriage of Dangerous Goods – Classification Packaging and Labelling) Regulations 1994. Table 35.2 shows the classification used. Hazard warning diamonds are also used for clear identification.

Table 35.2   Classification of waste substances during transport

Class 1	Explosives subject to the Classification and Labelling of Explosives Regulations 1983 (SI 1983 No. 1140)
Class 2	Gases, subdivided as: • 2.1: flammable • 2.2: non-flammable, non-toxic and non-corrosive • 2.3: poisonous (including substances which are poisonous via their corrosive effect)
Class 3	Flammable liquids, liquids with flashpoint under 61°C. Between 35°C and 61°C, the substance must also be combustible in order to be classified as a flammable liquid under CDG–CPL
Class 4	Flammable solids, readily combustible or self-reactive substances, certain desensitised explosives, substances liable to spontaneous combustion and substances which on contact with water or damp air give off flammable gas in dangerous quantities
Class 5	Oxidising substances and organic peroxides
Class 6.1	Poisonous (toxic) substances that are liable to cause death or serious injury to human health if inhaled, ingested or absorbed through the skin
Class 6.2	Infectious substances. Also subject to various official recommendations, e.g. Health Services Advisory Committee guidance
Class 7	Radioactive materials subject to the Radioactive Substances (Carriage by Road) (Great Britain) Regulations 1974 (SI 1974 No. 1735), as amended
Class 8	Corrosive substances which by chemical action will cause severe damage to living tissue or will materially damage or destroy the mode of transport in case of leakage
Class 9	Other dangerous substances, miscellaneous substances which have been found to present a danger not covered by other Classes, e.g. asbestos

Chemicals (Hazard Information and Packaging or Supply) Regulations (CHIP)

CHIP Regulations cover the classification and labelling of chemicals, substances and preparations which may create risk to health. The risks are classified into the following groups:

E	Explosive
O	Oxidising (ecothermic)
F+	Extremely flammable
F	Highly flammable
T+	Very toxic
T	Toxic
Xn	Harmful
C	Corrosive
Xi	Irritant
Xn	Sensitising
T	Carcinogenic
T	Mutagenic
T	Toxic for reproduction
N	Dangerous for environment

The regulations provide guidance on specific classification labelling and identification. Certain groups are provided with category ratings in accordance with the likelihood of health effects where:

Category 1: Known likelihood.
Category 2: Sufficient evidence to provide a strong assumption.
Category 3: Cause for concern.

35.14 Control of Substances Hazardous to Health (COSHH)

These Regulations require a risk assessment to be carried out on all substances that are capable of causing harm to health. The regulations give information on: assessments; prevention and control of exposure; use, maintenance and testing of control measures; monitoring; health surveillance; information, instruction and training for staff; and exposure limits. Substances are classified according to the exposure limits which are expressed as maximum exposure limits (MEL) and occupational exposure limits (OES).

35.15 Waste management audits

Objectives should be agreed before a waste management audit commences. An audit report should be produced to clearly and constructively benchmark current activities and make suitable environmental recommendations together with life-cycle costings where appropriate. A senior representative of the process/operation should be allocated to work with the audit team to ensure that all options are evaluated.

Audits should review the following:

❑ Company/departmental policies.
❑ Communications and training.
❑ Raw materials procurement, types and alternatives.

❑   Energy efficiency, consumption and use.
❑   Specific processes, alternative technologies and effectiveness.
❑   Wastes and discharges.
❑   Transport and distribution systems.
❑   Accidents and emergencies.

The output of the audit will:

❑   Demonstrate compliance with legislation.
❑   Demonstrate efficiency of business activities.
❑   Predict likely future controls.
❑   Benchmark achievements with good practice.
❑   Determine the means to maintain environmental and commercial competitiveness.
❑   Establish confidences of employees, customers and enhance the public image of the organisation.

35.16 Targets

Waste management targets are set either by legislation or by the practical limits set by enforcing agents. Compliance with these targets should mitigate against possible prosecutions by the enforcement agencies.

Various limits exist for the disposal of waste products, all of which are governed by various Acts of legislation such as Hazardous Waste Regulations, Trade Effluent consents, Water Industry Regulations, Environmental Protection Act, Clean Air Act, Environment Act, Waste Management Licensing Regulations, etc.

The legislation is enforced by precedent law (i.e. previous case law) and does not simply list the contaminant limits which products must achieve. Legislation uses phrases such as:

'...... release of any substance from prescribed processes into any environmental medium .....'

'....... capable (by reason of the quantity or concentrations involved) of causing harm to man or any other living organisms supported by the environment .....'

'.....take all reasonable precautions and exercise all due diligence to avoid....'

It is therefore necessary to interpret safe limits which hopefully will not result in further prosecutions. Many limits are stipulated by specific consents agreed with local regulatory authorities but even these do not necessarily guarantee that future prosecutions will not arise.

Waste disposal regulations are strengthening and practical limits must be set which will minimise pending legislation driven mainly from Europe.

Many limits are set for many waste streams – including:

❑ NO_x emission levels.
❑   CO emission levels.
❑   Packaging recycling, recovery and construction.
❑   Reductions of controlled waste to landfill sites.
❑   Recycling strategies.

❏   Waste minimisation.
❏   Water quality.
❏   Foul waste.
❏   Water quality.

35.17 Legislation

Organisations operating in the UK are required to meet certain legislative requirements with respect to waste issues. From 1 April 1996, the Environment Agency (EA) became responsible for regulation. The EA combines the activities of the National Rivers Authority (NRA), Her Majesty's Inspectorate of Pollution (HMIP) and the Local Waste Regulation Authorities (WRAs). This ensures an integrated and consistent approach to water, air and land pollution.

The Scottish Environment Protection Agency (SEPA) is responsible for regulation in Scotland.

The Integrated Pollution Prevention Control (IPPC) European Directive encourages business and industry to reduce the impact of their activities on the environment. Major industries such as cement manufacture, chemical plants, food and drink manufacturers will be covered by this legislation.

Hazardous Waste Regulations

This replaces the Special Waste Regulations and covers any waste that is harmful to human life, harmful to the environment or is difficult to handle. An additional 200 types of waste were added to the listings – including batteries, sodium lights, oils, paint, ink, chemical waste and solvents. The Regulations require a process based on the principle of 'cradle to grave' with a full audit document trail of transfer and consignment notes. There is a requirement to ensure greater segregation, pre-treatment and categorisation of waste by the producer.

Premises that produce more than 200 kg per year of hazardous waste must be registered with the Environment Agency (EA), and this registration must be on an annual basis.

Waste Electrical and Electronic Equipment Regulations

Waste Electrical and Electronic Equipment Regulations (WEEE) concerns the safe and controlled disposal of electrical and electronic components that run on less than 1000 V AC (or 1500 V DC) electrical supplies. This includes:

❏   Large and small household appliances.
❏   IT and telecommunication equipment.
❏   TVs, videos, hi-fis.
❏   Lighting, electrical and electronic tools.
❏   Toys, leisure and sports equipment.
❏   Automatic dispensers.
❏   Medical devices.
❏   Monitoring and control equipment.
❏   Automatic dispensers.

36 Catering and Hospitality Services

36.1 Introduction

The UK contract catering industry is a typical oligopoly. That is to say it is dominated by four organisations: Compass Group, Sodexho, Aramark and Elior (aka Avenance) and populated by a large number (over 3600) of significantly smaller companies. The two largest companies, Compass Groups and Sodhexo, operate over 3500 contracts each, Aramark and Elior operate approximately 1000 and 700 contracts, respectively, whereas a medium-sized contractor operates up to 300 contracts. The majority of contractors operate under 50 sites each.

Given this large number of catering contractors, it is inevitable that the market is well served by national, regional and local operators, as well as specialist operators working in a particular niche, such as director's dining, or schools. The FM has therefore to select the most appropriate contractor that suits the organisation's catering strategy.

This number in the market place gives the purchaser a huge choice. However, it is important to carry out some pre-qualification to ensure that only companies who are experienced in catering for the specific needs of the client organisation, whether this is a café, vending or client dining rooms, are invited to tender. Additionally, each contractor must be able to support the geographic location of the client site satisfactorily.

Typical catering services required by an organisation include:

❑ Vending.
❑ Staff restaurant.
❑ Fine dining.
❑ Staff café.
❑ Mobile catering services.
❑ Hospitality.
❑ Retail.
❑ BBQs.
❑ Events.
❑ Restaurants and cafes open to the public – such as in shopping centres, retail organisations and multi-tenanted premises.

Whilst the majority of 'food at work' operations in the UK are operated by catering contractors, there are some organisations that still directly employ their own catering staff. These organisations may choose this option due to financial or other strategic reasons. The greater proportion of self-operation is within the education and leisure sector. To manage and operate a catering operation directly the client will require the following:

❑ A suitably qualified and experienced catering manager, with a team of qualified staff.
❑ A reporting structure and accountability for operations to the FM.

- ❑ Supplier accreditation and purchasing systems.
- ❑ Accounts and auditing systems.
- ❑ Payroll administration (increased headcount).
- ❑ Knowledge of the extensive Food Safety Legislation, including registration of premises and services with the local Environmental Health Office.

Setting up these systems to suit the unique needs of a catering operation can be time and resource consuming.

The main advantage of an in-house operation is that the client retains direct control over the image and style of catering provided. Any profit made from catering outlets is also retained by the client organisation.

The main disadvantage of an in-house operation is that the client is directly responsible for all capital investment and any operational losses incurred. The risks of the operation remain with the client. Additionally, the catering department can be relatively isolated from other catering operations and management, which can lead to a lack of the creative and qualitative input necessary to keep the food offers up to date and maintain customer interest.

36.2 Contracted-out catering services

When selecting a catering contractor, it is necessary to carry out some background investigations relating to potential caterers. Typical questions include:

- ❑ Who do they currently cater for?
- ❑ What the support and service is like?
- ❑ Is the business growing or in decline?
- ❑ Are they growing so fast that it would affect their support for their new customers or for their existing cusomers?
- ❑ Have there been any significant developments or re-organisation in their company recently?
- ❑ What is the extent of catering expertise, and how do they keep their staff up to date with their qualifications and skills?

Networking among fellow FMs can give a useful insight into the nature of the contractors and a list of those who will suit a company's catering profile. Another valuable source of information is a catering consultant. A list of reputable consultancies can be obtained from the Hotel and Catering International Management Association (HCIMA) or the Food Service Consultants Society International (FCSI).

The main advantages to contracting out the catering service are as follows:

- ❑ Financial risk can be the responsibility of the caterer. (It must be noted that where they do take full financial responsibility, if the operation is not profitable, a caterer will withdraw from a contract, thus reverting the ultimate risk to the client.)
- ❑ The contractor can be a source of capital investment, which is generally amortised through the profit and loss account over a number of mutually agreed years. (It should be noted that this finance is in the form of a loan and its size will have a direct affect on the subsidy.)

❑ The food offer and service is kept up to date (depending on the supplier chosen).
❑ The contractor provides employee training, motivation, promotion and cross-pollination of ideas from other operations.
❑ The responsibility of administering the accounts including recruitment, payroll and financial accounting is removed from the client.
❑ The client's headcount is reduced.
❑ Introduction of specialist catering sector control systems, account packages and reports.

The main disadvantages of outsourcing are as follows:

❑ Control, in the form of food style, service opening times, staffing levels and tariffs may have to be compromised depending upon the level of financial responsibility the client wishes the contractor to take.
❑ The contractor will require income from the operation either in the form of net profit or a management fee thus increasing the cost to the client.
❑ Where they take complete financial responsibility, a contractor will withdraw from a contract if losses are incurred, thus leaving an impaired operating infrastructure.

36.3 Contract types

A basic knowledge of how catering contractors generate income helps in the understanding of the usual catering contracts in operation.

Generally, contractors earn income in two primary ways, either via a management fee and/or retained supplier discounts. Typically, their earnings from these two sources will range from 2.5% to 10% of contract turnover, depending on the size of contract. (Contract turnover in this case is calculated as subsidy less management fee, plus cash sales.)

A management fee is the most common way for a contractor to earn income. Usually, a sum is agreed annually between the client and contractor and is charged on the monthly catering trading account.

Contractors can also earn revenue from supplier discounts. Catering contractors negotiate with suppliers to deliver goods to their contract sites. The price will be based on the cost of the goods to the supplier plus the cost of delivery, associated administration and profit. In addition there will be a markup on this to cover 'discounts' returned to the catering contractor. They are variously known as drop discounts, volume-related discounts, royalties, loyalty bonus, overriding discounts and retained rebates.

The earnings from supplier discounts can be considerable—up to 50% of the volume of some types of produce. However, as client companies have become more aware of this practice there has been a trend towards sharing some, if not all of the income with clients or moving to 'net into unit' purchasing. As the name suggests, net into unit purchasing is when produce is invoiced at catering site level at the lowest price without any margin for return to the catering contractor. This transparency improves the trust and relationship between catering contractor and client.

One must be aware that contractors need to earn a minimum from a contract, so if their income from supplier discounts is diminished it will generally necessitate an increase in management fee. However, the advantage of having income shown as management fee

Table 36.1   Costs of catering in a cost-plus contract (in £s)

Cost of food	400,000
Cost of labour	300,000
Cost of sundry items	30,000
Cost of fee	50,000
Total	**780,000**
Less sales of food	500,000
Difference = Subsidy	**280,000**

is that it is transparent and comparable between contractors, unlike that earned from discounts. This is useful for comparison when in a tender situation.

'Cost-Plus' contract

Under this arrangement, the client pays all the operating costs such as food, labour and sundries plus, as the name suggests, a management fee to the contractor to supply and process these materials/skills as shown in Table 36.1. Any cash received is processed by the contractor and credited against the costs.

The subsidy in this case is £280,000 per annum. However, the total of the subsidy depends on the tariff charged for the food. Indeed, some companies issue the food for free to their staff. If this were the case in Table 36.1, the subsidy would be £780,000 per annum.

It can be seen that the element of risk in terms of cost rests firmly with the client. As a consequence of paying the costs and shouldering the risk, the client also retains control over elements such as service levels and menu tariff.

Fixed price contract

A fixed price contract is at the other end of the spectrum to a 'cost-plus' contract. Its most basic form is where an annual cost of catering is agreed between parties at the commencement of the contract. The client pays equal monthly instalments to the contractor for the term of the contract. It is then up to the contractor to provide the service and generate an element of profit within the total cost agreed.

An example of this is given in Table 36.2. In this case, the client pays the catering contractor £52,500 per month (£630,000 divided by 12 months). Any profit generated would be retained by the contractor.

The element of risk rests with the contractor and as such they may retain a high degree of control over the menu range, tariff, services levels and opening times after they have been awarded the contract.

Hybrid contract

The structure of this contract is based on the 'cost-plus' model. The earning potential of the contractor can increase or decrease based on their performance in both financial elements such as:

❑   Sales volumes.
❑   Gross profit targets.
❑   Labour and sundry costs.

Table 36.2   Costs of catering in a fixed price contract (in £s)

Cost of food	400,000
Cost of labour	200,000
Cost of sundry items	30,000
Total fixed cost	**630,000**
Less sales of food	670,000
Difference = Profit to contractor	**40,000**

and on qualitative elements such as:

❑   Menu range.
❑   Service levels.
❑   Staff appearance.
❑   Health and safety standards.

An agreed percentage of the base management fee is 'put at risk'. This is usually between 25% and 50%. Each of the elements listed earlier is weighted according to the importance attached to that element. Each is scored and the result is then reconciled, usually once a quarter and the fee adjusted upwards or downwards accordingly.

Nil subsidy

The method of how a *subsidy* is calculated is illustrated earlier. *Nil subsidy* refers to a site where all overhead costs such as food, labour, sundries and contractor earnings are recovered by the gross profit earned from sales. On occasion the caterer is also required to recover the rent, rates and energy costs.

This sounds like the perfect solution for many client organisations. However, before committing to this route for the catering strategy, it is worth understanding that there are certain prerequisites for this type of operation to be successful. Specifically:

❑   A high volume of customers is needed to generate high volume sales.
❑   A tariff which achieves a high gross profit, usually controlled by the caterer, is required. This has to be of sufficient mark-up to cover all the raw material, labour and sundry costs.
❑   A style of catering service which minimises the labour costs will be chosen by the contractor.

Often a nil subsidy contract operates on the 'fixed price' model, whereby the fixed price is based on the client not incurring any subsidy.

36.4 Catering strategy

The most crucial question the organisation must ask itself is why provide catering for staff at all. In order to get the best value from the catering service and therefore catering contractor, the organisation must be clear why they are providing catering to their staff. As with nearly all aspects of running a business if there is a clear policy, the subsequent decisions further down the process are made a lot easier.

The reasons for providing catering are many and varied. For instance, some companies provide a main meal at no cost to their employees as part of their remuneration package. In this case, it may be that the provision of a catering service is seen as a greater value than the cash alternative of a higher salary. Another company may provide a service because they are located in an isolated area and do not wish staff to leave the premises. Some companies use dining and hospitality services as a business development and customer relationship tool and maintain very high standard dining rooms for client entertaining.

36.5 Catering objectives

Once there is a clear picture of why the company is providing a catering service, a more detailed scenario of exactly how it is to be operated can be formed. For example, the following sample of questions can be used to build up a picture of the service a company wishes to provide.

Range and style of services

❑   Is there to be a full service restaurant or a pre-prepared and made-to-order sandwich service?
❑   What is the range of food to be provided?
❑   Is there a comprehensive range of hospitality services required?
❑   How are beverages to be supplied (vended, over-the-counter or by trolley service)?

Tariff policies

❑   Is the tariff designed to return a gross profit, to recover just the cost of food and VAT or free issue?
❑   If a gross profit is to be generated, what level is appropriate or achievable?
❑   What effect will different gross profit targets have on the tariff across a range of items?
❑   If the service is free issue what is the daily allowance per person?
❑   Are the hospitality service costs absorbed centrally or recharged to individual cost centres? If so, what costs are recharged?

Financial objectives

The financial outcome of the catering service, be it a subsidy or a profit, will be driven by the range of services and the tariff policy adopted. For example, if a policy of free issue meals is adopted, the cost to the organisation will be considerably higher. Conversely, a gross profit will reduce the subsidy.

If it is a green field site, the specification can be formed from scratch. If it is an existing service, each area can be reviewed in light of new business objectives.

36.6 Catering specification

An example of a specification is given in Figure 36.1. It is recommended that the document be in the form of an output rather than an input specification. The reason for this is twofold, namely:

❑   It specifies each service required without pre-empting the actual food/service offer.
❑   It elicits bespoke responses from the contractors which identifies how they would approach the contract.

Management of agreed on site catering and associated facilities in accordance with relevant legislation and the Food and Hygiene Act.

Contractor is responsible for:

- The provision and maintenance of all catering service vehicles.
- The provision of uniforms for staff.
- Obtaining all necessary licences and certificates for the operation of catering services.
- Marketing all catering services to the staff.
- Initiatives, for example themed restaurant events, to increase and maintain the customer base.
- Cleaning all catering facilities including, but not limited to, restaurants, kitchens, retail outlets and vehicles.
- The management of the maintenance and the provision of scheduled maintenance of the equipment.

Client is responsible for the provision and maintenance of:

- Premises.
- Restaurant furniture.
- Restaurant serving counters.
- Kitchen furniture including equipment excluding light equipment.
- Relevant utilities to the premises.
- The provision of light equipment (including, but not limited to, crockery, cutlery, serving trays, etc.).

Prices charged for all food and drink are to be agreed with the client representative, except for hospitality meals, beverages and snacks which shall be billed as tariff services in accordance with the tariff price list agreed between client and contractor.

The typical range of food provided by each catering service is illustrated in the attached schedule. The contractor will maintain equivalence with this range.

Management of on-site restaurant facilities dispensing a choice of hot and cold meals, snacks and drinks, in accordance with restaurant opening hours.

Provision of mobile catering facilities in accordance with hours of operation stated.

Provision of hospitality services providing hot and cold buffet meals, beverages and snacks.

Provision of retail outlets, dispensing confectionery, newspapers, hot and cold beverages and other miscellaneous items, in accordance with normal working opening hours.

Management of vending. Subject to the prior agreement of the client representative, the contractor may provide vending machines at locations on sites as per schedule.

Management of bottled water. The provision of bottled water and cups, dispensers and their maintenance will be billed as a demand service to the customer department.

The range of food and drink offered by the hospitality service and the restaurant service at each site is shown in the attached schedule. The range must remain comparable with that shown at all times and may only be reduced with the prior permission of the client representative.

Special event catering, outside the scope of the hospitality service, is a demand service.

Figure 36.1   Example catering specification

Ultimately, this arrangement will help differentiate between the contractors and facilitate a decision as to who should be awarded the contract.

The detail for each service should include information such as:

❑   Name of service.
❑   Times required.
❑   Potential customer numbers.
❑   Menu range.
❑   Service standard required.
❑   Tariff policy.

An example is shown in Figure 36.2.

The specification process will need to be repeated for all the services. This could possibly include services for the breakfast, lunch, supper and night restaurant, meeting rooms, vending (beverage, snack, food and soft drinks), and client, directors' and managers' dining rooms.

The drafting of the current service specification is usually a good time to review whether the organisation wishes to continue a service at all or in a different format.

Two examples could be as follows:

❑   A dining room where meals have been silver-served and the wish is to move to the more in-vogue plated service.
❑   The introduction of a made-to-order sandwich bar instead of pre-prepared bought-in sandwiches.

Lunch Service

Monday to Friday	12 noon to 1.30 pm	
Shift A	12 noon to 12.30 pm	50 employees
Shift B	12.30 pm to 1 pm	60 employees
Shift C	1 pm to 1.30 pm	70 employees

Menu to include the following as a minimum:

2 Hot Main Courses
2 Vegetables
1 Potato Dish
A Selection of 4 Salad Entrees
A Daily Selection of 4 Plain and 2 Composite Salads
A Selection of 6 Pre-prepared Sandwiches and Filled Rolls
1 Hot Sweet
1 Cold Sweet
Soft Drinks, Confectionery and Proprietary Snacks

Please propose a tariff that will recover the cost of food, VAT and 30% gross profit

---

Figure 36.2   Lunch service

36.7 Catering costs

The lowest cost does not always represent the best value for money. In evaluating the written and financial response, some means must be devised to identify which is the optimum bid.

The simplest way is to break down the elements of the document into component parts (see Table 36.3) as follows:

❑ Food.
❑ Labour.
❑ Miscellaneous.
❑ Management fee.

Each bid should be interrogated systematically for service/product quality versus cost in each category relevant to your specific site. The criteria used will vary from site to site and will depend on the service level specified. A range of questions need to be asked:

❑ Are the proposed sales volumes/gross profit/cost per head achievable?
❑ Was this demonstrated on the site(s) visited?
❑ Does the tender response match the tender specification?

Table 36.3   General catering cost elements

Category	Area	Element
Food	Staff restaurant	Proposed menus
		Sales volumes
		Food cost
		Gross profit
	Hospitality	Proposed menus
		Food cost
	Vending	Cup cost
Labour	Management staff	Each area can be evaluated as follows:
		Number
		Weekly hours
	Chefs	Hourly rates
	Other kitchen staff	Total cost
	Service staff	
Miscellaneous	Disposables	Each area should be scrutinised for appropriate volume and unit cost
	Cleaning materials	
	Uniforms	
	Laundry	
	Stationery	
	Merchandising materials	
Management fee	Fee at risk	Fee proposals should be weighed against which is
	Benefit of a longer contract	the most appropriate response in these criteria.
	Area support	
	Head office resource	
	Training support	

Negotiations

Once a preferred contractor has been selected for the catering services, the final details of the contract must be negotiated. The points to discuss and agree at this stage could include:

❑ Final operating budget. (Service requirements or volumes can change during a catering tender exercise.)
❑ Contractor earnings and any appropriate incentive schemes.
❑ TUPE details and their implications on the budget and contract.
❑ Payment terms.
❑ Invoice layout and supporting documentation requirements.

If applicable, the FM will also need to express any requirements concerning the lead-in time and handover details between contractors.

Additionally, it is good practice to debrief the unsuccessful contractors.

36.8 Catering services review

Once the contract is in place it is important to ensure that the contractor is providing the service as promised. It is usual to conduct reviews of two areas of the operation:

❑ Financial performance.
❑ Operational performance.

Financial key performance indicators

Most catering operations have a limited number of KPIs. They can be summarised as follows:

❑ Sales.
❑ Gross profit.
❑ Labour costs.
❑ Miscellaneous costs.

Sales

Sales are an effective measure of the effectiveness of the service. Typically, the higher the sales volume, the more popular the service.

Sales levels are influenced by many factors, such as:

❑ The catering services required in the specification.
❑ The tariffs agreed and set with the catering contractor.
❑ The location of the catering outlets and facilities.
❑ Effectiveness of the catering operation.

Typical measures could be:

❑ Effectiveness of marketing and merchandising.
❑ Food quality.
❑ Selection of food provided.

❏ Effectiveness of service.
❏ Image of the facility.

Gross profit

Gross profit can be defined as the difference between sales and the cost of food only. It is a measurement of the efficiency of the caterer in food production. It is typically best expressed as a percentage, as the percentage should remain broadly constant regardless of the sales volumes.

It can be affected by the following:

❏ The tariff policy as set by the client.
❏ The effectiveness of the caterer's purchasing.
❏ The effectiveness of the caterer's on-site control systems.

The latter two areas are therefore those on which the client should focus when managing their caterer.

Labour costs

This cost is often similar to the cost of food, so it is important that it should be carefully managed.

Once it is established through a competitive process what the optimum staffing levels and rates of pay should be for a given operation, there should be minimal changes to the cost of staffing a catering operation. Typical reasons for variations arising once a contract has been set up may include:

❏ Unexpected/unbudgeted high sickness levels requiring expensive replacement staff.
❏ Problems with staff retention resulting in excessive use of expensive agency staff to cover the vacancies whilst recruiting for new staff.
❏ Poor original forecasting of staffing requirement.
❏ Additional services required by the client.

Miscellaneous costs

This is a series of low cost categories that can sensibly be grouped together for easy monitoring. Typical headings in the catering budget include:

❏ Cleaning materials.
❏ Disposables.
❏ Uniform and laundry.
❏ Secure cash collection.
❏ Contractor charges for computer systems.
❏ Deep cleaning.

Once budgets are set for these areas, there should be minimal changes. All are largely dependent on effective contractor control, although the cost of disposables can be affected by client customer behaviour, especially on sites where there is a high proportion of take-away food.

Miscellaneous costs can also be measured as a percentage of sales, because they may vary with sales volumes.

Operational key performance indicators

The greatest problem associated with measuring performance is that it is an inexact science and will always be subjective. The client has to set up an effective means of communicating their qualitative expectations with the caterer so that they can be properly aligned. An SLA may be used.

The most practical means of doing this is to split the SLA into a number of sections that can be separately measured as follows:

❑ Food quality
  o Freshly prepared (i.e. not convenience).
  o Batch cooking (i.e. cooking small batches immediately prior to service).
  o Fat content of meat.
  o Proportion of main ingredient to supplementary ingredients in made-up dishes.
  o Appropriate portion sizes.
  o Use of seasonal ingredients and dishes.
❑ Food presentation
  o How carefully is the food arranged on the serving dish?
  o Has the most appropriate serving dish been used to enhance the appearance of the food?
  o Is the dish garnished where necessary?
  o Is the garnishing relevant to the dish and does it continue to look attractive throughout service?
  o Are appropriate accompaniments for each menu dish available?
  o Is sufficient (i.e. neither too much nor too little) food displayed throughout service?
❑ Menu variety and content
  o Is the menu structure appropriate to the demands of personnel on site?
  o Is the menu well balanced in terms of colour, texture, cooking method, taste, ingredients and country of origin?
  o Is there always a healthy choice available?
  o Is there a good choice of imaginative vegetarian food available?
  o Are there regularly new dishes featured on the menu?
  o Are all items clearly and accurately described on the menu?
  o Is the spelling correct?
  o Is the menu clearly displayed as appropriate throughout the building, in the restaurant and at the point of sale?
❑ Standard of service
  o Are all catering personnel briefed prior to service as to the content of all menu dishes?
  o Are staff correctly and smartly attired?
  o Are staff helpful, friendly and smiling?
  o Is response to questions swift and efficient?
❑ Marketing and merchandising
  o How effectively is the food displayed to maximise sales and gross profitability?
  o Is every item available for sale clearly priced and described at the point of sale?
  o How well is professionally produced point of sale material used to maximise sales?
  o Are there regular, changing special promotions?
  o What is the caterer doing to maintain interest in the catering facilities?
  o Are catering staff effective in maximising sales through customer liaison?

❑ Customer response
   o Are customer surveys regularly completed and are they acted on?
   o Are customer comment books/cards always available and are comments acted on?
   o Are there any repeated complaints that do not appear to have been acted on?
❑ Cleaning standards
   o Do both front and back of house areas appear clean?
   o Are all items of equipment being properly cleaned?
   o Is a cleaning schedule clearly displayed and is it completed and signed by a member of the catering management team?
   o Has the caterer completed a formal hygiene audit within the past 3 months?
   o Are staff being trained in key health, safety and hygiene practices?

Incentives

The financial and operational KPIs described earlier can easily be linked to an incentive scheme to allow the catering contractor to earn more in return for excellent performance (which could be self-funding when linked to financial KPIs) and to be penalised financially for poor performance.

36.9 Food hygiene

All operations that are classed as food businesses in the UK are governed by food safety legislation. The regulations concerning food hygiene affect food handlers, premises, storage of food and temperature control of food. Food premises must be registered. FMs who manage catering in-house or contract caterers need to be aware of the issues involved shown in Table 36.4.

Food poisoning and food-related illnesses arise from poor food handling practices. The pathogens that may cause bacterial infection are:

❑ Campylobacter.
❑ Salmonella.
❑ *E. coli*.

Table 36.4   Duties in food hygiene and food safety

Employer duties	Employee duties
Train all staff to level consistent with responsibilities	Comply with all food safety legislation
Keep records of training	Maintain a high standard of personal hygiene
Monitor suppliers	Wear protective clothing
Implement a form of HACCP or food safety programme	Wash hands correctly and frequently
Ensure compliance with all food safety legislation	Report to line manager if they know or suspect they are suffering or carrying a disease that may contaminate food
	Undertake food safety training

❑   *Clostridium perfringens.*
❑   Listeria.
❑   *Bacillus cereus.*
❑   *Staphylococcus aureus.*

The common causes of food poisoning and illnesses are:

❑   Not cooking food adequately.
❑   Preparation of food earlier than required, and kept at room temperature.
❑   Cross-contamination.
❑   Not thoroughly thawing frozen raw foods such as meat and poultry.
❑   Inadequate temperature controlled storage space.
❑   Infected food handlers.
❑   Infected raw food from unsafe suppliers.

Bacteria is destroyed by heating the food to above 63°C. Chilling and freezing slows the growth of bacteria. Refrigerators need to operate below 8°C to keep the food between 5°C and 8°C. Freezers will operate at − 18°C. Temperature probes are used to check food temperatures both in the fridges and freezers and also at the counters during service. Records must be kept of the temperatures. Sample portions of all food may also be kept for up to 24 hours after service, as part of food safety procedures.

36.10 Legislation

FMs need to be familiar with the legislation that applies to catering and food services, including:

❑   Food Safety and Hygiene legislation.
❑   Food Premises and Licensing legislation.

37 Quality Management

Quality management (QM) has developed over the past 60 years as countries and organisations have endeavoured to remain competitive in a global economy. The father of quality, W. Deming, encouraged the Japanese to adopt a systematic statistical approach to problem solving in the post-war rebuilding of Japan. This approach later became known as the Deming or PDCA (Plan, Do, Check, Action) cycle. He encouraged senior managers to become actively involved in their company's quality improvement programmes. His theories place great importance and responsibility on management, both at the individual, company and society level. Other quality concepts were introduced by others such as Juran, Shingo, Crosby, Feigenbaum and Ishikawa – these concepts include the quality spirals, zero defects, poka-yoke, fishbone diagram and quality circles.

37.1 Quality

Quality means basic nature or character. In recent years, the noun 'quality' has been used incorrectly to indicate a degree of excellence or superiority, such as 'quality managed facilities'. The word quality really needs a qualifying adjective such as high or low to indicate benchmarks of achievement. However, the terms quality management, quality control and quality assurance are now fully established in business management jargon. It is, however, still important in FM contexts to ensure that quality is a relative concept rather than absolute.

37.2 Quality management (QM)

Quality management is a business management programme that connects separate components of a business into an integrated whole. There are many examples of QM programmes, but essentially they are all concerned with rethinking how things are done so that quality is inherent in the products and services. There are several fundamental inputs, as shown in Table 37.1.

Quality management can be defined as 'the culture of an organisation committed to customer satisfaction through continuous improvement'.

It is an ongoing continuous process involving:

- ❑ Focus on the customer.
- ❑ Focus on process.
- ❑ Measurement of process.
- ❑ Commitment by top management.

Table 37.1   Fundamental inputs to a quality management system

Leadership	Quality must start at the top of an organisation. Leadership is the most important driving force behind a successful quality programme.
Education	The team involved will need to understand the principles of QM. This may involve participation in a workshop, looking at the effectiveness of customer interactions and customer service.
Communication	The successful deployment of QM will rely on good communications. A variety of tools can be used including posters, internal publication media, bulletin boards, videos, visual media, events with guest speakers, handbooks and so on. Success stories with individual staff are particularly useful to communicate the commitment of management.
Participation	Good management skills in training, nurturing and knowing when to stand back are required to empower the team in a QM programme. The FM front-line team must be empowered to make quality improvements as they know how to improve their services more than anyone else. Good staff working in front-line roles will naturally want to please, and want to provide a quality service or product to their customer.
Assessment	To understand how the QM process is going, a comprehensive set of measurements are required, together with periodic review.

The customer in a QM context is the customer of each step in the production chain of an organisation's services or products. Suppliers in the chain are also customers, so every part of the organisation needs to recognise their internal and external customer.

Quality management is about doing the right things right, first time and every time. If an organisation can reduce errors by improving the way things are done, there are many benefits such as:

❑ Providing a clear business focus.
❑ Improved efficiency.
❑ Increased customer satisfaction.
❑ Improved communications.
❑ Increased cash flow and the potential for profit.
❑ Less waste.
❑ Better use of resources.
❑ Improved staff morale.
❑ Enhanced reputation.

37.3 Continuous improvement

Most quality systems are built on the concept of continuous improvement or 'kaizen'. The following steps are required to achieve ongoing continuous improvement:

❑ Eliminate needless process steps.
❑ Continually seek and implement refinements.
❑ Eliminate defects.
❑ Reduce the process cycle, such as the speed of response.
❑ Design a systematic quality programme.

37.4 Quality systems and procedures

Analysis of business requirements to ensure that both products and services are designed consistently to achieve excellent quality is needed. Using a systematic process, and application of quality control measures, further improvements will achieve the desired quality.

Quality control is defined by Feigenbaum as 'An effective system for co-ordinating the quality maintenance and quality improvement efforts of the various groups in an organisation so as to enable production at the most economical levels which allow for full customer satisfaction.'

Various QM schemes have been developed, as shown below.

- ❑ Total quality management (TQM).
- ❑ European Foundation of Quality Management (EFQM) (also known as Business Excellence Model).
- ❑ Six Sigma.

It is suggested that the following principles are necessary to implement QM:

- ❑ The organisation needs to commit long term to continuous improvement.
- ❑ Adopt a 'right first time' culture.
- ❑ Help staff to understand customer/supplier relationships.
- ❑ Do not judge suppliers on price alone – look at the total cost.
- ❑ Adopt modern management methods and empower staff – eliminate fear in the workplace.
- ❑ Break down barriers between departments by improving communications and teamwork.

37.5 Total quality management

Total quality management is a business philosophy that focuses on quality throughout an organisation. It aims to deliver complete customer satisfaction, benefits to all staff and benefits to society as a whole.

The focus

Total quality management focuses on getting things right first time, and frequently involves an overhaul in the way an organisation manages staff, suppliers and processes. It also influences the way they interact with customers. The company needs to go back to basics and ask the following questions:

- ❑ What is the purpose as a business?
- ❑ What are the values?
- ❑ What's the mission and vision?
- ❑ What are the factors that affect whether the mission is achieved?

The building blocks of TQM

Total quality management is a way of thinking about business processes, people and systems to ensure things are done right first time.

Processes
Each business process is made up of a series of actions that satisfy the customer's needs and expectations. Each area of an organisation has many processes. It is important to look at each action – and its result – to assess what is needed to do to improve quality.

People
While a TQM strategy comes from senior management, it is the staff who carry out the business activities day to day who have true responsibility for performance and quality. Their buy-in is critical, so managers need to make sure they understand the long-term goal of total quality and the reasons for any new ways of working. It is also important to keep staff informed of any improvements they've achieved – to provide impetus for further improvements.

Staff need to see commitment from the top down – managers leading by example – and need to feel the whole company is embracing TQM. Managers need to promote the right climate for business improvement, encouraging staff to come up with ideas for innovation and problem solving.

Management systems
Total quality management often entails a change in company culture and working practices. It is essential to have a system in place to manage and sustain these changes.

Performance measurement
An effective review of how the organisation currently works is needed as the baseline for future measurement. This will highlight bottlenecks, bad service and other quality issues. Data is collected regularly to measure and check if the new desired level of performance is being achieved. Techniques such as brainstorming and tools such as cause and effect graphs can identify which areas are a priority for improvement.

Commitment
Total quality management must start at the top with commitment from the executive or board. Senior managers must consistently demonstrate their commitment to quality. Companies need a sound quality policy, supported by plans and resources to implement it. Leaders must take responsibility for preparing, reviewing and monitoring the policy – and this is an ongoing responsibility. Managers must ensure everyone understands – and signs up to – the quality policy.

Leadership
Effective leadership starts with the development of a mission statement, followed by a strategy, which is translated into action plans through the organisation. Key requirements for effective leadership include:

❑ Developing and promoting corporate beliefs and objectives, often in the form of a mission statement or company vision.
❑ Acting as role models for a culture of total quality.
❑ Developing effective strategies and plans for achieving total quality.
❑ Reviewing the QM system.
❑ Communicating the quality message and motivating staff to sign up for total quality.

Table 37.2   Fundamental concepts in the EFQM

Results orientation	Excellence is achieving results that delight all the organisation's stakeholders
Customer focus	Excellence is creating sustainable customer value.
Leadership and constancy of purpose	Excellence is visionary and inspirational leadership, coupled with constancy of purpose.
Management by processes and facts	Excellence is managing the organisation through a set of interdependent and interrelated systems, processes and facts.
People development and involvement	Excellence is maximising the contribution of employees through their development and involvement.
Continuous learning, innovation and improvement	Excellence is challenging the status quo and effecting change by utilising learning to create innovation and improvement opportunities.
Partnership development	Excellence is developing and maintaining value-adding partnerships.
Corporate social responsibility	Excellence is exceeding the minimum regulatory framework in which the organisation operates and to strive to understand and respond to the expectations of their stakeholders in society.

Culture

The culture in any organisation is made up of prevailing beliefs, norms and rules. New corporate strategy will take into account the company culture. Most companies recognise that they need co-operation at all levels, and a culture of good teamwork, to drive through major change such as a new QM system.

37.6 Business Excellence Model – European Foundation of Quality Management

This model is based on principles known as the Fundamental Concepts as shown in Table 37.2.

The model has a checklist to compare the way an organisation performs against best practice guidelines. It looks at leadership, business strategy, people management, partnerships, resources and business processes. It also covers relationships with the customer, staff and the wider community and society. Organisations are expected to use the checklist for self-assessment of performance against the standards of EFQM.

37.7 Six Sigma

Six Sigma aims to maximise customer satisfaction and minimise defects. In statistical terms, the purpose of Six Sigma is to reduce process variation so that virtually all the products or services provided meet or exceed customer expectations. This is defined as being only 3.4 defects per million occurrences. Six Sigma was developed by Motorola in the 1980s but has its roots in statistical process control (SPC), which first appeared in the 1920s.

Table 37.3   The five steps in Six Sigma

1	DEFINE	A serious problem is identified and a project team is formed and given the responsibility and resources for solving the problem.
2	MEASURE	Data that describes accurately how the process is working currently is gathered and analysed in order to produce some preliminary ideas about what might be causing the problem.
3	ANALYSE	Based upon these preliminary ideas, theories are generated as to what might be causing the problem and, by testing these theories, root causes are identified.
4	IMPROVE	Root causes are removed by means of designing and implementing changes to the offending process.
5	CONTROL	New controls are designed and implemented to prevent the original problem from returning and to hold the gains made by the improvement.

There are three basic elements to Six Sigma:

  (i) process improvement;
 (ii) process design/redesign;
(iii) process management.

A five-step approach is used in each stage as shown in Table 37.3.

37.8 Quality standards and accreditation schemes

FMs should be familiar with the quality standards and accreditation schemes that apply to the built environment. These include British Standards (BS 5750), International standards (ISO 9000), Investors in People (IiP) and BREEAM. Most of these standards are awarded to the organisations via self-certification or an external assessor.

Quality assurance is a systematic method of organising activities.

❑ Plan what you do.
❑ Do what you plan.
❑ Record what you have done.

It does not necessarily imply quality, just management processes and systems in place. Once a standard and a system are defined, measurements will be required on a regular basis. Typical measurements include:

❑ Availability.
❑ Capacity.
❑ Reliability.
❑ Flexibility.
❑ Timeliness.
❑ Usability.
❑ Accuracy.
❑ Satisfaction.

❑   Responsiveness.
❑   Completeness.

The most common measurement tool is benchmarking. Benchmarking can be internal, competitive, functional or generic. However, it is important to consider that benchmarking in itself can be a time-consuming and labour-intensive process that does not provide solutions, just ideas. Benchmarking is a continuous activity and offers a process of learning from both the organisation and others.

37.9 Standards

There are number of standards and accreditation schemes applicable to quality in FM. Here are just a few:

BS 4778/ISO 8402
BS 5750/ISO 9000 and ISO 9004
BS 5750 part 1/ISO 9001
BS 5750 part 2/ISO 9002
BS 5750 part 3/ISO 9003
ISO 14001
PAS 11000 Collaborative Business Relationships

ISO 9000

ISO 9000 is an internationally accepted programme for certifying QM systems. Launched in 1987, ISO 9000 is a group of QM standards laid down by the International Organisation for Standardisation. Originally, it grew out of the British Standards Institute's BS 5750 system.

The ISO 9000 standards are built around business processes, with a strong emphasis on improvement and a focus on meeting the needs of customers.

The ISO 9000 model contains eight QM principles, on which to base an efficient, effective and adaptable QMS as shown in Table 37.4. The principles reflect best practice and are designed to enable a continual improvement of the business, its efficiency and its capability of responding to customer needs and expectations.

The family of ISO 9000 Standards for QMSs comprises:

❑   ISO 9000:2000 – QMSs – Fundamentals and vocabulary. This is an introduction to the ISO 9000 family.
❑   ISO 9001:2000 – QMSs – Requirements. This is the core member of the ISO 9000 family, as it specifies the key requirements of an efficient, effective and adaptable QMS.
❑   ISO 9004:2000 – Guidelines for performance improvement. This focuses on performance improvement.

These standards originated from a regular 6-year review and are intended to be generic and adaptable to all kinds of organisations. They are also now more closely aligned with the requirements of the EFQM Business Excellence Model.

Ideally, the ISO 9001:2000 and ISO 9004:2000 standards should be to be used together, but, if required, they can be used independently.

Table 37.4   The eight ISO standard quality principles

1	**Customer focus**	Organisations depend on their customers and therefore should understand current and future customer needs, should meet customer requirements and should strive to exceed customer expectations. Customer needs and expectations must be determined and converted into product requirements.
2	**Leadership**	Good leaders establish unity of purpose, direction and the internal environment for their organisation. They formulate an appropriate quality policy and ensure that measurable objectives are established for the organisation. They create the environment in which people can become fully involved in achieving these objectives. They also demonstrate that they are committed to developing, sustaining and improving the QMS.
3	**Involvement of people**	People at all levels are the essence of an organisation and their full involvement enables their abilities to be used for the organisation's benefit. Managers must ensure that there is involvement of the people at all levels in the organisation. They must make the people aware of the importance of meeting customer requirements, and their responsibilities, as individuals, for doing this. They must also ensure that the people are competent on the basis of appropriate training and experience.
4	**Process approach**	A desired result is achieved more efficiently when related resources and activities are managed as a process. Consequently, an effective QMS must have, at its core, a process approach, with each process transforming one or more inputs to create an output of value to the customer. Successful, quality organisations will have identified a set of core business processes that define those activities that directly add value to the product or service for the external customer, and a set of supporting processes that are required to maintain the effectiveness of those core processes.
5	**Systems approach to management**	Identifying, understanding and managing a system of interrelated processes for a given objective contribute to the effectiveness and efficiency of the organisation. These processes must be thoroughly understood and managed so that the most efficient use is made of available resources. This in turn will ensure that the needs of all the stakeholders – customers, employees, shareholders and the community – are met.
6	**Continual improvement**	This is a permanent objective of any organisation. Customer satisfaction is a constantly moving entity, so an effective QMS must take this into account. For this to be achieved, attention needs to be given to both the voice of the customer and the employee – through complaint analysis, opinion surveys and regular contacts and through measurement, monitoring and analysis of both process and product data.
7	**Factual approach to decision making**	Effective decisions are based upon the logical, intuitive analysis of data and information (i.e. they are based upon the facts).
8	**Mutually beneficial supplier relationships**	Relationships between an organisation and its suppliers enhance the ability of both organisations to create value. Each organisation is just one of the links in a much larger supply chain. Consequently, in order to serve the long-term needs of the community and the organisation itself, mutually beneficial relationships need to exist at all points in the supply chain.

ISO 9001:2000 Standard

The ISO 9001:2000 Standard specifies the requirements for QMS that can be used by organisations for internal application, contractual purposes or certification. The approach is made up of four processes:

(i)   management responsibility;
(ii) resource management;
(iii) product realisation;
(iv) measurement, analysis, improvement.

The standard recognises that customer requirements are the main input to the QM process, and that customer satisfaction is the main output of the QM process. Consequently, it is vital to any organisation that the level of customer satisfaction is continually evaluated and fed back into the QM process so that it can be used to assess whether customer requirements have been met. If not, then an improvement process can be initiated.

Accreditation

Most organisations that develop and implement QMSs based on ISO 9001:2000 will have their systems approved by an independent certification body to reinforce inhouse disciplines and to demonstrate compliance to customers and purchasers. There are number of pros and cons of implementing the ISO 9000 QMS as shown in Table 37.5.

ISO 14001

This standard provides a framework for environmental management. The main driver for the development of this environmental management system was the Rio Summit in 1992. This standard specifies a framework of control against which the organisation is certified by an external verifier. The standard will help an organisation to achieve continuous improvement in regard to the environmental impacts.

Table 37.5   Advantages and disadvantages of ISO 9000

Advantages	Disadvantages
A document system	More records to keep
Clear roles and responsibilities	More work, less discretion, policing of activities
Expectations known	Emphasis on regulation
Pride from accreditation	Another award for the boss
Instructions are in writing	Procedures, procedures and yet more procedures
Product quality more consistent, avoid rejects	The same product
Production efficiencies, cost savings	Cost of training and trained staff and the system itself
Improves supply quality	The demands from customers increase, as they want even more from their suppliers
Enhances customer loyalty	Suppliers forced to comply may resent the bureaucracy
Export marketing easier	

Investors in People (IiP)

The IiP standard is a framework for delivering business improvement through people. It is available for all sizes and types of organisation. The aim of the IiP standard is to help organisations improve the way they work and how they value their employees. Organisations have to meet the same criteria – or 'indicators' – as other organisations, but the standard recognises that each business will meet them in their own way. IiP recognise that organisations use different means to achieve success through their people. It does not prescribe any one method but provides a framework to find the most suitable means for achieving success through people.

The IiP standard uses the principles of PDCA – Plan, Do, Check, Act. The principles that make up the standard are:

- ❑ A strategy for improving the performance of the organisation is clearly defined and understood.
- ❑ Learning and development is planned to achieve the organisation's objectives.
- ❑ Strategies for managing people are designed to promote equality of opportunity in the development of the organisation's people.
- ❑ The capabilities managers need to lead, manage and develop people effectively are clearly defined and understood.

The above principles are supported by the following actions to ensure the performance of the organisation:

- ❑ Managers are effective in leading, managing and developing people.
- ❑ People's contribution to the organisation is recognised and valued.
- ❑ People are encouraged to take ownership and responsibility by being involved in decision making.
- ❑ People learn and develop effectively.

The impact of the IiP investment in the organisation can be demonstrated in that:

- ❑ Investment in people improves the performance of the organisation.
- ❑ Improvements are continually made to the way people are managed and developed.

37.10 Benchmarking

The dictionary definition of a benchmark is 'something which serves as a standard by which others may be measured or judged'. A number of other definitions of benchmarking include:

'Benchmarking is the process of comparing a product, service, process – indeed any activity or object – with other samples from a peer group, with a view to identifying "best buy" or "best practice" and targeting oneself to emulate it.' (*Facilities Economics* by Bernard Williams Associates)

'Benchmarking is the process of continuously measuring and comparing one's business processes against comparable processes in leading organisations to obtain information that will help the organisation identify and implement improvements.' (*The Benchmarking Handbook* by B. Andersen and P. G. Petersen)

'A continuous, systematic process for evaluating the products, services and work processes of organisations that are recognised as representing best practice for the purpose of organisational improvement.' (*The Benchmarking Book* by Michael J. Spendolini).

Companies embarking on QM need to measure their current performance as a standard to compare future performance. Benchmarking is the ideal way of doing this. Types of benchmarking are shown in Table 37.6.

Benchmarking involves collecting and analysing data from across the organisation – it could be financial data such as annual pre-tax profit, or non-financial data such as the level of customer complaints. The main issues to be considered in benchmarking are:

❑ It is a time-consuming and labour-intensive process. It does not provide solutions but is a focused search for ideas.
❑ The focus of benchmarking is continual improvement. It is not a once-only event.
❑ It is a process of investigation and learning from others that provides valuable data to translate into information for decision making.

Benchmarking partnerships can be formed between non-competitive customers, suppliers and other organisations. Advantages of external benchmarking are numerous – including the potential of discovering useful and transferable innovative practices and the

Table 37.6   Types of benchmarking

	Type	Description	Advantages	Disadvantages
1	Internal	Assess company's operations, comparing activities across business. Comparison between the same, or similar activities in different departments, operating units, locations or even different countries if the organisation is a multi-national.	Data in a standardised format is easy to collect, facilitate good intra-organisational results.	Has a limited focus, may not reflect good practice in a wider sense.
2	Competitive	Comparing your product or business activity to a competitor's. You can look at product quality, value for money, market share, etc. This compares direct competitors selling to the same customer base. It focuses on the best competitors, not on the average or below.	The information is relevant to the business operations, comparable practices can be compared.	Data collection difficulties, genuine co-operation may not be easy to achieve, business ethics may also be a problem.
3	Functional	Compare core business activities within the same industry, for example 'selling insurance', or compare performance with industry leaders.	Sector issues become known, best practice established.	Identification of leaders, confidentiality, competitive issues.
4	Generic	Compare general business activities that are not related to a specific industry, for example purchasing or outsourcing catering service.	Establishes comparators in general services.	Inability to know if comparisons are relevant.

Table 37.7   Soft data questions

Customers	Suppliers	Staff
What do we need to do better to give you the best service?	What skills do you feel we need to invest in if we are to work together for future success?	What training do you need to improve service to customers and colleagues?
What skills and technology do you feel we need if we are to work together for future success?	What do we need to do better to help us get the best service from you as a supplier?	What do you want the business to provide you with to help you do your job more efficiently?

development of professional networks and access to relevant databases. Disadvantages are that it may be difficult, or even impossible, to successfully transfer practices appropriate for one business environment into another business environment. It is a time-consuming process that may not reward the organisation with commensurate benefits.

Some key measurements for benchmarking are:

❑ Not Right First Time – it measures the number of defective products.
❑ Value of Supplies delivered on time against Value of Bought in Materials – indicates the ability of suppliers to deliver on time. A higher figure indicates the use of reliable suppliers.
❑ Research and Development spend against Turnover – shows the company's level of investment in future products and services.
❑ Total Training Days per total number of Employees – shows how much the company is investing in training.

Soft data

To back up the hard data collected on performance, 'soft' data is also needed to show whether the organisation is satisfying stakeholder needs and expectations. Stakeholders are staff, customers, suppliers and investors. Questionnaires can be a useful tool for gathering this kind of information. Table 37.7 shows typical questions to be asked.

Review

Techniques can be used in the review:

❑ Brainstorming.
❑ Cause and effect diagrams.

Implementation

Use a four-step action plan as shown in Table 37.8.

37.11 FM benchmarking

An FM policy should indicate output and input performance levels, with benchmark cost and service delivery targets. Performance can be described as the capability of

Table 37.8   The four steps in the implementation of a benchmarking exercise

Plan	Collect	Analyse	Improve
Agree roles and responsibilities	Ensure everyone understands the need for data collection	Make sure the data is meaningful	Set targets that are realistic but stretching
Decide which business activity to benchmark	Ensure everyone is recording data in a standard way	Decide how to produce regular reports	Devise an alternative way of doing things
Document how the activity is currently carried out		Develop a comparison matrix to compare the current performance with future performance	Look at factors that may prevent change
Decide what data to collect and how to collect it			Draw up a plan to implement changes

the FM team, together with agreed objectives and standards, plus the behaviour of all parties.

FMs need credible performance tools to gain visibility in their organisations. The outputs of their endeavours should be published. Most FMs have plenty of information about their activities; however, the key issue is turning this information into knowledge and ultimately intelligence. It requires creativity and the right ingredients to get the best out of the raw data.

So for many FMs, the use of SLAs, KPIs and key performance measures are part of the benchmarking toolkit to demonstrate added value to the core business. Table 37.9 shows some examples.

Table 37.9   Benchmarking examples in FM

Financial	Product	Service
Capital and revenue costs	Availability of spares	Customer complaints – volume and frequency
Cost per metre^2	Warranties	Mean time to respond
Cost per person	Guarantees	Mean time to repair or fix
Cost per workspace	Optional extras/features	Mean time to contact the customer
Depreciation rates	Mean time to failure	No. of suggestions
Expenditure as a percentage of depreciation	Spares availability and cost	Image considerations, e.g. user perception of contact personnel
Direct and indirect labour costs	Specification	Quality of the original workmanship
Leasing costs	Location of equipment	Maintenance policy of the benchmarking comparator or partner
Repair costs	Age of the component/element/ system being benchmarked	Hours in use

Table 37.10   FM benchmarking metrics

Quantity	How many?
Quality	How good?
Duration/timescale	How long?
Frequency	How often?
Financial	How much it costs or earns?
Perception	What people are saying?
Actions	What people are doing?
Process	How are people doing it?

Performance can be measured by using one or more of the metrics shown in Table 37.10.

Office cost benchmarks

There are several benchmark schemes used in FM, including:

❑ The Frisque programme, developed by BWA Facilities Consultancy.
❑ BMI, the building cost information service at the RICS.
❑ Property Week/Johnson Controls Index.
❑ Occupiers Property Databank.
❑ OSCAR, office service charge analysis report, developed by Jones Lang LaSalle.
❑ AMIS FM and AMIS FM-PLUS.
❑ Compliance reports/RIDDOR statistics/accident rates.
❑ Annual reports – Financial, CSR, and Operating Review.

Key performance indicators

The first step is to find out what the KPIs are in the organisation. Many companies now report annually on energy consumption, recycling initiatives, staff development and community projects. These are all areas in which the FM team can provide data and information. The FM team needs to identify any business KPI that it can directly impact, and give priority to these. The next step in setting up a benchmarking programme is determining who should be involved in the process. The team may comprise finance, helpdesk and operational staff members. There is no single solution to this process, as there is no universal approach to managing facilities. Every organisation has differing needs, and understanding these needs is critical to getting the best fit between the facilities and the organisation, and the selection of the appropriate KPIs for the business.

Typical KPIs in most organisations include:

❑ Turnover.
❑ Profit.
❑ Operating expenditure.
❑ Customer satisfaction.
❑ Output volume.

The FM needs to determine what metrics in their sphere of influence have a direct impact or relationship to the top organisational KPIs. They need to understand the measurement philosophy and requirements of the organisational KPIs so that the FM measurements are feeding into these, and are compatible. The FM must find out what, who and whose behaviours are being measured. They need to know what processes are used in providing key KPI data, and most importantly, who owns the data and the KPI.

It is vital that the performance measurement system has a clarity of purpose. FMs need to ask themselves:

❑ What is the purpose of the measurement and KPIs. (What will happen to the information and what decisions or actions could arise?)
❑ Who needs to receive the information obtained from the KPI or benchmarking system. (Who will read the information, and what format is required?)
❑ Who has responsibility for collection of the data. (Do the suppliers and contractors buy-into the system, and provide information in the right format?)

Without this information, it is impossible to define how the performance measurement system will operate. The best performance measurement or benchmarking processes are simple and enable sharing for easy comparison and analysis.

Remember that good measurement systems, with considered and accurate reports, will influence how the FM is perceived in that organisation, so don't waste the opportunity to impress others. Consider who is the audience, and ensure that the results are published in a format to suit the readers.

Benchmarking data must be accurate, with assumptions clearly stated. Year-on-year trend information is significant as this gives a direction in the value of the FM services. It is important to be constant with the metrics, so use one protocol or standard. For example, it is common to find the space data varies depending on the measurement protocol, so just stick to one protocol throughout the benchmarking system.

It is sometimes easier to just focus on the language of accountants and finance for benchmarking, but remember that many behavioural drivers are not measured in monetary values. Metrics which measure quality and delivery are just as important to FMs. This will measure the contribution of FM, rather than just what it does. However, the advantage of KPIs and benchmarks produced in 'accounting language' are that they are easier for external comparison with other external organisations.

In an ideal organisation, everybody's objectives should be linked, and this makes the establishment of performance measurement systems easier. This should include the FM service partners, especially if they are needed to provide credible data for the performance measurement system.

There is a danger in measuring only what can be measured, and ignoring the rest. This can result in only doing what can be measured. For some FMs, the only aspect of their service that is measured is that which is needed for contract compliance. Adopting a focus on SLAs and KPIs may lead to a very narrow view of what FM is about, and restricts the potential of FMs to progress from being the problem fixers to the value adders. There is a risk that creativity and innovation is stifled if too much time is focused on benchmarking.

A final note of caution – the difficulty with all measurement is that it is only at the time of measurement that the data is accurate.

38 Document Management Services

38.1 Corporate information

Information is everywhere – every word on every page, and in every file on every computer in every language on every desk, in every office, business, building, street, city, country and continent. Information lies at the heart of every organisation. Some have information that is very sensitive; for others, information is time-sensitive and critical. Some retain too little information; some have so much that they can't hope to use a fraction of it. Some don't know what information they have, while others can't access or share theirs. Most don't manage information well; others don't even realise it needs managing.

A rigorous corporate information strategy enables organisations to be more successful by:

❑ Improving profitability, because it helps to win new business and retain the existing customers.
❑ Enhancing the customer experience, because information can be exchanged with them.
❑ Reducing the potential risk by protection of the integrity of their brand, and compliance to legalisation and governance regulations.

38.2 Document management

Document management is concerned with the distribution, storage and retrieval of documents. There will usually be many different types of document. Some may exist on paper only and others may be stored in an electronically readable format.

Definition

Document management can be defined as the ability to efficiently access documents. Document management is the management of information – the information found in letters, faxes, invoices, orders and computer listings – in fact all documents. This process is vital to all companies. The efficient control of paperwork is the key to success in today's increasingly competitive business markets. It is also necessary in today's more litigious society to provide due diligence and evidence in defence of an organisation's or employee's actions.

Purpose

The purpose of document management is to make available any document required by the people who need it, when they need it. The document is an important asset, yet many of these valuable assets are stored unsecured and inaccessible.

Origination of documents

There is a wide range of word processing, graphic and desktop publishing software which users can use to produce in-house documents and visual aids. For more prestige documents, such as brochures and external reports, dedicated graphic designers may be required to use their professional design skills.

The document trail

Document management begins with the originator creating a document. Soft copies can be sent and received electronically. However, many external documents still continue their journey via the postal system. The document trail ends in the off-site archive store, or confidential waste contractor's premises.

38.3 Mail

The mailroom is responsible for the mail operation in an organisation. Any organisation needs a process of mail distribution. Normally this involves letters and other packages being distributed internally and externally. Despite new technologies, the processes are more or less routine in many organisations, although RFID technology is now available for larger organisations to track the larger items within an organisation. Table 38.1 shows the procedures typically in place.

The mailroom is one of the main points for incoming and outgoing information. The Internet and email is the other main point for information exchange and is likely to replace traditional postal services for many documents.

Table 38.1   Mailroom procedures

Incoming mail	Outgoing mail
Only accept packages for listed employees	Use an identifiable return address
Only accept packages from authorised postal delivery personnel with identification	Use the opportunity to promote your organisation, products and services or company logo on the outgoing mail
Create an audit trail for each piece of mail	Consider window envelopes, postcards, preprinted tape to seal packages
Make provisions for valuable incoming items	Use tamper-evident seals to improve security of outgoing valuable mail
Train staff to identify the characteristics of suspect packages, such as grease marks, smells, unexpected destinations, style of writing, mismatched names and addresses or size and shape of package	Samples and other products need to be in a sealed poly-bag, and contents identified on the envelope
Keep outgoing mail in a separate secure area until collected	
Make provisions and have a recording system for undeliverable packages	

For many staff in an organisation, the mailroom is a hidden service. Safety and security considerations for employees, customers, suppliers are now increasingly important.

UK postal market

This market is now de-regulated to allow licensed postal businesses to provide an alternative to the Royal Mail. Royal Mail will continue to provide one collection and delivery of first- and second-class mail each day at a standard price. FMs can now choose from a wide variety of service providers. There are many businesses working in the postal market.

'Pricing in Proportion (PIP)' is a new pricing strategy for mail services that takes into account size as well as weight of the item.

Functions of mailroom staff

Mailroom staff often have many roles depending on the size of the organisation. These roles can be performed by a dedicated person(s) or they may be combined with other functions in the organisation. The successful service to building occupants will depend greatly on their local knowledge, and building effective internal customer relationships. The mailroom functions of the mailroom staff are summarised below:

❑ Opening, collating, referencing and distributing internal mail. In some organisations, this may include scanning or digitising the incoming mail, and then distributing via email/intranet/company system.
❑ Collating, packaging, stamping, recording and posting or despatching outgoing mail.

Workload

On average, one mailroom operative is able to service the mail of around 250–400 employees. Obviously this does depend on the level of sorting, the locations, the horizontal and vertical access of the building(s) and the frequency of distribution rounds within the organisation. Other general duties may also be added such as:

❑ Stationery supplies.
❑ General consumables.
❑ Building safety checks.
❑ General porterage.
❑ Meeting room management.
❑ Small office moves.
❑ Reprographics.
❑ Top-up of local copier centres.
❑ Noticeboard management.

Mailroom design

The design of the mailroom is fundamental to its efficiency. Racking systems are often used, and there are many proprietary mailroom equipment suppliers specialising in this market. Many of these suppliers will provide a layout and design service. Criteria to be considered in the design include:

❑ Space between aisles.
❑ Space for sorting operations.
❑ Space for packaging operations.

- ❑ Location for specialised equipment such as:
  - ○ Space for parking of trolleys (lightweight and designed for mail/goods handling).
  - ○ X-ray equipment.
  - ○ Franking machine.
  - ○ Intelligent weighing equipment.
  - ○ Electric letter openers.
  - ○ Direct envelope printers.
  - ○ Access control.
  - ○ Security controls (such as CCTV).

Audit

In assessing the mail needs of an organisation, an audit may be undertaken, asking questions such as:

- ❑ What is the level of risk posed to your business in terms of the volume of send and received mail and the potential cost of a security incident?
- ❑ What are the standards and SLAs to ensure good mail service performance?
- ❑ Do important items get to the right person at the specified time?
- ❑ Do the services include courier booking, item tracking, secure delivery?
- ❑ What are the costs of the service, and is the service considered value for money?
- ❑ Can the costs be analysed into distribution categories, e.g. post, courier, overnight services, etc.?
- ❑ Are there opportunities to combine the service with other parts of the organisation such as: goods-in deliveries; consumables (e.g. stationery) purchase and issue; or printing and reprographics?
- ❑ Does the service need to be in a particular building or location?
- ❑ How secure is the service?
- ❑ Can the service be outsourced to a specialist operator?

Security of mail

Guidelines to improve the security of the mail include:

- ❑ Ensure that there is a designated supervisor or manager in charge.
- ❑ All staff should have training and refresher training in security procedures.
- ❑ The location of the mailroom is critical to its effectiveness and efficiency. Most mail rooms are located on the ground floor of a building. It must be accessible to all users, including the external couriers and postal delivery organisations.
- ❑ Employ a range of security measures such as:
  - ○ Access control.
  - ○ Intrusion alarms.
  - ○ Surveillance cameras.
  - ○ X-ray screening.
- ❑ Have a robust disaster recovery plan and ensure that there are clear responsibilities for the mailroom team. Actions required of the staff must be understood. Training and refreser training of the staff should include actions to take with both hoax or real breaches of security.
- ❑ Conduct full employee security checks to check their past employment and criminal records.

Outgoing mail

It is common practice for outgoing mail to be stamped using a metered franking machine. This will allow all outgoing mail to be identified with the organisation, and makes tracing easier. Preprinted envelopes can also be used. Access to the franking machine may need to be controlled, so that only authorised items can be sent. Organisations may have strict policies on personal post and the cross-charging of the services back to each department or user. Departments can be allocated a unique code to track their mail, that can be written in pencil on the envelope. Some organisations may advise staff that all post will be sent second class unless marked otherwise. A simple 1 or 2 in the top right area in pencil could be sufficient to implement this simple procedure.

Franking

Franking is an easy, flexible way to pay for any amount of UK or overseas postage. However, the payment is made in advance of actually consuming the service. An organisation can either hire or buy a franking machine, and Royal Mail will issue a franking machine licence, which states the terms and conditions for using that equipment. All franking machine customers are required to adhere to these terms and conditions and Royal Mail has the right to withdraw a licence if they are not met. It gives the outgoing mail a more professional look.

Costs are reduced for franking customers, when compared to normal stamps. Organisations can make significant savings with discounts on first- and second-class mail. The credit limit on the machine can be topped up over the phone.

Franked mail must be posted on the date shown and before the last collection time (local opening times and latest acceptance times will apply). Franked letters must be segregated by class or service in bundles facing and oriented the same way using designated pouches. Pouches, trays and containers are provided to customers free of charge. Specialist suppliers will provide late posting envelopes and low volume envelopes.

Outsourcing mail services

Reasons may include operational efficiency, cost savings or security. Outsourcing may be done on the client premises or at a remote location. A range of services can be provided via external specialist organisations such as:

❑ Mailroom management services – Customised on- or off-site mailroom solutions to save business time and money.
❑ Mailroom consultancy services – Experts to advise how mailroom operations can be improved.
❑ Pre-sorted delivery – The external contractor will pre-sort the mail so it can be processed faster when it arrives.
❑ Security screening – Expert mail screening to minimise the risk of in-house staff receiving threatening or potentially harmful items in the mail.
❑ Secure mail opening services – Post can be opened and any potentially dangerous mail processed in a safe, off-site environment to prevent the risk of harmful substances being received.
❑ Mail opening services – Mail can be opened and sorted to meet an organisation's exact requirements so it arrives ready to be processed.

38.4 Reprographics

Different organisations will have different printing and document copying requirements. If a central reprographics service is provided to all occupants, then it may come under the FM's remit or alternatively it may be part of the Information Technology or Information Management department. In educational establishments, it often comes under the Library or Learning Resources team. Services can include:

- Self-service printing and photocopying.
- Printing and copying.
- Sending faxes.
- Book binding (thermal, comb, planax, etc.).
- Laminating.

Finishing

Finishing services are those aspects of document reproduction that complete the final product. Most reprographics functions in large organisations or an outsourced contractor will provide a full finishing service. The options may include:

- Folding.
- Collating/stapling.
- Booklet making.
- Binding.
- Padding.
- Numbering.
- Perforating.
- Two or four hole drilling of documents.
- Guillotine work.

38.5 Photocopiers

A copier works because of one basic principle of physics: opposite charges attract. Inside a copier there is a special drum which is charged with a form of static electricity. Inside the copier there is also a very fine black powder known as toner. The drum, charged with static electricity, can attract the toner particles.

There are three things about the drum and the toner that make a copier work.

- The drum can be selectively charged, so that only parts of it attract toner. In a copier, an 'image' in static electricity is made on the surface of the drum. The white or blank parts of the document to be copied will not attract the toner, as these will not create static electricity; whereas the dark or printed areas will create the charge and attract the toner. The way this selectivity is accomplished in a copier is with light – this is why it is called a photocopier!
- Somehow the toner has to get onto the drum and then onto a sheet of paper. The drum selectively attracts toner. The sheet of paper is then charged with static electricity and it pulls the toner off the drum.

❏   The toner is heat sensitive, so the loose toner particles are attached (fused) to the paper with heat as soon as they come off the drum.

The end result is a photocopy of the original document.

Photocopiers can come in many different sizes and functionality, from high volume photocopiers that are capable of more than 30,000 photocopies per month, right down to personal photocopiers with capacities of less than 2000 photocopies per month. Most photocopiers are equipped with an impressive range of options and facilities. The selection of copiers may be judged on these criteria:

❏   Quality.
❏   Productivity.
❏   Creativity (the features and functions).
❏   Reliablity.
❏   Size.
❏   Price.

Built-in electronic controls will automatically adjust the settings such as toner, temperature, humidity and exposure. Remote diagnostics offer effective maintenance by the supplier. Many organisation now set the default to two-sided copying to reduce the paper used.

Purchase options

Issues that are important to consider in the procurement of a copier include:

❏   Monthly volume.
❏   Expected growth of the business.
❏   Needs for colour.
❏   Space available.
❏   Quality of copies required.
❏   Extent of collating.
❏   Speed of output.
❏   Sizes of output – A4 or others such as A3.
❏   Use of features such as enlarge, reduce, margins, etc.

Leasing

Leasing is a well-established, tax-efficient method of financing a wide variety of capital equipment. Values can range from one to many thousands of pounds. Practically every sector of the British economy takes advantage of leasing, from small- and medium-sized enterprises (SMEs) through to large multinational organisations. Many organisations will have leasing arrangements for their photocopying and multifunction device (MFD) equipment.

Leasing is a contract between a finance company and a customer, giving the customer use of the equipment on payments of rentals over a period. The advantage of leasing equipment is that the organisation can make a series of regular (usually 3 monthly) payments, instead of a large capital outlay to buy the equipment.

The cash flow and tax relief benefits of leasing provide a very strong case against cash purchase. When an organisation buys equipment outright the capital invested becomes, in effect, tied up in a depreciating asset that loses its value. Copiers and cars are both examples of equipment that have rapid depreciation rates. Leasing on the other hand allows the organisation to use resources for other business-related purposes or opportunities. The rental fee remains the same for the term of the agreement. The rental amounts may change during the leasing term if there are changes in the taxation regimes, treatment of leases in accounts, or the organisation negotiates an upgrade or downgrade of equipment with the supplier.

Title to the goods remains with the finance provider, which means the equipment does not show on the company balance sheets as an asset, therefore not needing to be depreciated over a fixed period. However, provisions do need to be made for the liabilities of the rental charges.

A leasing facility allows businesses to keep up with changes in technology as the original installation can be altered either during or at the end of the lease period. The normal reason for this is due to a customer's expansion of business and their changing needs.

The majority of copiers are leased, although low volume personal copiers may be purchased outright. The types of lease or rental plans are:

❏ Copy plan – The machine is rented, with an additional charge made for the number of actual copies made.
❏ Service plan – The machine is rented with an agreed number of copies per month or quarter, with a quarterly service charge on top.
❏ Rental only – The machine is rented, with additional callout fees to fix the machine being charged at cost.

Photocopier leasing versus buying a copier

Every organisation is different but photocopier leasing is very popular with many organisations.

Advantages:

❏ Costs for the copier are certain and are known in advance.
❏ The copier cannot be withdrawn once the contract is signed and its conditions complied with.
❏ No need to tie up capital in fixed assets such as a photocopier.
❏ Allowances, depreciation and other calculations are not needed, since leasing is concerned only with rentals.
❏ Leasing provides a medium-term source of capital which may not be available elsewhere.
❏ Leasing provides a hedge against inflation as the use of the asset is obtained immediately – payments are made out of future funds and are made in fixed money terms, with real costs falling as inflation increases.
❏ Possibility of immediate acquisition of cost-saving equipment.

Disadvantages:

❏ It is generally not possible to dispose of the photocopier before the end of the lease.
❏ The copier is not owned.
❏ Funds must be found to pay the lease throughout its duration.

❏   Overall the lease costs over the full term are greater then the original purchase price.
❏   The interest rate charged on the funds in the lease may be greater than loans or over-drafts for funds obtained elsewhere.

High volume photocopiers

High volume digital photocopiers are designed for high speed, high volume usage. These photocopiers are designed for busy reprographic departments, professional printers and large corporate organisations where quality cannot be compromised by speed or quantity – the last copy out is as good as the first copy out and the original document. Features will typically include:

❏   Up to A3 format.
❏   Photocopy/print speed of over 40 pages per minute.
❏   Average monthly volume of 30,000 photocopies/prints or more.
❏   Faxing, network printing, scanning, iFax and Internet access facilities.

Medium volume photocopiers

Medium volume digital photocopiers are designed for medium speed and volume usage. Features typically include:

❏   Up to A3 format.
❏   Entry into automatic double siding (Duplex).
❏   Photocopy/print speed of between 20 and 40 photocopies/prints per minute.
❏   Average monthly volume of between 10,000 and 30,000 photocopies/prints or more.
❏   Faxing, network printing, scanning and iFax.

Low volume photocopiers

Low volume digital photocopiers are designed for the small office where the need for speed and/or volume is not a major consideration. Durability and quality of output is paramount. Features typically include:

❏   A4 only and up to A3 paper formats.
❏   Single-sided photocopying/printing (Simplex).
❏   Photocopy speed up to 20 prints per minute.
❏   Average monthly volume up to 10,000 photocopies.
❏   Electronic sorting and staple finishing, and fax options.

Personal photocopiers

Personal photocopiers are designed for the individual professional and small business with an occasional photocopying requirement. Features typically include:

❏   A4 photocopies.
❏   Maximum monthly volume of less than 2000 photocopies/prints.
❏   Facilities/options include automatic document feeder, printing, scanning and faxing.

38.6 Printers

There is a wide range of printer types available to suit budget and quality of print output required. These include:

- ❏ Dot matrix.
- ❏ Laserjet.
- ❏ Inkjet.
- ❏ Photo printer.

Dot matrix

Dot matrix printers produce characters and illustrations by striking pins against an ink ribbon to print closely spaced dots in the appropriate shape. Dot matrix printers do not produce high-quality output. However, they can print to multi-page forms (i.e. carbon copies), something laser and inkjet printers cannot do. Dot matrix printers vary in two important characteristics:

 (i) Speed – Given in characters per second (cps), the speed can vary from about 50 to over 500 cps. Most dot matrix printers offer different speeds depending on the quality of print desired.
(ii) Print quality – Determined by the number of pins (the mechanisms that print the dots), it can vary from 9 to 24. The best dot matrix printers (24 pins) can produce near letter-quality type, although you can still see a difference if you look closely.

Laserjet

A laser printer is a common type of computer printer that produces high quality printing, and is able to produce both text and graphics. The three major advantages of laser printers over inkjets are sharper text, lower cost per page and much faster print speed, since the entire page is imaged at one time.

Inkjet

Inkjet printers are the most common type of computer printer for the general consumer. Inkjets are usually inexpensive, quiet, reasonably fast and many models can produce high quality output.

Photo printer

A photo printer is specifically designed to print high quality digital photos on photo paper. These printers usually have a very high number of nozzles and are capable of printing droplets as small as 1 picolitre.

Photo printers may have digital media readers (memory cards) to conveniently print pictures without a computer. Some can also print directly from a camera, or a camera in a docking station, that supports the ability.

There is a growing trend to remove individual printers and replace with MFDs located in central areas. The advantages are numerous and include:

- ❏ Optimises equipment use.
- ❏ Central paper store for one piece of equipment.

❑   Encourages users to move, get up and walk around to release the tension of working at computer screens.
❑   Incorporates greater functionality such as fax, multiple copies, double-sided, etc.
❑   Less assets to be tested in the PAT electrical tests.
❑   Saves space at the workstation.

38.7 Multi-function devices

A multi-function device (MFD) combines the convenience and quality of a laser printer with the advanced paper handling and finishing features of a photocopier. These devices are becoming more common, and have reduced the need for individual fax and copy machines. In addition they have also reduced the need for individual desktop printers.

Although outwardly a photocopier, MFDs are fast network laser printers with a scanner attachment to provide the copying function and a hard disk to store print jobs. The ability to print to the MFD from the PC means that many of the features associated with photo-copying – duplexing, collating, stapling – are now available through a software application running on the internal computer network.

Printing is on a MFD as simple as printing to any of the laser printers on the network. The MFD will be given a unique name and be visible in the available printer list.

MFD features

These include:

❑   Multiple page to single sheet printing, e.g. put up to 16 pages on a single side of A4.
❑   Duplex printing – Printing to both sides of a single sheet.
❑   Stapling.
❑   Punching.
❑   A4 – A3 enlargement, A3 – A4 reduction.
❑   Multiple paper sources (e.g. print first page on different coloured paper, slip sleets).
❑   Watermarking – print background text onto every page.
❑   Locked printing – Allows a print job to be sent to the copier with a unique copier ID number. The job is not printed until the correct ID number is entered at the copier control panel.
❑   Sample printing – Allows the user to print only the first copy of a multiple-set print job for proofing purposes.
❑   Ability to handle copy and print jobs simultaneously.
❑   Scanning – allows the creation of PDF copies of documents to be made, saved and sent to email accounts.
❑   Faxing – allows a document to be faxed to another fascimile destination.

38.8 Facsimile (fax) machines

Fax machines use telecommunications technology to transfer copies of documents, using affordable devices over the telephone network. A fax machine is essentially an image scanner, a modem and a computer printer combined into a highly specialised package. The scanner converts the content of a physical document into a digital image, the modem

Table 38.2   Types of fax machines

Inkfilm	Inkfilm fax machines that are ideal for the home user with built-in fax machines and answerphones with fast modem speeds.
Inkjet	With fully featured all-in-one inkjet fax machines allowing you to print, fax, PC fax, copy and scan in colour from one compact unit. They offer exceptional performance across a wide range of functions and are ideally suited to any office environment.
Laser	Laser fax machines offer fast and economical laser functionality. With the inclusion of a large memory, important information will not be lost. They also boast one-touch dial locations, Super G3 modems, speed dialling and compact designs.

sends the image data over a phone line and the printer at the other end makes a duplicate of the original document.

Fax machines with additional electronic features can connect to computers, can be used to scan documents into a computer and to print documents from the computer. Such high-end devices are similar in functionality to multifunction printers and cost more than fax machines.

However, although most businesses still maintain some kind of fax capability, the technology appears increasingly replaced with the Internet.

There are several different indicators of fax capabilities:

- ❑ Group – there are four groups of fax machines.
- ❑ Class – computer modems are often designated by a particular fax class, which indicates how much processing is offloaded from the computer's CPU to the fax modem. There are different fax classes, including Class 1, Class 2 and Intel CAS.
- ❑ Data transmission rate – several different telephone line modulation techniques are used by fax machines. They are negotiated during the fax-modem handshake, and the fax devices will use the highest data rate that both fax devices support.
- ❑ Conformance with ITU-T (formerly CCITT) recommendations.

Fax machines from the 1970s to the 1990s often used direct thermal printers as their printing technology, but since the mid-1990s there has been a transition towards thermal transfer printers, inkjet printers and laser printers. Table 38.2 shows the range of fax machines available.

38.9 Electronic document management system (EDMS)

Electronic document management systems (EDMS) allows a document to be filed under multiple references and therefore be retrievable under different search criteria. A global library can list all relevant documents on an individual's computer screen. Hard copy documents can safely and inexpensively be stored off site allowing the business to access and recover these original documents in the event that there is corruption or a systems failure.

The benefits of EDMS are many and include:

□   Saving time finding documents.
□   Saving space on bulky storage facilities.
□   Reduce risk from fire or flood.
□   Reduce risk from business interruption whilst documents are retrieved.
□   Facilitate sharing of information across an organisation.
□   Reduce overall costs of document management.
□   Improved business processing time and service to customers.

Software

There is a range of document management software packages to suit a wide range of users to provide the capability to capture, index, store, retrieve, distribute and otherwise manage documents. To choose the most appropriate one, the FM needs to determine:

□   Number of documents.
□   Size of documents.
□   Methods of origination.
□   Number of documents produced per month.
□   Number of user of a document.
□   Location of users.
□   Flow of documents within the organisation.
□   Current storage.
□   Current formats of documents.
□   Required storage and retention times for documents.

Scanners

There is a broad range of high speed, high performance document scanners that combine reliable high quality image input with easy operation and maintenance. To benefit from an EDMS, the organisation will need to convert its paper-based information from hard copies via scanning technology to soft digital files. This can be costly and time-consuming. Organisations will need to determine how much of the archive and current documents are to be scanned into the EDMS, making information management more efficient and less time consuming.

38.10 Audio visual equipment

The range of equipment to satisfy audio visual requirements in a business includes:

□   Plasma screens – Ideal for multimedia applications – can be vertically or horizontally mounted and ideal as updateable digital signage or for an endless array of multi-media applications. The ultra-thin display offers a wide viewing angle of more than 160° and has a system that senses ambient lighting conditions and adjusts brightness and gradation accordingly.

❑ LCD TV.

❑ Projectors – Features to be considered include contrast ration, resolution, lamplife, warranty for both the unit and the lamps, lumens, weight of unit.

❑ Interactive whiteboards – These products are ideal for meetings, brainstorming, scheduling, training, real-time communication and creative presentations. Products range from simple boards that connect to:

   o the PC so the users can write or draw on its surface and electronically capture their notes in full colour;

   o any data projector and it instantly becomes a touchscreen board;

   o both PC and projector for a complete interactive system which responds to touch for annotation and application navigation. The projected images, complete with user notes and annotations, can then be captured and stored for electronic hard-copy distribution.

❑ Fully integrated top of the range products can be connected to a computer and LCD projector, allowing users to control Microsoft Windows applications directly from the supplied utility software and electronic pens. This additional functionality eliminates notetaking during meetings; information can be uploaded and emailed as an attached file. Most of the built-in printer versions allow for immediate distribution of notes to the audience. With appropriate additional software, these products may also provide a cost-effective real-time teleconferencing solution.

❑ Portable interactive devices – There are a range of devices available. The Mimio range of products uses ultrasound to convert white boards and flipcharts into interactive devices. The position of the marker stylus and eraser is tracked. Another product, the Cleverpad, is a wireless tablet fitted with Bluetooth techno-logy to allow many surfaces to be made interactive. These interactive Bluetooth pads will enable any meeting participant to contribute to a presentation from anywhere in the room.

❑ Screens – These can be either free-standing or fitted in a variety of ways in a room. For example, they can be mounted on tripods, wall mounted, ceiling mounted, be a table top version or pull-up from a base unit. There are a variety of sizes available. Screens can be manual or electrically operated. The surface needs to be matt white. It is usually advisable to fix clear notices that the screens must not be written on.

❑ Accessories – These may include stands, trolleys, security boxes for projectors, over-head projectors (OHPs), flipchart stands, white boards, ceiling mounting kit.

38.11 Archives

All organisations will have materials, documents and other materials that will require storage. An organisation needs to identify the various types of documents used in its business, and provide guidelines on the storage time, reminders for destruction, procedures for retrieval, and storage formats. British Standard BS ISO 15489 gives information on document management and archiving. An archive can be set up on site, or externally in cheaper premises. An archiving service can be provided by specialist contractors. This will include a destruction and retrieval service. Some organisations will identify diferent levels of storage – e.g. short-, medium- and long-term; or shallow (for documents that may be accessed once or twice a year) and deep (for documents that have not been accessed for 2 years). A proactive archive service will be monitoring retrieval rates to determine whether documents could be moved to cheaper (deeper) storage, and also when documents are nearing their predicted destruction time in order to progressively reduce the cost of time-term shortage of documents that are too old and have no value to the organisation.

An archive policy will help employees to appreciate what they need to do and the procedures that they need to follow. The policy may also be linked to a central filing scheme. Most company documents need to be kept for a period of 7 years from its year of origination. This is because it can take up to 6 years for a legal claim to be made for breach of contract. In addition, the Companies Act and the VAT Act will require organisations to keep documents for prescriptive periods of time. Documents that will require particular attention include insurance policies, contracts, employee records, leases and purchase orders. If an organisation is operating in the public sector, then there is likely to be a Records Manager appointed, who will have a responsibility under the Freedom of Information Act, to respond to requests for documents and information from the public. All organisations must comply with the Data Protection Act, and this too will influence how documents are retained a in safe and secure storage medium.

Index

Note: Page numbers in **bold** refer to the main sources of information.

A List of Abbreviations appears on page xxiii for further reference.